GO!

with Microsoft®

Word 2010
Comprehensive

**Shelley Gaskin,
Robert L. Ferrett, and
Carol Martin**

Prentice Hall

Boston   Columbus   Indianapolis   New York   San Francisco   Upper Saddle River
Amsterdam   Cape Town   Dubai   London   Madrid   Milan   Munich   Paris   Montreal   Toronto
Delhi   Mexico City   Sao Paulo   Sydney   Hong Kong   Seoul   Singapore   Taipei   Tokyo

Associate VP/Executive Acquisitions Editor, Print:
  Stephanie Wall
Editorial Project Manager: Laura Burgess
Editor in Chief: Michael Payne
Product Development Manager: Eileen Bien Calabro
Development Editor: Jennifer Lynn
Editorial Assistant: Nicole Sam
Director of Marketing: Kate Valentine
Marketing Manager: Tori Olson Alves
Marketing Coordinator: Susan Osterlitz
Marketing Assistant: Darshika Vyas
Senior Managing Editor: Cynthia Zonneveld
Associate Managing Editor: Camille Trentacoste
Production Project Manager: Mike Lackey
Operations Director: Alexis Heydt
Operations Specialist: Natacha Moore

Senior Art Director: Jonathan Boylan
Cover Photo: © Ben Durrant
Text and Cover Designer: Blair Brown
Manager, Cover Visual Research & Permissions:
  Karen Sanatar
Manager, Rights and Permissions: Zina Arabia
AVP/Director of Online Programs, Media: Richard Keaveny
AVP/Director of Product Development, Media: Lisa Strite
Media Project Manager, Editorial: Alana Coles
Media Project Manager, Production: John Cassar
Full-Service Project Management: PreMediaGlobal
Composition: PreMediaGlobal
Printer/Binder: Quad/Graphics-Taunton
Cover Printer: Lehigh-Phoenix Color
Text Font: Bookman Light

Credits and acknowledgments borrowed from other sources and reproduced, with permission, in this textbook appear on appropriate page within text. Photos appearing in Word chapters 1 and 2 supplied by Robert Ferrett and used with permission.

Microsoft® and Windows® are registered trademarks of the Microsoft Corporation in the U.S.A. and other countries. Screen shots and icons reprinted with permission from the Microsoft Corporation. This book is not sponsored or endorsed by or affiliated with the Microsoft Corporation.

Library of Congress Cataloging-in-Publication Data
Go! with Microsoft Word 2010 / Shelley Gaskin ... [et al.].
    p. cm.
  Includes index.
  ISBN-13: 978-0-13-509798-4
  ISBN-10: 0-13-509798-3
 1. Microsoft Office.   2. Business—Computer programs.   I. Gaskin, Shelley.
  HF5548.4.M525G6254 2011
  005.5—dc22

                                        2010019688

10 9 8 7 6 5 4 3 2

Prentice Hall
is an imprint of

www.pearsonhighered.com

ISBN 10: 0-13-509798-3
ISBN 13: 978-0-13-509798-4

Brief Contents

Contents

Word

Chapter 1   Creating Documents with Microsoft Word 2010

Chapter 2 Using Tables and Templates to Create Resumes and Cover Letters 105

Chapter 5   Creating Web Pages and Using Advanced Proofing Options 281

Chapter 6 Building Documents from Reusable Content and Revising Documents Using Markup Tools ... 339

Chapter 9   Creating Standardized Forms and Managing Documents............. 511

Chapter 10   Working with Long Documents.... 571

Chapter 11   Embedding and Linking Objects and Using Macros............. 635

Chapter 12 Integrating Word with PowerPoint and Modifying the Document Layout 693

GO! System Contributors

We thank the following people for their hard work and support in making the *GO!* System all that it is!

Instructor Resource Authors

Adickes, Erich	Parkland College	Holly, Terri	Indian River State College
Baray, Carrie	Ivy Tech Community College	Jacob, Sherry	Kentucky Community and Technical College
Bornstein, Abigail	City College of San Francisco		
Bowman, Valeria	National College	Landenberger, Toni	Southeast Community College-Nebraska
Callahan, Michael	Lone Star College		
Clausen, Jane	Western Iowa Tech Community College	Leinbach, Andrea	Harrisburg Area Community College
Cleary, Kevin	University at Buffalo	Lutz, Mary	Southwestern Illinois College
Colucci, William	Montclair State University	McMahon, Richard	University of Houston—Downtown
Crossley, Connie	Cincinnati State Technical and Community College	Miller, Abigail	Gateway Community and Technical College
Damanti, Lori		Miller, Sandra	Wenatchee Valley College
Edington, Barbara	St. Francis College	Monson, Shari	Black Hawk College
Emrich, Stefanie	Metropolitan Community College of Omaha, Nebraska	Neal, Ruth	Navarro College
		Niebur, Katherine	Dakota County Technical College
Faix, Dennis	Harrisburg Area Community College	Nowakowski, Anthony	Buffalo State
Hadden, Karen	Western Iowa Tech Community College	Pierce, Tonya	Ivy Tech Community College
		Reynolds, Mark	Lone Star College
Hammerle, Patricia	Indiana University/Purdue University at Indianapolis	Roselli, Diane	Harrisburg Area Community College
		Shing, Chen-Chi	Radford University
Hicks, Janette	Binghamton University/State University of New York	St. John, Steve	Tulsa Community College
		Sterr, Jody	Blackhawk Technical College
Hines, James	Tidewater Community College	Thompson, Joyce	Lehigh Carbon Community College
Holland, Susan	Southeast Community College-Nebraska	Tucker, William	Austin Community College
		Volker, Bonita	Tidewater Community College
Hollingsworth, Mary Carole	Georgia Perimeter College	Walters, Kari	Louisiana State University

Technical Editors

Matthew Bisi	Sarah Evans	Joyce Nielsen	Jan Snyder
Mary Corcoran	Adam Layne	Janet Pickard	Sam Stamport
Lori Damanti	Elizabeth Lockley	Sean Portnoy	Mara Zebest
Barbara Edington			

Student Reviewers

Albinda, Sarah Evangeline	Phoenix College	Frye, Alicia	Phoenix College
Allen, John	Asheville-Buncombe Tech Community College	Gadomski, Amanda	Northern Michigan University
		Gassert, Jennifer	Harrisburg Area Community College
Alexander, Steven	St. Johns River Community College	Gross, Mary Jo	Kirkwood Community College
Alexander, Melissa	Tulsa Community College	Gyselinck, Craig	Central Washington University
Bolz, Stephanie	Northern Michigan University	Harrison, Margo	Central Washington University
Berner, Ashley	Central Washington University	Hatt, Patrick	Harrisburg Area Community College
Boomer, Michelle	Northern Michigan University		
Busse, Brennan	Northern Michigan University	Heacox, Kate	Central Washington University
Butkey, Maura	Central Washington University	Hedgman, Shaina	Tidewater College
Cates, Concita	Phoenix College	Hill, Cheretta	Northwestern State University
Charles, Marvin	Harrisburg Area Community College	Hochstedler, Bethany	Harrisburg Area Community College Lancaster
Christensen, Kaylie	Northern Michigan University	Homer, Jean	Greenville Technical College
Clark, Glen D. III	Harrisburg Area Community College	Innis, Tim	Tulsa Community College
		Jarboe, Aaron	Central Washington University
Cobble, Jan N.	Greenville Technical College	Key, Penny	Greenville Technical College
Connally, Brianna	Central Washington University	Klein, Colleen	Northern Michigan University
Davis, Brandon	Northern Michigan University	Lloyd, Kasey	Ivy Tech Bloomington
Davis, Christen	Central Washington University	Moeller, Jeffrey	Northern Michigan University
De Jesus Garcia, Maria	Phoenix College	Mullen, Sharita	Tidewater Community College
Den Boer, Lance	Central Washington University	Nelson, Cody	Texas Tech University
Dix, Jessica	Central Washington University	Nicholson, Regina	Athens Tech College
Downs, Elizabeth	Central Washington University	Niehaus, Kristina	Northern Michigan University
Elser, Julie	Harrisburg Area Community College	Nisa, Zaibun	Santa Rosa Community College
		Nunez, Nohelia	Santa Rosa Community College
Erickson, Mike	Ball State University	Oak, Samantha	Central Washington University

Contributors continued

Oberly, Sara	Harrisburg Area Community College Lancaster	Schmadeke, Kimberly	Kirkwood Community College
Oertii, Monica	Central Washington University	Shafapay, Natasha	Central Washington University
Palenshus, Juliet	Central Washington University	Shanahan, Megan	Northern Michigan University
Pohl, Amanda	Northern Michigan University	Sullivan, Alexandra Nicole	Greenville Technical College
Presnell, Randy	Central Washington University	Teska, Erika	Hawaii Pacific University
Reed, Kailee	Texas Tech University	Torrenti, Natalie	Harrisburg Area Community College
Ritner, April	Northern Michigan University	Traub, Amy	Northern Michigan University
Roberts, Corey	Tulsa Community College	Underwood, Katie	Central Washington University
Rodgers, Spencer	Texas Tech University	Walters, Kim	Central Washington University
Rodriguez, Flavia	Northwestern State University	Warren, Jennifer L.	Greenville Technical College
Rogers, A.	Tidewater Community College	Wilson, Kelsie	Central Washington University
Rossi, Jessica Ann	Central Washington University	Wilson, Amanda	Green River Community College
Rothbauer, Taylor	Trident Technical College	Wylie, Jimmy	Texas Tech University
Rozelle, Lauren	Texas Tech University		

Series Reviewers

Abraham, Reni	Houston Community College	Buell, C	Central Oregon Community College
Addison, Paul	Ivy Tech Community College	Burns, Christine	Central New Mexico Community College
Agatston, Ann	Agatston Consulting Technical College	Byars, Pat	Brookhaven College
Akuna, Valeria, Ph.D.	Estrella Mountain Community College	Byrd, Julie	Ivy Tech Community College
Alexander, Melody	Ball Sate University	Byrd, Lynn	Delta State University, Cleveland, Mississippi
Alejandro, Manuel	Southwest Texas Junior College	Cacace, Richard N.	Pensacola Junior College
Alger, David	Tidewater Community College Chesapeake Campus	Cadenhead, Charles	Brookhaven College
Allen, Jackie	Rowan-Cabarrus Community College	Calhoun, Ric	Gordon College
Ali, Farha	Lander University	Cameron, Eric	Passaic Community College
Amici, Penny	Harrisburg Area Community College	Canine, Jill	Ivy Tech Community College of Indiana
Anderson, Patty A.	Lake City Community College	Cannamore, Madie	Kennedy King
Andrews, Wilma	Virginia Commonwealth College, Nebraska University	Cannon, Kim	Greenville Technical College
Anik, Mazhar	Tiffin University	Carreon, Cleda	Indiana University—Purdue University, Indianapolis
Armstrong, Gary	Shippensburg University	Carriker, Sandra	North Shore Community College
Arnold, Linda L.	Harrisburg Area Community College	Casey, Patricia	Trident Technical College
Ashby, Tom	Oklahoma City Community College	Cates, Wally	Central New Mexico Community College
Atkins, Bonnie	Delaware Technical Community College	Chaffin, Catherine	Shawnee State University
Aukland, Cherie	Thomas Nelson Community College	Chauvin, Marg	Palm Beach Community College, Boca Raton
Bachand, LaDonna	Santa Rosa Community College	Challa, Chandrashekar	Virginia State University
Bagui, Sikha	University of West Florida	Chamlou, Afsaneh	NOVA Alexandria
Beecroft, Anita	Kwantlen University College	Chapman, Pam	Wabaunsee Community College
Bell, Paula	Lock Haven College	Christensen, Dan	Iowa Western Community College
Belton, Linda	Springfield Tech. Community College	Clay, Betty	Southeastern Oklahoma State University
Bennett, Judith	Sam Houston State University	Collins, Linda D.	Mesa Community College
Bhatia, Sai	Riverside Community College	Cone, Bill	Northern Arizona University
Bishop, Frances	DeVry Institute—Alpharetta (ATL)	Conroy-Link, Janet	Holy Family College
Blaszkiewicz, Holly	Ivy Tech Community College/Region 1	Conway, Ronald	Bowling Green State University
Boito, Nancy	HACC Central Pennsylvania's Community College	Cornforth, Carol G.	WVNCC
Borger-Boglin, Grietje L.	San Antonio College/Northeast Lakeview College	Cosgrove, Janet	Northwestern CT Community
		Courtney, Kevin	Hillsborough Community College
		Coverdale, John	Riverside Community College
Branigan, Dave	DeVry University	Cox, Rollie	Madison Area Technical College
Bray, Patricia	Allegany College of Maryland	Crawford, Hiram	Olive Harvey College
Britt, Brenda K.	Fayetteville Technical Community College	Crawford, Sonia	Central New Mexico Community College
Brotherton, Cathy	Riverside Community College	Crawford, Thomasina	Miami-Dade College, Kendall Campus
Brown, Judy	Western Illinois University	Credico, Grace	Lethbridge Community College
Buehler, Lesley	Ohlone College	Crenshaw, Richard	Miami Dade Community College, North
		Crespo, Beverly	Mt. San Antonio College

Crooks, Steven	Texas Tech University	Guthrie, Rose	Fox Valley Technical College
Crossley, Connie	Cincinnati State Technical Community College	Hahn, Norm	Thomas Nelson Community College
Curik, Mary	Central New Mexico Community College	Haley-Hunter, Deb	Bluefield State College
		Hall, Linnea	Northwest Mississippi Community College
De Arazoza, Ralph	Miami Dade Community College		
Danno, John	DeVry University/Keller Graduate School	Hammerschlag, Dr. Bill	Brookhaven College
		Hansen, Michelle	Davenport University
Davis, Phillip	Del Mar College	Hayden, Nancy	Indiana University—Purdue University, Indianapolis
Davis, Richard	Trinity Valley Community College		
Davis, Sandra	Baker College of Allen Park	Hayes, Theresa	Broward Community College
Dees, Stephanie D.	Wharton County Junior College	Headrick, Betsy	Chattanooga State
DeHerrera, Laurie	Pikes Peak Community College	Helfand, Terri	Chaffey College
Delk, Dr. K. Kay	Seminole Community College	Helms, Liz	Columbus State Community College
Denton, Bree	Texas Tech University		
Dix, Jeanette	Ivy Tech Community College	Hernandez, Leticia	TCI College of Technology
Dooly, Veronica P.	Asheville-Buncombe Technical Community College	Hibbert, Marilyn	Salt Lake Community College
		Hinds, Cheryl	Norfolk State University
Doroshow, Mike	Eastfield College	Hines, James	Tidewater Community College
Douglas, Gretchen	SUNYCortland	Hoffman, Joan	Milwaukee Area Technical College
Dove, Carol	Community College of Allegheny		
Dozier, Susan	Tidewater Community College, Virginia Beach Campus	Hogan, Pat	Cape Fear Community College
		Holland, Susan	Southeast Community College
Driskel, Loretta	Niagara Community College	Holliday, Mardi	Community College of Philadelphia
Duckwiler, Carol	Wabaunsee Community College		
Duhon, David	Baker College	Hollingsworth, Mary Carole	Georgia Perimeter College
Duncan, Mimi	University of Missouri-St. Louis	Hopson, Bonnie	Athens Technical College
Duthie, Judy	Green River Community College	Horvath, Carrie	Albertus Magnus College
Duvall, Annette	Central New Mexico Community College	Horwitz, Steve	Community College of Philadelphia
Ecklund, Paula	Duke University	Hotta, Barbara	Leeward Community College
Eilers, Albert	Cincinnati State Technical and Community College	Howard, Bunny	St. Johns River Community
		Howard, Chris	DeVry University
Eng, Bernice	Brookdale Community College	Huckabay, Jamie	Austin Community College
Epperson, Arlin	Columbia College	Hudgins, Susan	East Central University
Evans, Billie	Vance-Granville Community College	Hulett, Michelle J.	Missouri State University
		Humphrey, John	Asheville Buncombe Technical Community College
Evans, Jean	Brevard Community College		
Feuerbach, Lisa	Ivy Tech East Chicago	Hunt, Darla A.	Morehead State University, Morehead, Kentucky
Finley, Jean	ABTCC		
Fisher, Fred	Florida State University	Hunt, Laura	Tulsa Community College
Foster, Nancy	Baker College	Ivey, Joan M.	Lanier Technical College
Foster-Shriver, Penny L.	Anne Arundel Community College	Jacob, Sherry	Jefferson Community College
		Jacobs, Duane	Salt Lake Community College
Foster-Turpen, Linda	CNM	Jauken, Barb	Southeastern Community
Foszcz, Russ	McHenry County College	Jerry, Gina	Santa Monica College
Fry, Susan	Boise State University	Johnson, Deborah S.	Edison State College
Fustos, Janos	Metro State	Johnson, Kathy	Wright College
Gallup, Jeanette	Blinn College	Johnson, Mary	Kingwood College
Gelb, Janet	Grossmont College	Johnson, Mary	Mt. San Antonio College
Gentry, Barb	Parkland College	Jones, Stacey	Benedict College
Gerace, Karin	St. Angela Merici School	Jones, Warren	University of Alabama, Birmingham
Gerace, Tom	Tulane University		
Ghajar, Homa	Oklahoma State University	Jordan, Cheryl	San Juan College
Gifford, Steve	Northwest Iowa Community College	Kapoor, Bhushan	California State University, Fullerton
Glazer, Ellen	Broward Community College	Kasai, Susumu	Salt Lake Community College
Gordon, Robert	Hofstra University	Kates, Hazel	Miami Dade Community College, Kendall
Gramlich, Steven	Pasco-Hernando Community College		
		Keen, Debby	University of Kentucky
Graviett, Nancy M.	St. Charles Community College, St. Peters, Missouri	Keeter, Sandy	Seminole Community College
		Kern-Blystone, Dorothy Jean	Bowling Green State
Greene, Rich	Community College of Allegheny County	Kerwin, Annette	College of DuPage
		Keskin, Ilknur	The University of South Dakota
Gregoryk, Kerry	Virginia Commonwealth State	Kinney, Mark B.	Baker College
Griggs, Debra	Bellevue Community College	Kirk, Colleen	Mercy College
Grimm, Carol	Palm Beach Community College	Kisling, Eric	East Carolina University

Kleckner, Michelle	Elon University	Marquez, Juan	Mesa Community College
Kliston, Linda	Broward Community College, North Campus	Martin, Carol	Harrisburg Area Community College
Knuth, Toni	Baker College of Auburn Hills	Martin, Paul C.	Harrisburg Area Community College
Kochis, Dennis	Suffolk County Community College	Martyn, Margie	Baldwin-Wallace College
Kominek, Kurt	Northeast State Technical Community College	Marucco, Toni	Lincoln Land Community College
		Mason, Lynn	Lubbock Christian University
Kramer, Ed	Northern Virginia Community College	Matutis, Audrone	Houston Community College
		Matkin, Marie	University of Lethbridge
Kretz, Daniel	Fox Valley Technical College	Maurel, Trina	Odessa College
Laird, Jeff	Northeast State Community College	May, Karen	Blinn College
		McCain, Evelynn	Boise State University
Lamoureaux, Jackie	Central New Mexico Community College	McCannon, Melinda	Gordon College
		McCarthy, Marguerite	Northwestern Business College
Lange, David	Grand Valley State	McCaskill, Matt L.	Brevard Community College
LaPointe, Deb	Central New Mexico Community College	McClellan, Carolyn	Tidewater Community College
		McClure, Darlean	College of Sequoias
Larsen, Jacqueline Anne	A-B Tech	McCrory, Sue A.	Missouri State University
Larson, Donna	Louisville Technical Institute	McCue, Stacy	Harrisburg Area Community College
Laspina, Kathy	Vance-Granville Community College		
		McEntire-Orbach, Teresa	Middlesex County College
Le Grand, Dr. Kate	Broward Community College	McKinley, Lee	Georgia Perimeter College
Lenhart, Sheryl	Terra Community College	McLeod, Todd	Fresno City College
Leonard, Yvonne	Coastal Carolina Community College	McManus, Illyana	Grossmont College
		McPherson, Dori	Schoolcraft College
Letavec, Chris	University of Cincinnati	Meck, Kari	HACC
Lewis, Daphne L, Ed.D.	Wayland Baptist University	Meiklejohn, Nancy	Pikes Peak Community College
Lewis, Julie	Baker College-Allen Park	Menking, Rick	Hardin-Simmons University
Liefert, Jane	Everett Community College	Meredith, Mary	University of Louisiana at Lafayette
Lindaman, Linda	Black Hawk Community College		
Lindberg, Martha	Minnesota State University	Mermelstein, Lisa	Baruch College
Lightner, Renee	Broward Community College	Metos, Linda	Salt Lake Community College
Lindberg, Martha	Minnesota State University	Meurer, Daniel	University of Cincinnati
Linge, Richard	Arizona Western College	Meyer, Colleen	Cincinnati State Technical and Community College
Logan, Mary G.	Delgado Community College		
Loizeaux, Barbara	Westchester Community College	Meyer, Marian	Central New Mexico Community College
Lombardi, John	South University		
Lopez, Don	Clovis-State Center Community College District	Miller, Cindy	Ivy Tech Community College, Lafayette, Indiana
Lopez, Lisa	Spartanburg Community College	Mills, Robert E.	Tidewater Community College, Portsmouth Campus
Lord, Alexandria	Asheville Buncombe Tech		
Lovering, LeAnne	Augusta Technical College	Mitchell, Susan	Davenport University
Lowe, Rita	Harold Washington College	Mohle, Dennis	Fresno Community College
Low, Willy Hui	Joliet Junior College	Molki, Saeed	South Texas College
Lucas, Vickie	Broward Community College	Monk, Ellen	University of Delaware
Luna, Debbie	El Paso Community College	Moore, Rodney	Holland College
Luoma, Jean	Davenport University	Morris, Mike	Southeastern Oklahoma State University
Luse, Steven P.	Horry Georgetown Technical College		
		Morris, Nancy	Hudson Valley Community College
Lynam, Linda	Central Missouri State University		
Lyon, Lynne	Durham College	Moseler, Dan	Harrisburg Area Community College
Lyon, Pat Rajski	Tomball College		
Macarty, Matthew	University of New Hampshire	Nabors, Brent	Reedley College, Clovis Center
MacKinnon, Ruth	Georgia Southern University	Nadas, Erika	Wright College
Macon, Lisa	Valencia Community College, West Campus	Nadelman, Cindi	New England College
		Nademlynsky, Lisa	Johnson & Wales University
Machuca, Wayne	College of the Sequoias	Nagengast, Joseph	Florida Career College
Mack, Sherri	Butler County Community College	Nason, Scott	Rowan Cabarrus Community College
Madison, Dana	Clarion University		
Maguire, Trish	Eastern New Mexico University	Ncube, Cathy	University of West Florida
Malkan, Rajiv	Montgomery College	Newsome, Eloise	Northern Virginia Community College Woodbridge
Manning, David	Northern Kentucky University		
Marcus, Jacquie	Niagara Community College	Nicholls, Doreen	Mohawk Valley Community College
Marghitu, Daniela	Auburn University		
Marks, Suzanne	Bellevue Community College	Nicholson, John R.	Johnson County Community College
Marquez, Juanita	El Centro College		

Nielson, Phil	Salt Lake Community College	Singer, Noah	Tulsa Community College
Nunan, Karen L.	Northeast State Technical Community College	Singer, Steven A.	University of Hawai'i, Kapi'olani Community College
O'Neal, Lois Ann	Rogers State University	Sinha, Atin	Albany State University
Odegard, Teri	Edmonds Community College	Skolnick, Martin	Florida Atlantic University
Ogle, Gregory	North Community College	Smith, Kristi	Allegany College of Maryland
Orr, Dr. Claudia	Northern Michigan University South	Smith, Patrick	Marshall Community and Technical College
Orsburn, Glen	Fox Valley Technical College	Smith, Stella A.	Georgia Gwinnett College
Otieno, Derek	DeVry University	Smith, T. Michael	Austin Community College
Otton, Diana Hill	Chesapeake College	Smith, Tammy	Tompkins Cortland Community Collge
Oxendale, Lucia	West Virginia Institute of Technology	Smolenski, Bob	Delaware County Community College
Paiano, Frank	Southwestern College	Smolenski, Robert	Delaware Community College
Pannell, Dr. Elizabeth	Collin College	Southwell, Donald	Delta College
Patrick, Tanya	Clackamas Community College	Spangler, Candice	Columbus State
Paul, Anindya	Daytona State College	Spangler, Candice	Columbus State Community College
Peairs, Deb	Clark State Community College	Stark, Diane	Phoenix College
Perez, Kimberly	Tidewater Community College	Stedham, Vicki	St. Petersburg College, Clearwater
Porter, Joyce	Weber State University	Stefanelli, Greg	Carroll Community College
Prince, Lisa	Missouri State University-Springfield Campus	Steiner, Ester	New Mexico State University
		Stenlund, Neal	Northern Virginia Community College, Alexandria
Proietti, Kathleen	Northern Essex Community College		
Puopolo, Mike	Bunker Hill Community College	St. John, Steve	Tulsa Community College
Pusins, Delores	HCCC	Sterling, Janet	Houston Community College
Putnam, Darlene	Thomas Nelson Community College	Stoughton, Catherine	Laramie County Community College
Raghuraman, Ram	Joliet Junior College	Sullivan, Angela	Joliet Junior College
Rani, Chigurupati	BMCC/CUNY	Sullivan, Denise	Westchester Community College
Reasoner, Ted Allen	Indiana University—Purdue	Sullivan, Joseph	Joliet Junior College
Reeves, Karen	High Point University	Swart, John	Louisiana Tech University
Remillard, Debbie	New Hampshire Technical Institute	Szurek, Joseph	University of Pittsburgh at Greensburg
Rhue, Shelly	DeVry University		
Richards, Karen	Maplewoods Community College	Taff, Ann	Tulsa Community College
Richardson, Mary	Albany Technical College	Taggart, James	Atlantic Cape Community College
Rodgers, Gwen	Southern Nazarene University	Tarver, Mary Beth	Northwestern State University
Rodie, Karla	Pikes Peak Community College	Taylor, Michael	Seattle Central Community College
Roselli, Diane Maie	Harrisburg Area Community College	Terrell, Robert L.	Carson-Newman College
Ross, Dianne	University of Louisiana in Lafayette	Terry, Dariel	Northern Virginia Community College
Rousseau, Mary	Broward Community College, South		
Rovetto, Ann	Horry-Georgetown Technical College	Thangiah, Sam	Slippery Rock University
Rusin, Iwona	Baker College	Thayer, Paul	Austin Community College
Sahabi, Ahmad	Baker College of Clinton Township	Thompson, Joyce	Lehigh Carbon Community College
Samson, Dolly	Hawaii Pacific University	Thompson-Sellers, Ingrid	Georgia Perimeter College
Sams, Todd	University of Cincinnati	Tomasi, Erik	Baruch College
Sandoval, Everett	Reedley College	Toreson, Karen	Shoreline Community College
Santiago, Diana	Central New Mexico Community College	Townsend, Cynthia	Baker College
		Trifiletti, John J.	Florida Community College at Jacksonville
Sardone, Nancy	Seton Hall University		
Scafide, Jean	Mississippi Gulf Coast Community College	Trivedi, Charulata	Quinsigamond Community College, Woodbridge
Scheeren, Judy	Westmoreland County Community College	Tucker, William	Austin Community College
		Turgeon, Cheryl	Asnuntuck Community College
Scheiwe, Adolph	Joliet Junior College	Turpen, Linda	Central New Mexico Community College
Schneider, Sol	Sam Houston State University		
Schweitzer, John	Central New Mexico Community College	Upshaw, Susan	Del Mar College
		Unruh, Angela	Central Washington University
Scroggins, Michael	Southwest Missouri State University	Vanderhoof, Dr. Glenna	Missouri State University-Springfield Campus
Sedlacek, Brenda	Tidewater Community College		
Sell, Kelly	Anne Arundel Community College	Vargas, Tony	El Paso Community College
Sever, Suzanne	Northwest Arkansas Community College	Vicars, Mitzi	Hampton University
		Villarreal, Kathleen	Fresno
Sewell, John	Florida Career College	Vitrano, Mary Ellen	Palm Beach Community College
Sheridan, Rick	California State University-Chico	Vlaich-Lee, Michelle	Greenville Technical College
Silvers, Pamela	Asheville Buncombe Tech	Volker, Bonita	Tidewater Community College
Sindt, Robert G.	Johnson County Community College	Waddell, Karen	Butler Community College

Contributors continued

Wahila, Lori (Mindy)	Tompkins Cortland Community College
Wallace, Melissa	Lanier Technical College
Walters, Gary B.	Central New Mexico Community College
Waswick, Kim	Southeast Community College, Nebraska
Wavle, Sharon M.	Tompkins Cortland Community College
Webb, Nancy	City College of San Francisco
Webb, Rebecca	Northwest Arkansas Community College
Weber, Sandy	Gateway Technical College
Weissman, Jonathan	Finger Lakes Community College
Wells, Barbara E.	Central Carolina Technical College
Wells, Lorna	Salt Lake Community College
Welsh, Jean	Lansing Community College Nebraska
White, Bruce	Quinnipiac University
Willer, Ann	Solano Community College
Williams, Mark	Lane Community College
Williams, Ronald D.	Central Piedmont Community College
Wilms, Dr. G. Jan	Union University
Wilson, Kit	Red River College
Wilson, MaryLou	Piedmont Technical College
Wilson, Roger	Fairmont State University
Wimberly, Leanne	International Academy of Design and Technology
Winters, Floyd	Manatee Community College
Worthington, Paula	Northern Virginia Community College
Wright, Darrell	Shelton State Community College
Wright, Julie	Baker College
Yauney, Annette	Herkimer County Community College
Yip, Thomas	Passaic Community College
Zavala, Ben	Webster Tech
Zaboski, Maureen	University of Scranton
Zlotow, Mary Ann	College of DuPage
Zudeck, Steve	Broward Community College, North
Zullo, Matthew D.	Wake Technical Community College

About the Authors

Shelley Gaskin, Series Editor, is a professor in the Business and Computer Technology Division at Pasadena City College in Pasadena, California. She holds a bachelor's degree in Business Administration from Robert Morris College (Pennsylvania), a master's degree in Business from Northern Illinois University, and a doctorate in Adult and Community Education from Ball State University. Before joining Pasadena City College, she spent 12 years in the computer industry where she was a systems analyst, sales representative, and Director of Customer Education with Unisys Corporation. She also worked for Ernst & Young on the development of large systems applications for their clients. She has written and developed training materials for custom systems applications in both the public and private sector, and has written and edited numerous computer application textbooks.

This book is dedicated to my students, who inspire me every day.

Robert L. Ferrett recently retired as the Director of the Center for Instructional Computing at Eastern Michigan University, where he provided computer training and support to faculty. He has authored or co-authored more than 70 books on Access, PowerPoint, Excel, Publisher, WordPerfect, Windows, Word, OpenOffice, and Computer Fundamentals. He has been designing, developing, and delivering computer workshops for more than three decades. Before writing for the *GO! Series*, Bob was a series editor for the Learn Series. He has a bachelor's degree in Psychology, a master's degree in Geography, and a master's degree in Interdisciplinary Technology from Eastern Michigan University. His doctoral studies were in Instructional Technology at Wayne State University.

I'd like to dedicate this book to my wife Mary Jane,
whose constant support has been so important all these years.

Carol L. Martin is a faculty member at Harrisburg Area Community College. She holds a bachelor's degree in Secondary Education—Mathematics from Millersville (PA) University and a master's degree in Training and Development from Pennsylvania State University. For over 35 years she has instructed individuals in the use of various computer applications. She has co-authored several training manuals for use in Pennsylvania Department of Education in-service courses and has written an Outlook textbook.

This book is dedicated to my husband Ron—a constant source
of encouragement and technical support; and to my delightful
grandsons, Tony and Josh, who keep me young at heart.

Teach the Course You Want in Less Time

A Microsoft® Office textbook designed for student success!

- **Project-Based** – Students learn by creating projects that they will use in the real world.

- **Microsoft Procedural Syntax** – Steps are written to put students in the right place at the right time.

- **Teachable Moment** – Expository text is woven into the steps—at the moment students need to know it—not chunked together in a block of text that will go unread.

- **Sequential Pagination** – Students have actual page numbers instead of confusing letters and abbreviations.

Student Outcomes and Learning Objectives – Objectives are clustered around projects that result in student outcomes.

Project Activities – A project summary stated clearly and quickly.

Project Files – Clearly shows students which files are needed for the project and the names they will use to save their documents.

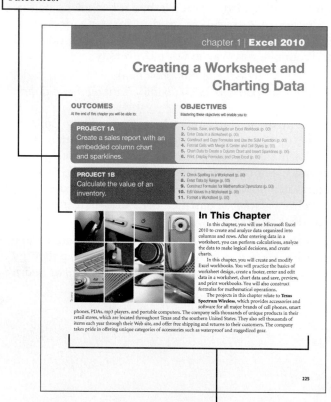

chapter 1 | **Excel 2010**

Creating a Worksheet and Charting Data

OUTCOMES
At the end of this chapter you will be able to:

OBJECTIVES
Mastering these objectives will enable you to:

PROJECT 1A
Create a sales report with an embedded column chart and sparklines.

1. Create, Save, and Navigate an Excel Workbook (p. 00)
2. Enter Data in a Worksheet (p. 00)
3. Construct and Copy Formulas and Use the SUM Function (p. 00)
4. Format Cells with Merge & Center and Cell Styles (p. 00)
5. Chart Data to Create a Column Chart and Insert Sparklines (p. 00)
6. Print, Display Formulas, and Close Excel (p. 00)

PROJECT 1B
Calculate the value of an inventory.

7. Check Spelling in a Worksheet (p. 00)
8. Enter Data by Range (p. 00)
9. Construct Formulas for Mathematical Operations (p. 00)
10. Edit Values in a Worksheet (p. 00)
11. Format a Worksheet (p. 00)

In This Chapter

In this chapter, you will use Microsoft Excel 2010 to create and analyze data organized into columns and rows. After entering data in a worksheet, you can perform calculations, analyze the data to make logical decisions, and create charts.

In this chapter, you will create and modify Excel workbooks. You will practice the basics of worksheet design, create a footer, enter and edit data in a worksheet, chart data and save, preview, and print workbooks. You will also construct formulas for mathematical operations.

The projects in this chapter relate to **Texas Spectrum Wireless**, which provides accessories and software for all major brands of cell phones, smart phones, PDAs, mp3 players, and portable computers. The company sells thousands of unique products in their retail stores, which are located throughout Texas and the southern United States. They also sell thousands of items each year through their Web site, and offer free shipping and returns to their customers. The company takes pride in offering unique categories of accessories such as waterproof and ruggedized gear.

225

Project 1A Sales Report with Embedded Column Chart and Sparklines

Project Activities

In Activities 1.01 through 1.16, you will create an Excel worksheet for Roslyn Thomas, the President of Texas Spectrum Wireless. The worksheet displays the first quarter sales of wireless accessories for the current year, and includes a chart to visually represent the data. Your completed worksheet will look similar to Figure 1.1.

Project Files

For Project 1A, you will need the following file:
New blank Excel workbook

You will save your workbook as:
Lastname_Firstname_1A_Quarterly_Sales

Project Results

Figure 1.1
Project 1A Quarterly Sales

226   Excel | Chapter 1: Creating a Worksheet and Charting Data

Scenario – Each chapter opens with a story that sets the stage for the projects the student will create.

Project Results – Shows students how their final outcome will appear.

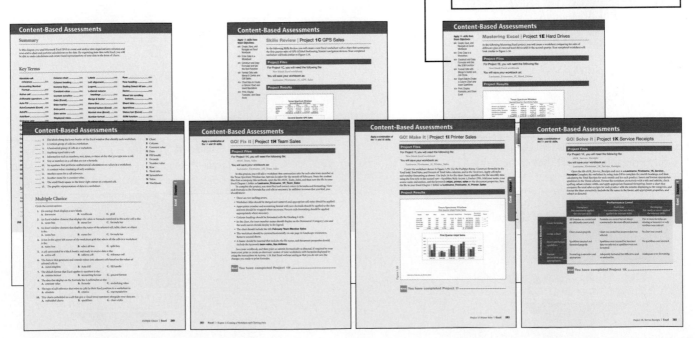

End-of-Chapter

Outcomes-Based Assessments – Assessments with open-ended solutions.

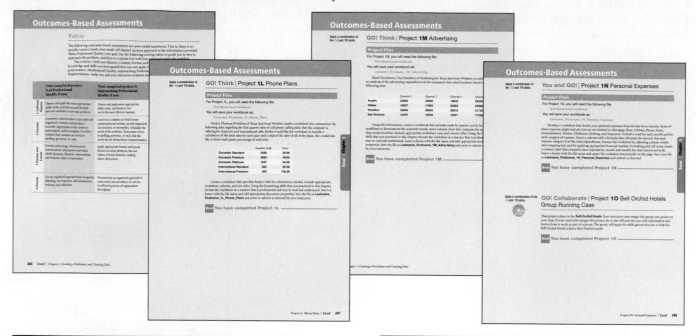

Task-Specific Rubric – A matrix specific to the **GO! Solve It** projects that states the criteria and standards for grading these defined-solution projects.

Outcomes Rubric – A matrix specific to the **GO! Think** projects that states the criteria and standards for grading these open-ended assessments.

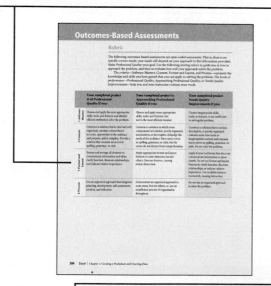

Student CD – All student data files readily available on a CD that comes with the book.

Student Videos – A visual and audio walk-through of every A and B project in the book (see sample images on following page).

Student Videos! – Each chapter comes with two videos that include audio, demonstrating the objectives and activities taught in the chapter.

Instructor Materials

All Instructor materials available on the IRCD

Annotated Instructor Edition - An instructor tool includes a full copy of the student textbook annotated with teaching tips, discussion topics, and other useful pieces for teaching each chapter.

Assignment Sheets – Lists all the assignments for the chapter. Just add in the course information, due dates, and points. Providing these to students ensures they will know what is due and when.

Scripted Lectures – Classroom lectures prepared for you.

Annotated Solution Files – Coupled with the assignment tags, these create a grading and scoring system that makes grading so much easier for you.

PowerPoint Lectures – PowerPoint presentations for each chapter.

Scoring Rubrics – Can be used either by students to check their work or by you as a quick check-off for the items that need to be corrected.

Syllabus Templates - For 8-week, 12-week, and 16-week courses.

Test Bank – Includes a variety of test questions for each chapter.

Companion Website – Online content such as the Online Study Guide, Glossary, and Student Data Files are all at **www.pearsonhighered.com/go**.

Using the Common Features of Microsoft Office 2010

OUTCOMES

At the end of this chapter you will be able to:

OBJECTIVES

Mastering these objectives will enable you to:

PROJECT 1A
Create, save, and print a Microsoft Office 2010 file.

1. Use Windows Explorer to Locate Files and Folders (p. 3)
2. Locate and Start a Microsoft Office 2010 Program (p. 6)
3. Enter and Edit Text in an Office 2010 Program (p. 9)
4. Perform Commands from a Dialog Box (p. 11)
5. Create a Folder, Save a File, and Close a Program (p. 13)
6. Add Document Properties and Print a File (p. 18)

PROJECT 1B
Use the Ribbon and dialog boxes to perform common commands in a Microsoft Office 2010 file.

7. Open an Existing File and Save It with a New Name (p. 22)
8. Explore Options for an Application (p. 25)
9. Perform Commands from the Ribbon (p. 26)
10. Apply Formatting in Office Programs (p. 32)
11. Use the Microsoft Office 2010 Help System (p. 43)
12. Compress Files (p. 44)

olly/Shutterstock

In This Chapter

In this chapter, you will use Windows Explorer to navigate the Windows folder structure, create a folder, and save files in Microsoft Office 2010 programs. You will also practice using the features of Microsoft Office 2010 that are common across the major programs that comprise the Microsoft Office 2010 suite. These common features include creating, saving, and printing files.

Common features also include the new Paste Preview and Microsoft Office Backstage view. You will apply formatting, perform commands, and compress files. You will see that creating professional-quality documents is easy and quick in Microsoft Office 2010, and that finding your way around is fast and efficient.

The projects in this chapter relate to **Oceana Palm Grill**, which is a chain of 25 casual, full-service restaurants based in Austin, Texas. The Oceana Palm Grill owners plan an aggressive expansion program. To expand by 15 additional restaurants in North Carolina and Florida by 2018, the company must attract new investors, develop new menus, and recruit new employees, all while adhering to the company's quality guidelines and maintaining its reputation for excellent service. To succeed, the company plans to build on its past success and maintain its quality elements.

Project 1A PowerPoint File

myitlab
Project 1A Training

In Activities 1.01 through 1.06, you will create a PowerPoint file, save it in a folder that you create by using Windows Explorer, and then print the file or submit it electronically as directed by your instructor. Your completed PowerPoint slide will look similar to Figure 1.1.

Project Files

For Project 1A, you will need the following file:

New blank PowerPoint presentation

You will save your file as:

Lastname_Firstname_1A_Menu_Plan

Project Results

Oceana Palm Grill Menu Plan

Prepared by Firstname Lastname
For Laura Hernandez

Figure 1.1
Project 1A Menu Plan

Objective 1 | Use Windows Explorer to Locate Files and Folders

A *file* is a collection of information stored on a computer under a single name, for example, a Word document or a PowerPoint presentation. Every file is stored in a *folder*—a container in which you store files—or a *subfolder*, which is a folder within a folder. Your Windows operating system stores and organizes your files and folders, which is a primary task of an operating system.

You *navigate*—explore within the organizing structure of Windows—to create, save, and find your files and folders by using the *Windows Explorer* program. Windows Explorer displays the files and folders on your computer, and is at work anytime you are viewing the contents of files and folders in a *window*. A window is a rectangular area on a computer screen in which programs and content appear; a window can be moved, resized, minimized, or closed.

Activity 1.01 | Using Windows Explorer to Locate Files and Folders

1 Turn on your computer and display the Windows *desktop*—the opening screen in Windows that simulates your work area.

> **Note** | Comparing Your Screen with the Figures in This Textbook
>
> Your screen will match the figures shown in this textbook if you set your screen resolution to 1024×768. At other resolutions, your screen will closely resemble, but not match, the figures shown. To view your screen's resolution, on the Windows 7 desktop, right-click in a blank area, and then click Screen resolution. In Windows Vista, right-click a blank area, click Personalize, and then click Display Settings. In Windows XP, right-click the desktop, click Properties, and then click the Settings tab.

2 In your CD/DVD tray, insert the **Student CD** that accompanies this textbook. Wait a few moments for an **AutoPlay** window to display. Compare your screen with Figure 1.2.

> *AutoPlay* is a Windows feature that lets you choose which program to use to start different kinds of media, such as music CDs, or CDs and DVDs containing photos; it displays when you plug in or insert media or storage devices.

> **Note** | If You Do Not Have the Student CD
>
> If you do not have the Student CD, consult the inside back flap of this textbook for instructions on how to download the files from the Pearson Web site.

Figure 1.2

AutoPlay window

Close button

Windows desktop (yours may vary in color and arrangement)

3 In the upper right corner of the **AutoPlay** window, move your mouse over—*point* to—the **Close** button ![close button], and then *click*—press the left button on your mouse pointing device one time.

4 On the left side of the **Windows taskbar**, click the **Start** button ⊕ to display the **Start menu**. Compare your screen with Figure 1.3.

> The *Windows taskbar* is the area along the lower edge of the desktop that contains the *Start button* and an area to display buttons for open programs. The Start button displays the *Start menu*, which provides a list of choices and is the main gateway to your computer's programs, folders, and settings.

Figure 1.3

Computer on Start menu

Start menu (your array of programs may vary)

Windows 7 taskbar

Start button

5 On the right side of the **Start menu**, click **Computer** to see the disk drives and other hardware connected to your computer. Compare your screen with Figure 1.4, and then take a moment to study the table in Figure 1.5.

> The *folder window* for *Computer* displays. A folder window displays the contents of the current folder, *library*, or device, and contains helpful parts so that you can navigate within Windows.

> In Windows 7, a library is a collection of items, such as files and folders, assembled from *various locations*; the locations might be on your computer, an external hard drive, removable media, or someone else's computer.

> The difference between a folder and a library is that a library can include files stored in *different locations*—any disk drive, folder, or other place that you can store files and folders.

Figure 1.4

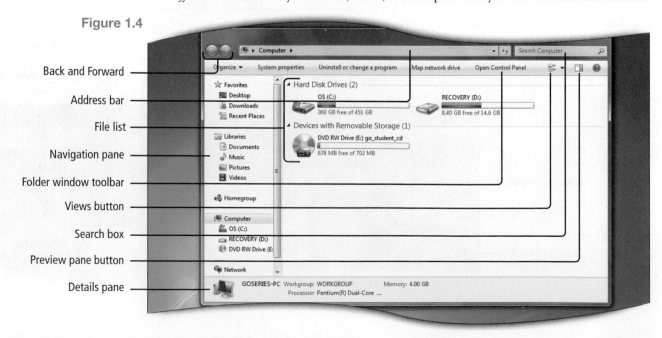

Back and Forward

Address bar

File list

Navigation pane

Folder window toolbar

Views button

Search box

Preview pane button

Details pane

Window Part	Use to:
Address bar	Navigate to a different folder or library, or go back to a previous one.
Back and Forward buttons	Navigate to other folders or libraries you have already opened without closing the current window. These buttons work in conjunction with the address bar; that is, after you use the address bar to change folders, you can use the Back button to return to the previous folder.
Details pane	Display the most common file properties—information about a file, such as the author, the date you last changed the file, and any descriptive *tags*, which are custom file properties that you create to help find and organize your files.
File list	Display the contents of the current folder or library. In Computer, the file list displays the disk drives.
Folder window for *Computer*	Display the contents of the current folder, library, or device. The Folder window contains helpful features so that you can navigate within Windows.
Folder window toolbar	Perform common tasks, such as changing the view of your files and folders or burning files to a CD. The buttons available change to display only relevant tasks.
Navigation pane	Navigate to, open, and display favorites, libraries, folders, saved searches, and an expandable list of drives.
Preview pane button	Display (if you have chosen to open this pane) the contents of most files without opening them in a program. To open the preview pane, click the Preview pane button on the toolbar to turn it on and off.
Search box	Look for an item in the current folder or library by typing a word or phrase in the search box.
Views button	Choose how to view the contents of the current location.

Figure 1.5

6 On the toolbar of the **Computer** folder window, click the **Views button arrow** —the small arrow to the right of the Views button—to display a list of views that you can apply to the file list. If necessary, on the list, click **Tiles**.

> The Views button is a *split button*; clicking the main part of the button performs a *command* and clicking the arrow opens a menu or list. A command is an instruction to a computer program that causes an action to be carried out.

> When you open a folder or a library, you can change how the files display in the file list. For example, you might prefer to see large or small *icons*—pictures that represent a program, a file, a folder, or some other object—or an arrangement that lets you see various types of information about each file. Each time you click the Views button, the window changes, cycling through several views—additional view options are available by clicking the Views button arrow.

Another Way

Point to the CD/DVD drive, right-click, and then click Open.

7 In the **file list**, under **Devices with Removable Storage**, point to your **CD/DVD Drive**, and then *double-click*—click the left mouse button two times in rapid succession—to display the list of folders on the CD. Compare your screen with Figure 1.6.

> When double-clicking, keep your hand steady between clicks; this is more important than the speed of the two clicks.

Figure 1.6

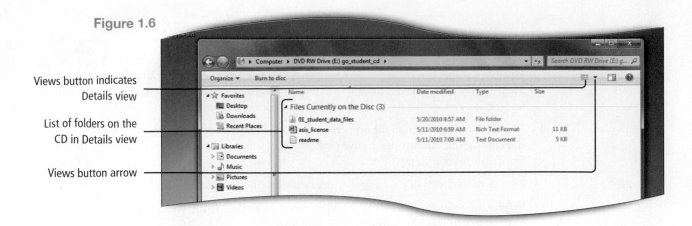

Views button indicates
Details view

List of folders on the
CD in Details view

Views button arrow

8 In the **file list**, point to the folder **01_student_data_files** and double-click to display the list of subfolders in the folder. Double-click to open the folder **01_common_features**. Compare your screen with Figure 1.7.

> The Student Resource CD includes files that you will use to complete the projects in this textbook. If you prefer, you can also copy the **01_student_data_files** folder to a location on your computer's hard drive or to a removable device such as a *USB flash drive*, which is a small storage device that plugs into a computer USB port. Your instructor might direct you to other locations where these files are located; for example, on your learning management system.

Figure 1.7

Address bar displays
sequence of folders

One folder in the
01_common_features
folder

9 In the upper right corner of the **Computer** window, click the **Close** button to redisplay your desktop.

Objective 2 | Locate and Start a Microsoft Office 2010 Program

Microsoft Office 2010 includes programs, servers, and services for individuals, small organizations, and large enterprises. A *program*, also referred to as an *application*, is a set of instructions used by a computer to perform a task, such as word processing or accounting.

Activity 1.02 | Locating and Starting a Microsoft Office 2010 Program

1 On the **Windows taskbar**, click the **Start** button to display the **Start** menu.

2 From the displayed **Start** menu, locate the group of **Microsoft Office 2010** programs on your computer—the Office program icons from which you can start the program may be located on your Start menu, in a Microsoft Office folder on the **All Programs** list, on your desktop, or any combination of these locations; the location will vary depending on how your computer is configured.

> *All Programs* is an area of the Start menu that displays all the available programs on your computer system.

3 Examine Figure 1.8, and notice the programs that are included in the Microsoft Office Professional Plus 2010 group of programs. (Your group of programs may vary.)

> *Microsoft Word* is a word processing program, with which you create and share documents by using its writing tools.

> *Microsoft Excel* is a spreadsheet program, with which you calculate and analyze numbers and create charts.

> *Microsoft Access* is a database program, with which you can collect, track, and report data.

> *Microsoft PowerPoint* is a presentation program, with which you can communicate information with high-impact graphics and video.

> Additional popular Office programs include *Microsoft Outlook* to manage e-mail and organizational activities, *Microsoft Publisher* to create desktop publishing documents such as brochures, and *Microsoft OneNote* to manage notes that you make at meetings or in classes and to share notes with others on the Web.

> The Professional Plus version of Office 2010 also includes *Microsoft SharePoint Workspace* to share information with others in a team environment and *Microsoft InfoPath Designer and Filler* to create forms and gather data.

Figure 1.8

All Programs menu

Microsoft Office folder

Programs in Microsoft
Office (your list may vary)

4 Click to open the program **Microsoft PowerPoint 2010**. Compare your screen with Figure 1.9, and then take a moment to study the description of these screen elements in the table in Figure 1.10.

Figure 1.9

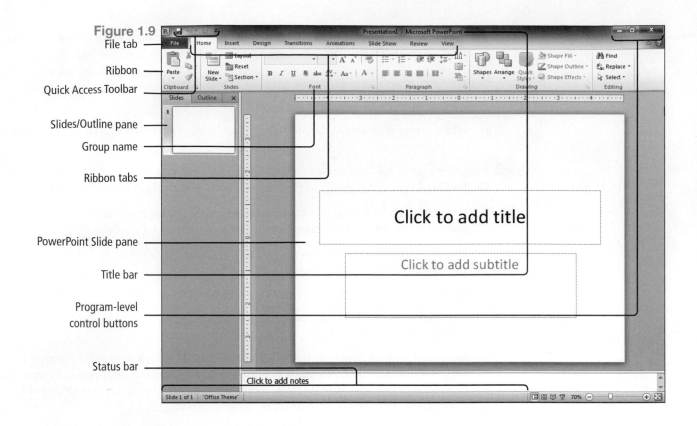

File tab
Ribbon
Quick Access Toolbar
Slides/Outline pane
Group name
Ribbon tabs
PowerPoint Slide pane
Title bar
Program-level control buttons
Status bar

Click to add title

Click to add subtitle

Click to add notes

Screen Element	Description
File tab	Displays Microsoft Office Backstage view, which is a centralized space for all of your file management tasks such as opening, saving, printing, publishing, or sharing a file—all the things you can do *with* a file.
Group names	Indicate the name of the groups of related commands on the displayed tab.
PowerPoint Slide pane	Displays a large image of the active slide in the PowerPoint program.
Program-level control buttons	Minimizes, restores, or closes the program window.
Quick Access Toolbar	Displays buttons to perform frequently used commands and resources with a single click. The default commands include Save, Undo, and Redo. You can add and delete buttons to customize the Quick Access Toolbar for your convenience.
Ribbon	Displays a group of task-oriented tabs that contain the commands, styles, and resources you need to work in an Office 2010 program. The look of your Ribbon depends on your screen resolution. A high resolution will display more individual items and button names on the Ribbon.
Ribbon tabs	Display the names of the task-oriented tabs relevant to the open program.
Slides/Outline pane	Displays either thumbnails of the slides in a PowerPoint presentation (Slides tab) or the outline of the presentation's content (Outline tab). In each Office 2010 program, different panes display in different ways to assist you.
Status bar	Displays file information on the left and View and Zoom on the right.
Title bar	Displays the name of the file and the name of the program. The program window control buttons—Minimize, Maximize/Restore Down, and Close—are grouped on the right side of the title bar.

Figure 1.10

Objective 3 | Enter and Edit Text in an Office 2010 Program

All of the programs in Office 2010 require some typed text. Your keyboard is still the primary method of entering information into your computer. Techniques to **edit**—make changes to—text are similar among all of the Office 2010 programs.

Activity 1.03 | Entering and Editing Text in an Office 2010 Program

1 In the middle of the PowerPoint Slide pane, point to the text *Click to add title* to display the [I] pointer, and then click one time.

The ***insertion point***—a blinking vertical line that indicates where text or graphics will be inserted—displays.

In Office 2010 programs, the mouse ***pointer***—any symbol that displays on your screen in response to moving your mouse device—displays in different shapes depending on the task you are performing and the area of the screen to which you are pointing.

2 Type **Oceana Grille Info** and notice how the insertion point moves to the right as you type. Point slightly to the right of the letter *e* in *Grille* and click to place the insertion point there. Compare your screen with Figure 1.11.

Figure 1.11

Insertion point

3 On your keyboard, locate and press the [Backspace] key to delete the letter *e*.

Pressing [Backspace] removes a character to the left of the insertion point.

4 Point slightly to the left of the *I* in *Info* and click one time to place the insertion point there. Type **Menu** and then press [Spacebar] one time. Compare your screen with Figure 1.12.

By ***default***, when you type text in an Office program, existing text moves to the right to make space for new typing. Default refers to the current selection or setting that is automatically used by a program unless you specify otherwise.

Figure 1.12

Menu inserted

5 Press [Del] four times to delete *Info* and then type **Plan**

> Pressing [Del] removes—deletes—a character to the right of the insertion point.

6 With your insertion point blinking after the word *Plan*, on your keyboard, hold down the [Ctrl] key. While holding down [Ctrl], press [←] three times to move the insertion point to the beginning of the word *Grill*.

> This is a **keyboard shortcut**—a key or combination of keys that performs a task that would otherwise require a mouse. This keyboard shortcut moves the insertion point to the beginning of the previous word.

> A keyboard shortcut is commonly indicated as [Ctrl] + [←] (or some other combination of keys) to indicate that you hold down the first key while pressing the second key. A keyboard shortcut can also include three keys, in which case you hold down the first two and then press the third. For example, [Ctrl] + [Shift] + [←] selects one word to the left.

7 With the insertion point blinking at the beginning of the word *Grill*, type **Palm** and press [Spacebar].

8 Click anywhere in the text *Click to add subtitle*. With the insertion point blinking, type the following and include the spelling error: **Prepered by Annabel Dunham**

9 With your mouse, point slightly to the left of the *A* in *Annabel*, hold down the left mouse button, and then **drag**—hold down the left mouse button while moving your mouse—to the right to select the text *Annabel Dunham*, and then release the mouse button. Compare your screen with Figure 1.13.

> The **Mini toolbar** displays commands that are commonly used with the selected object, which places common commands close to your pointer. When you move the pointer away from the Mini toolbar, it fades from view.

> To **select** refers to highlighting, by dragging with your mouse, areas of text or data or graphics so that the selection can be edited, formatted, copied, or moved. The action of dragging includes releasing the left mouse button at the end of the area you want to select. The Office programs recognize a selected area as one unit, to which you can make changes. Selecting text may require some practice. If you are not satisfied with your result, click anywhere outside of the selection, and then begin again.

Figure 1.13

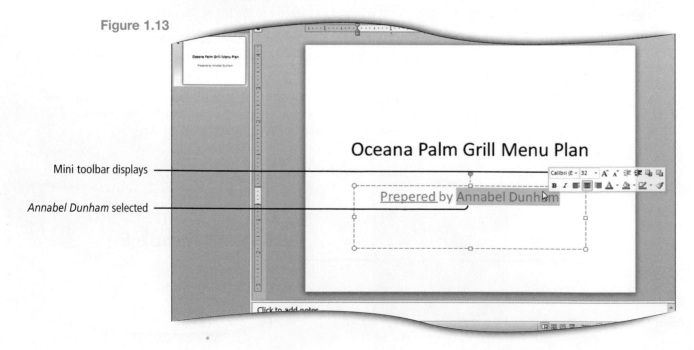

Mini toolbar displays

Annabel Dunham selected

10 With the text *Annabel Dunham* selected, type your own firstname and lastname.

In any Windows-based program, such as the Microsoft Office 2010 programs, selected text is deleted and then replaced when you begin to type new text. You will save time by developing good techniques to select and then edit or replace selected text, which is easier than pressing the [Del] key numerous times to delete text that you do not want.

11 Notice that the misspelled word *Prepered* displays with a wavy red underline; additionally, all or part of your name might display with a wavy red underline.

Office 2010 has a dictionary of words against which all entered text is checked. In Word and PowerPoint, words that are *not* in the dictionary display a wavy red line, indicating a possible misspelled word or a proper name or an unusual word—none of which are in the Office 2010 dictionary.

In Excel and Access, you can initiate a check of the spelling, but wavy red underlines do not display.

12 Point to *Prepered* and then ***right-click***—click your right mouse button one time.

The Mini toolbar and a ***shortcut menu*** display. A shortcut menu displays commands and options relevant to the selected text or object—known as ***context-sensitive commands*** because they relate to the item you right-clicked.

Here, the shortcut menu displays commands related to the misspelled word. You can click the suggested correct spelling *Prepared*, click Ignore All to ignore the misspelling, add the word to the Office dictionary, or click Spelling to display a ***dialog box***. A dialog box is a small window that contains options for completing a task. Whenever you see a command followed by an ***ellipsis*** (…), which is a set of three dots indicating incompleteness, clicking the command will always display a dialog box.

13 On the displayed shortcut menu, click **Prepared** to correct the misspelled word. If necessary, point to any parts of your name that display a wavy red underline, right-click, and then on the shortcut menu, click Ignore All so that Office will no longer mark your name with a wavy underline in this file.

More Knowledge | **Adding to the Office Dictionary**

The main dictionary contains the most common words, but does not include all proper names, technical terms, or acronyms. You can add words, acronyms, and proper names to the Office dictionary by clicking Add to Dictionary when they are flagged, and you might want to do so for your own name and other proper names and terms that you type often.

Objective 4 | Perform Commands from a Dialog Box

In a dialog box, you make decisions about an individual object or topic. A dialog box also offers a way to adjust a number of settings at one time.

Activity 1.04 | Performing Commands from a Dialog Box

1 Point anywhere in the blank area above the title *Oceana Palm Grill Menu Plan* to display the ⬚ pointer.

2 Right-click to display a shortcut menu. Notice the command *Format Background* followed by an ellipsis (…). Compare your screen with Figure 1.14.

Recall that a command followed by an ellipsis indicates that a dialog box will display if you click the command.

Figure 1.14

Shortcut menu ⎯⎯⎯⎯

Ellipsis following command ⎯⎯⎯⎯

3 Click **Format Background** to display the **Format Background** dialog box, and then compare your screen with Figure 1.15.

Figure 1.15

Fill selected ⎯⎯⎯⎯

Format Background dialog box ⎯⎯⎯⎯

Options related to the background fill ⎯⎯⎯⎯

4 On the left, if necessary, click **Fill** to display the **Fill** options.

Fill is the inside color of an object. Here, the dialog box displays the option group names on the left; some dialog boxes provide a set of tabs across the top from which you can display different sets of options.

5 On the right, under **Fill**, click the **Gradient fill** option button.

The dialog box displays additional settings related to the gradient fill option. An *option button* is a round button that enables you to make one choice among two or more options. In a gradient fill, one color fades into another.

6 Click the **Preset colors arrow**—the arrow in the box to the right of the text *Preset colors*—and then in the gallery, in the second row, point to the fifth fill color to display the ScreenTip *Fog*.

A *gallery* is an Office feature that displays a list of potential results. A *ScreenTip* displays useful information about mouse actions, such as pointing to screen elements or dragging.

7 Click **Fog**, and then notice that the fill color is applied to your slide. Click the **Type arrow**, and then click **Rectangular** to change the pattern of the fill color. Compare your screen with Figure 1.16.

Figure 1.16

Gradient fill option
button selected

Rectangular displays

Close button

8 At the bottom of the dialog box, click **Close**.

> As you progress in your study of Microsoft Office, you will practice using many dialog boxes and applying dramatic effects such as this to your Word documents, Excel spreadsheets, Access databases, and PowerPoint slides.

Objective 5 | Create a Folder, Save a File, and Close a Program

A *location* is any disk drive, folder, or other place in which you can store files and folders. Where you store your files depends on how and where you use your data. For example, for your classes, you might decide to store primarily on a removable USB flash drive so that you can carry your files to different locations and access your files on different computers.

If you do most of your work on a single computer, for example your home desktop system or your laptop computer that you take with you to school or work, store your files in one of the Libraries—Documents, Music, Pictures, or Videos—provided by your Windows operating system.

Although the Windows operating system helps you to create and maintain a logical folder structure, take the time to name your files and folders in a consistent manner.

Activity 1.05 | Creating a Folder, Saving a File, and Closing a Program

A PowerPoint presentation is an example of a file. Office 2010 programs use a common dialog box provided by the Windows operating system to assist you in saving files. In this activity, you will create a folder on a USB flash drive in which to store files. If you prefer to store on your hard drive, you can use similar steps to store files in your My Documents folder in your Documents library.

1 Insert a USB flash drive into your computer, and if necessary, **Close** [x] the **AutoPlay** dialog box. If you are not using a USB flash drive, go to Step 2.

> As the first step in saving a file, determine where you want to save the file, and if necessary, insert a storage device.

2 At the top of your screen, in the title bar, notice that *Presentation1 – Microsoft PowerPoint* displays.

> Most Office 2010 programs open with a new unsaved file with a default name—*Presentation1*, *Document1*, and so on. As you create your file, your work is temporarily stored in the computer's memory until you initiate a Save command, at which time you must choose a file name and location in which to save your file.

3 In the upper left corner of your screen, click the **File tab** to display **Microsoft Office Backstage** view. Compare your screen with Figure 1.17.

> Microsoft Office *Backstage view* is a centralized space for tasks related to *file* management; that is why the tab is labeled *File*. File management tasks include, for example, opening, saving, printing, publishing, or sharing a file. The *Backstage tabs*—*Info*, *Recent*, *New*, *Print*, *Save & Send*, and *Help*—display along the left side. The tabs group file-related tasks together.

> Above the Backstage tabs, *Quick Commands*—*Save*, *Save As*, *Open*, and *Close*—display for quick access to these commands. When you click any of these commands, Backstage view closes and either a dialog box displays or the active file closes.

> Here, the *Info tab* displays information—*info*—about the current file. In the center panel, various file management tasks are available in groups. For example, if you click the Protect Presentation button, a list of options that you can set for this file that relate to who can open or edit the presentation displays.

> On the Info tab, in the right panel, you can also examine the *document properties*. Document properties, also known as *metadata*, are details about a file that describe or identify it, such as the title, author name, subject, and keywords that identify the document's topic or contents. On the Info page, a thumbnail image of the current file displays in the upper right corner, which you can click to close Backstage view and return to the document.

More Knowledge | Deciding Where to Store Your Files

Where should you store your files? In the libraries created by Windows 7 (Documents, Pictures, and so on)? On a removable device like a flash drive or external hard drive? In Windows 7, it is easy to find your files, especially if you use the libraries. Regardless of where you save a file, Windows 7 will make it easy to find the file again, even if you are not certain where it might be.

In Windows 7, storing all of your files within a library makes sense. If you perform most of your work on your desktop system or your laptop that travels with you, you can store your files in the libraries created by Windows 7 for your user account—Documents, Pictures, Music, and so on. Within these libraries, you can create folders and subfolders to organize your data. These libraries are a good choice for storing your files because:

- From the Windows Explorer button on the taskbar, your libraries are always just one click away.
- The libraries are designed for their contents; for example, the Pictures folder displays small images of your digital photos.
- You can add new locations to a library; for example, an external hard drive, or a network drive. Locations added to a library behave just like they are on your hard drive.
- Other users of your computer cannot access your libraries.
- The libraries are the default location for opening and saving files within an application, so you will find that you can open and save files with fewer navigation clicks.

Figure 1.17

Save command

Information about the
file you are working on

Info tab selected

Backstage tabs,
Info tab active

Groups

Indicates unsaved file
with default name

Document Properties

Screen thumbnail

4 Above the **Backstage tabs**, click **Save** to display the **Save As** dialog box.

Backstage view closes and the Save As dialog box, which includes a folder window and an area at the bottom to name the file and set the file type, displays.

When you are saving something for the first time, for example a new PowerPoint presentation, the Save and Save As commands are identical. That is, the Save As dialog box will display if you click Save or if you click Save As.

> **Note** | Saving Your File
>
> After you have named a file and saved it in your desired location, the Save command saves any changes you make to the file without displaying any dialog box. The Save As command will display the Save As dialog box and let you name and save a new file based on the current one—in a location that you choose. After you name and save the new document, the original document closes, and the new document—based on the original one—displays.

5 In the **Save As** dialog box, on the left, locate the **navigation pane**; compare your screen with Figure 1.18.

By default, the Save command opens the Documents library unless your default file location has been changed.

Figure 1.18

Save As dialog box
Address bar

Default save location

Navigation pane

File list (yours will vary)

File name box

Save as type defaults to
PowerPoint Presentation

6 On the right side of the **navigation pane**, point to the **scroll bar**. Compare your screen with Figure 1.19.

A *scroll bar* displays when a window, or a pane within a window, has information that is not in view. You can click the up or down scroll arrows—or the left and right scroll arrows in a horizontal scroll bar—to scroll the contents up or down or left and right in small increments.

You can also drag the *scroll box*—the box within the scroll bar—to scroll the window in either direction.

Figure 1.19

Vertical scroll arrows
Vertical scroll box
Vertical scroll bar
Horizontal scroll bar
Horizontal scroll arrows
Horizontal scroll box

7 Click the **down scroll arrow** as necessary so that you can view the lower portion of the **navigation pane**, and then click the icon for your USB flash drive. Compare your screen with Figure 1.20. (If you prefer to store on your computer's hard drive instead of a USB flash drive, in the navigation pane, click Documents.)

Figure 1.20

Drive letter of your USB flash drive (yours will vary)
New folder button
File list on USB flash drive (yours may contain files or folders)
USB flash drive selected (yours will vary)

8 On the toolbar, click the **New folder** button.

In the file list, a new folder is created, and the text *New folder* is selected.

9 Type **Common Features Chapter 1** and press [Enter]. Compare your screen with Figure 1.21.

In Windows-based programs, the [Enter] key confirms an action.

Figure 1.21

New folder

10 In the **file list**, double-click the name of your new folder to open it and display its name in the **address bar**.

11 In the lower portion of the dialog box, click in the **File name** box to select the existing text. Notice that Office inserts the text at the beginning of the presentation as a suggested file name.

12 On your keyboard, locate the ⃞ key. Notice that the Shift of this key produces the underscore character. With the text still selected, type **Lastname_Firstname_1A_ Menu_Plan** Compare your screen with Figure 1.22.

> You can use spaces in file names, however some individuals prefer not to use spaces. Some programs, especially when transferring files over the Internet, may not work well with spaces in file names. In general, however, unless you encounter a problem, it is OK to use spaces. In this textbook, underscores are used instead of spaces in file names.

Figure 1.22

File name box indicates your file name

Save as type box indicates *PowerPoint Presentation*

Save button

13 In the lower right corner, click **Save**; or press ⃞Enter⃞. See Figure 1.23.

> Your new file name displays in the title bar, indicating that the file has been saved to a location that you have specified.

Figure 1.23

File name in title bar

14 In the text that begins *Prepared by*, click to position the insertion point at the end of your name, and then press ⃞Enter⃞ to move to a new line. Type **For Laura Hernandez**

15 Click the **File tab** to display **Backstage** view. At the top of the center panel, notice that the path where your file is stored displays. Above the Backstage tabs, click **Close** to close the file. In the message box, click **Save** to save the changes you made and close the file. Leave PowerPoint open.

> PowerPoint displays a message asking if you want to save the changes you have made. Because you have made additional changes to the file since your last Save operation, an Office program will always prompt you to save so that you do not lose any new data.

Objective 6 | Add Document Properties and Print a File

The process of printing a file is similar in all of the Office applications. There are differences in the types of options you can select. For example, in PowerPoint, you have the option of printing the full slide, with each slide printing on a full sheet of paper, or of printing handouts with small pictures of slides on a page.

Activity 1.06 | Adding Document Properties and Printing a File

> **Alert! | Are You Printing or Submitting Your Files Electronically?**
>
> If you are submitting your files electronically only, or have no printer attached, you can still complete this activity. Complete Steps 1-9, and then submit your file electronically as directed by your instructor.

1 In the upper left corner, click the **File tab** to display **Backstage** view. Notice that the **Recent tab** displays.

> Because no file was open in PowerPoint, Office applies predictive logic to determine that your most likely action will be to open a PowerPoint presentation that you worked on recently. Thus, the Recent tab displays a list of PowerPoint presentations that were recently open on your system.

2 At the top of the **Recent Presentations** list, click your **Lastname_Firstname_1A_ Menu_Plan** file to open it.

3 Click the **File tab** to redisplay **Backstage** view. On the right, under the screen thumbnail, click **Properties**, and then click **Show Document Panel**. In the **Author** box, delete the existing text, and then type your firstname and lastname. Notice that in PowerPoint, some variation of the slide title is automatically inserted in the Title box. In the **Subject** box, type your Course name and section number. In the **Keywords** box, type **menu plan** and then in the upper right corner of the **Document Properties** panel, click the **Close the Document Information Panel** button ⊠.

> Adding properties to your documents will make them easier to search for in systems such as Microsoft SharePoint.

Another Way

Press Ctrl + P or Ctrl + F2 to display the Print tab in Backstage view.

4 Redisplay **Backstage** view, and then click the **Print tab**. Compare your screen with Figure 1.24.

> On the Print tab in Backstage view, in the center panel, three groups of printing-related tasks display—Print, Printer, and Settings. In the right panel, the *Print Preview* displays, which is a view of a document as it will appear on the paper when you print it.

> At the bottom of the Print Preview area, on the left, the number of pages and arrows with which you can move among the pages in Print Preview display. On the right, *Zoom* settings enable you to shrink or enlarge the Print Preview. Zoom is the action of increasing or decreasing the viewing area of the screen.

Figure 1.24

Your default printer
(yours may differ)

Three groups of
printing-related tasks:
Print, Printer, Settings

Print tab selected
in Backstage view

Print Preview (yours may
display in shades of gray if a
non-color printer is attached)

Color (yours may
differ if a non-color
printer is attached)

Zoom tools

Page navigation arrows

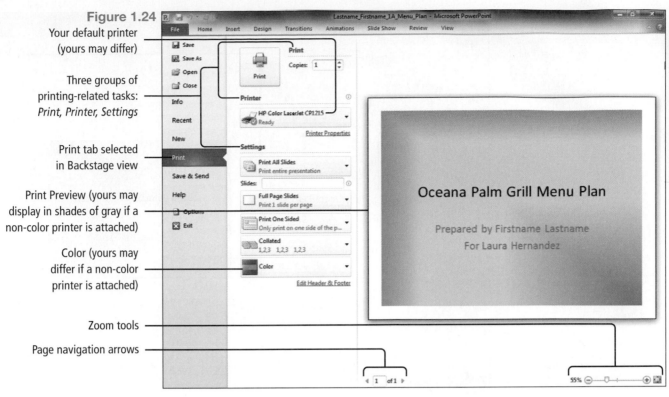

5 Locate the **Settings group**, and notice that the default setting is to **Print All Slides** and to print **Full Page Slides**—each slide on a full sheet of paper.

6 Point to **Full Page Slides**, notice that the button glows orange, and then click the button to display a gallery of print arrangements. Compare your screen with Figure 1.25.

Figure 1.25

Gallery of possible
print arrangements

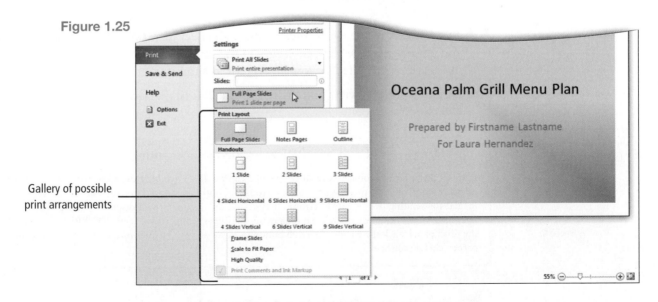

7 In the displayed gallery, under **Handouts**, click **1 Slide**, and then compare your screen with Figure 1.26.

The Print Preview changes to show how your slide will print on the paper in this arrangement.

Figure 1.26

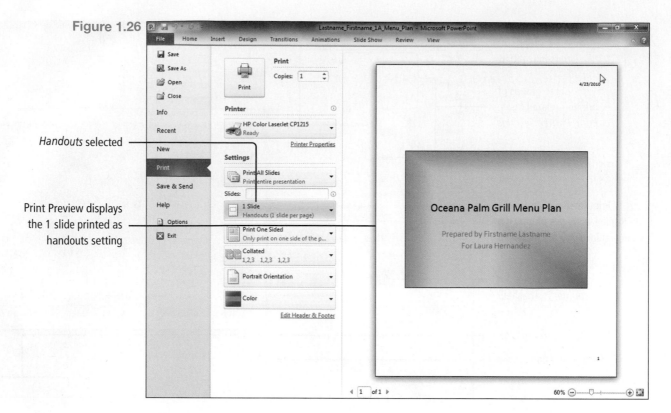

Handouts selected

Print Preview displays
the 1 slide printed as
handouts setting

8 To submit your file electronically, skip this step and move to Step 9. To print your slide, be sure your system is connected to a printer, and then in the **Print group**, click the **Print** button. On the Quick Access Toolbar, click **Save** 🔲, and then move to Step 10.

> The handout will print on your default printer—on a black and white printer, the colors will print in shades of gray. Backstage view closes and your file redisplays in the PowerPoint window.

9 To submit your file electronically, above the **Backstage tabs**, click **Close** to close the file and close **Backstage** view, click **Save** in the displayed message, and then follow the instructions provided by your instructor to submit your file electronically.

Another Way

In the upper right corner of your PowerPoint window, click the red Close button.

10 Display **Backstage** view, and then below the **Backstage tabs**, click **Exit** to close your file and close PowerPoint.

More Knowledge | Creating a PDF as an Electronic Printout

From Backstage view, you can save an Office file as a **PDF file**. **Portable Document Format** (PDF) creates an image of your file that preserves the look of your file, but that cannot be easily changed. This is a popular format for sending documents electronically, because the document will display on most computers. From Backstage view, click Save & Send, and then in the File Types group, click Create PDF/XPS Document. Then in the third panel, click the Create PDF/XPS button, navigate to your chapter folder, and then in the lower right corner, click Publish.

End **You have completed Project 1A** ————————————————

Project 1B Word File

Project Activities

In Activities 1.07 through 1.16, you will open, edit, save, and then compress a Word file. Your completed document will look similar to Figure 1.27.

Project Files

For Project 1B, you will need the following file:

cf01B_Cheese_Promotion

You will save your Word document as:

Lastname_Firstname_1B_Cheese_Promotion

Project Results

Memo

TO: Laura Mabry Hernandez, General Manager

FROM: Donna Jackson, Executive Chef

DATE: December 17, 2014

SUBJECT: Cheese Specials on Tuesdays

To increase restaurant traffic between 4:00 p.m. and 6:00 p.m., I am proposing a trial cheese event in one of the restaurants, probably Orlando. I would like to try a weekly event on Tuesday evenings where the focus is on a good selection of cheese.

I envision two possibilities: a selection of cheese plates or a cheese bar—or both. The cheeses would have to be matched with compatible fruit and bread or crackers. They could be used as appetizers, or for desserts, as is common in Europe. The cheese plates should be varied and diverse, using a mixture of hard and soft, sharp and mild, unusual and familiar.

I am excited about this new promotion. If done properly, I think it could increase restaurant traffic in the hours when individuals want to relax with a small snack instead of a heavy dinner.

The promotion will require that our employees become familiar with the types and characteristics of both foreign and domestic cheeses. Let's meet to discuss the details and the training requirements, and to create a flyer that begins something like this:

Oceana Palm Grill Tuesday Cheese Tastings

Lastname_Firstname_1B_Cheese_Promotion

Figure 1.27
Project 1B Cheese Promotion

Objective 7 | Open an Existing File and Save It with a New Name

In any Office program, use the Open command to display the *Open dialog box*, from which you can navigate to and then open an existing file that was created in that same program.

The Open dialog box, along with the Save and Save As dialog boxes, are referred to as *common dialog boxes*. These dialog boxes, which are provided by the Windows programming interface, display in all of the Office programs in the same manner. Thus, the Open, Save, and Save As dialog boxes will all look and perform the same in each Office program.

Activity 1.07 | Opening an Existing File and Saving it with a New Name

In this activity, you will display the Open dialog box, open an existing Word document, and then save it in your storage location with a new name.

1 Determine the location of the student data files that accompany this textbook, and be sure you can access these files.

> For example:
>
> If you are accessing the files from the Student CD that came with this textbook, insert the CD now.
>
> If you copied the files from the Student CD or from the Pearson Web site to a USB flash drive that you are using for this course, insert the flash drive in your computer now.
>
> If you copied the files to the hard drive of your computer, for example in your Documents library, be sure you can locate the files on the hard drive.

2 Determine the location of your **Common Features Chapter 1** folder you created in Activity 1.05, in which you will store your work from this chapter, and then be sure you can access that folder.

> For example:
>
> If you created your chapter folder on a USB flash drive, insert the flash drive in your computer now. This can be the same flash drive where you have stored the student data files; just be sure to use the chapter folder you created.
>
> If you created your chapter folder in the Documents library on your computer, be sure you can locate the folder. Otherwise, create a new folder at the computer at which you are working, or on a USB flash drive.

3 Using the technique you practiced in Activity 1.02, locate and then start the **Microsoft Word 2010** program on your system.

> **Another Way**
>
> In the Word (or other program) window, press Ctrl + F12 to display the Open dialog box.

4 On the Ribbon, click the **File tab** to display **Backstage** view, and then click **Open** to display the **Open** dialog box.

5 In the **navigation pane** on the left, use the scroll bar to scroll as necessary, and then click the location of your student data files to display the location's contents in the **file list**. Compare your screen with Figure 1.28.

> For example:
>
> If you are accessing the files from the Student CD that came with your book, under Computer, click the CD/DVD.
>
> If you are accessing the files from a USB flash drive, under Computer, click the flash drive name.
>
> If you are accessing the files from the Documents library of your computer, under Libraries, click Documents.

Figure 1.28

Open dialog box

Scroll bar in
navigation pane

Navigation pane

CD/DVD selected
(or location of your
student files)

Another Way

Point to a folder name,
right-click, and then
from the shortcut
menu, click Open.

6 Point to the folder **01_student_data_files** and double-click to open the folder. Point
to the subfolder **01_common_features**, double-click, and then compare your screen
with Figure 1.29.

Figure 1.29

File list displays
the contents of the
01_common_features folder

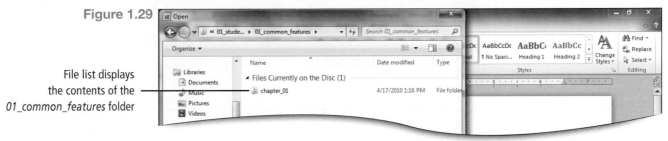

Another Way

Click one time to select
the file, and then press
Enter or click the Open
button in the lower
right corner of the
dialog box.

7 In the **file list**, point to the **chapter_01** subfolder and double-click to open it. In the
file list, point to Word file **cf01B_Cheese_Promotion** and then double-click to open
and display the file in the Word window. On the Ribbon, on the **Home tab**, in the
Paragraph group, if necessary, click the **Show/Hide** button ¶ so that it is active—
glowing orange. Compare your screen with Figure 1.30.

On the title bar at the top of the screen, the file name displays. If you opened the document
from the Student CD, (*Read-Only*) will display. If you opened the document from another
source to which the files were copied, (*Read-Only*) might not display. ***Read-Only*** is a property
assigned to a file that prevents the file from being modified or deleted; it indicates that you
cannot save any changes to the displayed document unless you first save it with a new name.

Figure 1.30

File name displays in the
title bar (*Read-only* will
display if opened from
the CD)

Show/Hide button active

Word document displays
in the Word window

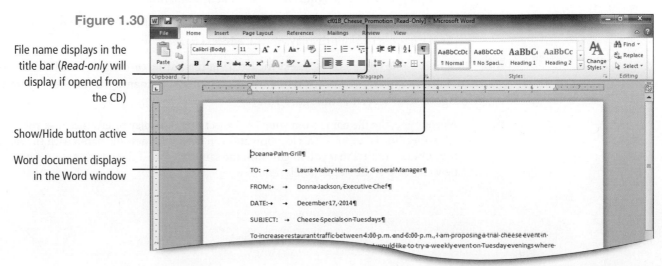

Alert! | Do You See a Message to Enable Editing or Enable Content?

In Office 2010, some files open in *Protected View* if the file appears to be from a potentially risky location, such as the Internet. Protected View is a new security feature in Office 2010 that protects your computer from malicious files by opening them in a restricted environment until you enable them. *Trusted Documents* is another security feature that remembers which files you have already enabled. You might encounter these security features if you open a file from an e-mail or download files from the Internet; for example, from your college's learning management system or from the Pearson Web site. So long as you trust the source of the file, click Enable Editing or Enable Content—depending on the type of file you receive—and then go ahead and work with the file.

Another Way

Press F12 to display the Save As dialog box.

8 Click the **File tab** to display **Backstage** view, and then click the **Save As** command to display the **Save As** dialog box. Compare your screen with Figure 1.31.

The Save As command displays the Save As dialog box where you can name and save a *new* document based on the currently displayed document. After you name and save the new document, the original document closes, and the new document—based on the original one—displays.

Figure 1.31

Save As dialog box

Navigation pane

Current file name selected

Default type is *Word Document*

9 In the **navigation pane**, click the location in which you are storing your projects for this chapter—the location where you created your **Common Features Chapter 1** folder; for example, your USB flash drive or the Documents library.

10 In the **file list**, double-click the necessary folders and subfolders until your **Common Features Chapter 1** folder displays in the **address bar**.

11 Click in the **File name** box to select the existing file name, or drag to select the existing text, and then using your own name, type **Lastname_Firstname_1B_Cheese_Promotion** Compare your screen with Figure 1.32.

As you type, the file name from your 1A project might display briefly. Because your 1A project file is stored in this location and you began the new file name with the same text, Office predicts that you might want the same or similar file name. As you type new characters, the suggestion is removed.

Figure 1.32

Your folder name in
address bar

File name box displays
your new file name

Save button

12 In the lower right corner of the **Save As** dialog box, click **Save**; or press Enter. Compare
your screen with Figure 1.33.

> The original document closes, and your new document, based on the original, displays
> with the name in the title bar.

Figure 1.33

New document
name in title bar

Insertion point at
beginning of document

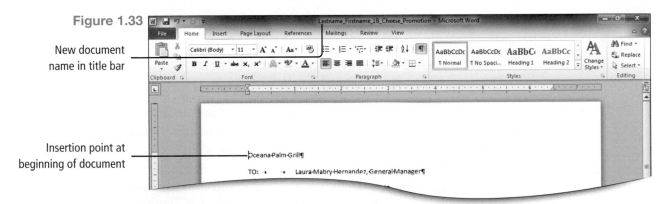

Objective 8 | Explore Options for an Application

Within each Office application, you can open an ***Options dialog box*** where you can
select program settings and other options and preferences. For example, you can set
preferences for viewing and editing files.

Activity 1.08 | Viewing Application Options

1 Click the **File tab** to display **Backstage** view. Under the **Help tab**, click **Options**.

2 In the displayed **Word Options** dialog box, on the left, click **Display**, and then on the
right, locate the information under **Always show these formatting marks on the screen**.

> When you press Enter, Spacebar, or Tab on your keyboard, characters display to represent
> these keystrokes. These screen characters do not print, and are referred to as ***formatting
> marks*** or ***nonprinting characters***.

3 Under **Always show these formatting marks on the screen**, be sure the last check box, **Show all formatting marks**, is selected—select it if necessary. Compare your screen with Figure 1.34.

Figure 1.34

Word Options dialog box

Display selected

Information about formatting marks

Check box selected

4 In the lower right corner of the dialog box, click **OK**.

Objective 9 | Perform Commands from the Ribbon

The **Ribbon**, which displays across the top of the program window, groups commands and features in a manner that you would most logically use them. Each Office program's Ribbon is slightly different, but all contain the same three elements: *tabs*, *groups*, and *commands*.

Tabs display across the top of the Ribbon, and each tab relates to a type of activity; for example, laying out a page. Groups are sets of related commands for specific tasks. Commands—instructions to computer programs—are arranged in groups, and might display as a button, a menu, or a box in which you type information.

You can also minimize the Ribbon so only the tab names display. In the minimized Ribbon view, when you click a tab the Ribbon expands to show the groups and commands, and then when you click a command, the Ribbon returns to its minimized view. Most Office users, however, prefer to leave the complete Ribbon in view at all times.

Activity 1.09 | Performing Commands from the Ribbon

1 Take a moment to examine the document on your screen.

This document is a memo from the Executive Chef to the General Manager regarding a new restaurant promotion.

2 On the Ribbon, click the **View tab**. In the **Show group**, if necessary, click to place a check mark in the **Ruler** check box, and then compare your screen with Figure 1.35.

> When working in Word, display the rulers so that you can see how margin settings affect your document and how text aligns. Additionally, if you set a tab stop or an indent, its location is visible on the ruler.

Figure 1.35

Quick Access Toolbar

Ruler selected

Button to minimize Ribbon

Rulers

3 On the Ribbon, click the **Home tab**. In the **Paragraph group**, if necessary, click the **Show/Hide** button ¶ so that it glows orange and formatting marks display in your document. Point to the button to display information about the button, and then compare your screen with Figure 1.36.

> When the Show/Hide button is active—glowing orange—formatting marks display. Because formatting marks guide your eye in a document—like a map and road signs guide you along a highway—these marks will display throughout this instruction. Many expert Word users keep these marks displayed while creating documents.

Figure 1.36

Show/Hide button glows orange

Paragraph group

ScreenTip for Show/Hide button

Paragraph mark

Tab mark

4 In the upper left corner of your screen, above the Ribbon, locate the **Quick Access Toolbar**.

> The **Quick Access Toolbar** contains commands that you use frequently. By default, only the commands Save, Undo, and Redo display, but you can add and delete commands to suit your needs. Possibly the computer at which you are working already has additional commands added to the Quick Access Toolbar.

5 At the end of the Quick Access Toolbar, click the **Customize Quick Access Toolbar** button ▾.

6 Compare your screen with Figure 1.37.

A list of commands that Office users commonly add to their Quick Access Toolbar displays, including *Open*, *E-mail*, and *Print Preview and Print*. Commands already on the Quick Access Toolbar display a check mark. Commands that you add to the Quick Access Toolbar are always just one click away.

Here you can also display the More Commands dialog box, from which you can select any command from any tab to add to the Quick Access Toolbar.

Figure 1.37

Customize Quick Access Toolbar

Popular commands to add

Existing commands checked

Displays *More Commands* dialog box

Another Way

Right-click any command on the Ribbon, and then on the shortcut menu, click Add to Quick Access Toolbar.

7 On the displayed list, click **Print Preview and Print**, and then notice that the icon is added to the **Quick Access Toolbar**. Compare your screen with Figure 1.38.

The icon that represents the Print Preview command displays on the Quick Access Toolbar. Because this is a command that you will use frequently while building Office documents, you might decide to have this command remain on your Quick Access Toolbar.

Figure 1.38

Icon for Print Preview command added to Quick Access Toolbar

8 In the first line of the document, be sure your insertion point is blinking to the left of the *O* in *Oceana*. Press [Enter] one time to insert a blank paragraph, and then click to the left of the new paragraph mark (¶) in the new line.

The ***paragraph symbol*** is a formatting mark that displays each time you press [Enter].

9 On the Ribbon, click the **Insert tab**. In the **Illustrations group**, point to the **Clip Art** button to display its ScreenTip.

Many buttons on the Ribbon have this type of ***enhanced ScreenTip***, which displays more descriptive text than a normal ScreenTip.

10 Click the **Clip Art** button.

The Clip Art ***task pane*** displays. A task pane is a window within a Microsoft Office application that enables you to enter options for completing a command.

11 In the **Clip Art** task pane, click in the **Search for** box, delete any existing text, and then type **cheese grapes** Under **Results should be:**, click the arrow at the right, if necessary click to *clear* the check mark for **All media types** so that no check boxes are selected, and then click the check box for **Illustrations**. Compare your screen with Figure 1.39.

Figure 1.39

Search term

Blank paragraph

12 Click the **Results should be arrow** again to close the list, and then if necessary, click to place a check mark in the **Include Office.com content** check box.

> By selecting this check box, the search for clip art images will include those from Microsoft's online collections of clip art at www.office.com.

13 At the top of the **Clip Art** task pane, click **Go**. Wait a moment for clips to display, and then locate the clip indicated in Figure 1.40.

Figure 1.40

Check box selected

Locate this image

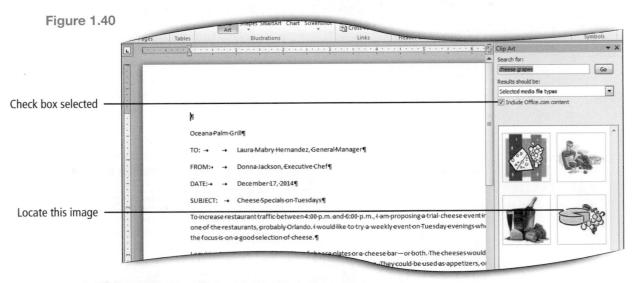

14 Click the image indicated in Figure 1.40 one time to insert it at the insertion point, and then in the upper right corner of the **Clip Art** task pane, click the **Close** ☒ button.

Alert! | **If You Cannot Locate the Image**

If the image shown in Figure 1.40 is unavailable, select a different cheese image that is appropriate.

---

15 With the image selected—surrounded by a border—on the Ribbon, click the **Home tab**, and then in the **Paragraph group**, click the **Center** button ☰. Click anywhere outside of the bordered picture to *deselect*—cancel the selection. Compare your screen with Figure 1.41.

Figure 1.41

Center button

Image inserted in
document and
centered horizontally

Oceana·Palm·Grill¶

TO: → → Laura·Mabry·Hernandez,·General·Manager¶

16 Point to the inserted clip art image, and then watch the last tab of the Ribbon as you click the image one time to select it.

> The *Picture Tools* display and an additional tab—the *Format* tab—is added to the Ribbon. The Ribbon adapts to your work and will display additional tabs—referred to as **contextual tabs**—when you need them.

17 On the Ribbon, under **Picture Tools**, click the **Format tab**.

Alert! | **The Size of Groups on the Ribbon Varies with Screen Resolution**

Your monitor's screen resolution might be set higher than the resolution used to capture the figures in this book. In Figure 1.42 below, the resolution is set to 1024 × 768, which is used for all of the figures in this book. Compare that with Figure 1.43 below, where the screen resolution is set to 1280 × 1024.

At a higher resolution, the Ribbon expands some groups to show more commands than are available with a single click, such as those in the Picture Styles group. Or, the group expands to add descriptive text to some buttons, such as those in the Arrange group. Regardless of your screen resolution, all Office commands are available to you. In higher resolutions, you will have a more robust view of the commands.

Figure 1.42

Picture Styles group at
1024 x 768 resolution

Arrange group at
1024 x 768 resolution

Figure 1.43

More styles show

Picture Styles at
1280 x 1024

Arrange group at
1280 x 1024

Expanded buttons

---

18 In the **Picture Styles group**, point to the first style to display the ScreenTip *Simple Frame, White*, and notice that the image displays with a white frame.

19 Watch the image as you point to the second picture style, and then to the third, and then to the fourth.

This is *Live Preview*, a technology that shows the result of applying an editing or formatting change as you point to possible results—*before* you actually apply it.

20 In the **Picture Styles group**, click the fourth style—**Drop Shadow Rectangle**—and then click anywhere outside of the image to deselect it. Notice that the Picture Tools no longer display on the Ribbon. Compare your screen with Figure 1.44.

Contextual tabs display only when you need them.

Figure 1.44

Picture Tools no longer
display on the Ribbon

Drop Shadow Rectangle
picture style applied
to image

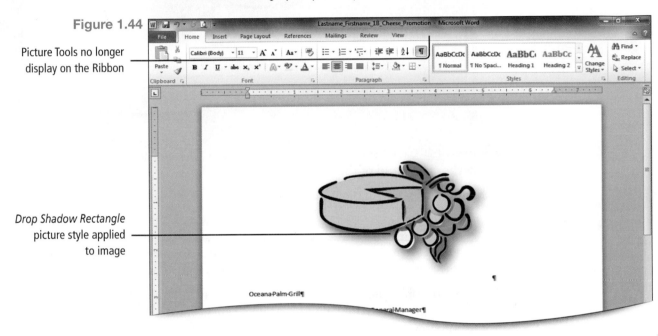

21 In the upper left corner of your screen, on the Quick Access Toolbar, click the **Save** button to save the changes you have made.

Activity 1.10 | Minimizing and Using the Keyboard to Control the Ribbon

Instead of a mouse, some individuals prefer to navigate the Ribbon by using keys on the keyboard. You can activate keyboard control of the Ribbon by pressing the Alt key. You can also minimize the Ribbon to maximize your available screen space.

1 On your keyboard, press the Alt key, and then on the Ribbon, notice that small labels display. Press N to activate the commands on the **Insert tab**, and then compare your screen with Figure 1.45.

Each label represents a *KeyTip*—an indication of the key that you can press to activate the command. For example, on the Insert tab, you can press F to activate the Clip Art task pane.

Figure 1.45

KeyTips indicate that
keyboard control
of the Ribbon is active

2 Press Esc to redisplay the KeyTips for the tabs. Then, press Alt again to turn off keyboard control of the Ribbon.

3 Point to any tab on the Ribbon and right-click to display a shortcut menu.

Here you can choose to display the Quick Access Toolbar below the Ribbon or minimize the Ribbon to maximize screen space. You can also customize the Ribbon by adding, removing, renaming, or reordering tabs, groups, and commands on the Ribbon, although this is not recommended until you become an expert Office user.

Another Way

Double-click the active tab; or, click the Minimize the Ribbon button at the right end of the Ribbon.

4 Click **Minimize the Ribbon**. Notice that only the Ribbon tabs display. Click the **Home tab** to display the commands. Click anywhere in the document, and notice that the Ribbon reverts to its minimized view.

Another Way

Double-click any tab to redisplay the full Ribbon.

5 Right-click any Ribbon tab, and then click **Minimize the Ribbon** again to turn the minimize feature off.

Most expert Office users prefer to have the full Ribbon display at all times.

6 Point to any tab on the Ribbon, and then on your mouse device, roll the mouse wheel. Notice that different tabs become active as your roll the mouse wheel.

You can make a tab active by using this technique, instead of clicking the tab.

Objective 10 | Apply Formatting in Office Programs

Formatting is the process of establishing the overall appearance of text, graphics, and pages in an Office file—for example, in a Word document.

Activity 1.11 | Formatting and Viewing Pages

In this activity, you will practice common formatting techniques used in Office applications.

1 On the Ribbon, click the **Insert tab**, and then in the **Header & Footer group**, click the **Footer** button.

2 At the top of the displayed gallery, under **Built-In**, click **Blank**. At the bottom of your document, with *Type text* highlighted in blue, using your own name type the file name of this document **Lastname_Firstname_1B_Cheese_Promotion** and then compare your screen with Figure 1.46.

> Header & Footer Tools are added to the Ribbon. A *footer* is a reserved area for text or graphics that displays at the bottom of each page in a document. Likewise, a *header* is a reserved area for text or graphics that displays at the top of each page in a document. When the footer (or header) area is active, the document area is inactive (dimmed).

Figure 1.46

Design tab added

Header & Footer Tools active

Document area inactive (dimmed) when footer area is active

Close Header and Footer button

Your file name

Footer area displays

3 On the Ribbon, on the **Design tab**, in the **Close group**, click the **Close Header and Footer** button.

4 On the Ribbon, click the **Page Layout tab**. In the **Page Setup group**, click the **Orientation** button, and notice that two orientations display—*Portrait* and *Landscape*. Click **Landscape**.

> In *portrait orientation*, the paper is taller than it is wide. In *landscape orientation*, the paper is wider than it is tall.

5 In the lower right corner of the screen, locate the **Zoom control** buttons.

> To *zoom* means to increase or decrease the viewing area. You can zoom in to look closely at a section of a document, and then zoom out to see an entire page on the screen. You can also zoom to view multiple pages on the screen.

6 Drag the **Zoom slider** to the left until you have zoomed to approximately *60%*. Compare your screen with Figure 1.47.

Figure 1.47

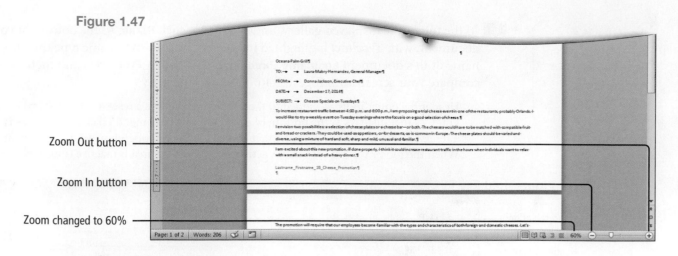

Zoom Out button

Zoom In button

Zoom changed to 60%

7 On the **Page Layout tab**, in the **Page Setup group**, click the **Orientation** button, and then click **Portrait**.

> Portrait orientation is commonly used for business documents such as letters and memos.

8 In the lower right corner of your screen, click the **Zoom In** button ⊕ as many times as necessary to return to the **100%** zoom setting.

> Use the zoom feature to adjust the view of your document for editing and for your viewing comfort.

9 On the Quick Access Toolbar, click the **Save** button 🔲 to save the changes you have made to your document.

Activity 1.12 | Formatting Text

1 To the left of *Oceana Palm Grill*, point in the margin area to display the 🔏 pointer and click one time to select the entire paragraph. Compare your screen with Figure 1.48.

> Use this technique to select complete paragraphs from the margin area. Additionally, with this technique you can drag downward to select multiple-line paragraphs—which is faster and more efficient than dragging through text.

Figure 1.48

Paragraph selected

2 On the Ribbon, click the **Home tab**, and then in the **Paragraph group**, click the **Center** button ≡ to center the paragraph.

> *Alignment* refers to the placement of paragraph text relative to the left and right margins. *Center alignment* refers to text that is centered horizontally between the left and right margins. You can also align text at the left margin, which is the default alignment for text in Word, or at the right margin.

3 On the **Home tab**, in the **Font group**, click the **Font button arrow** Calibri (Body). At the top of the list, point to **Cambria**, and as you do so, notice that the selected text previews in the Cambria font.

> A *font* is a set of characters with the same design and shape. The default font in a Word document is Calibri, which is a *sans serif* font—a font design with no lines or extensions on the ends of characters.

> The Cambria font is a *serif* font—a font design that includes small line extensions on the ends of the letters to guide the eye in reading from left to right.

> The list of fonts displays as a gallery showing potential results. For example, in the Font gallery, you can see the actual design and format of each font as it would look if applied to text.

4 Point to several other fonts and observe the effect on the selected text. Then, at the top of the **Font** gallery, under **Theme Fonts**, click **Cambria**.

> A *theme* is a predesigned set of colors, fonts, lines, and fill effects that look good together and that can be applied to your entire document or to specific items.

> A theme combines two sets of fonts—one for text and one for headings. In the default Office theme, Cambria is the suggested font for headings.

5 With the paragraph *Oceana Palm Grill* still selected, on the **Home tab**, in the **Font group**, click the **Font Size button arrow** 11, point to **36**, and then notice how Live Preview displays the text in the font size to which you are pointing. Compare your screen with Figure 1.49.

Figure 1.49

Font Size button

Font button

Font Size list

Pointing to 36 pt font size

Oceana Palm Grill centered, Cambria font applied

6 On the displayed list of font sizes, click **20**.

> Fonts are measured in *points*, with one point equal to 1/72 of an inch. A higher point size indicates a larger font size. Headings and titles are often formatted by using a larger font size. The word *point* is abbreviated as *pt*.

7 With *Oceana Palm Grill* still selected, on the **Home tab**, in the **Font group**, click the **Font Color button arrow** A. Under **Theme Colors**, in the seventh column, click the last color—**Olive Green, Accent 3, Darker 50%**. Click anywhere to deselect the text.

8 To the left of *TO:*, point in the left margin area to display the 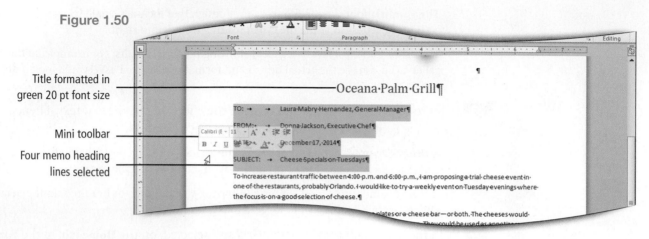 pointer, hold down the left mouse button, and then drag down to select the four memo headings. Compare your screen with Figure 1.50.

Use this technique to select complete paragraphs from the margin area—dragging downward to select multiple-line paragraphs—which is faster and more efficient than dragging through text.

Figure 1.50

Title formatted in green 20 pt font size

Mini toolbar

Four memo heading lines selected

9 With the four paragraphs selected, on the Mini toolbar, click the **Font Color** button ![A], which now displays a dark green bar instead of a red bar.

The font color button retains its most recently used color—Olive Green, Accent 3, Darker 50%. As you progress in your study of Microsoft Office, you will use other buttons that behave in this manner; that is, they retain their most recently used format.

The purpose of the Mini toolbar is to place commonly used commands close to text or objects that you select. By selecting a command on the Mini toolbar, you reduce the distance that you must move your mouse to access a command.

10 Click anywhere in the paragraph that begins *To increase*, and then *triple-click*—click the left mouse button three times—to select the entire paragraph. If the entire paragraph is not selected, click in the paragraph and begin again.

11 With the entire paragraph selected, on the Mini toolbar, click the **Font Color button arrow** ![A], and then under **Theme Colors**, in the sixth column, click the first color—**Red, Accent 2**.

It is convenient to have commonly used commands display on the Mini toolbar so that you do not have to move your mouse to the top of the screen to access the command from the Ribbon.

12 Select the text *TO:* and then on the displayed Mini toolbar, click the **Bold** button ![B] and the **Italic** button ![I].

Font styles include bold, italic, and underline. Font styles emphasize text and are a visual cue to draw the reader's eye to important text.

13 On the displayed Mini toolbar, click the **Italic** button ![I] again to turn off the Italic formatting. Notice that the Italic button no longer glows orange.

A button that behaves in this manner is referred to as a *toggle button*, which means it can be turned on by clicking it once, and then turned off by clicking it again.

14 With *TO:* still selected, on the Mini toolbar, click the **Format Painter** button. Then, move your mouse under the word *Laura*, and notice the mouse pointer. Compare your screen with Figure 1.51.

> You can use the *Format Painter* to copy the formatting of specific text or of a paragraph and then apply it in other locations in your document.

> The pointer takes the shape of a paintbrush, and contains the formatting information from the paragraph where the insertion point is positioned. Information about the Format Painter and how to turn it off displays in the status bar.

Figure 1.51

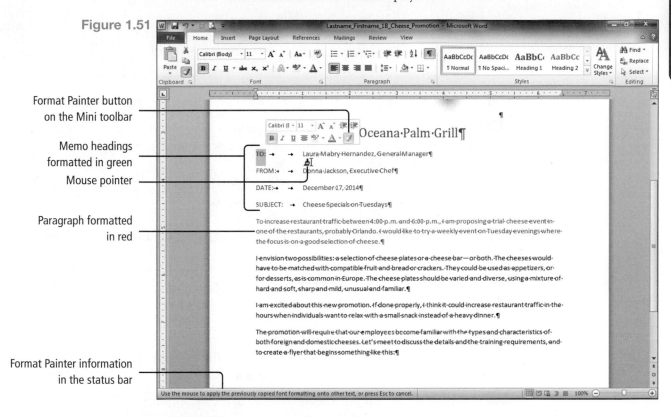

Format Painter button on the Mini toolbar

Memo headings formatted in green

Mouse pointer

Paragraph formatted in red

Format Painter information in the status bar

15 With the pointer, drag to select the text *FROM:* and notice that the Bold formatting is applied. Then, point to the selected text *FROM:* and on the Mini toolbar, *double-click* the **Format Painter** button.

16 Select the text *DATE:* to copy the Bold formatting, and notice that the pointer retains the shape.

> When you *double-click* the Format Painter button, the Format Painter feature remains active until you either click the Format Painter button again, or press Esc to cancel it—as indicated on the status bar.

17 With Format Painter still active, select the text *SUBJECT:*, and then on the Ribbon, on the **Home tab**, in the **Clipboard group**, notice that the **Format Painter** button is glowing orange, indicating that it is active. Compare your screen with Figure 1.52.

Figure 1.52

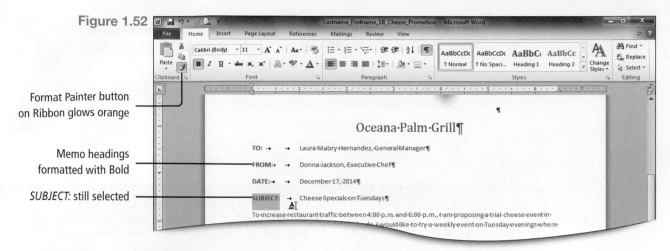

Format Painter button
on Ribbon glows orange

Memo headings
formatted with Bold

SUBJECT: still selected

18 Click the **Format Painter** button ✒ on the Ribbon to turn the command off.

19 In the paragraph that begins *To increase*, triple-click again to select the entire paragraph. On the displayed Mini toolbar, click the **Bold** button **B** and the **Italic** button *I*. Click anywhere to deselect.

20 On the Quick Access Toolbar, click the **Save** button 🖫 to save the changes you have made to your document.

Activity 1.13 | Using the Office Clipboard to Cut, Copy, and Paste

The **Office Clipboard** is a temporary storage area that holds text or graphics that you select and then cut or copy. When you **copy** text or graphics, a copy is placed on the Office Clipboard and the original text or graphic remains in place. When you **cut** text or graphics, a copy is placed on the Office Clipboard, and the original text or graphic is removed—cut—from the document.

After cutting or copying, the contents of the Office Clipboard are available for you to **paste**—insert—in a new location in the current document, or into another Office file.

1 Hold down Ctrl and press Home to move to the beginning of your document, and then take a moment to study the table in Figure 1.53, which describes similar keyboard shortcuts with which you can navigate quickly in a document.

To Move	Press
To the beginning of a document	Ctrl + Home
To the end of a document	Ctrl + End
To the beginning of a line	Home
To the end of a line	End
To the beginning of the previous word	Ctrl + ←
To the beginning of the next word	Ctrl + →
To the beginning of the current word (if insertion point is in the middle of a word)	Ctrl + ←
To the beginning of a paragraph	Ctrl + ↑
To the beginning of the next paragraph	Ctrl + ↓
To the beginning of the current paragraph (if insertion point is in the middle of a paragraph)	Ctrl + ↑
Up one screen	PgUp
Down one screen	PageDown

Figure 1.53

Another Way

Right-click the selection, and then click Copy on the shortcut menu; or, use the keyboard shortcut Ctrl + C.

2 To the left of *Oceana Palm Grill*, point in the left margin area to display the 🔗 pointer, and then click one time to select the entire paragraph. On the **Home tab**, in the **Clipboard group**, click the **Copy** button 📋.

> Because anything that you select and then copy—or cut—is placed on the Office Clipboard, the Copy command and the Cut command display in the Clipboard group of commands on the Ribbon.

> There is no visible indication that your copied selection has been placed on the Office Clipboard.

3 On the **Home tab**, in the **Clipboard group**, to the right of the group name *Clipboard*, click the **Dialog Box Launcher** button 🔲, and then compare your screen with Figure 1.54.

> The Clipboard task pane displays with your copied text. In any Ribbon group, the *Dialog Box Launcher* displays either a dialog box or a task pane related to the group of commands.

> It is not necessary to display the Office Clipboard in this manner, although sometimes it is useful to do so. The Office Clipboard can hold 24 items.

Figure 1.54

Copy button
Dialog Box Launcher in Clipboard group
Clipboard task pane displays
Selected text on the Office Clipboard

4 In the upper right corner of the **Clipboard** task pane, click the **Close** button ❌.

Another Way

Right-click, on the shortcut menu under Paste Options, click the desired option button.

5 Press Ctrl + End to move to the end of your document. Press Enter one time to create a new blank paragraph. On the **Home tab**, in the **Clipboard group**, point to the **Paste** button, and then click the *upper* portion of this split button.

> The Paste command pastes the most recently copied item on the Office Clipboard at the insertion point location. If you click the lower portion of the Paste button, a gallery of Paste Options displays.

6 Click the **Paste Options** button 📋 that displays below the pasted text as shown in Figure 1.55.

> Here you can view and apply various formatting options for pasting your copied or cut text. Typically you will click Paste on the Ribbon and paste the item in its original format. If you want some other format for the pasted item, you can do so from the *Paste Options gallery*.
>
> The Paste Options gallery provides a Live Preview of the various options for changing the format of the pasted item with a single click. The Paste Options gallery is available in three places: on the Ribbon by clicking the lower portion of the Paste button—the Paste button arrow; from the Paste Options button that displays below the pasted item following the paste operation; or, on the shortcut menu if you right-click the pasted item.

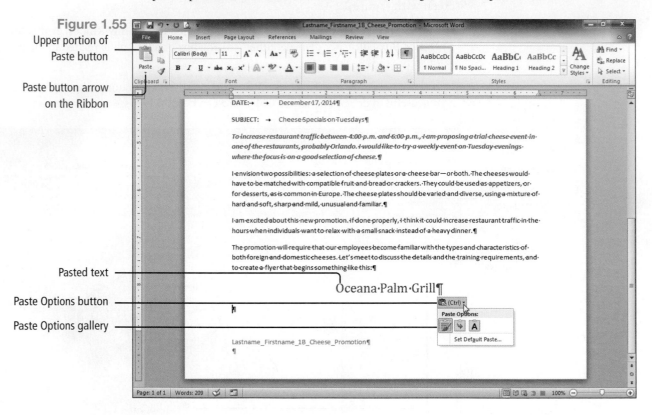

Figure 1.55

Upper portion of Paste button

Paste button arrow on the Ribbon

Pasted text

Paste Options button

Paste Options gallery

7 In the displayed **Paste Options** gallery, *point* to each option to see the Live Preview of the format that would be applied if you clicked the button.

> The contents of the Paste Options gallery are contextual; that is, they change based on what you copied and where you are pasting.

8 Press [Esc] to close the gallery; the button will remain displayed until you take some other screen action.

9 Press [Ctrl] + [Home] to move to the top of the document, and then click the **cheese image** one time to select it. While pointing to the selected image, right-click, and then on the shortcut menu, click **Cut**.

> Recall that the Cut command cuts—removes—the selection from the document and places it on the Office Clipboard.

Another Way

On the Home tab, in the Clipboard group, click the Cut button; or, use the keyboard shortcut [Ctrl] + [X].

10 Press Del one time to remove the blank paragraph from the top of the document, and then press Ctrl + End to move to the end of the document.

11 With the insertion point blinking in the blank paragraph at the end of the document, right-click, and notice that the **Paste Options** gallery displays on the shortcut menu. Compare your screen with Figure 1.56.

Figure 1.56

Paste Options on shortcut menu

12 On the shortcut menu, under **Paste Options**, click the first button—**Keep Source Formatting**.

13 Click the picture to select it. On the **Home tab**, in the **Paragraph group**, click the **Center** button.

14 Above the cheese picture, click to position the insertion point at the end of the word *Grill*, press Spacebar one time, and then type **Tuesday Cheese Tastings** Compare your screen with Figure 1.57.

Figure 1.57

Heading

Picture inserted and centered

Activity 1.14 | Viewing Print Preview and Printing a Word Document

1 Press Ctrl + Home to move to the top of your document. Select the text *Oceana Palm Grill*, and then replace the selected text by typing **Memo**

2 Display **Backstage** view, on the right, click **Properties**, and then click **Show Document Panel**. Replace the existing author name with your first and last name. In the **Subject** box, type your course name and section number, and then in the **Keywords** box, type **cheese promotion** and then **Close** ✕ the **Document Information Panel**.

Another Way

Press [Ctrl] + [F2] to display Print Preview.

3 On the Quick Access Toolbar, click **Save** 🖫 to save the changes you have made to your document.

4 On the Quick Access Toolbar, click the **Print Preview** button 🔍 that you added. Compare your screen with Figure 1.58.

Figure 1.58

Memo typed

If no printer is attached to your system, OneNote is the default printer

Print tab active in Backstage view

Print Preview (if you have a non-color printer as your default printer, the preview may display in shades of gray)

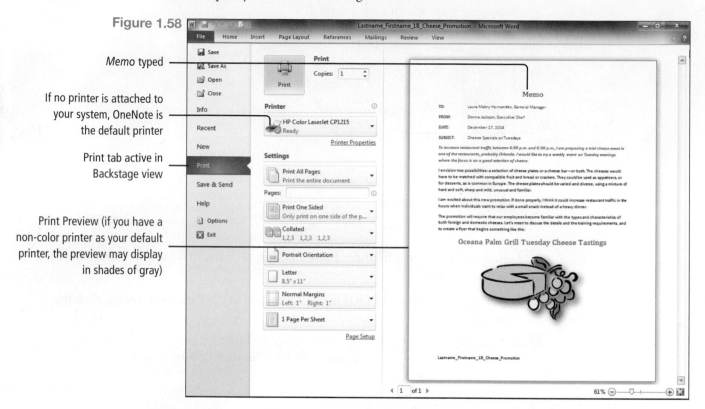

5 Examine the **Print Preview**. Under **Settings**, notice that in **Backstage** view, several of the same commands that are available on the Page Layout tab of the Ribbon also display.

> For convenience, common adjustments to Page Layout display here, so that you can make last-minute adjustments without closing Backstage view.

6 If you need to make any corrections, click the Home tab to return to the document and make any necessary changes.

> It is good practice to examine the Print Preview before printing or submitting your work electronically. Then, make any necessary corrections, re-save, and redisplay Print Preview.

7 If you are directed to do so, click Print to print the document; or, above the Info tab, click Close, and then submit your file electronically according to the directions provided by your instructor.

> If you click the Print button, Backstage view closes and the Word window redisplays.

8 On the Quick Access Toolbar, point to the **Print Preview icon** 🔍 you placed there, right-click, and then click **Remove from Quick Access Toolbar**.

> If you are working on your own computer and you want to do so, you can leave the icon on the toolbar; in a lab setting, you should return the software to its original settings.

9 At the right end of the title bar, click the program **Close** button 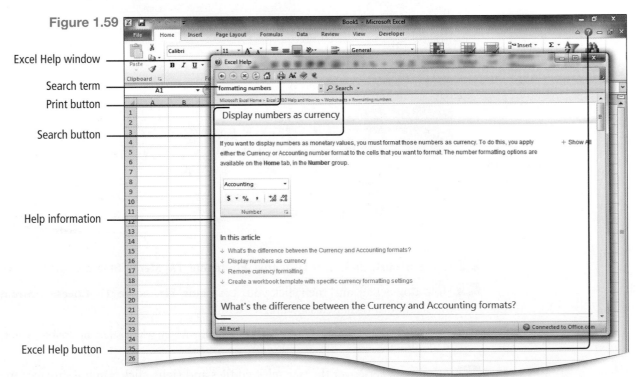 .

10 If a message displays asking if you want the text on the Clipboard to be available after you quit Word, click **No**.

> This message most often displays if you have copied some type of image to the Clipboard. If you click Yes, the items on the Clipboard will remain for you to use.

Objective 11 | Use the Microsoft Office 2010 Help System

Within each Office program, the Help feature provides information about all of the program's features and displays step-by-step instructions for performing many tasks.

Activity 1.15 | Using the Microsoft Office 2010 Help System in Excel

In this activity, you will use the Microsoft Help feature to find information about formatting numbers in Excel.

> **Another Way**
> Press [F1] to display Help.

1 **Start** the **Microsoft Excel 2010** program. In the upper right corner of your screen, click the **Microsoft Excel Help** button.

2 In the **Excel Help** window, click in the white box in upper left corner, type **formatting numbers** and then click **Search** or press [Enter].

3 On the list of results, click **Display numbers as currency**. Compare your screen with Figure 1.59.

Figure 1.59

Excel Help window
Search term
Print button
Search button
Help information
Excel Help button

4 If you want to do so, on the toolbar at the top of the **Excel Help** window, click the Print button to print a copy of this information for your reference.

5 On the title bar of the Excel Help window, click the **Close** button [X]. On the right side of the Microsoft Excel title bar, click the **Close** button [X] to close Excel.

Objective 12 | Compress Files

A *compressed file* is a file that has been reduced in size. Compressed files take up less storage space and can be transferred to other computers faster than uncompressed files. You can also combine a group of files into one compressed folder, which makes it easier to share a group of files.

Activity 1.16 | Compressing Files

In this activity, you will combine the two files you created in this chapter into one compressed file.

1 On the Windows taskbar, click the **Start** button ⊕, and then on the right, click **Computer**.

2 On the left, in the **navigation pane**, click the location of your two files from this chapter—your USB flash drive or other location—and display the folder window for your **Common Features Chapter 1** folder. Compare your screen with Figure 1.60.

Figure 1.60

Address bar displays path

Your chapter files in file list (your name displays)

Folder window for your chapter folder

Location selected in navigation pane (your location may vary)

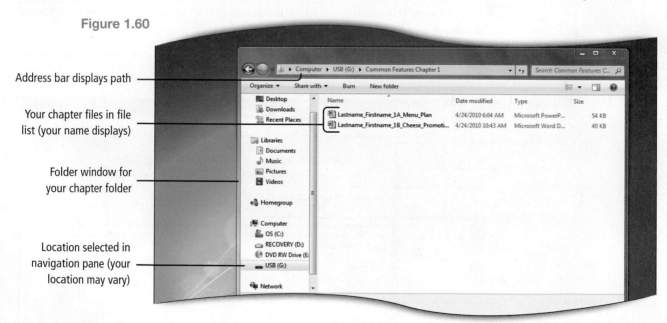

3 In the **file list**, click your **Lastname_Firstname_1A_Menu_Plan** file one time to select it.

4 Hold down [Ctrl], and then click your **Lastname_Firstname_1B_Cheese_Promotion** file to select both files. Release [Ctrl].

In any Windows-based program, holding down [Ctrl] while selecting enables you to select multiple items.

5 Point anywhere over the two selected files and right-click. On the shortcut menu, point to **Send to**, and then compare your screen with Figure 1.61.

Figure 1.61

Two files selected

Send to submenu

Shortcut menu
(yours may vary)

6 On the shortcut submenu, click **Compressed (zipped) folder**.

Windows creates a compressed folder containing a *copy* of each of the selected files. The folder name is the name of the file or folder to which you were pointing, and is selected—highlighted in blue—so that you can rename it.

7 Using your own name, type **Lastname_Firstname_Common_Features_Ch1** and press Enter.

The compressed folder is now ready to attach to an e-mail or share in some other electronic format.

8 **Close** ✕ the folder window. If directed to do so by your instructor, submit your compressed folder electronically.

More Knowledge | Extracting Compressed Files

Extract means to decompress, or pull out, files from a compressed form. When you extract a file, an uncompressed copy is placed in the folder that you specify. The original file remains in the compressed folder.

End **You have completed Project 1B** ————————————

Content-Based Assessments

Summary

In this chapter, you used Windows Explorer to navigate the Windows file structure. You also used features that are common across the Microsoft Office 2010 programs.

Key Terms

Content-Based Assessments

Matching

Match each term in the second column with its correct definition in the first column by writing the letter of the term on the blank line in front of the correct definition.

_____ 1. A collection of information stored on a computer under a single name.

_____ 2. A container in which you store files.

_____ 3. A folder within a folder.

_____ 4. The program that displays the files and folders on your computer.

_____ 5. The Windows menu that is the main gateway to your computer.

_____ 6. In Windows 7, a window that displays the contents of the current folder, library, or device, and contains helpful parts so that you can navigate.

_____ 7. In Windows, a collection of items, such as files and folders, assembled from various locations that might be on your computer.

_____ 8. The bar at the top of a folder window with which you can navigate to a different folder or library, or go back to a previous one.

_____ 9. An instruction to a computer program that carries out an action.

_____ 10. Small pictures that represent a program, a file, a folder, or an object.

_____ 11. A set of instructions that a computer uses to perform a specific task.

_____ 12. A spreadsheet program used to calculate numbers and create charts.

_____ 13. The user interface that groups commands on tabs at the top of the program window.

_____ 14. A bar at the top of the program window displaying the current file and program name.

_____ 15. One or more keys pressed to perform a task that would otherwise require a mouse.

A Address bar

B Command

C File

D Folder

E Folder window

F Icons

G Keyboard shortcut

H Library

I Microsoft Excel

J Program

K Ribbon

L Start menu

M Subfolder

N Title bar

O Windows Explorer

Multiple Choice

Circle the correct answer.

1. A small toolbar with frequently used commands that displays when selecting text or objects is the:
   A. Quick Access Toolbar   **B.** Mini toolbar   **C.** Document toolbar

2. In Office 2010, a centralized space for file management tasks is:
   A. a task pane   **B.** a dialog box   **C.** Backstage view

3. The commands Save, Save As, Open, and Close in Backstage view are located:
   A. above the Backstage tabs   **B.** below the Backstage tabs   **C.** under the screen thumbnail

4. The tab in Backstage view that displays information about the current file is the:
   A. Recent tab   **B.** Info tab   **C.** Options tab

5. Details about a file, including the title, author name, subject, and keywords are known as:
   A. document properties   **B.** formatting marks   **C.** KeyTips

6. An Office feature that displays a list of potential results is:
   A. Live Preview   **B.** a contextual tab   **C.** a gallery

7. A type of formatting emphasis applied to text such as bold, italic, and underline, is called:

   A. a font style   **B.** a KeyTip   **C.** a tag

8. A technology showing the result of applying formatting as you point to possible results is called:

   A. Live Preview   **B.** Backstage view   **C.** gallery view

9. A temporary storage area that holds text or graphics that you select and then cut or copy is the:

   A. paste options gallery   **B.** ribbon   **C.** Office clipboard

10. A file that has been reduced in size is:

    A. a compressed file   **B.** an extracted file   **C.** a PDF file

Creating Documents with Microsoft Word 2010

OUTCOMES

At the end of this chapter you will be able to:

OBJECTIVES

Mastering these objectives will enable you to:

PROJECT 1A
Create a flyer with a picture.

1. Create a New Document and Insert Text (p. 51)
2. Insert and Format Graphics (p. 53)
3. Insert and Modify Text Boxes and Shapes (p. 58)
4. Preview and Print a Document (p. 62)

PROJECT 1B
Format text, paragraphs, and documents.

5. Change Document and Paragraph Layout (p. 67)
6. Create and Modify Lists (p. 73)
7. Set and Modify Tab Stops (p. 78)
8. Insert a SmartArt Graphic (p. 80)

Joy Brown/Shutterstock

In This Chapter

In this chapter, you will use Microsoft Word, which is one of the most common programs found on computers and one that almost everyone has a reason to use. You will use many of the new tools found in Word 2010. When you learn word processing, you are also learning skills and techniques that you need to work efficiently on a computer. You can use Microsoft Word to perform basic word processing tasks such as writing a memo, a report, or a letter. You can also use Word to complete complex word processing tasks, such as creating sophisticated tables, embedding graphics, writing blogs, creating publications, and inserting links into other documents and the Internet. Word is a program that you can learn gradually, and then add more advanced skills one at a time.

The projects in this chapter relate to **Laurel College**. The college offers this diverse geographic area a wide range of academic and career programs, including associate degrees, certificate programs, and non-credit continuing education and personal development courses. The college makes positive contributions to the community through cultural and athletic programs and partnerships with businesses and nonprofit organizations. The college also provides industry-specific training programs for local businesses through its growing Economic Development Center.

Project 1A Flyer

Project Activities

In Activities 1.01 through 1.12, you will create a flyer announcing a new rock climbing class offered by the Physical Education Department at Laurel College. Your completed document will look similar to Figure 1.1.

Project Files

For Project 1A, you will need the following files:

New blank Word document
w01A_Fitness_Flyer
w01A_Rock_Climber

You will save your document as:

Lastname_Firstname_1A_Fitness_Flyer

Project Results

Figure 1.1
Project 1A Fitness Flyer

Objective 1 | Create a New Document and Insert Text

When you create a new document, you can type all of the text, or you can type some of the text and then insert additional text from another source.

Activity 1.01 | Starting a New Word Document and Inserting Text

1 **Start** Word and display a new blank document. On the **Home tab**, in the **Paragraph group**, if necessary click the Show/Hide button ¶ so that it is active (glows orange) to display the formatting marks. If the rulers do not display, click the View tab, and then in the Show group, select the Ruler check box.

2 Type **Rock Climbing 101** and then press Enter two times. As you type the following text, press the Spacebar only one time at the end of a sentence: **Increase your fitness level by learning basic rock climbing using the new Laurel College Gymnasium rock climbing wall. The Physical Education Department is offering Rock Climbing 101 as part of its Recreational Fitness Program.**

As you type, the insertion point moves to the right, and when it approaches the right margin, Word determines whether the next word in the line will fit within the established right margin. If the word does not fit, Word moves the entire word down to the next line. This feature is called *wordwrap* and means that you press Enter *only* when you reach the end of a paragraph—it is not necessary to press Enter at the end of each line of text.

Note | Spacing Between Sentences

Although you might have learned to add two spaces following end-of-sentence punctuation, the common practice now is to space only one time at the end of a sentence.

---

3 Press Enter one time. Take a moment to study the table in Figure 1.2 to become familiar with the default document settings in Microsoft Word, and then compare your screen with Figure 1.3.

When you press Enter, Spacebar, or Tab on your keyboard, characters display in your document to represent these keystrokes. These characters do not print and are referred to as *formatting marks* or *nonprinting characters*. These marks will display throughout this instruction.

Default Document Settings in a New Word Document

Setting	Default format
Font and font size	The default font is Calibri and the default font size is 11.
Margins	The default left, right, top, and bottom page margins are 1 inch.
Line spacing	The default line spacing is 1.15, which provides slightly more space between lines than single spacing does—an extra 1/6 of a line added between lines than single spacing.
Paragraph spacing	The default spacing after a paragraph is 10 points, which is slightly less than the height of one blank line of text.
View	The default view is Print Layout view, which displays the page borders and displays the document as it will appear when printed.

Figure 1.2

Figure 1.3

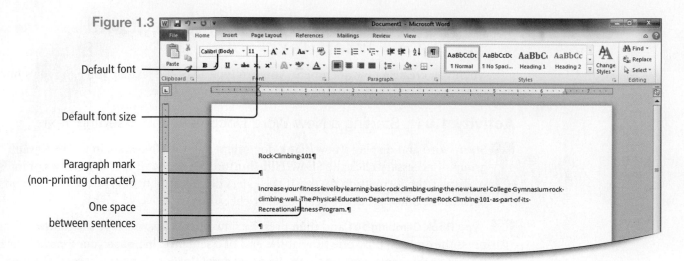

Default font

Default font size

Paragraph mark
(non-printing character)

One space
between sentences

4 On the Ribbon, click the **Insert tab**. In the **Text group**, click the **Object button arrow**, and then click **Text from File**.

> **Alert! | Does the Object Dialog Box Display?**
>
> If the Object dialog box displays, you probably clicked the Object *button* instead of the Object *button arrow*. Close the Object dialog box, and then in the Text group, click the Object button arrow, as shown in Figure 1.4. Click *Text from File*, and then continue with Step 5.

Another Way

Open the file, copy the required text, close the file, and then paste the text into the current document.

5 In the **Insert File** dialog box, navigate to the student files that accompany this textbook, locate and select **w01A_Fitness_Flyer**, and then click **Insert**. Compare your screen with Figure 1.4.

A *copy* of the text from the w01A_Fitness_Flyer file displays at the insertion point location; the text is not removed from the original file.

Figure 1.4

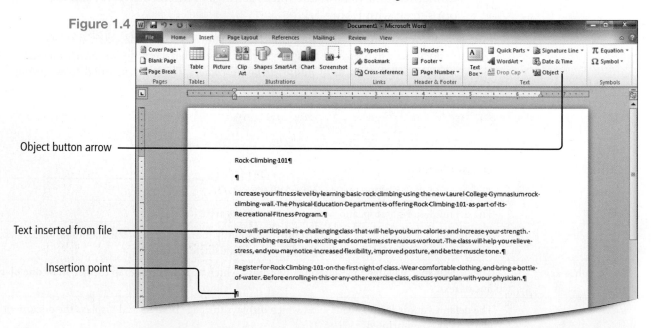

Object button arrow

Text inserted from file

Insertion point

6 On the **Quick Access Toolbar**, click the **Save** button. In the **Save As** dialog box, navigate to the location where you are saving your files for this chapter, and then create and open a new folder named **Word Chapter 1** In the **File name** box, replace the existing text with **Lastname_Firstname_1A_Fitness_Flyer** and then click **Save**.

Objective 2 | Insert and Format Graphics

To add visual interest to a document, insert *graphics*. Graphics include pictures, clip art, charts, and *drawing objects*—shapes, diagrams, lines, and so on. For additional visual interest, you can convert text to an attractive graphic format; add, resize, move, and format pictures; and add an attractive page border.

Activity 1.02 | Formatting Text Using Text Effects

Text effects are decorative formats, such as shadowed or mirrored text, text glow, 3-D effects, and colors that make text stand out.

1 Including the paragraph mark, select the first paragraph of text—*Rock Climbing 101*. On the **Home tab**, in the **Font group**, click the **Text Effects** button.

2 In the displayed **Text Effects** gallery, in the first row, point to the second effect to display the ScreenTip *Fill - None, Outline - Accent 2* and then click this effect.

3 With the text still selected, in the **Font group**, click in the **Font Size** box to select the existing font size. Type **60** and then press Enter.

> When you want to change the font size of selected text to a size that does not display in the Font Size list, type the number in the Font Size button box and press Enter to confirm the new font size.

4 With the text still selected, in the **Paragraph group**, click the **Center** button to center the text. Compare your screen with Figure 1.5.

Figure 1.5

Text Effects button

Center button glowing orange indicates centering applied

Text effects applied to title (title selected)

5 With the text still selected, in the **Font group**, click the **Text Effects** button. Point to **Shadow**, and then under **Outer**, in the second row, click the third style—**Offset Left**.

6 With the text still selected, in the **Font group**, click the **Font Color button arrow**. Under **Theme Colors**, in the fourth column, click the first color—**Dark Blue, Text 2**.

7 Click anywhere in the document to deselect the text, and then compare your screen with Figure 1.6.

Figure 1.6

Title color changed and shadow added

Rock·Climbing·101¶

¶

Increase·your·fitness·level·by·learning·basic·rock·climbing·using·the·new·Laurel·College·Gymnasium·rock·
...artment·is·offering·Rock·Climbing·101·as·part·of·its·

8 **Save** 💾 your document.

Activity 1.03 | Inserting and Resizing Pictures

1 In the paragraph that begins *Increase your fitness*, click to position the insertion point at the beginning of the paragraph.

2 On the **Insert tab**, in the **Illustrations group**, click the **Picture** button. In the **Insert Picture** dialog box, navigate to your student data files, locate and click **w01A_Rock_Climber**, and then click **Insert**.

> Word inserts the picture as an ***inline object***; that is, the picture is positioned directly in the text at the insertion point, just like a character in a sentence. Sizing handles surround the picture indicating it is selected.

3 If necessary, scroll to view the entire picture. Notice the round and square sizing handles around the border of the selected picture, as shown in Figure 1.7.

> The round corner sizing handles resize the graphic proportionally. The square sizing handles resize a graphic vertically or horizontally only; however, sizing with these will distort the graphic. A green rotate handle, with which you can rotate the graphic to any angle, displays above the top center sizing handle.

Figure 1.7

Center sizing handle

Rotate handle

Corner sizing handles

4 At the lower right corner of the picture, point to the round sizing handle until the ⬉ pointer displays. Drag upward and to the left until the bottom of the graphic is aligned at approximately **4 inches on the vertical ruler**. Compare your screen with Figure 1.8. Notice that the graphic is proportionally resized.

Figure 1.8

Picture resized ——

4-inch mark on the vertical ruler ——

Another Way

Click the Undo button to undo the change.

5 On the **Format tab**, in the **Adjust group**, click the **Reset Picture button arrow** 🖼, and then click **Reset Picture & Size**.

6 In the **Size group**, click the **Shape Height spin box up arrow** as necessary to change the height of the picture to **4.5"**. Scroll down to view the entire picture on your screen, compare your screen with Figure 1.9, and then **Save** 💾 your document.

When you use the Height and Width *spin boxes* to change the size of a graphic, the graphic will always resize proportionally; that is, the width adjusts as you change the height and vice versa.

Figure 1.9

Picture height increased to 4.5 inches

Activity 1.04 | Wrapping Text Around a Picture

Graphics inserted as inline objects are treated like characters in a sentence, which can result in unattractive spacing. You can change an inline object to a *floating object*—a graphic that can be moved independently of the surrounding text characters.

1 Be sure the picture is selected—you know it is selected if the sizing handles display.

2 On the **Format tab**, in the **Arrange group**, click the **Wrap Text** button to display a gallery of text wrapping arrangements.

> *Text wrapping* refers to the manner in which text displays around an object.

3 From the gallery, click **Square** to wrap the text around the graphic, and then notice the *anchor* symbol to the left of the first line of the paragraph. Compare your screen with Figure 1.10.

> Select square text wrapping when you want to wrap the text to the left or right of the image. When you apply text wrapping, the object is always associated with—anchored to—a specific paragraph.

Figure 1.10

Wrap Text button

Anchor symbol

Text wrapped around picture

4 **Save** 💾 your document.

Activity 1.05 | Moving a Picture

1 Point to the rock climber picture to display the ✛ pointer.

2 Hold down Shift and drag the picture to the right until the right edge of the picture aligns at approximately **6.5 inches on the horizontal ruler**. Notice that the picture moves in a straight line when you hold down Shift. Compare your screen with Figure 1.11.

Figure 1.11

Right edge aligned with right margin

Top edge aligned with top of paragraph

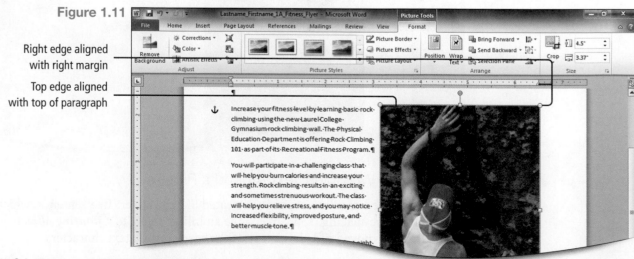

3 If necessary, press any of the arrow keys on your keyboard to *nudge*—move in small increments—the picture in any direction so that the text wraps to match Figure 1.11. **Save** 💾 your document.

Activity 1.06 | Applying Picture Styles and Artistic Effects

Picture styles include shapes, shadows, frames, borders, and other special effects with which you can stylize an image. *Artistic effects* are formats that make pictures look more like sketches or paintings.

1 Be sure the rock climber picture is selected. On the **Format tab**, in the **Picture Styles group**, click the **Picture Effects** button. Point to **Soft Edges**, and then click **5 Point**.

> The Soft Edges feature fades the edges of the picture. The number of points you choose determines how far the fade goes inward from the edges of the picture.

2 On the **Format tab**, in the **Adjust group**, click the **Artistic Effects** button. In the first row of the gallery, point to, but do not click, the third effect—**Pencil Grayscale**.

> Live Preview displays the picture with the *Pencil Grayscale* effect added.

3 In the second row of the gallery, click the third effect—**Paint Brush**. Notice that the picture looks like a painting, rather than a photograph, as shown in Figure 1.12. **Save** 💾 your document.

Figure 1.12

Paint Brush artistic effect applied to picture

Activity 1.07 | Adding a Page Border

Page borders frame a page and help to focus the information on the page.

1 Click anywhere outside the picture to deselect it. On the **Page Layout tab**, in the **Page Background group**, click the **Page Borders** button.

2 In the **Borders and Shading** dialog box, under **Setting**, click **Box**. Under **Style**, scroll down the list about a third of the way and click the heavy top line with the thin bottom line—check the **Preview** area to be sure the heavier line is the nearest to the edges of the page.

3 Click the **Color arrow**, and then in the fourth column, click the first color—**Dark Blue, Text 2**.

4 Under **Apply to**, be sure *Whole document* is selected, and then compare your screen with Figure 1.13.

Figure 1.13

Page Borders button

Page border preview

Box setting

Border style

Border color

5 At the bottom of the **Borders and Shading** dialog box, click **OK**.

6 Press Ctrl + Home to move to the top of the document, and then compare your page border with Figure 1.14. **Save** 💾 your document.

Figure 1.14

Page Border
added to document

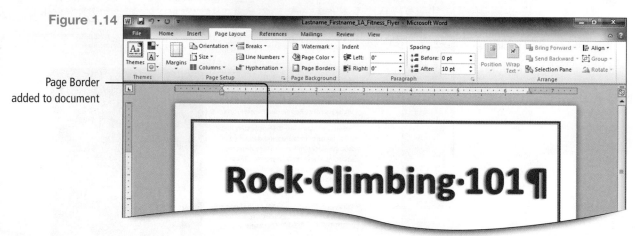

Objective 3 | Insert and Modify Text Boxes and Shapes

Word provides predefined *shapes* and *text boxes* that you can add to your documents. A shape is an object such as a line, arrow, box, callout, or banner. A text box is a movable, resizable container for text or graphics. Use these objects to add visual interest to your document.

Activity 1.08 | Inserting a Shape

1 Press ⬇ one time to move to the blank paragraph below the title. Press Enter four times to make space for a text box, and notice that the picture anchored to the paragraph moves with the text.

2 Press Ctrl + End to move to the bottom of the document, and notice that your insertion point is positioned in the empty paragraph at the end of the document.

3 Click the **Insert tab**, and then in the **Illustrations group**, click the **Shapes** button to display the gallery. Compare your screen with Figure 1.15.

Figure 1.15

Shapes button

Rounded Rectangle shape

Shapes gallery

4 Under **Rectangles**, click the second shape—**Rounded Rectangle**, and then move your pointer. Notice that the ⊞ pointer displays.

5 Position the ⊞ pointer just under the lower left corner of the picture, and then drag down approximately **1 inch** and to the right edge of the picture.

6 Point to the shape and right-click, and then from the shortcut menu, click **Add Text**.

7 With the insertion point blinking inside the shape, point inside the shape and right-click, and then on the Mini toolbar, change the **Font Size** to **16**, and be sure **Center** ≡ alignment is selected.

8 Click inside the shape again, and then type **Improve your strength, balance, and coordination** If necessary, use the lower middle sizing handle to enlarge the shape to view your text. Compare your screen with Figure 1.16. **Save** 🔲 your document.

Figure 1.16

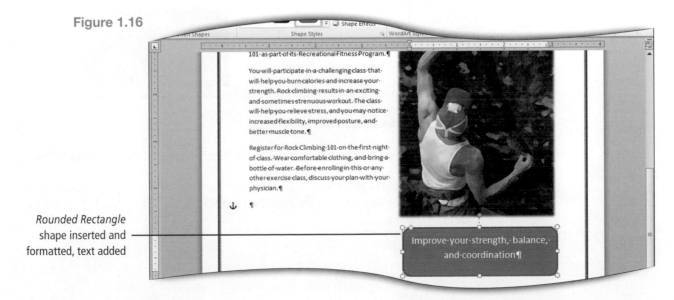

Rounded Rectangle shape inserted and formatted, text added

Activity 1.09 | Inserting a Text Box

A text box is useful to differentiate portions of text from other text on the page. You can move a text box anywhere on the page.

1 Press `Ctrl` + `Home` to move to the top of the document.

2 On the **Insert tab**, in the **Text group**, click the **Text Box** button. At the bottom of the gallery, click **Draw Text Box**.

3 Position the ⊞ pointer below the letter *k* in *Rock*—at approximately **1.5 inches on the vertical ruler**. Drag down and to the right to create a text box approximately **1.5 inches** high and **3 inches** wide—the exact size and location need not be precise.

4 With the insertion point blinking in the text box, type the following, pressing `Enter` after each line to create a new paragraph:

> **Meets Tuesdays and Thursdays, 7-9 p.m.**
>
> **Begins September 13, ends December 16**
>
> **College Gymnasium, Room 104**

5 Compare your screen with Figure 1.17.

Figure 1.17

Text box with inserted text

6 **Save** 💾 your document.

Activity 1.10 | Moving, Resizing, and Formatting Shapes and Text Boxes

1 In the text box you just created in the upper portion of the flyer, select all of the text. From the Mini toolbar, change the **Font Size** to **14**, apply **Bold** **B**, and then **Center** ≡ the text.

2 On the **Format tab**, in the **Size group**, if necessary, click the **Size** button. Click the **Shape Height spin arrows** as necessary to set the height of the text box to **1.2″**. Click the **Shape Width spin arrows** as necessary to set the width of the text box to **4″**.

3 In the **Shape Styles group**, click the **Shape Effects** button. Point to **Shadow**, and then under **Outer**, in the first row, click the first style—**Offset Diagonal Bottom Right**.

4 In the **Shape Styles group**, click the **Shape Outline button arrow**. In the fourth column, click the first color—**Dark Blue, Text 2** to change the color of the text box border.

5 Click the **Shape Outline button arrow** again, point to **Weight**, and then click **3 pt**.

6 Click anywhere in the document to deselect the text box. Notice that with the text box deselected, you can see all the measurements on the horizontal ruler.

7 Click anywhere in the text box and point to the text box border to display the pointer. By dragging, visually center the text box vertically and horizontally in the space below the *Rock Climbing 101* title. Then, if necessary, press any of the arrow keys on your keyboard to nudge the text box in precise increments to match Figure 1.18.

Figure 1.18

Text formatted and centered in text box, shadow added, border color and weight changed

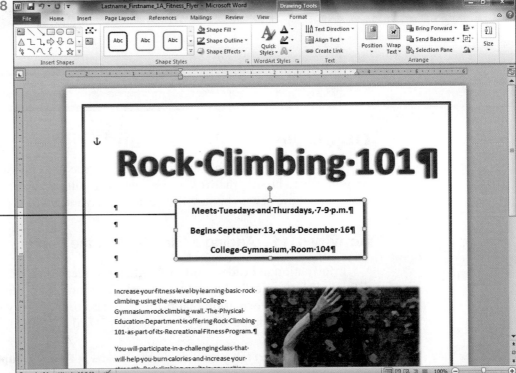

8 Press Ctrl + End to move to the bottom of the document. Click on the border of the rounded rectangular shape to select it.

9 On the **Format tab**, in the **Size group**, if necessary, click the **Size** button. Click the **Shape Height spin arrows** as necessary to change the height of the shape to **0.8″**.

10 In the **Shape Styles group**, click the **Shape Fill button arrow**, and then at the bottom of the gallery, point to **Gradient**. Under **Dark Variations**, in the third row click the first gradient—**Linear Diagonal - Bottom Left to Top Right**.

11 In the **Shape Styles group**, click the **Shape Outline button arrow**. In the sixth column, click the first color—**Red, Accent 2**.

12 Click the **Shape Outline button arrow** again, point to **Weight**, and then click **1 1/2 pt**. Click anywhere in the document to deselect the shape. Compare your screen with Figure 1.19, and then **Save** 💾 your document.

Figure 1.19

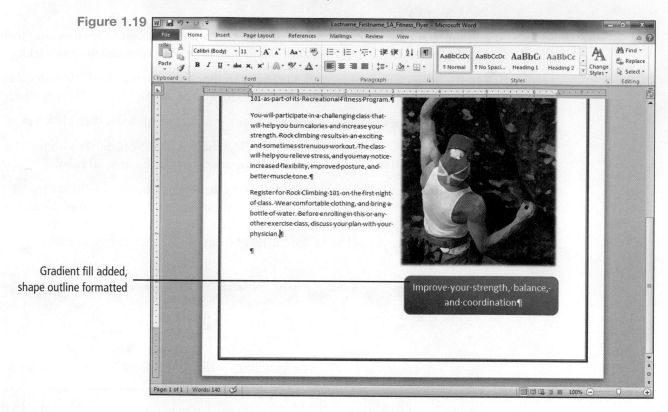

Gradient fill added, shape outline formatted

Objective 4 | Preview and Print a Document

While you are creating your document, it is useful to preview your document periodically to be sure that you are getting the result you want. Then, before printing, make a final preview to be sure the document layout is what you intended.

Activity 1.11 | Adding a File Name to the Footer

Information in headers and footers helps to identify a document when it is printed or displayed electronically. Recall that a header is information that prints at the top of every page; a footer is information that prints at the bottom of every page. In this textbook, you will insert the file name in the footer of every Word document.

Another Way

At the bottom edge of the page, right-click; from the shortcut menu, click Edit Footer.

1 Click the **Insert tab**, and then, in the **Header & Footer group**, click the **Footer** button.

2 At the bottom of the **Footer** gallery, click **Edit Footer**.

The footer area displays with the insertion point blinking at the left edge, and on the Ribbon, the Header & Footer Tools display and add the Design tab.

3 On the **Design tab**, in the **Insert group**, click the **Quick Parts** button, and then click **Field**. In the **Field** dialog box, under **Field names**, use the vertical scroll bar to examine the items that you can insert in a header or footer.

A *field* is a placeholder that displays preset content such as the current date, the file name, a page number, or other stored information.

4 In the **Field names** list, scroll as necessary to locate and then click **FileName**. Compare your screen with Figure 1.20.

Figure 1.20

Quick Parts button

Field dialog box

FileName field

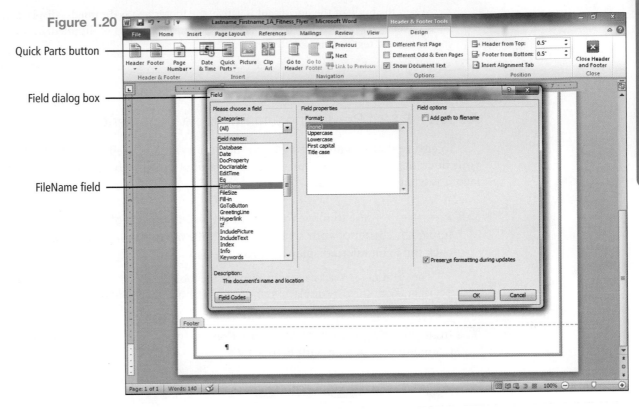

5 In the lower right corner of the **Field** dialog box, click **OK**, and then compare your screen with Figure 1.21.

Figure 1.21

Document text and image dimmed when footer is open

File name in footer

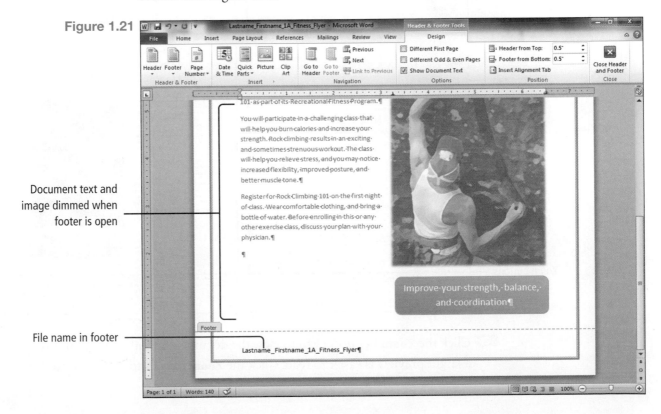

Another Way

Double-click anywhere in the document to close the footer area.

6 On the **Design tab**, at the far right in the **Close group**, click the **Close Header and Footer** button.

> When the body of the document is active, the footer text is dimmed—displays in gray. Conversely, when the footer area is active, the footer text is not dimmed; instead, the document text is dimmed.

7 **Save** 💾 your document.

Activity 1.12 | Previewing and Printing a Document

To ensure that you are getting the result you want, it is useful to periodically preview your document. Then, before printing, make a final preview to be sure the document layout is what you intended.

Another Way

Press Ctrl + F2 to display Print Preview.

1 Press Ctrl + Home to move the insertion point to the top of the document. In the upper left corner of your screen, click the **File tab** to display **Backstage** view, and then click the **Print tab** to display the **Print Preview**.

> The Print tab in Backstage view displays the tools you need to select your settings. On the right, Print Preview displays your document exactly as it will print; the formatting marks do not display.

2 In the lower right corner of the **Print Preview**, notice the zoom buttons that display. Compare your screen with Figure 1.22.

Figure 1.22

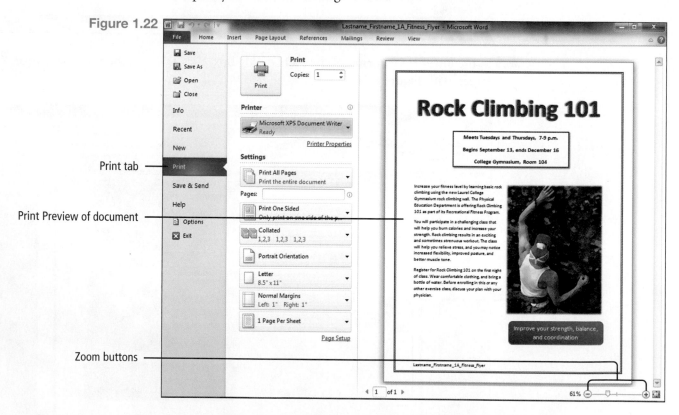

Print tab

Print Preview of document

Zoom buttons

3 Click the **Zoom In** button ⊕ to view the document at full size, and notice that a larger preview is easier to read. Click the **Zoom Out** button ⊖ to view the entire page.

4 Click the **Info tab**. On the right, under the screen thumbnail, click **Properties**, and then click **Show Document Panel**.

Here you can adjust the document properties.

5 In the **Author** box, delete any text and then type your firstname and lastname. In the **Subject** box type your course name and section number, and in the **Keywords** box type **fitness, rock climbing Close** the Document Panel.

6 **Save** 🖫 your document. To print, display **Backstage** view, and then on the **navigation bar**, click **Print**. In the **Settings** group, be sure the correct printer is selected, and then in the **Print group**, click the **Print** button. Or, submit your document electronically as directed by your instructor.

7 In **Backstage** view, click **Exit** to close the document and exit Word.

End **You have completed Project 1A** ——————————————————

Project 1B Information Handout

myitlab
Project 1B Training

Project Activities

In Activities 1.13 through 1.23, you will format and add lists to an information handout that describes student activities at Laurel College. Your completed document will look similar to Figure 1.23.

Project Files

For Project 1B, you will need the following file:

w01B_Student_Activities

You will save your document as:

Lastname_Firstname_1B_Student_Activities

Project Results

Every spring, students vote for the President, Vice President, Treasurer, Secretary, and Student Trustee for the following year. Executive Officers work with the college administration to manage campus activities and to make changes to policies and procedures. For example, the Student Trustee is a

...th consists of elected members from the
...college budget, and employee hiring.
...the Board to vote for a proposal to
...ocations in Laurelton and outlying areas.

...clubs and academic organizations vote for
...on information and applications on the
...mpus and in the student newspaper.

...f interests, including academic, political,
...currently in existence at Laurel College. A
...oin a club, you may enjoy being a member
...or you may decide to take a leadership role

...fice in the Campus Center, Room CC208, or
...d complete the form online. Clubs accept
...e following are the first meeting dates and

... October 8, 2:00 p.m., Room CC214
...ctober 5, 5:00 p.m., Computer Café
...7, 3:00 p.m., Field House, Room 2A
... October 6, 2:00 p.m., Room CC212
...6, 4:00 p.m., Math Tutoring Lab, L35
... October 8, 3:00 p.m., Room CC214
...4, 5:30 p.m., Photo Lab, Foster Hall
...........October 8, 5:00 p.m., Room L24
... October 7, 4:30 p.m., Room CC214
...October 4, 3:00 p.m., Little Theater

...listed here, are great, but your goals are
...ng a degree or certificate. Maybe you want
...ou leave Laurel College. Whatever your
...ur education, work experience, and
...lly ones in which you had a leadership role,

Associated Students of Laurel College

Student Activities
Government **Clubs**

Get Involved in Student Activities

Your experience at Laurel College will be richer and more memorable if you get involved in activities that take you beyond the classroom. You will have the opportunity to meet other students, faculty, and staff members and will participate in organizations that make valuable contributions to your college and to the community.

Consider becoming involved in student government or joining a club. You might take part in activities such as these:

✓ Volunteering to help with a blood drive
✓ Traveling to a foreign country to learn about other cultures
✓ Volunteering to assist at graduation
✓ Helping to organize a community picnic
✓ Planning and implementing advertising for a student event
✓ Meeting with members of the state legislature to discuss issues that affect college students—for example, tuition costs and financial aid

Student Government

As a registered student, you are eligible to attend meetings of the Executive Officers of the Associated Students of Laurel College. At the meetings, you will have the opportunity to learn about college issues that affect students. At the conclusion of each meeting, the Officers invite students to voice their opinions. Eventually, you might decide to run for an office yourself. Running for office is a three-step process:

1. Pick up petitions at the Student Government office.
2. Obtain 100 signatures from current students.
3. Turn in petitions and start campaigning.

Lastname_Firstname_1B_Student_Activities

Figure 1.23
Project 1B Student Activities

Objective 5 | Change Document and Paragraph Layout

Document layout includes *margins*—the space between the text and the top, bottom, left, and right edges of the paper. Paragraph layout includes line spacing, indents, and tabs. In Word, the information about paragraph formats is stored in the paragraph mark at the end of a paragraph. When you press the Enter, the new paragraph mark contains the formatting of the previous paragraph, unless you take steps to change it.

Activity 1.13 | Setting Margins

1 **Start** Word. From **Backstage** view, display the **Open** dialog box. From your student files, locate and open the document **w01B_Student_Activities**. On the **Home tab**, in the **Paragraph group**, be sure the **Show/Hide** button ¶ is active—glows orange—so that you can view the formatting marks.

2 From **Backstage** view, display the **Save As** dialog box. Navigate to your **Word Chapter 1** folder, and then **Save** the document as **Lastname_Firstname_1B_Student_Activities**

3 Click the **Page Layout tab**. In the **Page Setup group**, click the **Margins** button, and then take a moment to study the buttons in the Margins gallery.

The top button displays the most recent custom margin settings, while the other buttons display commonly used margin settings.

4 At the bottom of the **Margins** gallery, click **Custom Margins**.

5 In the **Page Setup** dialog box, press Tab as necessary to select the value in the **Left** box, and then, with *1.25"* selected, type **1**

This action will change the left margin to 1 inch on all pages of the document. You do not need to type the inch (") mark.

6 Press Tab to select the margin in the **Right** box, and then type **1** At the bottom of the dialog box, notice that the new margins will apply to the **Whole document**. Compare your screen with Figure 1.24.

Figure 1.24

Margins button

Left and Right margins changed

Changes applied to entire document

Another Way

Click the View tab, and then in the Show group, select the Ruler check box.

7 Click **OK** to apply the new margins and close the dialog box. If the ruler below the Ribbon is not displayed, at the top of the vertical scroll bar, click the View Ruler button 🔲.

8 Scroll to view the bottom of **Page 1** and the top of **Page 2**. Notice that the page edges display, and the page number and total number of pages display on the left side of the status bar.

9 Near the bottom edge of **Page 1**, point anywhere in the margin area, right-click, and then click **Edit Footer** to display the footer area.

10 On the **Design tab**, in the **Insert group**, click the **Quick Parts** button, and then click **Field**. In the **Field** dialog box, under **Field names**, locate and click **FileName**, and then click **OK**.

11 Double-click anywhere in the document to close the footer area, and then **Save** 🔲 your document.

Activity 1.14 | Aligning Text

Alignment refers to the placement of paragraph text relative to the left and right margins. Most paragraph text uses *left alignment*—aligned at the left margin, leaving the right margin uneven. Three other types of paragraph alignment are: *center alignment*— centered between the left and right margins; *right alignment*—aligned at the right margin with an uneven left margin; and *justified alignment*—text aligned evenly at both the left and right margins. See the table in Figure 1.25.

Paragraph Alignment Options

Alignment	Button	Description and Example
Align Text Left	▤	Align Text Left is the default paragraph alignment in Word. Text in the paragraph aligns at the left margin, and the right margin is uneven.
Center	▤	Center alignment aligns text in the paragraph so that it is centered between the left and right margins.
Align Text Right	▤	Align Text Right aligns text at the right margin. Using Align Text Right, the left margin, which is normally even, is uneven.
Justify	▤	The Justify alignment option adds additional space between words so that both the left and right margins are even. Justify is often used when formatting newspaper-style columns.

Figure 1.25

1 Scroll to position the middle of **Page 2** on your screen, look at the left and right margins, and notice that the text is justified—both the right and left margins of multiple-line paragraphs are aligned evenly at the margins. On the **Home tab**, in the **Paragraph group**, notice that the **Justify** button 🔲 is active.

2 In the paragraph that begins *Every spring, students vote*, in the first line, look at the space following the word *Every*, and then compare it with the space following the word *Trustee* in the second line. Notice how some of the spaces between words are larger than others.

To achieve a justified right margin, Word adjusts the size of spaces between words in this manner, which can result in unattractive spacing in a document that spans the width of a page. Many individuals find such spacing difficult to read.

Another Way

On the Home tab, in the Editing group, click the Select button, and then click Select All.

3 Press Ctrl + A to select all of the text in the document, and then on the **Home tab**, in the **Paragraph group**, click the **Align Text Left** button.

4 Press Ctrl + Home. At the top of the document, in the left margin area, point to the left of the first paragraph—*Associated Students of Laurel College*—until the pointer displays, and then click one time to select the paragraph. On the Mini toolbar, change the **Font Size** to **26**.

Use this technique to select entire lines of text.

5 Point to the left of the first paragraph—*Associated Students of Laurel College*—to display the pointer again, and then drag down to select the first two paragraphs, which form the title and subtitle of the document.

6 On the Mini toolbar, click the **Center** button to center the title and subtitle between the left and right margins, and then compare your screen with Figure 1.26.

Figure 1.26

Title centered and font size set to 26

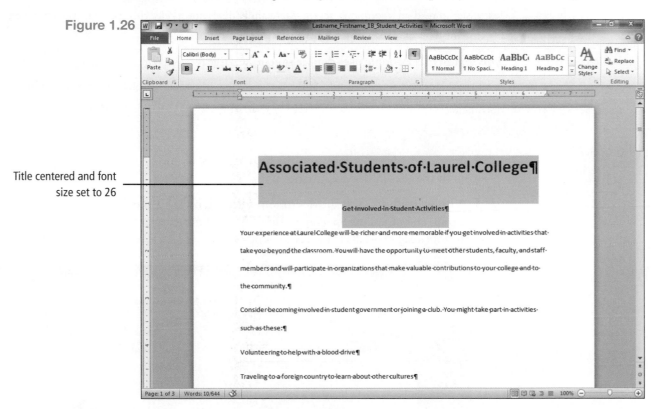

7 Scroll down to view the bottom of **Page 1**, and then locate the first bold subheading—*Student Government*. Point to the left of the paragraph to display the pointer, and then click one time.

8 With *Student Government* selected, use your mouse wheel or the vertical scroll bar to bring the lower portion of **Page 2** into view. Locate the subheading *Clubs*. Move the pointer to the left of the paragraph to display the pointer, hold down Ctrl, and then click one time.

Two subheadings are selected; in Windows-based programs, you can hold down Ctrl to select multiple items.

9 On the Mini toolbar, click the **Center** button to center both subheadings, and then click **Save**.

Activity 1.15 | Changing Line Spacing

Line spacing is the distance between lines of text in a paragraph. Three of the most commonly used line spacing options are shown in the table in Figure 1.27.

Line Spacing Options

Alignment	Description, Example, and Information
Single spacing	**This text in this example uses single spacing**. Single spacing was once the most commonly used spacing in business documents. Now, because so many documents are read on a computer screen rather than on paper, single spacing is becoming less popular.
Multiple 1.15 spacing	**This text in this example uses multiple 1.15 spacing**. The default line spacing in Microsoft Word 2010 is 1.15, which is equivalent to single spacing with an extra 1/6 line added between lines to make the text easier to read on a computer screen. Many individuals now prefer this spacing, even on paper, because the lines of text appear less crowded.
Double spacing	**This text in this example uses double spacing**. College research papers and draft documents that need space for notes are commonly double-spaced; there is space for a full line of text between each document line.

Figure 1.27

1 Press Ctrl + Home to move to the beginning of the document. Press Ctrl + A to select all of the text in the document.

2 With all of the text in the document selected, on the **Home tab**, in the **Paragraph group**, click the **Line Spacing** button, and notice that the text in the document is double spaced—**2.0** is checked. Compare your screen with Figure 1.28.

Figure 1.28

Document text double-spaced

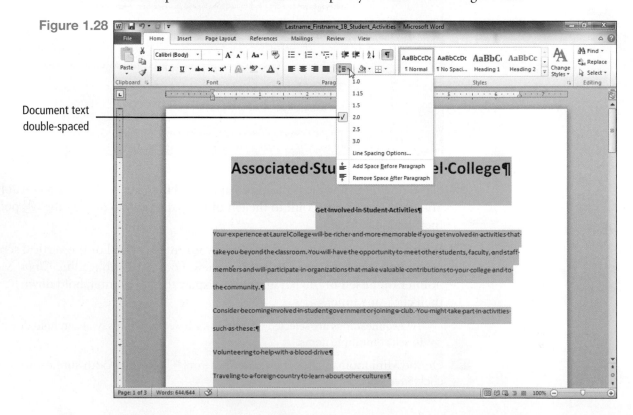

3 On the **Line Spacing** menu, click the *second* setting—**1.15**—and then click anywhere in the document. Compare your screen with Figure 1.29, and then **Save** 🖫 your document.

Double spacing is most commonly used in research papers and rough draft documents. Recall that 1.15 is the default line spacing for new Word documents. Line spacing of 1.15 has slightly more space between the lines than single spacing. On a computer screen, spacing of 1.15 is easier to read than single spacing. Because a large percentage of Word documents are read on a computer screen, 1.15 is the default spacing for a new Word document.

Figure 1.29

Line spacing changed to 1.15

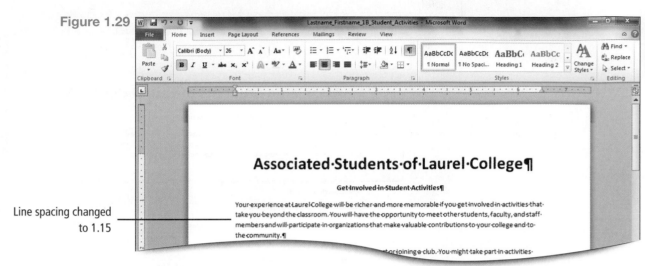

Activity 1.16 | Indenting Text and Adding Space After Paragraphs

Common techniques to distinguish paragraphs include adding space after each paragraph, indenting the first line of each paragraph, or both.

1 Below the title and subtitle of the document, click anywhere in the paragraph that begins *Your experience.*

2 On the **Home tab**, in the **Paragraph group**, click the **Dialog Box Launcher** 🖬.

3 In the **Paragraph** dialog box, on the **Indents and Spacing tab**, under **Indentation**, click the **Special arrow**, and then click **First line** to indent the first line by 0.5″, which is the default indent setting. Compare your screen with Figure 1.30.

Figure 1.30

First line indent applied

4 Click **OK**, and then click anywhere in the next paragraph, which begins *Consider becoming*. On the ruler under the Ribbon, drag the **First Line Indent** button ▽ to **0.5 inches on the horizontal ruler**, and then compare your screen with Figure 1.31.

Figure 1.31

First line Indent button ——

First lines indented ——

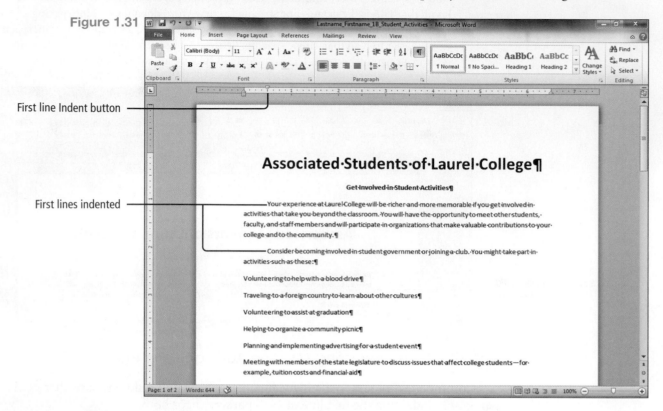

Another Way

On either the Home tab or the Page Layout tab, display the Paragraph dialog box from the Paragraph group, and then under Spacing, click the spin box arrows as necessary.

5 By using either of the techniques you just practiced, or by using the Format Painter, apply a first line indent of **0.5″** in the paragraph that begins *As a registered* to match the indent of the remaining paragraphs in the document.

6 Press Ctrl + A to select all of the text in the document. Click the **Page Layout tab**, and then in the **Paragraph group**, under **Spacing**, click the **After spin box down arrow** one time to change the value to **6 pt**.

> To change the value in the box, you can also select the existing number, type a new number, and then press Enter. This document will use 6 pt spacing after paragraphs.

7 Press Ctrl + Home, and then compare your screen with Figure 1.32.

Figure 1.32

Spacing After set to 6 pt ——

8 Scroll to view the lower portion of **Page 1**. Select the subheading *Student Government*, including the paragraph mark following it, hold down [Ctrl], and then select the subheading *Clubs*.

9 With both subheadings selected, in the **Paragraph group**, under **Spacing**, click the **Before up spin box arrow** two times to set the **Spacing Before** to **12 pt**. Compare your screen with Figure 1.33, and then **Save** 🖫 your document.

> This action increases the amount of space above each of the two subheadings, which will make them easy to distinguish in the document. The formatting is applied only to the two selected paragraphs.

Figure 1.33
Spacing before set to 12 pt.

12-point spacing before paragraphs

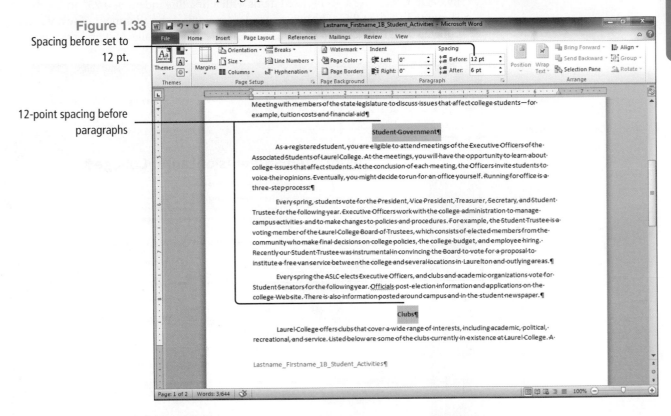

Objective 6 | Create and Modify Lists

To display a list of information, you can choose a ***bulleted list***, which uses ***bullets***—text symbols such as small circles or check marks—to introduce each item in a list. You can also choose a ***numbered list***, which uses consecutive numbers or letters to introduce each item in a list.

Use a bulleted list if the items in the list can be introduced in any order; use a numbered list for items that have definite steps, a sequence of actions, or are in chronological order.

Activity 1.17 | Creating a Bulleted List

1 In the upper portion of **Page 1**, locate the paragraph that begins *Volunteering to help*, and then point to this paragraph from the left margin area to display the 𝄃 pointer. Drag down to select this paragraph and the next five paragraphs.

2 On the **Home tab**, in the **Paragraph group**, click the **Bullets** button ▤▾ to change the selected text to a bulleted list.

> The spacing between each of the bulleted points changes to the spacing between lines in a paragraph—in this instance, 1.15 line spacing. The spacing after the last item in the list is the same as the spacing after each paragraph—in this instance, 6 pt. Each bulleted item is automatically indented.

3 On the ruler, point to the **First Line Indent** button ▽ and read the ScreenTip, and then point to the **Hanging Indent** button △. Compare your screen with Figure 1.34.

> By default, Word formats bulleted items with a first line indent of 0.25″ and adds a Hanging Indent at 0.5″. The hanging indent maintains the alignment of text when a bulleted item is more than one line, for example, the last bulleted item in this list.

Figure 1.34

Hanging Indent button on ruler

Bulleted list

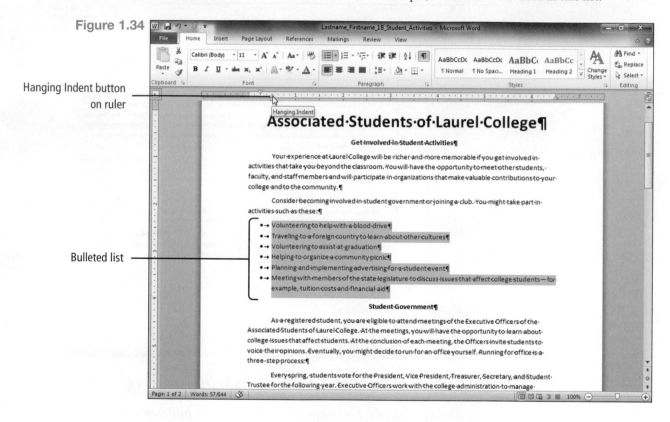

4 Scroll down to view **Page 2**. By using the ⟰ pointer from the left margin area, select all of the paragraphs that indicate the club names and meeting dates, beginning with *Chess Club* and ending with *Theater Club*.

5 In the **Paragraph group**, click the **Bullets** button ▤▾, and then **Save** 🖫 your document.

Activity 1.18 | Creating a Numbered List

1 Scroll to view **Page 1**, and then under the subheading *Student Government*, in the paragraph that begins *As a registered student*, click to position the insertion point at the *end* of the paragraph following the colon. Press [Enter] to create a blank paragraph.

2 Notice that the paragraph is indented, because the First Line Indent from the previous paragraph carried over to the new paragraph.

3 To change the indent formatting for this paragraph, on the ruler, drag the **First Line Indent** button to the left so that it is positioned directly above the lower button. Compare your screen with Figure 1.35.

First Line Indent button

Paragraph with no first line indent

Figure 1.35

4 Being sure to include the period, type **1.** and press Spacebar.

Word determines that this paragraph is the first item in a numbered list and formats the new paragraph accordingly, indenting the list in the same manner as the bulleted list. The space after the number changes to a tab, and the AutoCorrect Options button displays to the left of the list item. The tab is indicated by a right arrow formatting mark.

Alert! | Activating Automatic Numbered Lists

If a numbered list does not begin automatically, display Backstage view, and then click the Options tab. On the left side of the Word Options dialog box, click Proofing. Under AutoCorrect options, click the AutoCorrect Options button. In the AutoCorrect dialog box, click the AutoFormat As You Type tab. Under *Apply as you type*, select the *Automatic numbered lists* check box, and then click OK two times to close both dialog boxes.

---

5 Click the **AutoCorrect Options** button, and then compare your screen with Figure 1.36.

From the displayed list, you can remove the automatic formatting here, or stop using the automatic numbered lists option in this document. You also have the option to open the AutoCorrect dialog box to *Control AutoFormat Options*.

AutoCorrect Options button

Figure 1.36

6 Click the **AutoCorrect Options** button again to close the menu without selecting any of the commands. Type **Pick up petitions at the Student Government office.** and press Enter. Notice that the second number and a tab are added to the next line.

7 Type **Obtain 100 signatures from current students.** and press Enter. Type **Turn in petitions and start campaigning.** and press Enter. Compare your screen with Figure 1.37.

Figure 1.37

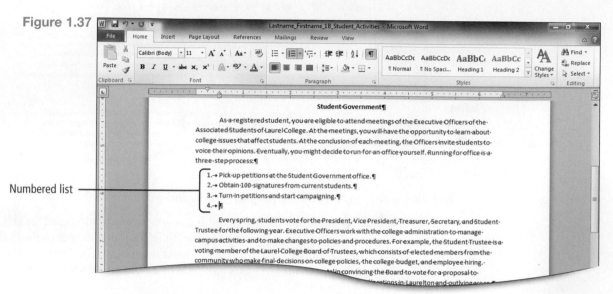

Numbered list

8 Press ←Bksp to turn off the list numbering. Then, press ←Bksp three more times to remove the blank paragraph. Compare your screen with Figure 1.38.

Figure 1.38

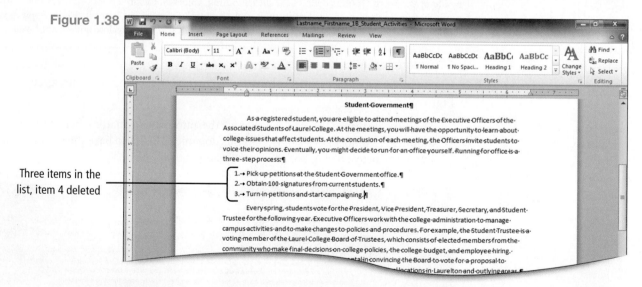

Three items in the list, item 4 deleted

9 **Save** 💾 your document.

More Knowledge | To End a List

To turn a list off, you can press ←Bksp, click the Numbering or Bullets button, or press Enter a second time. Both list buttons—Numbering and Bullets—act as *toggle buttons*; that is, clicking the button one time turns the feature on, and clicking the button again turns the feature off.

Activity 1.19 | Customizing Bullets

1 Press [Ctrl] + [End] to move to the end of the document, and then scroll up as necessary to display the bulleted list containing the list of clubs.

2 Point to the left of the first list item to display the pointer, and then drag down to select all the clubs in the list—the bullet symbols are not highlighted.

3 Point to the selected list and right-click. From the shortcut menu, point to **Bullets**, and then compare your screen with Figure 1.39.

Figure 1.39

Check mark bullet

4 Under **Bullet Library**, click the **check mark** symbol. If the check mark is not available, choose another bullet symbol.

> **Another Way**
>
> On the Home tab, in the Clipboard group, click the Format Painter button.

5 With the bulleted list still selected, right-click over the list, and then on the Mini toolbar, click the **Format Painter** button.

6 Use the vertical scroll bar or your mouse wheel to scroll to view **Page 1**. Move the pointer to the left of the first item in the bulleted list to display the pointer, and then drag down to select all of the items in the list and to apply the format of the second bulleted list to this list. Compare your screen with Figure 1.40, and then **Save** your document.

Figure 1.40

Bullet symbol changed

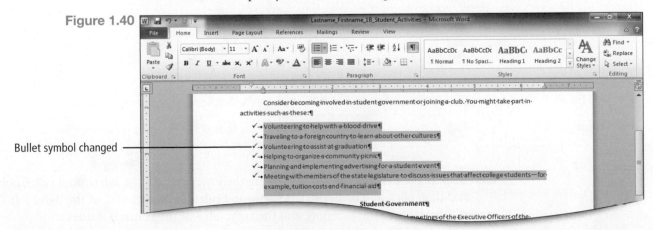

Objective 7 | Set and Modify Tab Stops

Tab stops mark specific locations on a line of text. Use tab stops to indent and align text, and use the Tab key to move to tab stops.

Activity 1.20 | Setting Tab Stops

1 Scroll to view the middle of **Page 2**, and then by using the pointer at the left of the first item, select all of the items in the bulleted list. Notice that there is a tab mark between the name of the club and the date.

The arrow that indicates a tab is a nonprinting formatting mark.

2 To the left of the horizontal ruler, point to the **Tab Alignment** button ⊑ to display the *Left Tab* ScreenTip, and then compare your screen with Figure 1.41.

Figure 1.41

Tab Alignment button
Left Tab ScreenTip
Tab mark

3 Click the **Tab Alignment** button ⊑ several times to view the tab alignment options shown in the table in Figure 1.42.

Tab Alignment Options

Type	Tab Alignment Button Displays This Marker	Description
Left	⊑	Text is left aligned at the tab stop and extends to the right.
Center	⊥	Text is centered around the tab stop.
Right	⊿	Text is right aligned at the tab stop and extends to the left.
Decimal	⊥	The decimal point aligns at the tab stop.
Bar	⏐	A vertical bar displays at the tab stop.
First Line Indent	▽	Text in the first line of a paragraph indents.
Hanging Indent	△	Text in all lines except the first line in the paragraph indents.
Left Indent	⊔	Moves both the First Line Indent and Hanging Indent buttons.

Figure 1.42

4 Display the **Left Tab** button ⊑. Along the lower edge of the horizontal ruler, point to and then click at **3 inches on the horizontal ruler**. Notice that all of the dates left align at the new tab stop location, and the right edge of the column is uneven.

5 Compare your screen with Figure 1.43, and then **Save** 🖫 your document.

Figure 1.43

Left tab mark in ruler —

Tabbed items aligned on left —

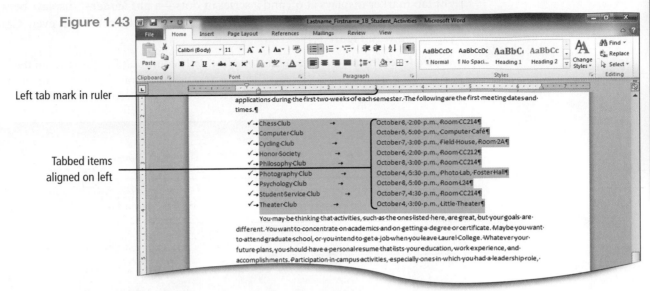

Activity 1.21 | Modifying Tab Stops

Tab stops are a form of paragraph formatting, and thus, the information about tab stops is stored in the paragraph mark in the paragraphs to which they were applied.

1 With the bulleted list still selected, on the ruler, point to the new tab marker, and then when the *Left Tab* ScreenTip displays, drag the tab marker to **3.5 inches on the horizontal ruler**.

In all of the selected lines, the text at the tab stop left aligns at 3.5 inches.

Another Way

On the Home tab, in the Paragraph group, click the Dialog Box Launcher. At the bottom of the Paragraph dialog box, click the Tabs button.

2 On the ruler, point to the tab marker to display the ScreenTip, and then double-click to display the **Tabs** dialog box.

3 In the **Tabs** dialog box, under **Tab stop position**, if necessary select *3.5"* and then type **6**

4 Under **Alignment**, click the **Right** option button. Under **Leader**, click the **2** option button. Near the bottom of the **Tabs** dialog box, click **Set**.

Because the Right tab will be used to align the items in the list, the tab stop at 3.5" is no longer necessary.

5 In the **Tabs** dialog box, in the **Tab stop position** box, click **3.5"** to select this tab stop, and then in the lower portion of the **Tabs** dialog box, click the **Clear** button to delete this tab stop, which is no longer necessary. Compare your screen with Figure 1.44.

Figure 1.44

Tab stop position —

Right tab selected —

Leader 2 selected —

6 Click **OK**. On the ruler, notice that the left tab marker at *3.5″* no longer displays, a right tab marker displays at *6″*, and a series of dots—a **dot leader**—displays between the columns of the list. Notice also that the right edge of the column is even. Compare your screen with Figure 1.45.

A **leader character** creates a solid, dotted, or dashed line that fills the space to the left of a tab character and draws the reader's eyes across the page from one item to the next. When the character used for the leader is a dot, it is commonly referred to as a dot leader.

Figure 1.45

Right tab marker

Tabbed items aligned right

Dot leader

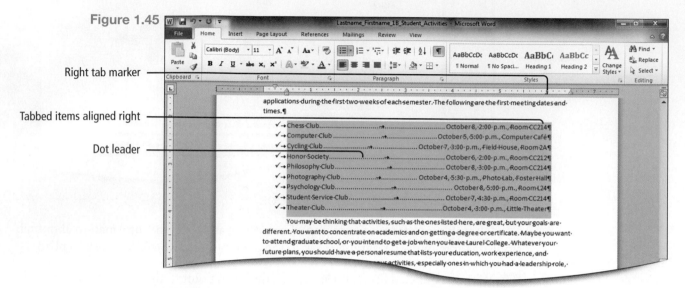

7 In the bulleted list that uses dot leaders, locate the *Honor Society* item, and then click to position the insertion point at the end of that line. Press [Enter] to create a new blank bullet item.

8 Type **Math Club** and press [Tab]. Notice that a dot leader fills the space to the tab marker location.

9 Type **October 6, 4:00 p.m., Math Tutoring Lab, L35** and notice that the text moves to the left to maintain the right alignment of the tab stop.

10 **Save** 💾 your document.

Objective 8 | Insert a SmartArt Graphic

SmartArt graphics are designer-quality visual representations of information, and Word provides many different layouts from which you can choose. A SmartArt graphic can communicate your messages or ideas more effectively than plain text and adds visual interest to a document or Web page.

Activity 1.22 | Inserting a SmartArt Graphic

1 Press [Ctrl] + [Home] to move to the top of the document. Press [End] to move to the end of the first paragraph—the title—and then press [Enter] to create a blank paragraph.

Because the paragraph above is 26 pt font size, the new paragraph mark displays in that size.

2 Click the **Insert tab**, and then in the **Illustrations group**, point to the **SmartArt** button to display its ScreenTip. Read the ScreenTip, and then click the button.

3 In the center portion of the **Choose a SmartArt Graphic** dialog box, scroll down and examine the numerous types of SmartArt graphics available.

4 On the left, click **Hierarchy**, and then in the first row, click the first graphic—**Organization Chart**.

At the right of the dialog box, a preview and description of the graphic displays.

5 Compare your screen with Figure 1.46.

Figure 1.46

SmartArt button

Preview of selected SmartArt

Hierarchy category

6 Click **OK**. If the pane indicating *Type your text here* does not display on the left side of the graphic, on the Design tab, in the Create Graphic group, click the Text Pane button. **Save** your document.

The SmartArt graphic displays at the insertion point location and consists of two parts—the graphic itself, and the Text Pane. On the Ribbon, the SmartArt Tools add the Design tab and the Format tab. You can type directly into the graphics, or type in the Text Pane. By typing in the Text Pane, you might find it easier to organize your layout.

Activity 1.23 | Modifying a SmartArt Graphic

1 In the SmartArt graphic, in the second row, click the border of the *[Text]* box to display a *solid* border and sizing handles, and then press Del. Repeat this procedure in the bottom row to delete the middle *[Text]* box.

Another Way

Close the Text Pane and type the text directly in the SmartArt boxes.

2 In the **Text Pane**, click in the top bulleted point, and then type **Student Activities** Notice that the first bulleted point aligns further to the left than the other points.

The *top-level points* are the main points in a SmartArt graphic. *Subpoints* are indented second-level bullet points.

3 Press ⬇. Type **Government** and then press ⬇ again. Type **Clubs** and then compare your screen with Figure 1.47.

Figure 1.47

SmartArt graphic

Text Pane

Top-level point

Subpoints

4 In the upper right corner of the **Text Pane**, click the **Close** button ☒.

5 Click the border of the SmartArt graphic—a pale border surrounds it. Click the **Format tab**, and then in the **Size group**, if necessary click the **Size** button to display the **Shape Height** and **Shape Width** boxes.

6 Set the **Height** to **2.5″** and the **Width** to **4.2″**, and then compare your screen with Figure 1.48.

Figure 1.48

Size button

Height and Width set

7 With the SmartArt graphic still selected, click the **Design tab**, and then in the **SmartArt Styles group**, click the **Change Colors** button. Under **Colorful**, click the second style—**Colorful Range - Accent Colors 2 to 3**.

8 On the **Design tab**, in the **SmartArt Styles group**, click the **More** button ⊡. Under **3-D**, click the first style—**Polished**. Compare your screen with Figure 1.49.

Figure 1.49

Polished style selected

SmartArt color and style changed

9 Click outside of the graphic to deselect it. Display **Backstage** view. On the right, under the screen thumbnail, click **Properties**, and then click **Show Document Panel**. In the **Author** box, delete any text and then type your firstname and lastname. In the **Subject** box, type your course name and section number, and in the **Keywords** box type **Student Activities, Associated Students Close** ☒ the Document Panel and **Save** 🖫 your document.

10 Display **Backstage** view, and then click **Print** to display **Print Preview**. At the bottom of the preview, click the **Next Page** ▶ and **Previous Page** ◀ buttons to move between pages. If necessary, return to the document and make any necessary changes.

11 As directed by your instructor, print your document or submit it electronically. **Close** ☒ Word.

More Knowledge | Changing the Bullet Level in a SmartArt Graphic

To increase or decrease the level of an item, on the Design tab, in the Create Graphic group, click either the Promote or the Demote button.

End **You have completed Project 1B**

Content-Based Assessments

Summary

In this chapter, you created and formatted documents using Microsoft Word 2010. You inserted and formatted graphics, created and formatted bulleted and numbered lists, and created and formatted text boxes. You also created lists using tab stops with dot leaders, and created and modified a SmartArt graphic.

Key Terms

Matching

Match each term in the second column with its correct definition in the first column by writing the letter of the term on the blank line in front of the correct definition.

_____ 1. Formats that make pictures look more like sketches or paintings.

_____ 2. A small box with an upward- and downward-pointing arrow that enables you to move rapidly through a set of values by clicking.

_____ 3. Small circles in the corners of a selected graphic with which you can resize the graphic proportionally.

_____ 4. The manner in which text displays around an object.

_____ 5. An object or graphic that can be moved independently of the surrounding text.

_____ 6. The process of using the arrow keys to move an object in small precise increments.

_____ 7. An object or graphic inserted in a document that acts like a character in a sentence.

_____ 8. Frames, shapes, shadows, borders, and other special effects that can be added to an image to create an overall visual style for the image.

_____ 9. Predefined drawing objects, such as stars, banners, arrows, and callouts, included with Microsoft Office, and that can be inserted into documents.

A Artistic effects

B Bullets

C Floating object

D Inline object

E Justified alignment

F Left alignment

G Line spacing

H Nudge

I Picture styles

J Shapes

K Sizing handles

L SmartArt

M Spin box

N Tab stop

O Text wrapping

_____ 10. A commonly used alignment of text in which text is aligned at the left margin, leaving the right margin uneven.

_____ 11. An alignment of text in which the text is evenly aligned on both the left and right margins.

_____ 12. The distance between lines of text in a paragraph.

_____ 13. Text symbols such as small circles or check marks that introduce items in a list.

_____ 14. A mark on the ruler that indicates the location where the insertion point will be placed when you press the Tab key.

_____ 15. A designer-quality graphic used to create a visual representation of information.

Multiple Choice

Circle the correct answer.

1. Characters that display on the screen to show the location of paragraphs, tabs, and spaces, but that do not print, are called:
   A. text effects
   B. bullets
   C. formatting marks

2. The placement of paragraph text relative to the left and right margins is referred to as:
   A. alignment
   B. spacing
   C. indents

3. The symbol that indicates to which paragraph an image is attached is:
   A. a small arrow
   B. an anchor
   C. a paragraph mark

4. A movable, resizable container for text or graphics is a:
   A. text box
   B. dialog box
   C. SmartArt graphic

5. A banner is an example of a predefined:
   A. paragraph
   B. format
   C. shape

6. A placeholder that displays preset content, such as the current date, the file name, a page number, or other stored information is:
   A. a leader
   B. a field
   C. a tab

7. The space between the text and the top, bottom, left, and right edges of the paper are referred to as:
   A. alignment
   B. margins
   C. spacing

8. A group of items in which items are displayed in order to indicate definite steps, a sequence of actions, or chronological order is a:
   A. numbered list
   B. bulleted list
   C. outline list

9. A series of dots following a tab that serve to guide the reader's eye is a:
   A. leader
   B. field
   C. shape

10. Tab stops are a form of:
    A. line formatting
    B. document formatting
    C. paragraph formatting

Content-Based Assessments

Apply 1A skills from these Objectives:

- ▣ Create a New Document and Insert Text
- ▣ Insert and Format Graphics
- ▣ Insert and Modify Text Boxes and Shapes
- ▣ Preview and Print a Document

Skills Review | Project **1C** Welcome Week

In the following Skills Review, you will create and edit a flyer for the Laurel College New Student Welcome Week. Your completed document will look similar to Figure 1.50.

Project Files

For Project 1C, you will need the following files:

New blank Word document
w01C_Welcome_Text
w01C_Welcome_Picture

You will save your document as:

Lastname_Firstname_1C_Welcome_Week

Project Results

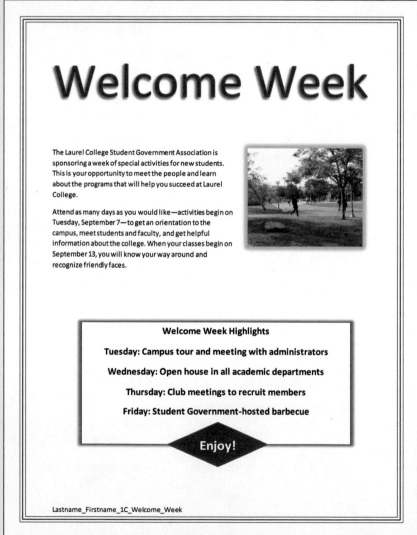

Figure 1.50

(Project 1C Welcome Week continues on the next page)

Skills Review | Project **1C** Welcome Week (continued)

1 **Start** Word and display a new blank document. On the **Home tab**, in the **Paragraph group**, be sure the **Show/Hide ¶** button is active so that you can view formatting marks. In the **Quick Access Toolbar**, click the **Save** button, navigate to your **Word Chapter 1** folder, and then **Save** the document as **Lastname_Firstname_1C_Welcome_Week**

a. Type **Welcome Week** and then press Enter two times.

b. Type **The Laurel College Student Government Association is sponsoring a week of special activities for new students. This is your opportunity to meet the people and learn about the programs that will help you succeed at Laurel College.**

c. Press Enter one time. Click the **Insert tab**. In the **Text group**, click the **Object button arrow**, and then click **Text from File**. Navigate to your student files, select the file **w01C_Welcome_Text**, and then at the bottom of the **Insert File** dialog box, click **Insert**. **Save** your document.

2 At the top of the document, in the left margin area, point to the left of the first paragraph—*Welcome Week*—until the pointer displays, and then click one time to select the paragraph. On the **Home tab**, in the **Font group**, click the **Text Effects** button. In the displayed **Text Effects** gallery, in the first row, click the fourth effect—**Fill - White, Outline - Accent 1**.

a. With the text still selected, in the **Font group**, click the **Font Size button arrow**, and then click **72**. In the **Paragraph group**, click the **Center** button.

b. With the text still selected, in the **Font group**, click the **Text Effects** button. Point to **Shadow**, and then under **Outer**, in the first row click the third style— **Offset Diagonal Bottom Left**. In the **Font group**, click the **Font Color button arrow**. Under **Theme Colors**, in the fourth column, click the first color— **Dark Blue, Text 2**.

c. In the paragraph that begins *The Laurel College*, click to position the insertion point at the beginning of the paragraph. On the **Insert tab**, in the **Illustrations group**, click the **Picture** button. From your student data files, **Insert** the file **w01C_Welcome_Picture**. On the **Format tab**, in the **Size group**, click the **Shape Height down spin arrow** as necessary to change the height of the picture to **2″**.

d. With the picture still selected, on the **Format tab**, in the **Arrange group**, click the **Wrap Text** button. From the **Wrap Text** gallery, click **Square**.

e. Hold down Shift and point anywhere in the picture to display the pointer. Drag the picture to align the right edge of the picture just to the left of the right margin.

f. On the **Format tab**, in the **Picture Styles group**, click the **Picture Effects** button. Point to **Glow**, and then under **Glow Variations**, in the third row, click the first style—**Blue, 11 pt glow, Accent color 1**. Nudge as necessary to match the picture position shown in Figure 1.50.

g. Click anywhere to deselect the picture. Click the **Page Layout tab**, and then in the **Page Background group**, click the **Page Borders** button. In the **Borders and Shading** dialog box, under **Setting**, click **Box**. Under **Style**, scroll down the list. About two-thirds down the list, click the style with a thin top and bottom line and a slightly thicker middle line.

h. Click the **Color arrow**, and then under **Theme Colors**, in the fourth column, click the first color— **Dark Blue, Text 2**. Click **OK**, and then **Save** your document.

3 Press Ctrl + End to move to the bottom of the document. On the **Insert tab**, in the **Text group**, click the **Text Box** button. At the bottom of the **Text Box** gallery, click **Draw Text Box**.

a. At the bottom of the document, position the pointer in an open area near the left margin, and then drag down and to the right to create a text box approximately **2.5 inches** high and **5.5 inches** wide; you need not be precise.

b. With the insertion point positioned in the text box, type the following:

Welcome Week Highlights

Tuesday: Campus tour and meeting with administrators

Wednesday: Open house in all academic departments

Thursday: Club meetings to recruit members

Friday: Student Government-hosted barbecue

(Project 1C Welcome Week continues on the next page)

c. In the text box, select all of the text. On the Mini toolbar, click the **Font Size button arrow**, and then click **14**. Click the **Bold** button, and then click the **Center** button.

d. On the **Format tab**, in the **Size group**, if necessary click the **Size** button. Click the **Shape Height spin arrows** as necessary to change the height of the text box to **2.5"**. Click the **Shape Width button up spin arrow** as necessary to widen the text box to **5.5"**.

e. In the **Shape Styles group**, click the **Shape Effects** button. Point to **Shadow**, and then under **Outer**, in the second row, click the second style—**Offset Center**. In the **Shape Styles group**, click the **Shape Outline button arrow**. Under **Theme Colors**, in the fourth column, click the first color—**Dark Blue, Text 2**.

f. If necessary, click anywhere inside the text box. Point to the text box border to display the ⬚ pointer. Drag the text box to align the left edge at approximately **0.5 inches on the horizontal ruler** and to align the top edge at approximately **5.5 inches on the vertical ruler**. You may have to click outside the text box several times to see the exact location on the rulers.

g. On the **Insert tab**, in the **Illustrations group**, click the **Shapes** button. Under **Basic Shapes**, in the first row, click the seventh shape—**Diamond**.

h. Position the ✛ pointer slightly under the text box and at approximately **2 inches on the horizontal ruler**. Drag down approximately **1 inch** and to the right approximately **2 inches**. On the **Format tab**, in the **Size group**, adjust the **Shape Height** to **0.9"** and the **Shape Width** to **2"**.

i. Right-click the new shape, and then click **Add Text**. Type **Enjoy!** and then select the text you typed. On the Mini toolbar, click the **Font Size button arrow**,

and then click **20**. Click the **Bold** button, and then if necessary, click the **Center** button.

j. On the **Format tab**, in the **Shape Styles group**, click the **Shape Fill button arrow**, and then under **Theme Colors**, in the fourth column, click the first color—**Dark Blue, Text 2**.

k. Point to the shape border until the ⬚ pointer displays, and then position the shape with its widest points aligned with the lower edge of the text box and approximately centered. As necessary, move the shape in small increments by pressing the arrow keys on your keyboard. Refer to Figure 1.50 for approximate placement. **Save** your document.

4 Click the **Insert tab**, and then, in the **Header & Footer group**, click the **Footer** button. At the bottom of the **Footer** gallery, click **Edit Footer**.

a. On the **Design tab**, in the **Insert group**, click the **Quick Parts** button, and then click **Field**. In the **Field names** list, scroll as necessary to locate and click **FileName**. Click **OK**, and then double-click anywhere in the document.

b. Press [Ctrl] + [Home] to move the insertion point to the beginning of the document. Display **Backstage** view. On the right, under the screen thumbnail, click **Properties**, and then click **Show Document Panel**. In the **Author** box, delete any text and then type your firstname and lastname. In the **Subject** box, type your course name and section number, and in the **Keywords** box type **Welcome Week**

c. **Close** the Document Panel. In **Backstage** view, click the **Print tab** to display the **Print Preview**. If necessary, return to the document to make any corrections or adjustments.

d. **Save** your document, print or submit electronically as directed by your instructor, and then **Close** Word.

End You have completed Project 1C ────────────

Apply 1B skills from these Objectives:

5. Change Document and Paragraph Layout
6. Create and Modify Lists
7. Set and Modify Tab Stops
8. Insert a SmartArt Graphic

Skills Review | Project **1D** Constitution

In the following Skills Review, you will edit the constitution of the Associated Students of Laurel College. Your completed document will look similar to Figure 1.51.

Project Files

For Project 1D, you will need the following file:

w01D_Constitution

You will save your document as:

Lastname_Firstname_1D_Constitution

Project Results

STUDENT GOVERNMENT CONSTITUTION

Associated Students of Laurel College

Executive Officers | Student Senate | Judicial Review Committee

We, the students of Laurel College, establish through this Constitution, a governing body to provide a means for student representation in college governance. We create a means for the expression of student opinion, the opportunity for the promotion of student rights, and the protection of the interests of individual students and of the student body as a whole.

ARTICLE I—General Provisions

Section 1 Name: The name of this organization shall be the Associated Students of Laurel College referred to as the ASLC.

Section 2 Membership: All students currently registered in one or more courses at Laurel College shall be members of the ASLC and shall have the right to an equal voice and vote.

Section 3 Structure: Three branches shall comprise the ASLC:

- Executive Branch...ASLC elected officers
- Legislative Branch ....Student Senate
- Judicial Branch .... Judicial Review Committee

ARTICLE II—Elections and Appointments

Section 1 Executive Branch: The elected Executive officers of the ASLC shall be the President, the Vice President, the Treasurer, the Secretary, and the Student Trustee.

Section 2 Legislative Branch: The Student Senate shall hold legislative powers. Senators elected by and representing the academic areas of the college and Senators elected by and representing student organizations shall serve in the Senate.

Lastname_Firstname_1D_Constitution

Section 3 Judicial Branch: The Judicial Review Committee shall be made up of students recommended by the Executive Vice President and appointed by the Executive President.

Figure 1.51

(Project 1D Constitution continues on the next page)

Content-Based Assessments

Skills Review | Project **1D** Constitution (continued)

1 **Start** Word. From your student files, locate and open the document **w01D_Constitution**. Display **Backstage** view, click **Save As**, and then navigate to your **Word Chapter 1** folder. **Save** the document as Lastname_Firstname_1D_Constitution

a. On the **Home tab**, in the **Paragraph group**, be sure the **Show/Hide** button is active so you can view formatting marks. Click the **Page Layout tab**. In the **Page Setup group**, click the **Margins** button, and then at the bottom of the **Margins** gallery, at the bottom of the list, click **Custom Margins**. In the **Page Setup** dialog box, in the **Top** box, type 1 Press Tab as necessary to select the values in the **Bottom**, **Left**, and **Right** boxes and change all margins to **1**. Click **OK**.

b. Press Ctrl + A to select all of the text in the document. On the **Home tab**, in the **Paragraph group**, click the **Align Text Left** button to change the alignment from justified to left aligned.

c. With all of the text still selected, on the **Home tab**, in the **Paragraph group**, click the **Line Spacing** button, and then click **1.15**. Click the **Page Layout tab**, and then in the **Paragraph group**, under **Spacing**, set **After** to **6 pt** spacing after each paragraph.

d. At the top of the document, click anywhere in the title, right-click, and then on the Mini toolbar, click **Center**. Near the top of **Page 1**, locate and select the paragraph that begins *ARTICLE 1*. Hold down Ctrl, and then use the vertical scroll bar to scroll through the document, and then select the other two paragraphs that begin *ARTICLE*. On the Mini toolbar, click **Center**.

e. With the three subheadings that begin *ARTICLE* still selected, on the **Page Layout tab**, in the **Paragraph group**, under **Spacing**, set **Before** to **12 pt**.

f. Scroll to view the bottom of **Page 1**, point anywhere in the bottom margin area, right-click, and then click **Edit Footer**. On the **Design tab**, in the **Insert group**, click the **Quick Parts** button, and then click **Field**. In the **Field names** list, scroll as necessary to locate and click **FileName**. Click **OK**, and then double-click anywhere in the document to exit the footer area.

2 Near the middle of **Page 1**, *above* the *ARTICLE II* subheading, locate the paragraph that begins *Executive Branch*, and then move the pointer into the left margin

area to display the pointer. Drag down to select this paragraph and the next two paragraphs. On the **Home tab**, in the **Paragraph group**, click the **Bullets** button.

a. Scroll to view the bottom of **Page 1**, and then locate the paragraph that begins *Completion of at least*. Select that paragraph and the next two paragraphs. On the **Home tab**, in the **Paragraph group**, click the **Numbering** button.

b. Locate the paragraph that begins *Section 4 Elections*. Click to position the insertion point at the *end* of that paragraph after the colon, and then press Enter.

c. Type **1.** and press Spacebar. Type **Completion of at least 12 credit hours at Laurel College** and then press Enter. Type the following text for items 2 and 3 in the list:

Minimum GPA of 2.75

Enrollment in at least six credit hours each semester in office

d. Near the middle of **Page 1**, select the three items in the bulleted list, right-click the list, and then point to **Bullets**. Under **Bullet Library**, click the **black square** symbol. If the black square is not available, choose another bullet symbol. **Save** your document.

3 Be sure the bulleted list is still selected. Point to the left tab marker at **2″ on the horizontal ruler**. When the *Left Tab* ScreenTip displays, double-click to open the **Tabs** dialog box.

a. Under **Tab stop position**, with *2″* selected, at the bottom of the dialog box, click **Clear** to delete this tab stop. Then, type **5.5** in the **Tab stop position** box.

b. Under **Alignment**, click the **Right** option button. Under **Leader**, click the **2** option button. At the bottom of the **Tabs** dialog box, click the **Set** button, and then click **OK**.

4 Press Ctrl + Home to move to the top of the document. Click at the end of the title, and then press Enter to insert a blank paragraph. Click the **Insert tab**, and then in the **Illustrations group**, click the **SmartArt** button.

a. In the **Choose a SmartArt Graphic** dialog box, on the left, click **Hierarchy**, and in the second row, click the fourth style—**Table Hierarchy**. At the bottom of the **Choose a SmartArt Graphic** dialog box, click **OK**. If necessary, on the Design tab, in the Create Graphic group, activate the Text Pane button.

(Project 1D Constitution continues on the next page)

Content-Based Assessments

Skills Review | Project **1D** Constitution (continued)

b. In the SmartArt graphic, in the second row, click the border of the first *[Text]* box, and then press Del. Press Del again to delete a second *[Text]* box. In the **Text Pane**, under **Type your text here** box, click in the last bulleted point. On the **Design tab**, in the **Create Graphic group**, click the **Promote** button to move the list item up one level.

c. In the **Text Pane**, click in the top bulleted point, type **Associated Students of Laurel College** and then press ↓. Type the following in the three remaining boxes:

Executive Officers

Student Senate

Judicial Review Committee

d. In the upper right corner of the **Text Pane**, click the **Close** button. Be sure the graphic is selected—a pale border surrounds the entire graphic, and then click the outside border one time. Click the **Format tab**, and then in the **Size group**, if necessary click the **Size** button. By clicking the spin box arrows, change the **Shape Height** to **2.6″** and the **Shape Width** to **6.5″**.

e. With the SmartArt graphic still selected, on the **Design tab**, in the **SmartArt Styles group**, click the **Change Colors** button. Scroll down, and then under **Accent 5**, click the second style—**Colored Fill - Accent 5**.

f. On the **Design tab**, in the **SmartArt Styles group**, click the **More** button. Under **3-D**, click the second style—**Inset**. Click anywhere in the document to deselect the graphic. Press Ctrl + Home to move the insertion point to the beginning of the document.

g. Display **Backstage** view, on the right, under the screen thumbnail, click **Properties**, and then click **Show Document Panel**. In the **Author** box, type your firstname and lastname. In the **Subject** box type your course name and section number, and in the **Keywords** box type **student constitution**

h. **Close** the Document Panel. Click **Save**. Display **Backstage** view and click the **Print tab**. Examine the **Print Preview**. Print or submit electronically as directed. **Close** Word.

End You have completed Project 1D ——————————————

Content-Based Assessments

Apply **1A** skills from these Objectives:

- **1** Create a New Document and Insert Text
- **2** Insert and Format Graphics
- **3** Insert and Modify Text Boxes and Shapes
- **4** Preview and Print a Document

Mastering Word | Project **1E** Retreat

In the following Mastering Word project, you will create a flyer announcing a retreat for the Associated Students of Laurel College Board. Your completed document will look similar to Figure 1.52.

Project Files

For Project 1E, you will need the following files:

New blank Word document
w01E_Retreat_Text
w01E_Retreat_Picture

You will save your document as:

Lastname_Firstname_1E_Retreat

Project Results

ASLC Board Retreat

College President Diane Gilmore is pleased to announce a retreat for the Board of the Associated Students of Laurel College.

Invitees include the ASLC Board, consisting of the Executive Officers and their appointed directors, Student Senators, Club Presidents, and members of the Judicial Review Committee. The retreat will be held at the Fogelsville campus of Penn State University on Friday, November 12.

The morning session will begin with a continental breakfast at 8:30 a.m., and will include presentations on effective ways to set and achieve goals. Lunch will be served at noon. The afternoon session will begin at 1:30 p.m., and will include small breakout sessions for the sharing and development of goals and a series of exercises to facilitate group interaction.

In addition to goal setting, the retreat is organized to provide a means for Board members to get to know one another. Students are so busy with courses, student government duties, and personal responsibilities that they rarely get to interact with other Board members outside of their immediate circles. The afternoon will be devoted to a series of exercises specially designed for this retreat. It will enable all participants to meet every other person in attendance and to exchange ideas. We have hired the well-known group, Mountain Retreat Planners, to conduct this portion of the program. They have some entertaining activities planned that will help break down barriers to becoming acquainted with other participants.

Prize drawings at lunch include concert tickets, college football jerseys, coffee mugs, and restaurant gift cards.

Lastname_Firstname_1E_Retreat

Figure 1.52

(Project 1E Retreat continues on the next page)

Content-Based Assessments

Mastering Word | Project **1E** Retreat (continued)

1 **Start** Word and display a new blank document. **Save** the document in your **Word Chapter 1** folder as **Lastname_Firstname_1E_Retreat** and then add the file name to the footer. Be sure the formatting marks and rulers display.

2 Type **ASLC Board Retreat** and press Enter two times. Type **College President Diane Gilmore is pleased to announce a retreat for the Board of the Associated Students of Laurel College.** Press Enter one time. **Insert** the file **w01E_Retreat_Text**.

3 Select the title *ASLC Board Retreat*. On the **Home tab**, in the **Font group**, display the **Text Effects** gallery, and then in the third row, apply the first effect—**Fill - White, Gradient Outline - Accent 1**. Change the **Font Size** to **56** pt. Apply a **Shadow** text effect using the first effect under **Outer—Offset Diagonal Bottom Right**. Change the **Font Color** to **Olive Green, Accent 3, Darker 25%**—in the seventh column, the fifth color.

4 Click to position the insertion point at the beginning of the paragraph that begins *College President*, and then from your student files, **Insert** the picture **w01E_Retreat_Picture**. Change the **Shape Height** of the picture to **2"**, and then set the **Wrap Text** to **Square**. Move the picture so that the right edge aligns with the right margin, and the top edge aligns with the top edge of the text that begins *College President*. Apply a **Film Grain Artistic Effect**—the third effect in the third row. From **Picture Effects**, add a **5 Point Soft Edge**.

5 Scroll to view the lower portion of the page. **Insert** a **Text Box** beginning at the left margin and at approximately **7 inches on the vertical ruler** that is approximately 1" high and 4.5" wide. Then, in the **Size group**, make the measurements exact by setting the **Height** to **1"** and the **Width** to **4.6"**. Type the following text in the text box:

> **Prize drawings at lunch include concert tickets, college football jerseys, coffee mugs, and restaurant gift cards.**

6 Select the text in the text box. Change the **Font Size** to **16** pt, apply **Bold**, and **Center** the text. Add a **Shape Fill** to the text box using the theme color **Olive Green, Accent 3, Lighter 40%**. Then apply a **Gradient** fill using the **Linear Right** gradient. Change the **Shape Outline** color to **White, Background 1**. Drag the text box as necessary to center it horizontally between the left and right margins, and vertically between the last line of text and the footer.

7 Display the **Document Panel**. Type your firstname and lastname in the **Author** box, your course name and section number in the **Subject** box, and then in the **Keywords** box type **retreat, ASLC**

8 **Close** the Document Panel. **Save** and preview your document, make any necessary adjustments, and then print your document or submit it electronically as directed. **Close** Word.

End **You have completed Project 1E**

Apply **1B** skills from these Objectives:

5 Change Document and Paragraph Layout

6 Create and Modify Lists

7 Set and Modify Tab Stops

8 Insert a SmartArt Graphic

Mastering Word | Project **1F** Cycling Trip

In the following Mastering Word project, you will create an informational handout about a planned trip by the Laurel College Cycling Club. Your completed document will look similar to Figure 1.53.

Project Files

For Project 1F, you will need the following file:

w01F_Cycling_Trip

You will save your document as:

Lastname_Firstname_1F_Cycling_Trip

Project Results

Figure 1.53

(Project 1F Cycling Trip continues on the next page)

Content-Based Assessments

Mastering Word | Project **1F** Cycling Trip (continued)

1 **Start** Word. From your student files open the document **w01F_Cycling_Trip**. **Save** the document in your **Word Chapter 1** folder as **Lastname_Firstname_1F_Cycling_Trip** Add the file name to the footer. Display formatting marks.

2 Display the **Page Setup** dialog box. Set the **Top** margin to **1.25"** and the other three margins to **1"**. Select all of the text in the document, including the title. Add **6 pt** spacing after all paragraphs. Change the **Line Spacing** to **1.15**. Change the alignment to **Align Text Left**. **Center** the document title—*Cycling Club Trip*.

3 Locate the paragraph that begins *Bicycle in good*. Select that paragraph and the three paragraphs that follow it. Create a bulleted list from the selected text. Use the shortcut menu to display bullet options, and change the bullet character to a **check mark** or another symbol if the check mark is unavailable.

4 Position the insertion point in the blank paragraph at the end of the document. Add a **Right** tab stop at **3.5"**. Display the **Tabs** dialog box and add a dot leader. **Set** the tab stop, and then add and **Set** another **Right** tab stop with a dot leader at **6.5"**.

5 Type the text shown in **Table 1**, pressing [Tab] between columns and [Enter] at the end of each line. Refer to Figure 1.53.

6 Select the first two lines in the tabbed list and change the **Space After** to **0 pt**. Near the top of the document, position the insertion point in the blank line below the title. Display the **Choose a SmartArt Graphic** dialog box, select the **Cycle** category, and then in the second row, select the first style—**Continuous Cycle**.

7 Display the **Text Pane**. Add the following cities in this order: **Allentown** and **Cemerton** and **Palmerton** and **Berlinsville** and **Pennsville**

8 **Close** the Text Pane. Click the SmartArt border. On the **Format tab**, set the **Shape Width** of the SmartArt graphic to **6.5"** and the **Shape Height** to **3"**. On the **Design tab**, from the **SmartArt Styles** gallery, apply the **Cartoon 3-D** style, and change the colors to the first color under **Colorful—Colorful – Accent Colors**.

9 Display the **Document Panel**, type your firstname and lastname in the **Author** box, your course name and section number in the **Subject** box, and then in the **Keywords** box type **cycling, cycling club**

10 **Close** the Document Panel. **Save** your document. Preview your document, check for and make any adjustments, and then print your document or submit it electronically as directed. **Close** Word.

Table 1

Thursday, October 7	3:00 p.m.	Field House Room B
Thursday, November 11	7:30 p.m.	Student Activities Center L-7
Thursday, December 9	5:00 p.m.	Little Theater

- - - ▸ (Return to Step 6)

End **You have completed Project 1F** ————————————————————

Content-Based Assessments

Apply a combination of 1A and 1B skills:

1 Create a New Document and Insert Text

2 Insert and Format Graphics

3 Insert and Modify Text Boxes and Shapes

4 Preview and Print a Document

5 Change Document and Paragraph Layout

6 Create and Modify Lists

7 Set and Modify Tab Stops

8 Insert a SmartArt Graphic

Mastering Word | Project **1G** Web Sites

In the following Mastering Word project, you will edit guidelines for club Web sites at Laurel College. Your completed document will look similar to Figure 1.54.

Project Files

For Project 1G, you will need the following files:

New blank Word document
w01G_Chess_Club_Picture
w01G_Web_Sites_Text

You will save your document as:

Lastname_Firstname_1G_Web_Sites

Project Results

Figure 1.54

(Project 1G Web Sites continues on the next page)

Content-Based Assessments

Mastering Word | Project **1G** Web Sites (continued)

1 **Start** Word and display a new blank document. Display formatting marks and rulers. **Save** the document in your **Word Chapter 1** folder as **Lastname_Firstname_ 1G_Web_Sites** Add the file name to the footer.

Type **Club Web Sites** and then press [Enter]. Select the title you just typed. From the **Text Effects** gallery, in the fourth row, apply the second effect—**Gradient Fill - Orange, Accent 6, Inner Shadow**, change the **Font Size** to **72** pt, and **Center** the title.

2 Click in the blank line below the title. Locate and insert the file **w01G_Web_Sites_Text**. *Except* for the document title, select all of the document text. **Align Text Left**, change the **Line Spacing** to **1.15**, and change the **Spacing After** to **6 pt**. Locate and **Center** the document subtitle that begins *Published by*.

3 In the middle of **Page 1**, under the subheading *Be sure that*, select the six paragraphs down to, but not including, the *General information* subheading. Format the selected text as a bulleted list. Near the bottom of **Page 1** and the top of **Page 2**, under the *Web Site Design Guidelines* subheading, select all of the paragraphs to the end of the document—not including the blank paragraph mark—and create another bulleted list.

4 Under the subheading that begins *General information*, select the six paragraphs and apply **Numbering** to create a numbered list.

Near the top of the document, position the insertion point to the left of the paragraph that begins The Web site. **Insert** the picture **w01G_Chess_Club_Picture**. Set the **Wrap Text** to **Square**. Decrease the picture **Width** to **2.7"**. From the **Picture Effects** gallery, apply the **Soft Edges** effect using **5 Point**.

5 Press [Ctrl] + [End] to move to the blank line at the end of the document. Type **For assistance, Student Computing Services hours are:** and then press [Enter]. Set a **Left** tab stop at **1.5"**. Display the **Tabs** dialog box. At **5"** add a **Right** tab stop with a **dot leader** and click **Set**. Click **OK** to close the dialog box, press [Tab] to begin, and then type the following information; be sure to press [Tab] to

begin each line and press [Tab] between the days and the times and press [Enter] at the end of each line:

Monday–Thursday	8 a.m. to 10 p.m.
Friday	8 a.m. to 5 p.m.
Saturday	8 a.m. to 12 noon

6 At the top of **Page 2**, position the insertion point to the left of the subheading *Web Site Design Guidelines*. Press [Enter] one time, and then click in the blank paragraph you just created. **Insert** a **SmartArt** graphic, and then from the **Process** group, select the **Basic Chevron Process**—in the fourth row, the third graphic. Click the border of the graphic, and then on the **Format tab**, set the **Shape Height** of the graphic to **1"** and the **Shape Width** of the graphic to **6.5"**. From the **Design tab**, display the **Text Pane**, and then type **Club** and **Web Site** and **New Members Close** the **Text Pane**. Change style to **3-D Inset** and the colors to **Colored Fill – Accent 6**, which is in the last set of colors.

7 At the bottom of **Page 2**, **Insert** a **Text Box** and set the height to **0.7"** and the width to **5"**. In the text box, type: **The Student Computing Services office is located in the Cedar Building, Room 114, call (215) 555-0932**.

Select the text in the text box. From the Mini toolbar, change the **Font Size** to **16** pt, apply **Bold**, and **Center** the text. Change the **Shape Fill** to **Orange, Accent 6, Darker 25%**. From the **Shape Effects** gallery, apply a **Circle Bevel**. By using the pointer, visually center the text box horizontally between the left and right margins and vertically between the tabbed list and the footer.

8 As the document properties, type your firstname and lastname in the **Author** box, your course name and section number in the **Subject** box, and then in the **Keywords** box type **Web sites, guidelines, Student Computing Services Save** your document, examine the Print Preview, check for and make any adjustments, and then print your document or submit it electronically as directed. **Close** Word.

End You have completed Project 1G

GO! Fix It | Project **1H** Guidelines

Project Files

For Project 1H, you will need the following file:

 w01H_Guidelines

You will save your document as:

 Lastname_Firstname_1H_Guidelines

From the student files that accompany this textbook, locate and open the file w01H_More_Guidelines, and then save the file in your Word Chapter 1 folder as **Lastname_Firstname_1H_Guidelines**

This document contains errors that you must find and correct. Read and examine the document, and then edit to correct any errors that you find and to improve the overall document format. Types of errors could include, but are not restricted to:

- Wasted space due to text not wrapping around pictures
- Inconsistent line spacing in paragraphs
- Inconsistent spacing between paragraphs
- Inconsistent paragraph indents
- Inconsistent indenting of lists
- Titles that do not extend across the page
- Text boxes that are too small
- Tabbed lists with wide spaces that do not contain leaders
- Spaces between paragraphs created using empty paragraphs rather than space after paragraphs

Things you should know to complete this project:

- Displaying formatting marks will assist in locating spacing errors.
- There are no errors in the fonts, although the title font size is too small.
- The final flyer should fit on one page.

Save your document and add the file name to the footer. In the Document Panel, type your firstname and lastname in the Author box and your course name and section number in the Subject box. In the Keywords box type **Web site guidelines** and then save your document and submit as directed.

End **You have completed Project 1H** ————————————

Content-Based Assessments

Apply a combination of the 1A and 1B skills.

GO! Make It | Project 1I Flyer

Project Files

For Project 1I, you will need the following files:

    w01I_Team_Building   w01I_Park_Picture

You will save your document as:

    Lastname_Firstname_1I_Team_Building

From the student files that accompany this textbook, locate and open the file w01I_Team_Building, and then save the file in your chapter folder as **Lastname_Firstname_1I_Team_Building**

Use the skills you have practiced, create the document shown in Figure 1.55. The title uses Gradient Fill – Blue, Accent 1, 48 pt. The SmartArt graphic uses the Radial Cycle with an Intense Effect style, is 3″ high and 6.5″ wide, has the Colorful Range – Accent Colors 2 to 3 applied. The w01I_Park_Picture picture has a 2.5 pt soft edge, and is 2.5″ wide. The page border uses Dark Blue, Text 2.

Add the file name to the footer; in the Document Panel, add your name and course information and the Keywords **team building**; save your document; and then submit as directed.

Project Results

Figure 1.55

End **You have completed Project 1I**

Content-Based Assessments

GO! Solve It | Project **1J** Food Drive

Project Files

For Project 1J, you will need the following file:

New blank Word document
w01J_Food_Drive

You will save your document as:

Lastname_Firstname_1J_Food_Drive

Create a new document and save it in your Word Chapter 1 folder as **Lastname_Firstname_1J_Food_Drive** Use the following information to create a flyer that includes a title that uses Text Effects, introductory text, two lists of an appropriate type, one text box, and a picture with appropriate formatting and text wrapping. Use your own picture or w01J_Food_Drive.

This Thanksgiving, the Associated Students of Laurel College is sponsoring a food drive for the local community. All college clubs are invited to participate. Results will be adjusted for club membership by measuring the results in pounds of food per member. Three kinds of food are acceptable: canned goods, non-perishable dry goods, and boxed or canned dry drink mixes, such as coffee, tea, or lemonade.

To participate, a club must follow this procedure: fill out a competition form, collect the goods, and then turn the food in on November 13. The address and telephone number for the ASLC is the Cedar Building, Room 222, Laurelton, PA 19100, (215) 555-0902.

Add the file name to the footer. To the Properties area, add your name, your course name and section number, and the keywords **food drive, clubs**

Performance Criteria	Performance Level		
	Exemplary: You consistently applied the relevant skills	**Proficient:** You sometimes, but not always, applied the relevant skills	**Developing:** You rarely or never applied the relevant skills
Create and format lists	Both lists use the proper list type and are formatted correctly.	One of the lists is formatted correctly.	Neither of the lists are formatted correctly.
Insert and format a picture	The picture is inserted and positioned correctly, and text is wrapped around the picture.	The picture is inserted but not formatted properly.	No picture is inserted.
Insert a text box	A text box with appropriate information is inserted and formatted.	A text box is adequately formatted but is difficult to read or unattractive.	No text box is inserted.
Insert introductory text	Introductory text explains the reason for the flyer, with no spelling or grammar errors.	Some introductory text is included, but does not contain sufficient information and/or includes spelling or grammar errors.	No introductory text, or insufficient introductory text.
Insert title using Text Effects	Text Effects title inserted and centered on the page.	Text Effects title is inserted, but not centered or formatted attractively on the page.	No Text Effects title is included.

End You have completed Project 1J

Content-Based Assessments

Apply a combination of the **1A** and **1B** skills..

GO! Solve It | Project **1K** Fitness Services

Project Files

For Project 1K, you will need the following files:

New blank Word document
w01K_Volleyball

You will save your document as:

Lastname_Firstname_1K_Fitness_Services

Create a new file and save it as **Lastname_Firstname_1K_Fitness Services** Use the following information to create a flyer that includes introductory text, a SmartArt graphic, a title that uses Text Effects, and a picture that has an artistic effect applied and uses text wrapping. Use your own picture or w01K_Volleyball.

The Associated Students of Laurel College sponsors fitness activities. These take place both on campus and off campus. The activities fall into two categories: Fitness Services and Intramural Sports. Fitness Services are noncompetitive activities, with the most popular being Kickboxing, Jogging, and Aerobics. The most popular Intramural Sports activities—which include competitive team and club sports—are Field Hockey, Volleyball, and Basketball.

Add the file name to the footer, and add your name, your course name and section number, and the keywords **fitness, sports** to the Properties area.

	Performance Level		
Performance Criteria	**Exemplary:** You consistently applied the relevant skills	**Proficient:** You sometimes, but not always, applied the relevant skills	**Developing:** You rarely or never applied the relevant skills
Insert title using Text Effects	Text Effects title inserted and centered on the page.	Text Effects title is inserted, but not centered on the page.	No Text Effects title is included.
Insert introductory text	Introductory text explains the reason for the flyer, with no spelling or grammar errors.	Some introductory text is included, but does not sufficiently explain the topic and/or includes spelling or grammar errors.	No or insufficient introductory text is included.
Insert and format a picture	The picture is inserted and positioned correctly, an artistic effect is applied, and text is wrapped around the picture.	The picture is inserted but not formatted properly.	No picture is inserted in the document.
Insert and format SmartArt	The SmartArt graphic displays both categories of fitness activities and examples of each type.	The SmartArt graphic does not display fitness activities by category.	No SmartArt graphic inserted.

End You have completed Project 1K ————————————

Outcomes-Based Assessments

Rubric

The following outcomes-based assessments are *open-ended assessments*. That is, there is no specific correct result; your result will depend on your approach to the information provided. Make *Professional Quality* your goal. Use the following scoring rubric to guide you in *how* to approach the problem and then to evaluate *how well* your approach solves the problem.

The *criteria*—Software Mastery, Content, Format and Layout, and Process—represent the knowledge and skills you have gained that you can apply to solving the problem. The *levels of performance*—Professional Quality, Approaching Professional Quality, or Needs Quality Improvements—help you and your instructor evaluate your result.

	Your completed project is of Professional Quality if you:	Your completed project is Approaching Professional Quality if you:	Your completed project Needs Quality Improvements if you:
1-Software Mastery	Choose and apply the most appropriate skills, tools, and features and identify efficient methods to solve the problem.	Choose and apply some appropriate skills, tools, and features, but not in the most efficient manner.	Choose inappropriate skills, tools, or features, or are inefficient in solving the problem.
2-Content	Construct a solution that is clear and well organized, contains content that is accurate, appropriate to the audience and purpose, and is complete. Provide a solution that contains no errors in spelling, grammar, or style.	Construct a solution in which some components are unclear, poorly organized, inconsistent, or incomplete. Misjudge the needs of the audience. Have some errors in spelling, grammar, or style, but the errors do not detract from comprehension.	Construct a solution that is unclear, incomplete, or poorly organized; contains some inaccurate or inappropriate content; and contains many errors in spelling, grammar, or style. Do not solve the problem.
3-Format and Layout	Format and arrange all elements to communicate information and ideas, clarify function, illustrate relationships, and indicate relative importance.	Apply appropriate format and layout features to some elements, but not others. Overuses features, causing minor distraction.	Apply format and layout that does not communicate information or ideas clearly. Do not use format and layout features to clarify function, illustrate relationships, or indicate relative importance. Use available features excessively, causing distraction.
4-Process	Use an organized approach that integrates planning, development, self-assessment, revision, and reflection.	Demonstrate an organized approach in some areas, but not others; or, uses an insufficient process of organization throughout.	Do not use an organized approach to solve the problem.

Outcomes-Based Assessments

Apply a combination of the **1A** and **1B** skills..

GO! Think | Project **1L** Academic Services

Project Files

For Project 1L, you will need the following file:

New blank Word document

You will save your document as:

Lastname_Firstname_1L_Academic_Services

The Services Coordinator of the Associated Students of Laurel College needs to create a flyer to inform students of academic services available at the ASLC office. Referrals are available for medical, legal, and counseling services, as well as tutoring and volunteer organizations. Among the services offered at the ASLC office are free printing (up to 250 pages per semester), help with minor legal issues, housing information, bicycle repair, minor computer repair, and help placing students with volunteer organizations.

Create a flyer with basic information about the services provided. Be sure the flyer is easy to read and understand and has an attractive design. If you need more information about student services available at other colleges, search the Web for **student government** and add whatever services you think might be (or should be) available at your college. Add appropriate information to the Document Panel. Save the document as **Lastname_Firstname_1L_Academic_Services** and submit it as directed.

 You have completed Project 1L ⎯⎯⎯⎯⎯⎯⎯⎯⎯⎯⎯⎯⎯⎯

Apply a combination of the **1A** and **1B** skills.

GO! Think | Project **1M** Campus Bookstore

Project Files

For Project 1M, you will need the following files:

New blank Word document
w01L_Campus_Bookstore

You will save your document as:

Lastname_Firstname_1M_Campus_Bookstore

The manager of the Laurel College Bookstore needs to create a flyer that can be handed out by the ASLC to students during Welcome Week. The bookstore gives students attending Welcome Week a discount of 20% on special items such as sweatshirts and other college-related clothing, coffee mugs, calendars, and similar items. Door prizes will also be awarded. The bookstore is open Monday and Thursday from 8 a.m. to 10 p.m., Tuesday and Wednesday from 8 a.m. to 8 p.m., and Friday from 8 a.m. to 5 p.m.

Using your own campus bookstore as an example, create a flyer that gives general information about the bookstore, provides one or more lists of items that are on sale, displays the picture w01M_ Campus_Bookstore, and has a highlighted area that gives the store hours.

Add appropriate information to the Document Panel. Save the document as **Lastname_Firstname_1M_Campus_Bookstore** and submit it as directed.

 You have completed Project 1M ⎯⎯⎯⎯⎯⎯⎯⎯⎯⎯⎯⎯⎯⎯

Outcomes-Based Assessments

Apply a combination of the 1A and 1B skills.

You and GO! | Project 1N Family Flyer

Project Files

For Project 1N, you will need the following file:

New blank Word document

You will save your document as

Lastname_Firstname_1N_Family_Flyer

In this project, you will create a one-page flyer that you can send to your family. Include any information that may interest your family members, such as work-related news, school events, vacation plans, and the activities and accomplishments of you, your spouse, your friends, or other family members. Choose any writing style that suits you—chatty, newsy, entertaining, or humorous.

To complete the assignment, be sure to include a title, at least one list, a picture, and either a SmartArt graphic or a text box or shape. Before you submit the flyer, be sure to check it for grammar and spelling errors, and also be sure to format the document in an attractive manner, using the skills you practiced in this chapter.

Save the file as **Lastname_Firstname_1N_Family_Flyer** Add the file name to the footer, and add your name, your course name and section number, and the keywords **flyer** and **family** to the Properties area. Submit your file as directed.

End **You have completed Project 1N** ———————————————————

Using Tables and Templates to Create Resumes and Cover Letters

OUTCOMES

At the end of this chapter you will be able to:

OBJECTIVES

Mastering these objectives will enable you to:

PROJECT 2A
Create a resume by using a Word table.

1. Create a Table (p. 107)
2. Add Text to a Table (p. 108)
3. Format a Table (p. 111)

PROJECT 2B
Create a cover letter and resume by using a template.

4. Create a New Document from an Existing Document (p. 120)
5. Change and Reorganize Text (p. 123)
6. Use the Proofing Options (p. 130)
7. Create a Document Using a Template (p. 134)

James Thew/Shutterstock

In This Chapter

Tables are useful for organizing and presenting data. Because a table is so easy to use, many individuals prefer to arrange tabular information in a Word table rather than setting a series of tabs. Use a table when you want to present rows and columns of information or to create a structure for a document such as a resume.

When using Word to write business or personal letters, use a commonly approved letter format. You will make a good impression on prospective employers if you use a standard business letter style when you are writing a cover letter for a resume. You can create a resume using one of the Microsoft resume templates included with Microsoft Office or available online.

The projects in this chapter relate to **Madison Staffing Services**. Many companies prefer to hire employees through a staffing service, so that both the employer and the employee can determine if the match is a good fit. Madison Staffing Services takes care of the details of recruiting, testing, hiring, and paying the employee. At the end of the employment assignment, neither the employer nor the employee is required to make a permanent commitment. Many individuals find full-time jobs with an employer for whom they initially worked through a staffing agency.

Project 2A Resume

Project Activities

In Activities 2.01 through 2.09, you will create a table to use as the structure for a resume for one of Madison Staffing Services' clients. Your completed document will look similar to Figure 2.1.

Project Files

For Project 2A, you will need the following file:

w02A_Experience

You will save your document as:

Lastname_Firstname_2A_Resume

Project Results

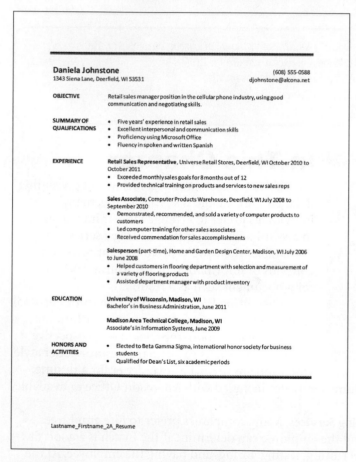

Figure 2.1
Project 2A Resume

Objective 1 | Create a Table

A *table* is an arrangement of information organized into rows and columns. The intersection of a row and a column in a table creates a box called a *cell* into which you can type. Tables are useful to present information in a logical and orderly manner.

Activity 2.01 | Creating a Table

1 Start **Word**, and in the new blank document, display formatting marks and rulers.

2 Click the **File tab**, and then in **Backstage** view, click **Save As**. In the **Save As** dialog box, navigate to the location where you are storing your projects for this chapter. Create a new folder named **Word Chapter 2**

3 **Save** the file in the **Word Chapter 2** folder as **Lastname_Firstname_2A_Resume**

4 Scroll to the end of the document, right-click near the bottom of the page, and then click **Edit Footer**. On the **Design tab**, in the **Insert group**, click the **Quick Parts** button, and then click **Field**.

5 Under **Field names**, scroll down, click **FileName**, and then click **OK**. **Close** the footer area.

6 On the **Insert tab**, in the **Tables group**, click the **Table** button. In the **Table** grid, in the fourth row, point to the second square, and notice that the cells display in orange and *2 × 4 Table* displays at the top of the grid. Compare your screen with Figure 2.2.

Figure 2.2

Table button
Table size
Pointer indicates table size
Preview of table

7 Click one time to create the table. Notice that formatting marks in each cell indicate the end of the contents of each cell and the mark to the right of each *row* indicates the row end. **Save** your document, and then compare your screen with Figure 2.3.

A table with four rows and two columns displays at the insertion point location, and the insertion point displays in the upper left cell. The table fills the width of the page, from the left margin to the right margin. On the Ribbon, Table Tools display and add two tabs—*Design* and *Layout*. Borders display around each cell in the table.

Figure 2.3

Table Tools
Indicates the end of a row
Indicates the end of cell contents

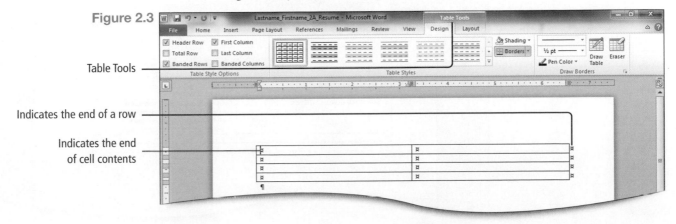

Objective 2 | Add Text to a Table

In a Word table, each cell behaves similarly to a document. For example, as you type in a cell, when you reach the right border of the cell, wordwrap moves the text to the next line. When you press Enter, the insertion point moves down to a new paragraph in the same cell. You can also insert text from another document into a table cell.

Activity 2.02 | Adding Text to a Table

There are numerous acceptable formats for resumes, many of which can be found in Business Communications textbooks. The layout used in this project is suitable for a recent college graduate and places topics in the left column and details in the right column.

1 Scroll up to view the top of the document. With the insertion point blinking in the first cell in the first row, type **OBJECTIVE** and then press Tab.

> Pressing Tab moves the insertion point to the next cell in the row, or, if the insertion point is already in the last cell in the row, pressing Tab moves the insertion point to the first cell in the following row.

2 Type **Retail sales manager position in the cellular phone industry, using good communication and negotiating skills.** Notice that the text wraps in the cell and the height of the row adjusts to fit the text.

3 Press Tab to move to the first cell in the second row. Type **SUMMARY OF QUALIFICATIONS** and then press Tab. Type the following, pressing Enter at the end of each line *except* the last line:

Five years' experience in retail sales

Excellent interpersonal and communication skills

Proficiency using Microsoft Office

Fluency in spoken and written Spanish

> The default font and font size in a table are the same as for a document—Calibri 11 pt. The default line spacing in a table is single spacing with no space before or after paragraphs, which differs from the defaults for a document.

4 **Save** your document, and then compare your screen with Figure 2.4.

Figure 2.4

Text typed in cells

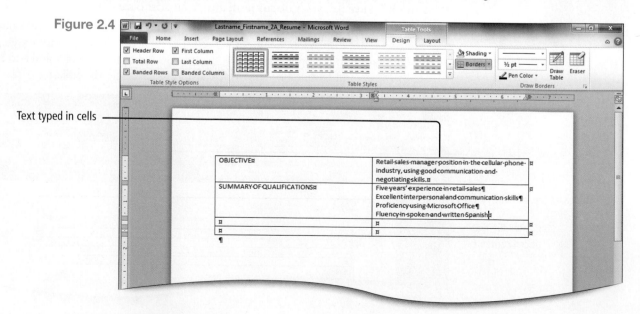

Activity 2.03 | Inserting Existing Text into a Table Cell

1 Press `Tab` to move to the first cell in the third row. Type **EXPERIENCE** and then press `Tab`.

2 Type the following, pressing `Enter` after each line:

> **Retail Sales Representative, Universe Retail Stores, Deerfield, WI October 2010 to October 2011**
>
> **Exceeded monthly sales goals for 8 months out of 12**
>
> **Provided technical training on products and services to new sales reps**

3 Be sure your insertion point is positioned in the second column to the left of the cell marker below *sales reps*. Compare your screen with Figure 2.5.

Figure 2.5

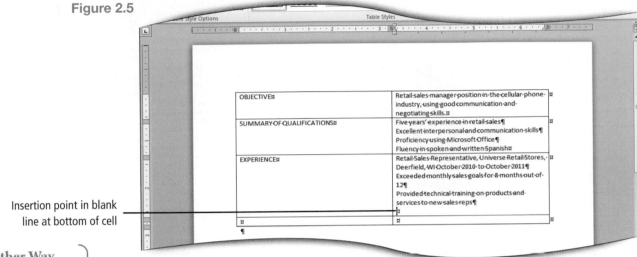

Insertion point in blank line at bottom of cell

Another Way

Open the second document and select the text you want. Copy the text, and then paste at the desired location.

4 On the **Insert tab**, in the **Text group**, click the **Object button arrow**, and then click **Text from File**. Navigate to your student files, select **w02A_Experience**, and then click **Insert**.

5 Press `Backspace` one time to remove the blank line at the end of the inserted text, and then compare your screen with Figure 2.6.

Figure 2.6

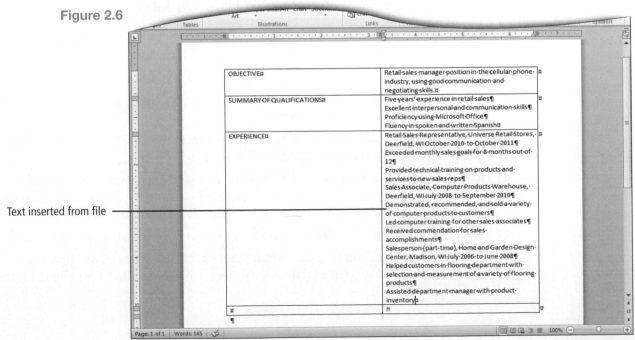

Text inserted from file

6 Press ⟮Tab⟯ to move to the first cell in the fourth row. Type **EDUCATION** and then press ⟮Tab⟯.

7 Type the following, pressing ⟮Enter⟯ at the end of each item *except* the last one:

> **University of Wisconsin, Madison, WI**
>
> **Bachelor's in Business Administration, June 2011**
>
> **Madison Area Technical College, Madison, WI**
>
> **Associate's in Information Systems, June 2009**

8 Compare your screen with Figure 2.7.

Figure 2.7

Text entered in new cell ————

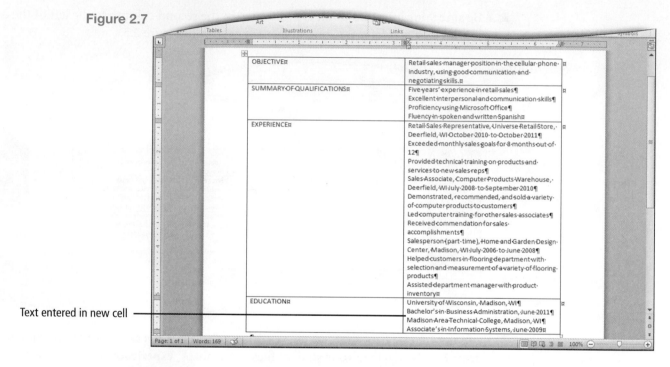

9 **Save** 🖫 your document.

Activity 2.04 | Creating Bulleted Lists in a Table

1 Scroll to view the top of your document, and then in the cell to the right of *SUMMARY OF QUALIFICATIONS*, select all of the text.

2 On the **Home tab**, in the **Paragraph group**, click the **Bullets** button ⌗.

> The selected text displays as a bulleted list. Using a bulleted list in this manner makes each qualification more distinctive.

3 In the **Paragraph group**, click the **Decrease Indent** button ⌗ one time to align the bullets at the left edge of the cell.

4 In the **Clipboard group**, double-click the **Format Painter** button. In the cell to the right of *EXPERIENCE*, select the second and third paragraphs—beginning *Exceeded* and *Provided*—to create the same style of bulleted list as you did in the previous step.

> When you double-click the Format Painter button, it remains active until you turn it off.

5 In the same cell, under *Sales Associate*, select the three paragraphs that begin *Demonstrated* and *Led* and *Received* to create another bulleted list aligned at the left edge of the cell.

6 With the Format Painter pointer still active, in the same cell, select the paragraphs that begin *Helped* and *Assisted* to create the same type of bulleted list.

7 Press [Esc] to turn off the Format Painter. Click anywhere in the table to deselect the text, and then compare your screen with Figure 2.8.

Figure 2.8

Bullets added to text ————

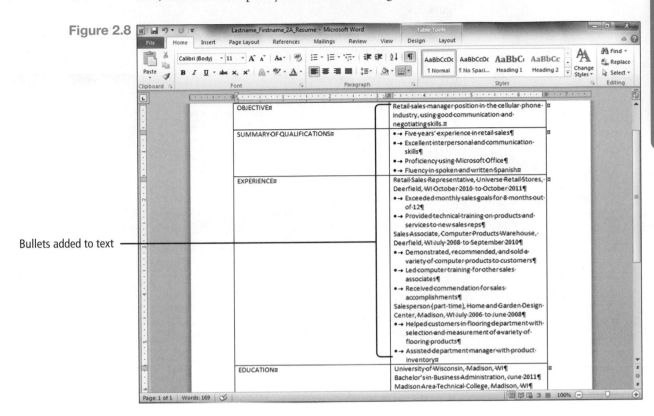

8 **Save** 💾 your document.

Objective 3 | Format a Table

Use Word's formatting tools to make your tables attractive and easy to read. Types of formatting you can add to a table include changing the row height and the column width, removing or adding borders, increasing or decreasing the paragraph or line spacing, or enhancing the text.

Activity 2.05 | Changing the Width of Table Columns

When you create a table, all of the columns are of equal width. In this activity, you will change the width of the columns.

1 In any row, point to the vertical border between the two columns to display the ⊹⊢ pointer.

2 Drag the column border to the left to approximately **1.25 inches on the horizontal ruler**.

3 Scroll to the top of the document. Notice that in the second row, the text *SUMMARY OF QUALIFICATIONS* wraps to two lines to accommodate the new column width.

4 If necessary, in the left column, click in any cell. On the Ribbon, under **Table Tools**, click the **Layout tab**.

5 In the **Cell Size group**, click the **Table Column Width button spin arrows** [1.37" ⬍] as necessary to change the width of the first column to **1.4"**. Compare your screen with Figure 2.9.

> After dragging a border with your mouse, use the Width button to set a precise measurement if necessary.

Figure 2.9

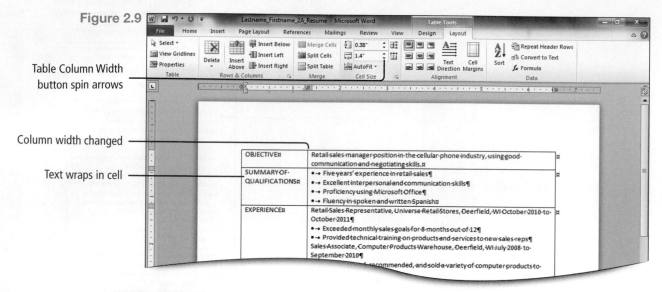

Table Column Width button spin arrows

Column width changed

Text wraps in cell

6 **Save** 🖫 your document.

More Knowledge | Changing Column Widths

You will typically get the best results if you change the column widths starting at the left side of the table, especially in tables with three or more columns. Word can also calculate the best column widths for you. To do this, select the table. Then, on the Layout tab, in the Cell Size group, click the AutoFit button and click AutoFit Contents.

Activity 2.06 | Adding Rows to a Table

You can add rows or columns anywhere in a table.

1 Scroll to view the lower portion of the table. In the last row of the table, click anywhere in the *second* cell that contains the educational information, and then press Tab.

> A new row displays at the bottom of the table. When the insertion point is in the last cell in the bottom row of a table, you can add a row by pressing the Tab key; the insertion point will display in the first cell of the new row.

2 Type **HONORS AND ACTIVITIES** and then press Tab.

3 Type the following, pressing Enter after the first item but not the second item:

Elected to Beta Gamma Sigma, international honor society for business students

Qualified for Dean's List, six academic periods

4 Select the text you typed in the last cell of the bottom row. On the **Home tab**, in the **Paragraph group**, click the **Bullets** button [≔ ▾], and then click the **Decrease Indent** button [⮜] one time to align the bullets at the left edge of the cell.

5 Scroll up to view the entire table, click anywhere in the table to deselect the text, and then compare your screen with Figure 2.10.

Figure 2.10

Row added to table ——

Bullets added to text ——

6 Click anywhere in the top row of the table.

7 On the **Layout tab**, in the **Rows & Columns group**, click the **Insert Above** button. Compare your screen with Figure 2.11.

A new row displays above the row that contained the insertion point, and the new row is selected.

Figure 2.11

Row inserted at top of table ——

8 **Save** your document.

Activity 2.07 | Merging Cells

The title of a table typically spans all of the columns. In this activity, you will merge cells so that you can position the personal information across both columns.

1 Be sure the two cells in the top row are selected; if necessary, drag across both cells to select them.

> **Another Way**
>
> Right-click the selected row and click Merge Cells on the shortcut menu.

2 On the **Layout tab**, in the **Merge group**, click the **Merge Cells** button.

The cell border between the two cells no longer displays.

3 With the merged cell still selected, on the **Home tab**, in the **Paragraph group**, click the **Dialog Box Launcher** to display the **Paragraph** dialog box.

4 In the **Paragraph** dialog box, on the **Indents and Spacing tab**, in the lower left corner, click the **Tabs** button to display the **Tabs** dialog box.

5 In the **Tabs** dialog box, under **Tab stop position**, type **6.5** and then under **Alignment**, click the **Right** option button. Click **Set**, and then click **OK** to close the dialog box.

6 Type **Daniela Johnstone** Hold down Ctrl and then press Tab. Notice that the insertion point moves to the right-aligned tab stop at 6.5″.

In a Word table, you must use Ctrl + Tab to move to a tab stop, because pressing Tab is reserved for moving the insertion point from cell to cell.

7 Type **(608) 555-0588** and then press Enter.

8 Type **1343 Siena Lane, Deerfield, WI 53531** Hold down Ctrl and then press Tab.

9 Type **djohnstone@alcona.net** and then compare your screen with Figure 2.12.

Figure 2.12

Right tab stop added to ruler

Cells merged in top row

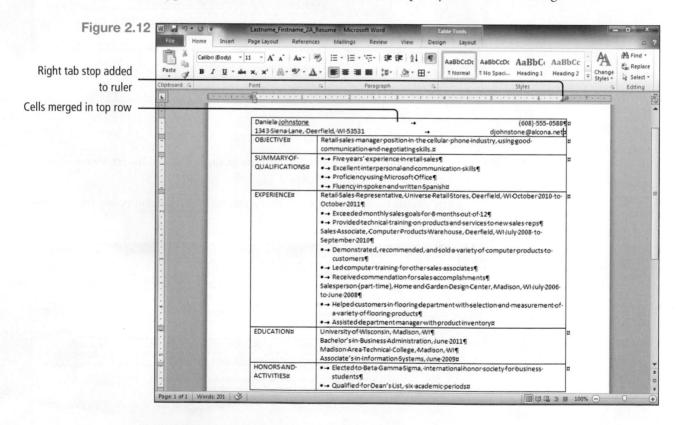

10 Save your document.

Activity 2.08 | Formatting Text in Cells

1 In the first row of the table, select the name *Daniela Johnstone*, and then on the Mini toolbar, apply **Bold** and change the **Font Size** to **16**.

2 Under *Daniela Johnstone*, click anywhere in the second line of text, which contains the address and e-mail address.

3 On the **Page Layout tab**, in the **Paragraph group**, click the **Spacing After up spin arrow** three times to add **18 pt** spacing between the first row of the table and the second row. Compare your screen with Figure 2.13.

These actions separate the personal information from the body of the resume and adds focus to the applicant's name.

Figure 2.13

Text formatted

18 pt space added after paragraph

4 Using the technique you just practiced, in the second column, click in the last paragraph of every cell and add **18 pt Spacing After** the last paragraph of all rows including the last row; a border will be added to the bottom of the table, and spacing will be needed between the last row and the border.

5 In the second row, point to the word *OBJECTIVE*, hold down the left mouse button, and then drag downward in the first column only to select all the headings in uppercase letters. On the Mini toolbar, click the **Bold** button **B**.

Note | Selecting Only One Column

When you drag downward to select the first column, a fast mouse might also begin to select the second column when you reach the bottom. If this happens, drag upward slightly to deselect the second column and select only the first column.

---

6 In the cell to the right of *EXPERIENCE*, without selecting the following comma, select *Retail Sales Representative* and then on the Mini toolbar, click the **Bold** button **B**.

7 In the same cell, apply **Bold** **B** to the other job titles—*Sales Associate* and *Salesperson*—but do not bold *(part time)*.

8 In the cell to the right of *EDUCATION*, apply **Bold** **B** to *University of Wisconsin, Madison, WI* and *Madison Area Technical College, Madison, WI*.

9 In the same cell, click anywhere in the line beginning *Bachelor's*. On the **Page Layout tab**, in the **Paragraph group**, click the **Spacing After up spin arrow** two times to add **12 pt** spacing after the paragraph.

10 In the cell to the right of *EXPERIENCE*, under *Retail Sales Representative*, click anywhere in the second bulleted item, and then add **12 pt Spacing After** the item.

11 In the same cell, repeat this process for the last bulleted item under *Sales Associate*.

12 Scroll to the top of the screen, and then compare your screen with Figure 2.14.

Figure 2.14

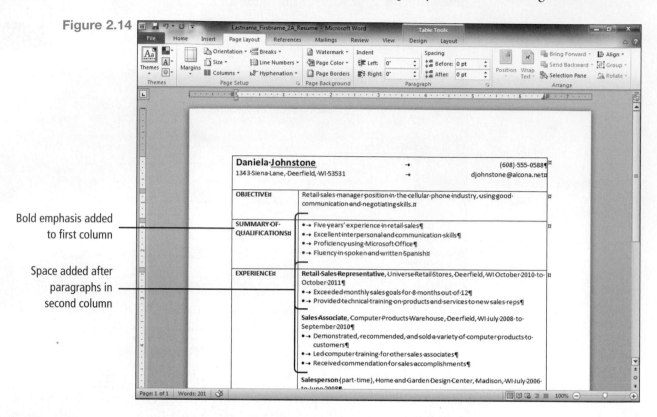

Bold emphasis added to first column

Space added after paragraphs in second column

13 Save 💾 your document.

Activity 2.09 | Changing the Table Borders

When you create a table, all of the cells have black borders. Most resumes do not display any cell borders. A border at the top and bottom of the resume, however, is attractive and adds a professional look to the document.

1 If necessary, press [Ctrl] + [Home] to move the insertion point to the top of the table, and then point slightly outside of the upper left corner of the table to display the **table move handle** ⊞.

2 With the 🡵 pointer, click one time to select the entire table, and notice that the row markers at the end of each row are also selected.

Shaded row markers indicate that the entire row is selected.

3 Click the **Design tab**. In the **Table Styles group**, click the **Borders button arrow**, and then click **No Border**.

The black borders no longer display; instead, depending on your setup, either no borders—the default setting—or nonprinting blue dashed borders display.

4 Click the **File tab** to display **Backstage** view, and then click the **Print tab** to preview the table. Notice that no borders display in the preview, as shown in Figure 2.15.

Figure 2.15

Document preview

All table borders removed

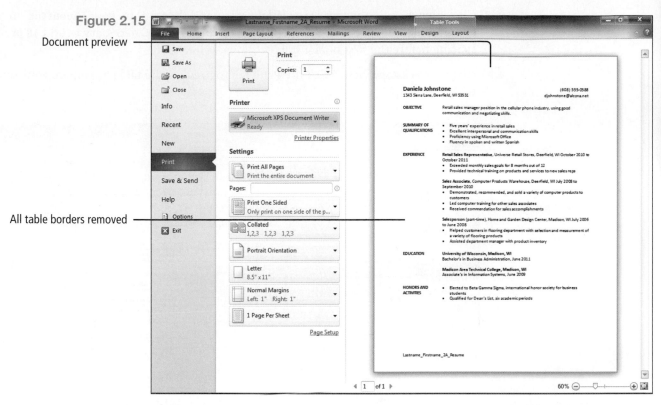

Another Way

Right-click the selected table, click Borders and Shading, and then click the Borders tab.

5 Click the **Design tab**; be sure the table is still selected. In the **Table Styles group**, click the **Borders button arrow**, and then at the bottom of the **Borders** gallery, click **Borders and Shading**.

6 Under **Setting**, click the **Custom** button. Under **Style**, scroll down about a third of the way and click the style with the thick upper line and the thin lower line.

Another Way

Click the top border button, which is one of the buttons that surround the Preview.

7 In the **Preview** box at the right, point to the *top* border of the small preview and click one time.

8 Under **Style**, click the style with the thin upper line and the thick lower line, and then in the **Preview** box, click the *bottom* border of the preview. Compare your screen with Figure 2.16.

Figure 2.16

Borders applied to table

Borders display in Preview

9 Click **OK**, click anywhere to cancel the selection, and then notice that there is only a small amount of space between the upper border and the first line of text.

10 Click anywhere in the text *Daniela Johnstone*, and then on the **Page Layout tab**, in the **Paragraph group**, click the **Spacing Before up spin arrow** as necessary to add **18 pt** spacing before the first paragraph.

11 Display **Backstage** view. Click the **Print tab** to preview the table. Compare your screen with Figure 2.17.

Figure 2.17

Top border

Spacing added above first paragraph

Bottom border

12 In **Backstage** view, click the **Info tab**. On the right, under the document thumbnail, click **Properties**, and then click **Show Document Panel**. In the **Author** box, delete any text and then type your firstname and lastname. In the **Subject** box, type your course name and section number, and in the **Keywords** box type **resume, Word table**

13 **Close** ⊠ the **Document Panel**. **Save** 🖫 and then print your document, or submit it electronically, as directed by your instructor. **Exit** Word.

End **You have completed Project 2A** ————————————————

Project 2B Cover Letter and Resume

myitlab
Project 2B Training

Project Activities

In Activities 2.10 through 2.22, you will create a letterhead, and then use the letterhead to create a cover letter. You will also create a short resume using a Microsoft template and save it as a Web page. Your completed documents will look similar to Figure 2.18.

Project Files

For Project 2B, you will need the following file:

w02B_Cover_Letter_Text

You will save your documents as:

Lastname_Firstname_2B_Letterhead
Lastname_Firstname_2B_Cover_Letter
Lastname_Firstname_2B_Brief_Resume
Lastname_Firstname_2B_HTML_Resume

Project Results

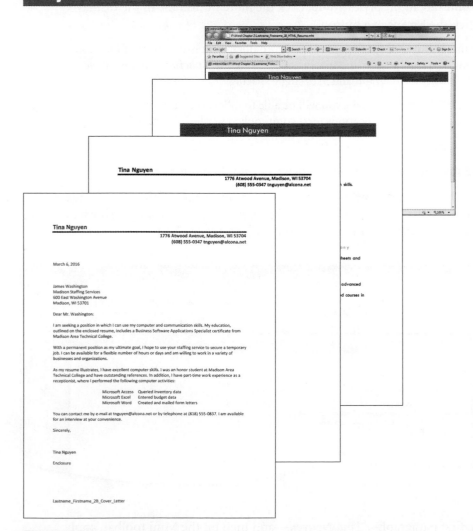

Figure 2.18
Project 2B Cover Letter and Resume

Objective 4 | Create a New Document from an Existing Document

A *template* is an *existing* document that you use as a starting point for a *new* document. The template document opens a copy of itself, unnamed, and then you use the structure—and possibly some content, such as headings—as the starting point for a new document.

All documents are based on a template. When you create a new blank document, it is based on Word's ***Normal template***, which serves as the starting point for all new Word documents.

Activity 2.10 | Creating a Letterhead

A ***letterhead*** is the personal or company information that displays at the top of a letter, and which commonly includes a name, address, and contact information. The term also refers to a piece of paper imprinted with such information at the top.

1 **Start** Word, and in the new blank document, be sure that formatting marks and rulers display.

2 On the **Home tab**, in the **Styles group**, click the **More** button ⊡. In the displayed gallery, click the **No Spacing** button.

> Recall that the default spacing for a new Word document is 10 points of blank space following a paragraph and line spacing of 1.15. The ***No Spacing style*** inserts *no* extra space following a paragraph and uses single spacing.
>
> By using the No Spacing style, you will be able to follow the prescribed format of a letter, which Business Communications texts commonly describe in terms of single spacing.

3 Type **Tina Nguyen** and then press Enter.

4 Type **1776 Atwood Avenue, Madison, WI 53704** and then press Enter.

5 Type **(608) 555-0347 tnguyen@alcona.net** and then press Enter. If the e-mail address changes to blue text, right-click the e-mail address, and then from the shortcut menu, click **Remove Hyperlink**. Compare your screen with Figure 2.19.

Figure 2.19

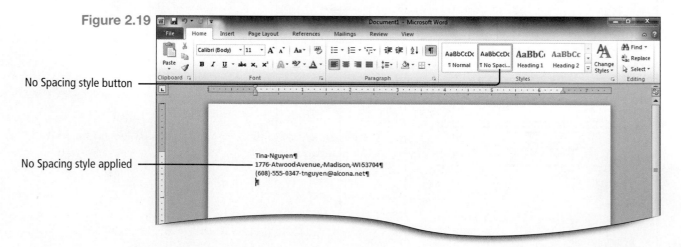

No Spacing style button

No Spacing style applied

6 Select the first paragraph—*Tina Nguyen*—and then on the Mini toolbar, apply **Bold** B and change the **Font Size** to **16**.

7 Select the second and third paragraphs. On the Mini toolbar, apply **Bold** B and change the **Font Size** to **12**.

Another Way

Press Ctrl + R to align text to the right.

8 With the two paragraphs still selected, on the **Home tab**, in the **Paragraph group**, click the **Align Text Right** button ≡.

9 Click anywhere in the first paragraph—*Tina Nguyen*. In the **Paragraph group**, click the **Borders button arrow** ▦▾, and then at the bottom, click **Borders and Shading**.

10 In the **Borders and Shading** dialog box, under **Style**, be sure the first style—a single solid line—is selected.

Another Way

Alternatively, click the bottom border button ▦.

11 Click the **Width arrow**, and then click **3 pt**. To the right, under **Preview**, click the bottom border of the diagram. Under **Apply to**, be sure *Paragraph* displays. Compare your screen with Figure 2.20.

Figure 2.20

Borders button arrow

3 pt line applied to bottom border

Width arrow

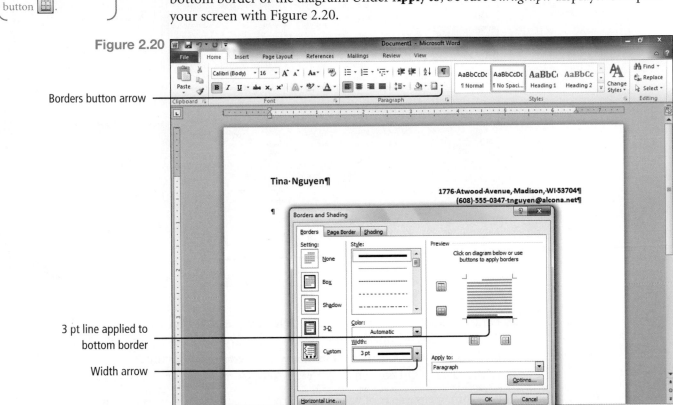

12 Click **OK** to display a 3 pt line below *Tina Nguyen*, which extends from the left margin to the right margin.

13 Display **Save As** dialog box, **Save** the document in your **Word Chapter 2** folder as **Lastname_Firstname_2B_Letterhead** and then add the file name to the footer.

14 Display **Backstage** view, click the **Info tab**, and then on the right, under the document thumbnail, click **Properties**. Click **Show Document Panel**. In the **Author** box, delete any text and then type your firstname and lastname. In the **Subject** box, type your course name and section number, and in the **Keywords** box type **personal letterhead**

15 **Close** × the **Document Panel**.

16 **Save** 🖫 your document. Display **Backstage** view, and then click **Close** to close the document but leave Word open. Hold this file until you complete this project.

Activity 2.11 | Creating a Document from an Existing Document

To use an existing document as the starting point for a new document, Word provides the ***New from existing*** command.

1 Click the **File tab** to display **Backstage** view, and then click **New** to display the new document options. Compare your screen with Figure 2.21.

> Here you can create a new document in a variety of ways, including from an existing document.

Figure 2.21

New from Existing template

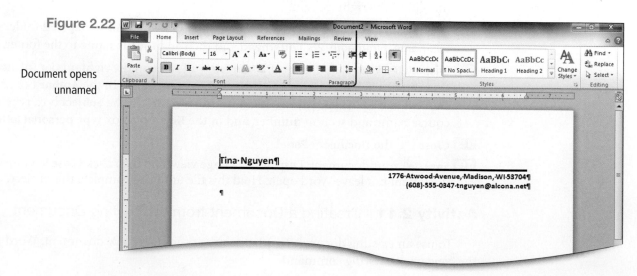

2 Under **Available Templates**, click the **New from existing** button. In the displayed **New from Existing Document** dialog box, if necessary, navigate to your **Word Chapter 2** folder, click your **Lastname_Firstname_2B_Letterhead** document to select it, and then in the lower right corner, click **Create New**. Compare your screen with Figure 2.22.

> Word opens a copy of your 2B_Letterhead document in the form of a new Word document—the title bar indicates *Document* followed by a number. You are not opening the original document, and changes that you make to this new document will not affect the contents of your 2B_Letterhead document.

Figure 2.22

Document opens unnamed

3 Display the **Save As** dialog box, and then navigate to your **Word Chapter 2** folder. **Save** the file as **Lastname_Firstname_2B_Cover_Letter**

> The personal information that you typed in the 2B_Letterhead Document Panel remains in the new document.

4 Scroll down to view the footer area, and notice that a footer displays.

> The footer displays because it was included in the document that you saved as a template. The *FileName* field does not automatically update to the new file name.

5 Point to the footer and right-click, and then click **Edit Footer**. Point to the highlighted footer text, right-click, and then from the shortcut menu, click **Update Field**. At the far right end of the Ribbon, click the **Close Header and Footer** button.

6 Save your document.

More Knowledge | Creating a Template File

You can also identify an original document so that your Windows operating system always knows that you want to create a new unnamed copy. To do so, save your document as a template file instead of a document. Word will then attach the dotx extension to the file, instead of the docx extension that is applied for a document, and will store the template file in a special location with other templates. Then, you can open the template from the New Document dialog box by clicking *My templates*.

Objective 5 | Change and Reorganize Text

Business letters follow a standard format and contain the following parts: the current date, referred to as the *date line*; the name and address of the person receiving the letter, referred to as the *inside address*; a greeting, referred to as the *salutation*; the text of the letter, usually referred to as the *body* of the letter; a closing line, referred to as the *complimentary closing*; and the *writer's identification*, which includes the name or job title (or both) of the writer, and which is also referred to as the *writer's signature block*.

Some letters also include the initials of the person who prepared the letter, an optional *subject line* that describes the purpose of the letter, or a list of *enclosures*—documents included with the letter.

Activity 2.12 | Recording AutoCorrect Entries

You can correct commonly misspelled words automatically by using Word's *AutoCorrect* feature. Commonly misspelled words—such as *teh* instead of *the*—are corrected using a built-in list that is installed with Office. If you have words that you frequently misspell, you can add them to the list for automatic correction.

1 Click the **File tab** to display **Backstage** view. On the **Help tab**, click **Options** to display the **Word Options** dialog box.

2 On the left side of the **Word Options** dialog box, click **Proofing**, and then under **AutoCorrect options**, click the **AutoCorrect Options** button.

3 In the **AutoCorrect** dialog box, click the **AutoCorrect tab**. Under **Replace**, type **resumee** and under **With**, type **resume**

> If another student has already added this AutoCorrect entry, a Replace button will display.

4 Click **Add**. If the entry already exists, click Replace instead, and then click Yes.

5 In the **AutoCorrect** dialog box, under **Replace**, type **computr** and under **With**, type **computer** and then compare your screen with Figure 2.23.

Figure 2.23

Replace box ——————

With box ——————

Add (or Replace) button ——————

6 Click **Add** (or Replace) and then click **OK** two times to close the dialog boxes.

Activity 2.13 | Creating a Cover Letter

There are a variety of accepted letter formats that you will see in reference manuals and Business Communication texts. The one used in this chapter is a block style cover letter taken from *Business Communication Today*.

1 Press Ctrl + End to move the insertion point to the blank line below the letterhead. Press Enter three times, and then type **March 16, 2016** to create the dateline.

> Most Business Communication texts recommend that the dateline be positioned at least 0.5 inch (3 blank lines) below the letterhead; or, position the dateline approximately 2 inches from the top edge of the paper.

2 Press Enter four times, which leaves three blank lines. Type the following inside address on four lines, but do not press Enter following the last line:

James Washington

Madison Staffing Services

600 East Washington Avenue

Madison, WI 53701

The recommended space between the dateline and inside address varies slightly among Business Communication texts and office reference manuals. However, all indicate that the space can be from one to 10 blank lines depending on the length of your letter.

3 Press Enter two times to leave one blank line. Compare your screen with Figure 2.24.

Figure 2.24

Three blank lines between letterhead and dateline

Dateline

Three blank lines between dateline and inside address

Inside address

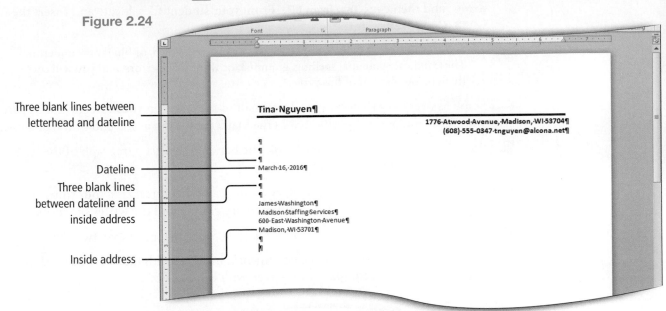

4 Type the salutation **Dear Mr. Washington:** and then press Enter two times.

Always leave one blank line above and below the salutation.

5 Type, exactly as shown, the following opening paragraph that includes an intentional word usage error: **I am seeking a position in witch I can use my** and press Spacebar. Type, exactly as shown, **computr** and then watch *computr* as you press Spacebar.

The AutoCorrect feature recognizes the misspelled word, and then changes *computr* to *computer* when you press Spacebar, Enter, or a punctuation mark.

6 Type the following, including the misspelled last word: **and communication skills. My education, outlined on the enclosed resumee** and then type **,** (a comma). Notice that when you type the comma, AutoCorrect replaces *resumee* with *resume*.

7 Press Spacebar. Complete the paragraph by typing **includes a Business Software Applications Specialist certificate from MATC.** Compare your screen with Figure 2.25.

Figure 2.25

Paragraphs are single spaced

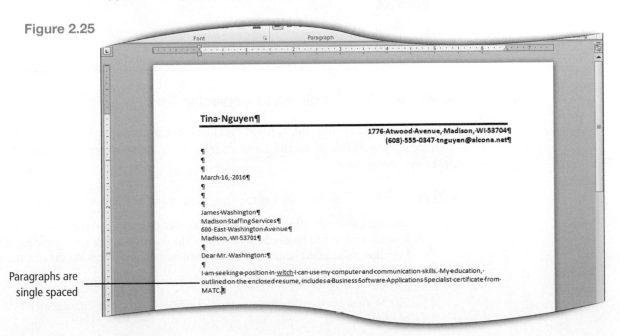

8 Press [Enter] two times. On the **Insert tab**, in the **Text group**, click the **Object button arrow**, and then click **Text from File**. From your student files, locate and **Insert** the file **w02B_Cover_Letter_Text**.

> Some of the words in the cover letter text display red, green, or blue wavy underlines. These indicate potential spelling, grammar, or word usage errors, and you will correct them before the end of this project.

9 Scroll as necessary to display the lower half of the letter on your screen, and be sure your insertion point is positioned in the blank paragraph at the end of the document.

10 Press [Enter] one time to leave one blank line between the last paragraph of the letter and the complimentary closing.

11 Type **Sincerely,** as the complimentary closing, and then press [Enter] four times to leave three blank lines between the complimentary closing and the writer's identification.

12 Type **Tina Nguyen** as the writer's identification, and then press [Enter] two times.

13 Type **Enclosure** to indicate that a document is included with the letter. **Save** 🖫 your document, and then compare your screen with Figure 2.26.

Figure 2.26

Wavy underlines indicate potential errors

Text inserted from another document

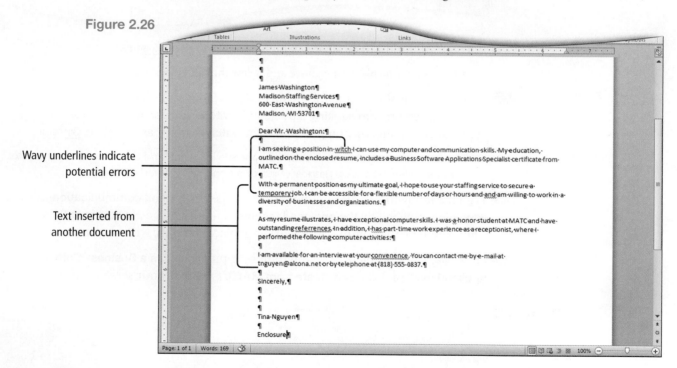

Activity 2.14 | Finding and Replacing Text

Use the Find command to locate text in a document quickly. Use the Find and Replace command to make the same change, or to make more than one change at a time, in a document.

1 Press [Ctrl] + [Home] to position the insertion point at the beginning of the document.

> Because a find operation—or a find and replace operation—begins from the location of the insertion point and proceeds to the end of the document, it is good practice to position the insertion point at the beginning of the document before initiating the command.

Another Way

Hold down [Ctrl] and press [F].

2 On the **Home tab**, in the **Editing group**, click the **Find** button.

> The Navigation Pane displays on the left side of the screen, with a search box at the top of the pane.

3 In the search box, type **ac** If necessary, scroll down slightly in your document to view the entire body text of the letter, and then compare your screen with Figure 2.27.

In the document, the search letters *ac* are selected and highlighted in yellow for all three words that contain the letters *ac* together. In the Navigation Pane, the three instances are shown in context—*ac* displays in bold.

Figure 2.27

Find button

Search term

Matches found in the document

4 In the search box, complete the word **accessible**.

One match for the search term displays in context in the Navigation Pane and is highlighted in the document.

5 In the document, point to the yellow highlighted word *accessible*, double-click, and then type **available** to replace the word. Notice that the list of results is now empty.

6 **Close** ☒ the **Navigation Pane**, and then on the **Home tab**, in the **Editing group**, click the **Replace** button.

7 In the **Find and Replace** dialog box, in the **Find what** box, replace the existing text by typing **MATC** In the **Replace with** box, type **Madison Area Technical College** and then compare your screen with Figure 2.28

Figure 2.28

Search term

Replacement text

8 In the lower left corner of the dialog box, click the **More** button to expand the dialog box, and then under **Search Options**, select the **Match case** check box.

The acronym *MATC* appears in the document two times. In a formal letter, the reader may not know what the acronym means, so you should include the full text instead of an acronym. In this instance, you must select the *Match case* check box so that the replaced text will match the case you typed in the Replace with box, and *not* display in all uppercase letters in the manner of *MATC*.

9 In the **Find and Replace** dialog box, click the **Replace All** button to replace both instances of *MATC*. Click **OK** to close the message box.

10 In the **Find and Replace** dialog box, clear the **Match case** check box, click the **Less** button, and then **Close** the dialog box.

The Find and Replace dialog box opens with the settings used the last time it was open. Thus, it is good practice to reset this dialog box to its default settings each time you use it.

11 **Save** 🖫 your document.

Activity 2.15 | Selecting and Moving Text to a New Location

By using Word's ***drag-and-drop*** feature, you can use the mouse to drag selected text from one location to another. Drag-and-drop is most effective when the text to be moved and the destination are on the same screen.

1 Take a moment to study the table in Figure 2.29 to become familiar with the techniques you can use to select text in a document quickly.

Selecting Text in a Document

To Select	Do This
A portion of text	Click to position the insertion point at the beginning of the text you want to select, hold down Shift, and then click at the end of the text you want to select. Alternatively, hold down the left mouse button and drag from the beginning to the end of the text you want to select.
A word	Double-click the word.
A sentence	Hold down Ctrl and click anywhere in the sentence.
A paragraph	Triple-click anywhere in the paragraph; or, move the pointer to the left of the line, into the margin area. When the 🔊 pointer displays, double-click.
A line	Move the pointer to the left of the line. When the 🔊 pointer displays, click one time.
One character at a time	Position the insertion point to the left of the first character, hold down Shift, and press ← or → as many times as desired.
A string of words	Position the insertion point to the left of the first word, hold down Shift and Ctrl, and then press ← or → as many times as desired.
Consecutive lines	Position the insertion point to the left of the first word, hold down Shift and press ↑ or ↓.
Consecutive paragraphs	Position the insertion point to the left of the first word, hold down Shift and Ctrl and press ↑ or ↓.
The entire document	Hold down Ctrl and press A. Alternatively, move the pointer to the left of any line in the document. When the 🔊 pointer displays, triple-click.

Figure 2.29

2 Be sure you can view the entire body of the letter on your screen. In the paragraph that begins *With a permanent position*, in the second line, locate and double-click *days*.

3 Point to the selected word to display the ⬚ pointer.

4 Drag to the right until the dotted vertical line that floats next to the pointer is positioned to the right of the word *hours* in the same line, as shown in Figure 2.30.

Figure 2.30

Word will be dragged to new location

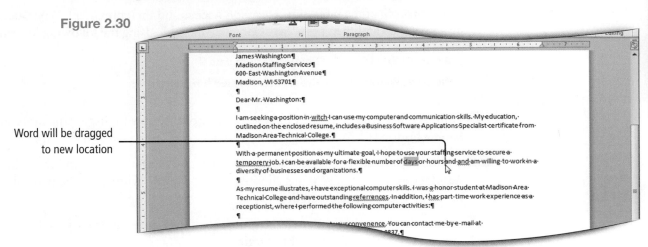

5 Release the mouse button to move the text. Select the word *hours* and drag it to the left of the word *or*—the previous location of the word *days*. Click anywhere in the document to deselect the text.

6 Examine the text that you moved, and add or remove spaces as necessary.

7 Hold down ⌈Ctrl⌋, and then in the paragraph that begins *I am available*, click anywhere in the first sentence to select the entire sentence.

8 Drag the selected sentence to the end of the paragraph by positioning the small vertical line that floats with the pointer to the left of the paragraph mark. Compare your screen with Figure 2.31.

Figure 2.31

Sentence moved to end of paragraph

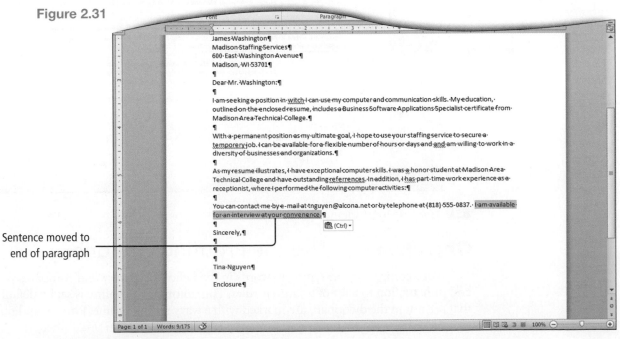

9 **Save** 🖫 your document.

Activity 2.16 | Inserting and Formatting a Table in a Document

1 Locate the paragraph that begins *As my resume*, and then click to position the insertion point in the blank line below that paragraph. Press Enter one time.

2 On the **Insert tab**, in the **Tables group**, click the **Table** button. In the **Table** grid, in the third row, click the second square to insert a 2 × 3 table.

3 In the first cell of the table, type **Microsoft Access** and then press Tab. Type **Queried inventory data** and then press Tab. Complete the table using the following information:

Microsoft Excel	**Entered budget data**
Microsoft Word	**Created and mailed form letters**

4 Point slightly outside of the upper left corner of the table to display the **table move handle** button ⊞. With the ⬚ pointer, click one time to select the entire table.

5 On the **Layout tab**, in the **Cell Size group**, click the **AutoFit** button, and then click **AutoFit Contents** to have Word choose the best column widths for the two columns based on the text you entered.

6 On the **Home tab**, in the **Paragraph group**, click the **Center** button ≡ to center the table between the left and right margins.

7 On the **Design tab**, in the **Table Styles group**, click the **Borders button arrow**, and then click **No Border**. Click anywhere to cancel the selection of the table, and then compare your screen with Figure 2.32.

> A light dashed line may display in place of the original table borders if your default settings have been changed.

Figure 2.32

Table inserted in letter ⎯⎯⎯⎯

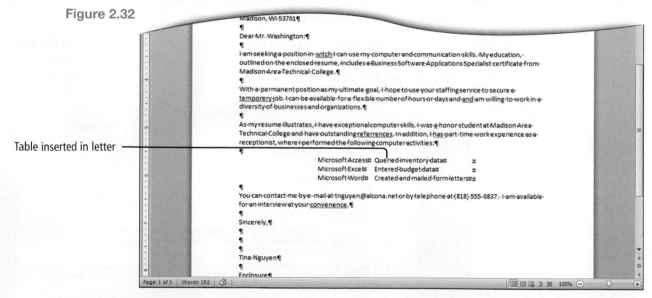

8 **Save** 🖫 your document.

Objective 6 | Use the Proofing Options

Word compares your typing to words in the Office dictionary and compares your phrases and punctuation to a list of grammar rules. This automatic proofing is set by default. Words that are not in the dictionary are marked with a wavy red underline. Phrases and punctuation that differ from the grammar rules are marked with a wavy green underline.

Word also compares commonly misused words with a set of word usage rules, and marks misused words with a wavy blue underline; for example the misuse of *their*, *there*, and *they're*. However, Word will not flag the word *sign* as misspelled even though you intended to type *sing a song* rather than *sign a song*, because both are words contained within Word's dictionary. Your own knowledge and proofreading skills are still required, even when using a sophisticated Word processing program like Word.

Activity 2.17 | Checking Spelling and Grammar Errors

There are two ways to respond to spelling and grammar errors flagged by Word. You can right-click a flagged word or phrase, and then from the shortcut menu choose a correction or action. Or, you can initiate the Spelling and Grammar command to display the Spelling and Grammar dialog box, which provides more options than the shortcut menus.

> **Alert! | Spelling and Grammar Checking**
>
> If you do not see any wavy red, green, or blue lines under words, the automatic spelling and/or grammar checking has been turned off on your system. To activate the spelling and grammar checking, display Backstage view, on the Help tab, click Options, click Proofing, and then under *When correcting spelling in Microsoft Office programs*, select the first four check boxes. Under *When correcting spelling and grammar in Word*, select the first four check boxes, and then click the Writing Style arrow and click Grammar Only. Under *Exceptions for*, clear both check boxes. To display the flagged spelling and grammar errors, click the Recheck Document button, and then close the dialog box.

1 Position the body of the letter on your screen, and then examine the text to locate green, red, and blue wavy underlines. Compare your screen with Figure 2.33.

A list of grammar rules applied by a computer program like Word can never be exact, and a computer dictionary cannot contain all known words and proper names. Thus, you will need to check any words flagged by Word with wavy underlines, and you will also need to proofread for content errors.

Figure 2.33

Blue wavy underline indicates potential word usage problem

Red wavy underline indicates potential spelling problem

Green wavy underline indicates potential grammar problem

2 In the lower left corner of your screen, in the status bar, locate and point to the ✏ icon to display the ScreenTip *Proofing errors were found. Click to correct.*

If this button displays, you know there are potential errors identified in the document.

3 In the paragraph that begins *With a permanent*, locate the word *temporery* with the wavy red underline. Point to the word and right-click to display the shortcut menu, and then compare your screen with Figure 2.34.

Figure 2.34

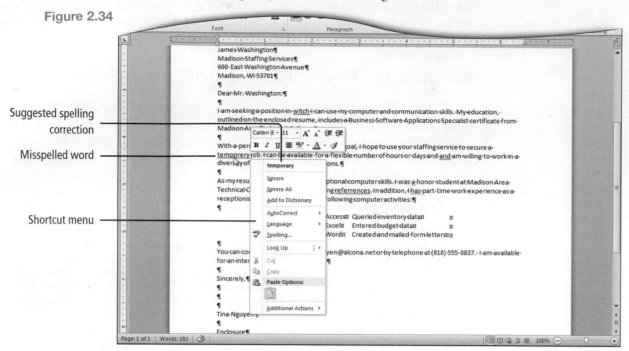

Suggested spelling correction

Misspelled word

Shortcut menu

4 On the shortcut menu, click **temporary** to correct the spelling error.

5 In the next line, locate the word *and* that displays with a wavy red underline, point to word and right-click, and then from the shortcut menu, click **Delete Repeated Word** to delete the duplicate word.

Another Way

Press F7 to start the Spelling & Grammar command.

6 Press Ctrl + Home to move the insertion point to the beginning of the document. Click the **Review tab**, and then in the **Proofing group**, click the **Spelling & Grammar** button to check the spelling and grammar of the text in the document. Compare your screen with Figure 2.35.

> The word *witch* is highlighted—a *Possible Word Choice Error*—and the sentence containing the potential error displays in the dialog box. A suggested change also displays.

Figure 2.35

Word usage error

Suggested correction

7 In the **Spelling and Grammar** dialog box, click the **Change** button to change to the correct usage *which*.

> The next marked word—a possible spelling error—displays.

8 Click the **Change** button to change *referrences* to *references*. Notice that the next error is a possible grammar error.

9 Click the **Change** button to change *a* to *an*. Continue the spelling and grammar check and change *has* to *have* and correct the spelling of *convenence*.

10 When Word indicates *The spelling and grammar check is complete*, click **OK**.

11 Save 💾 your document.

Activity 2.18 | Using the Thesaurus

A *thesaurus* is a research tool that lists *synonyms*—words that have the same or similar meaning to the word you selected.

1 Scroll so that you can view the body of the letter. In the paragraph that begins *With a permanent*, at the end of the second line, locate and right-click the word *diversity*.

2 On the shortcut menu, point to **Synonyms**, and then compare your screen with Figure 2.36.

> A list of synonyms displays; the list will vary in length depending on the selected word.

Figure 2.36

List of synonyms

3 From the list of synonyms, click **variety** to replace *diversity* with *variety*.

4 In the paragraph that begins *As my resume*, point to the word *exceptional*, right-click, point to **Synonyms**, and then at the bottom of the shortcut menu, click **Thesaurus** to display the **Rescarch** task pane.

5 In the **Research** task pane, under **Thesaurus**, point to the non-bold word *excellent*, and then click the **arrow**. Compare your screen with Figure 2.37.

Figure 2.37

Synonym

Selected word

6 On the menu, click **Insert**, and then **Close** ☒ the **Research** task pane.

> *excellent* replaces the word *exceptional*.

7 Display **Backstage** view and click the **Info tab**. On the right, under the document thumbnail, click **Properties**, and then click **Show Document Panel**. In the **Author** box, type your firstname and lastname. Be sure your course name and section number display in the **Subject** box, and as the **Keywords**, replace any existing text with **cover letter**

8 Close ☒ the **Document Panel**.

9 Save 🖫, and then display **Backstage** view. Click **Close** to close the document but leave Word open. Hold this file until you complete this project.

Objective 7 | Create a Document Using a Template

Microsoft provides pre-designed templates for letters, resumes, invoices, and other types of documents. Recall that when you open a template, it opens unnamed so that you can reuse it as often as you need to do so.

Activity 2.19 | Locating and Opening a Template

If you need to create a short resume quickly, or if you need ideas about how to format your resume, Microsoft Word provides pre-designed resume templates. Some templates are available on your computer; many more are available online. After opening a template, you can add text as indicated, modify the layout and design, and add or remove resume elements.

1 Close any open documents, and then from **Backstage** view, click **New**.

2 Under **Available Templates**, click **Sample templates**.

3 Under **Available Templates**, scroll toward the bottom of the window, and then click **Median Resume**. Notice that a preview of the *Median Resume* template displays on the right. Compare your screen with Figure 2.38.

Figure 2.38

Preview of template

Selected template

4 In the lower right corner, click the **Create** button.

> The template opens a copy of itself in the form of a new Word document—the title bar indicates *Document* followed by a number. Recall that you are not opening the template itself, and that changes you make to this new document will not affect the contents of the template file.

5 Display the **Save As** dialog box. **Save** the document in your **Word Chapter 2** folder as **Lastname_Firstname_2B_Brief_Resume** and then add the file name to the footer—called the *First Page Footer* in this template.

6 **Save** 🖫 your document.

Activity 2.20 | Replacing Template Placeholder Text

After you save the template file as a Word document, you can begin to substitute your own information in the indicated locations. You can also remove unneeded resume elements that are included with the template.

1 Click on the picture, and notice that a Picture Tool tab is added to the Ribbon.

2 Click the **Layout tab**, and then in the **Table group**, click the **View Gridlines** button to display non-printing table borders.

> This template consists of two Word tables, and the name in the first row of the upper table displays either the user name or the text *[Type your name]* in square brackets.

3 At the top of the upper table, click the **Resume Name tab arrow**, and then compare your screen with Figure 2.39.

There are two styles available with the Median template—with or without a photo. You should not include a picture on a resume unless physical appearance is directly related to the job for which you are applying—for example, for a job as an actor or a model.

Figure 2.39

Resume Name tab arrow

Two styles available

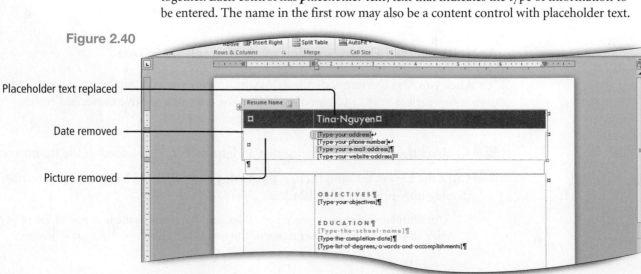

4 In the **Resume Name** gallery, click the first style—**Name**—to switch to the style with no picture.

5 In the first row of the table, select the displayed text—typically the name of your computer as indicated in your Windows operating system—and replace the text by typing **Tina Nguyen**

Another Way

Select the entire row, right-click, and then from the shortcut menu, click Delete Rows.

6 In the second row, click anywhere in the date control *[Select the Date]*. On the Ribbon, click the **Layout tab**. In the **Rows & Columns group**, click the **Delete** button, and then click **Delete Rows**.

Text surrounded by brackets is called a *content control*. There are several different types of content controls, including date, picture, and *text controls*. Most of the controls in this template are text controls. Because resumes do not typically include a date, you can delete this row.

7 Click anywhere in the content control *[Type your address]*. Compare your screen with Figure 2.40.

For the name and address at the top of the document, all of the text controls are grouped together. Each control has *placeholder text*, text that indicates the type of information to be entered. The name in the first row may also be a content control with placeholder text.

Figure 2.40

Placeholder text replaced

Date removed

Picture removed

8 Complete the personal information by using the following information:

[Type your address]	**1776 Atwood Avenue, Madison, WI 53704**
[Type your phone number]	**(608) 555-0347**
[Type your e-mail address]	**tnguyen@alcona.net**
[Type your website address]	(leave this blank)

9 In the lower table, click in the *[Type your objectives]* control, and then type **To obtain a position using my computer and communications skills.**

10 Complete the **Education** section by using the following information:

[Type the school name]	**Madison Area Technical College**
[Type the completion date]	**June 2015**
[Type list of degrees, awards and accomplishments] *(type three separate lines)*	**Business Computing Specialist certificate** **Dean's List, four semesters** **President, Community Service Club**

11 Complete the **Experience** section by using the following information:

[Type the job title]	**Office Assistant (part-time)**
[Type the company name]	**The Robinson Company**
[Type the start date]	**September 2014**
[Type the end date]	**present**
[Type list of job responsibilities]	**Data entry and report generation using company spreadsheets and databases.**

12 Click in the *[Type list of skills]* control, type **Proficiency using Word, Excel, and Access (completed advanced courses in Microsoft Office programs)** and then press Enter.

13 As the second bulleted point, type **Excellent written and verbal communications (completed courses in Business Communications, PowerPoint, and Speech)** and then compare your screen with Figure 2.41. **Save** your document.

Figure 2.41

Placeholder text replaced ⟶

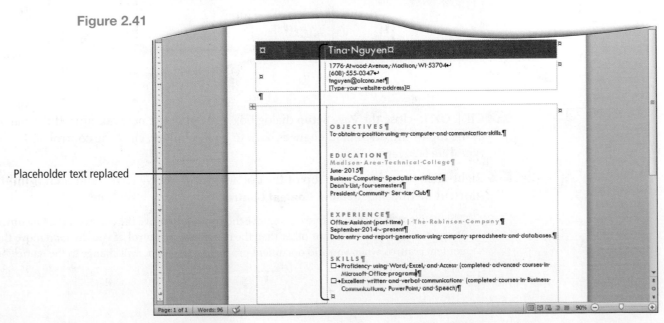

Activity 2.21 | Removing Template Controls and Formatting the Resume

1 Near the top of the document, point to the text control that you did not use—*[Type your website address]*. Right-click the control, and then from the shortcut menu, click **Remove Content Control**. Press $\boxed{\text{Backspace}}$ as necessary to position the insertion point at the end of the e-mail address. Select the three lines with the address, phone, and e-mail information. On the Mini toolbar, notice that the text size is *11.5*. Click the **Font Size button arrow**, and then click **12**.

2 Click anywhere in lower table—the table with the *Objectives* row at the top—and then point to the upper left corner of the active table to display the **move table handle**. Click one time to select the lower table.

3 On the Mini toolbar, change the **Font Size** to **12** to match the table above.

4 Click anywhere to cancel the selection. On the **Page Layout tab**, in the **Page Setup group**, click the **Margins** button, and then click **Custom Margins**. Change the **Top** margin to **1.5** and the **Left** and **Right** margins to **1** to make this short resume better fill the page. Compare your screen with Figure 2.42.

Figure 2.42

New margins

5 Click **OK** to close the **Page Setup** dialog box and apply the new margins. If the name at the top of the document changes back to a placeholder, click the control and type **Tina Nguyen**

6 Right-click the name at the top of the document—*Tina Nguyen*—and then from the shortcut menu, click **Remove Content Control**.

> This action will leave the name but remove the control. Remove the control if the Document Properties will have an author other than the name in this control. If you do *not* remove the content control, when you add document properties, the name will change to the name you type in the Author box.

7 Press Ctrl + F2 to display the Print Preview in **Backstage** view. Click the **Info tab**. On the right, under the document thumbnail, click **Properties**, and then click **Show Document Panel**. In the **Author** box, delete any text and then type your firstname and lastname. In the **Subject** box, type your course name and section number, and in the **Keywords** box, type **short resume, template**

8 **Close** ☒ the **Document Panel**. **Save** 🖫 your document, and then hold this file until you complete this project. Leave the resume displayed on your screen.

Activity 2.22 | Saving a Resume as a Web Page

You can save your resume as a Web page. This enables you to post the Web page on your own Web site or on Web space provided by your college. It also enables you to send the resume as an e-mail attachment that can be opened using any Web browser.

1 With your **2B_Brief_Resume** still open on your screen, click **Save** 🖫 to be sure the current version of the document is saved.

2 Display the **Save As** dialog box. In the lower portion of the **Save As** dialog box, click the **Save as type arrow**, and then click **Single File Web Page**.

A *Single File Web Page* is a document saved using the *Hypertext Markup Language (HTML)*. HTML is the language used to format documents that can be opened using a Web browser such as Internet Explorer.

3 In the **Save As** dialog box, in the **File name** box, type **Lastname_Firstname_2B_HTML_ Resume** Click **Save**, and then click **Yes** if a message box displays. Notice that the Web page displays in Word.

4 Display **Backstage** view. On the right, click **Properties**, and then click **Advanced Properties**. In the **Properties** dialog box, on the **Summary tab**, in the **Subject** box, be sure your course name and section number display. In the **Author** box, be sure your first and last names display. In the **Keywords** box, replace the existing text with **HTML** Click **OK**, and then click the **Home tab**. **Save** 🖫 the document; print or submit electronically as directed.

5 **Exit** Word. From the **Start** menu 🔵, click **Computer**. Navigate to your **Word Chapter 2** folder, and then double-click your **Lastname_Firstname_2B_HTML_Resume** file to open the resume in your Web browser. Compare your screen with Figure 2.43.

Figure 2.43

Resume displayed in a Web browser

6 **Close** ☒ your Web browser. As directed by your instructor, print or submit electronically the four files from this project—2B_Letterhead, 2B_Cover_Letter, 2B_Brief_Resume, and 2B_HTML_Resume.

End **You have completed Project 2B** ——————

Content-Based Assessments

Summary

In this chapter, you created a table, and then used the table to create a resume. You created a letterhead template, and then created a document using a copy of the letterhead template. You created a cover letter for the resume, moved text, corrected spelling and grammar, and used the built-in thesaurus. Finally, you created a short resume using a template, and also saved the resume as a Web page.

Key Terms

Matching

Match each term in the second column with its correct definition in the first column by writing the letter of the term on the blank line in front of the correct definition.

_____ 1.   An arrangement of information organized into rows and columns.

_____ 2.   The box at the intersection of a row and column in a table.

_____ 3.   A document structure that opens a copy of itself, opens unnamed, and is used as the starting point for another document.

_____ 4.   The template that serves as a basis for all new Word documents.

_____ 5.   The personal or company information that displays at the top of a letter.

_____ 6.   The Word style that inserts no extra space following a paragraph and uses single spacing.

_____ 7.   The first line in a business letter that contains the current date and that is positioned just below the letterhead if a letterhead is used.

_____ 8.   The name and address of the person receiving a letter and positioned below the date line.

_____ 9.   The greeting line of a letter.

_____ 10. A parting farewell in a letter.

_____ 11. The name and title of the author of a letter, placed near the bottom of the letter under the complimentary closing.

_____ 12. The optional line following the inside address in a business letter that states the purpose of the letter.

A AutoCorrect

B Cell

C Complimentary closing

D Date line

E Drag and drop

F Enclosures

G Inside address

H Letterhead

I No Spacing

J Normal template

K Salutation

L Subject line

M Table

N Template

O Writer's identification

_____ 13. Additional documents included with a business letter.

_____ 14. A Word feature that corrects common spelling errors as you type, for example changing _teh_ to _the_.

_____ 15. A technique by which you can move, by dragging, selected text from one location in a document to another.

Multiple Choice

Circle the correct answer.

1. When you create a table, the width of all of cells in the table is:
   A. equal   B. proportional   C. 1 inch

2. To indicate words that might be misspelled because they are not in Word's dictionary, Word flags text with:
   A. blue wavy underlines   B. green wavy underlines   C. red wavy underlines

3. To indicate possible grammar errors, Word flags text with:
   A. blue wavy underlines   B. green wavy underlines   C. red wavy underlines

4. To indicate possible errors in word usage, Word flags text with:
   A. blue wavy underlines   B. green wavy underlines   C. red wavy underlines

5. A research tool that provides a list of words with similar meanings is:
   A. a thesaurus   B. a dictionary   C. an encyclopedia

6. A word with the same or similar meaning as another word is:
   A. an acronym   B. a search term   C. a synonym

7. In a template, an area indicated by placeholder text into which you can add text, pictures, dates, or lists is a:
   A. text control   B. content control   C. quick control

8. A document saved in HTML, which can be opened using a Web browser, is a:
   A. Web page   B. template   C. resume

9. Using drag-and-drop to move text is most useful when both the text and the destination are on the same:
   A. document   B. section   C. screen

10. To locate specific text in a document quickly, use the:
    A. Find command   B. Replace command   C. Locate command

Content-Based Assessments

Skills Review | Project **2C** Student Resume

In the following Skills Review, you will use a table to create a resume for Joshua Green. Your completed resume will look similar to Figure 2.44.

Project Files

For Project 2C, you will need the following files:

New blank Word document
w02C_Skills
w02C_Experience

You will save your document as:

Lastname_Firstname_2C_Student_Resume

Project Results

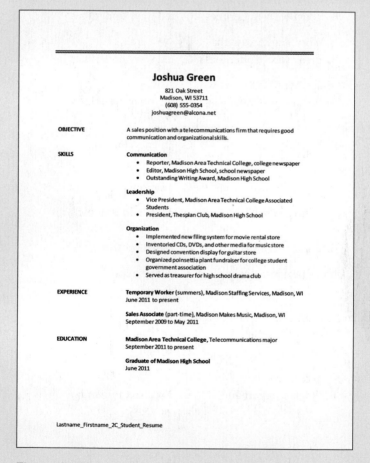

Joshua Green

821 Oak Street
Madison, WI 53711
(608) 555-0354
joshuagreen@alcona.net

OBJECTIVE	A sales position with a telecommunications firm that requires good communication and organizational skills.
SKILLS	**Communication** • Reporter, Madison Area Technical College, college newspaper • Editor, Madison High School, school newspaper • Outstanding Writing Award, Madison High School **Leadership** • Vice President, Madison Area Technical College Associated Students • President, Thespian Club, Madison High School **Organization** • Implemented new filing system for movie rental store • Inventoried CDs, DVDs, and other media for music store • Designed convention display for guitar store • Organized poinsettia plant fundraiser for college student government association • Served as treasurer for high school drama club
EXPERIENCE	**Temporary Worker** (summers), Madison Staffing Services, Madison, WI June 2011 to present **Sales Associate** (part-time), Madison Makes Music, Madison, WI September 2009 to May 2011
EDUCATION	**Madison Area Technical College**, Telecommunications major September 2011 to present **Graduate of Madison High School** June 2011

Lastname_Firstname_2C_Student_Resume

Figure 2.44

(Project 2C Student Resume continues on the next page)

Content-Based Assessments

Skills Review | Project 2C Student Resume (continued)

1 **Start** Word. In the new blank document, be sure that formatting marks and rulers display. **Save** the document in your **Word Chapter 2** folder as **Lastname_Firstname_2C_Student_Resume**

a. Add the file name to the footer, and then close the footer area. Click the **Insert tab**, and then in the **Tables group**, click the **Table** button. In the **Table** grid, in the fourth row, click the second square to insert a **2 × 4** table.

b. In the first cell of the table, type **Joshua Green** and then press Enter. Type the following text, pressing Enter after each line *except* the last line:

821 Oak Street

Madison, WI 53711

(608) 555-0354

joshuagreen@alcona.net

c. Press ↓ to move to the first cell in the second row. Type **SKILLS** and then press ↓ to move to the first cell in the third row.

d. Type **EXPERIENCE** and then press ↓. Type **EDUCATION**

e. In the first cell, if the e-mail address displays in blue, right-click the e-mail address, and then from the shortcut menu, click **Remove Hyperlink**. **Save** your document

2 Click in the cell to the right of *SKILLS*, and then type the following, pressing Enter after each item:

Communication
Reporter, Madison Area Technical College, college newspaper
Editor, Madison High School, school newspaper
Outstanding Writing Award, Madison High School

a. With the insertion point in the new line at the end of the cell, click the **Insert tab**. In the **Text group**, click the **Object button arrow**, and then click **Text from File**.

b. Navigate to your student files, select **w02C_Skills**, and then click **Insert**. Press Backspace one time to remove the blank line.

c. Click in the cell to the right of *EXPERIENCE*, and then insert the file **w02C_Experience**. Press Backspace one time to remove the blank line.

d. Click in the cell to the right of *EDUCATION*, and then type the following, pressing Enter after all *except* the last item:

Madison Area Technical College, Telecommunications major

September 2011 to present

Graduate of Madison High School

June 2011

3 Click anywhere in the top row of the table. Click the **Layout tab**, and then in the **Rows & Columns group**, click the **Insert Below** button. Type **OBJECTIVE** and then press Tab.

a. Type **A sales position with a telecommunications firm that requires good communication and organizational skills.**

b. In any row, point to the vertical border between the two columns to display the ⟷ pointer. Drag the column border to the left to approximately **1.75 inches on the horizontal ruler**.

c. Click anywhere in the left column. Click the **Layout tab**. In the **Cell Size group**, in the **Table Column Width** box, if necessary, type **1.75** and press Enter.

d. In the first row of the document, drag across both cells to select them. On the **Layout tab**, in the **Merge group**, click the **Merge Cells** button. Right-click the selected cell, and then from the Mini toolbar, click the **Center** button.

e. In the top row, select the first paragraph of text—*Joshua Green*. From the Mini toolbar, increase the **Font Size** to **20** and apply **Bold**.

f. In the second row, point to the word *OBJECTIVE*, hold down the left mouse button, and then drag down to select the row headings in uppercase letters. On the Mini toolbar, click the **Bold** button. **Save** your document.

4 Click in the cell to the right of *OBJECTIVE*. On the **Page Layout tab**, in the **Paragraph group**, click the **Spacing After up spin arrow** three times to change the spacing to **18 pt**.

a. In the cell to the right of *SKILLS*, apply **Bold** to the words *Communication*, *Leadership*, and *Organization*. Then, under each bold heading in the cell, select the lines of text, and create a bulleted list.

b. In the first two bulleted lists, click in the last bullet item, and then on the **Page Layout tab**, in the **Paragraph group**, set the **Spacing After** to **12 pt**.

(Project 2C Student Resume continues on the next page)

Content-Based Assessments

c. In the last bulleted list, click in the last bullet item, and then set the **Spacing After** to **18 pt**.

d. In the cell to the right of *EXPERIENCE*, apply **Bold** to *Temporary Worker* and *Sales Associate*. Click in the line *June 2011 to present* and apply **Spacing After** of **12 pt**. Click in the line *September 2009 to May 2011* and apply **Spacing After** of **18 pt**.

e. In the cell to the right of *EDUCATION*, apply **Bold** to *Madison Area Technical College* and *Graduate of Madison High School*.

f. In the same cell, click in the line *September 2011 to present* and apply **Spacing After** of **12 pt**.

g. In the first row, click in the last line—*joshuagreen@alcona.net*—and then change the **Spacing After** to **18 pt**. Click in the first line—*Joshua Green*—and set the **Spacing Before** to **30 pt** and the **Spacing After** to **6 pt**.

5 Point to the upper left corner of the table, and then click the displayed **table move handle** button ⊞ to select the entire table. On the **Design tab**, in the **Table Styles group**, click the **Borders button arrow**, and then click **No Border**.

a. On the **Design tab**, in the **Table Styles group**, click the **Borders button arrow** again, and then at the bottom of the gallery, click **Borders and Shading**. In the **Borders and Shading** dialog box, under **Setting**, click **Custom**. Under **Style**, scroll down slightly, and then click the style with two equal lines.

b. Click the **Width arrow**, and then click **1 1/2 pt**. Under **Preview**, click the top border of the preview box, and then click **OK**.

c. Click the **File tab** to display **Backstage** view, and then click the **Print tab** to display the Print Preview.

d. Click the **Info tab**. On the right side, under the document thumbnail, click **Properties**, and then click **Show Document Panel**.

e. In the **Author** box, delete any text and then type your firstname and lastname. In the **Subject** box, type your course name and section number, and in the **Keywords** box type **resume, table**

f. **Close** the **Document Panel. Save** 🖫 and then, as directed by your instructor, print your document or submit it electronically. **Exit** Word.

End **You have completed Project 2C** ────────────

Content-Based Assessments

Apply 2B skills from these Objectives:

- **4** Create a New Document from an Existing Document
- **5** Change and Reorganize Text
- **6** Use the Proofing Options
- **7** Create a Document Using a Template

Skills Review | Project **2D** Ross Letter

In the following Skills Review, you will create a letterhead, and then create a new document from the letterhead to create a resume cover letter. You will also create a short resume using a Microsoft template and save it as a Web page. Your completed documents will look similar to Figure 2.45.

Project Files

For Project 2D, you will need the following files:

> New blank Word document
> w02D_Letter_Text
> Equity Resume Template from Word's installed templates

You will save your documents as:

> Lastname_Firstname_2D_Ross_Letterhead
> Lastname_Firstname_2D_Ross_Letter
> Lastname_Firstname_2D_Resume
> Lastname_Firstname_2D_Web_Resume

Project Results

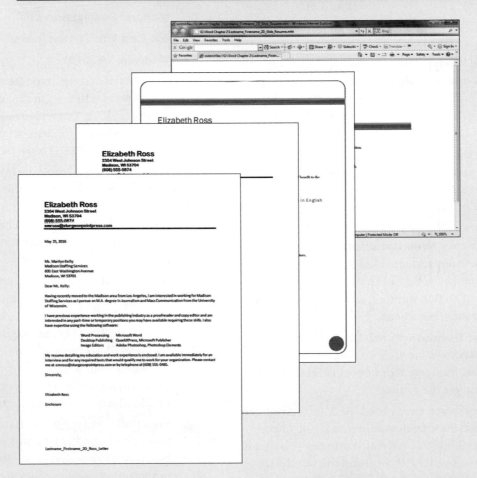

Figure 2.45

(Project 2D Ross Letter continues on the next page)

Content-Based Assessments

1 **Start** Word. In the new blank document, be sure that formatting marks and rulers display. On the **Home tab**, in the **Styles group**, click the **No Spacing** button.

   a. Type **Elizabeth Ross** and then press Enter. Type **2304 West Johnson Street** and press Enter. Type **Madison, WI 53704** and then press Enter.

   b. Type **(608) 555-0874** and then press Enter. Type **emross@sturgeonpointpress.com** and then press Enter three times. If the e-mail address changes to blue text, right-click the e-mail address, and then click Remove Hyperlink.

   c. Select all five lines of the personal information, but do not select the blank paragraphs. From the Mini toolbar, change the **Font** to **Arial Rounded MT Bold**. Select the first paragraph—*Elizabeth Ross*—and then on the Mini toolbar, apply **Bold** and change the **Font Size** to **20**.

   d. Click anywhere in the fifth line of text—the e-mail address. On the **Home tab**, in the **Paragraph group**, click the **Borders button arrow**, and then click **Borders and Shading**. Under **Style**, click the first style—a single solid line. Click the **Width arrow**, and then click **3 pt**. In the **Preview** area, click the bottom border, and then click **OK**.

   e. Display **Backstage** view, and then click **Save As**. Save the document in your **Word Chapter 2** folder as **Lastname_Firstname_2D_Ross_Letterhead**

   f. Add the file name to the footer, and then close the footer area. Display **Backstage** view, click **Properties**, and then click **Show Document Panel**. In the **Author** box, delete any text and then type your firstname and lastname. In the **Subject** box, type your course name and section number, and in the **Keywords** box, type **personal letterhead**

   g. **Close** the **Document Panel**. **Save** your document. From **Backstage** view, click **Close** to close the document but leave Word open. Hold this file until you complete the project.

2 From **Backstage** view, click **New**. Under **Available Templates**, click **New from existing**. Navigate to your **Word Chapter 2** folder, click your **Lastname_Firstname_2D_Ross_Letterhead** document, and then in the lower right corner, click **Create New**. From **Backstage** view, click **Save As**. Navigate to your **Word Chapter 2** folder, and **Save** the file as **Lastname_Firstname_2D_Ross_Letter**

Double-click the footer, right-click the file name, and then click **Update Field**. Close the footer area.

   a. From **Backstage** view, display the **Word Options** dialog box. In the **Word Options** list, click **Proofing**, and then under **AutoCorrect options**, click the **AutoCorrect Options** button.

   b. In the **AutoCorrect** dialog box, click the **AutoCorrect tab**. Under **Replace**, type **expereince** and under **With**, type **experience** Click **Add**. If the entry already exists, click Replace instead, and then click Yes. Click **OK** two times to close the dialog boxes.

   c. Press Ctrl + End, type **May 25, 2016** and then press Enter four times. Type the following inside address using four lines:

     Ms. Marilyn Kelly

     Madison Staffing Services

     600 East Washington Avenue

     Madison, WI 53701

   d. Press Enter two times, type **Dear Ms. Kelly:** and then press Enter two times. On the **Insert tab**, in the **Text group**, click the **Object button arrow**, and then click **Text from File**. From your student files, locate and insert the file **w02D_Letter_Text**.

   e. Scroll to view the lower portion of the page, and be sure your insertion point is in the empty paragraph mark at the end. Press Enter, type **Sincerely,** and then press Enter four times. Type **Elizabeth Ross** and press Enter two times. Type **Enclosure** and then **Save** your document.

   f. Near the bottom of the document, locate the paragraph that begins *I am available* and click to position the insertion point at the beginning of the paragraph. Type **My resume detailing my education and work** Press Spacebar and then type the misspelled word **expereince** Press Spacebar and notice that AutoCorrect corrects the misspelling. Type **is enclosed.** and then press Spacebar.

   g. Press Ctrl + Home. On the **Home tab**, in the **Editing group**, click the **Replace** button. In the **Find what** box, type **association** In the **Replace with** box, type **organization** and then click **Replace All**. Click **OK** to close the message box, and then **Close** the **Find and Replace** dialog box.

(Project 2D Ross Letter continues on the next page)

Content-Based Assessments

h. In the paragraph that begins *I have previous*, double-click *experience*. Point to the selected word to display the ⬚ pointer, and then drag the word to the left of *working*. Adjust spacing as necessary.

i. Below the paragraph that begins *I have previous*, position the insertion point in the second blank line. On the **Insert tab**, in the **Tables group**, click the **Table** button. In the **Table** grid, in the third row, click the second square to insert a 2 × 3 table. Type the following information in the table:

Word Processing	Microsoft Word
Desktop Publishing	QuarkXPress, Microsoft Publisher
Image Editors	Adobe Photoshop, Photoshop Elements

j. Point outside of the upper left corner and click the **table move handle** button to select the entire table. On the **Layout tab**, in the **Cell Size group**, click the **AutoFit** button, and then click **AutoFit Contents**. On the **Home tab**, in the **Paragraph group**, click the **Center** button. On the **Design tab**, in the **Table Styles group**, click the **Borders button arrow**, and then click **No Border**. **Save** your document.

3 If you do not see any wavy red and green lines under words, refer to the Alert in Activity 2.17 to enable the default settings for automatic proofing.

a. In the paragraph that begins *Having lately*, in the second line, locate and right-click the phrase *an M.A. degrees*, and then from the shortcut menu, click *an M.A. degree*. In the same paragraph, locate and right-click *Journlism*. From the shortcut menu, click *Journalism*.

b. Press Ctrl + Home. On the **Review tab**, in the **Proofing group**, click the **Spelling & Grammar** button. In the **Spelling and Grammar** dialog box, click the **Change** button to change *are* to *am*. For the misspelled word *expertis*, under **Suggestions**, be sure *expertise* is selected, and then click **Change**.

c. **Change** *qualifie* to *qualify*, and then click **OK** to close the message box.

d. Near the top of the document, in the paragraph that begins *Having lately*, right-click *lately*. In the shortcut menu, point to **Synonyms**, and then click *recently*. In the same line, right-click *region*, and replace it with the synonym *area*.

e. Display **Backstage** view, click **Properties**, and then click **Show Document Panel**. Type your firstname and lastname as the **Author** and your course number and section as the **Subject**. In the **Keywords** box, replace any existing text with **cover letter Close** the **Document Panel**. **Save** your document. From **Backstage** view, **Close** the document but leave Word open. Hold this file until you complete the project.

4 Display **Backstage** view, and then click **New**. Under **Available Templates**, click **Sample templates**. Locate and click **Equity Resume**. In the lower right corner, click **Create**.

a. **Save** the document in your **Word Chapter 2** folder as **Lastname_Firstname_2D_Resume** and then add the file name to the footer—called *First Page Footer* in this template. At the top of the resume, select the text in the first control, which displays the name of the computer at which you are working. Replace this text by typing **Elizabeth Ross** Right-click the name, and then from the shortcut menu, click **Remove Content Control**.

b. Click the *[Type your phone number]* control, and then type **(608) 555-0874** Click the *[Type your address]* control, type **2304 West Johnson Street** and press Enter. Type **Madison, WI 53703**

c. Click the *[Type your e-mail address]* control, and then type **emross@sturgeonpointpress.com** Right-click the *[Type your website]* control, and then from the shortcut menu, click **Remove Content Control**. Press Backspace to remove the *website* line.

d. Click the *[Type the objectives]* control, and then type **A copy editing or proofreading position where my editing and advanced computer skills will be of benefit to the organization.**

e. Under *Education*, click the *[Type the completion date]* control, and then type **University of Wisconsin-Milwaukee, May 2015** Click the *[Type the degree]* control, and then type **Bachelor of Arts in English** For the *[Type list of accomplishments]* bulleted list, type:

Dean's list, six terms

Harriet McArthur Creative Writing Award

(Project 2D Ross Letter continues on the next page)

Skills Review | Project **2D** Ross Letter (continued)

Assistant Editor of college newspaper

3.8 GPA

f. Under *Experience*, enter the text shown in **Table 1** below.

g. Click the *[Type list of skills]* control and type **Word** Press Enter, and then type two additional bullet points with **QuarkXPress** and **Adobe Photoshop**

h. Display **Backstage** view, click **Properties**, and then click **Show Document Panel**. Type your firstname and lastname as the **Author**. In the **Subject** box, type your course and section number. In the **Keywords** box, **resume, template Close** the **Document Panel**.

i. **Save** your document.

j. Display **Backstage** view, click **Save As**, and then in the **Save as type** box, click **Single File Web Page**. Navigate to your **Word Chapter 2** folder. In the **File name** box,

type **Lastname_Firstname_2D_Web_Resume** Click **Save**.

k. Display **Backstage** view, click **Properties**, and then click **Advanced Properties**. In the **Properties** dialog box, be sure your name displays in the *Author* box, and then in the **Keywords** box, add **HTML** to the list of keywords. Click **OK** and **Save** your document.

l. **Exit** Word. From the **Start** menu, click **Computer** (or My Computer). Navigate to your **Word Chapter 2** folder, and then double-click your **2D_Web_Resume** file to open the resume in your Web browser. **Close** the Web browser. As directed by your instructor, print or submit electronically the four files that are the results of this project—2D_Ross_Letterhead, 2D_Ross_Letter, 2D_Resume, and 2D_Web_Resume.

Table 1

[Type the start date]	**May 2012**
[Type the end date]	**Present-**
[Type the job title]	**Senior Copy Editor**
[Type the company name]	**Sturgeon Point Press**
[Type the company address]	**Milwaukee, WI**
[Type job responsibilities]	**Produced final edited copy of books, technical manuals, and pamphlets; supervised three copy editors.**

(Return to Step 4-g)

End **You have completed Project 2D** ——————————————————

Content-Based Assessments

Apply **2A** skills from these Objectives:
1 Create a Table
2 Add Text to a Table
3 Format a Table

Mastering Word | Project **2E** Job Listings

In the following Mastering Word project, you will create an announcement for new job postings at Madison Staffing Services. Your completed document will look similar to Figure 2.46.

Project Files

For Project 2E, you will need the following files:

New blank Word document
w02E_New_Jobs

You will save your document as:

Lastname_Firstname_2E_Job_Listings

Project Results

Madison Staffing Services

Job Alert! New Health Care Listings Just Added!

January 7

Madison Staffing Services has just added several new jobs in the Health Care Industry for the week of January 7. These listings are just in, so apply now to be one of the first candidates considered!

For further information about any of these new jobs, or a complete listing of jobs that are available through Madison Staffing Services, please call Marilyn Kelly at (608) 555-0386 or visit our Web site at www.madisonstaffing.com.

New Health Care Listings for the Week of January 7

Job Title	Type	Location
Computer Developer	Radiology Office	Dane County
Executive Assistant	Medical Records	Deerfield
Insurance Biller	Dental Office	Madison
Office Assistant	Health Clinic	Madison

To help prepare yourself before applying for these jobs, we recommend that you review the following articles on our Web site at www.madisonstaffing.com.

Topic	Article Title
Research	Working in Health Care
Interviewing	Interviewing in Health Care

Lastname_Firstname_2E_Job_Listings

Figure 2.46

(Project 2E Job Listings continues on the next page)

Content-Based Assessments

Mastering Word | Project 2E Job Listings (continued)

1 **Start** Word and display a new blank document; display formatting marks and rulers. **Save** the document in your **Word Chapter 2** folder as **Lastname_Firstname_2E_Job_Listings** and then add the file name to the footer.

2 Type **Madison Staffing Services** and press Enter. Type **Job Alert! New Health Care Listings Just Added!** and press Enter. Type **January 7** and press Enter two times. **Insert** the file **w02E_New_Jobs**.

3 At the top of the document, select and **Center** the three title lines. Select the title *Madison Staffing Services* and change the **Font Size** to **20** pt and apply **Bold**. Apply **Bold** to the second and third title lines. Locate the paragraph that begins *For further information*, and then below that paragraph, click to position the insertion point in the second blank paragraph. **Insert** a **3 × 4** table. Enter the following:

Job Title	Type	Location
Executive Assistant	Medical Records	Deerfield
Insurance Biller	Dental Office	Madison
Office Assistant	Health Clinic	Madison

4 In the table, click anywhere in the second row, and then insert a row above. Add the following information so that the job titles remain in alphabetic order:

Computer Developer	Radiology Office	Dane County

5 Select the entire table. On the **Layout tab**, in the **Cell Size group**, use the **AutoFit** button to **AutoFit**

Contents. With the table still selected, **Center** the table. With the table still selected, on the **Page Layout tab**, add **6 pt Spacing Before** and **6 pt Spacing After**.

6 With the table still selected, remove all table borders, and then add a **Custom 1 pt** solid line top border and bottom border. Select all three cells in the first row, apply **Bold**, and then **Center** the text. Click anywhere in the first row, and then insert a new row above. Merge the three cells in the new top row, and then type **New Health Care Listings for the Week of January 7** Notice that the new row keeps the formatting of the row from which it was created.

7 At the bottom of the document, **Insert** a **2 × 3** table. Enter the following:

Topic	Article Title
Research	Working in Health Care
Interviewing	Interviewing in Health Care

8 Select the entire table. On the **Layout tab**, in the **Cell Size group**, use the **AutoFit** button to **AutoFit Contents**. On the **Home tab**, **Center** the table. On the **Page Layout tab**, add **6 pt Spacing Before** and **6 pt Spacing After**.

9 With the table still selected, remove all table borders, and then add a **Custom 1 pt** solid line top border and bottom border. Select the cells in the first row, apply **Bold**, and then **Center** the text.

10 In the **Document Panel**, add your name and course information and the **Keywords new listings, health care Save** and then print or submit the document electronically as directed. **Exit** Word.

End **You have completed Project 2E**

Content-Based Assessments

Apply **2B** skills from these Objectives:

4 Create a New Document from an Existing Document

5 Change and Reorganize Text

6 Use the Proofing Options

7 Create a Document Using a Template

Mastering Word | Project **2F** Job Tips

In the following Mastering Word project, you will create a fax and a memo that includes job tips for Madison Staffing Services employees. Your completed documents will look similar to Figure 2.47.

Project Files

For Project 2F, you will need the following files:

w02F_Memo_Heading
w02F_Memo_Text
Origin Fax template from Word's installed templates

You will save your documents as:

Lastname_Firstname_2F_Job_Tips
Lastname_Firstname_2F_Fax

Project Results

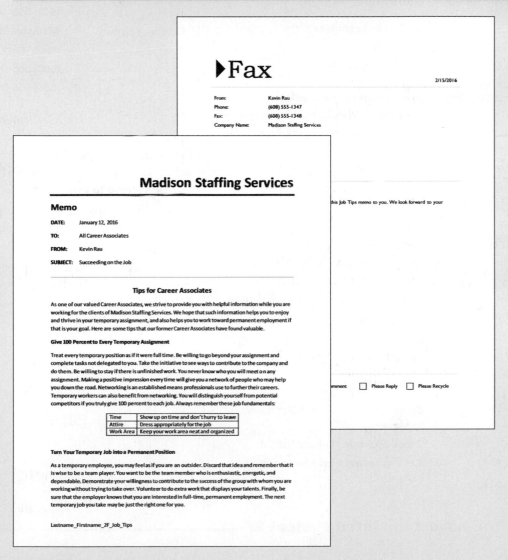

Figure 2.47

(Project 2F Job Tips continues on the next page)

Content-Based Assessments

Mastering Word | Project **2F** Job Tips (continued)

1 **Start** Word; display rulers and formatting marks. In **Backstage** view, create a **New** document using the **New from existing** template. In the **New from Existing Document** dialog box, navigate to your student files, click **w02F_Memo_Heading**, and then click **Create New**.

2 Display the **Document Panel**, add your name and course information and the **Keywords memo, associates**

3 **Save** the document in your **Word Chapter 2** folder as **Lastname_Firstname_2F_Job_Tips** Add the file name to the footer.

4 At the top of your document, in the *DATE* paragraph, click to the right of the tab formatting mark, and then type **January 12, 2016** Use a similar technique to add the following information:

TO:	**All Career Associates**
FROM:	**Kevin Rau**
SUBJECT:	**Succeeding on the Job**

5 Position the insertion point in the blank paragraph below the memo heading. **Insert** the file **w02F_Memo_Text** and press Backspace to remove the blank line at the end of the selected text.

6 Select and **Center** the title *Tips for Career Associates.* By using either the **Spelling and Grammar** dialog box, or by right-clicking selected words, correct all spelling, grammar, and word usage errors.

7 In the first line of the paragraph that begins *Treat every*, locate and right-click *provisional*. Use the shortcut menu to change the word to the synonym *temporary*. In the second line of the same paragraph, change *donate* to the synonym *contribute*.

8 At the end of the paragraph that begins *Treat every temporary*, create a blank paragraph. **Insert** at **2 × 3** table, and then type the following information:

Time	Show up on time and don't hurry to leave
Attire	Dress appropriately for the job
Work Area	Keep your work area neat and organized

9 Select the entire table. **AutoFit Contents** and **Center** the table. Display **Backstage** view and preview the document. **Save** and **Close** the document but leave Word open. Hold this file until you complete this project.

10 From **Sample templates**, create a document based on the **Origin Fax** template. Save the document in your **Word Chapter 2** folder as **Lastname_Firstname_2F_Fax** and then add the file name to the footer—called the *First Page Footer* in this template.

11 Click the *Pick a date* placeholder, type **2/15/2016** and then type the following for the remaining controls:

From:	**Kevin Rau**
Phone:	**(608) 555-1347**
Fax:	**(608) 555-1348**
Company Name:	**Madison Staffing Services**
To:	**Jane Westerfield**
Phone:	**(608) 555-0034**
Fax:	**(608) 555-0035**

12 Locate and right-click *Kevin Rau*; remove the content control. Delete the lower *Company Name* text and remove the control to its right. In the *Type comments* control, type **Jane: I know you are on leave, so I thought I would fax this Job Tips memo to you. We look forward to your return.**

13 In the **Document Panel**, add your name and course information and the **Keywords job tips, fax Save** the document.

14 As directed by your instructor, print or submit electronically the two files that are the results of this project. **Exit** Word.

End You have completed Project 2F

Content-Based Assessments

Apply **2A** and **2B** skills
from these Objectives:

1. Create a Table
2. Add Text to a Table
3. Format a Table
4. Create a New Document from an Existing Document
5. Change and Reorganize Text
6. Use the Proofing Options
7. Create a Document Using a Template

Mastering Word | Project **2G** Job Letter

In the following Mastering Word project, you will create a new document from an existing document, format a table, and then create a fax cover using a template. Your completed documents will look similar to Figure 2.48.

Project Files

For Project 2G, you will need the following files:

w02G_Letter_Text
w02G_Letterhead
w02G_Resume
Equity Fax template from Word's installed templates

You will save your documents as:

Lastname_Firstname_2G_Job_Letter
Lastname_Firstname_2G_Resume
Lastname_Firstname_2G_Fax

Project Results

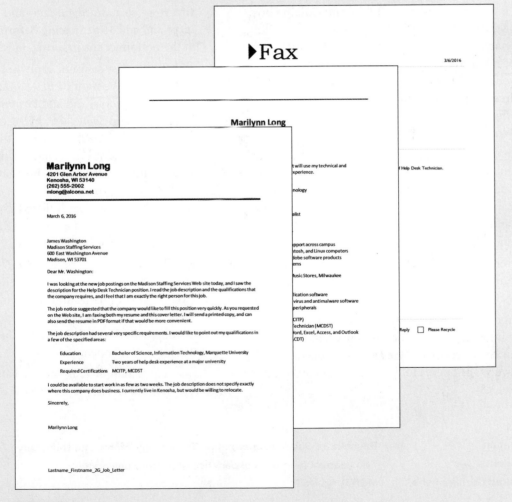

Figure 2.48

(Project 2G Job Letter continues on the next page)

Mastering Word | Project **2G** Job Letter (continued)

1 **Start** Word and display rulers and formatting marks. By using the **New from existing** template, create a document from the file **w02G_Letterhead**. **Save** the document in your **Word Chapter 2** folder as **Lastname_Firstname_2G_Job_Letter** Add the file name to the footer. Move to the end of the document, and then on the **Home tab**, apply the **No Spacing** style. Type **March 6, 2016** and then press Enter four times. Type the following:

> **James Washington**
> **Madison Staffing Services**
> **600 East Washington Avenue**
> **Madison, WI 53701**

2 Press Enter two times, type **Dear Mr. Washington:** and press Enter two times. **Insert** the text from the file **w02G_Letter_Text** and remove the blank line at the bottom of the selected text.

3 Move to the top of the document, and then by using either the **Spelling and Grammar** dialog box, or by right-clicking selected words, correct spelling, grammar, and word usage errors. In the paragraph that begins *I was looking,* in the third line, locate and right-click *corporation.* Use the shortcut menu to open the **Thesaurus** and change the word to the synonym *company.* In the same line, change *correct* to the synonym *right.*

4 In the paragraph that begins *I currently,* select the first sentence of the paragraph and drag it to the end of the same paragraph. In the second blank line below the paragraph that begins *The job description,* **Insert** a **2 × 3** table, and then type the text shown in **Table 1** below.

5 Select the entire table. **AutoFit Contents**, **Center** the table, remove the table borders, and then add **3 pt** spacing before and after by typing **3** in the **Spacing** boxes and pressing Enter.

6 In the **Document Panel**, add your name and course information and the **Keywords job letter** Preview the document. **Save** and **Close** the document but leave Word open. Hold the file until you complete this project.

7 From your student files, open **w02G_Resume**. **Save** the document in your **Word Chapter 2** folder as **Lastname_Firstname_2G_Resume** Add the file name to the footer.

8 **Insert** a new second row in the table. In the first cell of the new row, type **OBJECTIVE** and then press Tab. Type **To obtain a Help Desk Technician position that will use my technical and communication skills and computer support experience.** In the same cell, add **12 pt Spacing After.**

9 Select the entire table. On the **Layout tab**, **AutoFit Contents**. Remove the table borders, and then display the **Borders and Shading** dialog box. With the table selected, create a **Custom** single solid line **1 1/2 pt** top border.

10 In the first row of the table, select both cells and then **Merge Cells**. **Center** the five lines and apply **Bold**. In the first row, select *Marilynn Long* and change the **Font Size** to **20 pt** and add **36 pt Spacing Before**. In the e-mail address at the bottom of the first row, add **24 pt Spacing After.**

11 In the first column, apply **Bold** to the four headings. In the cell to the right of *EDUCATION,* **Bold** the names of the two schools, and add **12 pt Spacing After** the two lines that begin *September.* In the cell to the right of *RELEVANT EXPERIENCE,* bold the names of the two jobs—*IT Help Desk Specialist* and *Computer Technician.* In the same cell, below the line that begins *January 2014,* apply bullets to the four lines that comprise the job duties. Create a similar bulleted list for the duties as a Computer Technician. Add **12 pt Spacing After** to the last line of each of the bulleted lists.

12 In the cell to the right of *CERTIFICATIONS,* select all four lines and create a bulleted list. In the **Document Panel**, add your name and course information and the **Keywords help desk resume** and then submit your document as directed. **Save** and **Close** the document but leave Word open.

13 From **Sample templates**, create a document based on the **Origin Fax** template. **Save** the document in your **Word**

Table 1

Education	Bachelor of Science, Information Technology, Marquette University
Experience	Two years of help desk experience at a major university
Required Certifications	MCITP, MCDST

(Return to Step 5)

(Project 2G Job Letter continues on the next page)

Content-Based Assessments

Mastering Word | Project **2G** Job Letter (continued)

Chapter 2 folder as **Lastname_Firstname_2G_Fax** and then add the file name to the footer—called a *First Page Footer* in this template.

14 Type the text shown in **Table 2** for the content controls.

15 Locate and right-click *Marilynn Long*; remove the content control. In the **Document Panel**, add your name and course information and the **Keywords fax cover page** As directed by your instructor, print or submit electronically the three files from this project. **Exit** Word.

Table 2

Pick a date	**3/6/2016**
From:	**Marilynn Long**
Phone:	**(608) 555-0967**
Fax:	**(608) 555-0966**
Company Name:	Remove this content control and row heading
To:	**James Washington, Recruiter**
Phone:	**(608) 555-0034**
Fax:	**(608) 555-0035**
Company Name	**Madison Staffing Services**
Comments:	**Two pages to follow that include my resume and a cover letter for the position of Help Desk Technician.**

(Return to Step 15)

End **You have completed Project 2G** ———————————————

GO! Fix It | Project **2H** New Jobs

In this project, you will construct a solution by applying any combination of the skills you practiced from the Objectives in Projects 2A and 2B.

Project Files

For Project 2H, you will need the following file:

w02H_New_Jobs

You will save your document as:

Lastname_Firstname_2H_New_Jobs

From the student files that accompany this textbook, locate and open the file w02H_New_Jobs, and then save the file in your Word Chapter 2 folder as **Lastname_Firstname_2H_New_Jobs**

This document contains errors that you must find and correct. Read and examine the document, and then edit to correct the errors that you find and to improve the overall document format. Types of errors could include, but are not restricted to:

- Spelling errors
- Grammar errors
- Word choice errors
- Duplicate words
- Unattractive table column widths
- Title not merged across the top row of the table
- Inconsistent spacing before and after paragraphs in the table

Things you should know to complete this project:

- Viewing the document in Print Preview will help identify some of the problems
- The Spelling and Grammar checker will be useful
- Adjust the column widths *before* merging the title

Save your document and add the file name to the footer. In the Document Panel, type your firstname and lastname in the Author box and your course name and section number in the Subject box. In the Keywords box type **job listings** and then save your document and submit as directed.

 You have completed Project 2H _____

Content-Based Assessments

Apply a combination of the **2A** and **2B** skills.

GO! Make It | Project 2I Training

Project Files

For Project 2I, you will need the following file:

New blank Word document

You will save your document as:

Lastname_Firstname_2I_Training

Start Word, and then save the file in your Word Chapter 2 folder as **Lastname_Firstname_ 2I_Training**

Use the skills you practiced in this chapter to create the table shown in Figure 2.49. The first row font is Cambria 16 pt, the remainder is Cambria 14 pt. The spacing after the first row is 36 pt, the spacing at the bottom of the rows is 12 pt.

Add the file name to the footer; in the Document Panel, add your name and course information and the Keywords **online training** Save your document, and then submit as directed.

Project Results

Selected Training Programs Available Online

Software	Program Title
Microsoft Word	• Create your first Word document I • Getting started with Word 2010 • Use the Navigation Pane to search and move around in your document • Create your first Word document II
Microsoft Excel	• Get to know Excel 2010: Create your first workbook • Charts I: How to create a chart in Excel • Get to know Excel 2010: Enter formulas • Sort data in a range or table

Lastname_Firstname_2I_Training

Figure 2.49

End You have completed Project 2I

Content-Based Assessments

Apply a combination of the **2A** and **2B** skills.

GO! Solve It | Project **2J** Job Postings

Project Files

For Project 2J, you will need the following files:

> New blank Word document
> w02J_Job_Postings

You will save your documents as:

> Lastname_Firstname_2J_Letterhead
> Lastname_Firstname_2J_Job_Postings

Print the w02J_Job_Postings document, and use the information to complete this project. Create a new company letterhead and save it in your Word Chapter 2 folder as **Lastname_Firstname_2J_Letterhead** Add the file name to the footer. Add your name, your course name and section number, and the keyword **letterhead** to the Properties area.

Create a new document based on the existing document you just created. The new document will be a list of new jobs posted by Madison Staffing Services. The job posting should include the letterhead, introductory text, and a table that includes the information about the new jobs that are currently available. The job list should be in table format. Use either two or three columns, and label the columns appropriately. Format the table, the table borders, and the text in an attractive, readable manner.

Save the document as **Lastname_Firstname_2J_Job_Postings** Add the file name to the footer, and add your name, your course name and section number, and the keywords **new jobs** to the Properties area. Submit your two files as directed.

	Performance Level		
	Exemplary: You consistently applied the relevant skills	**Proficient:** You sometimes, but not always, applied the relevant skills	**Developing:** You rarely or never applied the relevant skills
Create and format a letterhead template	The text in the letterhead is appropriately formatted, the company name stands out, and the spacing between paragraphs is attractive.	The letterhead is complete, but the line spacing or text formatting is not appropriate for a letterhead.	The spacing and formatting is not appropriate for a letterhead.
Insert a table	The inserted table has the appropriate number of columns and rows to display the information.	The table is not structured to effectively display the information.	No table is inserted in the document.
Format the table structure	Table column widths fit the information, extra space is added between the rows, and borders are attractively formatted.	The column widths do not reflect the amount of information in the column, and the spacing between the cells is insufficient.	Table displays only default column widths and spacing.
Format the text in the table	Important text is highlighted and formatted appropriately, making the text easy to read and interpret.	Some text formatting is added, but the formatting does not highlight the important information.	No text formatting is included.

Performance Element (vertical label on left)

End **You have completed Project 2J**

Content-Based Assessments

Apply a combination of the **2A** and **2B** skills.

GO! Solve It | Project **2K** Agenda

Project Files

For Project 2K, you will need the following file:

Agenda template from Word's Online templates

You will save your document as:

Lastname_Firstname_2K_Agenda

Create a new document based on an agenda template—such as the *Formal meeting agenda* template—from the Agenda templates at Microsoft Office Online. Save the agenda as **Lastname_ Firstname_2K_Agenda** Use the following information to prepare an agenda for a Madison Staffing Services meeting.

The meeting will be chaired by Marilyn Kelly and will be the monthly meeting of the company administrators—Kevin Rau, Marilyn Kelly, Andre Randolph, Susan Nguyen, and Charles James. The meeting will be held on March 15, 2016, at 3:00 p.m. The old business (open issues) include 1) expanding services into the printing and food service industries; 2) recruitment at the UW-Madison and MATC campuses; and 3) the addition of a part-time trainer. The new business will include 1) recruitment at the University of Wisconsin, Milwaukee; 2) rental of office space in or around Milwaukee; 3) purchase of new computers for the training room; and 4) renewal of snow removal service contract.

Add the file name to the footer, and add your name, your course name and section number, and the keywords **agenda, monthly administrative meeting** to the Properties area. Submit as directed.

		Performance Level		
		Exemplary: You consistently applied the relevant skills	Proficient: You sometimes, but not always, applied the relevant skills	Developing: You rarely or never applied the relevant skills
Performance Element	Select an agenda template	Agenda template is appropriate for the information provided for the meeting.	Agenda template is used, but does not fit the information provided.	No template is used for the agenda.
	Add appropriate information to the template	All information is inserted in the appropriate places. All unused controls are removed.	All information is included, but not in the appropriate places, and not all of the unused controls are removed.	Information is missing and unused placeholders are not removed.
	Format template information	All text in the template is properly aligned and formatted.	All text is included, but alignment or formatting is inconsistent.	No additional formatting has been added.

End You have completed Project 2K

Outcomes-Based Assessments

Rubric

The following outcomes-based assessments are *open-ended assessments*. That is, there is no specific correct result; your result will depend on your approach to the information provided. Make *Professional Quality* your goal. Use the following scoring rubric to guide you in *how* to approach the problem and then to evaluate *how well* your approach solves the problem.

The *criteria*—Software Mastery, Content, Format and Layout, and Process—represent the knowledge and skills you have gained that you can apply to solving the problem. The *levels of performance*—Professional Quality, Approaching Professional Quality, or Needs Quality Improvements—help you and your instructor evaluate your result.

	Your completed project is of Professional Quality if you:	Your completed project is Approaching Professional Quality if you:	Your completed project Needs Quality Improvements if you:
1-Software Mastery	Choose and apply the most appropriate skills, tools, and features and identify efficient methods to solve the problem.	Choose and apply some appropriate skills, tools, and features, but not in the most efficient manner.	Choose inappropriate skills, tools, or features, or are inefficient in solving the problem.
2-Content	Construct a solution that is clear and well organized, contains content that is accurate, appropriate to the audience and purpose, and is complete. Provide a solution that contains no errors in spelling, grammar, or style.	Construct a solution in which some components are unclear, poorly organized, inconsistent, or incomplete. Misjudge the needs of the audience. Have some errors in spelling, grammar, or style, but the errors do not detract from comprehension.	Construct a solution that is unclear, incomplete, or poorly organized; contains some inaccurate or inappropriate content; and contains many errors in spelling, grammar, or style. Do not solve the problem.
3-Format and Layout	Format and arrange all elements to communicate information and ideas, clarify function, illustrate relationships, and indicate relative importance.	Apply appropriate format and layout features to some elements, but not others. Overuse features, causing minor distraction.	Apply format and layout that does not communicate information or ideas clearly. Do not use format and layout features to clarify function, illustrate relationships, or indicate relative importance. Use available features excessively, causing distraction.
4-Process	Use an organized approach that integrates planning, development, self-assessment, revision, and reflection.	Demonstrate an organized approach in some areas, but not others; or, use an insufficient process of organization throughout.	Do not use an organized approach to solve the problem.

Outcomes-Based Assessments

Apply a combination of the **2A** and **2B** skills.

GO! Think | Project **2L** Workshops

Project Files

For Project 2L, you will need the following files:

New blank Word document
w02L_Workshop_Information

You will save your document as:

Lastname_Firstname_2L_Workshops

Madison Staffing Services offers a series of workshops for its employee-clients. Any temporary employee who is available during the workshop hours can attend the workshops and there is no fee. Currently, the company offers three-session workshops covering Excel and Word, a two-session workshop covering Business Communication, and a one-session workshop covering *Creating a Resume*.

Print the w02L_Workshop_Information file and use the information to complete this project. Create an announcement with a title, an introductory paragraph, and a table listing the workshops and the topics covered in each workshop. Use the file w02L_Workshop_Information for help with the topics covered in each workshop. Format the table cells appropriately. Add an appropriate footer and information to the Document Panel. Save the document as **Lastname_Firstname_2L_Workshops** and submit it as directed.

End **You have completed Project 2L** ——————————————

Apply a combination of the **2A** and **2B** skills.

GO! Think | Project **2M** Planner

Project Files

For Project 2M, you will need the following files:

Weekly appointment sheet template from Word's Online templates
w02M_Workshop_Information

You will save your document as:

Lastname_Firstname_2M_Planner

To keep track of workshops provided to employees, the trainer fills out a weekly schedule. Each workshop lasts two hours. Print the w02M_Workshop_Information file and use part or all of the information to complete this project.

Create a new document using a template, for example the *Weekly appointment sheet* template found in the Planners category in the online template list. Create a template for a week, and include the first part of each workshop series, along with the Creating a Resume workshop. Customize the template as necessary to include *Room* and *Workshop* titles for each day of the week. The computer skills workshops are held in the Lab, the others are held in Room 104. The trainer always schedules the hour before each workshop for preparation. Fill out the workshop schedule and use your choice of formatting to indicate that the workshops cover a two-hour period. Add appropriate information to the Document Panel. Save the document as **Lastname_Firstname_2M_Planner** and submit it as directed.

End **You have completed Project 2M** ——————————————

Outcomes-Based Assessments

You and GO! | Project **2N** Personal Resume

Project Files

For Project 2N, you will need the following file:

New blank Word document

You will save your documents as

Lastname_Firstname_2N_Personal_Resume
Lastname_Firstname_2N_Cover_Letter

Locate and print the information for a job for which you would like to apply, and then create your own personal resume using a table and a cover letter. Include any information that is appropriate, including your objective for a specific job, your experience, skills, education, honors, or awards. Create your own letterhead and cover letter, using the cover letter you created in Project 2B as a guide.

To complete the assignment, be sure to format the text appropriately, resize the table columns in the resume to best display the information, and check both documents for spelling and grammar errors.

Save the resume as **Lastname_Firstname_2N_Personal_Resume** and the cover letter as **Lastname_Firstname_2N_Personal_Cover_Letter** Add the file name to the footer, and add your name, your course name and section number, and the keywords **my resume** and **cover letter** to the Properties area. Submit your file as directed.

End **You have completed Project 2N** ——————————————

Creating Research Papers, Newsletters, and Merged Mailing Labels

OUTCOMES

At the end of this chapter you will be able to:

OBJECTIVES

Mastering these objectives will enable you to:

PROJECT 3A

Create a research paper that includes citations and a bibliography.

1. Create a Research Paper (p. 165)
2. Insert Footnotes in a Research Paper (p. 167)
3. Create Citations and a Bibliography in a Research Paper (p. 172)

PROJECT 3B

Create a multiple-column newsletter and merged mailing labels.

4. Format a Multiple-Column Newsletter (p. 181)
5. Use Special Character and Paragraph Formatting (p. 186)
6. Create Mailing Labels Using Mail Merge (p. 189)

prism68/Shutterstock

In This Chapter

Microsoft Word provides many tools for creating complex documents. For example, Word has tools that enable you to create a research paper that includes citations, footnotes, and a bibliography. You can also create multiple-column newsletters, format the nameplate at the top of the newsletter, use special character formatting to create distinctive title text, and add borders and shading to paragraphs to highlight important information.

In this chapter, you will edit and format a research paper, create a two-column newsletter, and then create a set of mailing labels to mail the newsletter to multiple recipients.

The projects in this chapter relate to **Memphis Primary Materials** located in the Memphis area. In addition to collecting common recyclable materials, the company collects and recycles computers, monitors, copiers and fax machines, cell phones, wood pallets, and compostable materials. The company's name comes from the process of capturing the "primary materials" of used items for reuse. Memphis Primary Materials ensures that its clients comply with all state and local regulations. They also provide training to clients on the process and benefits of recycling.

Project 3A Research Paper

myitlab
Project 3A Training

Project Activities

In Activities 3.01 through 3.07, you will edit and format a research paper that contains an overview of recycling activities in which businesses can engage. This paper was created by Elizabeth Freeman, a student intern working for Memphis Primary Metals, and will be included in a customer information packet. Your completed document will look similar to Figure 3.1.

Project Files

For Project 3A, you will need the following file:

w03A_Green_Business

You will save your document as:

Lastname_Firstname_3A_Green_Business

Project Results

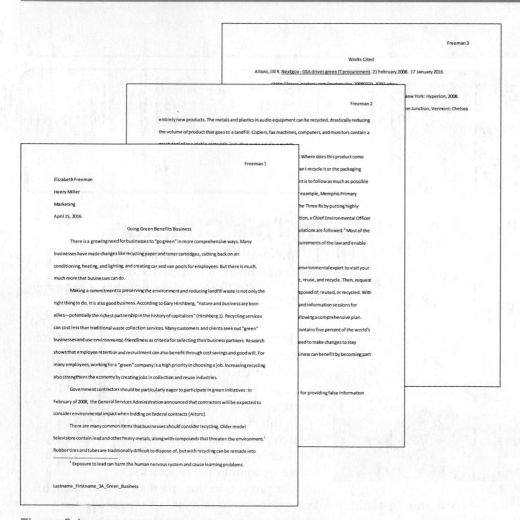

Figure 3.1
Project 3A Green Business

Objective 1 | Create a Research Paper

When you write a research paper or a report for college or business, follow a format prescribed by one of the standard *style guides*—a manual that contains standards for the design and writing of documents. The two most commonly used styles for research papers are those created by the *Modern Language Association (MLA)* and the *American Psychological Association (APA)*; there are several others.

Activity 3.01 | Formatting Text and Page Numbers in a Research Paper

When formatting the text for your research paper, refer to the standards for the style guide that you have chosen. In this activity, you will create a research paper using the MLA style. The MLA style uses 1-inch margins, a 0.5″ first line indent, and double spacing throughout the body of the document, with no extra space above or below paragraphs.

1 **Start** Word. From your student files, locate and open the document **w03A_Green_Business**. If necessary, display the formatting marks and rulers. In the location where you are storing your projects for this chapter, create a new folder named **Word Chapter 3** and then save the file in the folder as **Lastname_Firstname_3A_Green_Business**

2 Press Ctrl + A to select the entire document. On the **Home tab**, in the **Paragraph group**, click the **Line and Paragraph Spacing** button, and then change the line spacing to **2.0**. On the **Page Layout tab**, in the **Paragraph group**, change the **Spacing After** to **0 pt**.

3 Press Ctrl + Home to deselect and move to the top of the document. Press Enter one time to create a blank line at the top of the document, and then click to position the insertion point in the blank line. Type **Elizabeth Freeman** and press Enter.

4 Type **Henry Miller** and press Enter. Type **Marketing** and press Enter. Type **April 15, 2016** and press Enter. Type **Going Green Benefits Business** Right-click anywhere in the line you just typed, and then on the Mini toolbar, click the **Center** button. Compare your screen with Figure 3.2.

Figure 3.2

Title centered

Text double-spaced

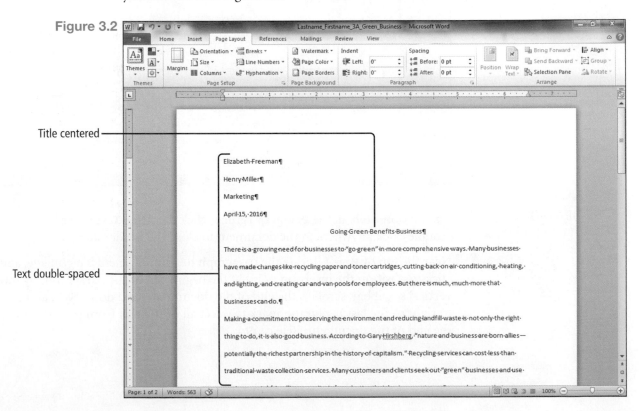

5 At the top of the **Page 1**, point anywhere in the white top margin area, right-click, and then click **Edit Header**. In the header area, type **Freeman** and then press Spacebar.

> Recall that the text you insert into a header or footer displays on every page of a document. Within a header or footer, you can insert many different types of information; for example, automatic page numbers, the date, the time, the file name, or pictures.

6 On the **Design tab**, in the **Header & Footer group**, click the **Page Number** button, and then point to **Current Position**. In the displayed gallery, under **Simple**, click **Plain Number**. Compare your screen with Figure 3.3.

> Word will automatically number the pages using this number format.

Figure 3.3

Page number field added to header

Last name in header

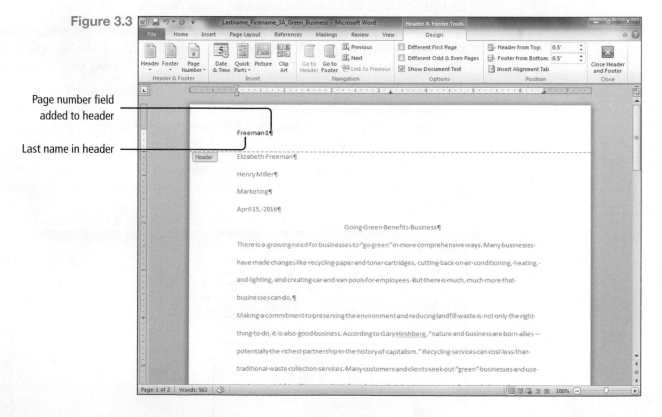

7 On the **Home tab**, in the **Paragraph group**, click the **Align Text Right** button. Double-click anywhere in the document to close the header area.

8 Near the top of **Page 1**, locate the paragraph beginning *There is a growing*, and then click to position the insertion point at the beginning of the paragraph. By moving the vertical scroll bar, scroll to the end of the document, hold down Shift, and then click to right of the last paragraph mark to select all of the text from the insertion point to the end of the document. Release Shift.

Another Way

Right-click the selected text, click Paragraph, on the Indents and Spacing tab, under Indentation, click the Special arrow, and then click First line. Under Indentation, in the By box, be sure 0.5" displays.

9 With the text selected, on the ruler, point to the **First Line Indent** button , and then drag the button to **0.5" on the horizontal ruler**. Compare your screen with Figure 3.4.

The MLA style uses 0.5-inch indents at the beginning of the first line of every paragraph. Indenting—moving the beginning of the first line of a paragraph to the right or left of the rest of the paragraph—provides visual cues to the reader to help divide the document text and make it easier to read.

Figure 3.4

First Line Indent button moved to 0.5" on the ruler

First line indented 0.5 inch

10 Click anywhere to deselect the text. Scroll to view the bottom of **Page 1**, point anywhere in the bottom white margin area, right-click, and then click **Edit Footer**. On the **Design tab**, in the **Insert group**, click the **Quick Parts** button, and then click **Field**. In the **Field** dialog box, under **Field names**, locate and click **FileName**, and then click **OK**.

The file name in the footer is *not* part of the research report format, but it is included in projects in this textbook so that you and your instructor can identify your work.

11 Double-click anywhere in the document to close the Footer area, and then **Save** your document.

More Knowledge | Suppressing the Page Number on the First Page

Some style guidelines require that the page number and other header and footer information on the first page be hidden from view—*suppressed*. To hide the information contained in the header and footer areas on Page 1 of a document, double-click in the header or footer area. Then, on the Design tab, in the Options group, select the Different First Page check box.

Objective 2 | Insert Footnotes in a Research Paper

Reports and research papers typically include information that you find in other sources, and these must be credited. Within report text, numbers mark the location of ***notes***—information that expands on the topic being discussed but that does not fit well in the document text. The numbers refer to ***footnotes***—notes placed at the bottom of the page containing the note, or to ***endnotes***—notes placed at the end of a document or chapter.

Activity 3.02 | Inserting Footnotes

Footnotes can be added as you type the document or after the document is complete. Word renumbers the footnotes automatically, so footnotes do not need to be entered in order, and if one footnote is removed, the remaining footnotes renumber automatically.

1 Scroll to view the top of **Page 2**. Locate the paragraph that begins *Consumers and businesses*. In the seventh line of text, toward the end of the line, click to position the insertion point to the right of the period after *followed*.

2 On the **References tab**, in the **Footnotes group**, click the **Insert Footnote** button.

Word creates space for a footnote in the footnote area at the bottom of the page and adds a footnote number to the text at the insertion point location. Footnote *1* displays in the footnote area, and the insertion point moves to the right of the number. A short black line is added just above the footnote area. You do not need to type the footnote number.

3 Type **Tennessee, for example, imposes penalties of up to $10,000 for providing false information regarding the recycling of hazardous waste.**

This is an explanatory footnote; the footnote provides additional information that does not fit well in the body of the report.

4 Click the **Home tab**, and then in the **Font group**, notice that the font size of the footer is *10 pt*. In the **Paragraph group**, click the **Line and Paragraph Spacing** button, and notice that the line spacing is *1.0*—single-spaced—even though the font size of the document text is 11 pt and the text is double-spaced, as shown in Figure 3.5.

Figure 3.5

Footnote text, single-spaced and 10 pt. font size

5 Scroll to view the bottom of **Page 1**, and then locate the paragraph that begins *There are many common*. At the end of the second line of text, click to position the insertion point to the right of the period following *environment*.

6 On the **References tab**, in the **Footnotes group**, click the **Insert Footnote** button. Type **Exposure to lead can harm the human nervous system and cause learning problems.** Notice that the footnote you just added becomes the new footnote *1*, as shown in Figure 3.6.

The first footnote is renumbered as footnote *2*.

Figure 3.6

Footnote number in text ─────────────

New footnote ─────────────

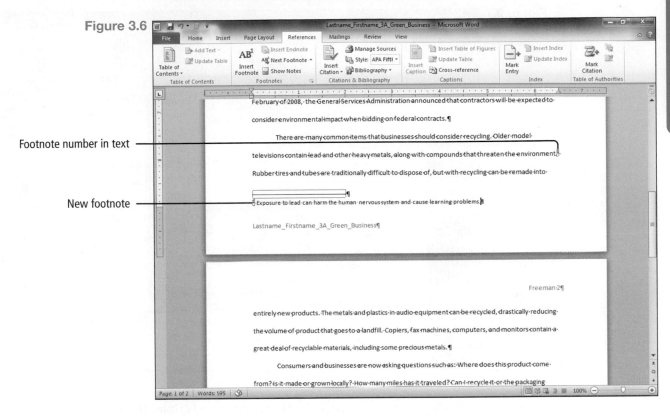

7 **Save** your document.

More Knowledge | Using Symbols Rather Than Numbers for Notes

Instead of using numbers to designate footnotes, you can use standard footnote symbols. The seven traditional symbols, available from the Footnote and Endnote dialog box, in order, are * (asterisk), † (dagger), ‡ (double dagger), § (section mark), || (parallels), ¶ (paragraph mark), and # (number or pound sign). This sequence can be continuous (this is the default setting), or can begin anew with each page.

Activity 3.03 | Modifying a Footnote Style

Microsoft Word contains built-in paragraph formats called *styles*—groups of formatting commands, such as font, font size, font color, paragraph alignment, and line spacing—which can be applied to a paragraph with one command.

The default style for footnote text is a single-spaced paragraph that uses a 10-point Calibri font and no paragraph indents. MLA style specifies double-spaced text in all areas of a research paper—including footnotes. According to the MLA style, first lines of footnotes must also be indented 0.5 inch and use the same font size as the report text.

1 Scroll to view the bottom of **Page 2**. Point anywhere in the footnote text and right-click, and then from the shortcut menu, click **Style**. Compare your screen with Figure 3.7.

The Style dialog box displays, listing the styles currently in use in the document, in addition to some of the word processing elements that come with special built-in styles. Because you right-clicked on the footnote text, the selected style is the Footnote Text style.

Figure 3.7

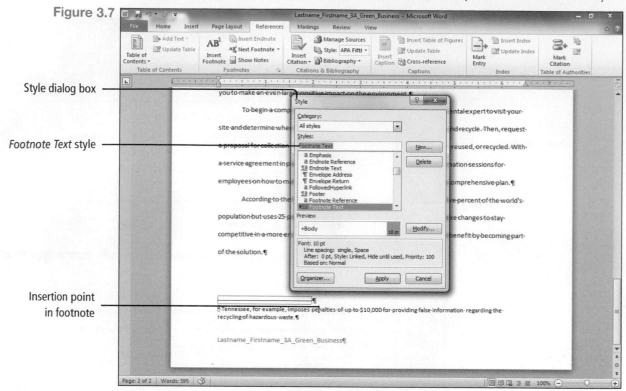

2 In the **Style** dialog box, click the **Modify** button to display the **Modify Style** dialog box.

3 In the **Modify Style** dialog box, locate the small **Formatting** toolbar in the center of the dialog box, click the **Font Size button arrow**, click **11**, and then compare your screen with Figure 3.8.

Figure 3.8

4 In the lower left corner of the dialog box, click the **Format** button, and then click **Paragraph**. In the **Paragraph** dialog box, under **Indentation**, click the **Special arrow**, and then click **First line**.

5 Under **Spacing**, click the **Line spacing** button arrow, and then click **Double**. Compare your dialog box with Figure 3.9.

Figure 3.9

First line indent selected

Line spacing set to *Double*

6 Click **OK** to close the **Paragraph** dialog box, click **OK** to close the **Modify Style** dialog box, and then click **Apply** to apply the new style. Notice that when you click Apply, the Style dialog box closes. Compare your screen with Figure 3.10.

Your inserted footnotes are formatted with the new Footnote Text paragraph style; any new footnotes that you insert will also use this format.

Figure 3.10

First line indented

Footnote text double-spaced

7 Scroll to view the bottom of **Page 1** to confirm that the new format was also applied to the first footnote, and then **Save** ⊞ your document.

Objective 3 | Create Citations and a Bibliography in a Research Paper

When you use quotations from, or detailed summaries of, other people's work, you must specify the source of the information. A *citation* is a note inserted into the text of a report or research paper that refers the reader to a source in the bibliography. Create a *bibliography* at the end of a document to list the sources referred to in the document. Such a list is typically titled *Works Cited* (in MLA style), *Bibliography*, *Sources*, or *References*.

Activity 3.04 | Adding Citations

When writing a long research paper, you will likely reference numerous books, articles, and Web sites. Some of your research sources may be referenced many times, others only one time. References to sources within the text of your research paper are indicated in an *abbreviated* manner. However, as you enter a citation for the first time, you can also enter the *complete* information about the source. Then, when you have finished your paper, you will be able to automatically generate the list of sources that must be included at the end of your research paper.

1 Press Ctrl + Home, and then locate the paragraph that begins *Making a commitment*. In the third line, following the word *capitalism*, click to position the insertion point to the right of the quotation mark.

> The citation in the document points to the full source information in the bibliography, which typically includes the name of the author, the full title of the work, the year of publication, and other publication information.

2 On the **References tab**, in the **Citations & Bibliography group**, click the **Style button arrow**, and then click **MLA Sixth Edition** (or the latest edition) to insert a reference using MLA style.

3 Click the **Insert Citation** button, and then click **Add New Source**. Be sure *Book* is selected as the **Type of Source**. Add the following information, and then compare your screen with Figure 3.11:

Author:	**Hirshberg, Gary**
Title:	**Stirring it Up: How to Make Money and Save the World**
Year:	**2008**
City:	**New York**
Publisher:	**Hyperion**

> In the MLA style, citations that refer to items on the *Works Cited* page are placed in parentheses and are referred to as **parenthetical references**—references that include the last name of the author or authors and the page number in the referenced source, which you add to the reference. No year is indicated, and there is no comma between the name and the page number.

Figure 3.11

MLA style selected

Source type

Citation information

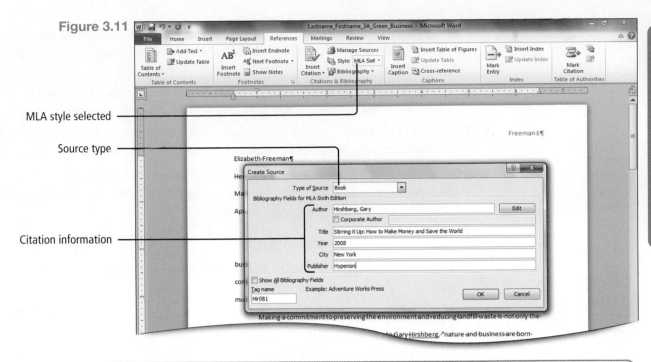

Note | Citing Corporate Authors

If the author of a document is identified as the name of an organization only, select the Corporate Author check box and type the name of the organization in the Corporate Author box.

4 Click **OK** to insert the citation. In the paragraph, point to *(Hirshberg)* and click one time to select the citation.

5 In the lower right corner of the box that surrounds the reference, point to the small arrow to display the ScreenTip *Citation Options*. Click this **Citation Options arrow**, and then from the list of options, click **Edit Citation**.

6 In the **Edit Citation** dialog box, under **Add**, in the **Pages** box, type **1** to indicate that you are citing from page 1 of this source. Compare your screen with Figure 3.12.

Figure 3.12

Page number

Parenthetical reference

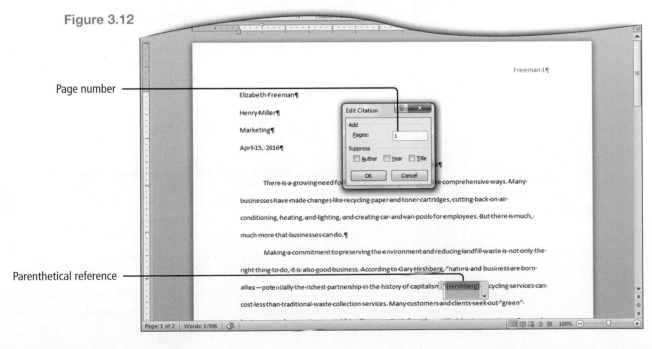

7 Click **OK** to display the page number of the citation. Click outside of the citation box to deselect it. Then type a period to the right of the citation, and delete the period to the left of the quotation mark.

> In the MLA style, if the reference occurs at the end of a sentence, the parenthetical reference always displays to the left of the punctuation mark that ends the sentence.

8 In the next paragraph, which begins *Government contractors*, click to position the insertion point at the end of the paragraph, but before the period.

9 In the **Citations & Bibliography group**, click the **Insert Citation** button, and then click **Add New Source**. Click the **Type of Source arrow**, scroll down as necessary, and then click **Web site**. Add the following information:

Author:	**Aitoro, Jill R.**
Name of Web Page:	**Nextgov - GSA drives green IT procurement**
Year:	**2008**
Month:	**February**
Day:	**21**
Year Accessed:	**2016**
Month Accessed:	**January**
Day Accessed:	**17**
URL:	**http://www.nextgov.com/nextgov/ng_20080221_8792.php**

10 Compare your screen with Figure 3.13, and then click **OK** to close the **Create Source** dialog box and add the citation.

> A parenthetical reference is added. Because the cited Web page has no page numbers, only the author name is used in the parenthetical reference.

Figure 3.13

Web site citation ———

Insertion point indicates location of parenthetical reference ———

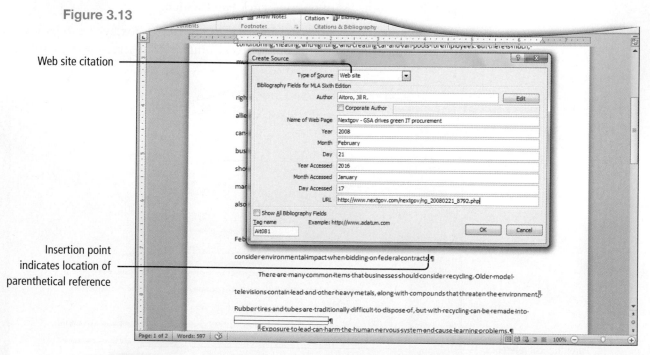

11 Near the top of **Page 2**, in the paragraph that begins *Consumers and businesses*, in the third line, click to position the insertion point following the word *toxic* to the left of the question mark.

12 In the **Citations & Bibliography group**, click the **Insert Citation** button, and then click **Add New Source**. Click the **Type of Source arrow**, if necessary scroll to the top of the list, click **Book**, and then add the following information:

Author:	**Scott, Nicky**
Title:	**Reduce, Reuse, Recycle: An Easy Household Guide**
Year:	**2007**
City:	**White River Junction, Vermont**
Publisher:	**Chelsea Green Publishing**

13 Click **OK**. Click the inserted citation to select it, click the **Citation Options arrow**, and then click **Edit Citation**.

14 In the **Edit Citation** dialog box, under **Add**, in the **Pages** box, type **7** to indicate that you are citing from page 7 of this source. Click **OK**.

15 On the **References tab**, in the **Citations & Bibliography group**, click the **Manage Sources** button. In the **Source Manager** dialog box, under **Current List**, click the third source and then compare your screen with Figure 3.14.

> The Source Manager dialog box displays. Other citations on your computer display in the Master List box. The citations for the current document display in the Current List box. Word maintains the Master List so that if you use the same sources regularly, you can copy sources from your Master List to the current document. A preview of the selected bibliography entry also displays at the bottom of the dialog box.

Figure 3.14

Sources used in this document

Other available sources (yours will vary)

Preview of selected citation

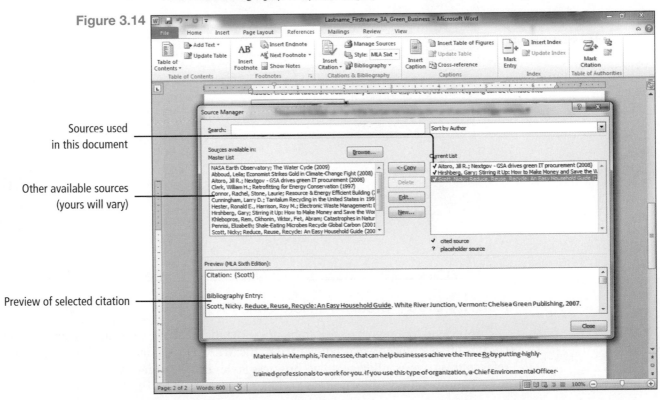

16 At the bottom of the **Source Manager** dialog box, click **Close**. Click anywhere in the document to deselect the parenthetical reference, and then **Save** your document.

Activity 3.05 | Inserting Page Breaks

In this activity you will insert a manual page break so that you can begin your bibliography on a new page.

1 Press `Ctrl` + `End` to move the insertion point to the end of the document. Notice that the insertion point displays at the end of the final paragraph, but above the footnote—the footnote is always associated with the page that contains the citation.

2 Press `Ctrl` + `Enter` to insert a manual page break.

A *manual page break* forces a page to end at the insertion point location, and then places any subsequent text at the top of the next page. Recall that the new paragraph retains the formatting of the previous paragraph, so the first line is indented.

3 On the ruler, point to the **First Line Indent** button ⬇, and then drag the **First Line Indent** button to the left to **0 inches on the horizontal ruler**.

4 Scroll as necessary to position the bottom of **Page 2** and the top of **Page 3** on your screen.

5 Compare your screen with Figure 3.15, and then **Save** 💾 your document.

A *page break indicator*, which shows where a manual page break was inserted, displays at the bottom of the Page 2, and the footnote remains on the page that contains the citation, even though it displays below the page break indicator.

Figure 3.15

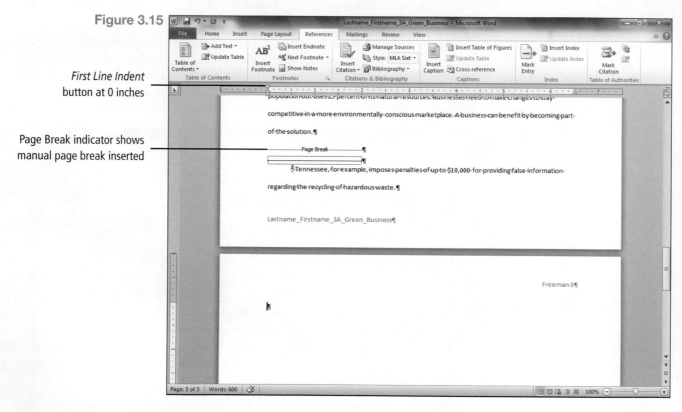

First Line Indent button at 0 inches

Page Break indicator shows manual page break inserted

Activity 3.06 | Creating a Reference Page

At the end of a report or research paper, include a list of each source referenced. *Works Cited* is the reference page heading used in the MLA style guidelines. Other styles may refer to this page as a *Bibliography* (Business Style) or *References* (APA Style). This information is always displayed on a separate page.

1 With the insertion point blinking in the first line of **Page 3**, type **Works Cited** and then press `Enter`. On the **References tab**, in the **Citations & Bibliography group**, in the **Style** box, be sure *MLA* displays.

2 In the **Citations & Bibliography group**, click the **Bibliography** button, and then near the bottom of the list, click **Insert Bibliography**.

3 Scroll as necessary to view the entire list of three references, and then click anywhere in the inserted text.

> The bibliography entries that you created display as a field, which is indicated by the gray shading when you click in the text. The field links to the Source Manager for the citations. The references display alphabetically by the author's last name.

4 In the bibliography, point to the left of the first entry—beginning *Aitoro, Jill*—to display the pointer. Drag down to select all three references.

5 On the **Home tab**, in the **Paragraph group**, change the **Line spacing** to **2.0**, and then on the **Page Layout tab**, in the **Paragraph group**, change the **Spacing After** to **0 pt**.

> The entries display according to MLA guidelines; the text is double-spaced, the extra space between paragraphs is removed, and each entry uses a *hanging indent*—the first line of each entry extends 0.5 inch to the left of the remaining lines of the entry.

6 At the top of **Page 3**, right-click the *Works Cited* title, and then click the **Center** button. Compare your screen with Figure 3.16, and then **Save** your document.

> In MLA style, the *Works Cited* title is centered.

Figure 3.16

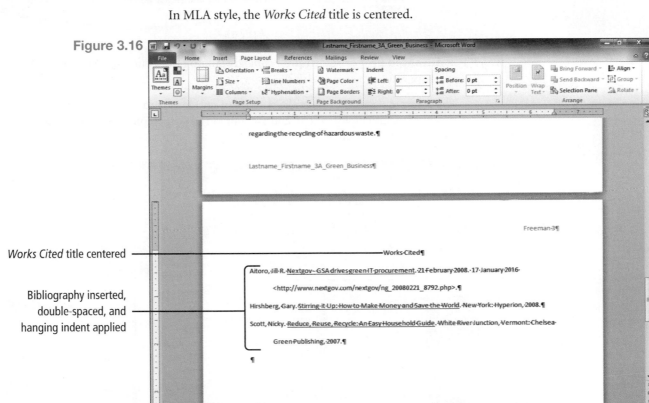

Works Cited title centered

Bibliography inserted, double-spaced, and hanging indent applied

Activity 3.07 | Managing Document Properties

Recall that document property information is stored in the Document Panel. An additional group of property categories is also available.

1 Display **Backstage** view. On the right, under the document thumbnail, click **Properties**, and then click **Show Document Panel** to display the **Document Panel**.

2 Type your name and course information, and then add the keywords **green business, research paper**

3 In the upper left corner of the **Document Panel**, click the **Document Properties** button, and then compare your screen with Figure 3.17.

Figure 3.17

Document Panel

Document Properties button

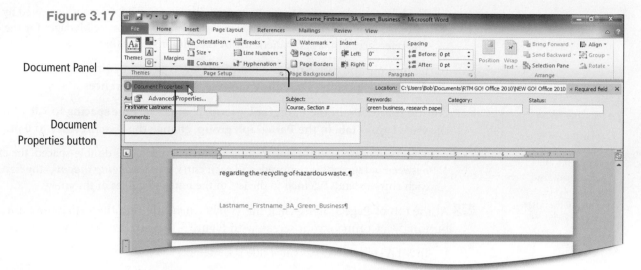

4 Click **Advanced Properties**. In the **Properties** dialog box, click the **Statistics tab**, and then compare your screen with Figure 3.18.

The document statistics show the number of revisions made to the document, the last time the document was edited, and the number of paragraphs, lines, words, and characters in the document.

Figure 3.18

Statistics tab

Document statistics (yours may vary)

5 In the **Properties** dialog box, click the **Summary tab**. Notice that not all of the categories are filled in, and also notice that there are categories on this tab that are not found in the Document Panel.

Some of the boxes may contain information from your computer system.

6 In the **Properties** dialog box, click in the **Title** box and type **Going Green Benefits Business**

7 Click in the **Manager** box and type **Henry Miller**

8 In the **Company** box, select and delete any existing text, and then type **Memphis Primary Materials**

9 Click in the **Category** box and type **Marketing Documents**

10 Click in the **Comments** box and type **Draft copy of a research report that will be included in the marketing materials packet**

Additional information categories are available by clicking the Custom tab.

11 Compare your screen with Figure 3.19, and then at the bottom of the **Properties** dialog box, click **OK**.

Figure 3.19

Summary tab

Properties not available on Document Information Panel

12 **Close** ☒ the **Document Panel**. Press Ctrl + F2 , and then examine the three pages of your document in **Print Preview**. Redisplay your document. If necessary, make any corrections or adjustments.

13 **Save** 🖫 your document, and then print or submit electronically as directed by your instructor. **Exit** Word.

End **You have completed Project 3A**

Project 3B Newsletter with Mailing Labels

myitlab
Project 3B Training

Project Activities

In Activities 3.08 through 3.17, you will edit a newsletter that Memphis Primary Materials sends to its list of customers and subscribers. Your completed documents will look similar to Figure 3.20.

Project Files

For Project 3B, you will need the following files:

New blank Word document
w03B_Memphis_Newsletter
w03B_Addresses

You will save your documents as:

Lastname_Firstname_3B_Memphis_Newsletter
Lastname_Firstname_3B_Mailing_Labels
Lastname_Firstname_3B_Addresses

Project Results

Figure 3.20
Project 3B Memphis Newsletter

Objective 4 | Format a Multiple-Column Newsletter

All newspapers and most magazines and newsletters use multiple columns for articles because text in narrower columns is easier to read than text that stretches across a page. Word has a tool with which you can change a single column of text into two or more columns, and then format the columns. If a column does not end where you want it to, you can end the column at a location of your choice by inserting a *manual column break*.

Activity 3.08 | Changing One Column of Text to Two Columns

Newsletters are usually two or three columns wide. When using 8.5 × 11-inch paper in portrait orientation, avoid creating four or more columns because they are so narrow that word spacing looks awkward, often resulting in one long word on a line by itself.

1 **Start** Word. From your student files, locate and open the document **w03B_Memphis_Newsletter**. If necessary, display the formatting marks and rulers. **Save** the file in your **Word Chapter 3** folder as **Lastname_Firstname_3B_Memphis_Newsletter** and then add the file name to the footer.

2 Select the first paragraph of text—*Memphis Primary Materials*. From the Mini toolbar, change the **Font** to **Arial Black** and the **Font Size** to **24**.

3 Select the first two paragraphs—the title and the Volume information and date. From the Mini toolbar, click the **Font Color button arrow** ▲▾, and then under **Theme Colors**, in the fifth column, click the last color—**Blue, Accent 1, Darker 50%**.

4 With the text still selected, on the **Home tab**, in the **Paragraph group**, click the **Borders button arrow**, and then at the bottom, click **Borders and Shading**.

5 In the **Borders and Shading** dialog box, on the **Borders tab**, click the **Color arrow**, and then under **Theme Colors**, in the fifth column, click the last color—**Blue, Accent 1, Darker 50%**.

> **Another Way**
>
> In the Preview area, click the Bottom Border button.

6 Click the **Width arrow**, and then click **3 pt**. In the **Preview** box at the right, point to the *bottom* border of the small preview and click one time. Compare your screen with Figure 3.21.

Figure 3.21

Preview of border

Color set to *Blue, Accent 1, Darker 50%*

Line width set to 3 pt

7 In the **Borders and Shading** dialog box, click **OK**.

The line visually defines the newsletter *nameplate*—the banner on the front page of a newsletter that identifies the publication.

8 Below the nameplate, beginning with the paragraph *Memphis Primary Materials: An Introduction*, select all of the text to the end of the document, which extends to two pages.

9 On the **Page Layout tab**, in the **Page Setup group**, click the **Columns** button. From the **Columns** gallery, click **Two**.

10 Scroll up to view the top of **Page 1**, and then compare your screen with Figure 3.22, and then **Save** 🖫 the document.

Word divides the text into two columns, and inserts a *section break* below the nameplate, dividing the one-column section of the document from the two-column section of the document. A *section* is a portion of a document that can be formatted differently from the rest of the document. A section break marks the end of one section and the beginning of another section. Do not be concerned if your columns do not break at the same line as shown in the figure.

Figure 3.22

Section break inserted

Text displays in two columns

Activity 3.09 | Formatting Multiple Columns

The uneven right margin of a single page-width column is easy to read. When you create narrow columns, justified text is sometimes preferable. Depending on the design and layout of your newsletter, you might decide to reduce extra space between paragraphs and between columns to improve the readability of the document.

1 With the two columns of text still selected, on the **Page Layout tab**, in the **Paragraph group**, click the **Spacing After down spin arrow** one time to change the spacing after to **6 pt**.

2 On the **Home tab**, in the **Paragraph group**, click the **Justify** button 📄.

3 Click anywhere in the document to deselect the text, and then compare your screen with Figure 3.23. **Save** 🖫 the document.

Figure 3.23

Column text justified ———

More Knowledge | Justifying Column Text

Although many magazines and newspapers still justify text in columns, there are a variety of opinions about whether to justify the columns, or to use left alignment and leave the right edge uneven. Justified text tends to look more formal and cleaner, but in a word processing document, it also results in uneven spacing between words. It is the opinion of some authorities that justified text is more difficult to read, especially in a page-width document. Let the overall look and feel of your newsletter be your guide.

Activity 3.10 | Inserting a Column Break

1 Scroll down to view the lower portion of the page. In the first column, locate the company address that begins with the paragraph *Memphis Primary Materials*, and then select that paragraph and the three following paragraphs, ending with the telephone number.

2 On the **Page Layout tab**, in the **Paragraph group**, click the **Spacing After down spin arrow** one time to change the spacing after to **0 pt**.

3 Select the three paragraphs that begin with *CEO* and end with *CFO*, and then in the **Paragraph group**, change the **Spacing After** to **0 pt**.

4 Near the bottom of the first column, click to position the insertion point at the beginning of the line that begins *Make Recycling*.

5 On the **Page Layout tab**, in the **Page Setup group**, click the **Breaks** button to display the gallery of Page Breaks and Section Breaks. Compare your screen with Figure 3.24.

Figure 3.24

Column break command

6 Under **Page Breaks**, click **Column**. Scroll to view the bottom of the first column.

A column break displays at the insertion point; text to the right of the insertion point moves to the top of the next column.

7 Compare your screen with Figure 3.25, and then **Save** the document.

A *column break indicator*—a dotted line containing the words *Column Break*—displays at the bottom of the column.

Figure 3.25

Manual column break inserted

Activity 3.11 | Inserting a Clip Art Image

Clip art images—predefined graphics included with Microsoft Office or downloaded from the Web—can make your document visually appealing and more interesting.

1 Press Ctrl + Home. On the **Insert tab**, in the **Illustrations group**, click the **Clip Art** button to display the **Clip Art** task pane on the right of your screen.

2 In the **Clip Art** task pane, click in the **Search for** box, and then replace any existing text with **environmental awareness** so that Word can search for images that contain the keywords *environmental* and *awareness*.

3 In the **Clip Art** task pane, click the **Results should be arrow**. Be sure the **Illustrations** check box is selected, and then click as necessary to clear the *Photographs, Videos,* and *Audio* check boxes. Click the **Results should be** arrow again to collapse the list. Be sure the **Include Office.com content** check box is selected.

4 In the **Clip Art** task pane, click the **Go** button. Locate the image of the three white arrows in a blue circle. Click on the image to insert it, and then compare your screen with Figure 3.26.

> Recall that when you insert a graphic, it is inserted as an inline object; that is, it is treated as a character in a line of text. Here, the inserted clip art becomes the first character in the nameplate.

Figure 3.26

Clip Art task pane

Search term

Selected image

Image inserted in document

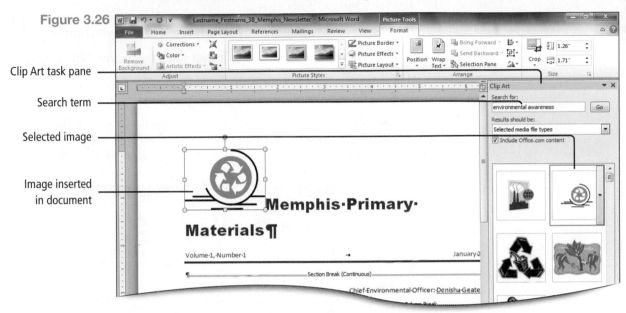

5 **Close** ☒ the **Clip Art** task pane. With the image still selected, on the **Format tab**, in the **Size group**, click in the **Shape Height** box, type **1** and then press Enter. In the **Arrange group**, click the **Wrap Text** button, and then click **Square**.

6 Point to the image to display the 🔼 pointer, and then drag the image to the right so that the bottom edge aligns slightly above *January 2016*, and the right side aligns with the right margin. Recall that you can press the arrow keys as necessary to move the image in small, precise increments.

7 Compare your screen with Figure 3.27, and then **Save** 🖫 the document.

Figure 3.27

Image resized

Text wrapping applied to image

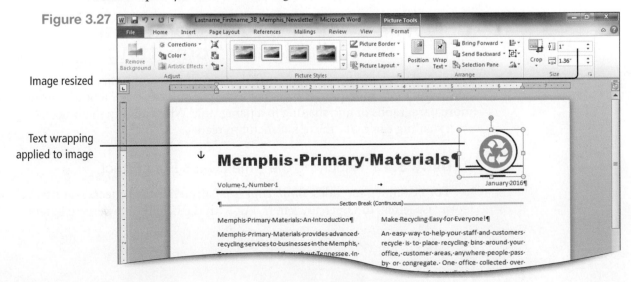

Activity 3.12 | Inserting a Screenshot

A **screenshot** is an image of an active window on your computer that you can paste into a document. Screenshots are especially useful when you want to insert an image of a Web site into a document you are creating in Word. You can insert a screenshot of any open window on your computer.

1 In the second column, click to position the insertion point at the beginning of the paragraph that begins *You can make.* Open your Internet browser, and then in the address bar type **www.epa.gov/osw/conserve/rrr** and press Enter. Maximize the browser window, if necessary.

2 From the taskbar, redisplay your **3B_Memphis_Newletter** document.

3 On the **Insert tab**, in the **Illustrations group**, click the **Screenshot** button.

All of your open windows display in the Available Windows gallery and are available to paste into the document.

4 In the **Screenshot** gallery, click the browser window that contains the EPA site to insert the screenshot at the insertion point, and notice that the image resizes to fit between the column margins. Compare your screen with Figure 3.28. **Save** the document.

Figure 3.28

Screenshot inserted in document

Objective 5 | Use Special Character and Paragraph Formatting

Special text and paragraph formatting is useful to emphasize text, and it makes your newsletter look more professional. For example, you can place a border around one or more paragraphs or add shading to a paragraph. When adding shading, use light colors; dark shading can make the text difficult to read.

Activity 3.13 | Applying the Small Caps Font Effect

For headlines and titles, **small caps** is an attractive font effect. The effect changes lowercase letters to uppercase letters, but with the height of lowercase letters.

1 At the top of the first column, select the paragraph *Memphis Primary Materials: An Introduction* including the paragraph mark.

2 Right-click the selected text, and then from the shortcut menu, click **Font**. In the **Font** dialog box, click the **Font color arrow**, and then under **Theme Colors**, in the fifth column, click the last color—**Blue, Accent 1, Darker 50%**.

3 Under **Font style**, click **Bold**. Under **Size**, click **18**. Under **Effects**, select the **Small caps** check box. Compare your screen with Figure 3.29.

> The Font dialog box provides more options than are available on the Ribbon and enables you to make several changes at the same time. In the Preview box, the text displays with the selected formatting options applied.

Figure 3.29

Small caps effect selected

Selected text

Preview of changes to text

4 Click **OK**. Right-click the selected text, and then on the Mini toolbar, click **Center** ☰.

5 With the text still selected, right-click, and then on the Mini toolbar, click the **Format Painter** button ✦. Then, with the ▲Ⅰ pointer, at the top of the second column, select the paragraph *Make Recycling Easy for Everyone!* to apply the same formats. Notice that the column title wraps placing a single word on the second line.

6 Position the insertion point to the right of the word *Recycling*, and then press Del to remove the space. Hold down Shift and then press Enter.

> Holding down Shift while pressing Enter inserts a ***manual line break***, which moves the text to the right of the insertion point to a new line while keeping the text in the same paragraph. A ***line break indicator***, in the shape of a bent arrow, indicates that a manual line break was inserted.

7 Compare your screen with Figure 3.30, and then **Save** 🖫 the document.

Figure 3.30

Manual line break inserted

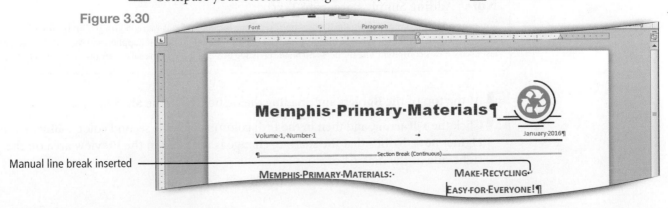

Activity 3.14 | Adding a Border and Shading to a Paragraph

Paragraph borders provide strong visual cues to the reader. Paragraph shading can be used with or without borders. When used with a border, light shading can be very effective in drawing the reader's eye to the text.

1 In the first column, in the paragraph that begins *We strive to grow*, click to position the insertion point at the end of the paragraph, and then press [Enter] one time.

2 At the bottom of the column, select the nine lines of company information, beginning with *Memphis Primary Materials* and ending with the paragraph that begins *Chief Environmental*. On the Mini toolbar, apply **Bold** [B] and **Center** [≡].

3 With the text still selected, on the **Home tab**, in the **Paragraph group**, click the **Borders button arrow** [▦ ▾], and then click **Borders and Shading**.

4 In the **Borders and Shading** dialog box, be sure the **Borders tab** is selected. Under **Setting**, click **Shadow**. If necessary, click the **Color arrow**, and then in the fifth column, click the last color—**Blue, Accent 1, Darker 50%**. Click the **Width arrow**, and then click **3 pt**. Compare your screen with Figure 3.31.

> In the lower right portion of the Borders and Shading dialog box, the *Apply to* box displays *Paragraph*. The *Apply to* box directs where the border will be applied—in this instance, the border will be applied only to the selected paragraphs.

Figure 3.31

Preview of paragraph border

Shadow border selected

Note | Adding Simple Borders to Text

You can add simple borders from the Borders button gallery, located in the Paragraph group. This button offers less control over the border appearance, however, because the line thickness and color applied will match whatever was last used on this computer. The Borders and Shading dialog box enables you to make your own custom selections.

---

5 At the top of the **Borders and Shading** dialog box, click the **Shading tab**.

6 Click the **Fill arrow**, and then in the fifth column, click the second color—**Blue, Accent 1, Lighter 80%**. Notice that the shading change is reflected in the Preview area on the right side of the dialog box.

7 At the bottom of the **Borders and Shading** dialog box, click **OK**. Click anywhere in the document to deselect the text, and then compare your screen with Figure 3.32.

Figure 3.32

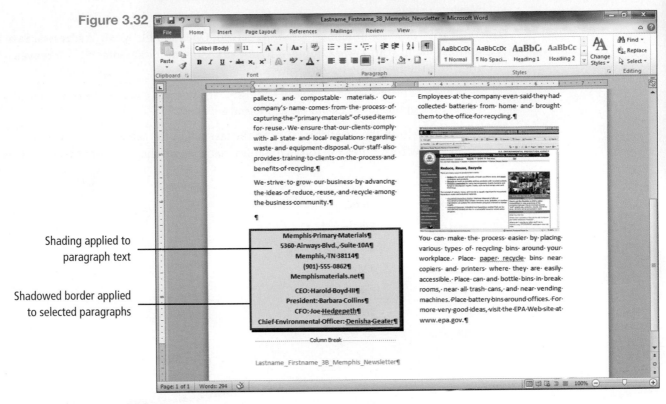

Shading applied to paragraph text

Shadowed border applied to selected paragraphs

8 From **Backstage** view, display the **Document Panel**.

9 In the **Author** box, delete any text and then type your firstname and lastname. In the **Subject** box, type your course name and section number, and in the **Keywords** box, type **newsletter, January Close** [x] the **Document Panel**.

10 Press Ctrl + F2 to view the **Print Preview**. **Close** the preview, make any necessary corrections, and then click **Save** [💾]. **Exit** Word; hold this file until you complete this Project.

Objective 6 | Create Mailing Labels Using Mail Merge

Word's *mail merge* feature joins a *main document* and a *data source* to create customized letters or labels. The main document contains the text or formatting that remains constant. For labels, the main document contains the formatting for a specific label size. The data source contains information including the names and addresses of the individuals for whom the labels are being created. Names and addresses in a data source might come from a Word table, an Excel spreadsheet, or an Access database.

The easiest way to perform a mail merge is to use the Mail Merge Wizard, which asks you questions and, based on your answers, walks you step by step through the mail merge process.

Activity 3.15 | Opening the Mail Merge Wizard Template

In this activity, you will open the data source for the mail merge, which is a Word table containing names and addresses.

1 **Start** Word and display a new blank document. Display formatting marks and rulers. **Save** the document in your **Word Chapter 3** folder as **Lastname_Firstname_3B_ Mailing_Labels**

2 With your new document open on the screen, **Open** the file **w03B_Addresses**. **Save** the address file in your **Word Chapter 3** folder as **Lastname_Firstname_3B_Addresses** and then add the file name to the footer.

> This document contains a table of addresses. The first row contains the column names. The remaining rows contain the names and addresses.

3 Click to position the insertion point in the last cell in the table, and then press Tab to create a new row. Enter the following information, and then compare your table with Figure 3.33:

First Name	**John**
Last Name	**Wisniewski**
Address 1	**1226 Snow Road**
Address 2	**#234**
City	**Lakeland**
State	**TN**
ZIP Code	**38002**

Figure 3.33

New record added to address list

4 **Save** , and then **Close** the table of addresses. Be sure your blank **Lastname_ Firstname_3B_Mailing_Labels** document displays.

5 Click the **Mailings tab**. In the **Start Mail Merge group**, click the **Start Mail Merge** button, and then click **Step by Step Mail Merge Wizard** to display the **Mail Merge** task pane.

6 Under **Select document type**, click the **Labels** option button. At the bottom of the task pane, click **Next: Starting document** to display Step 2 of 6 of the Mail Merge Wizard.

7 Under **Select starting document**, be sure **Change document layout** is selected, and then under **Change document layout**, click **Label options**.

8 In the **Label Options** dialog box, under **Printer information**, click the **Tray arrow**, and then click **Default tray (Automatically Select)**—the exact wording may vary depending on your printer, but select the *Default* or *Automatic* option—to print the labels on regular paper rather than manually inserting labels in the printer.

9 Under **Label information**, click the **Label vendors arrow**, and then click **Avery US Letter**. Under **Product number**, scroll about halfway down the list, and then click **5160 Easy Peel Address Labels**. Compare your screen with Figure 3.34.

> The Avery 5160 address label is a commonly used label. The precut sheets contain three columns of 10 labels each—for a total of 30 labels per sheet.

Figure 3.34

Label vendor

Product number

Label options

10 At the bottom of the **Label Options** dialog box, click **OK**. If a message box displays, click OK to set up the labels. At the bottom of the task pane, click **Next: Select recipients**.

> The label page is set up with three columns and ten rows. The label borders may or may not display on your screen, depending on your settings. Here in Step 3 of the Mail Merge Wizard, you must identify the recipients—the data source. For your recipient data source, you can choose to use an existing list—for example, a list of names and addresses that you have in an Access database, an Excel worksheet, a Word table, or your Outlook contacts list. If you do not have an existing data source, you can type a new list at this point in the wizard.

11 If gridlines do not display, click the **Layout tab**. In the **Table group**, click the **View Gridlines** button, and then notice that each label is outlined with a dashed line. If you cannot see the right and left edges of the page, in the status bar, click the **Zoom Out** button ⊖ as necessary to see the right and left edges of the label sheet on your screen.

12 Under **Select recipients**, be sure the **Use an existing list** option button is selected. Under **Use an existing list**, click **Browse**.

13 Navigate to your **Word Chapter 3** folder, select your **Lastname_Firstname_3B_ Addresses** file, and then click **Open** to display the **Mail Merge Recipients** dialog box.

> In the Mail Merge Recipients dialog box, the column headings are formed from the text in the first row of your Word table of addresses. Each row of information that contains data for one person is referred to as a *record*. The column headings—for example, *Last_Name* and *First_Name*—are referred to as *fields*. An underscore replaces the spaces between words in the field name headings.

14 Compare your screen with Figure 3.35.

Figure 3.35

Mail Merge Recipients dialog box →

Gridlines indicate label borders →

Path containing your file name →

Activity 3.16 | Completing the Mail Merge Wizard

You can add or edit names and addresses while completing the Mail Merge Wizard. You can also match your column names with preset names used in Mail Merge.

1 In the lower left portion of the **Mail Merge Recipients** dialog box, in the **Data Source** box, click the path that contains your file name. Then, at the bottom of the **Mail Merge Recipients** dialog box, click **Edit**.

2 In the upper right corner of the **Data Form** dialog box, click **Add New**. In the blank record, type the following, pressing Tab to move from field to field, and then compare your **Data Form** dialog box with Figure 3.36.

First_Name	**Susan**
Last_Name	**Ballard**
Address_1	**1251 Parker Road**
Unit:	
City	**Memphis**
State	**TN**
ZIP_Code	**38123**

Figure 3.36

New record →

Edit button →

3 In the lower right corner of the **Data Form** dialog box, click **Close**. Scroll to the end of the recipient list to confirm that the record for *Susan Ballard* that you just added is in the list. At the bottom of the **Mail Merge Recipients** dialog box, click **OK**.

4 At the bottom of the **Mail Merge** task pane, click **Next: Arrange your labels**.

5 Under **Arrange your labels**, click **Address block**. In the **Insert Address Block** dialog box, under **Specify address elements**, examine the various formats for names. If necessary, under *Insert recipient's name in this format*, select the *Joshua Randall Jr.* format. Compare your dialog box with Figure 3.37.

Figure 3.37

Format selected

Preview of address block

Match Fields button

6 In the lower right corner of the **Insert Address Block** dialog box, click **Match Fields**.

If your field names are descriptive, the Mail Merge program will identify them correctly, as is the case with most of the information in the *Required for Address Block* section. However, the Address 2 field is unmatched—in the source file, this column is named *Unit*.

7 Scroll down and examine the dialog box, and then compare your screen with Figure 3.38.

Figure 3.38

Address 2 unmatched

8 Click the **Address 2 arrow**, and then from the list of available fields, click **Unit** to match the Mail Merge field with the field in your data source.

9 At the bottom of the **Match Fields** dialog box, click **OK**. At the bottom of the **Insert Address Block** dialog box, click **OK**.

> Word inserts the Address block in the first label space surrounded by double angle brackets. The *AddressBlock* field name displays, which represents the address block you saw in the Preview area of the Insert Address Block dialog box.

10 In the task pane, under **Replicate labels**, click **Update all labels** to insert an address block in each label space for each subsequent record.

11 At the bottom of the task pane, click **Next: Preview your labels**. Notice that for addresses with four lines, the last line of the address is cut off.

12 Press Ctrl + A to select all of the label text, click the **Page Layout tab**, and then in the **Paragraph group**, click in the **Spacing Before** box. Type **3** and press Enter.

13 Click in any label to deselect, and notice that 4-line addresses are no longer cut off. Compare your screen with Figure 3.39.

Figure 3.39

Preview of mailing labels

14 At the bottom of the task pane, click **Next: Complete the merge**.

> Step 6 of the Mail Merge task pane displays. At this point you can print or edit your labels, although this is done more easily in the document window.

15 Save your labels, and then Close the **Mail Merge** task pane.

Activity 3.17 | Previewing and Printing the Mail Merge Document

If you discover that you need to make further changes to your labels, you can still make them even though the Mail Merge task pane is closed.

1 Add the file name to the footer, close the footer area, and then move to the top of Page 2. Click anywhere in the empty table row, click the **Layout tab**, in the **Rows & Columns group**, click the **Delete** button, and then click **Delete Rows**.

> Adding footer text to a label sheet replaces the last row of labels on a page with the footer text, and moves the last row of labels to the top of the next page. In this instance, a blank second page is created, which you can delete by deleting the blank row.

2 Press Ctrl + F2 to display the **Print Preview**. Notice that the labels do not display in alphabetical order.

3 Click the **Mailings tab**, and then in the **Start Mail Merge group**, click the **Edit Recipient List** button to display the list of names and addresses.

4 In the **Mail Merge Recipients** dialog box, click the **Last_Name** field heading, and notice that the names are sorted alphabetically by the recipient's last name.

> Mailing labels are often sorted by either last name or by ZIP Code.

5 Click the **Last_Name** field heading again, and notice that the last names are sorted in descending order. Click the **Last_Name** field one more time to return to ascending order, and then click **OK**. Press Ctrl + Home, and then compare your screen with Figure 3.40.

Figure 3.40

Labels in alphabetical order

6 From **Backstage** view, display the **Document Panel**. In the **Author** box, delete any text and then type your firstname and lastname. In the **Subject** box, type your course name and section number, and in the **Keywords** box type **newsletter mailing labels** **Close** ☒ the **Document Panel**.

7 Click **Save** 🖫. Display **Backstage** view, and then click the **Print tab**. Examine the **Print Preview** on the right side of the window.

8 As directed by your instructor, print or submit electronically.

> If you print, the labels will print on whatever paper is in the printer; unless you have preformatted labels available, the labels will print on a sheet of paper. Printing the labels on plain paper enables you to proofread the labels before you print them on more expensive label sheets.

9 **Close** the document, click **Yes** to save the data source, and then if necessary, click **Save** to save the labels.

10 In addition to your labels and address document, print or submit your **3B_Memphis_Newsletter** document as directed. **Exit** Word.

 You have completed Project 3B

Content-Based Assessments

Summary

In this chapter, you created a research paper using the MLA style. You added a header, footnotes, citations, and a bibliography, and changed the footnote style. You created a newsletter that used multiple columns. You added a column break, a page break, and a manual line break. You added special font effects, and added a border and shading to a paragraph. Finally, you used the Mail Merge Wizard to create a set of mailing labels for the newsletter.

Key Terms

Matching

Match each term in the second column with its correct definition in the first column by writing the letter of the term on the blank line in front of the correct definition.

_____ 1. A manual that contains standards for the design and writing of documents.

_____ 2. One of two commonly used style guides for formatting research papers.

_____ 3. An image of an active window on your computer that you can paste into a document.

_____ 4. In a research paper, information that expands on the topic, but that does not fit well in the document text.

_____ 5. In a research paper, a note placed at the bottom of the page.

_____ 6. In a research paper, a note placed at the end of a document or chapter.

_____ 7. A list of cited works in a report or research paper, also referred to as *Works Cited*, *Sources*, or *References*, depending upon the report style.

_____ 8. In the MLA style, a list of cited works placed at the end of a research paper or report.

_____ 9. A group of formatting commands, such as font, font size, font color, paragraph alignment, and line spacing that can be applied to a paragraph with one command.

_____ 10. A note, inserted into the text of a research paper that refers the reader to a source in the bibliography.

_____ 11. In the MLA style, a citation that refers to items on the *Works Cited* page, and which is placed in parentheses; the citation includes the last name of the author or authors, and the page number in the referenced source.

A American Psychological Association (APA)

B Bibliography

C Citation

D Endnote

E Footnote

F Hanging indent

G Manual column break

H Manual page break

I Note

J Page break indicator

K Parenthetical reference

L Screenshot

M Style

N Style guide

O Works Cited

Content-Based Assessments

_____ 12. The action of forcing a page to end and placing subsequent text at the top of the next page.

_____ 13. A dotted line with the text *Page Break* that indicates where a manual page break was inserted.

_____ 14. An indent style in which the first line of a paragraph extends to the left of the remaining lines, and that is commonly used for bibliographic entries.

_____ 15. An artificial end to a column to balance columns or to provide space for the insertion of other objects.

Multiple Choice

Circle the correct answer.

1. Column text that is aligned to both the left and right margins is referred to as:
   A. centered
   B. justified
   C. indented

2. The banner on the front page of a newsletter that identifies the publication is the:
   A. heading
   B. nameplate
   C. title

3. A portion of a document that can be formatted differently from the rest of the document is a:
   A. tabbed list
   B. paragraph
   C. section

4. A font effect, commonly used in titles, that changes lowercase text into uppercase letters using a reduced font size is:
   A. Small Caps
   B. Level 2 Head
   C. Bevel

5. To end a line before the normal end of the line, without creating a new paragraph, hold down the Shift key while pressing the:
   A. Enter key
   B. Ctrl key
   C. Alt key

6. The nonprinting symbol that displays where a manual line break is inserted is the:
   A. short arrow
   B. bent arrow
   C. anchor

7. In mail merge, the document that contains the text or formatting that remains constant is the:
   A. data source
   B. mailing list
   C. main document

8. In mail merge, the list of variable information, such as names and addresses, that is merged with a main document to create customized form letters or labels is the:
   A. data source
   B. mailing list
   C. main document

9. In mail merge, a row of information that contains data for one person is a:
   A. record
   B. field
   C. label

10. To perform a mail merge using Word's step-by-step guided process, use the:
    A. Mail Merge Template
    B. Mail Merge Management Source
    C. Mail Merge Wizard

Content-Based Assessments

Apply **3A** skills from these Objectives:

◻ Create a Research Paper

◻ Insert Footnotes in a Research Paper

◻ Create Citations and a Bibliography in a Research Paper

Skills Review | Project **3C** Recycling Report

In the following Skills Review, you will format and edit a research paper for Memphis Primary Materials. The research topic is recycling in the natural environment. Your completed document will look similar to Figure 3.41.

Project Files

For Project 3C, you will need the following file:

w03C_Recycling_Report

You will save your document as:

Lastname_Firstname_3C_Recycling_Report

Project Results

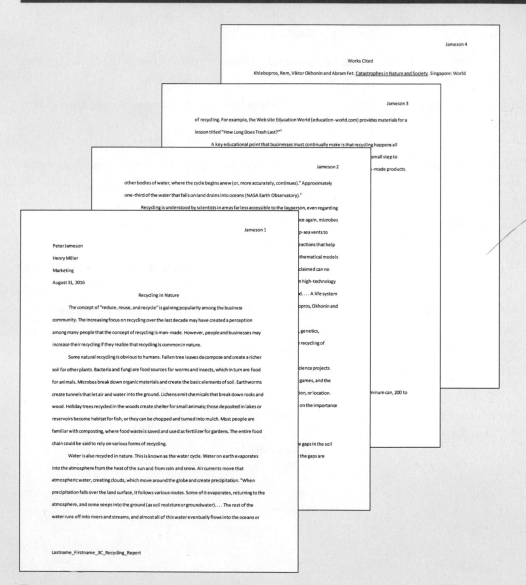

Figure 3.41

(Project 3C Recycling Report continues on the next page)

Content-Based Assessments

Skills Review | Project **3C** Recycling Report (continued)

1 **Start** Word. From your student files, locate and open the document **w03C_Recycling_Report**. Display the formatting marks and rulers. **Save** the file in your **Word Chapter 3** folder as **Lastname_Firstname_3C_Recycling_Report**

a. Press Ctrl + A. On the **Home tab**, in the **Paragraph group**, click the **Line spacing** button, and then change the line spacing to **2.0**. On the **Page Layout tab**, in the **Paragraph group**, change the **Spacing After** to **0 pt**.

b. Press Ctrl + Home, press Enter to create a blank line at the top of the document, and then click to position the insertion point in the blank line. Type **Peter Jameson** and then press Enter. Type **Henry Miller** and then press Enter. Type **Marketing** and then press Enter. Type **August 31, 2016** and then press Enter.

c. Type **Recycling in Nature** and then right-click anywhere in the title you just typed. From the Mini toolbar, **Center** the title.

d. Near the top of **Page 1**, locate the paragraph beginning *The concept of*, and then click to position the insertion point at the beginning of the paragraph. Scroll to the end of the document, hold down Shift, and then click to the right of the last paragraph mark to select all of the text from the insertion point to the end of the document. On the horizontal ruler, drag the **First Line Indent** button to **0.5″**.

e. On **Page 1**, point to the top margin area and right-click. Click **Edit Header**. In the header area, type **Jameson** and then press Spacebar.

f. On the **Design tab**, in the **Header & Footer group**, click the **Page Number** button, and then point to **Current Position**. In the displayed gallery, under **Simple**, click **Plain Number**. On the **Home tab**, in the **Paragraph group**, click the **Align Text Right** button.

g. Click the **Design tab**, and then in the **Navigation group**, click the **Go to Footer** button. In the **Insert group**, click the **Quick Parts** button, and then click **Field**. In the **Field** dialog box, under **Field names**, locate and click **FileName**, and then click **OK**.

h. Double-click anywhere outside the footer area. **Save** your document.

2 Scroll to view the top of **Page 2**, locate the paragraph that ends *drains into oceans*, and then click to position the insertion point to the right of the period following *oceans*. On the **References tab**, in the **Footnotes group**, click the **Insert Footnote** button.

a. Type **Groundwater is found in two layers of the soil, the "zone of aeration," where gaps in the soil are filled with both air and water, and, further down, the "zone of saturation," where the gaps are completely filled with water.**

b. In the lower half of **Page 2**, locate the paragraph that begins *School students*. Click to position the insertion point at the end of the paragraph and insert a footnote.

c. As the footnote text, type **A wool sock will last one year in a landfill; a soup can, 80 to 100 years; an aluminum can, 200 to 500 years; and plastic rings from a six–pack of cans, 450 years. Save** your document.

d. At the bottom of **Page 2**, right-click anywhere in either footnote. From the shortcut menu, click **Style**. In the **Style** dialog box, click the **Modify** button. In the **Modify Style** dialog box, locate the small Formatting toolbar in the center of the dialog box, click the **Font Size button arrow**, and then click **11**.

e. In the lower left corner of the dialog box, click the **Format** button, and then click **Paragraph**. In the **Paragraph** dialog box, under **Indentation**, click the **Special arrow**, and then click **First line**. Under **Spacing**, click the **Line spacing button arrow**, and then click **Double**.

f. Click **OK** to close the **Paragraph** dialog box, click **OK** to close the **Modify Style** dialog box, and then click **Apply** to apply the new style. Notice that the second footnote moves to **Page 3**. **Save** your document.

3 Scroll to view the top of **Page 2**, and then locate the footnote marker at the end of the second line of text. Click to position the insertion point to the left of the period at the end of the paragraph.

a. On the **References tab**, in the **Citations & Bibliography group**, click the **Style button arrow**, and then click **MLA** to insert a reference using MLA style. Click the **Insert Citation** button, and then click **Add New Source**. Click the **Type of Source arrow**,

(Project 3C Recycling Report continues on the next page)

Content-Based Assessments

and then click **Web site**. Select the **Corporate Author** check box, and then add the following information (type the URL on one line):

Corporate Author:	**NASA Earth Observatory**
Name of Web Page:	**The Water Cycle**
Year:	**2009**
Month:	**March**
Day:	**3**
Year Accessed:	**2016**
Month Accessed:	**May**
Day Accessed:	**24**
URL:	**http://earthobservatory.nasa.gov/ Features/Water/water_2.php**

b. Click **OK** to insert the citation. In the next paragraph, which begins *Recycling is understood,* in the fifth line, click to position the insertion point to the right of the quotation mark. In the **Citations & Bibliography group**, click the **Insert Citation** button, and then click **Add New Source**. Click the **Type of Source arrow**, click **Journal Article**, and then add the following information (type the Title on one line):

Author:	**Pennisi, Elizabeth**
Title:	**Shale-Eating Microbes Recycle Global Carbon**
Journal Name:	**Science**
Year:	**2001**
Pages:	**1043**

c. Click **OK**. In the text, click to select the citation, click the **Citation Options arrow**, and then click **Edit Citation**. In the **Edit Citation** dialog box, under **Add**, in the **Pages** box, type **1043** and then click **OK**. Add a period to the right of the citation and delete the period to the left of the quotation mark.

d. In the same paragraph, position the insertion point at the end of the paragraph. In the **Citations & Bibliography group**, click the **Insert Citation** button, and then click **Add New Source**. Click the **Type of**

Source arrow, click **Book**, and then add the following information (type the Author information on one line):

Author:	**Khlebopros, Rem; Okhonin, Viktor; Fet, Abram**
Title:	**Catastrophes in Nature and Society**
Year:	**2007**
City:	**Singapore**
Publisher:	**World Scientific Publishing Company**

e. Click **OK**. Click to select the citation, click the **Citation Options arrow**, and then click **Edit Citation**. In the **Edit Citation** dialog box, under **Add**, in the **Pages** box, type **111** Click **OK**. Add a period to the right of the citation and delete the period to the left of the quotation mark.

f. Press Ctrl + End to move the insertion point to the end of the document. Press Ctrl + Enter to insert a manual page break. On the ruler, drag the **First Line Indent** button to the left to **0 inches on the horizontal ruler**.

g. Type **Works Cited** and then press Enter. On the **References tab**, in the **Citations & Bibliography group**, be sure **MLA** displays in the **Style** box. In the **Citations & Bibliography group**, click the **Bibliography** button, and then click **Insert Bibliography**.

h. In the bibliography, move the pointer to the left of the first entry—beginning *Khlebopros*—to display the pointer. Drag down to select all three references. On the **Home tab**, in the **Paragraph group**, set the **Line spacing** to **2.0**. On the **Page Layout tab**, set the **Spacing After** to **0 pt**.

i. Right-click the *Works Cited* title, and then from the Mini toolbar, click the **Center** button. **Save** your document.

4 From **Backstage** view, display the **Document Panel**, type your name and course information, and then add the keywords **recycling, nature, research paper** In the upper left corner of the panel, click the **Document Properties** button, and then click **Advanced Properties**.

(Project 3C Recycling Report continues on the next page)

Content-Based Assessments

Skills Review | Project **3C** Recycling Report (continued)

a. In the **Properties** dialog box, click the **Summary tab**.
In the **Properties** dialog box, fill in the following
information:

Title:	**Recycling in Nature**
Manager:	**Henry Miller**
Company:	**Memphis Primary Materials**
Comments:	**Draft of a new white paper research report on recycling**

b. At the bottom of the **Properties** dialog box, click
OK. **Close** the **Document Panel**. **Save** your document.
View the Print Preview, and then print or submit
electronically as directed by your instructor. **Exit**
Word.

End You have completed Project 3C

Content-Based Assessments

Apply **3B** skills from these Objectives:

- **4** Format a Multiple-Column Newsletter
- **5** Use Special Character and Paragraph Formatting
- **6** Create Mailing Labels Using Mail Merge

Skills Review | Project **3D** Company Newsletter

In the following Skills Review, you will format a newsletter for Memphis Primary Materials, and then create a set of mailing labels for the newsletter. Your completed documents will look similar to Figure 3.42.

Project Files

For Project 3D, you will need the following files:

New blank Word document
w03D_Company_Newsletter
w03D_Addresses

You will save your documents as:

Lastname_Firstname_3D_Company_Newsletter
Lastname_Firstname_3D_Addresses
Lastname_Firstname_3D_Labels

Project Results

Figure 3.42

(Project 3D Company Newsletter continues on the next page)

Content-Based Assessments

Skills Review | Project **3D** Company Newsletter (continued)

1 **Start** Word. From your student files, open the document **w03D_Company_Newsletter**. **Save** the file in your **Word Chapter 3** folder as **Lastname_Firstname_3D_Company_Newsletter** and then add the file name to the footer.

a. Select the first paragraph of text—*Memphis Primary Materials*. From the Mini toolbar, change the **Font** to **Arial Black** and the **Font Size** to **24**. Select the title you just formatted. Click the **Font Color button arrow**, and then under **Theme Colors**, in the seventh column, click the fifth color—**Olive Green, Accent 3, Darker 25%**.

b. Select the second paragraph. On the **Home tab**, in the **Paragraph group**, click the **Borders button arrow**, and then click **Borders and Shading**. In the **Borders and Shading** dialog box, click the **Color arrow**, and then under **Theme Colors**, in the seventh column, click the fifth color—**Olive Green, Accent 3, Darker 25%**. Click the **Width arrow**, and then click **3 pt**. In the **Preview** area, click the *bottom* border of the Preview and then click **OK**.

c. Below the nameplate, locate the paragraph that begins *Recycle Your Mobile*, and then select all of the text from that point to the end of the document. On the **Page Layout tab**, in the **Page Setup group**, click the **Columns** button, and then click **Two**.

d. With the text still selected, in the **Paragraph group**, set **Spacing After** to **6 pt**. On the **Home tab**, in the **Paragraph group**, click the **Justify** button. Click anywhere in the document to deselect the text, and then **Save** the newsletter.

e. Press [Ctrl] + [Home]. On the **Insert tab**, in the **Illustrations group**, click the **Clip Art** button. In the **Clip Art** task pane, click in the **Search for** box, and then type **conservation**

f. In the **Clip Art** task pane, click the **Results should be arrow**, and be sure that only the **Illustrations** check box is selected. Be sure the **Include Office.com content** check box is selected, and then click **Go**. Locate the image of three green arrows, as shown in Figure 3.42, and then click on the image.

g. On the **Format tab**, in the **Size group**, click in the **Shape Height** box, type **1** and then press [Enter]. In the **Arrange group**, click the **Wrap Text** button, and then click **Square**. **Close** the Clip Art task pane, and then drag the image to the location shown in Figure 3.42.

h. In the second column, position the insertion point at the beginning of the paragraph that begins *By managing costs*. Open your Web browser. In the address bar, type **www.energy.gov** and then press [Enter]. Maximize the browser window. Use the taskbar to return to your Word document.

i. On the **Insert tab**, in the **Illustrations group**, click the **Screenshot** button. In the gallery, click the DOE screenshot to insert it. **Close** your Web browser, and then **Save** your document.

2 At the top of the first column, select the paragraph that begins *Recycle Your Mobile*. Be sure to include the paragraph mark. Right-click the selected text, and then click **Font**. In the **Font** dialog box, click the **Font color arrow**, and then under **Theme Colors**, in the seventh column, click the last color—**Olive Green, Accent 3, Darker 50%**. Under **Font style**, click **Bold**. Under **Size**, click **14**. Under **Effects**, select the **Small caps** check box.

a. In the **Font** dialog box, click **OK**. Right-click the selected text, and then click the **Center** button. In the title you just formatted, click to position the insertion point to the right of *Phone*, and then press [Del] to remove the space. Hold down [Shift], and then press [Enter] to insert a manual line break.

b. Select and right-click the title you just formatted, and then on the Mini toolbar, click the **Format Painter** button. Near the middle of the first column, select the paragraph that begins *A New World* to apply the same formatting.

c. At the bottom of the second column, in the paragraph that begins *For further*, select the entire paragraph. On the Mini toolbar, apply **Bold**.

d. With the text still selected, on the **Home tab**, in the **Paragraph group**, click the **Borders button arrow**, and then click **Borders and Shading**. In the **Borders and Shading** dialog box, be sure the **Borders tab** is selected. Under **Setting**, click **Box**. Click the **Width arrow**, and then click **3 pt**. If necessary, click the **Color arrow**, and then in the seventh column, click the fifth color—**Olive Green, Accent 3, Darker 25%**.

e. At the top of the **Borders and Shading** dialog box, click the **Shading tab**. Click the **Fill arrow**, and then in the seventh column, click the second color—**Olive Green, Accent 3, Lighter 80%**. At the bottom of the **Borders and Shading** dialog box, click **OK**. Click anywhere in the document to deselect the text.

(Project 3D Company Newsletter continues on the next page)

Content-Based Assessments

f. Near the bottom of the first column, in the paragraph that begins *Information and communications*, click to position the insertion point at the beginning of the sixth line. On the **Page Layout tab**, in the **Page Setup group**, click the **Breaks** button. Under **Page Breaks**, click **Column**.

g. From **Backstage** view, display the **Document Panel**, type your name and course information. Add the keywords **newsletter, energy** and then **Close** the **Document Panel**. **Save** the document, view the Print Preview, and then **Exit** Word. Hold this file until you complete this project.

3 **Start** Word and display a new blank document. Display formatting marks and rulers. **Save** the document in your **Word Chapter 3** folder as **Lastname_Firstname_3D_Labels Open** the file **w03D_Addresses Save** the address file in your **Word Chapter 3** folder as **Lastname_Firstname_3D_Addresses** and then add the file name to the footer.

a. Click to position the insertion point in the last cell in the table, and then press ⟨Tab⟩ to create a new row. Enter the following new record:

First Name	Eldon
Last Name	Aarons
Address 1	5354 Thornewood Dr.
Unit	#2B
City	Memphis
State	TN
ZIP Code	38112

b. **Save**, and then **Close** the table of addresses; be sure your blank **Lastname_Firstname_3D_Labels** document displays. Click the **Mailings tab**. In the **Start Mail Merge group**, click the **Start Mail Merge** button, and then click **Step by Step Mail Merge Wizard**. Under **Select document type**, click the **Labels** option button.

c. At the bottom of the task pane, click **Next: Starting document**. Under **Select starting document**, be sure **Change document layout** is selected, and then under **Change document layout**, click **Label options**.

d. In the **Label Options** dialog box, under **Printer information**, click the **Tray arrow**, and then click **Default tray (Automatically Select)**.

e. Under **Label information**, click the **Label vendors arrow**, and then click **Avery US Letter**. Under **Product number**, scroll about halfway down the list, and then click **5160**. At the bottom of the **Label Options** dialog box, click **OK**. At the bottom of the task pane, click **Next: Select recipients**.

f. Under **Select recipients**, be sure the **Use an existing list** option button is selected. Under **Use an existing list**, click **Browse**. Navigate to your **Word Chapter 3** folder, select your **Lastname_Firstname_3D_Addresses** file, and then click **Open**. At the bottom of the **Mail Merge Recipients** dialog box, click **OK**, and then in the **Mail Merge** task pane, click **Next: Arrange your labels**.

g. Under **Arrange your labels**, click **Address block**. If necessary, in the **Insert Address Block** dialog box, under **Insert recipient's name in this format**, select the **Joshua Randall Jr.** format.

h. Click **Match Fields**. Click the **Address 2 arrow**, and then click **Unit**. Click **OK** two times.

i. In the task pane, under **Replicate labels**, click **Update all labels**. Click **Next: Preview your labels**. Press ⟨Ctrl⟩ + ⟨A⟩ to select all of the label text, and then on the **Page Layout tab**, click in the **Spacing Before** box, type **4** and press ⟨Enter⟩ to ensure that the four-line addresses will fit on the labels. **Save** your labels, and then **Close** the **Mail Merge** task pane.

4 Add the file name to the footer, and then close the footer area. Click in the bottom empty row of the table, click the **Layout tab**, in the **Rows & Columns group**, click **Delete**, and then click **Delete Rows**. From **Backstage** view, display the **Document Panel**, type your name and course information, and then add the keywords **newsletter mailing labels Close** the **Document Panel**.

a. Print or submit electronically your 3D_Company_Newsletter, 3D_Addresses, and 3D_Labels documents.

b. **Close** the document, click **Save** to save the labels, and then **Exit** Word.

 You have completed Project 3D ──────────────

Content-Based Assessments

Apply **3A** skills from these Objectives:

1. Create a Research Paper
2. Insert Footnotes in a Research Paper
3. Create Citations and a Bibliography in a Research Paper

Mastering Word | Project **3E** Hazards

In the following Mastering Word project, you will edit and format a research paper for Memphis Primary Materials, the topic of which is hazardous materials in electronic waste. Your completed document will look similar to Figure 3.43.

Project Files

For Project 3E, you will need the following file:

w03E_Hazards

You will save your document as:

Lastname_Firstname_3E_Hazards

Project Results

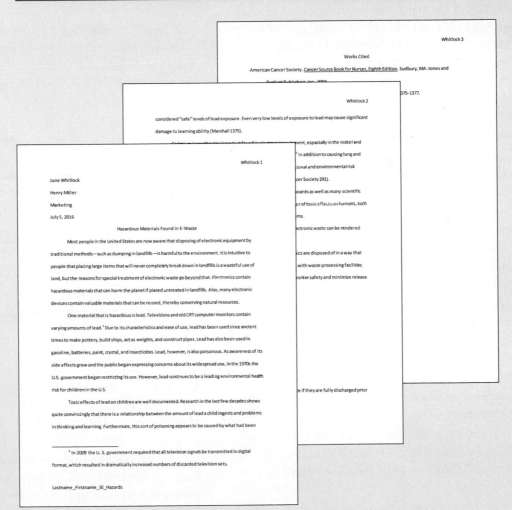

Figure 3.43

(Project 3E Hazards continues on the next page)

Content-Based Assessments

Mastering Word | Project 3E Hazards (continued)

1 **Start** Word. From your student files open the document **w03E_Hazards**. **Save** the document in your **Word Chapter 3** folder as **Lastname_Firstname_3E_Hazards** Display the header area, type **Whitlock** and then press Spacebar. Display the **Page Number gallery**, and then in the **Current Position**, add the **Plain Number** style. Apply **Align Text Right** formatting to the header. Add the file name to the footer.

2 Return to the beginning of the document, press Enter to insert a blank line, click in the blank line, type **June Whitlock** and then press Enter. Type **Henry Miller** and press Enter. Type **Marketing** and press Enter. Type **July 5, 2016**

3 Select all of the text in the document. Change the **Line Spacing** to **2.0**, and change the **Spacing After** to **0 pt**. Deselect the text, right-click anywhere in the title *Hazardous Materials Found in E-Waste*, and then **Center** the title.

Starting with the paragraph that begins *Most people*, select the text from that point to the end of the document, and then set the **First Line Indent** to **0.5"**.

4 Near the middle of **Page 1**, in the paragraph that begins *One material*, in the second line, click to position the insertion point to the right of the period following *lead*, and then add the following footnote:

> **In 2009 the U.S. government required that all television signals be transmitted in digital format, which resulted in dramatically increased numbers of discarded television sets.**

On **Page 2**, in the paragraph that begins *Cadmium is another*, in the second line, click to position the insertion point to the right of the period following *devices*, and then add the following footnote:

> **Newer lithium batteries are not considered hazardous waste if they are fully discharged prior to disposal.**

5 Right-click anywhere in the footnote, modify the **Style** to set the **Font Size** to **11**, and then change the **Format** of paragraphs to add a **First line** indent and use double-spacing.

Near the bottom of **Page 1**, locate the paragraph that begins *Toxic effects*, and then click position the insertion

point to the left of the period at the end of the paragraph, which displays at the top of **Page 2**. In the **MLA** format, add the following **Journal Article** citation (type the Title on one line):

Author:	**Marshall, Eliot**
Title:	**EPA May Allow More Lead in Gasoline**
Journal Name:	**Science**
Year:	**1982**
Pages:	**1375–1377**

6 Near the top of **Page 2**, locate the paragraph that begins *Cadmium*, and then click to position the insertion point to the left of the period at the end of the paragraph. Add the following **Book** citation, using a **Corporate Author** (type the Title on one line):

Corporate Author:	**American Cancer Society**
Title:	**Cancer Source Book for Nurses, Eighth Edition**
Year:	**2004**
City:	**Sudbury, MA**
Publisher:	**Jones and Bartlett Publishers, Inc.**

Select the *Marshall* citation and add the page number **1375** At the end of the next paragraph, select the *American Cancer Society* citation and add the page number **291**

7 Move to the end of the document, and then insert a manual page break to create a new page. Change the **First Line Indent** to **0"**. Add a **Works Cited** title, and then **Insert Bibliography**. Select the two references, apply **Double** line spacing, and then remove spacing after the paragraphs. **Center** the *Works Cited* title.

Display the **Document Panel** and add your name and course information and the keywords **hazardous materials Save** your document. Display the Print Preview, make any necessary adjustments, and then print or submit electronically as directed. **Exit** Word.

 End You have completed Project 3E ——————————

Content-Based Assessments

Apply 3B skills from these Objectives:

4 Format a Multiple-Column Newsletter

5 Use Special Character and Paragraph Formatting

6 Create Mailing Labels Using Mail Merge

Mastering Word | Project **3F** Spring Newsletter

In the following Mastering Word project, you will format a newsletter for Memphis Primary Materials, and then create a set of mailing labels for the newsletter. Your completed documents will look similar to Figure 3.44.

Project Files

For Project 3F, you will need the following files:

New blank Word document
w03F_Spring_Newsletter
w03F_Addresses

You will save your documents as:

Lastname_Firstname_3F_Spring_Newsletter
Lastname_Firstname_3F_Labels

Project Results

Figure 3.44

(Project 3F Spring Newsletter continues on the next page)

Content-Based Assessments

Mastering Word | Project 3F Spring Newsletter (continued)

1 **Start** Word. Open **w03F_Spring_Newsletter**, and then save it in your **Word Chapter 3** folder as **Lastname_Firstname_3F_Spring_Newsletter** Add the file name to the footer. Display the rulers and formatting marks.

Select the first line of text—*Memphis Primary Materials*. Change the **Font** to **Arial Black**, the **Font Size** to **24**, and the **Font Color** to **Orange, Accent 6, Darker 25%**.

Select the second line of text—the date and volume. Change the **Font Color** to **Orange, Accent 6, Darker 25%**. Display the **Borders and Shading** dialog box, and then add an **Orange, Accent 6, Darker 25%, 3 pt** line below the selected text.

2 Click at the beginning of the newsletter title. Display the **Clip Art** task pane, search for **recycle earth** and then insert the image of the orange and tan recycle arrows. Change the **Height** to **1** and then apply **Square** text wrapping. Close the **Clip Art** task pane. Drag the image to the location shown in Figure 3.44.

Starting with the paragraph that begins *CARE enough*, select all of the text from that point to the end of the document. Change the **Spacing After** to **6 pt**, format the text in two columns, and apply the **Justify** alignment.

3 At the top of the first column, select the paragraph *CARE Enough to Recycle*. From the **Font** dialog box, change the **Font Size** to **20**, apply **Bold**, add the **Small caps** effect, and change the **Font color** to **Orange, Accent 6, Darker 25%**. **Center** the paragraph. Near the bottom of the same column, apply the same formatting to the paragraph that begins *Hazards of Old*. Add a manual line break between *Old* and *Home*.

Move to the blank line at the bottom of the second column. Open your Web browser and open the **www.epa.gov/ozone/partnerships/rad/** Web site. Maximize the browser window and return to your Word document. Insert a **Screenshot** of the EPA Web page. **Close** your Web browser.

4 Select the two lines of text above the inserted screenshot. **Center** the text and apply **Bold**. Add a **Shadow** border, change the **Color** to **Tan, Background 2, Darker 25%**, the **Width** to **1 1/2 pt**, and then on the **Shading tab** of the dialog box, apply a **Fill** of **Tan, Background 2** shading—in the third column, the first color.

Display the **Document Panel** and add your name, course information, and the **Keywords Spring newsletter** Display the **Print Preview**, return to your document and make any necessary corrections, and then **Save** and **Close** the document. Hold this document until you complete the project.

5 Display a **New** blank document. **Save** the document in your **Word Chapter 3** folder as **Lastname_Firstname_3F_Labels** On the **Mailings tab**, start the **Step by Step Mail Merge Wizard**.

In **Step 1**, select **Labels** as the document type. In **Step 2**, set **Label options** to use the **Auto default** tray (yours may vary) and **Avery US Letter 5160**.

In **Step 3**, use an existing list, browse to select **w03F_Addresses**. In **Step 4**, add an **Address block** to the labels, use the *Joshua Randall Jr.* format, and then **Match Fields** by matching *Address 2* to *Unit*.

Update all labels and **Preview**. Select all of the label text, and then on the **Page Layout tab**, click in the **Spacing Before** box, type **4** and press Enter to ensure that the four-line addresses will fit on the labels. On the **Layout tab**, in the **Table group**, if necessary click **View Gridlines** to check the alignment of the labels.

Complete the merge, and then **Close** the **Mail Merge** task pane. Delete the last two empty rows of the table, and then add the file name to the footer.

6 Display the **Document Panel**, and then add your name and course information and the keywords **mailing labels** Display the **Print Preview**, return to your document and make any necessary corrections, and then **Save**. Print or submit electronically your two files that are the results of this project—3F_Spring_Newsletter and 3F_Labels. **Exit** Word.

End You have completed Project 3F ――――――――――――――

Content-Based Assessments

Apply 3A and 3B skills from these Objectives:

1. Create a Research Paper
2. Insert Footnotes in a Research Paper
3. Create Citations and a Bibliography in a Research Paper
4. Format a Multiple-Column Newsletter
5. Use Special Character and Paragraph Formatting
6. Create Mailing Labels Using Mail Merge

Mastering Word | Project 3G Economics

In the following Mastering Word project, you will edit and format a newsletter and a research paper for Memphis Primary Materials on the topic of environmental economics. Your completed documents will look similar to Figure 3.45.

Project Files

For Project 3G, you will need the following files:

New blank Word document
w03G_Economics
w03G_Addresses
w03G_April_Newsletter

You will save your documents as:

Lastname_Firstname_3G_Economics
Lastname_Firstname_3G_April_Newsletter
Lastname_Firstname_3G_Labels

Project Results

Figure 3.45

(Project 3G Economics continues on the next page)

Mastering Word | Project **3G** Economics (continued)

1 **Start** Word. Open the document **w03G_April_Newsletter**, and then save the document in your **Word Chapter 3** folder as **Lastname_Firstname_3G_April_Newsletter** Add the file name to the footer. Starting with the paragraph that begins *Research on Environmental Economics*, select all of the text from that point to the end of the document—the document text extends to two pages. Set the **Spacing After** to **6 pt**, format the selected text as two columns, and set the alignment to **Justify**.

2 Near the bottom of the first column, in the paragraph that begins *Maine has already*, click to position the insertion point to the left of the sixth line, which begins *pollutants would*. Insert a column break. At the top of the first column, select the paragraph *Research on Environmental Economics*.

Display the **Font** dialog box, set the **Font Size** to **14**, apply **Bold**, set the **Font color** to **Dark Blue, Text 2**, and then add the **Small caps** effect. **Center** the paragraph. Use the Format Painter to copy the formatting and then apply the same formatting to the paragraph *The Hard Costs of Pollution* located near the bottom of the first column and to *Environmental Economics Conference* in the second column.

3 At the bottom of the second column, select the last two paragraphs of text. From the **Borders and Shading** dialog box, apply a **1 1/2 pt**, **Shadow** border using the **Dark Blue, Text 2** color, and then on the **Shading tab**, apply a **Fill** of **Dark Blue, Text 2, Lighter 80%**.

In the second column, click to position the insertion point at the beginning of the paragraph that begins *Memphis Primary Materials is a cosponsor*. Display the **Clip Art** task pane. Search for **conference** and limit your search to **Illustrations**. **Insert** the image shown in Figure 3.45, apply **Top and Bottom** text wrapping, decrease the **Height** of the image to **1"**, and position the image as shown. **Close** the Clip Art task pane.

Display the **Document Panel** and add your name and course information and the **Keywords April newsletter** **Save** and then **Close** the document. Hold this file until you complete this project.

4 From your student files, open the document **w03G_Economics**, and then save it in your **Word Chapter 3** folder as **Lastname_Firstname_3G_Economics** Display the header area, type **Jaworski** and then press [Spacebar]. In the **Header & Footer group**, add a **Plain Number** from the

Current Position gallery. Apply **Align Text Right** formatting to the header. Move to the footer area and add the file name to the footer.

Select all of the text in the document. Change the **Line Spacing** to **2.0**, and change the **Spacing After** to **0**. Near the top of the document, **Center** the title *Environmental Economics and Business*. Beginning with the text below the centered title, select the text from that point to the end of the document, and then set a **First Line Indent** at **0.5"**.

5 At the bottom of **Page 1**, in the paragraph that begins *Environmental economics also*, in the second line, click to position the insertion point to the right of the comma following *Protocol*, and then insert the following footnote:

> **The Kyoto Protocol is an international agreement under the UN Framework Convention on Climate Change that went into effect in 2005.**

In the next paragraph, which begins *In the United States*, in the second line, position the insertion point to the right of the period following *Economics*, and then insert the following footnote:

> **The NCEE offers a centralized source of technical expertise to the EPA, as well as other federal agencies, Congress, universities, and other organizations.**

Right-click in the footnote, and then modify the style to set the **Font Size** to **11** and the format of the paragraph to include a **First line** indent and double-spacing. **Save** your document.

6 Near the bottom of **Page 1**, in the paragraph that begins *Environmental economists*, position the insertion point to the left of the period at the end of the paragraph. Using **MLA** format, add the following **Article in a Periodical** citation (type the Title on one line):

Author:	Abboud, Leila
Title:	**Economist Strikes Gold in Climate-Change Fight**
Periodical Title:	**The Wall Street Journal**
Year:	**2008**
Month:	**March**
Day:	**13**

(Project 3G Economics continues on the next page)

Content-Based Assessments

Mastering Word | Project **3G** Economics (continued)

Select the *Abboud* citation and add the page number **A1** Near the middle of **Page 2**, in the paragraph that begins *In the United States*, click to position the insertion point to the left of the period at the end of the paragraph. Add the following **Book** citation in **MLA** format (type the Title on one line):

Author:	Tietenberg, Tom; Folmer, Henk, Editors
Title:	The International Yearbook of Environmental Resource Economics, 2006/2007
Year:	2006
City:	Northampton, MA
Publisher:	Edward Elgar Publishers

7 Select the *Tietenberg* citation and add the page number **1** Insert a manual page break at the end of the document. On the new **Page 3**, on the ruler, set the **First Line Indent** to **0"**. Type **Works Cited** and then press Enter.

On the **References tab**, in the **Citations & Bibliography group**, be sure *MLA* displays in the **Style** box. Insert the bibliography. Select the inserted references, set the **Line Spacing** to **2.0**, and then set **Spacing After** to **0 pt**. Center the *Works Cited* title.

Display the **Document Panel** and add your name and course information and the **Keywords environmental**

economics Display the **Print Preview** to check your document, make any necessary adjustments, **Save**, and then **Close** the document. Hold this file until you complete this project.

8 Display a **New** blank document. **Save** the document in your **Word Chapter 3** folder as **Lastname_Firstname_3G_Labels** On the **Mailings tab**, start the **Step by Step Mail Merge Wizard**. In **Step 1**, select **Labels** as the document type. In **Step 2**, set **Label options** to use the **Auto default** tray (yours may vary) and **Avery US Letter 5160**. If you cannot see the gridlines, on the **Layout tab**, in the **Table group**, click **View Gridlines**. In **Step 3**, use an existing list, browse to select **w03G_Addresses**, and then click **OK**.

In **Step 4**, add an **Address block** to the labels, use the *Joshua Randall Jr.* format, and then **Match Fields** by matching *Address 2* to *Unit*. **Update all labels** and then **Preview**. Select all of the label text, and then on the **Page Layout tab**, click in the **Spacing Before** box, type **4** and press Enter. Complete the merge, and then **Close** the **Mail Merge** task pane. Delete the last two empty rows of the table, and then add the file name to the footer, which adds an additional page.

Display the **Document Panel**, and then add your name, course information, and the keywords **mailing labels** Click **Save**. Print or submit electronically your three files that are the results of this project—3G_Economics, 3G_April_Newsletter, and 3G_Labels. **Exit** Word.

End You have completed Project 3G ———————————————

Content-Based Assessments

GO! Fix It | Project 3H Metals Report

Project Files

For Project 3H, you will need the following file:

w03H_Metals_Report

You will save your document as:

Lastname_Firstname_3H_Metals_Report

From the student files that accompany this textbook, locate and open the file w03H_Metals_Report, and then save the file in your Word Chapter 3 folder as **Lastname_Firstname_3H_Metals_Report**

This document contains errors that you must find and correct. Read and examine the document, and then edit to correct any errors that you find and to improve the overall document format. Types of errors could include, but are not restricted to:

- Formatting does not match MLA style guidelines that you practiced in the chapter
- Incorrect header format
- Incorrect spacing between paragraphs
- Incorrect paragraph indents
- Incorrect line spacing
- Incorrect footnote format
- Incorrectly formatted reference page

Things you should know to complete this project:

- Displaying formatting marks will assist in locating spacing errors.
- There are no errors in the parenthetical references in the document.
- There are no errors in the information in the footnotes or bibliographical references.

Save your document and add the file name to the footer. In the Document Panel, add your name, course information, and the keywords **valuable metals, recycling** Save your document and submit as directed.

End **You have completed Project 3H** ————————————————————

Content-Based Assessments

Apply a combination of the **3A** and **3B** skills.

GO! Make It | Project 3I Green Newsletter

Project Files

For Project 3I, you will need the following files:

New blank Word document   w03I_Kids
w03I_Competition

You will save your document as:

Lastname_Firstname_3I_Green_Newsletter

Start with a new Word document, and then save the file in your chapter folder as **Lastname_Firstname_3I_Green_Newsletter** Create the document shown in Figure 3.46. Create a nameplate, and then insert the files w03I_Competition and w03I_Kids. The title is Arial Black, 24 pt, Dark Blue, Text 2. Other titles and borders are Dark Blue, Text 2. The two titles in the columns are Calibri, 16 pt. The clip art image can be found by using the search term **recycle** and the screenshot can be found at the Web address in the last line of the newsletter.

Add the file name to the footer; in the Document Panel, add your name and course information and the Keywords **green, campuses, kids** Save your document and submit as directed.

Project Results

Memphis Primary Materials

Volume 1, Number 4   April 2016

THE COMPETITIVE SPIRIT OF GREEN

One way to increase people's willingness to reuse and recycle is to invoke their spirit of competition—and prizes do not hurt either. College campuses are proving this by participating in the America's Greenest Campus competition.

America's Greenest Campus is a nationwide contest, with the goal of reducing the carbon footprint of entire campus populations across the country.

Partnering with Smart Power and the U.S. Department of Energy, the winning campus will receive a donation of $10,000. As of February 2009, the University of Maryland has reduced its CO2 emissions by 2% and George Mason University by 3%.

Students, faculty, and staff are encouraged to recycle, turn off lights, reduce heating and air conditioning, and engage in many other small and large changes that can help the environment. Treehugger.com calls the contest, "the NCAA of sustainability."

Another college competition for environmentalism is RecycleMania. Designed to encourage colleges and universities to reduce waste, the competition collects reports on recycling and trash over a 10-week period. This competition thinks of colleges and universities as small cities that consume large amounts of resources and generate a lot of solid waste. Participating campuses are ranked by categories such as "least amount of waste per capita." Weekly results are distributed to the participants so they can benchmark against their competition and step up their efforts.

With growing awareness of the need to reduce, reuse, and recycle among students, expect some competition if you are part of a campus community!

CLEANUP IS FOR KIDS

Cleaning up the planet isn't just for college students. Younger students often have a desire to get involved with environmental activities, and there is no shortage of resources.

Start at the website of the Environmental Protection Agency. They provide resources like Cleanup for Kids, a Web site of the National Oceanic and Atmospheric Administration (NOAA), which makes the hazards of oil spills real through science demonstrations. The brochure, *Environmental Protection Begins With You*, outlines examples of community volunteer projects in which students can participate.

Learn more at the EPA website:
http://www.epa.gov/highschool/waste.htm

Lastname_Firstname_3I_Green_Newsletter

Figure 3.46

End You have completed Project 3I

Content-Based Assessments

GO! Solve It | Project **3J** Municipal Newsletter

Project Files

For Project 3J, you will need the following file:

New blank Word document

You will save your document as:

Lastname_Firstname_3J_Municipal_Newsletter

Memphis Primary Materials writes an informational newsletter for customers. Create a new document and save it in your Word Chapter 3 folder as **Lastname_Firstname_3J_Municipal_Newsletter** Use the following information to create a newsletter that includes a nameplate, multiple columns, at least two articles with article titles formatted so that they stand out, at least one clip art image, one screenshot, and one paragraph that includes a border and shading.

This issue (Volume 1, Number 6—June 2016) will focus on municipal solid waste—the waste generated by householders and small businesses. This category of waste does not include hazardous, industrial, or construction waste. The articles you write can be on any topic regarding municipal waste, and might include an introduction to the topic and a discussion of recycling in the U.S. or in the Memphis community. You will need to research this topic on the Web. A good place to start is www.epa.gov, which has many articles on solid municipal waste, and also provides links to further articles on the topic. You might also consider doing a Web search for the term **municipal solid waste recycling**

Add the file name to the footer. To the Document Panel, add your name, your course name and section number, and the keywords **municipal solid waste recycling**

Performance Level			
Performance Element	**Exemplary:** You consistently applied the relevant skills	**Proficient:** You sometimes, but not always, applied the relevant skills	**Developing:** You rarely or never applied the relevant skills
Create and format nameplate	The nameplate includes both the company name and the date and volume information, and is formatted attractively.	One or more of the nameplate elements are done correctly, but other items are either omitted or not formatted properly.	The newsletter does not include a nameplate.
Insert at least two articles in multiple-column format	The newsletter contains at least two articles, displayed in multiple columns that are well written and are free of grammar and spelling errors.	The newsletter contains only one article, or the text is not divided into two columns, or there are spelling and grammar errors in the text.	The newsletter contains only one article, the article is not divided into multiple columns, and there are spelling and grammar errors.
Insert and format at least one clip art image	An appropriate clip art image is included. The image is sized and positioned appropriately.	A clip art image is inserted, but is either inappropriate, or is formatted or positioned poorly.	No clip art image is included.
Border and shading added to a paragraph	One or more paragraphs display an attractive border with shading that enables the reader to read the text.	A border or shading is displayed, but not both; or, the shading is too dark to enable the reader to easily read the text.	No border or shading is added to a paragraph.
Insert a screenshot	A screenshot is inserted in one of the columns; the screenshot is related to the content of the article.	A screenshot is inserted in the document, but does not relate to the content of the article.	No screenshot is inserted.

End You have completed Project 3J

Content-Based Assessments

Apply a combination of the **3A** and **3B** skills.

GO! Solve It | Project **3K** Paper Report

Project Files

For Project 3K, you will need the following file:

New blank Word document

You will save your document as:

Lastname_Firstname_3K_Paper_Report

Create a new file and save it as **Lastname_Firstname_3K_Paper_Report** Use the following information to create a report written in the MLA format. The report should include at least two footnotes, at least two citations, and should include a *Works Cited* page.

Memphis Primary Materials writes and distributes informational reports on topics of interest to the people of Memphis. This report will be written by Sarah Stanger for the head of Marketing, Henry Miller. Information reports are provided as a public service of the company, and are distributed free of charge.

The topic of the report is recycling and reuse of paper and paper products. The report should contain an introduction, and then details about how much paper is used, what it is used for, the increase of paper recycling over time, and how paper products can be recycled or reused. A good place to start is www.epa.gov, which has many articles on paper use and recycling, and also provides links to further articles on the topic. You might also consider doing a Web search for the terms **paper recycling**

Add the file name to the footer, and add your name, your course name and section number, and the keywords **paper products, recycling** to the Document Panel.

Performance Element	Performance Level		
	Exemplary: You consistently applied the relevant skills	**Proficient:** You sometimes, but not always, applied the relevant skills	**Developing:** You rarely or never applied the relevant skills
Format the header and heading	The last name and page number are right-aligned in the header, and the report has a four-line heading and a centered title.	The header and heading are included, but are not formatted according to MLA style guidelines.	The header or heading is missing or incomplete.
Format the body of the report	The report is double-spaced, with no space after paragraphs. The first lines of paragraphs are indented 0.5".	Some, but not all, of the report formatting is correct.	The majority of the formatting does not follow MLA guidelines.
Footnotes are included and formatted correctly	Two or more footnotes are included, and the footnote text is 11 pt, double-spaced, and the first line of each footnote is indented.	The correct number of footnotes is included, but the footnotes are not formatted properly.	No footnotes are included.
Citations and bibliography are included and formatted according to MLA guidelines	At least two citations are included in parenthetical references, with page numbers where appropriate, and the sources are included in a properly formatted Works Cited page.	Only one citation is included, or the citations and sources are not formatted correctly.	No citations or Works Cited page are included.

End You have completed Project 3K

Outcomes-Based Assessments

Rubric

The following outcomes-based assessments are *open-ended assessments*. That is, there is no specific correct result; your result will depend on your approach to the information provided. Make *Professional Quality* your goal. Use the following scoring rubric to guide you in *how* to approach the problem, and then to evaluate *how well* your approach solves the problem.

The *criteria*—Software Mastery, Content, Format and Layout, and Process—represent the knowledge and skills you have gained that you can apply to solving the problem. The *levels of performance*—Professional Quality, Approaching Professional Quality, or Needs Quality Improvements—help you and your instructor evaluate your result.

	Your completed project is of Professional Quality if you:	Your completed project is Approaching Professional Quality if you:	Your completed project Needs Quality Improvements if you:
1-Software Mastery	Choose and apply the most appropriate skills, tools, and features and identify efficient methods to solve the problem.	Choose and apply some appropriate skills, tools, and features, but not in the most efficient manner.	Choose inappropriate skills, tools, or features, or are inefficient in solving the problem.
2-Content	Construct a solution that is clear and well organized, contains content that is accurate, appropriate to the audience and purpose, and is complete. Provide a solution that contains no errors in spelling, grammar, or style.	Construct a solution in which some components are unclear, poorly organized, inconsistent, or incomplete. Misjudge the needs of the audience. Have some errors in spelling, grammar, or style, but the errors do not detract from comprehension.	Construct a solution that is unclear, incomplete, or poorly organized; contains some inaccurate or inappropriate content; and contains many errors in spelling, grammar, or style. Do not solve the problem.
3-Format and Layout	Format and arrange all elements to communicate information and ideas, clarify function, illustrate relationships, and indicate relative importance.	Apply appropriate format and layout features to some elements, but not others. Overuse features, causing minor distraction.	Apply format and layout that does not communicate information or ideas clearly. Do not use format and layout features to clarify function, illustrate relationships, or indicate relative importance. Use available features excessively, causing distraction.
4-Process	Use an organized approach that integrates planning, development, self-assessment, revision, and reflection.	Demonstrate an organized approach in some areas, but not others; or, use an insufficient process of organization throughout.	Do not use an organized approach to solve the problem.

Outcomes-Based Assessments

Apply a combination of the **3A** and **3B** skills.

GO! Think | Project **3L** Jobs Newsletter

Project Files

For Project 3L, you will need the following file:

New blank Word document

You will save your document as:

Lastname_Firstname_3L_Jobs_Newsletter

The marketing manager of Memphis Primary Materials needs to create the next issue of the company's monthly newsletter (Volume 1, Number 7—July 2016), which will focus on "green jobs." Green jobs are jobs associated with environmentally friendly companies or are positions with firms that manufacture, sell, or install energy-saving or resource-saving products.

Use the following information to create a newsletter that includes a nameplate, multiple columns, at least two articles with article titles formatted so that they stand out, at least one clip art image, one screenshot, and one paragraph that includes a border and shading.

The articles you write can be on any topic regarding green jobs, and might include an introduction to the topic, information about a recent (or future) green job conference, and a discussion of green jobs in the United States. You will need to research this topic on the Web. A good place to start is www.epa.gov. You might also consider doing a Web search for the terms **green jobs** or **green jobs conference**

Add the file name to the footer. Add appropriate information to the Document Panel. Save the document as **Lastname_Firstname_3L_Jobs_Newsletter** and submit it as directed.

 You have completed Project 3L ⸻⸻⸻⸻⸻

Apply a combination of the **3A** and **3B** skills.

GO! Think | Project **3M** Construction Report

Project Files

For Project 3M, you will need the following file:

New blank Word document

You will save your document as:

Lastname_Firstname_3M_Construction_Report

As part of the ongoing research provided on environment topics by the staff of Memphis Primary Materials, the Marketing Director, Henry Miller, has asked a summer intern, James Bodine, to create a report on recycling and reuse in the construction and demolition of buildings.

Create a new file and save it as **Lastname_Firstname_3M_Construction_Report** Use the following information to create a report written in the MLA format. The report should include at least two footnotes, at least two citations, and should include a *Works Cited* page.

The report should contain an introduction, and then details about, for example, how much construction material can be salvaged from existing buildings, how these materials can be reused in future buildings, and how materials can be saved and recycled on new building projects. A good place to start is www.epa.gov, which has a number of articles on recycling and reuse of materials during construction and demolition. You might also consider doing a Web search for the terms **construction recycling** or **demolition recycling** or **construction and demolition**

Add the file name to the footer. Add appropriate information to the Document Panel and submit it as directed.

 You have completed Project 3M ⸻⸻⸻⸻⸻

Outcomes-Based Assessments

You and GO! | Project **3N** College Newsletter

Project Files

For Project 3N, you will need the following file:

> New blank Word document

You will save your document as

> Lastname_Firstname_3N_College_Newsletter

In this project, you will create a one-page newsletter. The newsletter should include at least one article describing your college and one article about an academic or athletic program at your college.

Be sure to include a nameplate, at least two articles, at least one clip art or screenshot image, and a bordered paragraph or paragraphs. Before you submit the newsletter, be sure to check it for grammar and spelling errors, and also be sure to format the newsletter in an attractive manner by using the skills you practiced in this chapter.

Save the file as **Lastname_Firstname_3N_College_Newsletter** Add the file name to the footer, and add your name, your course name and section number, and the keywords **newsletter** and **college** to the Document Panel. Save and submit your file as directed.

End **You have completed Project 3N** ——————————————————

Business Running Case

Razvan CHIRNOAGA/Shutterstock

This project relates to **Front Range Action Sports**, which is one of the country's largest retailers of sports gear and outdoor recreation merchandise. The company has large retail stores in Colorado, Washington, Oregon, California, and New Mexico, in addition to a growing online business. Major merchandise categories include fishing, camping, rock climbing, winter sports, action sports, water sports, team sports, racquet sports, fitness, golf, apparel, and footwear.

In this project, you will apply skills you practiced from the Objectives in Word Chapters 1-3. You will assist Irene Shviktar, the Vice President of Marketing, to edit and create documents for a National Sales Meeting that will precede a Winter Sports Expo sponsored by Front Range Action Sports. The first document is a cover letter from the vice president to the company president. The letter will accompany a packet of materials for the meeting and the expo, which includes a brief resume for the guest speaker, a flyer that will announce the expo, a newsletter for employees, a research paper on the history and development of skis, and a set of name tags for a group of employees attending the national sales meeting. Your completed documents will look similar to Figure 1.1.

Project Files

For Project BRC1, you will need the following files:

> New blank Word document
> wBRC1_Cover_Letter_Text
> wBRC1_Newsletter
> wBRC1_Career_Text
> wBRC1_Ski_Research
> wBRC1_Addresses
> wBRC1_Flyer_Text
> wBRC1_Downhill_Racing
> wBRC1_Powder_Skiing

You will save your documents as:

> Lastname_Firstname_BRC1_Cover_Letter
> Lastname_Firstname_BRC1_Newsletter
> Lastname_Firstname_BRC1_Resume
> Lastname_Firstname_BRC1_Ski_Research
> Lastname_Firstname_BRC1_Name_Tags
> Lastname_Firstname_BRC1_Flyer

Project Results

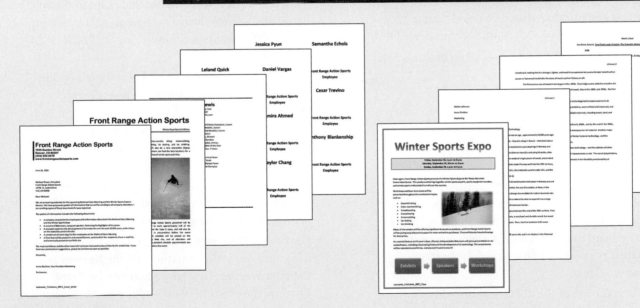

Figure 1.1

Business Running Case

Front Range Action Sports

1 **Start** Word and display a new document. Display rulers and formatting marks. In the location where you are storing your projects, create a new folder named **Front Range Action Sports** or navigate to this folder if you have already created it. **Save** the new document as **Lastname_Firstname_BRC1_Cover_Letter** Add the file name to the footer. Apply the **No Spacing** style to the document, and then type the following to form a letterhead:

Front Range Action Sports

1926 Quebec Street

Denver, CO 80207

(303) 555-0970

www.frontrangeactionsports.com

a. Press [Enter] to create a blank line below the letterhead. If the Web address changes to blue, right-click the address, and then from the shortcut menu, remove the hyperlink.

b. Select the letterhead text, but not the blank line. Change the **Font** to **Arial Rounded MT Bold**. Select the first line, and increase the **Font Size** to **28 pt** Change the **Font Size** of the remaining four lines to **12 pt**. Select all five lines of the letterhead, display the **Borders and Shading** dialog box, and then create a **6 pt**, **Black** border on the left side of the selected text.

c. Enter the following information using business letter format:

June 26, 2016

Michael Dixon, President

Front Range Action Sports

12756 St. Aubin Drive

Vail, CO 81658

d. Press [Enter] two times. With the insertion point in the second blank line below the inside address, **Insert** the text from the file **wBRC1_Cover_Letter_Text**, and then remove the blank line at the bottom of the selected text.

e. Move to the top of the document, and then by using either the **Spelling and Grammar** dialog box, or by right-clicking selected words, correct the *three* spelling, grammar, and word usage errors. Ignore proper names. In the paragraph that begins *If you have any*, select the first sentence and move it to the end of the paragraph.

f. In the middle of the document, select the five paragraphs beginning with *A company newsletter*, and create a bulleted list. In the fourth bullet, select the text *national sales meeting*, and then on the **Home tab**, in the **Font group**, click the **Change Case** button [Aa▾], and then click **Capitalize Each Word**.

g. Display the **Document Panel**, add your name, course information, and the **Keywords expo, national sales meeting** View your document in **Print Preview,** make any necessary adjustments, **Save** and **Close** your document, and then hold this file until you complete the project.

2 From your student files, open **wBRC1_Newsletter**, and then **Save** it in your **Front Range Action Sports** folder as **Lastname_Firstname_BRC1_Newsletter** Add the file name to the footer.

a. Select the first paragraph of text—*Front Range Action Sports*. Change the **Font** to **Arial Rounded MT Bold**, the **Font Size** to **36**, and **Center** the text. Select the second paragraph of text, display the **Borders and Shading** dialog box, and then add a **Black**, **3 pt** line below the selected text.

b. Starting with the paragraph that begins *National Sales*, select all of the text from that point to the end of the document. Change the **Spacing After** to **6 pt**, format the text in two columns, and apply the **Justify** alignment.

c. At the top of the first column, select the paragraph *National Sales Meeting*. From the **Font** dialog box, change the **Font Size** to **20**, apply **Bold**, add the **Small caps** effect, and then **Center** the paragraph. Near the bottom of the same column, apply the same formatting to the paragraph *Winter Sports Expo*.

d. In the blank line above the last paragraph of the newsletter, **Insert** the picture **wBRC1_Powder_Skiing**. Set the **Width** of the picture to **3"**.

e. Display the **Document Panel**, and then add your name and course information and the **Keywords Expo newsletter** View your document in **Print Preview,** make any necessary adjustments, **Save** and **Close** your document, and then hold this file until you complete the project.

3 Display a new blank document and **Save** it in your **Front Range Action Sports** folder as **Lastname_Firstname_BRC1_Resume** Add the file name to the footer. **Insert** a **2 × 3** table.

(Business Running Case: Front Range Action Sports continues on the next page)

Business Running Case

Front Range Action Sports (continued)

a. In the first cell of the table, type on four lines:

Robert Lewis

1227 Aspen Lake Trail

Vail, CO 81657

www.boblewisskis.com

b. In the second row, in the first cell, type **CAREER HIGHLIGHTS** In the cell to the immediate right, **Insert** the text from the file **wBRC1_Career_Text**, and then press Backspace to remove the blank line at the bottom of the inserted text.

c. In the third row, in the first cell, type **EDUCATION** In the cell to the right, type Mr. Lewis' educational information as follows:

University of Colorado

Ph.D. in Psychology

University of Colorado

M.S. in Psychology

University of Minnesota

B.S. in Psychology

d. Insert a new row at the bottom of the table. In the first cell of the new row, type **CONSULTANT** and then in the cell to the right, type the following:

U.S. Junior Ski Team

U.S. National Ski Team

Special Olympics

e. Apply **Bold** to the headings *CAREER HIGHLIGHTS*, *EDUCATION*, and *CONSULTANT*. Drag the vertical border between the two columns to approximately **1.5 inches on the horizontal ruler**.

f. In the first row, **Merge** the two cells, and then **Center** the text. Select *Robert Lewis*, increase the font size to **24 pt**, apply **Bold**, and then add **12 pt** spacing **Before** the text. If necessary, remove the hyperlink from the Web address. Select the Web address and add **18 pt** spacing after the text.

g. Create a bulleted list for the items below *SKIING* and below *COACHING*. In the cells to the right of *EDUCATION* and *CONSULTANT*, add **12 pt** spacing **After** the last item in each cell. Add **12 pt** spacing **After** *Ph.D. in Psychology* and *M.S. in Psychology*. Apply **Bold** to the three paragraphs that begin *University*.

h. Select the table, and then remove all borders. From the **Borders and Shading** dialog box, add a **3 pt** border to the top and bottom of the table. Change the top

margin to **1.5"**. To the **Document Panel**, add your name, course information, and the **Keywords Robert Lewis resume** View your document in **Print Preview,** make any necessary adjustments, **Save** and then **Close** your document. Hold this file until you complete the project.

4 From your student files, open the document **wBRC1_ Ski_Research**. **Save** the document in your **Front Range Action Sports** folder as **Lastname_Firstname_BRC1_ Ski_Research** Display the header area, type **Johnson** and then press Spacebar. Display the **Page Number gallery**, and then in the **Current Position**, add the **Plain Number** style. Apply **Align Text Right** formatting to the header. Add the file name to the footer.

a. In the blank line at the beginning of the document, type **Walter Johnson** and then press Enter. Type **Irene Shviktar** and press Enter. Type **Marketing** and press Enter. Type **June 5, 2016**

b. Select all of the text in the document. Change the **Line Spacing** to **2.0**, and then change the **Spacing After** to **0 pt**. Click anywhere in the title that begins *The Evolution* and then **Center** the title.

c. Beginning with the paragraph that begins *The use of skis*, select the text from that point to the end of the document. Indent the first line of each selected paragraph to **0.5"**.

d. Near the top of **Page 1**, in the paragraph that begins *The use of skis*, in the third line, position the insertion point to the right of the period following *wood*, and then insert the following footnote:

The oldest known ski and pole is more than 4,000 years old, and is on display in the National Ski Hall of Fame and Museum in Ishpeming, Michigan.

e. Select the footnote text, change the **Font Size** to **11 pt**, add a **First Line Indent** of **0.5"**, and set **Line spacing** to **2.0"**.

f. In the paragraph that begins *The use of skis*, position the insertion point to the left of the period at the end of the paragraph. Using the **MLA** format, insert the following **Book** citation:

Author: **Huntford, Roland**

Title: **Two Planks and a Passion: The Dramatic History of Skiing**

Year: **2008**

City: **New York**

Publisher: **Continuum Press**

(Business Running Case: Front Range Action Sports continues on the next page)

Business Running Case

Front Range Action Sports (continued)

g. In the text, select the *Huntford* citation and insert the page numbers **4-6** Position the insertion point to the left of the period at the end of the document. Add the following **Web site** citation:

Author:	**Lund, Morten; Masia, Seth**
Name of Web Page:	**A Short History of Skis**
Year Accessed:	**2016**
Month Accessed:	**May**
Day Accessed:	**25**
URL:	**www.skiinghistory.org**

h. At the end of the document, insert a manual page break to create a new page. Change the **First Line Indent** to 0". Add a **Works Cited** title, display the **Bibliography** gallery, and then at the bottom of the gallery, click **Insert Bibliography**. Select the two references, remove the space after the paragraphs, and change the line spacing to **2.0**. **Center** the *Works Cited* title.

i. Press $\boxed{\text{Ctrl}}$ + $\boxed{\text{A}}$ to move to the top of the document, and then on the **Review tab**, in the **Proofing group**, click **Spelling & Grammar**. Ignore proper names, change *polyethelene* to *polyethylene*, and correct the subject-verb agreement between *have* and *has* in the last paragraph. Display the **Document Panel** and add your name and course information and the **Keywords ski history, ski research** View your document in **Print Preview** and make any necessary adjustments. **Save** and **Close** your document, and hold this file until you complete the project.

5 Display a **New** blank document. Start the **Step by Step Mail Merge Wizard** and select **Labels** as the document type. In **Step 2**, set **Label options** to use the **Auto default** tray (yours may vary) and **Avery US Letter 74541 Clip Style Name Badges**. In **Step 3**, **Use an existing list**, browse to select **wBRC1_Addresses**, click **Open**, and then click **OK**. This is a Name Badge label, and the steps differ slightly from the steps for creating mailing labels.

a. In **Step 4**, on the Ribbon, in the **Write & Insert Fields group**, click the **Insert Merge Field button arrow**, click **First_Name** field, press $\boxed{\text{Spacebar}}$, and then repeat for the **Last_Name** field. Press $\boxed{\text{Enter}}$ six times.

b. Type **Front Range Action Sports** and press $\boxed{\text{Enter}}$. Type **Employee** Select the first line of the label—

<<First_Name>> <<Last_Name>>. Change the **Font Size** to **24**, apply **Bold**, and then **Center** the text. Select the last two lines of text, change the **Font Size** to **18**, apply **Bold**, and then **Center** the text. In the **Mail Merge** task pane, click **Update all labels**, and then move to step 5—**Preview your labels**.

c. **Complete the merge**. On the **Mailings tab**, in the **Finish group**, click the **Finish & Merge** button, and then click **Edit Individual Documents**. Merge **All** of the records. **Save** the resulting document in your **Front Range Action Sports** folder as **Lastname_ Firstname_BRC1_Name_Tags** and then if necessary, close the Mail Merge task pane. Add the file name to the footer. Preview the labels in **Print Preview** and make any necessary adjustments.

d. Display the **Document Panel**, and then add your name and course information and the **Keywords name tags, expo Save** and close your label document. **Close** the original document without saving. Hold this file until you complete the project.

6 From your student files, open **wBRC1_Flyer_Text**, and then **Save** it in your **Front Range Action Sports** folder as **Lastname_Firstname_BRC1_Flyer** Add the file name to the footer.

a. Select the title *Winter Sports Expo*, and apply a **Gradient Fill - Blue, Accent 1 Text Effect**—in the third row, the fourth effect. Increase the **Font Size** to **56** point, and then **Center** the title. Select the two paragraphs below the title that begin *Friday* and *Saturday*, and then change the **Spacing After** to **0**. Select the three paragraphs below the title—the three days and times—and then **Center** and apply **Bold**.

b. With the three paragraphs still selected, display the **Borders and Shading** dialog box. Apply a **Box** border using theme color **Blue, Accent 1** and a **3 pt** border, and add **Shading** using theme color **Blue, Accent 1, Lighter 80%**. Apply a **Page Border** using the **Box** setting, and the theme color **Blue, Accent 1** with a **Weight** of **6 pt**.

c. Format the seven sport topics—beginning with *Downhill skiing*—as a bulleted list, and then click anywhere to deselect the bulleted list. **Insert** the picture **wBRC1_Downhill_Racing**. Change the **Width** of the picture to **3.5"**, and then set **Wrap Text** to **Square**. Move the picture so that the right edge

(Business Running Case: Front Range Action Sports continues on the next page)

Front Range Action Sports (continued)

aligns with the right margin, and the top edge aligns with the top edge of the text that begins *Workshops and how-to*. Apply a **Picture Effect** using the **Soft Edge** of **10 point**.

d. Move to the end of the document and press ⏎Enter two times. Display the **Choose a SmartArt Graphic** dialog box, select **Process**, and then choose the first style—**Basic Process**. Click the border of the SmartArt graphic to deselect the first box. On the **Format tab**, set the **Width** of the SmartArt graphic to **6.5"** and the **Height** to **1"**; or, drag the SmartArt graphic sizing handles to change the width to **6.5"** and the height to **1"**.

In the three boxes, add the following text in this order: **Exhibits** and **Speakers** and **Workshops** On the **Design tab**, apply the **3-D Polished** style. Click anywhere outside of the SmartArt to deselect it. Display your document in **Print Preview** and make any necessary adjustments.

e. Display the **Document Panel** and add your name and course information and the **Keywords expo, flyer Save** and **Close** the document. Submit the six files that you created in this project—the cover letter, newsletter, resume, research paper, name tag labels, and flyer—as directed by your instructor. **Exit** Word.

End **You have completed Business Running Case 1** ———————————

Using Styles and Creating Multilevel Lists and Charts

OUTCOMES

At the end of this chapter you will be able to:

OBJECTIVES

Mastering these objectives will enable you to:

PROJECT 4A

Edit a handout using Quick Styles and arrange text into an organized list.

1. Apply and Modify Quick Styles (p. 227)
2. Create New Styles (p. 230)
3. Manage Styles (p. 232)
4. Create a Multilevel List (p. 236)

PROJECT 4B

Change a style set, and create and format a chart.

5. Change the Style Set and Paragraph Spacing of a Document (p. 244)
6. Insert a Chart and Enter Data into a Chart (p. 247)
7. Change a Chart Type (p. 253)
8. Format a Chart (p. 254)

© Steve Murray / Alamy

In This Chapter

In this chapter you will apply styles, create multilevel lists, and display numerical data in charts. You can draw attention to text by using formatting tools. The theme and style set features in Word provide a simple way to coordinate colors, fonts, and effects used in a document. For example, if you publish a monthly newsletter, you can apply styles to article headings and modify lists to ensure all editions of the newsletter maintain a consistent and professional look.

Charts display numerical data in a visual format. You can use charts to show a comparison among items, to show the relationship of each part to a whole, or to show trends over time. Formatting chart elements adds interest and assists the reader in interpreting the displayed data.

The projects in this chapter relate to **Lehua Hawaiian Adventures**. Named for the small, crescent-shaped island that is noted for its snorkeling and scuba diving, Lehua Hawaiian Adventures offers exciting but affordable adventure tours. Hiking tours go off the beaten path to amazing remote places on the islands. If you prefer to ride into the heart of Hawaii, try the cycling tours. Lehua Hawaiian Adventures also offers Jeep tours. Whatever you prefer—mountain, sea, volcano—our tour guides are experts in the history, geography, culture, and flora and fauna of Hawaii.

Project 4A Customer Handout

myitlab
Project 4A Training

Project Activities

In Activities 4.1 through 4.10, you will create a handout for Lehua Hawaiian Adventures customers who are interested in scuba diving tours. You will use styles and multilevel list formats so that the document is attractive and easy to read. Your completed document will look similar to Figure 4.1.

Project Files

For Project 4A, you will need the following file:

w04A_Customer_Handout

You will save your document as:

Lastname_Firstname_4A_Customer_Handout

Project Results

Lehua Hawaiian Adventures

Requirements for Scuba Diving Trips

Lehua Hawaiian Adventures offers several tours that include scuba diving. For any tours where equipment will be rented, facilitators must ensure that several pieces of safety equipment are available for each participant.

Please notify us when you book a tour if you would like us to supply any of the following scuba gear for you. We are happy to do so at a reasonable price.

Equipment

1. **Air Tank**
   - The air tank holds high-pressure breathing gas. Typically, each diver needs just one air tank. Contrary to common perception, the air tank does not hold pure oxygen; rather, it is filled with compressed air that is about 21 percent oxygen and 79 percent nitrogen.
     - Examples: Aluminum, steel, pony
2. **Buoyancy Compensator**
   - The buoyancy compensator controls the overall buoyancy of the diver so that descending and ascending can be controlled.
     - Examples: Wings, stab jacket, life jacket
3. **Regulator**
   - A regulator controls the pressure of the breathing gas supplied to the diver to make it safe and comfortable to inhale.
     - Examples: Constant flow, twin-hose
4. **Weights**
   - Weights add just enough weight to help the diver descend rather than float. The right amount of weight will not cause the diver to sink.
     - Examples: Weight belt, integrated weight systems

Attire

1. **Dry Suits**
   - A dry suit is intended to insulate and protect the diver's skin. Dry suits are different from wet suits in that they prevent water from entering the suits.
     - Examples: Membrane, neoprene, hybrid
2. **Wet Suits**
   - A wet suit insulates and protects, whether in cool or warm water. Wet suits differ from dry suits in that a small amount of water gets between the suit and the diver's skin.
     - Examples: Two millimeter, 2.5 millimeter, 3 millimeter, 5 millimeter, 7 millimeter, Titanium

Lastname_Firstname_4A_Customer_Handout

Figure 4.1
Project 4A Customer Handout

Objective 1 | Apply and Modify Quick Styles

A **style** is a group of formatting commands, such as font, font size, font color, paragraph alignment, and line spacing. You can retrieve a style by name and apply it to text with one click.

Using styles to format text has several advantages over using **direct formatting**—the process of applying each format separatcly; for example, bold, then font size, then font color, and so on. Styles are faster to apply, result in a consistent look, and can be automatically updated in all instances in a document, which can be especially useful in long documents.

Activity 4.01 | Applying Quick Styles

Quick Styles are combinations of formatting options that work together and look attractive together. A collection of frequently used Quick Styles is available from the Quick Styles gallery on the Ribbon. Each Quick Style option has a name—for example, *Subtitle* or *Heading 1*. A Quick Style can be applied to any selected text.

1 **Start** Word. Click the **File tab** to display **Backstage** view, and then click **Open**. From your student files, locate and open the document **w04A_Customer_Handout**.

2 Click the **File tab**, and then click **Save As**. In the **Save As** dialog box, navigate to the location where you are saving your files for this chapter. Create a new folder named **Word Chapter 4 Save** the document as **Lastname_Firstname_4A_Customer_Handout**

3 Scroll to the bottom of **Page 1**, right-click in the footer area, click **Edit Footer**, and then using **Quick Parts**, insert the file name. **Close** the footer area. If necessary, display the rulers and formatting marks.

4 Press Ctrl + Home to move to the top of the document. If *Lehua* is flagged as a spelling error, point to the first occurrence, right-click, and then click **Ignore All**.

5 On the **Home tab**, in the **Styles group**, notice that the **Normal** style is selected—outlined in orange. Compare your screen with Figure 4.2.

The **Normal Quick Style** is the default style for new documents and includes default styles and customizations that determine the basic look of a document. For example, the Normal Quick Style includes the Calibri font, 11 point font size, multiple line spacing at 1.15, and 10 pt spacing after a paragraph.

Figure 4.2

Normal style selected

Styles group

6 Including the paragraph mark, select the first paragraph, which forms the title of the document. On the **Home tab**, in the **Styles group**, click the **More** button ⊡ to display the **Quick Styles** gallery. Point to the **Quick Style** named **Title**, and then compare your screen with Figure 4.3.

> Live Preview displays how the text will look with this style applied.

Figure 4.3

Normal style

Title style

Quick Styles gallery—
your view may differ

Live Preview shows
how style will display

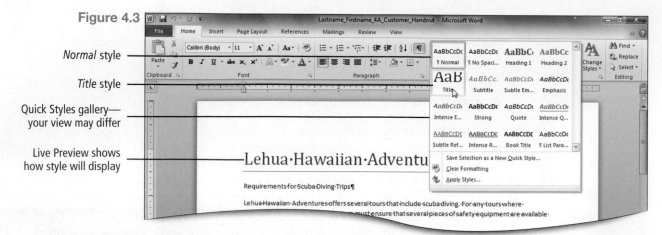

7 Click the **Title** style, and then click anywhere in the document to deselect the title.

> The Title style includes the 26 point Cambria font, a dark blue font color, and a line that spans the width of the document.

8 Select the second paragraph, which begins *Requirements for* and is the subtitle of the document. In the **Styles group**, click the **More** button ⊡, and then from the displayed **Quick Styles** gallery, click the **Subtitle** style.

> The Subtitle style includes the 12 point Cambria font, italic emphasis, and a blue font color.

9 Select the third and fourth paragraphs, beginning with *Lehua Hawaiian Adventures offers* and ending with the text *at a reasonable price*. In the **Styles group**, click the **More** button ⊡, and then from the displayed **Quick Styles** gallery, click the **Emphasis** style. Click anywhere to deselect the text, and then compare your screen with Figure 4.4.

Figure 4.4

Title style applied

Subtitle style applied

Emphasis style applied

10 **Save** 💾 your document.

Activity 4.02 | Modifying Quick Styles

You are not limited to the exact formatting of a Quick Style—you can change it to suit your needs. For example, you might like the effect of a Quick Style with the exception of the font size. If you plan to use such a customized style repeatedly in a document, it's a good idea to modify the style to look exactly the way you want it, and then save it as a *new* Quick Style.

1 Select the heading *Equipment*. Using the technique you practiced, display the **Quick Styles** gallery, and then click the **Heading 1** style.

> The Heading 1 style includes the 14 point Cambria font, bold emphasis, a blue font color, and 24 pt spacing before the paragraph.
>
> A small black square displays to the left of the paragraph indicating that the Heading 1 style also includes the *Keep with next* and *Keep lines together* formatting—Word commands that keep a heading with its first paragraph of text on the same page, or prevent a single line from displaying by itself at the bottom of a page or at the top of a page.

2 With the paragraph selected, on the displayed Mini toolbar, change the **Font Size** to **16**.

3 Click the **Page Layout tab**, and then in the **Paragraph group**, change the **Spacing Before** to **12 pt**.

4 With the paragraph still selected, click the **Home tab**. Display the **Quick Styles** gallery, and then right-click the **Heading 1** style to display a shortcut menu. Compare your screen with Figure 4.5.

Figure 4.5

Heading 1 style

Font size changed to 16

Shortcut menu

Selected text

5 From the displayed shortcut menu, click **Update Heading 1 to Match Selection**, and then click anywhere to deselect the text.

> By updating the heading style, you ensure that the next time you apply the Heading 1 style in *this* document, it will retain these new formats. In this manner, you can customize a style. The changes to the Heading 1 style are stored *only* in this document and will not affect the Heading 1 style in any other documents.

6 Scroll down to view the lower portion of **Page 1**, and then select the heading *Attire*. In the **Styles group**, click **Heading 1**, and notice that the *modified* **Heading 1** style is applied to the paragraph. Click anywhere in the document to deselect the text. **Save** 💾 your document.

Activity 4.03 | Changing the Theme

Recall that a theme is a predefined combination of colors, fonts, and effects; the *Office* theme is the default setting. Quick Styles use the color scheme, font scheme, and effects associated with the current theme. If you change the theme, the Quick Styles adopt the fonts, colors, and effects of the new theme.

1 Press `Ctrl` + `Home`. Click the **Page Layout tab**, and then in the **Themes group**, click the **Themes** button.

2 Point to various themes and notice the changes in your document.

> Live Preview enables you to see the effect a theme has on text with Quick Styles applied.

3 Scroll as necessary, click the **Metro** theme, and then compare your screen with Figure 4.6.

> The Metro theme's fonts, colors, and effects display in the document. All the Quick Styles now use the Metro theme.

Figure 4.6

Title style in Metro theme

Subtitle style in Metro theme

Emphasis style in Metro theme

Heading 1 style in Metro theme

Normal style in Metro theme

4 Select the subtitle, which begins *Requirements for*, and then on the Mini toolbar, apply **Bold** B and change the **Font Size** to **18**. **Save** 💾 your document.

> In this handout, this emphasis on the subtitle is useful. Because the handout has no other subtitles and you will not be applying this style again in this document, it is not necessary to modify the actual style.

Objective 2 | Create New Styles

You can create a new style based on formats that you specify. For example, if you frequently use a 12 pt Verdana font with bold emphasis and double spacing, you can create a style to apply those settings to a paragraph with a single click, instead of using multiple steps each time you want that specific formatting. Any new styles that you create are stored with the document and are available any time the document is open.

Activity 4.04 | Creating New Styles

1 Select the paragraph that begins *Examples: Aluminum*, and then on the Mini toolbar, change the **Font Size** to **12** and apply **Bold** B and **Italic** *I*.

2 With the paragraph still selected, click the **Home tab**, and then in the **Styles group**, click the **More** button ⏷ to display the **Quick Styles** gallery. In the lower portion of the gallery, click **Save Selection as a New Quick Style**.

3 In the **Create New Style from Formatting** dialog box, in the **Name** box, type **Examples** Compare your screen with Figure 4.7.

> Select a name for your new style that will remind you of the type of text to which the style applies. A preview of the style displays in the Paragraph style preview box.

Figure 4.7

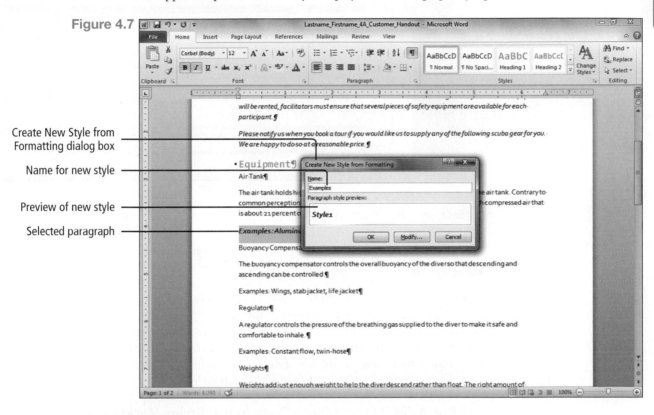

Create New Style from Formatting dialog box

Name for new style

Preview of new style

Selected paragraph

4 Click **OK** to add your *Examples* style to the available styles for this document and display it in the Quick Styles gallery.

5 Scroll down as necessary and select the paragraph that begins *Examples: Wings*. In the **Quick Styles** gallery, click the **Examples** style to apply the new style.

6 Using the technique you just practiced, select the four remaining paragraphs that begin *Examples:*, and then apply the **Examples** style. Click anywhere to deselect the text, and then compare your screen with Figure 4.8.

Figure 4.8

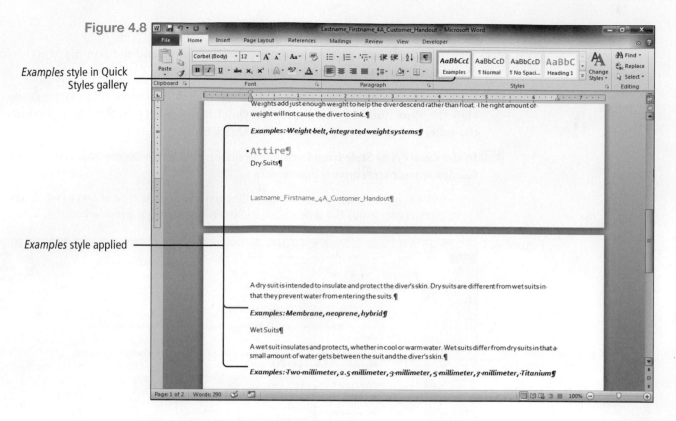

Examples style in Quick Styles gallery

Examples style applied

7 **Save** 📄 your document.

Objective 3 | Manage Styles

You can accomplish most of the tasks related to applying, modifying, and creating styles easily by using the Quick Styles gallery. However, if you create and modify many styles in a document, you will find it useful to work in the ***Styles window***. The Styles window is a pane that displays a list of styles and contains tools to manage styles. Additionally, by viewing available styles in the Styles window, you can see the exact details of all the formatting included with each style.

Activity 4.05 | Modifying a Style in the Styles Window

1 Press Ctrl + Home, and then click anywhere in the title *Lehua Hawaiian Adventures*. On the **Home tab**, in the lower right corner of the **Styles group**, click the **dialog box launcher button** 🔲 to display the **Styles** window. Compare your screen with Figure 4.9.

The Styles window displays the same group of available styles found in the Quick Styles gallery, including the new *Examples* style that you created.

Figure 4.9

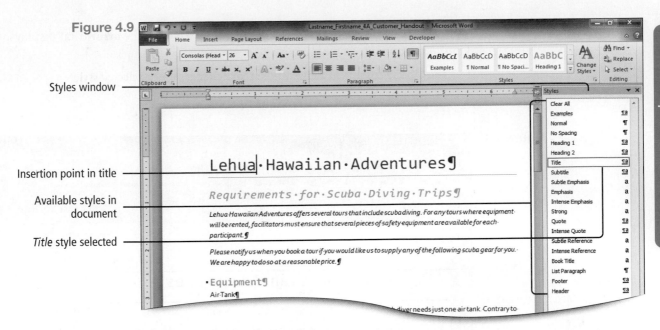

Styles window

Insertion point in title

Available styles in document

Title style selected

2 In the **Styles** window, point to **Title** to display a ScreenTip with the details of the formats associated with this style. In the displayed ScreenTip, under **Style**, notice that *Style Linked* is indicated.

By displaying a style's ScreenTip in this manner, you can verify all the information associated with the style.

3 Move your mouse pointer 🔖 into the document to close the ScreenTip. In the **Styles** window, examine the symbols to the right of each style, as shown in Figure 4.10.

A *character style*, indicated by the symbol **a**, contains formatting characteristics that you apply to text—for example, font name, font size, font color, bold emphasis, and so on.

A *paragraph style*, indicated by the symbol ¶, includes everything that a character style contains *plus* all aspects of a paragraph's appearance—for example, text alignment, tab stops, line spacing, and borders.

A *linked style*, indicated by the symbol ¶a, behaves as either a character style or a paragraph style, depending on what you select.

List styles, which apply formats to a list, and *table styles*, which apply a consistent look to the borders, shading, and so on of a table, are also available but do not display here.

Figure 4.10

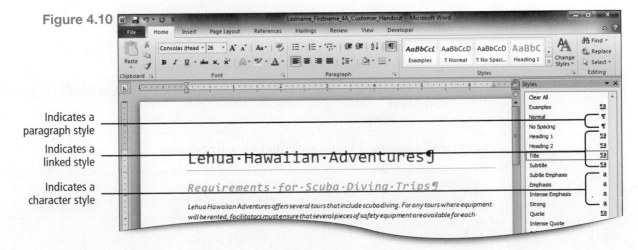

Indicates a paragraph style

Indicates a linked style

Indicates a character style

Another Way

In the **Quick Styles** gallery, right-click the style name, and then click **Modify**.

4 In the **Styles** window, point to **Heading 1**, and then click the **arrow** that displays. Compare your screen with Figure 4.11.

The Modify command allows you to make changes to the selected style.

Figure 4.11

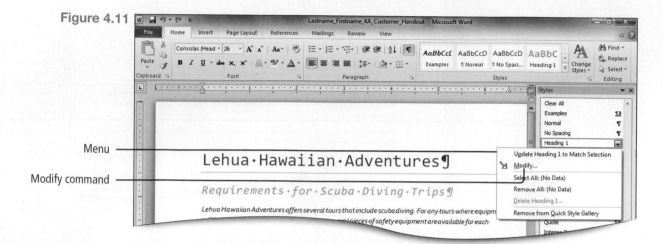

Menu

Modify command

5 From the displayed menu, click **Modify** to display the **Modify Style** dialog box. In the **Modify Style** dialog box, under **Formatting**, click the **Underline** button ⊔ to add underline emphasis to the style. Compare your screen with Figure 4.12.

Figure 4.12

Modify Style dialog box

Heading 1 style

Underline selected

6 Click **OK** to close the dialog box. Scroll as necessary, and then notice that both headings—*Equipment* and *Attire*—are underlined.

7 In the upper right corner of the **Styles** window, click the **Close** button ✕. **Save** 🖫 your document.

More Knowledge | Using Styles in Other Documents

By default, styles that you create are stored in the current document only. However, you can make the style available in other documents. To do so, in the Modify Style dialog box, select the New documents based on this template option button at the bottom of the screen, which deselects the Only in this document option button.

Activity 4.06 | Clearing Formats

There may be instances where you wish to remove all formatting from existing text—for example, when you want to create a multilevel list.

Another Way

Display the **Styles** window, and then at the top of the window, click the **Clear All** command.

1 Scroll to view the upper portion of **Page 1**, and then select the paragraph that begins *Examples: Aluminum*. On the **Home tab**, in the **Font group**, click the **Clear Formatting** button. Compare your screen with Figure 4.13.

The Clear Formatting command removes all formatting and applied styles from the selected text. The text returns to the *Normal* style for the current theme.

Figure 4.13

Clear Formatting button

Normal indicated for selected text after formatting cleared

Selected text cleared of formatting

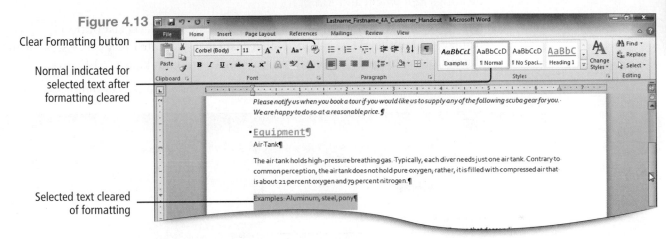

2 In the **Styles group**, point to the **Examples** style, and then right-click. From the displayed shortcut menu, click **Update Examples to Match Selection**.

The Examples style is removed from all text in the document. In this manner, you can clear the formatting for all instances with the applied style in the document.

3 **Save** your document.

Activity 4.07 | Removing a Quick Style

If a style that you created is no longer needed, you can remove it from the Quick Styles gallery.

1 In the **Styles group**, display the **Quick Styles** gallery. Right-click **Examples**, and then click **Remove from Quick Style Gallery**.

The Examples style is removed from the Quick Styles gallery. The style is no longer needed because all the paragraphs that are examples of scuba gear will be included in the multilevel list. Although the Examples style is removed from the Quick Styles gallery, it is not deleted from the document.

> **More Knowledge | Removing Built-in Styles**
>
> Built-in styles are predefined in Word, displaying in the Quick Styles gallery whenever you open a new document. Although you can remove a built-in style from a single document, the built-in style is not deleted from the Word program; the built-in style will be available in all other documents.

2 **Save** your document.

Objective 4 | Create a Multilevel List

When a document includes a list of items, you can format the items as a bulleted list, as a numbered list, or as a *multilevel list*. Use a multilevel list when you want to add a visual hierarchical structure to the items in the list.

Activity 4.08 | Creating a Multilevel List

1 On **Page 1**, scroll to position the heading *Equipment* near the top of your screen. Beginning with the paragraph *Air Tank*, select the 12 paragraphs between the headings *Equipment* and *Attire*.

2 On the **Home tab**, in the **Paragraph group**, click the **Multilevel List** button to display the **Multilevel List** gallery. Under **List Library**, locate the ❖, ➤, ■ style, which is the multilevel bullet list style. Compare your screen with Figure 4.14.

Word provides several built-in styles for multilevel lists. You can customize any style.

Figure 4.14

Multilevel List gallery ———

Selected text ———

Multilevel bullet list style ———

3 Click the **multilevel bullet list** style. Compare your screen with Figure 4.15.

All the items in the list display at the top level; the items are not visually indented to show different levels.

Figure 4.15

Multilevel bullet list format applied ———

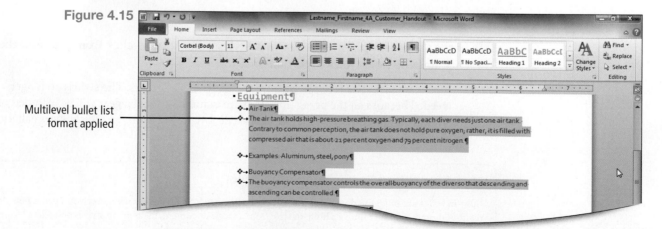

4 Click anywhere in the second list item, which begins *The air tank*. In the **Paragraph group**, click the **Increase Indent** button one time, and then compare your screen with Figure 4.16.

The list item displays at the second level, which uses the ➤ symbol. The Increase Indent button demotes an item to a lower level; the Decrease Indent button promotes an item to a higher level. To change the list level using the Increase Indent button or Decrease Indent button, it is not necessary to select the entire paragraph.

Figure 4.16

List item demoted to second level

5 Click in the third item in the list, which begins *Examples: Aluminum*. In the **Paragraph group**, click the **Increase Indent** button two times, and then compare your screen with Figure 4.17.

The list item displays at the third level, which uses the ■ symbol.

Figure 4.17

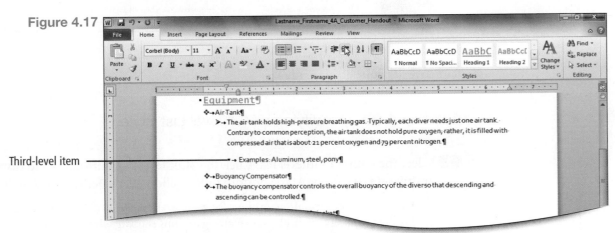

Third-level item

6 Using the technique you just practiced, continue setting levels for the remainder of the multilevel list as follows: Apply the second-level indent for the descriptive paragraphs that begin *The buoyancy*, *A regulator*, and *Weights add*. Apply the third-level indent for the paragraphs that begin *Examples*.

More Knowledge | Selecting List Items

To select several items in a document that are *contiguous*—adjacent to one another—click the first item, hold down [Shift], and then click the last item. To select several items that are *noncontiguous*—not adjacent to one another—hold down [Ctrl], and then click each item. After items are selected, you can format all the selected items at the same time.

7 Compare your screen with Figure 4.18. If necessary, adjust your list by using the Increase Indent or Decrease Indent buttons so that your list matches the one shown in Figure 4.18.

Figure 4.18

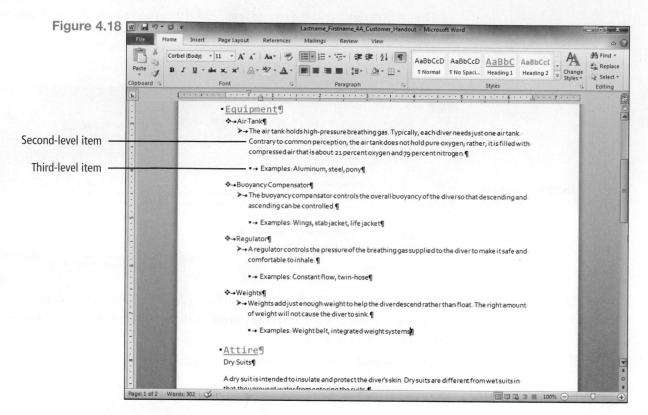

Second-level item

Third-level item

8 Save 🖫 your document.

Activity 4.09 | Modifying a Multilevel List Style

1 Select the entire multilevel list. Click the **Multilevel List** button 🔽 to display the **Multilevel List** gallery. At the bottom of the gallery, click **Define New List Style**.

Here you select formatting options for each level in your list. By default, the Define New List Style dialog box displays formatting options starting with the *1st level*.

2 Under **Properties**, in the **Name** box, type **Equipment List** Under **Formatting**, in the small toolbar above the preview area, to the right of *Bullet:* ❖, click the **Numbering Style arrow**.

3 In the displayed list, scroll to the top of the list, and then click the **1, 2, 3** style. Click the **Font Color arrow**, which currently displays black, and then in the fifth column, click the fifth color—**Green, Accent 1, Darker 25%**. Compare your screen with Figure 4.19.

The numbering style and font color change will be applied only to first-level items. The style changes are visible in the preview area.

Figure 4.19

Name box indicates *Equipment List*

Apply formatting to arrow

Font Color arrow

Numbering Style arrow

Preview area

4 Under **Formatting**, click the **Apply formatting to arrow**, and then click **2nd level**. Click the **Font Color arrow**, and then in the fifth column, click the fifth color—**Green, Accent 1, Darker 25%**—to change the bullet color for the second-level items.

5 Click the **Apply formatting to arrow**, and then click **3rd level**. Click the **Font Color arrow**, and then in the fifth column, click the first color—**Green, Accent 1**.

Another Way

If you know a symbol's character code, in the **Symbol** dialog box, select the number that displays in the **Character code** box, and then type the desired number.

6 Click the **Insert Symbol** button Ω. In the **Symbol** dialog box, click the **Font arrow** and display the **Wingdings** font, if necessary, and then scroll to the top of the icons list. In the sixth row, click the twelfth symbol—✿. Compare your screen with Figure 4.20.

The character code for this symbol—123—displays in the Character code box.

Figure 4.20

Symbol dialog box

Wingdings font

Flower symbol selected

Character code 123

7 Click **OK** to apply the flower symbol and close the **Symbol** dialog box.

This action changes both the bullet and bullet color for third-level items in your list.

8 In the **Define New List Style** dialog box, notice the preview of your changes, and then click **OK** to close the dialog box. Click anywhere to deselect the text, and then compare your screen with Figure 4.21.

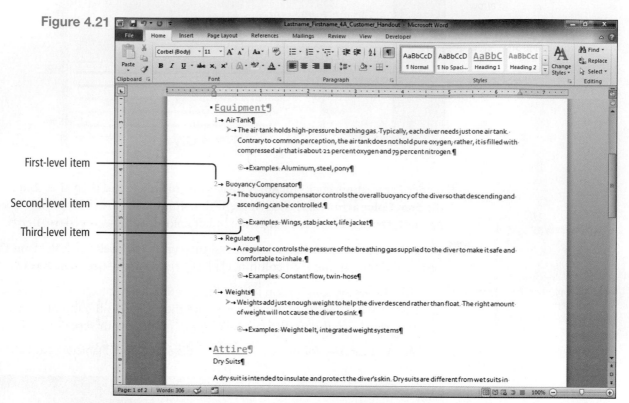

Figure 4.21

First-level item
Second-level item
Third-level item

9 Select the entire list. With all 12 paragraphs selected, click the **Page Layout tab**, and then in the **Paragraph group**, change the **Spacing After** to **0 pt**. **Save** your document.

Activity 4.10 | Applying the Current List Style

After you define a new list style, you can apply the style to other similar items in your document.

1 Scroll to position the heading *Attire* near the top of your screen. Beginning with the paragraph *Dry Suits*, select the remaining paragraphs in the document, including the paragraph that begins *Examples* on **Page 2**.

2 Click the **Home tab**. In the **Paragraph group**, click the **Multilevel List** button, and then click the style under **Current List**. Click anywhere to deselect the text, and then compare your screen with Figure 4.22.

The current list style formats each paragraph as a first-level item.

Figure 4.22

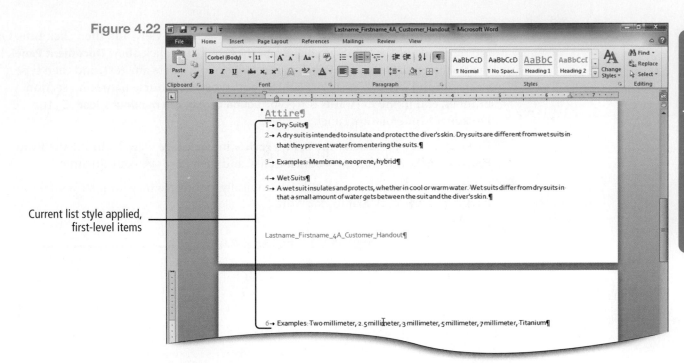

Current list style applied,
first-level items

3 Under the **Attire** heading, select the two descriptive paragraphs that begin *A dry suit* and *A wet suit*, and then click the **Increase Indent** button 🔲 one time. Select the two paragraphs that begin *Examples*, and then click the **Increase Indent** button 🔲 two times. Deselect the text, and then compare your screen with Figure 4.23.

Figure 4.23

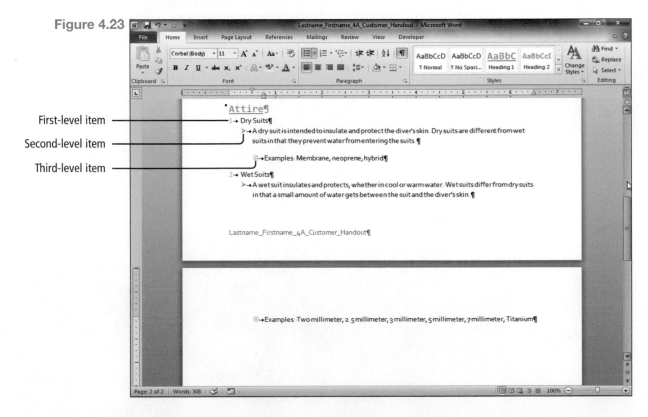

First-level item

Second-level item

Third-level item

4 Select the entire list. With all six paragraphs selected, click the **Page Layout tab**, and then in the **Paragraph group**, change the **Spacing After** to **0 pt**. Click anywhere to deselect the list.

5 Press `Ctrl` + `Home`. Click the **File tab** to display **Backstage** view, and then click **Info**. On the right side of the window, click **Properties**, and then click **Show Document Panel**. In the **Document Information Panel**, in the **Author** box, delete any text, and then type your first and last names. In the **Subject** box, type your course name and section number, and in the **Keywords** box, type **scuba diving, trip handout Close** `×` the Document Information Panel.

6 Press `Ctrl` + `F2` to display the **Print Preview** in **Backstage** view. Examine the **Print Preview**, make any necessary adjustments, and then **Save** 🖫 your document.

7 Print your document or submit it electronically as directed by your instructor. From **Backstage** view, click **Exit** to exit Word.

End **You have completed Project 4A** ——————————————

Project 4B Planning Memo with a Chart

Project 4B Training

Project Activities

In Activities 4.11 through 4.20, you will edit a memo to all thc company tour guides regarding the planning session. The Tour Operations Manager of Lehua Hawaiian Adventures is preparing for a planning session in which he and other key decision makers will discuss the types of tours the company will offer in the coming year. They want to use information gathered from customer research to provide an appropriate mix of tour types that will appeal to a wide audience. You will add a chart to illustrate plans for tour types in the coming year. Your completed document will look similar to Figure 4.24.

Project Files

For Project 4B, you will need the following file:

w04B_Planning_Memo

You will save your document as:

Lastname_Firstname_4B_Planning_Memo

Project Results

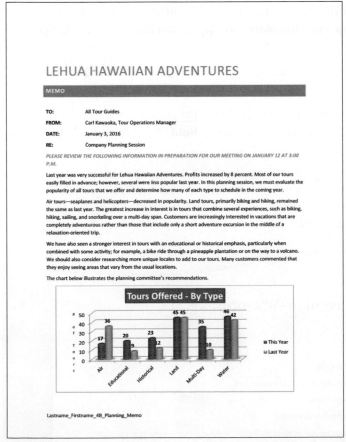

Figure 4.24
Project 4B Planning Memo

Objective 5 | Change the Style Set and Paragraph Spacing of a Document

Recall that formatting commands that are grouped together comprise a style. Likewise, styles that are grouped together comprise a *style set*. A style set is a group of styles that is designed to work together. A style set is useful when you want to change the look of *all* the styles in a document in one step rather than modifying individual styles. The styles grouped together in each style set reflect the font scheme and color scheme of the current theme, including paragraph spacing formats.

Activity 4.11 | Formatting a Memo

A *memo*, also referred to as a *memorandum*, is a written message to someone working in the same organization. Among organizations, memo formats vary, and there are many acceptable memo formats. Always consult trusted references or the preferences set by your organization when deciding on the proper formats for your professional memos.

1 **Start** Word. From your student files, locate and open the file **w04B_Planning_Memo**.

2 Save the document in your **Word Chapter 4** folder as **Lastname_Firstname_4B_Planning_Memo** Scroll to the bottom of the page, right-click in the footer area, click **Edit Footer**, and then using **Quick Parts**, insert the file name. **Close** the footer area. If necessary, display the rulers and formatting marks.

3 Press Ctrl + Home. If *Lehua* or *Kawaoka* are flagged as spelling errors, point to the first occurrence of each, right-click, and then click **Ignore All**.

4 Select the first paragraph of the document—*Lehua Hawaiian Adventures*. On the **Home tab**, in the **Styles group**, click the **More** button ⏷, and then from the **Quick Styles** gallery, click **Title**.

5 Select the second paragraph—the heading *MEMO*, and then from the **Quick Styles** gallery, apply the **Heading 1** style.

6 Select the text *TO:*—include the colon—hold down Ctrl, and then select the text *FROM:*, *DATE:*, and *RE:*. On the Mini toolbar, apply **Bold** B to these four memo headings.

7 Select the paragraph that begins *Please review*. In the **Styles group**, click the **More** button ⏷ to display the **Quick Styles** gallery. By using the ScreenTips, locate and then click the **Intense Reference** style. Click anywhere to deselect the text. **Save** 🖫 your document. Compare your screen with Figure 4.25.

Figure 4.25

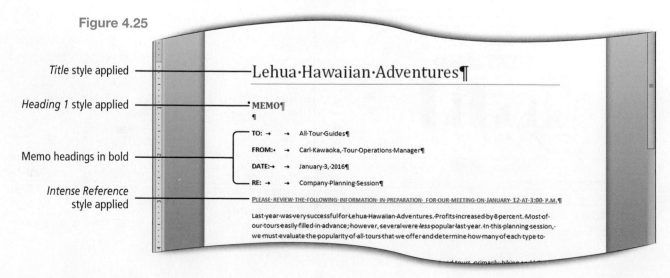

- *Title* style applied — Lehua·Hawaiian·Adventures¶
- *Heading 1* style applied — MEMO¶
- Memo headings in bold — TO: → → All·Tour·Guides¶
  FROM:→ → Carl·Kawaoka,·Tour·Operations·Manager¶
  DATE:→ → January·3,·2016¶
  RE: → → Company·Planning·Session¶
- *Intense Reference* style applied — PLEASE·REVIEW·THE·FOLLOWING·INFORMATION·IN·PREPARATION·FOR·OUR·MEETING·ON·JANUARY·12·AT·3:00·P.M.¶
  Last·year·was·very·successful·for·Lehua·Hawaiian·Adventures.·Profits·increased·by·8·percent.·Most·of·our·tours·easily·filled·in·advance;·however,·several·were·less·popular·last·year.·In·this·planning·session,·we·must·evaluate·the·popularity·of·all·tours·that·we·offer·and·determine·how·many·of·each·type·to

Activity 4.12 | Changing the Style Set

By changing a style set, you can apply a group of styles to a document in one step.

1 In the **Styles group**, click the **Change Styles** button, and then point to **Style Set**. Compare your screen with Figure 4.26.

> All available style sets are listed by name in the Style Set menu; there are 13 predefined style sets. The default style set is *Word 2010*.

Figure 4.26

Change Styles button

Style Set command

Available style sets

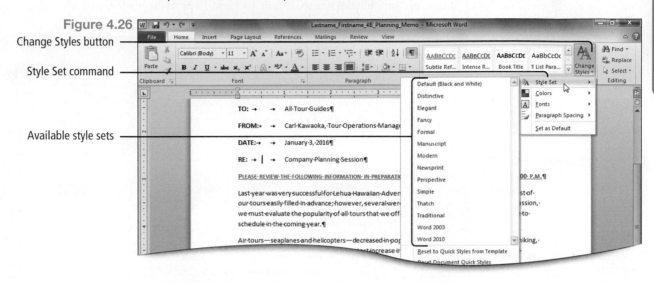

2 From the **Style Set** menu, point to **Fancy**, and notice that **Live Preview** displays how the text would look with this style set applied.

3 From the **Style Set** menu, click **Modern**, compare your screen with Figure 4.27, and then **Save** 💾 your document.

> *Modern* is the name of a particular style set. Applying *Modern* causes styles—such as Title, Heading 1, and Intense Reference—to display a different format.

Figure 4.27

Title style

Heading 1 style

Intense Reference style

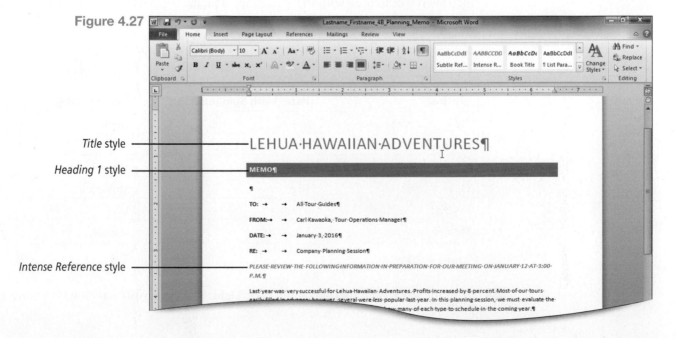

Activity 4.13 | Changing the Paragraph Spacing of a Document

Built-in paragraph spacing formats allow you to change the paragraph spacing and line spacing for an entire document in one step.

1 In the **Styles group**, click the **Change Styles** button, and then point to **Paragraph Spacing**. Under **Style Set**, point to **Modern**. Compare your screen with Figure 4.28.

Word provides six built-in styles for paragraph spacing. The *Modern* style set uses paragraph spacing that includes line spacing of 1.15 and 10 pt spacing before and after a paragraph.

Figure 4.28

Currently selected style set is *Modern*

ScreenTip indicates line spacing and paragraph spacing

Available paragraph spacing formats

Paragraph Spacing command

2 From the **Paragraph Spacing** menu, point to **Double**. Notice the **ScreenTip** that describes the paragraph spacing format and that **Live Preview** displays how the document would look with this paragraph spacing format applied. Take a moment to study the table shown in Figure 4.29.

Paragraph Spacing Formats		
Option	**Paragraph Spacing After**	**Line Spacing**
No Paragraph Spacing	0	Single
Compact	4 pt	Single
Tight	6 pt	Multiple 1.15
Open	10 pt	Multiple 1.15
Relaxed	6 pt	1.5
Double	8 pt	Double

Figure 4.29

3 From the **Paragraph Spacing** menu, click **Tight**. Compare your screen with Figure 4.30.

Figure 4.30

Tight paragraph
format applied

Paragraph Spacing
After set to 6 pt

Line Spacing set to 1.15

4 Save your document.

Objective 6 | Insert a Chart and Enter Data into a Chart

A ***chart*** is a visual representation of ***numerical data***—numbers that represent facts. Word provides the same chart tools that are available in Excel. A chart that you create in Word is stored in an Excel worksheet, and the worksheet is saved with the Word document. Excel, which is part of Microsoft Office 2010, is a spreadsheet application that makes calculations on numbers. An Excel worksheet is a set of cells, identified by row and column headings, that is part of a spreadsheet. Charts make numbers easier for the reader to understand.

Activity 4.14 | Selecting a Chart Type

1 Press Ctrl + End, and then press Enter one time. Compare your screen with Figure 4.31.

Figure 4.31

New blank paragraph

2 Click the **Insert tab**, and then in the **Illustrations group**, click the **Chart** button to display the **Insert Chart** dialog box. Take a moment to examine the chart types described in the table shown in Figure 4.32.

> Eleven chart types display on the left side of the Insert Chart dialog box. The most commonly used chart types are column, line, pie, bar, and area.

Commonly Used Chart Types Available in Word	
Chart Type	**Purpose of Chart**
Column, *Bar*	Show comparison among related data
Pie	Show proportion of parts to a whole
Line, *Area*	Show trends over time

Figure 4.32

3 On the left side of the **Insert Chart** dialog box, click **Bar**. In the right pane, under **Bar**, click the fourth style—**Clustered Bar in 3-D**. Compare your screen with Figure 4.33.

> A bar chart is a good choice because this data will *compare* the number of tours offered in two different years.

Figure 4.33

Insert Chart dialog box

Bar chart types

Clustered Bar in 3-D

4 Click **OK** to insert the chart in your document and open the related Excel worksheet. Compare your screen with Figure 4.34.

> The chart displays on page 2 of your Word document. Excel opens in a split window and displays sample data in a worksheet.

> The process of inserting a chart in your document in this manner is referred to as *embedding*—the object, in this case a chart, becomes part of the Word document. When you edit the data in Excel, the chart in your Word document updates automatically.

Figure 4.34

Excel worksheet window
Columns
Rows
Sample data
Chart displays on page 2

Activity 4.15 | Entering Chart Data

You can replace the sample data in the Excel worksheet with specific tour data for your chart.

1 In the Excel worksheet window, point to the box where **column B** and **row 1** intersect— referred to as cell **B1**—and click one time. Compare your screen with Figure 4.35.

> A *cell* is the location where a row and column intersect. The cells are named by their column and row headings. For example, cell B1, containing the text *Series 1*, is in column B and row 1.

Figure 4.35

Column B
Row 1
Cell B1

2 With cell **B1** selected, type **This Year** and then press ⬚Tab⬚. With cell **C1** selected, type **Last Year** and then click cell **A2**—which displays the text *Category 1*.

3 With cell **A2** selected, type **Air** and then press ⬚Tab⬚ to move to cell **B2**. Type **17** and then press ⬚Tab⬚. In cell **C2**, type **36** and then press ⬚Tab⬚ two times to move to **row 3**.

> As you enter data in the Excel worksheet, the chart is automatically updated in the Word document. When entering a large amount of data in a cell, it may not fully display. If necessary, the data worksheet or chart can be modified to display the data completely.

4 Using the technique you just practiced, and without changing any values in **column D**, type the following data:

	This Year	Last Year	Series 3
Air	17	36	2
Educational	**13**	**9**	2
Historical	**17**	**12**	3
Land	**45**	**45**	5
Multi-Day	**35**	**10**	
Water	**46**	**42**	

5 Compare your screen with Figure 4.36.

> A blue line—the **data range border**—surrounds the cells that display in the chart. The group of cells surrounded by the blue border is referred to as the **chart data range**— the range of data that Excel will use to create the chart.

Figure 4.36

Current chart data range

Chart data range border

Instruction for resizing

6 In the **Excel** worksheet, point to the lower right corner of the blue border to display the ⬚↖⬚ pointer, and then drag to the left to select only cells **A1** through **C7**. Compare your screen with Figure 4.37.

Figure 4.37

Blue border surrounds only cells A1 through C7

Bars in chart display area

7 In the upper right corner of the **Excel** window, click the **Close** button, and then **Save** your Word document. Scroll if necessary to display the chart, on **Page 2** of your document. Compare your screen with Figure 4.38.

The *chart area* refers to the entire chart and all its elements. The categories—the tour type names—display on the *vertical axis*, which is also referred to as the *Y-axis*. The scale, based on the numerical data, displays on the *horizontal axis*, which is also referred to as the *X-axis*.

Data markers, the bars in the chart, are the shapes representing each of the cells that contain data, referred to as the *data points*. A *data series* consists of related data points represented by a unique color. For example, this chart has two data series—*This Year* and *Last Year*. The *legend* identifies the colors assigned to each data series or category.

Figure 4.38

Chart area

Data marker

Vertical axis or Y-axis

Data series—includes all bars of the same color

Horizontal axis or X-axis

Legend

Activity 4.16 | Editing Data

You can edit data points to update a chart.

1 Be sure your chart is selected; if necessary, click the chart border to select it. Compare your screen with Figure 4.39.

> With the chart selected, the Chart Tools display and three additional tabs display on the Ribbon—*Design*, *Layout*, and *Format*—to provide commands with which you can modify and format chart elements.

Figure 4.39

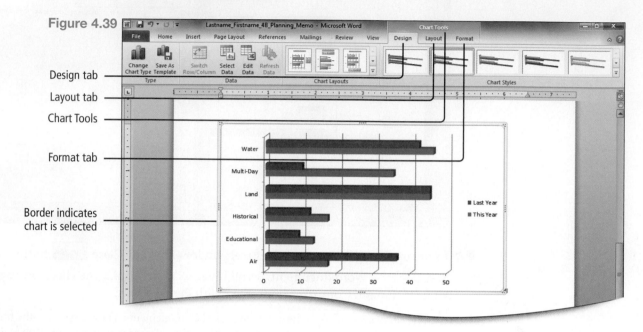

Design tab
Layout tab
Chart Tools
Format tab
Border indicates chart is selected

2 On the **Design tab**, in the **Data group**, click the **Edit Data** button to redisplay the embedded Excel worksheet.

3 In the **Excel worksheet**, click cell **B3**, and then type **20** Click cell **B4**, and then type **23** Press Enter.

> Word automatically updates the chart to reflect these data point changes.

4 **Close** the Excel window, and then **Save** your Word document. Compare your screen with Figure 4.40.

Figure 4.40

Data points updated

Objective 7 | Change a Chart Type

A chart commonly shows one of three types of relationships—a comparison among data, the proportion of parts to a whole, or trends over time. You may decide to alter a chart type—for example, change a bar chart to a column chart—so that the chart displays more attractively in the document.

Activity 4.17 | Changing the Chart Type

The data in the Tour Types chart compares tour numbers for two years and is appropriately represented by a bar chart. A column chart is also appropriate to compare data.

1 With the chart selected, on the **Design tab**, in the **Type group**, click the **Change Chart Type** button.

2 In the displayed **Change Chart Type** dialog box, on the left, click **Column**, and then on the right, under **Column**, in the second row, click the first chart type—**Clustered Cylinder**. Click **OK**, and then compare your screen with Figure 4.41.

The category names display in alphabetical order on the horizontal axis; the number scale displays on the vertical axis.

Figure 4.41

Clustered Cylinder chart

Vertical axis

Horizontal axis

3 Save 🔲 your document.

Objective 8 | Format a Chart

You can modify, add, or delete chart elements such as the chart title, data labels, and text boxes. You can also format a chart to change its size and color.

Activity 4.18 | Adding Chart Elements

Add chart elements to help the reader understand the data in your chart. For example, you can add a title to the chart and to individual axes, or add *data labels*, which display the value represented by each data marker.

1 Click the **Layout tab**. In the **Labels group**, click the **Chart Title** button, and then from the displayed menu, click **Above Chart**.

> A text box containing the text *Chart Title* displays above the chart.

2 In the text box, select the text *Chart Title*, and then type **Tours Offered - By Type**

3 On the **Layout tab**, in the **Labels group**, click the **Axis Titles** button, point to **Primary Vertical Axis Title**, and then click **Vertical Title**.

> The text *Axis Title* displays in a text box to the left of the vertical axis.

4 Select the text *Axis Title*, type **# of Tours** and then notice that the text displays vertically in the text box.

5 Click in an empty corner inside the chart to deselect the vertical text box. On the **Layout tab**, in the **Labels group**, click the **Data Labels** button, and then click **Show**. Compare your screen with Figure 4.42. **Save** 🔲 your document.

> The data point values display above each data marker column in the chart. In addition to the scale on the vertical axis, data labels are helpful for the reader to understand the values represented by the columns.

Figure 4.42

Chart title

Vertical axis title

Data labels

Activity 4.19 | Changing the Chart Style and Formatting Chart Elements

A *chart style* refers to the overall visual look of a chart in terms of its graphic effects, colors, and backgrounds; for example, you can have flat or beveled columns, colors that are solid or transparent, and backgrounds that are dark or light.

1 With the chart selected, click the **Design tab**. In the **Chart Styles group**, click the **More** button. In the displayed **Chart Styles** gallery, in the fourth row, click the fourth chart style—**Style 28**. Compare your screen with Figure 4.43.

Figure 4.43

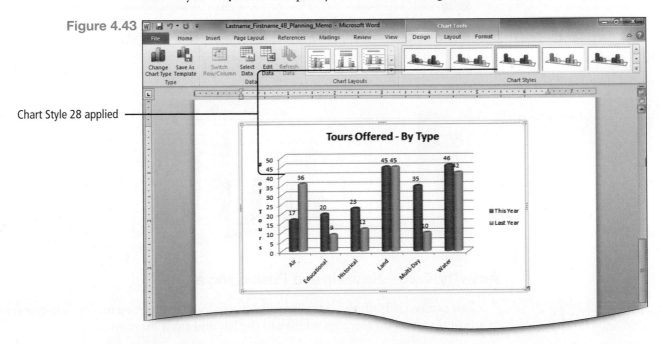

Chart Style 28 applied

2 Select the chart title text. Click the **Format tab**, and then in the **Shape Styles group**, click the **More** button. In the displayed **Shape Styles** gallery, in the second row, click the third style—**Colored Fill – Red, Accent 2**. Click in an empty corner of the chart to deselect the chart title. Compare your screen with Figure 4.44.

Figure 4.44

Chart Title with shape style applied

3 To the left of the vertical axis, select the text *# of Tours*. On the Mini toolbar, click the **Font Color button arrow** ![A], and then in the sixth column, click the fifth color—**Red, Accent 2, Darker 25%**.

4 Above the **Air** columns, click **17** to select the data labels for each data marker in the *This Year* data series.

5 Point to **17** and right-click, and then on the Mini toolbar, click **Bold** ![B].

All the numbers in the *This Year* data series display with bold.

6 Using the technique you just practiced, apply **Bold** ![B] to the data labels in the *Last Year* data series. Compare your screen with Figure 4.45, and then **Save** ![disk] your document.

Figure 4.45

Data labels display in bold

Vertical axis title formatted with red font

Activity 4.20 | Resizing and Positioning a Chart

You can resize both the chart area and the individual chart elements. You can also position the chart on the page relative to the left and right margins.

1 Click in an empty corner inside the chart so that the chart, and not the data labels, is selected. On the **Format tab**, in the **Size group**, click the **Shape Height spin box down arrow** to **2.7"**. Scroll up as necessary to view your document.

> The resized chart moves to the bottom of the first page. Resizing a chart might also require specific chart elements to be resized or repositioned.

2 To the left of the vertical axis, select the text *# of Tours*. On the Mini toolbar, change the **Font Size** to **8**. Click in an empty corner of the chart to deselect the text.

3 Click the **Home tab**. In the **Paragraph group**, click the **Center** button ≡ to center the chart between the left and right margins. Compare your screen with Figure 4.46.

Figure 4.46

Chart centered horizontally

Vertical axis title resized

Chart displays on Page 1

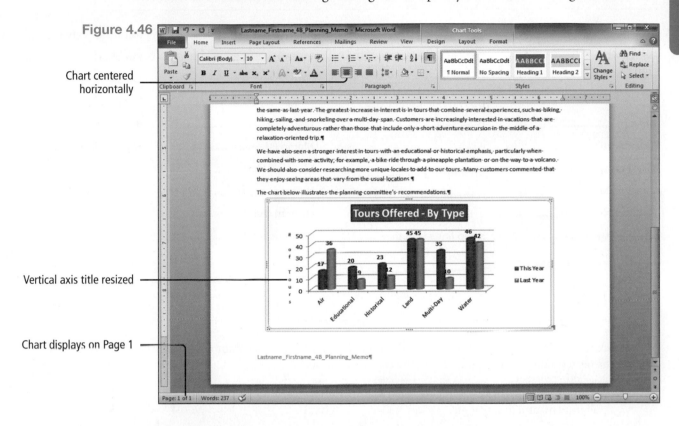

4 Press Ctrl + Home. In **Backstage** view, click **Info**. On the right side of the window, click **Properties**, and then click **Show Document Panel** to display the **Document Information Panel**. In the **Author** box, delete any text, and then type your first and last names. In the **Subject** box, type your course name and section number, and in the **Keywords** box, type **planning memo, tours data Close** ✕ the Document Information Panel.

5 Press Ctrl + F2 to display the **Print Preview** in **Backstage** view. Examine the **Print Preview**, and make any necessary adjustments. **Save** 🔲 your document.

6 Print your document or submit it electronically as directed by your instructor. Click the **File tab**, and then click **Exit** to exit Word.

End You have completed Project 4B ⸻

Content-Based Assessments

Summary

In this chapter, you used predefined styles, and created your own styles, to apply uniform formatting in a document. You also customized a multilevel list to organize information and inserted and edited a chart to display numerical data in a graphical format within a Word document.

Key Terms

Area chart 248	**Data labels** 254	**Keep with next** 229	**Paragraph style** 233
Bar chart 248	**Data markers** 251	**Legend**............................251	**Pie chart** 248
Cell................................249	**Data points** 251	**Line chart** 248	**Quick Styles** 227
Character style 233	**Data range border** 250	**Linked style**....................233	**Style**.................................227
Chart 247	**Data series** 251	**List style** 233	**Style set**...........................244
Chart area 251	**Direct formatting** 227	**Memo (Memorandum)**....244	**Styles window**.................232
Chart data range 250	**Embedding** 249	**Multilevel list**..................236	**Table style** 233
Chart style......................255	**Horizontal axis**	**Noncontiguous** 237	**Vertical axis (Y-axis)** 251
Column chart 248	**(X-axis)**........................251	**Normal Quick Style** 227	
Contiguous 237	**Keep lines together** 229	**Numerical data** 247	

Matching

Match each term in the second column with its correct definition in the first column by writing the letter of the term on the blank line in front of the correct definition.

_____ 1. A group of formatting commands, such as font, font size, font color, paragraph alignment, and line spacing.

_____ 2. The process of applying each format separately to text—for example, bold, then font size, then font color, and so on.

_____ 3. Combinations of formatting options that work together and look attractive together.

_____ 4. A formatting feature that keeps a heading with its first paragraph of text on the same page.

_____ 5. A formatting feature that prevents a single line from displaying by itself at the bottom of a page or at the top of a page.

_____ 6. A pane that displays a list of styles and contains tools to manage styles.

_____ 7. A style, indicated by the symbol **a**, that contains formatting characteristics that you apply to text—for example, font name, font size, font color, bold emphasis, and so on.

_____ 8. A style, indicated by the symbol ¶, that includes everything that a character style contains, plus all aspects of a paragraph's appearance—for example, text alignment, tab stops, or line spacing.

A Area

B Bar

C Cell

D Character style

E Chart

F Direct formatting

G Keep lines together

H Keep with next

I Memo

J Multilevel

K Paragraph style

L Quick Styles

M Style

N Style set

O Styles window

Content-Based Assessments

_____ 9.   A list in which the items display in a visual hierarchical structure.

_____ 10. A group of styles that are designed to work together.

_____ 11. A written message sent to someone working in the same organization.

_____ 12. A visual representation of numerical data.

_____ 13. A chart type used to show a comparison among related data.

_____ 14. A chart type used to show trends over time.

_____ 15. In Excel, the location where a row and column meet.

Multiple Choice

Circle the correct answer.

1. What is the default style in Word for new documents that determines the basic look of document?
   A. Word Quick Style
   B. Normal Template Style
   C. Normal Quick Style

2. A style, indicated by the symbol ¶a, that behaves as either a character style or a paragraph style is:
   A. an embedded style
   B. a linked style
   C. a Quick Style

3. Numbers that represent facts are referred to as:
   A. numerical data
   B. data points
   C. information

4. To show a comparison among related data, use a:
   A. pie chart
   B. line chart
   C. column chart

5. The process of inserting an object, such as a chart, into a Word document so that it becomes part of the document is:
   A. embedding
   B. linking
   C. attaching

6. In Excel, the group of cells that is used to create a chart is the:
   A. cell range
   B. chart data range
   C. chart point range

7. The Y-axis that displays along the left side of a chart is also referred to as the:
   A. primary axis
   B. horizontal axis
   C. vertical axis

8. The shapes in a chart that represent each of the cells that contain data are:
   A. data labels
   B. data markers
   C. chart styles

9. The part of a chart that identifies the colors assigned to each data series or category is the:
   A. legend
   B. vertical axis
   C. horizontal axis

10. The overall visual look of a chart in terms of its graphic effects, colors, and backgrounds is the:
    A. chart format
    B. chart style
    C. chart theme

Content-Based Assessments

Apply **4A** skills from these Objectives:

1 Apply and Modify Quick Styles
2 Create New Styles
3 Manage Styles
4 Create a Multilevel List

Skills Review | Project **4C** Training Classes

In the following Skills Review, you will add styles and a multilevel list format to a document that describes training classes for Lehua Hawaiian Adventures tour guides. Your completed document will look similar to Figure 4.47.

Project Files

For Project 4C, you will need the following file:

w04C_Training_Classses

You will save your document as:

Lastname_Firstname_4C_Training_Classes

Project Results

Lehua Hawaiian Adventures

In an effort to remain the premier adventure travel company in Hawaii and increase the number of tours we offer annually, *Lehua Hawaiian Adventures* is holding several tour guide training classes. Guides who have focused on a specific area of expertise, such as biking or snorkeling, will have the exciting opportunity to branch out into other types of tours.

Classes will be conducted by *Lehua Hawaiian Adventures* tour guides and other experts from around the country. Please contact Carl Kawaoka, Tour Operations Manager, to reserve a space in a session.

1 Basic Coastal Sailing

> Learn to handle a sailboat safely, including equipment, communication, knots, and traffic rules. Also learn the specifics of sailing safely in the waters around the Hawaiian Islands. Coast Guard equipment requirements, anchoring techniques, sail handling, chart reading, weather response, and more will be taught in this course by local sailing champion Grace McPherson.
> - Dates offered: September 23, October 2

2 Horseback Riding

> Craig Weston, a horseback tour guide in Hawaii for more than 10 years, will demonstrate how to use saddles and other equipment, teach about horse behavior, trailer loading and transportation, equipment, safety, and how to deal with common problems that can occur on a horseback riding adventure.
> - Dates offered: September 2, October 1

3 Intermediate Sea Kayaking

> This course assumes that you already have some basic sea kayaking experience. Topics will include advanced strokes, rescues, bracing and rolling, navigation, and how to handle moderate to rough water conditions. Cliff Lewis, head kayaking guide for *Lehua Hawaiian Adventures*, will teach this course.
> - Dates offered: September 30, October 29

4 Wilderness Survival

> Philip Thurman, our own expert, will teach about general safety, accident prevention, emergency procedures, and how to handle hypothermia and dehydration. This is important information that we hope you will never need to use.
> - Dates offered: September 16, October 15

Lastname_Firstname_4C_Training_Classes

Figure 4.47

(Project 4C Training Classes continues on the next page)

Content-Based Assessments

1 **Start** Word. From your student files, open the file **w04C_Training_Classes**. **Save** the document in your **Word Chapter 4** folder as **Lastname_Firstname_4C_ Training_Classes** Scroll to the bottom of the page, right-click in the footer area, click **Edit Footer**, and then using **Quick Parts**, insert the file name. **Close** the footer area.

a. If any proper names are flagged as a spelling error, point to the first occurrence, right-click, and then click **Ignore All**.

b. Select the first paragraph, and in the **Styles group**, click the **More** button. In the **Quick Styles** gallery, click **Title**.

c. In the second paragraph, in the second line, select the text *Lehua Hawaiian Adventures*. Display the **Quick Styles** gallery, and then click the **Strong** style.

d. With *Lehua Hawaiian Adventures* selected, right-click the selection, and then on the Mini toolbar, click the **Font Color button arrow**. In the fifth column, click the first color—**Blue, Accent 1**.

e. With the text still selected, display the **Quick Styles** gallery, right-click the **Strong** style, and then from the displayed shortcut menu, click **Update Strong to Match Selection**.

f. In the third paragraph, in the first line, select the text *Lehua Hawaiian Adventures* and apply the **Strong** style. Using the same technique, in the eleventh paragraph that begins *This course*, in the third line, select *Lehua Hawaiian Adventures*—do not include the comma—and then apply the **Strong** style.

2 On the **Page Layout tab**, in the **Themes group**, click the **Themes** button, and then click the **Flow** theme.

a. Including the paragraph mark, select the fourth paragraph of the document—*Basic Coastal Sailing*. On the Mini toolbar, apply **Bold**. On the **Home tab**, in the **Paragraph group**, click the **Shading button arrow**, and then in the last column, click the fourth color—**Lime, Accent 6, Lighter 40%**.

b. With the paragraph still selected, display the **Quick Styles** gallery, and then click **Save Selection as a New Quick Style**. In the **Name** box, type **Class Title** and then click **OK**.

c. Scroll down as necessary, select the paragraph *Horseback Riding*, and then apply the **Class Title** style.

d. Using the same technique, apply the **Class Title** style to the paragraphs *Intermediate Sea Kayaking* and *Wilderness Survival*.

3 Press [Ctrl] + [Home]. On the **Home tab**, in the **Styles group**, click the **dialog box launcher** button to display the **Styles** window.

a. In the **Styles** window, point to **Strong**, click the **arrow** that displays, and then click **Modify**.

b. In the **Modify Style** dialog box, under **Formatting**, click the **Italic** button. Click **OK** to close the dialog box and update all instances of the **Strong** style. **Close** the **Styles** window.

4 Click to position the insertion point to the left of the paragraph *Basic Coastal Sailing*, and then from this point, select all remaining text in the document.

a. On the **Home tab**, in the **Paragraph group**, click the **Multilevel List** button. Under **List Library**, locate and then click the ❖, ➢, ◼ style.

b. Click in the first paragraph following *Basic Coastal Sailing*, and then in the **Paragraph group**, click the **Increase Indent** button one time. Click in the second paragraph following *Basic Coastal Sailing*, which begins *Dates*, and then click the **Increase Indent** button two times. Under *Horseback Riding*, *Intermediate Sea Kayaking*, and *Wilderness Survival*, format the paragraphs in the same manner.

5 Select the entire multilevel list. Click the **Multilevel List** button to display the **Multilevel List** gallery. At the bottom of the gallery, click **Define New List Style**.

a. Name the style **Training Class** Under **Formatting**, in the **Apply formatting to** box, be sure **1st level** displays. In the small toolbar above the preview area, click the **Numbering Style arrow**, and in the displayed list, scroll to locate and then click the **1, 2, 3** style.

b. Under **Formatting**, click the **Apply formatting to arrow**, and then click **2nd level**. In the small toolbar above the preview area, make certain the **Bullet:** ➢ style displays. Click the **Font Color arrow**, and then in the last column, click the fifth color—**Lime, Accent 6, Darker 25%**. Click **OK** to close the dialog box.

6 Press [Ctrl] + [Home]. Click the **File tab** to display **Backstage** view, and then click **Info**. On the right side of the window, click **Properties**, and then click **Show**

(Project 4C Training Classes continues on the next page)

Content-Based Assessments

Document Panel to display the **Document Information Panel**. In the **Author** box, delete any text, and then type your first and last names. In the **Subject** box, type your course name and section number, and then in the **Keywords** box, type **training classes, description Close** the Document Information Panel.

7 Press Ctrl + F2 to display the **Print Preview** in **Backstage** view. **Examine** the **Print Preview**, and make any necessary adjustments. **Save** your changes. Print your document or submit electronically as directed by your instructor. From **Backstage** view, **Exit** Word.

 You have completed Project 4C ————————————————

Content-Based Assessments

Apply 4B skills from these Objectives:

- **5** Change the Style Set and Paragraph Spacing of a Document
- **6** Insert a Chart and Enter Data into a Chart
- **7** Change a Chart Type
- **8** Format a Chart

Skills Review | Project **4D** Strategy Session

In the following Skills Review, you will create a memo for Katherine Okubo, President of Lehua Hawaiian Adventures, which details the company's financial performance and provides strategies for the upcoming year. Your completed document will look similar to Figure 4.48.

Project Files

For Project 4D, you will need the following file:

w04D_Strategy_Session

You will save your document as:

Lastname_Firstname_4D_Strategy_Session

Project Results

Figure 4.48

(Project 4D Strategy Session continues on the next page)

Skills Review | Project **4D** Strategy Session (continued)

1 **Start** Word. From your student files, locate and open the file **w04D_Strategy_Session**. Save the document in your **Word Chapter 4** folder as **Lastname_Firstname_4D_Strategy_Session** Scroll to the bottom of **Page 1**, right-click in the footer area, click **Edit Footer**, and then using **Quick Parts**, insert the file name. **Close** the footer area.

a. If *Lehua* and *Okubo* are flagged as spelling errors, point to the first occurrence, right-click, and then click **Ignore All**.

b. Select the first paragraph of the document—*Lehua Hawaiian Adventures*. Display the **Quick Styles** gallery, and then click **Title**. Select the second paragraph, the heading *Memo*, and then from the **Quick Styles** gallery, apply the **Heading 1** style.

c. Select the memo heading *TO:*—include the colon—hold down (Ctrl), and then select the memo headings *FROM:*, *DATE:*, and *RE:*. On the Mini toolbar, click **Bold**.

d. Select the paragraph *Tour Summary*, hold down (Ctrl), and then select the paragraphs *Local Industry Assessment* and *Customer Feedback*. From the **Quick Styles** gallery, apply the **Heading 2** style.

e. In the **Styles group**, click the **Change Styles** button, point to **Style Set**, and then click **Fancy**. In the **Styles group**, click the **Change Styles** button, point to **Paragraph Spacing**, and then click **Relaxed**.

2 On **Page 1**, below *Tour Summary*, locate the paragraph that begins *In order to provide*. Place your insertion point at the end of the paragraph, and then press (Enter).

a. On the **Insert tab**, in the **Illustrations group**, click the **Chart** button to display the **Insert Chart** dialog box.

b. On the left side of the **Insert Chart** dialog box, click **Column**, if necessary. On the right, under **Column**, in the first row, click the fourth chart type—**3-D Clustered Column**—and then click **OK**.

3 In the Excel worksheet window, click cell **B1**, type **Male** and then press (Tab). With cell **C1** selected, type **Female** and then click cell **A2**.

a. With cell **A2** selected, type **2013** and then press (Tab) to move to cell **B2**. Type **36** and then press (Tab). In cell **C2**, type **32** and then press (Tab) two times to move to **row 3**.

b. Using the technique you just practiced, and without changing any values in **column D**, type the following data:

	Male	Female	Series 3
2013	36	32	2
2014	47	39	2
2015	52	43	3

c. Point to the lower right corner of the blue border to display the ⬈ pointer, and then drag to the left to select only cells **A1** through **C5**.

d. Point to the lower right corner of the blue border to display the ⬈ pointer, and then drag up to select only cells **A1** through **C4**.

e. In the upper right corner of the Excel window, click the **Close** button, and then **Save** your Word document. Scroll as necessary to view the chart on **Page 2** of your document.

4 If necessary, click in an empty area of the chart to select it. On the **Design tab**, in the **Data group**, click the **Edit Data** button to redisplay the embedded Excel worksheet.

a. In the Excel worksheet, click cell **C4**, and then type **45** Press (Enter), and then **Close** the Excel window.

b. With the chart selected, on the **Design tab**, in the **Type group**, click the **Change Chart Type** button.

c. In the **Change Chart Type** dialog box, on the left, click **Bar**, and then on the right under **Bar**, in the first row, click the first chart type—**Clustered Bar**. Click **OK**.

5 On the **Layout tab**, in the **Labels group**, click the **Chart Title** button, and then from the displayed menu, click **Above Chart**. Select the text *Chart Title*, and then type **Tour Summary**

a. On the **Layout tab**, in the **Labels group**, click the **Axis Titles** button, point to **Primary Horizontal Axis Title**, and then click **Title Below Axis**. Select the text *Axis Title*, and then type **Average Age**

b. Click in an empty corner inside the chart to deselect the axis title. On the **Layout tab**, in the **Labels group**, click the **Data Labels** button, and then click **Outside End**.

c. With the chart selected, on the **Design tab**, in the **Chart Styles group**, click the **More** button to display

(Project 4D Strategy Session continues on the next page)

Content-Based Assessments

Skills Review | Project **4D** Strategy Session (continued)

the **Chart Styles** gallery. In the first row, click the third chart style—**Style 3**.

d. Select the chart title text. On the **Format tab**, in the **Shape Styles group**, click the **More** button to display the **Shape Styles** gallery. In the third row, click the second style—**Light 1 Outline, Colored Fill – Blue, Accent 1**.

e. Click in an empty corner of the chart so that the chart, and not the title, is selected. On the **Format tab**, in the **Size group**, click the **Shape Height spin box down arrow** to **2.7"** to display the chart on **Page 1** of the document.

f. Click the **Home tab**. In the **Paragraph group**, click the **Center** button.

6 Press Ctrl + Home. Click the **File tab** to display **Backstage** view, and then click **Info**. On the right side of the window, click **Properties**, and then click **Show Document Panel** to display the **Document Information Panel**. In the **Author** box, delete any text, and then type your first and last names. In the **Subject** box, type your course name and section number, and in the **Keywords** box, type **strategy session, memo Close** the Document Information Panel.

7 Press Ctrl + F2 to display the **Print Preview** in **Backstage** view. Examine the **Print Preview**, and make any necessary adjustments. **Save** your document. Print your document or submit electronically as directed by your instructor. From **Backstage** view, **Exit** Word.

End **You have completed Project 4D** _____

Content-Based Assessments

Apply **4A** skills from these Objectives:

1 Apply and Modify Quick Styles
2 Create New Styles
3 Manage Styles
4 Create a Multilevel List

Mastering Word | Project **4E** Trip Tips

In the following Mastering Word project, you will create a handout for Carl Kawaoka, Tour Operations Manager of Lehua Hawaiian Adventures, which details tips for tour participants. Your completed document will look similar to Figure 4.49.

Project Files

For Project 4E, you will need the following file:

> w04E_Trip_Tips

You will save your document as:

> Lastname_Firstname_4E_Trip_Tips

Project Results

Lehua Hawaiian Adventures

Tips for a Successful Trip

> *Health and Safety*

- Remember to bring any prescription medications or supplements that you take regularly.
- Consider bringing disposable contact lenses for the trip.
- Eat healthy throughout the trip, and be sure you get plenty of protein and carbohydrates.
- Drink lots of water.
- Let your tour guide know if you feel ill.
- Wash your hands regularly.
- On an uphill hike, take shorter steps.

> *Packing Suggestions*

- Pack appropriately for the temperature, weather conditions, and type of trip.
- For water trips, bring rubber shoes.
- For hiking trips, be sure your shoes are broken in.
- Bring a small notebook to record your thoughts during the trip.
- A pair of lightweight binoculars will help you get a better view from a distance.
- Leave your mobile phone and other electronic devices behind.
- Bring extra camera batteries and film or memory cards.
- Leave your perfume or cologne at home. Some animals have particularly sensitive noses.

> *Other Tips*

- Wear subdued clothing to blend in with the scenery; you'll be more likely to get closer to wildlife.
- Remember to turn off your camera's auto flash when photographing animals.
- For certain trips, be sure you have the appropriate skills that are required.

Enjoy Your Adventure!

> *Plan Ahead*

- Research your options.
- Visit our Web site.
- Make reservations early.

Lastname_Firstname_4E_Trip_Tips

Figure 4.49

(Project 4E Trip Tips continues on the next page)

Content-Based Assessments

Mastering Word | Project **4E** Trip Tips (continued)

1 **Start** Word. From your student files, open the document **w04E_Trip_Tips**. **Save** the file in your **Word Chapter 4** folder as **Lastname_Firstname_4E_Trip_Tips** Insert the file name in the footer. For any proper names flagged as spelling errors, right-click, and **Ignore All**.

2 Select the first paragraph—*Lehua Hawaiian Adventures*, and then apply the **Title** style. Select the second paragraph that begins *Tips for*, apply the **Heading 2** style, change the **Font Size** to **16**, and then change the **Spacing After** to **6 pt**. Display the **Quick Styles** gallery, right-click **Heading 2**, and then click **Update Heading 2 to Match Selection**.

3 Scroll to view **Page 2**, and then select the paragraph *Enjoy your Adventure!* Apply the **Heading 2** style. Change the document **Theme** to **Opulent**.

4 Near the top of **Page 1**, select the third paragraph, *Health and Safety*, apply **Italic**, and change the **Font Color** to **Pink, Accent 1, Darker 25%**—in the fifth column, the fifth color. With the text selected, display the **Quick Styles** gallery. Click **Save Selection as a New Quick Style**, and then name the new style **Tip Heading** Apply the **Tip Heading** style to the paragraphs *Packing Suggestions*, *Other Tips*, and *Plan Ahead*. **Modify** the **Tip Heading** style by applying **Bold**.

5 Select the block of text beginning with *Health and Safety* and ending with *that are required* on **Page 2**. Apply a **Multilevel List** with the ❖, ➢, ▪ style. Select the paragraphs below each tip heading, and **Increase Indent** one time.

6 Select the entire list, and then display the **Define New List Style** dialog box. Name the list style **Tips List** If necessary, change the **1st level** to **Bullet: ➢** and set the **Font Color** to **Pink, Accent 1**—in the fifth column, the first color. Set the **2nd level** to **Bullet: ▪**. Be sure the bullet ▪ displays in black. Click **OK**.

7 At the bottom of **Page 1**, beginning with *Plan Ahead*, select the last four paragraphs. Apply the **Tips List** multilevel list style. Select the last three paragraphs, and then click **Increase Indent** one time.

8 From **Backstage** view, click **Properties**, and then click **Show Document Panel**. In the **Document Information Panel**, in the **Author** box, type your name. In the **Subject** box, type your course name and section, and in the **Keywords** box, type **trip tips, multilevel list**

9 Check your document in **Print Preview**, and then make any necessary corrections. **Save** your document, and then print the document or submit electronically as directed by your instructor. **Exit** Word.

 You have completed Project 4E ——————————————————————

Content-Based Assessments

- **5** Change the Style Set and Paragraph Spacing of a Document
- **6** Insert a Chart and Enter Data into a Chart
- **7** Change a Chart Type
- **8** Format a Chart

Mastering Word | Project **4F** Hiking FAQ

In the following Mastering Word project, you will create a document that provides frequently asked questions (FAQs) and includes a chart about hiking trips offered by Lehua Hawaiian Adventures. Your completed document will look similar to Figure 4.50.

Project Files

For Project 4F, you will need the following file:

w04F_Hiking_FAQ

You will save your document as:

Lastname_Firstname_4F_Hiking_FAQ

Project Results

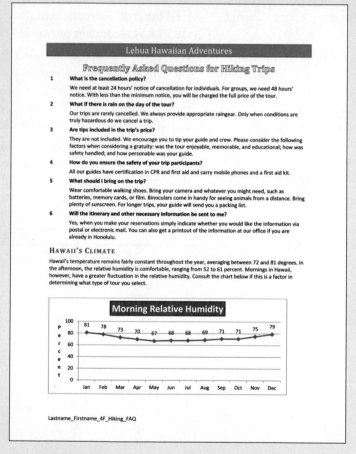

Figure 4.50

(Project 4F Hiking FAQ continues on the next page)

Content-Based Assessments

Mastering Word | Project 4F Hiking FAQ (continued)

1 **Start** Word. From your student files, open the file **w04F_Hiking_FAQ**, and then save the document in your **Word Chapter 4** folder as **Lastname_Firstname_4F_ Hiking_FAQ** Insert the file name in the footer. For any proper names flagged as spelling errors, right-click, and **Ignore All**.

2 Format the first paragraph—the title *Lehua Hawaiian Adventures*—with the **Heading 1** style. Change its **Font Size** to **16**, and then **Center** the title. Select the second paragraph, apply the **Heading 2** style, and then **Center** the paragraph. Select the paragraph *Hawaii's Climate*, and then apply the **Heading 3** style. Change the **Style Set** to **Thatch**. Change the **Paragraph Spacing** style to **Compact**. Select all the numbered paragraphs, and then apply **Bold**. For each single paragraph following a numbered paragraph, click the **Increase Indent** button one time.

3 Move the insertion point to the end of the document, and then press Enter two times. **Insert** a **Clustered Column** chart, and then beginning in cell **B1**, and without changing any values in **column C** or **column D**, type the following data, pressing Tab to move from one cell to the next. Note: As you type, the displayed instructions will automatically move to a new row.

4 Select the chart data range **A1** through **B13**, and then **Close** Excel. Change the chart type to a **Line** chart using the **Line with Markers** style. Display **Data Labels Above** the data points. Add a **Primary Vertical Axis Title** in the style **Vertical Title** with the text **Percent** and **Delete** the legend.

5 Change the chart style to **Style 4**. Format the chart title as a shape style, using the **Colored Fill – Red, Accent 2 Shape Style**. Change the **Shape Height** of the chart to **2.4"**.

6 Display the **Document Information Panel**, add your name, course name and section, and the keywords **FAQ, hiking** Check your document in **Print Preview**, and then make any necessary corrections. **Save** your document, and then print the document or submit electronically as directed by your instructor. **Exit** Word.

	Morning Relative Humidity	Series 2	Series 3
Jan	81	2.4	2
Feb	78	4.4	2
Mar	73	1.8	3
Apr	70	2.8	5
May	67		
Jun	68		
Jul	68		
Aug	69		
Sep	71		
Oct	71		
Nov	75		
Dec	79		

End You have completed Project 4F

Content-Based Assessments

Mastering Word | Project **4G** Expense Reduction (continued)

1 **Start** Word. From your student files, open the file **w04G_Expense_Reduction**, and then save the document in your **Word Chapter 4** folder as **Lastname_Firstname_4G_Expense_Reduction** Insert the file name in the footer. For any proper names flagged as spelling errors, right-click, and **Ignore All**.

2 Apply the **Title** style to the first paragraph. Apply the **Strong** style to *MEMO*, and then change the **Font Size** to **26**. Select *TO:*—include the colon—and then apply **Bold** and change the **Font Color** to **Dark Blue, Text 2**. Save the selection as a new Quick Style with the name **Memo Heading** and then apply the new style to *FROM:*, *DATE:*, and *SUBJECT:*.

3 Change the **Style Set** to **Modern**, and then change the **Paragraph Spacing** style to **Relaxed**. On **Page 1**, beginning with the heading *TO:*, change the **Font Size** of all the remaining text to **11**. Select the text on **Page 2**, and apply a **Multilevel List** with the format **1., a., i.**. For the paragraphs beginning *Mobile phone*, *Reduction*, *Focus*, *Research*, *Evaluate*, and *Utilize*, **Increase Indent** one time.

4 Select the entire list, and then display the **Define New List Style** dialog box. Name the style **Reduction List** Change the **2nd level** letter style to **A, B, C, …**.

5 Position the insertion point at the end of the document. **Insert** a **Pie in 3-D** chart. Type the following chart data:

Projected Savings in Dollars	
Employee	15,000
Operations	43,000
Marketing	26,000

6 Select the chart data range **A1** through **B4**, and then **Close** Excel. Display **Data Labels** in the **Center** position on the data points. Format the data labels with **Bold** emphasis and a **Font Size** of **12**. **Center** the chart horizontally on the page.

7 Display the **Document Information Panel**, add your name, course name and section, and the keywords **expenses, reduction** Check your document in **Print Preview**, and then make any necessary corrections. **Save** your document, and then print or submit electronically as directed. **Exit** Word.

End **You have completed Project 4G** ——————————————

Content-Based Assessments

GO! Fix It | Project **4H** New Tours

Project Files

For Project 4H, you will need the following file:

w04H_New_Tours

You will save your document as:

Lastname_Firstname_4H_New_Tours

In this project, you will edit a flyer from James Gilroy, a guide for Lehua Hawaiian Adventures, to tour guides indicating new tours and tour popularity by gender. From the student files that accompany this textbook, open the file **w04H_New_Tours**, and then save the file in your **Word Chapter 4** folder as **Lastname_Firstname_4H_New_Tours**

To complete the project, you must make changes to the file including formatting text, formatting a multilevel list, and editing a chart. Correct the following:

- The title should have an appropriate style applied.
- The remaining paragraphs should be formatted as a logical multilevel list of two basic tour types—*Full Day Tours* and *Half Day Tours*.
- A custom list style should be created and applied to the first-level list items.
- The chart data for *One Week* should display as 30 percent for *Men* and 10 percent for *Women*.
- The chart title should display as *Tour Popularity by Gender*, a legend should display at the bottom, and the chart type should be Clustered Column with an appropriate chart style applied.

Things you should know to complete this project:

- Displaying formatting marks will assist in formatting the document.
- The final document should fit on one page.

Save your document and add the file name to the footer. In the Document Information Panel, type your first and last names in the Author box and your course name and section number in the Subject box. In the Keywords box, type **new tours, tour popularity** Save your file, and then print or submit electronically as directed by your instructor.

 You have completed Project 4H ———————————————

Content-Based Assessments

Apply a combination of the **4A** and **4B** skills.

GO! Make It | Project **4I** Newsletter

Project Files

For Project 4I, you will need the following file:

w04I_Newsletter

You will save your document as:

Lastname_Firstname_4I_Newsletter

From the student files that accompany this textbook, open the file **w04I_Newsletter** and create the document shown in Figure 4.52. Use the Office theme and Word 2010 style set. Apply existing styles to the date and three tour headings. Create a new style and apply it to the four article headings. Apply any other text and paragraph formatting as shown and insert the chart using the percentages as the data in column B. Add your name, your course name and section number, and the keywords **newsletter, chart** to the document properties. Save the file in your **Word Chapter 4** folder as **Lastname_Firstname_4I_Newsletter** and then print or submit electronically as directed by your instructor.

Project Results

Figure 4.52

Lehua Hawaiian Adventures

1250 Punchbowl Street ○ Honolulu, HI 96813 ○ 808-555-0754 ○ www.lehua-adventure.com

Spring Edition

Customer Trip Ideas

We recently surveyed you to ask what trips you'd like to see added to our upcoming schedule. While many of you responded that our selection was already sufficient, we did receive lots of great ideas. We've decided to add a few of your ideas to this year's adventures. See the chart below that summarizes the voting results.

NEW: MANOA WATERFALL ADVENTURE
Hike to the Manoa Waterfall, the tallest accessible waterfall on Oahu. See rainforests, giant ferns, beautiful waterfalls, streams, and unique animals along the way.

NEW: SHARK ADVENTURE TOUR
Travel three miles off Oahu's shore to the shark grounds. You'll get into a shark cage with windows that are so clear you'll feel like the sharks are coming right in with you. No diving experience is required.

NEW: UNDERWATER PHOTOGRAPHY CLASS
Learn the basics of underwater photography as you dive two miles off Oahu's shore. The primary focus will be on taking pictures of fish.

New Tour Guides

We'd like to introduce two of our newest guides.
Sam Glaser grew up in Visalia, California, and moved to Honolulu a few years ago after getting a Botany degree. Hiking has always been a hobby of his, and he's backpacked throughout the islands. He is eager to pass on his extensive knowledge of Hawaii's culture, plants, animals, and history with you and enjoys sharing his passion for the outdoors with others.
Leah Parker grew up on the island of Oahu and has always loved the natural world. She spent her time hiking, diving, surfing, camping, and biking. Leah has a degree in Marine Science and Zoology from the University of Hawaii. She is excited to guide you in discovering Hawaii's natural beauty and splendor.

Kayaking Lessons Available

Whether you're a beginner or experienced, we have begun offering kayaking lessons for any skill set. If you are taking one of our multi-day kayaking trips, why not schedule a lesson the day before to take your skills to the next level? Even if you are a proficient paddler, we can design a custom class for you that will teach you some specifics about kayaking in Hawaiian waters.

Surfing Lessons Available

Whether you're interested in long board or short board surfing, our instructors are happy to pass their skills on to you. This would also be a great activity for a family or group. We guarantee that you will stand during your first lesson.

Voting Results

- 17%
- 22%
- 38%
- 23%

■ Culture
■ Scenery
■ Skill Classes
■ Wildlife

Lastname_Firstname_4I_Newsletter

End You have completed Project 4I

GO! Solve It | Project **4J** Custom Adventure

Project Files

For Project 4J, you will need the following file:

w04J_Custom_Adventure

You will save your document as:

Lastname_Firstname_4J_Custom_Adventure

Open the file **w04J_Custom_Adventure** and save it as **Lastname_Firstname_4J_Custom_Adventure** in your **Word Chapter 4** folder. Change the style set, and apply existing styles to the first two and last two paragraphs of the document. Create a new style for *Choose an Island*, and apply the style to *Choose Your Favorite Activities* and *Develop Your Skills*. Define a multilevel list style and apply the style to all lists in the document. Adjust paragraph and text formats to display the information appropriately in a one-page document. Include the file name in the footer, add appropriate document properties, and print your document or submit electronically as directed by your instructor.

		Performance Level		
		Exemplary: You consistently applied the relevant skills	Proficient: You sometimes, but not always, applied the relevant skills	Developing: You rarely or never applied the relevant skills
Performance Element	Change style set and apply existing styles	All existing styles are applied correctly using an appropriate style set.	Existing styles are applied correctly but an appropriate style set is not used.	One or more styles are not applied properly.
	Create a style	A new style is created and applied properly.	A new style is created but not applied properly.	A new style is not created.
	Create a multilevel list	A multilevel list style is created and applied correctly.	A multilevel list style is applied correctly but the default style is used.	A multilevel list style is not applied correctly.
	Format attractively and appropriately	Document formatting is attractive and appropriate.	The document is adequately formatted but is unattractive or difficult to read.	The document is formatted inadequately.

End You have completed Project 4J

Content-Based Assessments

Apply a combination of the **4A** and **4B** skills.

GO! Solve It | Project **4K** Fall Newsletter

Project Files

For Project 4K, you will need the following file:

w04K_Fall_Newsletter

You will save your document as:

Lastname_Firstname_4K_Fall_Newsletter

Open the file **w04K_Fall Newsletter** and save it as **Lastname_Firstname_4K_Fall_Newsletter** to your **Word Chapter 4** folder. Apply appropriate styles to the first five paragraphs of the document. Create and apply styles for the four article headings and three trip titles. Apply a multilevel list style to the trip titles and their descriptions. Change the chart type to display the proportion of parts to a whole. Modify and format the chart so that it clearly explains the represented data. Make other formatting changes to create a one-page document. Include the file name in the footer, add appropriate document properties, and print your document or submit electronically as directed by your instructor.

Performance Element		**Performance Level**		
		Exemplary: You consistently applied the relevant skills	**Proficient:** You sometimes, but not always, applied the relevant skills	**Developing:** You rarely or never applied the relevant skills
	Apply existing styles	All existing styles are applied correctly.	Some existing styles are not applied correctly.	No existing styles are applied.
	Create and apply new styles	Two new styles are created and applied properly.	Only one new style is created, or new styles are not applied properly.	No new styles are created.
	Apply a multilevel list style	The multilevel list style is applied correctly.	The multilevel list style is applied but no second level items are created.	The multilevel list style is not applied.
	Modify a chart	The chart is changed to a pie chart, and data labels and legend display.	The chart is modified but incorrect chart type is used or data labels and legend do not display.	The chart is not modified.
	Format attractively and appropriately	Document formatting is attractive and appropriate.	The document is adequately formatted but is unattractive or difficult to read.	The document is formatted inadequately.

End You have completed Project 4K

Outcomes-Based Assessments

Rubric

The following outcomes-based assessments are *open-ended assessments*. That is, there is no specific correct result; your result will depend on your approach to the information provided. Make *Professional Quality* your goal. Use the following scoring rubric to guide you in *how* to approach the problem and then to evaluate *how well* your approach solves the problem.

The *criteria*—Software Mastery, Content, Format and Layout, and Process—represent the knowledge and skills you have gained that you can apply to solving the problem. The *levels of performance*—Professional Quality, Approaching Professional Quality, or Needs Quality Improvements—help you and your instructor evaluate your result.

	Your completed project is of Professional Quality if you:	Your completed project is Approaching Professional Quality if you:	Your completed project Needs Quality Improvements if you:
1-Software Mastery	Choose and apply the most appropriate skills, tools, and features and identify efficient methods to solve the problem.	Choose and apply some appropriate skills, tools, and features, but not in the most efficient manner.	Choose inappropriate skills, tools, or features, or are inefficient in solving the problem.
2-Content	Construct a solution that is clear and well organized, contains content that is accurate, appropriate to the audience and purpose, and is complete. Provide a solution that contains no errors in spelling, grammar, or style.	Construct a solution in which some components are unclear, poorly organized, inconsistent, or incomplete. Misjudge the needs of the audience. Have some errors in spelling, grammar, or style, but the errors do not detract from comprehension.	Construct a solution that is unclear, incomplete, or poorly organized; contains some inaccurate or inappropriate content; and contains many errors in spelling, grammar, or style. Do not solve the problem.
3-Format and Layout	Format and arrange all elements to communicate information and ideas, clarify function, illustrate relationships, and indicate relative importance.	Apply appropriate format and layout features to some elements, but not others. Overuse features, causing minor distraction.	Apply format and layout that does not communicate information or ideas clearly. Do not use format and layout features to clarify function, illustrate relationships, or indicate relative importance. Use available features excessively, causing distraction.
4-Process	Use an organized approach that integrates planning, development, self-assessment, revision, and reflection.	Demonstrate an organized approach in some areas, but not others; or, use an insufficient process of organization throughout.	Do not use an organized approach to solve the problem.

Outcomes-Based Assessments

Apply a combination of the 4A and 4B skills.

GO! Think | Project **4L** Training Memo

Project Files

For Project 4L, you will need the following file:

New blank Word document

You will save your document as:

Lastname_Firstname_4L_Training_Memo

Carl Kawaoka, Tour Operations Manager, wants to send a memo to all tour guides concerning upcoming training opportunities.

Date	Training	Location	Length
June 6	Horseback Riding	Hamilton Stables	4 hours
June 17	Orienteering	Kapiolani Regional Park	8 hours
June 29	Basic Coastal Sailing	Waikiki Beach	6 hours
July 7	Intermediate Sea Kayaking	Waimea Bay	5 hours

Using this information, create the memo. Include a multilevel list for the four training sessions. Insert a chart to compare class length. Format the entire memo in a manner that is professional and easy to read and understand. Save the file as **Lastname_Firstname_4L_Training_Memo** Insert the file name in the footer and add appropriate document properties. Print or submit as directed.

End You have completed Project 4L

Outcomes-Based Assessments

Apply a combination of the 4A and 4B skills.

GO! Think | Project **4M** Waterfalls Handout

Project Files

For Project 4M, you will need the following file:

New blank Word document

You will save your document as:

Lastname_Firstname_4M_Waterfalls_Handout

Lehua Hawaiian Adventures is promoting a three-day tour of Hawaii's waterfalls. The tour includes hiking, riding in a four-wheel drive vehicle, and a helicopter ride. Available dates are June 20, July 15, and August 3. Cost is $1,500, which includes hotel and a daily continental breakfast.

Waterfall	Location	Access	Height in feet
Akaka Falls	Big Island	Paved Road	422
Hi'ilawe Falls	Big Island	Paved road	1600
Wai'ilikahi Falls	Big Island	Helicopter	1080
Opaekaa Falls	Kauai	Visible from overlook	151
Waipo'o Falls	Kauai	Visible from overlook	800
Makahiku Falls	Maui	Hiking trail	180
Waimoku Falls	Maui	Hiking trail	400

Create the promotional handout. Include a multilevel list using the waterfall, location, and access data shown. Insert a chart to compare the waterfall heights by location. Format the flyer, list, and chart in a manner that is professional and easy to read and understand. Save the file as **Lastname_Firstname_4M_Waterfalls_Handout** Insert the file name in the footer and add appropriate document properties. Print or submit electronically as directed.

 End **You have completed Project 4M** ————————————————

Outcomes-Based Assessments

Apply a combination of the 4A and 4B skills.

You and GO! | Project **4N** Cover Letter

Project Files

For Project 4N, you will need the following file:

New blank Word document

You will save your document as:

Lastname_Firstname_4N_Cover_Letter

Create a cover letter to be sent with a resume to potential employers. Add a multilevel list that includes the types of college courses you have taken, such as Computer Applications, English, Mathematics, and Psychology. Below each course type, list the names of specific courses. Insert a chart that displays the total number of credit hours earned for each subject. Format the letter, multilevel list, and chart appropriately to create a professional appearance. Save the file as **Lastname_Firstname_4N_Cover_Letter** Insert a footer with the file name, and add appropriate document properties. Print the document or submit electronically as directed.

 You have completed Project 4N _____

Creating Web Pages and Using Advanced Proofing Options

OUTCOMES
At the end of this chapter you will be able to:

OBJECTIVES
Mastering these objectives will enable you to:

PROJECT 5A
Create a Web page from a Word document.

1. Create a Web Page from a Word Document (p. 283)
2. Insert and Modify Hyperlinks in a Web Page (p. 289)
3. Create a Blog Post (p. 296)

PROJECT 5B
Use proofing tools and save a document in RTF format.

4. Locate Word Settings to Personalize Word 2010 (p. 301)
5. Collect and Paste Images and Text (p. 303)
6. Locate Supporting Information (p. 306)
7. Use Advanced Find and Replace and Proofing Options (p. 311)
8. Save in Other File Formats (p. 316)

kwest/Shutterstock

In This Chapter

In this chapter you will use text, graphic, and document formatting features in Word to create a professional-looking Web page that includes hyperlinks. You will also create a blog post, which can contain text, images, and links to related blogs or Web pages.

You will also examine Word settings so that you can use Word in the most productive way for you. You will locate information on the Internet by using research features, translate foreign-language text, and use the Office Clipboard to collect and organize information. Finally, you will save documents in other useful formats.

The projects in this chapter relate to **Texas Spectrum Wireless**, which provides accessories and software for all major brands of cell phones, smart phones, PDAs, MP3 players, and laptop computers. The company sells thousands of unique products in their retail stores, which are located throughout Texas and the southern United States. They also sell thousands of items each year through their Web site, and offer free shipping and returns to their customers. The company takes pride in offering unique categories of accessories such as waterproof and ruggedized gear.

Project 5A Web Page

myitlab
Project 5A Training

Project Activities

In Activities 5.01 through 5.12, you will assist Eliott Verschoren, Vice President of Marketing for Texas Spectrum Wireless, in creating a new home page for the online store and a new blog post for the company's customer service blog. Your completed documents will look similar to Figure 5.1.

Project Files

For Project 5A, you will need the following files:

w05A_Home_Page
w05A_Features_Guide

You will save your documents as:

Lastname_Firstname_5A_Home_Page
Lastname_Firstname_5A_Features_Guide
Lastname_Firstname_5A_Blog_Post

Project Results

Figure 5.1
Project 5A Home Page

Objective 1 | Create a Web Page from a Word Document

You can create a **Web page** from a Word document. A Web page is a file coded in **HyperText Markup Language**—referred to as **HTML**—that can be viewed on the Internet by using a **Web browser**. A Web browser—also referred to as just a **browser**—is software that interprets HTML files, formats them into Web pages, and then displays them. HTML is a markup language that communicates color and graphics in a format that all computers can understand.

Activity 5.01 | Saving a Document as a Web Page

For a Word document to display in a browser, you must save it in HTML. In this activity, you will save a Word document in the Web Page format so it can be added to the company's Web site.

1 **Start** Word. From your student files, locate and open the file **w05A_Home_Page**. If necessary, display formatting marks and rulers.

2 Click the **File tab**, and then click **Save As**. In the **Save As** dialog box, navigate to the location where you are saving your files for this chapter. Create a new folder named **Word Chapter 5** In the lower portion of the **Save As** dialog box, click the **Save as type arrow**, and then in the displayed list, click **Web Page**.

> In this project, you will use the **Web Page format**, a file type that saves a Word document as an HTML file, with some elements of the Web page in a folder, separate from the Web page. This format is useful if you want to access individual elements, such as pictures, separately.

3 Near the bottom of the dialog box, click the **Change Title** button, and then in the displayed **Enter Text** dialog box, in the **Page title** box, type **Texas Spectrum Wireless** Compare your screen with Figure 5.2.

> By creating this title, when the document is viewed as a Web page with a browser, *Texas Spectrum Wireless* will display on the title bar. Because Internet search engines locate the content of Web pages by title, it is important to create a title that describes the content of the Web page.

Figure 5.2

Page title

Save as type indicates *Web Page*

Change Title button

4 Click **OK**. In the displayed **Save As** dialog box, in the **File name** box, type **Lastname_Firstname_5A_Home_Page** and then click **Save**. Compare your screen with Figure 5.3.

Because you saved the document as a Web Page, the document displays in Web Layout view, and on the status bar, the Web Layout button is active. The Zoom level may change to display text according to the size of your screen.

Figure 5.3

Zoom level—yours may differ

Web Layout button active

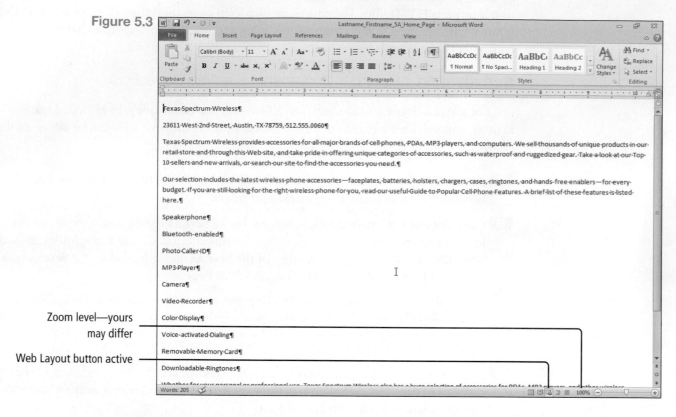

5 On the **Insert tab**, in the **Header & Footer group**, click the **Footer** button. At the bottom of the displayed list, click **Edit Footer**, and then use **Quick Parts** to insert the file name in the footer.

In Web Layout view, headers and footers do not display on the screen, so you used this alternative method to insert the footer.

6 On the **Design tab**, in the **Close group**, click the **Close Header and Footer** button. Save your document.

Activity 5.02 | Applying Background Color

In this activity, you will format text and change the background color of the document so that when it is viewed as a Web page, an attractive background color displays.

1 Select the first paragraph of the document—the company name *Texas Spectrum Wireless*. On the Mini toolbar, apply **Bold** B , and then change the **Font Size** to **48**.

2 Select the second paragraph—the company address and telephone number. Apply **Bold** B , and then change the **Font Size** to **24**.

3 Select the first and second paragraphs, and then click the **Center** button. Click anywhere to deselect the text, and then compare your screen with Figure 5.4.

Figure 5.4

Text formatted and centered

Text wrapping may vary

4 Beginning with the paragraph that begins *Texas Spectrum Wireless provides*, select all the remaining text in the document, and then change the **Font Size** to **14**.

5 At the beginning of the third paragraph, select the text *Texas Spectrum Wireless*. Apply **Bold**, click the **Font Color button arrow**, and then under **Theme Colors**, in the sixth column, click the last color—**Red, Accent 2, Darker 50%**.

6 Press Ctrl + End. In the paragraph that begins *Whether*, select the text *Texas Spectrum Wireless*. Apply **Bold**, and then click the **Font Color** button.

7 Select the last paragraph, apply **Bold**, and then deselect the text.

8 On the **Page Layout tab**, in the **Page Background group**, click the **Page Color** button, and then in the fifth column, click the third color—**Blue, Accent 1, Lighter 60%**. **Save** your document, and then compare your screen with Figure 5.5.

Figure 5.5

Blue page color applied

Red font color and bold applied

Bold applied

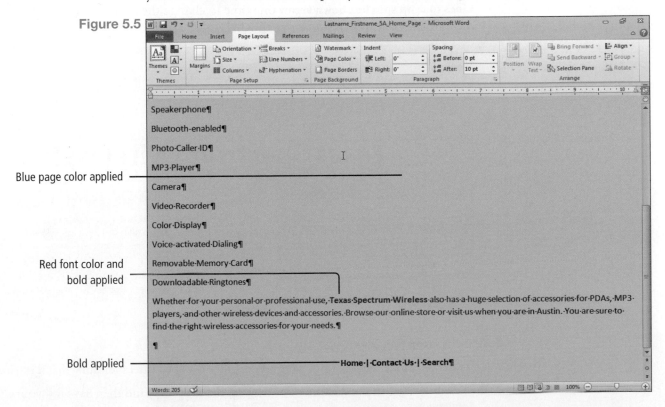

Activity 5.03 | Inserting a Drop Cap in Text

A *drop cap* is a large capital letter at the beginning of a paragraph that formats text in a visually distinctive manner.

1 At the beginning of the third paragraph in the document, select the red letter *T*. On the **Insert tab**, in the **Text group**, click the **Drop Cap** button, and then click **Drop Cap Options**. Compare your screen with Figure 5.6.

Here you can select either the *dropped* position, which enlarges the letter and drops it into the text, or the *in margin* position, which drops the enlarged letter into the left margin. The Drop Cap dialog box provides a visual example of each position.

Figure 5.6

In margin example

Dropped example

Selected letter

2 In the **Drop Cap** dialog box, under **Position**, click **Dropped**. Under **Options**, click the **Lines to drop spin box down arrow** one time to change the number of lines by which to drop to **2** lines. Compare your screen with Figure 5.7.

Figure 5.7

Dropped position selected

Height—in lines—of drop cap

3 In the **Drop Cap** dialog box, click **OK**.

Resize handles display around the border of the dropped letter indicating that it is selected.

4 Click anywhere in the document to deselect the drop cap, and then **Save** 🖫 your document.

Activity 5.04 | Sorting Paragraphs

Use the *Sort* command to alphabetize selected text or to order numerical data. *Ascending* refers to sorting alphabetically from A to Z or ordering numerically from the smallest to the largest. *Descending* refers to sorting alphabetically from Z to A or ordering numerically from the largest to smallest.

1 Scroll to display the ten paragraphs that comprise the cell phone features—beginning with *Speakerphone* and ending with *Downloadable Ringtones*. Click to position the insertion point to the left of *Speakerphone*, and then select the ten paragraphs.

2 On the **Home tab**, in the **Paragraph group**, click the **Sort** button $\downarrow$ to display the **Sort Text** dialog box. Compare your screen with Figure 5.8.

Here you can select what you want to sort by, which in this instance is *Paragraphs*; the type of data to sort, which in this instance is *Text*; and the type of sort—ascending or descending.

Figure 5.8

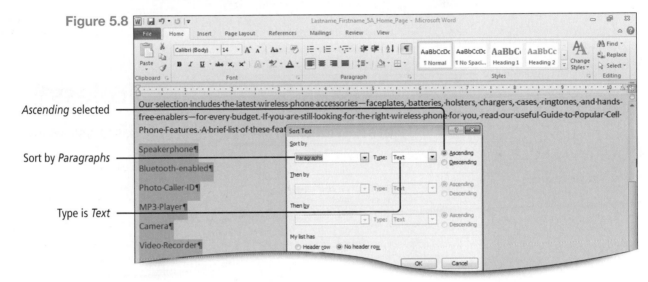

Ascending selected

Sort by *Paragraphs*

Type is *Text*

3 Click **OK** to accept the default settings. Notice the paragraphs are arranged alphabetically.

4 With the paragraphs still selected, in the **Paragraph group**, click the **Bullets** button $\equiv$, and then click anywhere to deselect the bulleted text. Compare your screen with Figure 5.9. **Save** $\blacksquare$ your document.

Figure 5.9

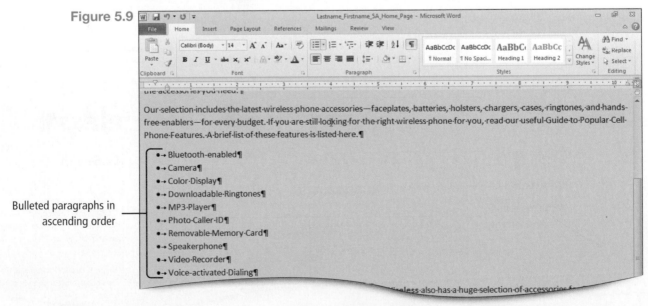

Bulleted paragraphs in ascending order

Activity 5.05 | Inserting a Horizontal Line

Word includes a variety of graphical horizontal lines that can add visual interest to and differentiate sections of a Web page.

1 Press Ctrl + Home. In the second paragraph, click to position the insertion point to the right of the last *0* in the telephone number.

2 Press Enter. On the **Home tab**, in the **Paragraph group**, click the **Border button arrow** , and then click **Borders and Shading**. In the **Borders and Shading** dialog box, if necessary, click the **Borders** tab, and then in the lower left corner, click the **Horizontal Line** button.

3 In the **Horizontal Line** dialog box, scroll down until a thick bright red line displays in the first column. Click the red line, and then compare your screen with Figure 5.10.

Figure 5.10

Horizontal Line dialog box

Bright red line

4 In the **Horizontal Line** dialog box, click **OK**. In your document, point to the red line, and then right-click. From the displayed shortcut menu, click **Format Horizontal Line**.

5 In the **Format Horizontal Line** dialog box, click the **Measure in arrow**, and then click **Percent**. Set the **Width** to **95%** and the **Height** to **8 pt**. Compare your screen with Figure 5.11.

Figure 5.11

Format Horizontal Line dialog box

Width set to 95%

Height set to 8 pt

Width measured as a percent

6 Click **OK**. Point to the line and right-click, and then from the displayed shortcut menu, click **Copy**.

7 In the blank paragraph immediately above the last paragraph of the document that begins *Home*, click to position the insertion point. Right-click, and from the displayed shortcut menu, under **Paste Options**, click the first button—**Keep Source Formatting** 📝—to insert a copy of the red line. **Save** 🖫 your document.

Objective 2 | Insert and Modify Hyperlinks in a Web Page

A Web browser—for example, *Internet Explorer* developed by Microsoft—can transfer files, play sound or video files that are embedded in Web pages, and follow *hyperlinks*—text, buttons, pictures, or other objects displayed on Web pages that, when clicked, access other Web pages, other sections of the active page, or another file.

Activity 5.06 | Inserting a Hyperlink

By inserting hyperlinks, individuals who view your Web page can move to other Web pages inside your *Web site* or to pages in another Web site. A Web site is a group of related Web pages published to a specific location on the Internet. The most common type of hyperlink is a *text link*—a link applied to a selected word or phrase. Text links usually display as blue underlined text.

1 Press [Ctrl] + [End], and notice that the last paragraph consists of a series of words and phrases.

> Web sites commonly have a *navigation bar*—a series of text links across the top or bottom of a Web page that, when clicked, link to another Web page in the same Web site.

Another Way

Alternatively, right-click the selected text, and then from the displayed shortcut menu, click **Hyperlink**.

2 Select the first word in the paragraph—*Home*—and then on the **Insert tab**, in the **Links group**, click the **Hyperlink** button. Compare your screen with Figure 5.12.

Figure 5.12

Hyperlink button

Text to display box indicates *Home*

Insert Hyperlink dialog box

Selected text

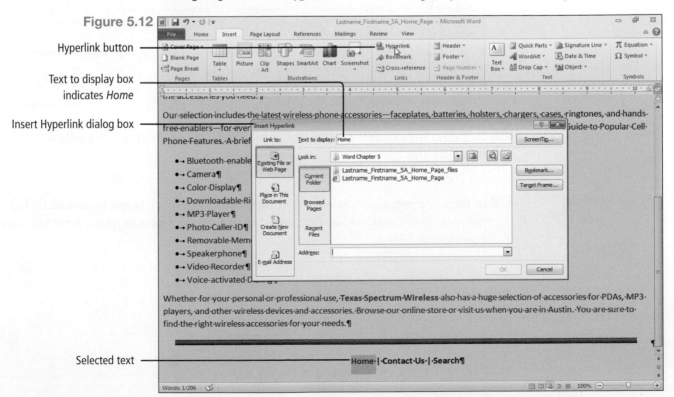

3 Under **Link to**, click **Existing File or Web Page**, if necessary. In the **Address** box, delete any existing text, and then type **www.txspectrum.com** If another address displays while you are typing, continue typing to replace it. When you are finished typing, if any other characters display, delete them.

As you type an Internet address, Word automatically inserts *http://*. An address may display in the Address box as you type. This is a result of the AutoComplete feature, which displays the most recently used Web address from your computer.

4 In the upper right corner, click the **ScreenTip** button. In the **Set Hyperlink ScreenTip** dialog box, in the **ScreenTip text** box, type **Texas Spectrum Wireless** Compare your screen with Figure 5.13.

Text that you type here will display as a ScreenTip when an individual viewing your site points to this hyperlink.

Figure 5.13

ScreenTip text

Address

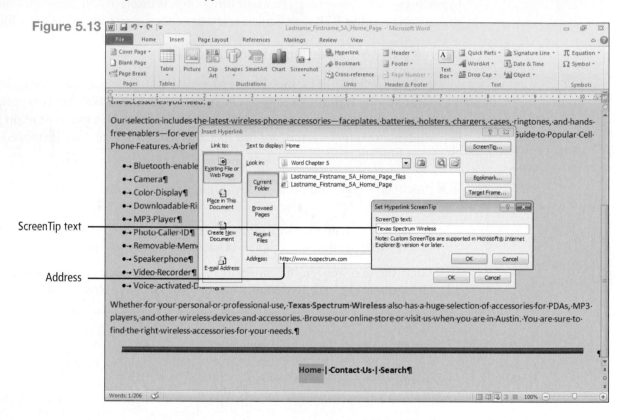

5 In the **Set Hyperlink ScreenTip** dialog box, click **OK**. In the **Insert Hyperlink** dialog box, click **OK**.

The hyperlink is recorded, and the selected text is blue and underlined.

6 In the same paragraph, select the word *Search*. Display the **Insert Hyperlink** dialog box, and in the **Address** box type **www.txspectrum.com/search** As the **ScreenTip text**, type **Search TSW**

7 Click **OK** two times to close the dialog boxes, and then compare your screen with Figure 5.14.

Figure 5.14

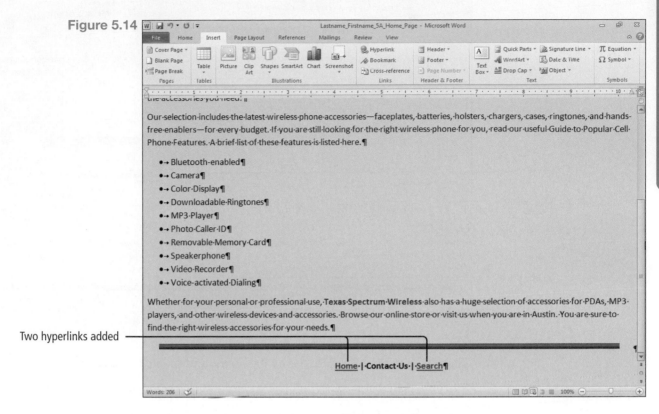

Two hyperlinks added

8 **Save** 💾 your document.

Activity 5.07 | Inserting a Hyperlink That Opens a New E-mail Message

Another common type of hyperlink is an *e-mail address link*, which opens a new message window so that an individual viewing your site can send an e-mail message.

1 At the end of the document, select the text *Contact Us*, and then display the **Insert Hyperlink** dialog box. Under **Link to**, click **E-mail Address**.

2 In the **E-mail address** box, type **jlovrick@txspectrum.com** As the **ScreenTip text**, type **Operations Manager** and then compare your screen with Figure 5.15.

As you type an e-mail address, Word automatically inserts *mailto:*. Other e-mail addresses may display in the Recently used e-mail addresses box.

Figure 5.15

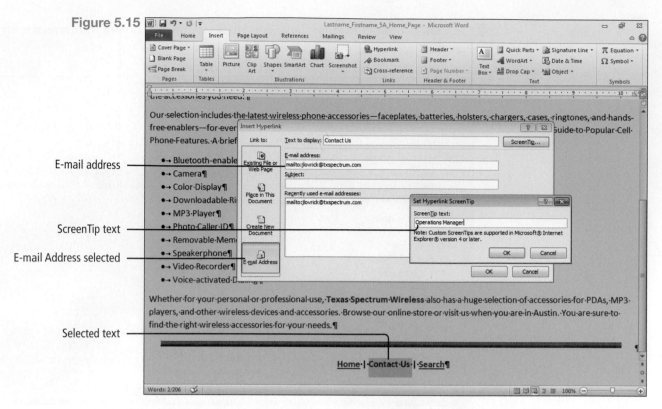

E-mail address

ScreenTip text

E-mail Address selected

Selected text

3 Click **OK** two times to close the dialog boxes, and then click **Save** 💾.

> The hyperlink is recorded, and the selected text changes to blue and is underlined.

Activity 5.08 | Creating a Web Page for an Internal Link

An ***internal link*** is a hyperlink that connects to another page in the same Web site. In this activity, you will create a second Web page for the Web site and create a link to this page from the home page.

1 Without closing your displayed **Lastname_Firstname_5A_Home_Page** document, from your student files, locate and open the file **w05A_Features_Guide**.

> Because you are currently working in Web Layout view, the document opens in Web Layout view.

2 Display **Backstage** view, and then click **Save As**. Navigate to your **Word Chapter 5** folder. Click the **Save as type arrow**, and then click **Web Page**.

3 Click the **Change Title** button to display the **Enter Text** dialog box, and then in the **Page title** box, type **Features Guide** Click **OK**. In the **Save As** dialog box, in the **File name** box, type **Lastname_Firstname_5A_Features_Guide** and then click **Save**.

> When viewed with a browser, *Features Guide* will display on the title bar.

4 On the **Insert tab**, in the **Header & Footer group**, click the **Footer** button, click **Edit Footer**, and then use **Quick Parts** to insert the file name in the footer. Close the footer area.

> Recall that when viewing documents in Web Layout view, footers do not display.

5 Display **Backstage** view. With the **Info** section selected, on the right under the document thumbnail, click **Properties**, and then click **Show Document Panel**. Below the Ribbon, under the displayed message *The Document Information Panel cannot show properties for this file type.*, click **View properties**. Notice the **Lastname_Firstname_5A_Features_Guide Properties** dialog box displays.

> When a document is saved as a Web Page, the Document Information Panel does not display.

6 If necessary, click the **Summary tab**. In the **Subject** box, type your course name and section number. In the **Author** box, delete any existing text, and type your first and last names. In the **Keywords** box, type **web site, features guide** Compare your screen with Figure 5.16.

Figure 5.16

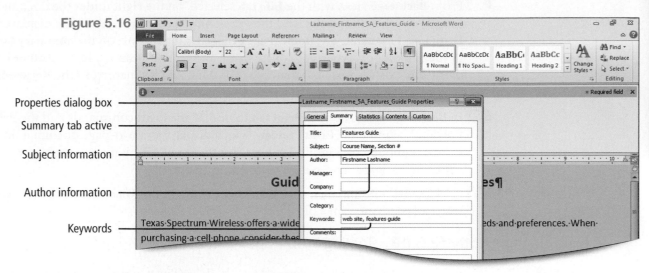

Properties dialog box

Summary tab active

Subject information

Author information

Keywords

7 Click **OK**, click **Save** , and then **Close** your **Lastname_Firstname_5A_Features_Guide** document.

8 With your **Lastname_Firstname_5A_Home_Page** document displayed, in the paragraph that begins *Our selection includes*, select the text *Guide to Popular Cell Phone Features*. On the **Insert tab**, in the **Links group**, click the **Hyperlink** button.

9 Under **Link to**, click **Existing File or Web Page**. In the **Look in** box, be sure that the name of your **Word Chapter 5** folder displays, and then in the list below, click your file—*not* the folder—named **Lastname_Firstname_5A_Features_Guide**. Compare your screen with Figure 5.17.

Figure 5.17

Your storage folder name

Existing File or Web Page selected

Your Lastname_Firstname_5A_Features_Guide file selected

10 Click the **ScreenTip** button, type **Features Guide** and then click **OK** two times to close the dialog boxes.

> The selected text displays in blue and is underlined.

11 From **Backstage** view, with the **Info tab** selected, on the right under the document thumbnail, click **Properties**, and then click **Advanced Properties**. In the displayed **Lastname_Firstname_5A_Home_Page Properties** dialog box, on the **Summary** tab, click in the **Subject** box, type your course name and section number. In the **Author** box, delete any existing text, and then type your first and last names. In the **Keywords** box, type **web site, home page** Click **OK**.

12 In **Backstage** view, click the **Print tab** to display the Print commands and the Print Preview. Examine the **Print Preview**, which displays as a two-page document in Word format without a background color. Click the **Home tab**, make any necessary adjustments, and then **Save** 🔲 your document.

13 Click the **File tab**, and then click **Exit** to exit Word. In the **Microsoft Word** message box, when asked if you want a picture to be available, click **No**.

Activity 5.09 │ Testing Web Pages in a Browser

In this activity, you will display and test the Texas Spectrum Wireless Web pages in your browser.

> **Alert!** │ **I Cannot Connect to the Internet**
>
> If the system on which you are working is not connected to the Internet, skip this activity and move to Activity 5.10.

1 From your taskbar, start **Windows Explorer**. Alternatively, click **Start** 🟢 , and then click **Computer**—or My Computer on Windows XP. Navigate to your **Word Chapter 5** folder, and then select your **Lastname_Firstname_5A_Home_Page** HTML document. Compare your screen with Figure 5.18.

Figure 5.18

Word Chapter 5 folder

File Type indicates HTML—your Windows Explorer view may vary

Your 5A_Home_Page HTML file selected

2 Double-click the file to open it in your browser.

> This textbook uses Internet Explorer as the default browser, but it is not necessary to use Internet Explorer. Because this file is an HTML file, it will display in any browser.

3 If necessary, scroll to the bottom of the Web page, and then point to the text *Home* to display the 🖑 pointer and the ScreenTip that you created. Compare your screen with Figure 5.19.

Figure 5.19

Internet Explorer—your
browser may vary

Document displayed in
browser—your hyperlink
colors may vary

ScreenTip for hyperlink

Pointer

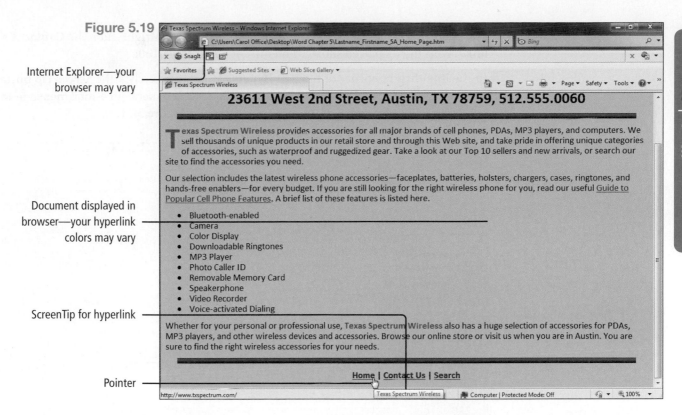

On the same line, point to the text *Contact Us* and *Search* to display the ScreenTips.

Locate and then click the **Guide to Popular Cell Phone Features** link to display the linked page. Compare your screen with Figure 5.20.

The browser displays the Features Guide Web page.

Figure 5.20

Back button—yours
may differ

Displayed Web page

In your browser, locate and then click the **Back** button to return to the previously displayed page.

Close the browser window. If necessary, close any Windows Explorer windows.

Activity 5.10 | Editing and Removing Hyperlinks

You can modify the hyperlinks in your Web page—for example, to change an address or ScreenTip—and you can also remove a hyperlink.

Start **Word**. From **Backstage** view, display the **Open** dialog box. Navigate to your **Word Chapter 5** folder, and then open your **Lastname_Firstname_5A_Home_Page** HTML file.

2 Press ⌈Ctrl⌋ + ⌈End⌋. In the navigation bar, point to and then right-click the **Contact Us** link. From the displayed shortcut menu, click **Edit Hyperlink**.

3 In the upper right corner of the **Edit Hyperlink** dialog box, click the **ScreenTip** button, and then edit the ScreenTip text to indicate **Click here to send an e-mail message to our Operations Manager** Compare your screen with Figure 5.21.

Figure 5.21

New ScreenTip text—
not all text may display

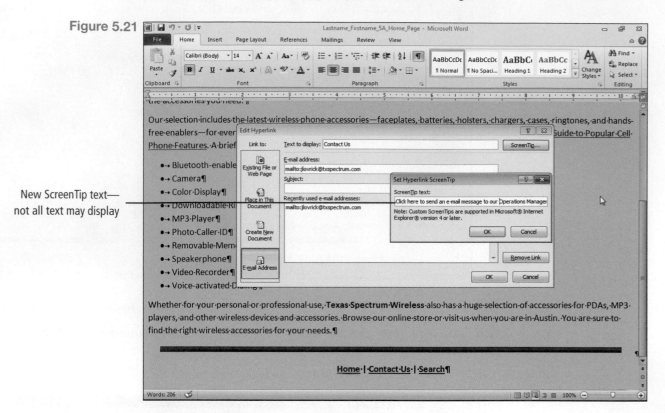

4 Click **OK** two times to close the dialog boxes.

5 In the navigation bar at the bottom of the document, point to and then right-click the **Search** link. From the shortcut menu, click **Remove Hyperlink**.

The link is removed, but the link can be added again at a later time when Texas Spectrum Wireless decides how customers will be able to search the site.

6 Press ⌈Ctrl⌋ + ⌈F2⌋ to display the **Print Preview** in **Backstage** view. Examine the **Print Preview**, click the **Home tab**, make any necessary adjustments, and then **Save** 🖫 your document.

The Print Preview displays in Print Layout view.

7 Open your **Lastname_Firstname_5A_Features_Guide** HTML file, view the **Print Preview**, and make any necessary adjustments.

8 **Save** 🖫 and then **Close** ❌ both documents. Leave Word open.

Objective 3 | Create a Blog Post

A **blog**, short for *Web log*, is a Web site that displays dated entries. Blogs are fast-changing Web sites and usually contain many hyperlinks—links to other blogs, to resource sites about the topic, or to photos and videos.

Blogs exist for both individuals and organizations. For example, a blog can function as an individual's personal journal or as a way for a business or organization to provide news on new products or information about customer service.

Microsoft employees post to a blog site about using Word. The site is a good example of a professional blog, and you can view it at http://blogs.msdn.com/microsoft_office_word/.

Activity 5.11 | Creating a Blog Post

A *blog post* is an individual article entered in a blog with a time and date stamp. Blog posts commonly display with the most recent post first. Texas Spectrum Wireless has a blog to address customer service questions. In this activity, you will create a new blog post for the customer service blog.

1 Click the **File tab**, click **New**, click **Blog post**, and then in the lower right portion of the screen, click **Create**. If the **Register a Blog Account** dialog box displays, click the **Register Later** button, and then compare your screen with Figure 5.22.

> A new document, formatted as a blog post, displays, and the Blog Post and Insert tabs display on the Ribbon. Here you can enter a title for the blog post and then type the text.
>
> Some of the commands are inactive until you register at an actual blog site.

Figure 5.22

Available tabs

New blog post document

2 Click the **File tab**, click **Save As**, and then in the **Save As** dialog box, navigate to your **Word Chapter 5** folder. In the **File name** box, type **Lastname_Firstname_5A_Blog_Post** and then click **Save**.

> This file is saved as a Word Document, not as an HTML file.

3 At the top of the document, click anywhere in the text **Enter Post Title Here** field to select the placeholder text, and then type **Learn to Use Your Bluetooth Headset**

4 Under the thin blue line, click in the body text area, and then type the following text:

> **Do you have one of our new Bluetooth headsets? We can help you learn all about it! Call us at 512-555-0060, send us an e-mail, download user guides from our Web site, or visit our Austin store for hands-on assistance.**

5 Select all the text you typed in the previous step, and then on the Mini toolbar, change the **Font** to **Verdana** and the **Font Size** to **16**. Save your blog post.

> Although it is not required, you can use Word's formatting tools to change the font, size, color, or alignment of text.

Activity 5.12 | Inserting Hyperlinks in a Blog Post

Blog posts are not limited to text. You can link to pictures, graphics, other Web sites, and to e-mail addresses.

Another Way

Alternatively, right-click the selected text, and then click Hyperlink.

1 In the last sentence, select the text *e-mail*. Click the **Insert tab**, and then in the **Links group**, click the **Hyperlink** button.

2 In the **Insert Hyperlink** dialog box, under **Link to**, click **E-mail Address**, if necessary. In the **E-mail address** box, type **jlovrick@txspectrum.com** Compare your screen with Figure 5.23.

Recall that when you create an e-mail hyperlink, Word automatically inserts *mailto:*. Because this is the same e-mail address you typed previously, it may display in the Recently used e-mail addresses box.

Figure 5.23

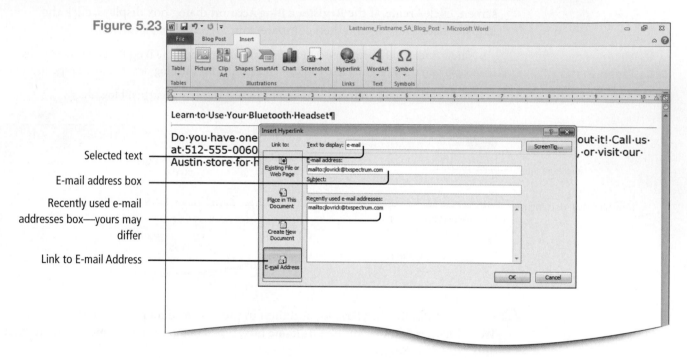

Selected text

E-mail address box

Recently used e-mail addresses box—yours may differ

Link to E-mail Address

3 Click **OK**. Notice that the text *e-mail* displays with hyperlink formatting.

4 In the last sentence, select the text *Web site*, and then create a hyperlink to link to an existing Web page. As the **Address,** type **www.txspectrum.com** When you are finished typing, if any other characters display, delete them. As the **ScreenTip**, type **Texas Spectrum Wireless** Click **OK** two times to close the dialog boxes.

5 Click to position your insertion point at the end of the paragraph, press Enter two times, and then type your first name and last name.

6 Select your name that you just typed. On the **Blog Post tab**, in the **Styles group**, click the **More** button ▼ , and then apply the **Heading 5** style. Click anywhere to deselect the text, and then compare your screen with Figure 5.24.

Figure 5.24

Learn·to·Use·Your·Bluetooth·Headset¶

Do·you·have·one·of·our·new·Bluetooth·headsets?·We·can·help·you·learn·all·about·it!·Call·us· at·512-555-0060,·send·us·an·e-mail,·download·user·guides·from·our·Web·site,·or·visit·our· Austin·store·for·hands-on·assistance.¶

Hyperlinks

¶

Your name formatted with the Heading 5 style

Firstname·Lastname¶

7 From **Backstage** view, display the **Document Information Panel**. In the **Author** box, type your first and last names, if necessary. In the **Subject** box, type your course name and section number, and then in the **Keywords** box, type **web page, blog, Bluetooth** Close ✕ the Document Information Panel.

8 **Save** 🖫 your document.

9 Print, or submit electronically, your two HTML files and your blog post as directed by your instructor. In **Backstage** view, click **Exit** to exit Word.

End You have completed Project 5A ——————————————

Project 5B FAQ List

Project Activities

In Activities 5.13 through 5.22, you will examine Word settings, gather supporting information, and use proofing options to create a draft version of the FAQ list. Additionally, you will save the file in a different format. Eliott Verschoren, Vice President of Marketing for Texas Spectrum Wireless, is compiling a list of Frequently Asked Questions, or FAQs, from customers who shop from the online site. He plans to include the information in a separate Web page on the company's Web site. Your completed documents will look similar to Figure 5.25.

Project Files

For Project 5B, you will need the following files:

> w05B_FAQ_List
> w05B_Images
> w05B_Packaging

You will save your documents as:

> Lastname_Firstname_5B_FAQ_List
> Lastname_Firstname_5B_FAQ_RTF

Project Results

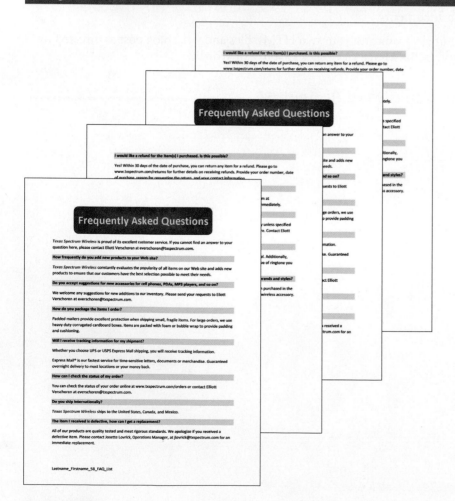

Figure 5.25
Project 5B FAQ List

Objective 4 | Locate Word Settings to Personalize Word 2010

When you install Microsoft Office, default settings are created for many features. For example, when you save a file, the default location that displays in the Save As dialog box is *Documents*. You can personalize Word by displaying and changing default settings in the **Word Options** dialog box. Word Options form a collection of settings that you can change if you have permission to do so. In the Word Options dialog box, you can also customize some Word features.

Activity 5.13 | Examining the Word Options Dialog Box

Most individuals are satisfied with the default settings in Word. If you find some defaults that you want to change to create a personalized work environment, use the Word Options dialog box to do so. In this activity, you will examine the default settings in the Word Options dialog box.

1 **Start** Word. From your student files, locate and then open the file **w05B_FAQ_List**. If necessary, display formatting marks and rulers.

2 Save the document in your **Word Chapter 5** folder as **Lastname_Firstname_5B_FAQ_List** Scroll to view the bottom of **Page 1**, and then using **Quick Parts**, insert the file name in the footer. Note: Names flagged as spelling errors will be addressed in a later activity.

3 Display **Backstage** view, and then on the left, click **Options** to display the **Word Options** dialog box.

> Recall that in an organizational environment such as a college or business, you may not have access or permission to change some or all of the settings.

4 Compare your screen with Figure 5.26, and then take a few moments to study the table in Figure 5.27 to examine the categories of Word options.

Figure 5.26

Word Options dialog box—your settings may vary

Options categories

Word Options

Category	Options
General	Set up Word for your personal way of working—for example, changing the color scheme—and personalize Word with your user name and initials.
Display	Control the way Word displays pages on the screen and prints.
Proofing	Control how Word corrects and formats your text—for example, how AutoCorrect and spell checker perform.
Save	Specify where you want to save your Word documents by default and set the AutoRecover time for saving information.
Language	Set the default language and add additional languages for editing documents.
Advanced	Control advanced features related to editing and printing.
Customize Ribbon	Add commands to existing tabs, create new tabs, and set up your own keyboard shortcuts.
Quick Access Toolbar	Customize the Quick Access Toolbar by adding commands.
Add-Ins	View and manage add-in programs that come with the Word software or ones that you add to Word.
Trust Center	Control privacy and security when working with files from other sources or when you share files with others.

Figure 5.27

5 Click **Cancel** to close the dialog box without changing any settings.

Activity 5.14 | Zooming from the View Tab

By changing the way in which documents display on your screen, you make your editing tasks easier and more efficient. For example, you can display multiple pages of a long document or increase the zoom level to make reading text easier or examine graphics more closely.

1 Press [Ctrl] + [Home] to move to the top of the document, if necessary, and then click at the end of the first paragraph—*FAQ*. Press [Enter] one time to insert a new blank paragraph.

2 Type **Texas Spectrum Wireless is proud of its excellent customer service. If you cannot find an answer to your question here, please contact Eliott Verschoren at everschoren@txspectrum.com.**

Another Way

Alternatively, you can use the Zoom slider on the status bar to change the Zoom percentage.

3 Click the **View tab**, and then in the **Zoom group**, click the **Zoom** button. In the **Zoom** dialog box, under **Zoom to**, click to select the **200%** option button, and then compare your screen with Figure 5.28.

Here you can select from among several preset zoom levels, select a specific number of pages to view at one time, or use the Percent box to indicate a specific zoom level.

Figure 5.28

Zoom dialog box

Zoom to options

Zoom Percent box

Select many pages to view at one time

4 Click **OK**, and notice that the document displays in a magnified view.

5 Scroll as necessary, and in the paragraph that begins *We welcome*, notice that the e-mail address has an extra *r* after the letter *p*—the text should be *txspectrum*. **Delete** the character *r*.

> A magnified view is useful when you want to make a close inspection of characters—for example, when typing e-mail addresses or scientific formulas.

6 On the **View tab**, in the **Zoom group**, click the **Two Pages** button to display **Page 1** and **Page 2** on your screen.

> The *Two Pages* zoom setting decreases the magnification to display two pages of a document. Although the text is smaller, you have an overall view of the page arrangement.

7 On the **View tab**, in the **Zoom group**, click the **100%** button to return to the default zoom setting. **Save** 💾 your document.

Objective 5 | Collect and Paste Images and Text

As you are writing, you may want to gather material—for example, text and pictures—related to your topic. This supporting information may be located in another document or on the Internet. Recall that you can use the Office Clipboard to collect a group of graphics or selected text blocks and then paste them into a document.

Activity 5.15 | Collecting Images and Text from Multiple Documents

In this activity, you will copy images and text from two different documents and then paste them into your current document.

1 On the **Home tab**, in the lower right corner of the **Clipboard group**, click the 🔲 button to display the **Clipboard** task pane. If necessary, at the top of the task pane, click the **Clear All** button to delete anything currently on the Clipboard.

2 Be sure that *only* your **Lastname_Firstname_5B_FAQ_List** document and the **Clipboard** task pane display; if necessary, close any other open windows. Then, from your student files, locate and open the file **w05B_Images**. If necessary, on the **Home tab**, in the **Clipboard group**, click the button to display the **Clipboard** task pane.

3 With the **w05B_Images** document displayed, scroll as necessary so that the **lightning bolt** graphic containing the letters *TSW* displays near the top of your screen. Right-click, and then from the shortcut menu, click **Copy**. Compare your screen with Figure 5.29.

> The image in your w05B_Images document displays on the Clipboard task pane.

Figure 5.29

Image stored on the Office Clipboard

4 Using the technique you just practiced, **Copy** the **Frequently Asked Questions** graphic to the Clipboard. **Close** the **w05B_Images** file.

> The copied images display on the Clipboard in your Lastname_Firstname_5B_FAQ_List document.

5 From your student files, open the file **w05B_Packaging**. If necessary, on the **Home tab**, in the **Clipboard group**, click the button to display the **Clipboard** task pane. Without selecting the paragraph mark at the end, select the entire paragraph text that begins *Padded mailers*, and then **Copy** the selection to the Clipboard.

> At the top of the Clipboard task pane, notice *3 of 24*, which indicates that 3 of 24 items are now on the Clipboard.

6 **Close** the **w05B_Packaging** document, and then notice the first few lines of the copied text display on the Clipboard. **Save** your document, and then compare your screen with Figure 5.30.

> When copying multiple items to the Clipboard, the most recently copied item displays at the top of the list.

Figure 5.30

Most recently copied item

Three items stored on the Clipboard

Activity 5.16 | Pasting Information from the Clipboard Task Pane

After you have collected text items or images on the Office Clipboard, you can paste them into a document in any order.

1 Press Ctrl + Home. Without selecting the paragraph mark, select only the text *FAQ*. In the **Clipboard** task pane, click the graphic *Frequently Asked Questions*.

> The graphic replaces the selected text.

2 Click the inserted graphic one time to select it, and then on the **Home tab**, in the **Paragraph group**, click the **Center** button.

3 Locate the sixth text paragraph of the document, which begins *Will I receive*. Click to position the insertion point to the left of the paragraph, press Enter, and then press ↑. In the new paragraph, type **How do you package the items I order?** and then press Enter.

4 In the **Clipboard** task pane, click the text entry that begins *Padded mailers* to paste the entire block of text at the insertion point. Compare your screen with Figure 5.31.

Figure 5.31

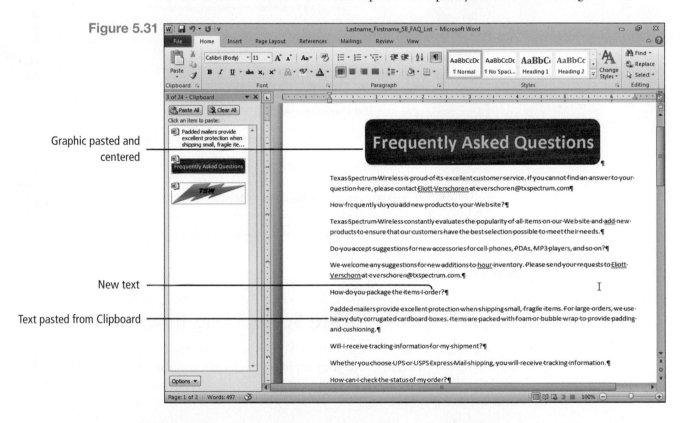

Graphic pasted and centered

New text

Text pasted from Clipboard

5 Press Ctrl + End to move to the end of the document, and then press Enter. In the **Clipboard** task pane, click the image containing the lightning bolt graphic to paste it at the insertion point, and then using the technique you practiced, **Center** it.

6 At the top of the **Clipboard** task pane, click the **Clear All** button to remove all items from the Office Clipboard, and then **Close** the **Clipboard** task pane.

7 Press Ctrl + Home. Locate and then select, including the paragraph mark, the paragraph that begins *How frequently*. Hold down Ctrl and then select the next question—the paragraph that begins *Do you accept*.

8 Continue to hold down Ctrl, and then select all the remaining paragraphs that end in a question mark, scrolling down with the scroll bar or **down scroll arrow** as necessary to move through the document.

Content-Based Assessments

Apply **4A** and **4B** skills from these Objectives:

1. Apply and Modify Quick Styles
2. Create New Styles
3. Manage Styles
4. Create a Multilevel List
5. Change the Style Set and Paragraph Spacing of a Document
6. Insert a Chart and Enter Data into a Chart
7. Change a Chart Type
8. Format a Chart

Mastering Word | Project **4G** Expense Reduction

In the following Mastering Word project, you will create a memo for Paulo Alvarez, Vice President of Finance for Lehua Hawaiian Adventures, which includes ideas for reducing expenses. Your completed document will look similar to Figure 4.51.

Project Files

For Project 4G, you will need the following file:

    w04G_Expense_Reduction

You will save your document as:

    Lastname_Firstname_4G_Expense_Reduction

Project Results

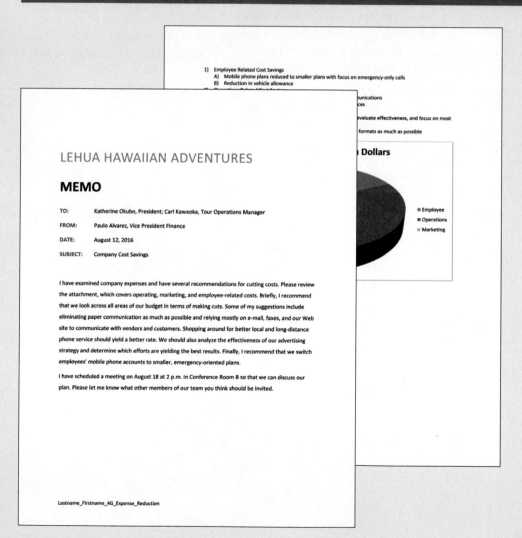

Figure 4.51

(Project 4G Expense Reduction continues on the next page)

9 With all the questions selected, apply **Bold** $\boxed{B}$. On the **Home tab**, in the **Paragraph group**, click the **Shading button arrow** $\boxed{\textcircled{\tiny$\triangle$}\cdot}$, and then in the fourth column, click the second color—**Dark Blue, Text 2, Lighter 80%**.

10 Click anywhere to deselect the text, scroll through the document to be sure you have shaded each question, and then scroll so that the Frequently Asked Questions graphic displays at the top of your screen. Compare your screen with Figure 5.32.

Figure 5.32

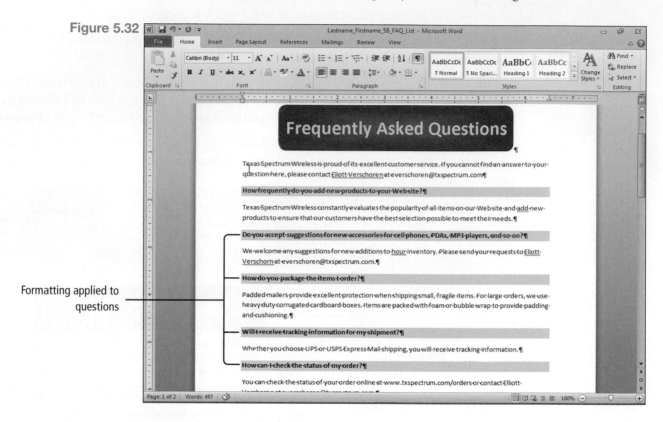

Formatting applied to questions

11 **Save** $\boxed{\textrm{H}}$ your document.

Objective 6 | Locate Supporting Information

While composing a document in Word, you can use the Research task pane to locate additional information about your topic. For example, you can look up additional facts on the Internet, replace words with synonyms to improve readability, or translate a phrase into another language.

Activity 5.17 | Using the Research Task Pane to Locate Information

In this activity, you will use the Research Sites and Thesaurus features in the Research task pane to search for additional information for and make changes to the FAQ list.

1 In the middle of **Page 1**, locate the paragraph that begins *Whether you choose*, and then click to position the insertion point at the end of the paragraph. Press [Enter] to add a blank paragraph.

2 Click the **Review tab**, and then in the **Proofing group**, click the **Research** button to display the **Research** task pane.

3 In the **Research** task pane, click in the **Search for** box, type **USPS Express** Under the **Search for** box, in the second box—the **Search location** box—click the **arrow**, point to **Bing**, and then compare your screen with Figure 5.33.

In the Search location box, you can specify the type of reference source from which you want to locate information. For example, you might want to use the Microsoft search engine Bing as a reference source.

> **Alert! | What If Bing Does Not Display?**
>
> If Bing does not display, you may be running an older version of Windows. Consult your instructor.

Figure 5.33

Search for box
Search location arrow

List of reference sources

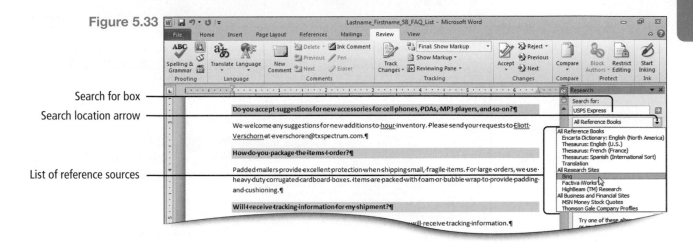

4 In the displayed list, click **Bing**. In the list of results, locate the item titled *USPS - Express Mail Overnight Guaranteed*, and then compare your screen with Figure 5.34.

The search results include Web sites containing information about your search term— *USPS Express*. Each item contains the title of the Web page, a brief summary of the Web page, and a link to the Web page. Because the information on Web sites changes often, the information on your screen may differ.

Figure 5.34

Web page title

Search results—yours may differ

Web page summary

Link to the Web page

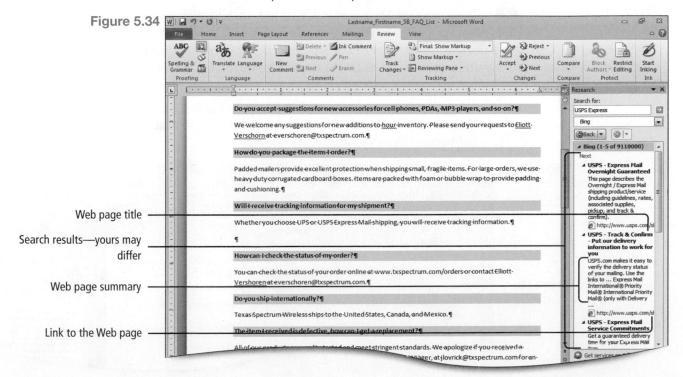

5 For the item titled *USPS - Express Mail Overnight Guaranteed*, click the related hyperlink to open your browser. If necessary, maximize your browser window. Locate and then select the entire paragraph that begins *Express Mail® is our fastest* and ends with *or your money back.* Compare your screen with Figure 5.35.

> A blue arrow, called an *accelerator*, displays when you select text in Internet Explorer 8. Because Web pages change frequently, consult your instructor if your results do not look similar to Figure 5.35.

Figure 5.35

Selected paragraph

Accelerator arrow—may not display in your browser

6 On the Web page, right-click the selection, and then from the shortcut menu, click **Copy. Close** [X] the browser window.

Alert! | If Your Browser Displays Differently

Depending on your operating system—Windows 7, Windows Vista, or Windows XP—you might need to open or close additional browser windows to locate the information from the USPS site.

---

7 In the **Lastname_Firstname_5B_FAQ List**, with the insertion point in the blank line below the paragraph that begins *Whether you choose*, right-click, and then from the shortcut menu, under **Paste Options**, click the second button—**Merge Formatting** [icon] —to insert the copied text in the document. Compare your screen with Figure 5.36.

> When you paste text from a source into a document, you will typically want to format the text in the same manner as the document into which you are pasting—the destination. The Merge Formatting option causes the pasted text to match the formatting in your Lastname_Firstname_5B_FAQ_List document.

Figure 5.36

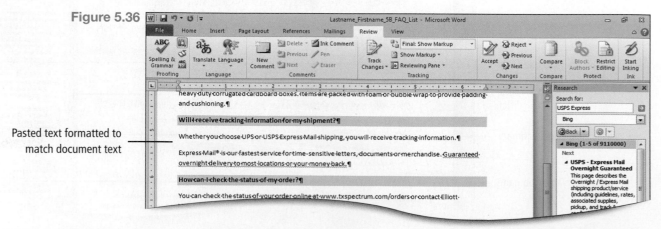

Pasted text formatted to match document text

> **Note | Be Careful of Copyright Issues**
>
> Nearly everything you find on the Internet is protected by copyright law, which protects authors of original works, including text, art, photographs, and music. If you want to use text or graphics that you find online, you will need to get permission. One of the exceptions to this law is the use of small amounts of information for educational purposes, which falls under Fair Use guidelines. As a general rule, however, if you want to use someone else's material, always get permission first.

8 In the lower portion of **Page 1**, in the paragraph that begins *All of our products*, point to and then right-click the word *stringent*. Point to **Synonyms**, and then click **Thesaurus**. Compare your screen with Figure 5.37.

> In the Research task pane, *stringent* displays in the Search for box, and synonyms for the word *stringent* display under Thesaurus.

Figure 5.37

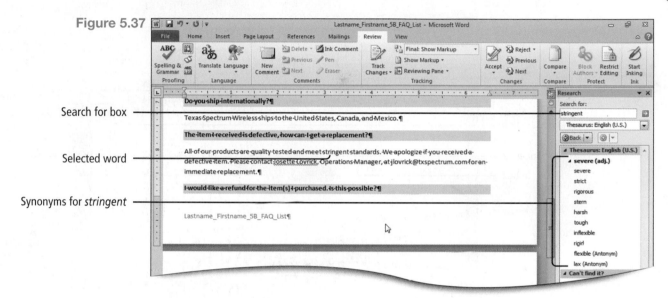

Search for box

Selected word

Synonyms for *stringent*

9 In the **Research** task pane, point to **rigorous**, click the displayed **arrow**, and then click **Insert** to replace *stringent* with *rigorous*.

> **Another Way**
>
> Alternatively, on the **Page Layout tab**, in the **Page Setup group**, click the **Breaks** button, and then under **Page Breaks**, click **Page**.

10 At the bottom of **Page 1**, click to position the insertion point to the left of the paragraph that begins *I would like*. Hold down [Ctrl], and then press [Enter], which is the keyboard shortcut to insert a page break. **Save** your document.

> Because the document contains questions and answers, it is good document design to keep the question and answer together on the same page.

> **More Knowledge | Using the Research Options Command**
>
> The option to add or remove research sources does not display in the Word Options dialog box; rather, this command is located at the bottom of the Research task pane. To add or remove a source, click Research Options, and then in the Research Options dialog box, select or clear its check box, and then click OK.

Activity 5.18 | Translating Text from the Research Task Pane

You can translate a word or phrase into a different language from the Research task pane. Because Texas Spectrum Wireless has customers outside of the United States, the FAQ will include text for Spanish-speaking and French-speaking customers that can eventually be linked to FAQ pages written in those languages. In this activity, you will add Spanish and French text to the FAQ list.

Another Way

Alternatively, on the **Review tab**, in the **Language group**, you can click the **Translate** button, and click **Translate Selected Text**.

1 On **Page 2**, locate the paragraph that begins *Our wireless accessories*, and then click to position the insertion point at the end of the paragraph.

2 Press Enter two times, type **FAQ** and then press Spacebar.

3 In the **Research** task pane, in the **Search for** box, delete any existing text if necessary, and then type **Spanish** In the **Search location** box, click the **arrow**, and then click **Translation**.

Here you can select the type of reference you want to search, including online references.

4 If necessary, under **Translation**, click the **From arrow**, and then click **English (U.S.)**. Click the **To box arrow**, and then click **Spanish (International Sort)**. Compare your screen with Figure 5.38.

The translated text—español—displays in the Translation area of the task pane.

Figure 5.38

Search for box
Search location
From box
To box
Translated text

5 In the lower portion of the **Research** task pane, select the translated text *español*, right-click, and then from the shortcut menu, click **Copy**. In your document, locate the paragraph *FAQ*, and then click to position the insertion point at the end of the paragraph. Right-click, and from the shortcut menu, under **Paste Options**, click the **Keep Text Only** [A] button. In the pasted text, select the first letter *e*, type **E** and then compare your screen with Figure 5.39.

Word uses a machine translation service—not a human being—to translate text, which can result in slight discrepancies in the translated phrases. The main idea is captured, but an accurate translation may differ slightly.

Figure 5.39

Translated text

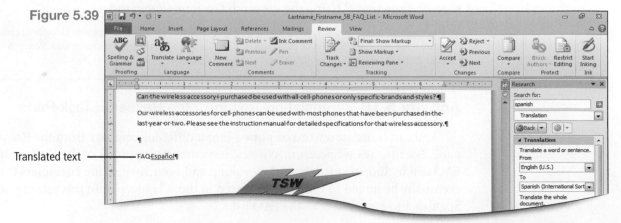

6 Position the insertion point at the end of the paragraph, press `Enter`, type **FAQ** and then press `Spacebar`.

7 In the **Research** task pane, in the **Search for** box, type **French** Click the **To box arrow**, and then click **French (France)**.

8 Using the technique you just practiced, insert the French text *français* at the insertion point location. Select the first letter *f*, and then type **F**

9 Select both paragraphs that begin *FAQ*, and then on the Mini toolbar, change the **Font Size** to **14**, and apply **Bold** `B`.

> Mr. Verschoren will develop specific FAQs in both languages to link here.

10 **Close** `×` the **Research** task pane, and then **Save** `🖫` your document.

More Knowledge | **Using the Translation Language Tools**

On the Review tab, in the Language group, you can choose your translation language, translate an entire document, translate selected text, or use the Mini Translator. The Mini Translator provides an instant translation when you point to a word or selected phrase. When you click the Play button in the Mini Translator, the text is read back to you.

Objective 7 | Use Advanced Find and Replace and Proofing Options

From the Find and Replace dialog box, you can locate occurrences of words that sound the same although spelled differently, find phrases that are capitalized in exactly the same way, and find different forms of a word—such as *work*, *worked*, and *working*.

Activity 5.19 | Using Find and Replace to Change Text Formatting

You can change the formatting of a word or phrase that is repeated throughout a document easily by using the Find and Replace dialog box. In this activity, you will change the formatting of the company name that displays numerous times in the FAQ list.

1 Press `Ctrl` + `Home`. On the **Home tab**, in the **Editing group**, click the **Replace** button to display the **Find and Replace** dialog box.

2 In the **Find what** box, type **Texas Spectrum Wireless** and then in the **Replace with** box, type the exact same text **Texas Spectrum Wireless**

3 Below the **Replace with** box, click the **More** button to expand this dialog box.

> The More button exposes advanced settings, such as formatting, with which you can refine this command.

4 Near the bottom of the **Find and Replace** dialog box, under **Replace**, click the **Format** button, and then in the displayed list, click **Font**.

5 In the displayed **Replace Font** dialog box, under **Font style**, click **Bold Italic**. Click the **Font color arrow**, and then in the sixth column, click the fifth color—**Red, Accent 2, Darker 25%**. Compare your screen with Figure 5.40.

Figure 5.40

Replace Font dialog box

Bold Italic selected

Font color displays

Preview of formatted text

6 Click **OK** to close the **Replace Font** dialog box, and then in the middle of the **Find and Replace** dialog box, click the **Replace All** button. When a **Microsoft Office Word** message displays indicating that you have made 4 replacements, click **OK**. Leave the expanded dialog box displayed.

> This action finds each instance of the text *Texas Spectrum Wireless*, and then replaces the font format with bold italic in the red color that you selected.

7 Click anywhere in the document, and then **Save** 🖫 the document.

Activity 5.20 | Using Wildcards in Find and Replace

Use a ***wildcard*** in the Find and Replace dialog box when you are uncertain of the exact term you want to find. A wildcard is a special character such as * or ? inserted with a Find what term. For example, searching a document for the term *b*k* could find *blink*, *book*, *brick*, or any other word in the document that begins with *b* and ends with *k*. Using a wildcard can save time when you do not know the specific characters in the search term. In this activity, you will use a wildcard to search for e-mail and Web page addresses that may be spelled incorrectly.

1 In the **Find and Replace** dialog box, in the **Find what** box, delete the existing text, and then type **V*n**

2 Press ⸢Tab⸣ to move to and select the text in the **Replace with** box, and then type **Verschoren** At the bottom of the **Find and Replace** dialog box, click the **No Formatting** button to remove the formatting settings from the previous activity.

3 Under **Search Options**, select the **Use wildcards** check box. Compare your screen with Figure 5.41.

> Mr. Verschoren's name may have been spelled incorrectly. By using the Find command to locate each instance that begins with *V* and ends with *n*, you can find, and then verify, the correct spelling of his name in every instance.

Figure 5.41

Find and Replace
dialog box

Find what box

Replace with box

Use wildcards selected

No Formatting button
dimmed

4 In the **Find and Replace** dialog box, click the **Less** button so that the dialog box is smaller. Then, click the **Find Next** button. The text *Verschoren* is selected in the document. If necessary, move the Find and Replace dialog box to view the selection.

This instance is spelled correctly—no changes are required.

5 In the **Find and Replace** dialog box, click the **Find Next** button again, and notice that this occurrence is not spelled correctly.

6 Click the **Replace** button, and then compare your screen with Figure 5.42.

The text *Verschoren* is now spelled correctly, and Word selects the next occurrence of text that begins with *V* and ends with *n*.

Figure 5.42

Corrected text

Next occurrence selected

7 The selected text *Vershoren* is incorrect; click **Replace** to correct the error, and move to the next occurrence.

8 The selected text *Verschoren* is spelled correctly. Click **Find Next** to move to the next occurrence. Notice a Microsoft Office Word message box indicates that you have searched the entire document.

9 Click **OK** to close the message box. In the **Find and Replace** dialog box, click the **More** button, click to deselect the **Use wildcards** check box, and then click the **Less** button to restore the dialog box to its default settings. **Close** [X] the **Find and Replace** dialog box.

10 **Save** 🔲 the document.

Activity 5.21 | Using the Spelling and Grammar Checker

Initiate the Spelling & Grammar command to check an entire document. In this activity, you will use the Spelling and Grammar dialog box to view additional options and correct the identified errors in the document.

1 Press [Ctrl] + [Home]. On the **Review tab**, in the **Proofing group**, click the **Spelling & Grammar** button.

The first suggested error—*Eliott*—displays.

> **Alert! | Spelling and Grammar Selections May Differ**
>
> Flagged errors depend on the Proofing settings in the Word Options area, or on the actions of others who might have used the computer at which you are working. Not all of the potential errors listed in this activity may display in your spelling and grammar check. Your document may also display errors not noted here. If you encounter flagged words or phrases that are not included here, take appropriate action.

2 If *Eliott* is indicated as a spelling error, in the **Spelling and Grammar** dialog box, click **Ignore All**.

All occurrences of *Eliott* are now ignored, and the word *Verschoren* displays in red as a potential spelling error.

3 If *Verschoren* is indicated as a spelling error, click **Ignore All**. Compare your screen with Figure 5.43.

All occurrences of *Verschoren* are now ignored, and the word *add* displays in green as a potential grammar error. Because it is a subject-verb agreement error, the word *adds* is suggested to fix the error.

Figure 5.43

Identified potential error

Subject-Verb Agreement problem

Suggested change

4 In the **Spelling and Grammar** dialog box, click the **Explain** button. In the displayed **Word Help** dialog box, read the displayed text.

When Word detects a potential grammatical error, you can read a detailed explanation of the problem.

5 **Close** ✖ the **Word Help** dialog box. In the **Spelling and Grammar** dialog box, if necessary, under **Suggestions**, select *adds*, and then click the **Change** button.

The correction is made and the next identified error is highlighted.

6 Near the bottom of the **Spelling and Grammar** dialog box, click the **Options** button to display the **Proofing** category of the **Word Options** dialog box.

7 In the **Word Options** dialog box, under **When correcting spelling and grammar in Word**, notice that the option **Use contextual spelling** is selected. Compare your screen with Figure 5.44.

When this option is selected, Word will flag potential word usage errors and display with a blue underline.

Figure 5.44

Word Options dialog box

Proofing category selected

Use contextual spelling selected

8 Click **OK** to close the **Word Options** dialog box.

9 In the **Spelling and Grammar** dialog box, if *hour* is highlighted as a contextual error, under **Suggestions**, select *our*, and then click the **Change** button. If *hour* is not identified as an error, proceed to Step 10.

In this case, Word identified *hour* as a word that is spelled correctly but used in the wrong context.

10 Click **Ignore All** as necessary to ignore the proper names *Josette* and *Lovrick*.

11 Continue to the end of the document, and click **Ignore Once** for the foreign words.

A message indicates that the spelling and grammar check is complete.

12 Click **OK** to close the message box. **Save** 🖫 the document.

Objective 8 | Save in Other File Formats

If you send a Word document to someone who uses a word processing program *other* than Microsoft Word, he or she may not be able to read the document. If you expect that your document must be read or edited in another word processing program, save your Word document in *Rich Text Format*, or *RTF*, which is a universal document format that can be read by nearly all word processing programs, and that retains most text and paragraph formatting. Saving a document in the RTF file format adds the *.rtf* extension to the document file name. An RTF file that you might receive can be easily converted to the Word file format.

Activity 5.22 | Saving a Document in RTF Format

When you save a Word document as an RTF file, all but the most complex formatting is translated into a format usable by most word processing programs. Eliott Verschoren is sending the FAQ list to his sales managers for review before saving it as a Web page. In this activity, you will save the FAQ list as an RTF file to ensure that all the managers can review the document.

1 Display **Backstage** view, and then display the **Document Information Panel**. In the **Author** box, delete any existing text, and then type your first and last names. In the **Subject** box, type your course name and section number, and in the **Keywords** box, type **faq list Close** ✕ the Document Information Panel, and then **Save** 🖫 your document.

> Recall that your document is saved with the default Word file format with the *.docx* file extension.

2 In **Backstage** view, click **Save As**. Navigate to your **Word Chapter 5** folder. In the lower portion of the displayed **Save As** dialog box, click the **Save as type arrow**, and then in the displayed list, click **Rich Text Format**.

3 In the **File name** box, type **Lastname_Firstname_5B_FAQ_RTF** Compare your screen with Figure 5.45.

Figure 5.45

Save in location—yours will differ

Save As dialog box

File name

Save as type

4 Click **Save**. Scroll to the bottom of **Page 1**, and then double-click the footer. Right-click the file name, and then from the shortcut menu, click **Update Field** to update the file name and format. **Close** the footer area.

5 Display **Backstage** view, click **Properties**, and then click **Advanced Properties**.

Because the document is saved as an RTF file, a Properties dialog box displays instead of the Document Information Panel.

6 Click the **Summary tab**, if necessary, and then in the **Keywords** box, position the insertion point to the right of the existing text and type **, rtf** Compare your screen with Figure 5.46.

Figure 5.46

Properties dialog box —

Summary tab —

Keywords revised —

7 Click **OK** to close the **Properties** dialog box, and then click **Save**. Print, or submit electronically, your two files as directed by your instructor. Click **Exit** to exit Word.

More Knowledge | Saving in PDF or XPS Formats

Microsoft Word enables you to save documents in other file formats such as PDF—Portable Document Format—and XPS—XML Paper Specification. Click the File tab, and then click Share. On the Send screen, under File Types, click Create PDF/XPS Document. On the displayed screen, click Create a PDF/XPS.

End **You have completed Project 5B** ————————————

Content-Based Assessments

Summary

In this chapter you saved documents as Web pages, added hyperlinks, and inserted a page background, a drop cap, and graphics. You created a blog post. You examined Word options to identify how you can personalize Word settings. To facilitate using the Office Clipboard to copy and paste text, you changed the view and zoom settings. You used the Research task pane to locate new information and advanced Find and Replace features to modify existing text. Finally, you saved a document in an RTF format.

Key Terms

Matching

Match each term in the second column with its correct definition in the first column by writing the letter of the term on the blank line in front of the correct definition.

_____ 1. A file coded in HTML that can be viewed using a browser.

_____ 2. The markup language that communicates color and graphics in a format that all computers can understand and that is used to display documents on the Internet.

_____ 3. The software that interprets files and displays them as Web pages.

_____ 4. The position of a drop cap when it is within the text of the paragraph.

_____ 5. The position of a drop cap when it is in the left margin of a paragraph.

_____ 6. The action of ordering data, usually in alphabetical or numeric order.

_____ 7. Text, buttons, or pictures that, when clicked, access other Web pages.

_____ 8. A group of related Web pages.

_____ 9. A hyperlink applied to a word or phrase.

_____ 10. A hyperlink that connects to another page in the same Web site.

_____ 11. A Web site that displays dated entries.

_____ 12. An individual article entered on a Web site with a time and date stamp.

_____ 13. A collection of settings you can change to personalize Word.

_____ 14. A Word feature used to find synonyms for selected text.

_____ 15. A file format that can be read by many word processing programs.

A Blog

B Blog post

C Dropped

D HTML

E Hyperlinks

F In margin

G Internal link

H RTF

I Sort

J Text link

K Thesaurus

L Web browser

M Web page

N Web site

O Word Options

Content-Based Assessments

Multiple Choice

Circle the correct answer.

1. The file type used to save a document in HTML format, with some elements saved in a separate folder, is:
   A. PDF
   B. Single File Web Page
   C. Web Page

2. A large, capital letter at the beginning of a paragraph that displays on several lines is:
   A. a drop cap
   B. a Quick Part
   C. an embedded cap

3. Numerical data that is arranged from largest to smallest is in:
   A. ascending order
   B. descending order
   C. reverse order

4. The Web browser developed by Microsoft is:
   A. Explorer
   B. Internet Explorer
   C. Windows Explorer

5. A series of text links across the top or bottom of a Web page is called the:
   A. command bar
   B. navigation bar
   C. site map

6. The hyperlink type that causes an e-mail message window to open when clicked is:
   A. a contact link
   B. an e-mail address link
   C. an e-mail message link

7. A zoom setting that decreases the magnification of a document is:
   A. Two Page
   B. 300%
   C. 200%

8. Copyrighted information may be used for educational purposes according to the:
   A. Copied Works guidelines
   B. Educational Research guidelines
   C. Fair Use guidelines

9. A special character such as * or ? that can be part of a search term is called a:
   A. search card
   B. search symbol
   C. wildcard

10. The term RTF stands for:
    A. Rich Text File
    B. Rich Text Format
    C. Rich Type Format

Content-Based Assessments

Apply **5A** skills from these Objectives:

1. Create a Web Page from a Word Document
2. Insert and Modify Hyperlinks in a Web Page
3. Create a Blog Post

Skills Review | Project **5C** Awards Information

In the following Skills Review, you will modify and add hyperlinks to the Web page containing nomination information for the Employee of the Year Award that is given to outstanding individuals at Texas Spectrum Wireless. You will also create a blog related to the nomination process. Your completed documents will look similar to Figure 5.47, although your text wrapping may vary.

Project Files

For Project 5C, you will need the following files:

w05C_Awards_Information
w05C_Nomination_Form

You will save your documents as:

Lastname_Firstname_5C_Awards_Information
Lastname_Firstname_5C_Nomination_Form
Lastname_Firstname_5C_Awards_Blog

Project Results

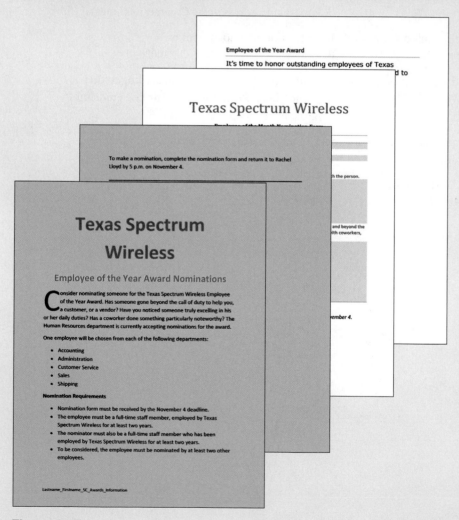

Figure 5.47

(Project 5C Awards Information continues on the next page)

Content-Based Assessments

1 **Start** Word, and then open the file **w05C_Awards_Information**. From **Backstage** view, display the **Save As** dialog box, navigate to your **Word Chapter 5** folder, and then click the **Save as type arrow**. In the displayed list, click **Web Page**. Near the bottom of the dialog box, click the **Change Title** button, and then in the displayed **Enter Text** dialog box, in the **Page title** box, type **Awards Information** Click **OK**. In the **File name** box, using your own name, type **Lastname_Firstname_5C_Awards_Information** and then press Enter.

a. On the **Insert tab**, in the **Header & Footer group**, click the **Footer** button, click **Edit Footer**, and then use **Quick Parts** to insert the file name. **Close** the footer area.

b. Select the first paragraph—*Texas Spectrum Wireless*. On the Mini toolbar, change the **Font Size** to **48**, apply **Bold** and **Center**. Click the **Font Color button arrow**, and then in the fifth column, click the fifth color—**Blue, Accent 1, Darker 25%**.

c. Select the second paragraph, which begins *Employee*. Change the **Font Size** to **24**, apply **Bold**, and then click **Center**. Click the **Font Color button arrow**, and then in the last column, click the fifth color—**Orange, Accent 6, Darker 25%**.

d. Select the remaining text in the document, and then change the **Font Size** to **14**.

2 On the **Page Layout tab**, in the **Page Background group**, click the **Page Color** button, and then in the fourth column, click the second color—**Dark Blue, Text 2, Lighter 80%**.

a. Click to position the insertion point to the left of the paragraph that begins *Consider*. On the **Insert tab**, in the **Text group**, click the **Drop Cap** button, and then click **Dropped**.

b. Click to position the insertion point to the left of the paragraph that begins *Administration*. Beginning with the paragraph *Administration*, select the five paragraphs that comprise the departments—ending with the paragraph *Customer Service*. On the **Home tab**, in the **Paragraph group**, click the **Sort** button. In the **Sort Text** dialog box, click **OK** to accept the default settings. With the paragraphs still selected, in the **Paragraph group**, click the **Bullets** button, and then click anywhere to deselect the list.

c. Select the paragraph *Nomination Requirements* and apply **Bold**. Click to position the insertion point to the left of the paragraph that begins *Nomination form must be*. Beginning with the paragraph *Nomination form*, select the four paragraphs that comprise the requirements—ending with the paragraph that begins *To be considered*. On the **Home tab**, in the **Paragraph group**, click the **Bullets** button, and then click anywhere to deselect. **Save** your changes.

3 In the paragraph that begins *To make a nomination*, click to position the insertion point to the right of the period at the end of the sentence, and then press Enter. On the **Home tab**, in the **Paragraph group**, click the **Border button arrow**, and then click **Horizontal Line**.

a. Point to the inserted line and right-click. From the shortcut menu, click **Format Horizontal Line**. In the **Format Horizontal Line** dialog box, change the **Height** to **2 pt**. Under **Color**, click the **arrow**, and then in the fourth column, click the fifth color—**Dark Blue, Text 2, Darker 25%**. Click **OK**, and then click anywhere to deselect the line. **Save** your changes.

b. From **Backstage** view, display the **Open** dialog box, and navigate to your student files. If necessary, click the Files of type arrow, and then click All Word Documents. Open the file **w05C_Nomination_Form**. From **Backstage** view, display the **Save As** dialog box, and then navigate to your **Word Chapter 5** folder. In the lower portion of the **Save As** dialog box, click the **Save as type arrow**, and then click **Web Page**.

c. Near the bottom of the dialog box, click the **Change Title** button, and then as the **Page title**, type **Nomination Form** Click **OK**, and then in the **File name** box, type **Lastname_Firstname_5C_Nomination_Form** Click **Save**.

d. On the **Insert tab**, in the **Header & Footer group**, click the **Footer** button, click **Edit Footer**, and then use **Quick Parts** to insert the file name in the footer. **Close** the footer area. In **Backstage** view, click **Properties**, and then click **Advanced Properties**. In the displayed dialog box, on the **Summary tab**, in the **Author** box, delete any existing text, and then type your first and last names. In the **Subject** box, type your course name and section number, and in the **Keywords** box, type **awards, nomination form** Click **OK**, click **Save**, and then **Close** the document.

(Project 5C Awards Information continues on the next page)

4 With your **Lastname_Firstname_5C_Awards_ Information** document displayed, press Ctrl + End. Select the text *Nomination Form*. On the **Insert tab**, in the **Links group**, click the **Hyperlink** button. In the **Insert Hyperlink** dialog box, under **Link to**, click **Existing File or Web Page**, if necessary.

a. In the **Look in** box, if necessary navigate to your **Word Chapter 5** folder, click your **Lastname_ Firstname_5C_Nomination_Form** document, and then click the **ScreenTip** button. In the **ScreenTip text** box, type **Nomination Form** and then click **OK** two times.

b. Select the text *Rachel Lloyd*, and then display the **Insert Hyperlink** dialog box. Under **Link to**, click **E-mail Address**. In the **E-mail address** box, type **rlloyd@txspectrum.com** As the **ScreenTip text**, type **Human Relations Director** Click **OK** two times.

c. At the bottom of the Web page, point to *Rachel Lloyd* to display the ScreenTip. Right-click the **Rachel Lloyd** hyperlink, and then from the shortcut menu, click **Edit Hyperlink**. Click the **ScreenTip** button, and then edit the **ScreenTip text** to indicate **Click here to send an e-mail message to Rachel Lloyd** Click **OK** two times, and then point to the **Rachel Lloyd** link to display the ScreenTip.

d. Press Ctrl + Home. In **Backstage** view, click **Properties**, and then click **Advanced Properties**. In the displayed dialog box, on the **Summary** tab, in the **Author** box, delete any existing text, and then type your first and last names. In the **Subject** box, type your course name and section number, and in the **Keywords** box, type **awards information, Web page** Click **OK**.

e. **Save** your changes, and **Close** the document.

5 If necessary, start **Word**. In **Backstage** view, click the **New tab**, click **Blog post**, and then on the right, click

Create. If the **Register a Blog Account** dialog box displays, click the **Register Later** button.

a. From **Backstage** view, display the **Save As** dialog box, navigate to your **Word Chapter 5** folder, name the file **Lastname_Firstname_5C_Awards_Blog** and then click **Save**.

b. Click anywhere in the **Enter Post Title Here** field to select the placeholder text, and then type **Employee of the Year Award** Click under the thin blue line in the body text area, and then type **It's time to honor outstanding employees of Texas Spectrum Wireless. Nominations must be submitted to Rachel Lloyd by 5 p.m. on November 4.**

c. Select all the body text, and then change the **Font** to **Verdana** and the **Font Size** to **16**. In the second sentence, select *Rachel Lloyd*. Click the **Insert tab**, and then in the **Links group**, click the **Hyperlink** button. Under **Link to**, click **E-mail Address**, and then in the **E-mail address** box, type **rlloyd@ txspectrum.com** Click **OK**.

d. Click to position your insertion point at the end of the paragraph, press Enter two times, and then type your first and last names.

e. From **Backstage** view, display the **Document Information Panel**. In the **Author** box, delete any existing text, and then type your first and last names. In the **Subject** box, type your course name and section number, and in the **Keywords** box, type **awards nominations, blog Close** the Document Information Panel. **Save** your document, and then **Exit** Word.

6 As directed by your instructor print, or submit electronically, the three files—the blog post and two Web pages—that are the results of this project.

End **You have completed Project 5C** ——————————

Content-Based Assessments

Skills Review | Project **5D** Outdoor Accessories

In the following Skills Review, you will create a document for Eliott Verschoren, Marketing Vice President of Texas Spectrum Wireless, which details the waterproof and ruggedized accessories sold by the company. Your completed documents will look similar to Figure 5.48.

Project Files

For Project 5D, you will need the following files:

w05D_Outdoor_Accessories
w05D_Product_Info
w05D_Product_Images

You will save your documents as:

Lastname_Firstname_5D_Outdoor_Accessories
Lastname_Firstname_5D_Accessories_RTF

Project Results

Texas Spectrum Wireless

Accessories for the Outdoor Enthusiast

Waterproof and Ruggedized

Like you, we at Texas Spectrum Wireless regularly use our cell phones, PDAs, MP3 players, and other wireless devices while engaged in outdoor activities. Also like you, we've had those unfortunate experiences where our devices have been dropped, doused with water, or scratched. Our waterproof items are treated or constructed so as to be impenetrable or unaffected by water. To ruggedize an item is to make something such as a piece of computer equipment capable of withstanding rough treatment.

We carry a complete line of waterproof and ruggedized accessories to protect your wireless devices. Browse our selection of waterproof and ruggedized accessories.

Camera Cases: These waterproof and ruggedized cases are perfect for use at the beach, on a boat, in the mountains, at a pool, or anytime you're carrying your camera and want extra protection.

Cell Phone Cases: These cover the cell phone screen with a thin membrane, but it remains fully usable without removing the case. These ruggedized cases offer protection from bumps, drops, and shocks.

MP3 Player Cases: If you're tired of bumping, scratching, and dropping your MP3 player, a ruggedized case will help keep it in great condition. These cases are available in many colors and patterns, so you can make a style statement while protecting your device.

Sports Headphones: Frequently used by swimmers and surfers, these waterproof headphones are completely submersible.

Wireless Headset System: These are ideal for swimming instructors, water aerobics, and other outdoor uses. It is lightweight and completely waterproof.

Wireless Speakers: These waterproof speakers will meet your outdoor audio needs anytime you will be near the water. Each speaker also comes equipped with a light for nighttime use. These are small and lightweight, but provide powerful sound.

We hope these accessories give you some added peace of mind, because we all know that accidents are a fact of life. If there is something missing that you would like to see, please contact us and we will try to add the item to our stock.

Lastname_Firstname_5D_Outdoor_Accessories

Figure 5.48

(Project 5D Outdoor Accessories continues on the next page)

Content-Based Assessments

1 **Start** Word. From your student files, open the file **w05D_Outdoor_Accessories**. In **Backstage** view, display the **Save As** dialog box, navigate to your **Word Chapter 5** folder, and then save the document as **Lastname_ Firstname_5D_Outdoor_Accessories**

a. At the bottom of **Page 1**, use **Quick Parts** to insert the file name in the footer.

b. Select the first three paragraphs, and then on the Mini toolbar, change the **Font Size** to **28**, apply **Bold**, and click **Center**. Click the **Font Color button arrow**, and then in the seventh column, click the first color—**Olive Green, Accent 3**.

c. On the **Home tab**, in the **Clipboard group**, click the **Dialog Box Launcher** to display the **Clipboard** task pane. If necessary, at the top of the task pane, click the **Clear All** button to delete anything on the Clipboard.

d. From your student files, open **w05D_Product_Images**. If necessary, display the **Clipboard** task pane. Point to the first graphic—a cell phone in water—right-click, and then click **Copy**. Copy the *rock* graphic using the same technique. **Close** the **w05D_Product_Images** file.

e. From your student files, open **w05D_Product_Info**. Press [Ctrl] + [A] to select all of the text, right-click the selected text, click **Copy**, and then **Close** the **w05D_Product_Info** file.

2 Click to position the insertion point to the left of the paragraph that begins *Like you*. In the **Clipboard** task pane, click the **water** graphic. Click the inserted graphic to select it. On the **Format tab**, in the **Arrange group**, click the **Wrap Text** button, and then click **Square**.

a. Click to position the insertion point to the left of the paragraph that begins *We hope*. In the **Clipboard** task pane, click the text entry that begins *Camera Cases* to paste the entire block of text at the insertion point.

b. With the insertion point still to the left of *We hope*, in the **Clipboard** task pane, click the **rock** graphic. Click to select the inserted graphic. On the **Format tab**, in the **Arrange group**, click the **Wrap Text** button, and then click **Square**. **Close** the **Clipboard** task pane. **Save** the document.

3 Scroll to view the top of the document. In the fourth paragraph, position the insertion point at the end of the paragraph—following the period after *scratched*. Press [Spacebar], type **Our waterproof items are** and then press [Spacebar].

a. On the **Review tab**, in the **Proofing group**, click the **Research** button to display the **Research** task pane on the right.

b. In the **Research** task pane, click in the **Search for** box, delete any text, and then type **waterproof** Under the **Search for** box, in the second box—the **Search location** box—click the **arrow**. In the displayed list, click **Encarta Dictionary: English (North America)**. Under **Encarta Dictionary**, locate the text *impervious to water*. Indented and immediately below the definition, select the text that begins *treated or constructed* and ends with *by water*. Right-click the selection and then from the shortcut menu, click **Copy**.

c. Click in your document at the point you stopped typing, right-click, and then from the shortcut menu, under **Paste Options**, click the **Keep Text Only** button to insert the copied text in the document. Type a period, and then press [Spacebar]. Type **To ruggedize an item is**

d. In the **Research** task pane, in the **Search for** box, replace *waterproof* with **ruggedize** and then press [Enter]. Under **Encarta Dictionary**, locate and then select the entire definition that begins *to make something* and ends with *rough treatment*. Right-click the selection and click **Copy**.

e. Click in your document at the point you stopped typing, right-click, and then under **Paste Options**, click the **Keep Text Only** button to insert the copied text in the document. Type a period. **Close** the **Research** task pane and click **Save**.

4 Press [Ctrl] + [Home]. On the **Home tab**, in the **Editing group**, click the **Replace** button to display the **Find and Replace** dialog box. In the **Find what** box, type **waterproof** and then in the **Replace with** box, type the exact same text **waterproof**

a. Below the **Replace with** box, click the **More** button. Under **Search Options**, select the **Match case** check box. At the bottom, under **Replace**, click the **Format** button, and then in the displayed list, click **Font**.

b. In the **Replace Font** dialog box, under **Font style**, click **Bold**. Click the **Font color arrow**, and then in the fifth column, click the first color—**Blue, Accent 1**.

c. Click **OK** to close the **Replace Font** dialog box, and then in the **Find and Replace** dialog box, click **Replace All**. When a **Microsoft Office Word** message displays indicating that you have made *7* replacements, click **OK**.

(Project 5D Outdoor Accessories continues on the next page)

Skills Review | Project **5D** Outdoor Accessories (continued)

d. Using the same technique, replace all instances of *ruggedized* and select **Match case**. For the replaced text, change the **Font style** to **Bold** and for the **Font color**, in the last column, click the first color—**Orange, Accent 6**. When a **Microsoft Office Word** message displays indicating that you have made *5* replacements, click **OK**.

e. In the **Find and Replace** dialog box, **Delete** the text in the **Find what** and **Replace with** boxes. Deselect **Match case**, click the **No Formatting** button, and then click the **Less** button. **Close** the **Find and Replace** dialog box.

5 Press Ctrl + Home. On the **Review tab**, in the **Proofing group**, click the **Spelling & Grammar** button.

a. For any contextual errors, select the suggestion if necessary, and then click **Change**. Click **Ignore Once** for all other errors. When a message indicates that the spelling and grammar check is complete, click **OK** to close the dialog box. Note: If Word does not identify *weave* and *their* as contextual errors, change the words to *we've* and *there* respectively.

b. From **Backstage** view, display the **Document Information Panel**. In the **Author** box, delete any existing text, and then type your first and last names.

In the **Subject** box, type your course name and section number, and in the **Keywords** box, type **waterproof, ruggedized Close** the Document Information Panel. **Save** your document.

c. From **Backstage** view, display the **Save As** dialog box. If necessary, navigate to your **Word Chapter 5** folder. In the lower portion of the **Save As** dialog box, click the **Save as type arrow**, and then in the displayed list, click **Rich Text Format**. In the **File name** box, type **Lastname_Firstname_5D_Accessories_RTF** and then click **Save**.

d. Scroll to the bottom of the document and double-click in the footer area. Right-click the file name, and then from the shortcut menu, click **Update Field**. **Close** the footer area.

e. Display **Backstage** view, click **Properties**, and then click **Advanced Properties**. Click the **Summary tab** if necessary, and then in the **Keywords** box, position the insertion point to the right of the existing text and type **, rtf** Click **OK** to close the **Properties** dialog box, and then **Save** your document.

6 As directed by your instructor, print or submit electronically the two files—the Word document and the RTF file—that are the results of this project. **Exit** Word.

End **You have completed Project 5D** —————————————

Mastering Word | Project **5E** Phone Accessories

In the following Mastering Word project, you will create a Web page for Eliott Verschoren, Marketing Vice President of Texas Spectrum Wireless, which describes the types of cell phone accessories available for purchase. You will also create a blog announcing savings on purchases. Your completed documents will look similar to Figure 5.49, although text wrapping may vary.

Project Files

For Project 5E, you will need the following files:

w05E_Phone_Accessories
w05E_Phone_Cases

You will save your documents as:

Lastname_Firstname_5E_Phone_Accessories
Lastname_Firstname_5E_Phone_Cases
Lastname_Firstname_5E_Newsletter_Offer

Project Results

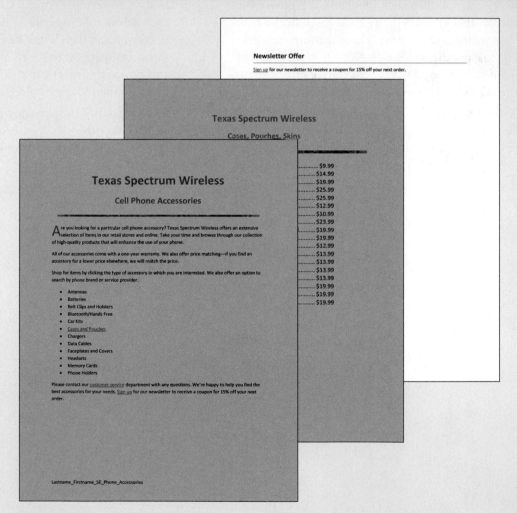

Figure 5.49

(Project 5E Phone Accessories continues on the next page)

Content-Based Assessments

Mastering Word | Project **5E** Phone Accessories (continued)

1 **Start** Word, open the document **w05E_Phone_Accessories**, display the **Save As** dialog box, and then navigate to your **Word Chapter 5** folder. Change the **Save as type** to **Web Page**, change the title to **Cell Phone Accessories** and then save the file as **Lastname_Firstname_5E_Phone_Accessories** Insert the file name in the footer.

2 Select the first paragraph, change the **Font Size** to **28**, apply **Bold** and **Center**, and then change the **Font Color** to **Olive Green, Accent 3, Darker 50%**. Select the second paragraph, change the **Font Size** to **20**, apply **Bold** and **Center**, and then change the **Font Color** to **Olive Green, Accent 3, Darker 50%**. Set the **Page Color** to **Tan, Background 2, Darker 25%**. Click to the left of the fourth paragraph that begins *Are you looking*. Insert a **Drop Cap**, change **Lines to drop** to **2**, and then change the **Font Color** of the dropped cap to **Olive Green, Accent 3, Darker 50%**.

3 Click in the third paragraph, which is blank, display the **Borders and Shading** dialog box, and then click the **Horizontal Line** button. In the fifth row, select the first line—shades of gold, green, and red. Change the **Width** of the line to **95%** and the **Height** to **10 pt**. Click to the left of the paragraph *Cases and Pouches*. Select the next 12 paragraphs, ending with *Memory Cards*. **Sort** the list in ascending order, and then apply bullets. **Save** your document.

4 Open the document **w05E_Phone_Cases**, display the **Save As** dialog box, navigate to your **Word Chapter 5** folder, and then change the **Save as type** to **Web Page**. Change the page title to **Cases and Pouches** and then save the file as **Lastname_Firstname_5E_Phone_Cases** Insert the file name in the footer.

5 Display the **Document Information Panel**, and then click **View Properties** to display the **Properties** dialog box. If necessary, click the **Summary tab**. In the **Author** box, type your first and last names. In the **Subject** box, type your course name and section number, and in the **Keywords** box type **cases, Web page Save** your changes and **Close** the document.

6 In your displayed **Lastname_Firstname_5E_Phone_Accessories** document, in the bulleted list, select the text *Cases and Pouches*. Insert a hyperlink to the existing file in your **Word Chapter 5** folder named **Lastname_Firstname_5E_Phone_Cases**. In the last paragraph of the document, select the text *customer service department*, and insert a hyperlink to the e-mail address **service@txspectrum.com** In the last sentence, select the text *Sign up*, and insert a hyperlink to the e-mail address **newsletter@txspectrum.com**

7 Display the **Document Information Panel**, and then click **View Properties** to display the **Properties** dialog box. If necessary, click the **Summary tab**. In the **Author** box, type your first and last names. In the **Subject** box, type your course name and section number, and in the **Keywords** box, type **accessories, Web page Close** the **Properties** dialog box. **Save** your changes and **Close** the document.

8 **Create** a new **Blog post**. If necessary, in the displayed message box, click **Register Later**. Save the document in your **Word Chapter 5** folder as **Lastname_Firstname_5E_Newsletter_Offer** In the **Enter Post Title Here** field, type **Newsletter Offer** In the body text area, type **Sign up for our newsletter to receive a coupon for 15% off your next order.** Select the text *Sign up*, and then insert a hyperlink to the e-mail address **newsletter@txspectrum.com** At the end of the typed text, press Enter two times, and then type your first and last names.

9 From **Backstage** view, display the **Document Information Panel**, type your name in the **Author** box, type your course name and section number in the **Subject** box, and as the **Keywords**, type **newsletter, blog Save** and **Close** the blog post.

10 Print, or submit electronically the three files—the blog post and two Web pages—as directed by your instructor. **Exit** Word.

End **You have completed Project 5E** ————————————

Mastering Word | Project **5F** Sale Flyer

In the following Mastering Word project, you will create an RTF document for Eliott Verschoren, Marketing Vice President of Texas Spectrum Wireless, which announces an upcoming sale. Your completed document will look similar to Figure 5.50.

Project Files

For Project 5F, you will need the following files:

w05F_Sale_Flyer
w05F_Sale_List

You will save your document as:

Lastname_Firstname_5F_Sale_Flyer

Project Results

Figure 5.50

(Project 5F Sale Flyer continues on the next page)

Content-Based Assessments

Mastering Word | Project **5F** Sale Flyer (continued)

1 **Start** Word, open the file **w05F_Sale_Flyer**, and then save it in your **Word Chapter 5** folder as a **Rich Text Format** file with the name **Lastname_Firstname_5F_Sale_Flyer** Insert the file name in the footer.

2 Display the **Clipboard** task pane, and then open the document **w05F_Sale_List**. If necessary, display the **Clipboard** task pane. **Copy** the **Texas Spectrum Wireless** graphic to the Clipboard. Beginning with the text *Available accessories*, select the remaining text in the document, and then **Copy** it to the Clipboard. **Close** the **w05F_Sale_List** file.

3 Click in the blank paragraph at the top of the document, and then from the **Clipboard** task pane, **Paste** the **Texas Spectrum Wireless** graphic. Click in the blank line following the paragraph that begins *For the month*, and then from the **Clipboard** task pane, paste the text that begins *Available accessories*. In the **Clipboard** task pane, **Clear All** entries, and then **Close** the **Clipboard** task pane.

4 Click at the end of the paragraph that begins *When ordering*, press [Spacebar], and then type **A ringtone is** Display the **Research** task pane, in the **Search for** box, type **ringtone** and then using the **Encarta Dictionary**, search for the definition. In the **Research** task pane, select and copy the text that begins *the sound that notifies* and ends with *a musical tune*. Paste the text in the document. Type a period.

5 At the top of the document, click to the right of *SALE*, and then press [Tab] two times. In the **Research** task pane, type **sale** and then translate the text to Spanish. Using the translation for *reduced prices*, copy and paste the translated text. Format the text as uppercase letters. Press [Tab] two times. Using the same technique, translate the text to French. Copy and paste the translated text, and then format the text as uppercase letters. **Close** the **Research** task pane.

6 Press [Ctrl] + [Home], and then display the **Find and Replace** dialog box. In the **Find what** box, type **smart phone** In the **Replace with** box, type **smart phone** Click the **More** button, and then change the **Font style** to **Bold**. Click **OK**, and then click **Replace All**. In the **Microsoft Office Word** message box, click **OK**. In the **Find and Replace** dialog box, click in the **Replace with** box, and then click the **No Formatting** button. Click the **Less** button, and then **Close** the **Find and Replace** dialog box.

7 Display **Backstage** view, click **Properties**, and then click **Advanced Properties**. On the **Summary** tab, as the **Title**, type **Sale Flyer** In the **Author** box, type your first and last names, as the **Subject**, type your course name and section number, and then as the **Keywords**, type **sale flyer, rtf**

8 **Save** your document, print or submit electronically as directed by your instructor, and then **Exit** Word.

End You have completed Project 5F ———————————

Apply **5A** and **5B** skills from these Objectives:

1. Create a Web Page from a Word Document
2. Insert and Modify Hyperlinks in a Web Page
3. Create a Blog Post
4. Locate Word Settings to Personalize Word 2010
5. Collect and Paste Images and Text
6. Locate Supporting Information
7. Use Advanced Find and Replace and Proofing Options
8. Save in Other File Formats

Mastering Word | Project **5G** Returns Policy

In the following Mastering Word project, you will create a Web page and blog post for Josette Lovrick, Operations Manager of Texas Spectrum Wireless, that explain the return and exchange policy for the company. Your completed documents will look similar to Figure 5.51, although text wrapping may vary.

Project Files

For Project 5G, you will need the following files:

> w05G_Returns_Policy
> w05G_Returns_Image
> w05G_Shipping_Policy

You will save your documents as:

> Lastname_Firstname_5G_Returns_Policy
> Lastname_Firstname_5G_Shipping_RTF
> Lastname_Firstname_5G_Returns_Blog

Project Results

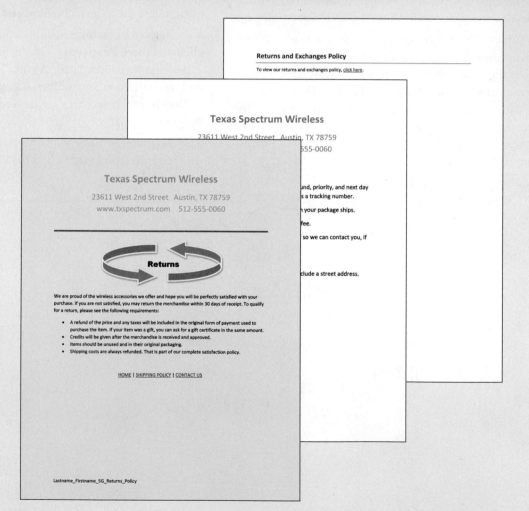

Returns and Exchanges Policy

To view our returns and exchanges policy, click here.

Texas Spectrum Wireless

23611 West 2nd Street   Austin, TX 78759

555-0060

und, priority, and next day
s a tracking number.

h your package ships.

fee.

so we can contact you, if

clude a street address.

Texas Spectrum Wireless

23611 West 2nd Street   Austin, TX 78759
www.txspectrum.com   512-555-0060

Returns

We are proud of the wireless accessories we offer and hope you will be perfectly satisfied with your purchase. If you are not satisfied, you may return the merchandise within 30 days of receipt. To qualify for a return, please see the following requirements:

- A refund of the price and any taxes will be included in the original form of payment used to purchase the item. If your item was a gift, you can ask for a gift certificate in the same amount.
- Credits will be given after the merchandise is received and approved.
- Items should be unused and in their original packaging.
- Shipping costs are always refunded. That is part of our complete satisfaction policy.

HOME | SHIPPING POLICY | CONTACT US

Lastname_Firstname_5G_Returns_Policy

Figure 5.51

(Project 5G Returns Policy continues on the next page)

Content-Based Assessments

Mastering Word | Project **5G** Returns Policy (continued)

1 **Start** Word, open the document **w05G_Returns_ Policy**, display the **Save As** dialog box, navigate to your **Word Chapter 5** folder, and then set the document type to **Web Page**. Change the title to **Returns and Exchanges** and then save the file as **Lastname_Firstname_5G_ Returns_Policy** Insert the file name in the footer.

2 Change the **Page Color** to **Aqua, Accent 5, Lighter 80%**. In the second paragraph, which is blank, display the **Borders and Shading** dialog box, and then insert a **Horizontal Line**, using the first style in the **Horizontal Line** dialog box. Format the line by changing the **Height** to **3 pt** and the **Color** to **Orange, Accent 6, Darker 50%**. Beginning with *Items*, select the next four paragraphs. **Sort** the list alphabetically and apply bullets. Display the **Clipboard** task pane and clear it if necessary.

3 Open the file **w05G_Returns_Image**. **Copy** the image to the Clipboard, and then **Close** the document. Open the file **w05G_Shipping_Policy**, display the **Save As** dialog box, navigate to your **Word Chapter 5** folder, set the file type to **Rich Text Format**, and then save as **Lastname_ Firstname_5G_Shipping_RTF** Add the file name to the footer. Select and then copy to the Clipboard the first three paragraphs—the company information.

4 Display the **Document Information Panel** and click **View Properties** to display the **Properties** dialog box. If necessary, click the **Summary tab**. In the **Author** box, type your first and last names. In the **Subject** box, type your course name and section number, and then in the **Keywords** box, type **shipping policy, RTF Save** and **Close** the document.

5 In your **5G_Returns_Policy** document, press [Ctrl] + [Home]. In the **Clipboard** task pane, paste the text in the document. In the blank paragraph below the horizontal line, paste the image, and then clear all items and **Close** the **Clipboard** task pane. At the bottom of the document, select *HOME*, and then insert a hyperlink to **www.txspectrum.com** In the same paragraph, select the text *SHIPPING POLICY*, and then insert a hyperlink to the file in your **Word Chapter 5** folder named **Lastname_ Firstname_5G_Shipping_RTF**. Select the text *CONTACT US*, and then insert a hyperlink to the e-mail address **service@txspectrum.com** Display the **Spelling and Grammar Checker**, and then take appropriate action to correct any errors.

6 Display the **Document Information Panel** and click **View Properties** to display the **Properties** dialog box. If necessary, click the **Summary tab**. As the **Author** type your first and last names, as the **Subject** type, your course name and section number, and then as the **Keywords**, type **returns, exchanges, Web page Save** and **Close** the document.

7 Create a new **Blog post**; if necessary, click **Register Later**. Save the blog post in your **Word Chapter 5** folder as **Lastname_Firstname_5G_Returns_Blog** As the title, type **Returns and Exchanges Policy** In the body text area, type **To view our returns and exchanges policy, click here.** Press [Enter] two times, and then type your name. Select the text *click here*, and then insert a hyperlink to your **Lastname_Firstname_5G_Returns_Policy** file.

8 Display the **Document Information Panel**. As the **Author**, type your first and last names. As the **Subject** type, your course name and section number, and then as the **Keywords**, type **returns, exchanges, blog Save** your blog post. Print or submit electronically your three files—the blog, the Web page, and the RTF document—as directed by your instructor. **Exit** Word.

End **You have completed Project 5G**

Content-Based Assessments

GO! Fix It | Project 5H Company Overview

Project Files

For Project 5H, you will need the following file:

w05H_Company_Overview

You will save your document as:

Lastname_Firstname_5H_Company_Overview

Open the file **w05H_Company_Overview**, save the file in your **Word Chapter 5** folder as a Web Page, change the page title to **About TSW** and then for the file name, type **Lastname_Firstname_5H_Company_Overview**

This document requires additional formatting and contains errors. Read and examine the document, and then make modifications to improve the overall appearance and correct the errors. Include the following changes and make any other necessary corrections:

- Use the Module theme.
- Apply the Title and Heading 1 styles to the first two paragraphs, respectively.
- Insert and format a drop cap as the first character in the third paragraph, dropped two lines and using the font color Gold, Accent 1.
- Set the page color to Green, Accent 4, Lighter 80%.
- For the horizontal line under the fourth paragraph, set the width to 95%.
- Sort the last five paragraphs of the document alphabetically.
- Replace all occurrences of *TSW* with *Texas Spectrum Wireless* using the Match Case option and Bold font style.
- Create hyperlinks for the last five paragraphs as follows:

Contact Us	**jlovrick@txspectrum.com**
Customer Service	**www.txspectrum.com/service**
Payment Methods	**www.txspectrum.com/payment**
Returns and Exchanges	**www.txspectrum.com/returns**
Shipping Policies	**www.txspectrum.com/shipping**

Things you should know to complete this project:

- Displaying formatting marks will assist in editing the document.
- There are no errors in fonts or font sizes.

Save your document, and add the file name to the footer. In the Document Information Panel, type your first and last names in the Author box and your course name and section number in the Subject box. In the Keywords box, type **Web page, overview** Save your document, and then print or submit electronically as directed by your instructor.

End **You have completed Project 5H** ———————————————

Content-Based Assessments

Apply a combination of the **5A** and **5B** skills.

GO! Make It | Project **5I** Screen Protectors

Project Files

For Project 5I, you will need the following file:

    w05I_Screen_Protectors

You will save your document as:

    Lastname_Firstname_5I_Screen_Protectors

From the student files that accompany this textbook, open the file **w05I_Screen_Protectors** and create the document shown in Figure 5.52. The page color is Blue, Accent 1, Lighter 60%. The three headings are centered and formatted with styles based on the Office theme. Use **www.txspectrum.com** and **yreynolds@txspectrum.com** for the Home and Contact Us hyperlinks. The displayed clip art is 1" high—if necessary, substitute another image. Add your name, your course name and section, and the keywords **screen protectors** to the document properties. Save the file in your **Word Chapter 5** folder as **Lastname_Firstname_5I_Screen_Protectors** Add the file name to the footer, and then print or submit electronically as directed by your instructor.

Project Results

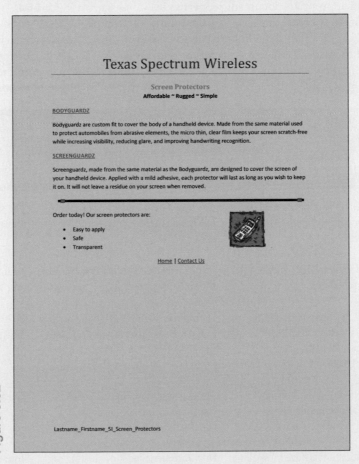

Figure 5.52

End You have completed Project 5I

Content-Based Assessments

GO! Solve It | Project **5J** Staff Increase

Project Files

For Project 5J, you will need the following files:

> New blank Word document
> w05J_Staff_Increase

You will save your files as:

> Lastname_Firstname_5J_Staff_Schedule
> Lastname_Firstname_5J_Staff_Increase

Create a new RTF document and save it as **Lastname_Firstname_5J_Staff_Schedule** in your **Word Chapter 5** folder. Use the following information to create an attractive document:

Sales Manager Yolanda Reynolds is sending a memo to President Roslyn Thomas with an *Employee Schedule for December* attached. The memo should explain that four additional sales associates must be scheduled at the Austin store during the holiday season for the following times: Monday through Friday 9 a.m. to 3 p.m. and 3 p.m. to 9 p.m., Saturday 10 a.m. to 6 p.m., and Sunday 11 a.m. to 5 p.m. Employees will work the same hours throughout December. No employee can be scheduled for two different time periods. Using fictitious employee names, arrange the time periods in an alphabetical list that includes the employee names as bulleted items.

Add appropriate document properties including the keywords **staff, schedule** Open the file **w05J_Staff_Increase** and save it as **Lastname_Firstname_5J_Staff_Increase** Using the existing text, add appropriate hyperlinks to the schedule you created and to contact Ms. Reynolds at yreynolds@txspectrum.com. Add appropriate properties including the keywords **staff, increase** Proofread the documents, correcting any errors. Insert the file names in the footers. Print both files—the RTF file and memo—or submit electronically as directed by your instructor.

Performance Element	Performance Level		
	Exemplary: You consistently applied the relevant skills	**Proficient:** You sometimes, but not always, applied the relevant skills	**Developing:** You rarely or never applied the relevant skills
Save in RTF format	The schedule is saved in RTF format with the appropriate file name.	The schedule is saved in RTF format, but has an incorrect file name.	The schedule is saved in the wrong format.
Insert lists	Sorted, bulleted lists are inserted in the schedule.	Lists are inserted in the schedule, but they are not sorted.	No lists are inserted in the schedule.
Insert hyperlinks	Hyperlinks are inserted in the memo for the schedule and contact information, using existing text.	Hyperlinks are inserted in the memo, but at the wrong locations or include incorrect text.	No hyperlinks are inserted in the memo.
Insert and format text	The schedule contains the correct information and is formatted attractively.	The schedule contains the correct information, but the format is not consistent or attractive.	The schedule does not contain the correct information.
Correct errors	Both documents have no spelling or grammar errors.	One document contains spelling or grammar errors.	Both documents contain spelling or grammar errors.

End You have completed Project 5J

Content-Based Assessments

Apply a combination of the **5A** and **5B** skills.

GO! Solve It | Project **5K** Wholesalers

Project Files

For Project 5K, you will need the following files:

> New blank Word document
> w05K_Benefits

You will save your file as:

> Lastname_Firstname_5K_Wholesalers

Create a new document and save it in your **Word Chapter 5** folder as a Web page, using **Wholesale Information** for the page title and the file name **Lastname_Firstname_5K_Wholesalers** Use the following information to create a document that includes at least one graphic, a sorted bulleted list, and hyperlinks to the company's home page and contact e-mail address.

Texas Spectrum Wireless is beginning a new venture—selling to wholesalers. Participation is limited to valid companies already in the business of reselling wireless phones or accessories. A company must register with Texas Spectrum Wireless to receive a wholesale account. New accounts are activated within 24 hours. The company will not set up reseller accounts for consumers. Information regarding benefits to wholesalers and contact information to register can be found in the student file **w05K_Benefits**.

Proofread the document, and correct any errors. Add the file name to the footer. In the Properties area, add your name, your course name and section number, and the keywords **wholesalers, Web page** Print your file, or submit electronically, as directed by your instructor.

	Performance Level		
	Exemplary: You consistently applied the relevant skills	**Proficient:** You sometimes, but not always, applied the relevant skills	**Developing:** You rarely or never applied the relevant skills
Insert and format text	Text explains the purpose of the document with no spelling or grammar errors.	Text explains the purpose, but the document contains spelling or grammar errors.	The purpose of the document is unclear due to insufficient text.
Insert list	A sorted, bulleted list is inserted.	A list is inserted, but it is not sorted.	No list is inserted in the document.
Insert hyperlinks	Hyperlinks are inserted for the company's home page and contact information.	Hyperlinks are inserted, but contain the wrong information.	No hyperlinks are inserted in the document.
Insert graphics	Graphics are inserted to create an attractive document.	Graphics are inserted, but do not enhance the appearance of the document.	No graphics are inserted in the document.
Save as Web page	The document is saved in Web Page format with the appropriate title.	The document is saved in Web Page format, but has an incorrect title.	The document is saved in the wrong format.

(left side label: Performance Element)

End You have completed Project 5K

Outcomes-Based Assessments

Rubric

The following outcomes-based assessments are *open-ended assessments*. That is, there is no specific correct result; your result will depend on your approach to the information provided. Make *Professional Quality* your goal. Use the following scoring rubric to guide you in *how* to approach the problem and then to evaluate *how well* your approach solves the problem.

The *criteria*—Software Mastery, Content, Format and Layout, and Process—represent the knowledge and skills you have gained that you can apply to solving the problem. The *levels of performance*—Professional Quality, Approaching Professional Quality, or Needs Quality Improvements—help you and your instructor evaluate your result.

	Your completed project is of Professional Quality if you:	Your completed project is Approaching Professional Quality if you:	Your completed project Needs Quality Improvements if you:
1-Software Mastery	Choose and apply the most appropriate skills, tools, and features and identify efficient methods to solve the problem.	Choose and apply some appropriate skills, tools, and features, but not in the most efficient manner.	Choose inappropriate skills, tools, or features, or are inefficient in solving the problem.
2-Content	Construct a solution that is clear and well organized, contains content that is accurate, appropriate to the audience and purpose, and is complete. Provide a solution that contains no errors in spelling, grammar, or style.	Construct a solution in which some components are unclear, poorly organized, inconsistent, or incomplete. Misjudge the needs of the audience. Have some errors in spelling, grammar, or style, but the errors do not detract from comprehension.	Construct a solution that is unclear, incomplete, or poorly organized; contains some inaccurate or inappropriate content; and contains many errors in spelling, grammar, or style. Do not solve the problem.
3-Format and Layout	Format and arrange all elements to communicate information and ideas, clarify function, illustrate relationships, and indicate relative importance.	Apply appropriate format and layout features to some elements, but not others. Overuse features, causing minor distraction.	Apply format and layout that does not communicate information or ideas clearly. Do not use format and layout features to clarify function, illustrate relationships, or indicate relative importance. Use available features excessively, causing distraction.
4-Process	Use an organized approach that integrates planning, development, self-assessment, revision, and reflection.	Demonstrate an organized approach in some areas, but not others; or, use an insufficient process of organization throughout.	Do not use an organized approach to solve the problem.

Outcomes-Based Assessments

Apply a combination of the **5A** and **5B** skills.

GO! Think | Project **5L** Phone Jewelry

Project Files

For Project 5L, you will need the following file:

New blank Word document

You will save your file as:

Lastname_Firstname_5L_Phone_Jewelry

The marketing director at Texas Spectrum Wireless wants to create a flyer to advertise their latest product line—cell phone bling, a variety of jewelry accessories. The categories include butterfly, tiger, seashore, carnation, and mountain. This document will be reviewed by others because it includes Spanish and French translations of the styles.

Create a flyer with basic information about the new product line. Include a brief paragraph describing cell phone bling and accessories. Use the Research task pane to locate the descriptive information, adding a hyperlink to the Web site where you obtained the data. Display the individual styles in an organized list. Use the Translation tool to create two additional style lists— in Spanish and French. Be sure the document has an attractive design and is easy to read. Correct all spelling and grammar errors, excluding the translated text.

Save the file in Rich Text Format, with the file name **Lastname_Firstname_5L_Phone_Jewelry** Add appropriate information in the Properties area, and then add the file name to the footer. Print your file, or submit electronically, as directed by your instructor.

 End You have completed Project 5L ———————————————

Apply a combination of the **5A** and **5B** skills.

GO! Think | Project **5M** Memory Cards

Project Files

For Project 5M, you will need the following files:

New blank Word document
w05M_TSW_Cards

You will save your file as:

Lastname_Firstname_5M_Memory_Cards

Eliott Verschoren, Marketing Vice President, wants to create a Web page advertising the different types of memory cards sold by Texas Spectrum Wireless. The Web page will include the company name, brief explanations of memory cards, SD cards, and microSD cards, and a list of specific cards available.

Create the Web page, using the Research task pane to find definitions for the types of cards. Open the document **w05M_TSW_Cards** to collect the information for the specific cards that are sold by the company. Be sure the Web page has an attractive design and is easy to read and understand. The list of memory cards should be arranged in a logical order. Include a hyperlink **sales@txspectrum.com** to contact the sales department. Correct all spelling and grammar errors.

Save the file as a Web Page, using **TSW Memory Cards** for the page title and **Lastname_Firstname_5M_Memory_Cards** for the file name. Add appropriate information to the Properties area, and add the file name to the footer. Print your file, or submit electronically, as directed by your instructor.

 End You have completed Project 5M ———————————————

Outcomes-Based Assessments

You and GO! | Project **5N** Personal Web Page

Project Files

For Project 5N, you will need the following file:

New blank Word document

You will save your files as:

Lastname_Firstname_5N_Personal_Webpage
Lastname_Firstname_5N_Courses

Create a personal Web page that includes information about yourself—such as family, school, interests, accomplishments, and goals. Save the file as a Web Page, using your name for the page title and **Lastname_Firstname_5N_Personal_Webpage** the file name. Add the file name to the footer. In the Properties area, add your name, your course name and section number, and the keywords **Web page** and **personal**

Create a second document that contains the courses you are taking this semester. For each course, include the name of the course, when it meets, and a brief description. Save this second document as an RTF file, with the file name **Lastname_Firstname_5N_Courses** Add the file name to the footer. In the Properties area, add your name, your course name and section number, and the keyword **course schedule**

On the Web page, be sure to include a page background, horizontal line, and hyperlinks to your college's Web site, your *5N_Courses* file, and an e-mail address link to contact you. Format the document in an attractive manner and check for spelling errors.

Print your two files, or submit electronically, as directed by your instructor.

End **You have completed Project 5N** ——————————————

Building Documents from Reusable Content and Revising Documents Using Markup Tools

OUTCOMES
At the end of this chapter you will be able to:

OBJECTIVES
Mastering these objectives will enable you to:

PROJECT 6A
Create reusable content and construct a document with building blocks and theme templates.

1. Create Building Blocks (p. 341)
2. Create and Save a Theme Template (p. 348)
3. Create a Document by Using Building Blocks (p. 351)

PROJECT 6B
Collaborate with others to edit, review, and finalize a document.

4. Use Comments in a Document (p. 358)
5. Track Changes in a Document (p. 363)
6. View Side by Side, Compare, and Combine Documents (p. 371)

newphotoservice/Shutterstock

In This Chapter

In this chapter you will use building blocks, which save time and give consistency to your documents. You can use predefined building blocks or create your own custom building blocks. To give documents a customized appearance, you can create a theme by defining the colors, fonts, and effects. You will create building blocks and a custom theme template, and then build a document from reusable content.

You will also use the Track Changes feature, which makes it easy to work with a team to collaborate on documents. Because several people may need to review a document, you can track changes made to a document and add comments. You will track changes and insert comments, review changes made by others, and accept or reject changes.

The projects in this chapter relate to the **Lakefield Public Library**, which serves the local community at three locations—the Main library, the East Branch, and the West Branch. The collection includes books, audio books, music CDs, videos and DVDs, and magazines and newspapers—for all ages. The library also provides sophisticated online and technology services, youth programs, and frequent appearances by both local and nationally known authors. The citizens of Lakefield support the Lakefield Public Library with local taxes, donations, and special events fees.

Project 6A Newsletter with Reusable Content and Custom Theme

myitlab
Project 6A Training

Project Activities

In Activities 6.01 through 6.08, you will assist Benedetta Herman, Director of Operations at Lakefield Public Library, in designing a custom look for documents that the library produces by creating a custom theme and building blocks for content that can be reused. Your completed documents will look similar to Figure 6.1.

Project Files

For Project 6A, you will need the following files:

Two new blank Word documents
w06A_February_Articles
w06A_Classes

You will save your files as:

Lastname_Firstname_6A_Building_Blocks
Lastname_Firstname_6A_Library_Theme—not shown in figure
Lastname_Firstname_6A_February_Newsletter

Project Results

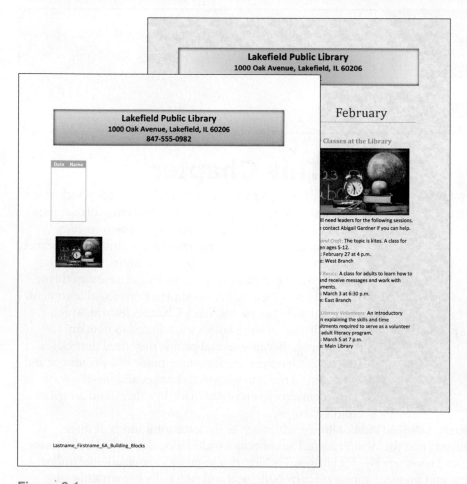

Figure 6.1
Project 6A February Newsletter

Objective 1 | Create Building Blocks

Building blocks are reusable pieces of content or other document parts—for example, headers, footers, page number formats—that are stored in galleries. The Headers gallery, the Footers gallery, the Page Numbers gallery, and the Bibliographies gallery, some of which you have already used, are all examples of building block galleries. You can also create your own building blocks for content that you use frequently.

Alert! | Completing This Project in One Working Session

If you are working in a college lab, plan to complete Project 6A in one working session. Building blocks are stored on the computer at which you are working. Thus, in a college lab, if you exit Word before completing the project, the building blocks might be deleted and will be unavailable for your use—you will have to re-create them. On your own computer, you can exit Word, and the building blocks will remain until you delete them.

Activity 6.01 | Creating a Building Block in the Text Box Gallery

Recall that a **text box** is a movable, resizable container for text or graphics. In this activity, you will create a distinctive text box building block that the library can use for any documents requiring the library's contact information.

1 **Start** Word. From **Backstage** view, display the **Save As** dialog box, navigate to the location where you are saving your files for this chapter, and then create a folder named **Word Chapter 6** Save the document as **Lastname_Firstname_6A_Building_Blocks** Using **Quick Parts**, insert the file name in the footer. If necessary, display the rulers and formatting marks.

2 On the **Insert tab**, in the **Text group**, click the **Text Box** button. Notice that predesigned, built-in building blocks display in the **Text Box** gallery. Click the first text box—**Simple Text Box**.

> A text box containing placeholder text displays at the top of your document. Text boxes can be formatted like other graphic elements in Word and saved as building blocks.

3 On the **Format tab**, in the **Shape Styles group**, click the **More** button . In the **Shape Styles** gallery, in the fourth row, click the second style—**Subtle Effect – Blue, Accent 1**.

4 On the **Format tab**, if the **Size group** is visible, change the **Shape Width** 1.37" to **6.5"**; otherwise, to the right of the **Arrange group**, click the **Size** button, and then change the **Shape Width** 1.37" to **6.5"**. Compare your screen with Figure 6.2.

> Depending on the resolution setting of your monitor, either the Size group or the Size button will display.

Figure 6.2

Format tab active

Subtle Effect – Blue, Accent 1 selected

Placeholder text

Text box inserted

Size button—your screen may differ

5 On the **Format tab**, in the **Shape Styles group**, click the **Shape Effects** button, and point to **Shadow**. Under **Inner**, in the second row, click the second style—**Inside Center**.

6 In the text box, type the following to replace the placeholder text: **Lakefield Public Library** Press Enter, and then type **1000 Oak Avenue, Lakefield, IL 60206** Press Enter, and then type **847-555-0982**

7 Select all three paragraphs, click the **Home tab**, and then in the **Styles group**, click the **No Spacing** style. Select the first paragraph, change the **Font Size** to **20**, and then apply **Bold** B and **Center** ≡. Select the second and third paragraphs, change the **Font Size** to **16**, and then apply **Bold** B and **Center** ≡. Notice the height of the text box automatically adjusts to accommodate the text.

8 Click in the first paragraph to cancel the selection. Click the outer edge of the text box so that none of the text is selected, but that the text box itself is selected and displays sizing handles. Compare your screen with Figure 6.3.

Figure 6.3

Sizing handles indicate text box is selected

Text entered and formatted

9 On the **Insert tab**, in the **Text group**, click the **Text Box** button, and then click **Save Selection to Text Box Gallery**. In the **Create New Building Block** dialog box, in the **Name** box, type **Library Information** Notice that the **Gallery** box displays *Text Boxes*.

By selecting the Text Boxes gallery, this building block will display in the gallery of other text box building blocks.

10 In the **Description** box, type **Use as the library contact information in newsletters, flyers, public meeting agendas, and other publications** Compare your screen with Figure 6.4.

Figure 6.4

Building block name

Create New Building Block dialog box

Building block will be stored in Text Boxes gallery

Description of building block

11 Click **OK** to close the dialog box and save the building block. **Save** 🖫 your document.

Activity 6.02 | Viewing Building Blocks in the Building Blocks Organizer

The *Building Blocks Organizer* enables you to view—in a single location—all of the available building blocks from all the different galleries.

1 On the **Insert tab**, in the **Text group**, click the **Quick Parts** button.

> *Quick Parts* refers to all of the reusable pieces of content that are available to insert into a document, including building blocks, document properties, and fields. Recall that you have used the Quick Parts button to insert the field containing the file name into footers.

2 From the displayed list, click **Building Blocks Organizer**. In the displayed **Building Blocks Organizer** dialog box, in the upper left corner, click **Name** to sort the building blocks alphabetically by name.

> Here you can view all of the building blocks available in Word. In this dialog box, you can also delete a building block, edit its properties—for example, change the name or description or gallery location—or select and insert it into a document.

3 By using the scroll bar in the center of the **Building Blocks Organizer** dialog box, scroll down until you see your building block that begins *Library*, and then click to select it. Compare your screen with Figure 6.5.

> You can see that Word provides numerous building blocks. In the preview area on the right, notice that under the preview of the building block, the name and description that you entered displays.

Figure 6.5

Building Blocks Organizer dialog box

Building Blocks sorted alphabetically by name

Library Information building block

Preview of selected building block

Name and description that you entered

4 In the lower right corner, click **Close**.

Activity 6.03 | Creating a Building Block in the Quick Tables Gallery

Quick Tables are tables that are stored as building blocks. Word includes many predesigned Quick Tables, and you can also create your own tables and save them as Quick Tables in the Quick Tables gallery. In this activity, you will modify an existing Quick Table and then save it as a new building block. Ms. Herman will use this table to announce staff birthdays in the quarterly newsletter and in the monthly staff bulletin.

1 Click anywhere outside of the text box to deselect it, and then point slightly under the lower left corner of the text box to display the ⌶▤ pointer at approximately **1.5 inches on the vertical ruler**, as shown in Figure 6.6.

The *click and type pointer* is the text select—I-beam—pointer with various attached shapes that indicate which formatting—left-aligned, centered, or right-aligned—will be applied when you double-click in a blank area of a document. In this case, if you double-click, a new paragraph will be inserted with a left-aligned format.

Figure 6.6

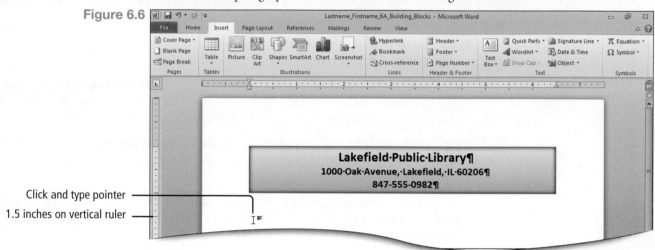

Click and type pointer
1.5 inches on vertical ruler

2 At approximately **1.5 inches on the vertical ruler**, double-click to insert a blank paragraph below the text box. Notice that two paragraph marks display below the text box. If you are not satisfied with your result, click Undo ↶ and begin again.

3 With the insertion point in the second blank paragraph, on the **Insert tab**, in the **Tables group**, click the **Table** button, and then at the bottom of the list, point to **Quick Tables**. In the **Quick Tables** gallery, scroll down to locate **Tabular List**, as shown in Figure 6.7.

Figure 6.7

Table button
Quick Tables gallery
Tabular List table
Scroll bar

4 Click **Tabular List**. In the first row of the table, click in the first cell, select the text *ITEM*, and then type **Date**

5 Press [Tab] to move to the second cell, and with *NEEDED* selected, type **Name** Select all the remaining cells of the table, and then press [Del]. Compare your screen with Figure 6.8.

> Because this table will be used as a building block to enter birthday information, the sample text is not needed.

Figure 6.8

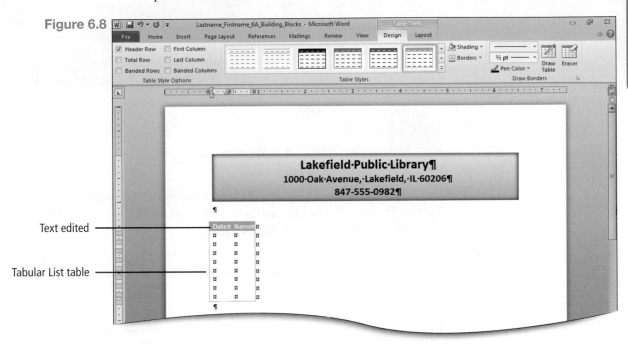

Text edited

Tabular List table

6 Click in the table, point slightly outside of the upper left corner of the table, and then click the **table move handle** 🖽 to select the entire table.

7 With the table selected, move your pointer to the left end of the horizontal ruler, and then point to the first **Move Table Column** marker to display the ↔ pointer, as shown in Figure 6.9.

Figure 6.9

Pointer

Move Table Column marker

Table selected

8 Drag the **Move Table Column** marker slightly to the right until the displayed vertical dotted line aligns with the left edge of the text box, as shown in Figure 6.10, and then release the left mouse button.

This action aligns the left edge of the table with the left edge of the text box.

Figure 6.10

Pointer

Dotted vertical line aligns with left edge of text box

9 With the table still selected, on the **Insert tab**, in the **Tables group**, click the **Table** button. In the displayed list, point to **Quick Tables**, and then at the bottom of the list, click **Save Selection to Quick Tables Gallery**.

10 In the **Create New Building Block** dialog box, in the **Name** box, type **Birthday Table** In the **Description** box, type **Use for staff birthdays in newsletters and bulletins** Compare your screen with Figure 6.11.

Figure 6.11

Name of new building block
Tables gallery indicated

Description

11 Click **OK** to save the table in the **Quick Tables** gallery. **Save** 💾 your document.

Activity 6.04 | Creating a Graphic Building Block

In this activity, you will modify an image and save it as a building block so that Benedetta Herman can use it in any document that includes information about library classes.

1 Click in the blank paragraph below the table, and then press Enter. On the **Insert tab**, in the **Illustrations group**, click the **Picture** button.

2 In the **Insert Picture** dialog box, navigate to your student files, select the file **w06A_Classes**, and then click **Insert**.

3 With the picture selected, on the **Format tab**, in the **Picture Styles group**, click the **Picture Effects** button, point to **Bevel**, and then under **Bevel**, in the first row, click the fourth bevel—**Cool Slant**.

4 On the **Format tab**, in the **Size group**, change the **Shape Width** [1.37"] to **1.3"**.

5 With the picture selected, click the **Insert tab**, and then in the **Text group**, click the **Quick Parts** button. From the displayed list, click **Save Selection to Quick Part Gallery**.

> By choosing the Save Selection to Quick Parts Gallery command, building blocks that you create are saved in the Quick Parts gallery and assigned to the General category. However, you can save the building block in any of the other relevant galleries, or create your own custom gallery. You can also create your own category if you want to do so.

6 In the **Create New Building Block** dialog box, in the **Name** box, type **Classes Picture** and then in the **Description** box, type **Use this picture in documents containing information about library classes.** Compare your screen with Figure 6.12.

> You can create and then select any content and save it as a building block in this manner.

Figure 6.12

Name of building block

Quick Parts gallery indicated

Description of new building block

Picture selected as the content to save as a building block

7 Click **OK** to close the dialog box and save the **Classes Picture** building block.

> Your new building block is saved, and you can insert it in a document by selecting it from the Quick Parts gallery.

8 On the **Insert tab**, in the **Text group**, click the **Quick Parts** button, and then point to **Classes Picture**. Compare your screen with Figure 6.13.

> Your picture displays under General in the Quick Parts gallery.

Figure 6.13

General category displays your picture

ScreenTip

Quick Parts button—your view may differ

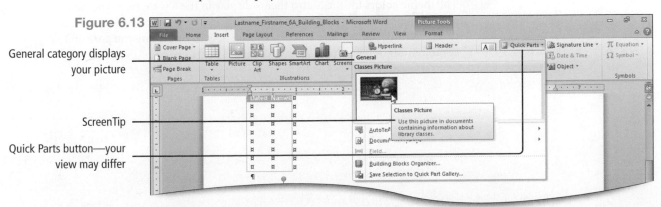

9 Click anywhere in the document to close the **Quick Parts** gallery.

10 Display the **Document Information Panel**. In the **Author** box, type your first and last names. In the **Subject** box, type your course name and section number, and in the **Keywords** box, type **library newsletter, building blocks Close** ☒ the Document Information Panel.

11 **Save** 🖫 your document, display **Backstage** view, and then **Close** the document. Leave Word open for the next activity.

> The purpose of this document is to submit a copy of your building blocks to your instructor. After the building blocks are stored in a gallery, they are saved on your system and no document is required unless you want to distribute your building blocks to someone else who would like to use the building blocks on his or her computer.

> **Alert!** | **What Happens If I Accidentally Close Word?**
>
> If you accidently close Word, in the dialog box regarding changes to building blocks, click Save to accept the changes.

Objective 2 | Create and Save a Theme Template

Recall that a *theme* is a predefined combination of colors, fonts, and effects that look good together and that you apply as a single selection. Word comes with a group of predefined themes, and the default theme is named *Office*. You can also create your own theme by selecting any combination of colors, fonts, and effects that, when saved, creates a *theme template*. A theme template, which stores a set of colors, fonts, and effects—lines and fill effects—can be shared with other Office programs, for example, Excel and PowerPoint.

Activity 6.05 | Customizing a Theme

In this activity, you will create a custom theme that the library will use for all documents.

1 Press Ctrl + N to display a new blank document.

2 On the **Page Layout tab**, in the **Themes group**, click the **Theme Colors** button 🔲. Under **Built-In**, take a moment to examine the groups of colors for each of the predefined themes, scrolling as needed.

3 From the list, click **Metro**. Click the **Theme Colors** button 🔲 again, and then at the bottom, click **Create New Theme Colors**. Compare your screen with Figure 6.14.

> The theme colors for the Metro theme display in the Create New Theme Colors dialog box. A set of theme colors contains four text and background colors, six accent colors, and two hyperlink colors. Here you can select a new color for any category and save the combination of colors with a new name.

Figure 6.14

Create New Theme Colors dialog box

Four text/background colors

Six accent colors

Two hyperlink colors

Colors for the selected theme—Metro—display

4 Click **Cancel** to keep the current group of color definitions. In the **Themes group**, click the **Theme Fonts** button [A].

Theme fonts contain a heading font—the upper font—and a body text font—the lower font. You can use an existing set of Built-In fonts for your new theme, or define new sets of fonts.

5 Under **Built-In**, click the **Office** font set. In the **Themes group**, click the **Theme Effects** button [⊙].

Theme effects are sets of lines and fill effects. Here you can see the lines and fill effects for each predefined theme. You cannot create your own set of theme effects, but you can choose any set of effects to combine with other theme colors and theme fonts.

6 Under **Built-In**, click **Flow** as the theme effects. Leave Word open—you will save your document in the next activity.

Your custom theme—a combination of the Metro colors, the Office fonts, and the Flow effects—is complete, with no further customization to the Metro color combination or the Office font combination.

Activity 6.06 | Saving a Theme Template

To use your custom theme in other Microsoft Office files, you can save it as a theme template.

1 In the **Themes group**, click the **Themes** button, and then at the bottom of the displayed list, click **Save Current Theme** to display the **Save Current Theme** dialog box. Compare your screen with Figure 6.15.

> By default, saving a new theme displays the Templates folder, which includes the Document Themes folder, containing separate folders for Theme Colors, Theme Effects, and Theme Fonts. The Save as type box specifies the file type *Office Theme*.
>
> If you save your theme in the Templates folder, it is available to the Office programs on the computer at which you are working. In a college or organization, you may not have permission to update this folder, but on your own computer, you can save your themes here if you want to do so.

Figure 6.15

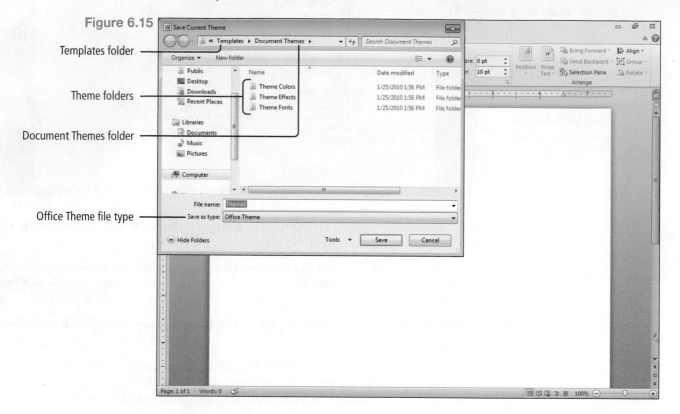

Templates folder

Theme folders

Document Themes folder

Office Theme file type

2 In the **Save Current Theme** dialog box, navigate to your **Word Chapter 6** folder. In the **File name** box, type **Lastname_Firstname_6A_Library_Theme** and then click **Save**.

> For the purposes of this instruction, you are saving the theme to your Word Chapter 6 folder.

3 In the **Themes group**, click the **Themes** button, and then click **Browse for Themes**. In the **Choose Theme or Themed Document** dialog box, navigate to your **Word Chapter 6** folder, right-click your file **Lastname_Firstname_6A_Library_Theme**, and from the shortcut menu, click **Properties**. Compare your screen with Figure 6.16.

> The Properties dialog box for the Theme displays. A Microsoft Office theme is saved with the file extension *.thmx*. By default, a theme template is set to open with PowerPoint; however, the theme can also be applied in Word or Excel.

Figure 6.16

Lastname_Firstname_
6A_Library_Theme
Properties dialog box

.thmx file extension

Open with PowerPoint

4 Close [×] the **Properties** dialog box, and then **Close** [×] the **Choose Theme or Themed Document** dialog box.

5 From **Backstage** view, **Close** the blank document on your screen without saving changes.

Objective 3 | Create a Document by Using Building Blocks

One of the benefits of creating building blocks and theme templates is that they can be used repeatedly to create individual documents. The building blocks ensure consistency in format and structure, and the theme template provides consistency in colors, fonts, and effects.

Activity 6.07 | Creating a Document Using Building Blocks

Benedetta Herman sends a monthly newsletter to all library staff. In this activity, you will create the February newsletter by using the building blocks that you created.

1 Press [Ctrl] + [N] to display a new blank document, and then save it in your **Word Chapter 6** folder as **Lastname_Firstname_6A_February_Newsletter** Scroll to the bottom of the page, and then using **Quick Parts**, insert the file name in the footer. If necessary, display the rulers and formatting marks.

2 On the **Page Layout tab**, in the **Themes group**, click the **Themes** button, and then click **Browse for Themes**. In the **Choose Theme or Themed Document** dialog box, navigate to your **Word Chapter 6** folder, and then click your file **Lastname_Firstname_6A_ Library_Theme**. Compare your screen with Figure 6.17.

Figure 6.17

Choose Theme or Themed Document dialog box

Selected theme file

3 Click **Open** to apply the theme, and notice that the colors on the buttons in the **Themes group** change to reflect the new theme.

4 On the **Page Layout tab**, in the **Page Background group**, click the **Page Color** button, and then click **Fill Effects**. In the **Fill Effects** dialog box, click the **Texture tab**, and then in the fourth row, click the third texture–**Parchment**. Compare your screen with Figure 6.18.

Figure 6.18

Library theme colors display on buttons in Themes group

Fill Effects dialog box

Texture tab

Parchment texture selected

5 Click **OK** to apply the textured background.

6 On the **Insert tab**, in the **Text group**, click the **Text Box** button. Scroll to the bottom of the **Text Box** gallery, and then under **General**, click your **Library Information** building block.

The theme colors of your custom theme are applied to the building block.

7 Click anywhere outside of the text box to deselect it, and then point slightly under the lower left corner of the text box to display the ⌶ pointer at approximately **1.5 inches on the vertical ruler**. Double-click to insert two blank paragraphs under the text box. If you are dissatisfied with your result, click **Undo** ↶.

8 On the **Home tab**, in the **Styles group**, click the **More** button ⏷ to display the **Styles** gallery, and then apply the **Title** style. Type **Staff Newsletter** press ⟦Tab⟧ two times, and then type **February** Select and then **Center** ≡ the paragraph you just typed.

9 Position the ⌶ pointer at the left margin at approximately **2.25 inches on the vertical ruler**, and then double-click to insert a new blank paragraph. In the **Styles group**, click the **More** button ⏷ , and then if necessary, apply the **Normal** style to the new paragraph. Select the paragraph mark, and then compare your screen with Figure 6.19.

Figure 6.19

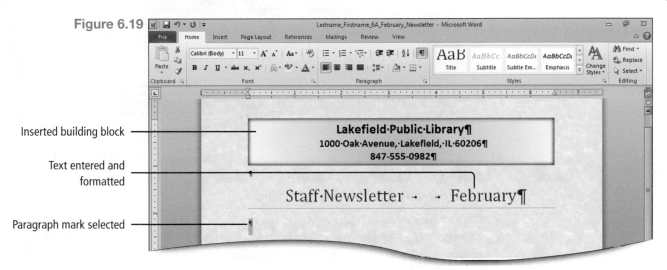

Inserted building block

Text entered and formatted

Paragraph mark selected

10 With the paragraph mark selected, on the **Page Layout tab**, in the **Page Setup group**, click the **Columns** button, and then click **Two**. Click to the left of the paragraph mark, and then compare your screen with Figure 6.20.

A continuous section break is inserted at the end of the previous paragraph. The remainder of the document will be formatted in two columns.

Figure 6.20

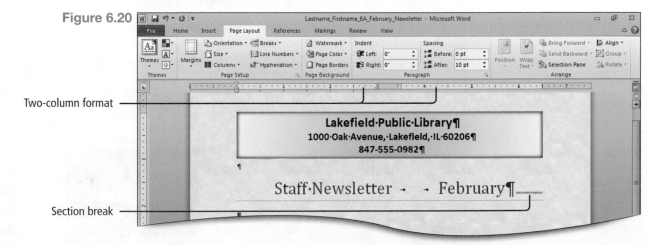

Two-column format

Section break

11 On the **Insert tab**, in the **Text group**, click the **Object button arrow**, and then click **Text from File**. In the **Insert File** dialog box, navigate to your student files, click **w06A_February_Articles**, and then click **Insert**. Compare your screen with Figure 6.21.

> Word inserts the text in two columns.

Figure 6.21

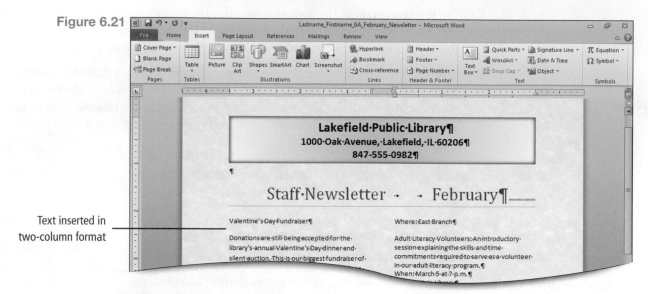

Text inserted in two-column format

12 Select the paragraph *Valentine's Day Fundraiser*. Press and hold Ctrl, and then select the paragraphs *Card Shower* and *New Classes at the Library*. On the **Home tab**, in the **Styles group**, click the **Heading 1** style.

13 In the *New Classes* section, being careful to include each colon, select the headings *Story and Craft:*, *E-mail Basics:*, and *Adult Literacy Volunteers:*, and then from the **Styles** gallery, apply the **Intense Emphasis** style.

14 In the first column, click to position the insertion point to the left of the paragraph that begins *We still need*. On the **Insert tab**, in the **Text group**, click the **Quick Parts** button. Under **General**, click the **Classes Picture** building block.

15 Click to select the picture, and then on the **Format tab**, in the **Size group**, change the **Shape Height** ☐ 1.5" ☐ to **1.85"**. Deselect the picture, and then compare your screen with Figure 6.22.

> The picture and the section titled "New Classes at the Library" move to the second column.

Figure 6.22

New Classes at the Library section moves to second column

Heading 1 style

Inserted picture

Intense Emphasis style

16 At the bottom of the first column, click at the end of the last paragraph—following *60206*—and then press Enter to insert a new paragraph.

17 Type **February Birthdays** and then press Enter. Select the text you just typed, and then from the **Styles** gallery, apply the **Heading 1** style.

18 Click in the blank paragraph below *February Birthdays*. On the **Insert tab**, in the **Tables group**, click the **Table** button, point to **Quick Tables**, scroll toward the bottom of the list, and then under **General**, click **Birthday Table**.

19 In the second row of the table, position the insertion point in the first cell, and then type **11** Press Tab, and then type **Mary Margolis** Using the same technique, type the following text in the table:

17	Antonio Ramirez
18	Lydia Zimmerman
20	Eleanor Robinson
27	Stefan Richards

20 Select the last three empty rows of the table. On the **Layout tab**, in the **Rows & Columns group**, click the **Delete** button, and then click **Delete Rows**.

21 Press Ctrl + End, and then select the blank paragraph mark at the bottom of the second column. With the paragraph mark selected, on the **Page Layout tab**, in the **Page Setup group**, click the **Columns** button, and then click **One**. Compare your screen with Figure 6.23, and then **Save** your document.

The existing text remains formatted in two columns; however, the bottom of the document returns to one column—full page width.

Figure 6.23

Section break inserted

New paragraph moves to left margin

Activity 6.08 | Managing Files and Restoring Settings

You can delete user-created building blocks and user templates if they are no longer needed. If you are sharing a computer with others, you should restore Word to its default settings. In this activity, you will delete the building blocks you created.

1 Click the **Insert tab**, and then in the **Text group**, click the **Quick Parts** button. Right-click the **Classes Picture** building block, and then on the shortcut menu, click **Organize and Delete**. Compare your screen with Figure 6.24.

> The Classes Picture building block is selected in the Building Blocks Organizer dialog box. A preview of the building block displays on the right. The name and description of the building block display below the preview.

Figure 6.24

Preview of selected building block

Name and description of selected building block

2 Click the **Delete** button. In the **Microsoft Office Word** dialog box, click **Yes** to confirm the deletion.

More Knowledge | Deleting Building Blocks

To delete a building block, you must have an open document. This allows the Quick Parts command to become active.

---

3 In the **Building Blocks Organizer** dialog box, in the upper left corner, click **Name** to sort the building blocks alphabetically by name.

4 By using the scroll bar in the center of the **Building Blocks Organizer** dialog box, scroll until you see your building block that begins *Birthday*, and then click to select it. Click the **Delete** button, and then click **Yes** to confirm the deletion.

5 Using the same technique, scroll to locate your building block that begins *Library*, and then **Delete** it. **Close** the **Building Blocks Organizer** dialog box.

6 Press Ctrl + Home. Display the **Document Information Panel**. In the **Author** box, delete any text, and then type your first and last names. In the **Subject** box, type your course name and section number, and in the **Keywords** box, type **library newsletter, February** **Close** ✕ the Document Information Panel.

7 **Save** 🖫 your document. Print your two Word documents—you cannot print the theme file—or submit all three files electronically as directed by your instructor. **Close** ✕ Word. In the dialog box regarding changes to building blocks, click **Save** to accept the changes.

End You have completed Project 6A ───────

Project 6B Events Schedule with Tracked Changes

Project Activities

In Activities 6.09 through 6.17, you will assist Abigail Gardner, Director of Programs and Youth Services, in using the markup tools in Word to add comments and make changes to a schedule of events. You will accept or reject each change, and then compare and combine your document with another draft version to create a final document. Your completed documents will look similar to Figure 6.25.

Project Files

For Project 6B, you will need the following files:

> w06B_Events_Schedule
> w06B_Schedule_Revisions

You will save your documents as:

> Lastname_Firstname_6B_Events_Schedule
> Lastname_Firstname_6B_Schedule_Combined

Project Results

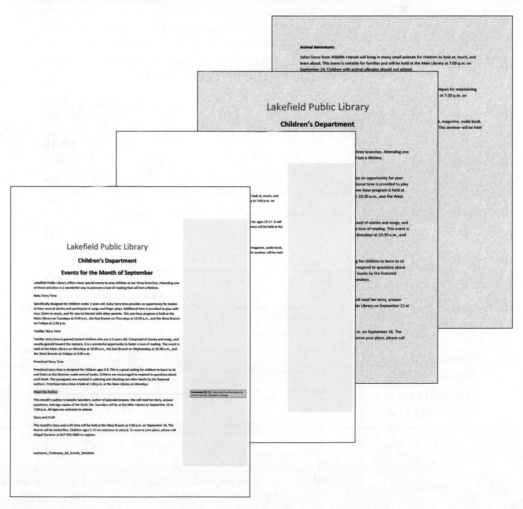

Figure 6.25
Project 6B Events Schedule

Objective 4 | Use Comments in a Document

Building a final document often involves more than one person. One person usually drafts the original and becomes the document *author*—or *owner*—and then others add their portions of text and comment on, or propose changes to, the text of others. A *reviewer* is someone who reviews and marks changes on a document.

A *comment* is a note that an author or reviewer adds to a document. Comments are a good way to communicate when more than one person is involved with the writing, reviewing, and editing process. Comments are like sticky notes attached to the document—they can be viewed and read by others, but are not part of the document text.

Activity 6.09 | Inserting Comments

For the library's monthly schedule of events, Abigail Gardner has created a draft document; edits and comments have been added by others. In this activity, you will insert a comment to suggest confirming a scheduled guest.

1 **Start** Word. From your student files, locate and open the file **w06B_Events_Schedule**. If necessary, display the rulers and formatting marks. Compare your screen with Figure 6.26.

The document displays with *revisions*—changes—shown as *markup*. Markup refers to the formatting Word uses to denote the revisions visually. For example, when a reviewer changes text, the original text displays with strikethrough formatting by default. When a reviewer inserts new text, the new text is underlined. The space to the right or left of the document is the nonprinting *markup area* where comments and formatting changes—for example, applying italic—display. The outline shape in which a comment or formatting change displays is referred to as a *balloon*. A *vertical change bar* displays in the left margin next to each line of text that contains a revision.

Figure 6.26

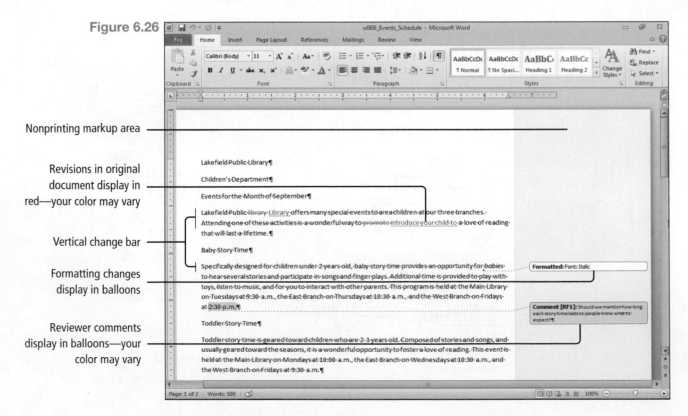

Nonprinting markup area

Revisions in original document display in red—your color may vary

Vertical change bar

Formatting changes display in balloons

Reviewer comments display in balloons—your color may vary

> **Note** | Balloons Might Display Instead of Strikethrough Formatting
>
> Depending on how Word was installed on the computer you are using, you may see balloons instead of strikethrough formatting for some revisions.

■2 From **Backstage** view, display the **Save As** dialog box, and then save the document in your **Word Chapter 6** folder as **Lastname_Firstname_6B_Events_Schedule** Using **Quick Parts**, insert the file name in the footer.

■3 Click the **Review tab**, and then in the **Tracking group**, notice that *Final: Show Markup* displays, indicating that the markup area is visible and proposed revisions display.

> Final: Show Markup is the default view, because you probably do not want to distribute a document that still contains comments or other markup. Thus, Word automatically displays any revisions or comments when you open a document.

■4 In the **Tracking group**, click the **Track Changes button arrow**. From the list, click **Change User Name**. Under **Personalize your copy of Microsoft Office**, on a piece of paper, make a note of the **User name** and **Initials**—if you are using your own computer, your own name and initials may display.

> The user name identifies the person who makes comments and changes in a document.

> **Alert!** | Changing the User Name and Initials
>
> In a college lab or organization, you may be unable to change the user name and initials, so make a note of the name and initials currently displayed so that you can identify your revisions in this document.

■5 If you are able to do so, in the **User name** box, delete any existing text, and then type your own first and last names. In the **Initials** box, delete any existing text, and then type your initials, if necessary. Compare your screen with Figure 6.27. If you are unable to make this change, move to Step 6.

Figure 6.27

Word Options dialog box

User name—change to your name if you are able to do so

Initials—change to your initials if you are able to do so

■6 Click **OK**. In the lower portion of **Page 1**, select the paragraph *Meet the Author*.

7 On the **Review tab**, in the **Comments group**, click the **New Comment** button, and notice that the comment balloon displays in the markup area with the user initials. Type **Check with Barry Smith to confirm that Ms. Saunders is coming.** Click anywhere outside of the comment, and then compare your screen with Figure 6.28.

> You can insert a comment at a specific location in a document or to selected text, such as an entire paragraph. Your initials—or those configured for the computer at which you are working—display at the beginning of the comment, followed by the number 3, which indicates that this is the third comment in the document. When a new comment is added to a document, existing comments are automatically renumbered. Each reviewer's comments are identified by a distinct color.

Figure 6.28

New Comment button

Comment number

Initials of person adding comment

Inserted comment— yours may differ

8 On the **Review tab**, in the **Tracking group**, click the **Show Markup** button, and then point to **Balloons**.

> The default setting is *Show Only Comments and Formatting in Balloons*. In this default setting, insertions and deletions *do not* display in balloons. Rather, insertions and deletions display directly in the text with insertions underlined and deletions struck out with a line. Comments and formatting *do* display in balloons.

9 Click anywhere in the document to close the **Balloons** menu. For the comment you just added, point to your initials, and notice that the comment displays as a ScreenTip—indicating the date and time the comment was created. Compare your screen with Figure 6.29.

Figure 6.29

ScreenTip displays the comment

Inserted comment

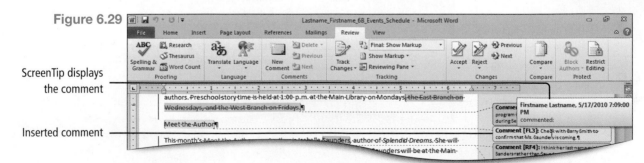

10 Scroll upward as necessary and locate **Comment [RF1]**, which begins *Should we mention*. Point to the question mark at the end of the comment text, and then click to position your insertion point after the question mark.

11 In the **Comments group**, click the **New Comment** button, and notice that a new comment displays in the markup area. Compare your screen with Figure 6.30.

> The comment includes your initials, the number *2*, and the additional characters *R1*, indicating that this is a *reply* to comment 1.

Figure 6.30

Comment [RF1]

New comment—your initials will differ

R1 indicates a reply to an existing comment

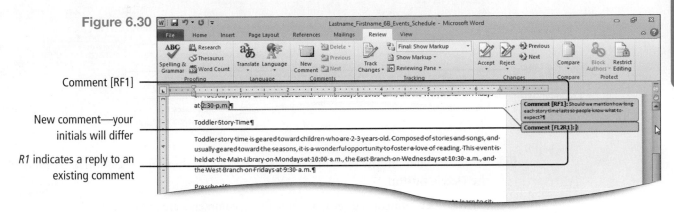

12 With the insertion point in the new comment, type **The program is scheduled for approximately one hour.** and then compare your screen with Figure 6.31.

Figure 6.31

New comment—your initials will differ

13 **Save** 🔲 your document.

Activity 6.10 | Editing and Deleting Comments

Typically, comments are temporary. One person inserts a comment, another person answers the question or clarifies the text based on the comment—and then the comments are removed before the document is final. In this activity, you will replace text in your comment and delete comments.

1 Locate the comment you inserted referencing **Barry Smith**, which was comment **4**. Delete the text *Barry Smith*, and then with the insertion point to the left of *to*, type **Caroline Marina** If necessary, press ⌷Spacebar⌷.

> In this manner, you can edit your comments.

2 Scroll as necessary to locate the **Comment [RF5]** that begins *I think her last name* and the following comment—**Comment [LT6]**. Compare your screen with Figure 6.32.

> Because the question asked in *Comment [RF5]* has been answered in *Comment [LT6]*, both comments can be deleted.

Figure 6.32

Comment [RF5]

Comment [LT6]

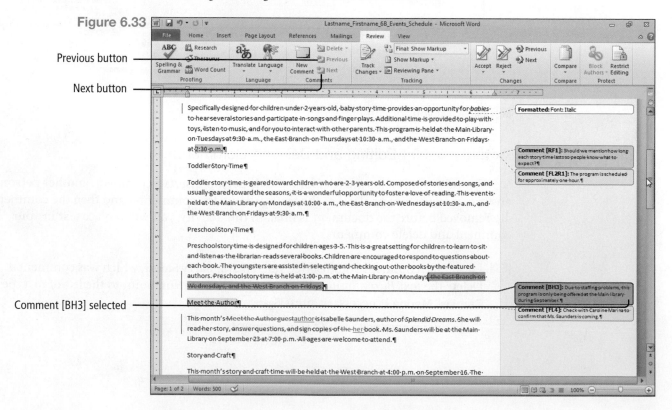

3 Click anywhere in the text for **Comment [RF5]**, and then in the **Comments group**, click the **Delete** button.

> When a comment is deleted, the remaining comments are renumbered.

4 Point to **Comment [LT5]**, right-click, and then from the shortcut menu, click **Delete Comment**.

> Use either technique to delete a comment.

5 Press Ctrl + Home. In the **Comments group**, click the **Next** button three times. In the markup area, notice that the balloon containing **Comment [BH3]** is selected. Compare your screen with Figure 6.33.

> In the Comments group, you can use the Next button and Previous button in this manner to navigate through the comments in a document.

Figure 6.33

Previous button

Next button

Comment [BH3] selected

6 With **Comment [BH3]** selected, right-click, and then click **Delete Comment**.

7 In the **Comments group**, click the **Next** button two times to select **Comment [BH4]**, and then using any technique you have practiced, **Delete** the comment.

8 Scroll as necessary, delete **Comment [RF4]**, and then delete **Comment [RF5]**—four comments remain. **Save** 💾 your document.

Objective 5 | Track Changes in a Document

When you turn on the ***Track Changes*** feature, Word makes a record of—*tracks*—the changes made to a document. As you revise the document, Word uses markup to visually indicate insertions, deletions, comments, formatting changes, and content that has moved.

Each reviewer's revisions and comments display in a different color. This is useful if, for example, you want to quickly scan only for edits made by a supervisor or only for edits made by a coworker. After the document has been reviewed by the appropriate individuals, you can locate the changes and accept or reject the revisions on a case-by-case basis or globally in the entire document.

Activity 6.11 | Managing Tracked Changes

In this activity, you will change the way insertions and comments display.

1 Press `Ctrl` + `Home` to move to the top of the document.

2 In the **Tracking group**, click the **Track Changes button arrow**, and then from the list, click **Change Tracking Options**. Take a moment to study Figure 6.34 and the table shown in Figure 6.35.

Here you can change how markup, moved text, table revisions, formatting changes, and balloons display.

Figure 6.34

Markup options

Moves options

Table cell highlighting options

Formatting options

Balloons options

Settings in the Track Changes Options Dialog Box	
Options	**Settings You Can Adjust**
Markup	Specify the format and color of inserted text, deleted text, and changed lines. By default, inserted text is underlined, deleted text displays with strikethrough formatting, and the vertical change bar displays on the outside border—left margin. Click an arrow to select a different format, and click the Color arrow to select a different color. By author, the default, indicates that Word will assign a different color to each person who inserts comments or tracks changes.
Moves	Specify the format of moved text. The default is green with double strikethrough in the moved content and a double underline below the content in its new location. To turn off this feature, clear the check box.
Table cell highlighting	Specify the color that will display in a table if cells are inserted, deleted, merged, or split.
Formatting	Specify the formatting and color of format changes, such as applying italic to a word. By default, no formatting is applied; instead, the formatting change displays in a balloon in the markup area, color coded by author. To turn off this feature, clear the check box.
Balloons	Specify the size and placement of balloons and whether lines should connect the balloon to text. You can also control balloon width and location for online viewing and for printing.

Figure 6.35

3 In the **Track Changes Options** dialog box, under **Balloons**, click the **Preferred width spin box down arrow** as necessary to change the width to **2.5"**. Click the **Margin arrow**, and then from the list, click **Left**.

This action will cause the balloons to display with a width of 2.5 inches and the markup area to display on the left instead of on the right.

4 Click **OK**, and then **Save** 🖫 your document.

Use the Track Changes Options dialog box in this manner to set Track Changes to display the way that works best for you.

Activity 6.12 | Using the Reviewing Pane

The *Reviewing Pane*, which displays in a separate scrollable window, shows all of the changes and comments that currently display in your document. In this activity, you will use the Reviewing Pane to view a summary of all changes and comments in the document.

1 On the **Review tab**, in the **Tracking group**, click the **Reviewing Pane button arrow**. From the list, click **Reviewing Pane Vertical**, and then compare your screen with Figure 6.36.

The Reviewing Pane displays at the left of the document. Optionally, you can display the Reviewing Pane horizontally at the bottom of the document window. The summary section at the top of the Reviewing Pane displays the exact number of visible tracked changes and comments that remain in your document. Recall that this document contains four comments.

Figure 6.36

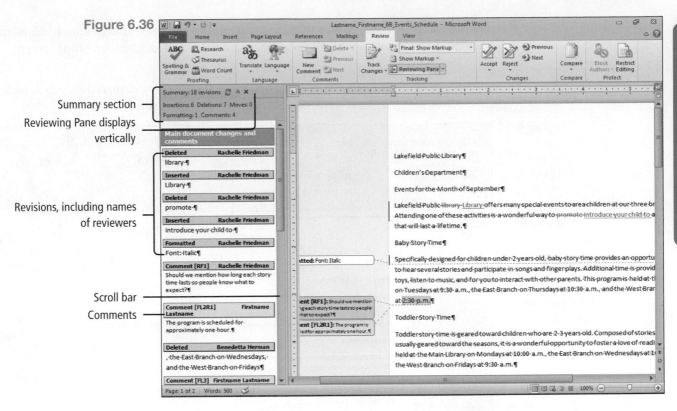

Summary section
Reviewing Pane displays vertically

Revisions, including names of reviewers

Scroll bar
Comments

2 Take a moment to read the comments in the **Reviewing Pane**.

In the Reviewing Pane, you can view each type of revision, the name of the reviewer associated with each item, and read long comments that do not fit within a comment bubble. The Reviewing Pane is also useful for ensuring that all tracked changes have been *removed* from your document when it is ready for final distribution.

3 At the top of the **Reviewing Pane**, click the **Close** button [×].

Activity 6.13 | Viewing Revisions in a Document

After one or more reviewers have made revisions and inserted comments, you can view the revisions in various ways. You can display the document in its original or final form, showing or hiding revisions and comments. Additionally, you can choose to view the revisions and comments by only some reviewers or view only a particular type of revision—for example, only formatting changes.

1 On the **Review tab**, in the **Tracking group**, locate the **Display for Review** box that displays the text *Final: Show Markup*. Click the **Display for Review arrow** to display a list.

Final view displays the document with all proposed changes included and comments hidden.

Final: Show Markup view, which is the default view, displays the final document with all revisions and comments visible.

Original view hides the tracked changes and shows the original, unchanged document with comments hidden.

Original: Show Markup view displays the original document with all revisions and comments visible.

2 On the list, click **Final**. Notice that all comments and marked changes are hidden, and the document displays with all proposed changes included. Compare your screen with Figure 6.37.

> When you are editing a document in which you are proposing changes, this view is useful because the revisions of others or the markup of your own revisions is not distracting.

Figure 6.37

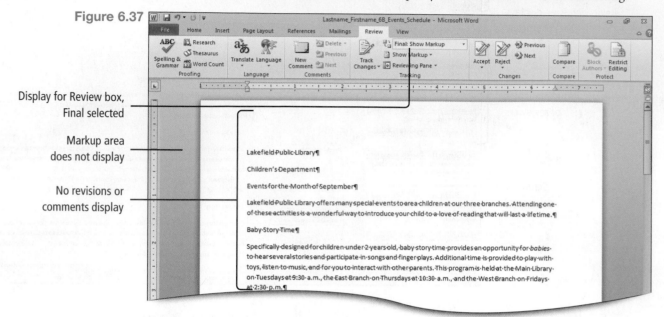

Display for Review box, Final selected

Markup area does not display

No revisions or comments display

3 In the **Tracking group**, click the **Display for Review arrow**, and then from the list, click **Final: Show Markup**.

> At the stage where you, the document owner, must decide which revisions to accept or reject, you will find this view to be the most useful.

4 In the **Tracking group**, click the **Show Markup** button. Point to **Reviewers** to see the name of each individual who proposed changes to this document. Compare your screen with Figure 6.38.

> Here you can turn off the display of revisions by one or more reviewers. For example, you might want to view only the revisions proposed by a supervisor—before you consider the revisions proposed by others—by clearing the check box for all reviewers except the supervisor.

> Here you can also determine which changes display by deselecting one or more check boxes. *Ink*, if displayed, refers to marks made directly on a document by using a stylus on a Tablet PC.

Figure 6.38

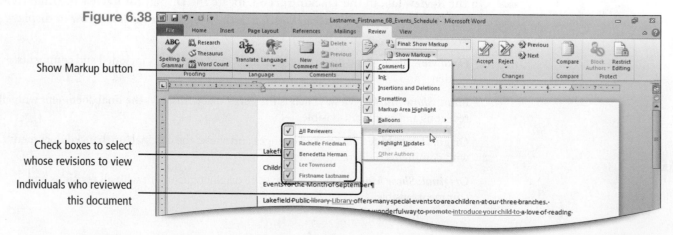

Show Markup button

Check boxes to select whose revisions to view

Individuals who reviewed this document

5 Click anywhere in the document to close the **Show Markup** menu and leave all revision types by all reviewers displayed.

Activity 6.14 | Turning on Track Changes

The Track Changes feature is turned off by default; you must turn on the feature each time you want to begin tracking changes in a document.

1 Press Ctrl + Home, if necessary, to move to the top of the document. In the **Tracking group**, click the upper portion of the **Track Changes** button to enable tracking; notice that the button glows orange to indicate that the feature is turned on.

2 Select the first paragraph—the text *Lakefield Public Library*. On the Mini toolbar, change the **Font Size** to **28**, apply **Center** ☰ alignment, and change the **Font Color** 🅰 to **Dark Blue, Text 2**—in the fourth column, the first color.

> As you make each change, the markup displays in the markup area, and the vertical change bar displays. The types of changes—formatted text and center alignment—are indicated in balloons, and lines point to the location of the revisions.

3 Click anywhere in the document to cancel the selection. Point to the formatted text, and then compare your screen with Figure 6.39.

> A ScreenTip displays, indicating who made the change, when it was made, and the type of change.

Figure 6.39

ScreenTip displays details

Lines point to location of changes

Markup indicating formatting changes

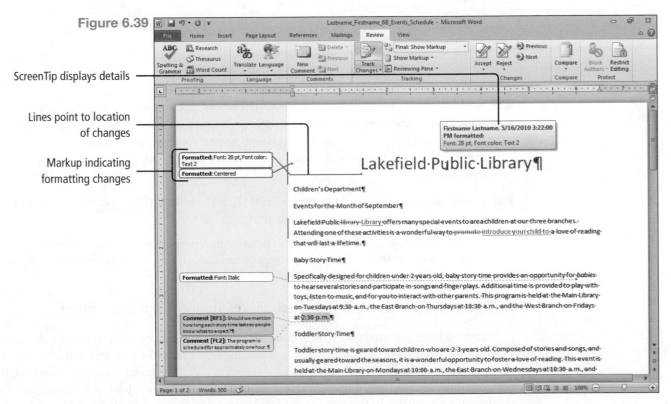

4 Select the second and third paragraphs, change the **Font Size** to **20**, apply **Bold** **B**, and then **Center** 〓 the paragraphs.

5 Select the paragraph heading *Baby Story Time*, hold down Ctrl, and then by using the **down scroll arrow** ▾, move through the document and select the remaining paragraph headings—*Toddler Story Time, Preschool Story Time, Meet the Author, Story and Craft, Animal Adventures, Internet Safety,* and *Seek and Find at the Library.* Apply **Bold** **B** to the selected headings.

6 Scrolling as necessary, locate the paragraph below *Baby Story Time* that begins *Specifically designed.* In the third line, click to place your insertion point to the left of *program,* type **one-hour** and then press Spacebar.

The inserted text is underlined and displays with your designated color.

7 Point to the inserted text, and then compare your screen with Figure 6.40.

A ScreenTip displays, showing the revision that was made, which reviewer made the change, and the date and time of the change.

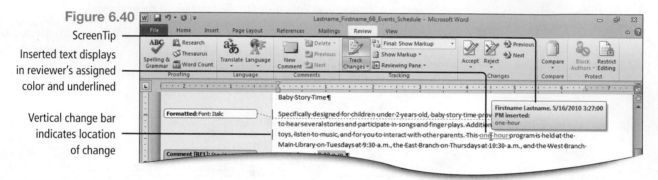

Figure 6.40
ScreenTip
Inserted text displays
in reviewer's assigned
color and underlined

Vertical change bar
indicates location
of change

8 Scroll to view **Page 2,** locate the paragraph below *Animal Adventures* that begins *Safari Steve,* and then click to place your insertion point at the end of the paragraph. Press Spacebar, and then type **Children with animal allergies should not attend.** Notice that the inserted text is underlined and displays with the same color as your previous insertion.

9 In the markup area, read **Comment [LT4].** Using any technique you practiced, **Delete Comment [LT4]. Save** 🖫 your document.

Having responded to this suggestion by inserting appropriate text, you can delete the comment. When developing important documents, having others review the document can improve its content and appearance.

Activity 6.15 | Accepting or Rejecting Changes in a Document

After all reviewers make their proposed revisions and add their comments, the document owner must decide which changes to accept and incorporate into the document and which changes to reject. Unlike revisions, it is not possible to accept or reject comments; instead, the document owner reads the comments, takes appropriate action or makes a decision, and then deletes each comment. In this activity, you will accept and reject changes to create a final document.

1 Press Ctrl + Home to move to the top of the document.

When reviewing comments and changes in a document, it is good practice to start at the beginning of the document to be sure you do not miss any comments or revisions.

2 On the **Review tab**, in the **Changes group**, click the **Next** button—be careful to select the **Next** button from the **Changes group**, *not* the **Comments group**. Notice the first paragraph is selected.

The Next button and the Previous button in the Changes group enable you to navigate from one revision or comment to the next or previous one.

3 In the **Changes group**, click the upper portion of the **Accept** button.

The text formatting is accepted for the first paragraph, the related balloon no longer displays in the markup area, and the next change—center alignment for the first three paragraphs—is selected. When reviewing a document, changes can be accepted or rejected individually, or all at one time.

Another Way

Right-click the selection, and on the shortcut menu, click **Accept**.

4 In the **Changes group**, click the upper portion of the **Accept** button to accept the alignment change.

The centering change is applied to all three paragraphs.

5 In the **Changes group**, click the **Accept** button to accept the text formatting for the second and third paragraphs.

6 In the next paragraph, point to the strikethrough text *library* and notice the ScreenTip that indicates Rachelle Friedman deleted *library*. Then, point to the underline directly below *Library* to display a ScreenTip. Compare your screen with Figure 6.41.

When a reviewer replaces text—for example, when Rachelle replaced *library* with *Library*—the inserted text displays with an underline and in the color designated for the reviewer. The original text displays with strikethrough formatting.

Figure 6.41

ScreenTip for inserted text

Strikethrough indicates original text—*library*

Underline indicates *Library* text inserted

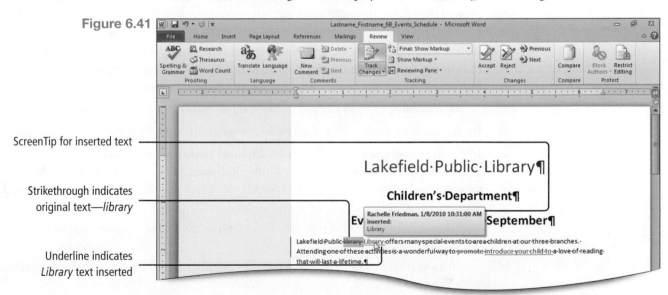

7 In the **Changes group**, click the **Accept** button two times to accept the deletion of *library* and the insertion of *Library*.

The next change, the deletion of *promote* is selected.

8 In the **Changes group**, click the **Reject** button, and then point to the selected text *introduce your child to*, to display a ScreenTip. Compare your screen with Figure 6.42.

> The original text *promote* is reinserted in the sentence. As the document owner, you decide which proposed revisions to accept; you are not required to accept every change in a document.

Figure 6.42

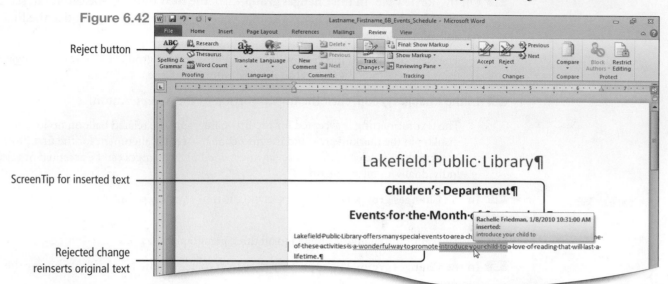

Reject button

ScreenTip for inserted text

Rejected change reinserts original text

9 Click the **Reject** button again to reject the insertion of *introduce your child to* and to select the next change.

10 Click the **Accept** button three times, and then notice that **Comment [RF1]**, suggesting that the program length be mentioned, is selected. Right-click the comment, and then click **Delete Comment**.

> Recall that you cannot accept or reject comments. Rather, you take appropriate action, and then delete the comment when it is no longer relevant. Because you entered text indicating the program length, you can delete the comment.

11 Delete the next comment, which is selected. Then, scroll down to quickly scan the remaining revisions in the document, and then in the **Changes group**, click the **Accept button arrow**. From the list, click **Accept All Changes in Document**.

> All remaining changes in the document are accepted.

12 In the **Tracking group**, click the **Track Changes** button to turn off tracking changes.

13 In the **Tracking group**, click the **Track Changes button arrow**, and then display the **Track Changes Options** dialog box. Under **Balloons**, click the **Preferred Width spin box up arrow** as necessary to reset the width to **3"**. Click the **Margin arrow**, and then click **Right**. Click **OK**.

> These actions restore the system to the default settings. One comment remains, and the markup area is still visible.

14 Scroll as necessary to verify the remaining comment, and then compare your screen with Figure 6.43.

Figure 6.43

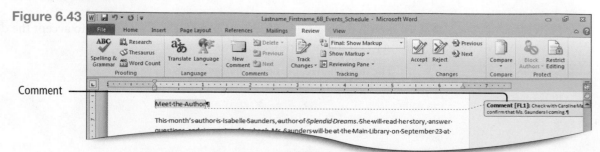

Comment

15 Display the **Document Information Panel**. In the **Author** box, delete any text, and then type your first and last names. In the **Subject** box, type your course name and section number, and in the **Keywords** box, type **events schedule, reviewed Close** ☒ the Document Information Panel.

16 **Save** 🖫 your document, and leave it open for the next activity.

Objective 6 | View Side by Side, Compare, and Combine Documents

It is not always possible for reviewers to make their comments and edits on a single Word file. Each reviewer might edit a copy of the file, and then the document owner must gather all of the files and combine all the revisions into a single final document. One method to examine the changes is to use the *View Side by Side* command. Using the View Side by Side command displays two open documents, in separate windows, next to each other on your screen.

Word has two other features, *Compare* and *Combine*, which enable you to view revisions in two documents and determine which changes to accept and which ones to reject. Compare is useful when reviewing differences between an original document and the latest version of the document. When using Compare, Word assumes all revisions were made by the same individual. The Combine feature enables you to review two different documents containing revisions—both based on an original document—and the individuals who made the revisions are identified.

Activity 6.16 | Using View Side by Side

Abigail Garner has received another copy of the original file, which contains revisions and comments from two additional reviewers—Angie Harper and Natalia Ricci. In this activity, you will use View Side by Side to compare the new document with the version you finalized in the previous activity.

1 With your file **Lastname_Firstname_6B_Events_Schedule** open and the insertion point displaying at the top of the document, navigate to your student files, and then locate and open the file **w06B_Schedule_Revisions**.

2 On the **View tab**, in the **Window group**, click the **View Side by Side** button to display both documents.

This view enables you to see if there have been any major changes to the original document that should be discussed by the reviewers before making revisions. Both documents contain the same basic text.

Alert! | Why Doesn't the Entire Window Display?

Depending upon your screen resolution, the entire window may not display.

---

3 In the **w06B_Schedule_Revisions** document, drag the horizontal scroll bar to the right so that you can see the markup area. Notice that both documents scroll. Compare your screen with Figure 6.44. Depending on your screen resolution, your view may differ.

Edits and comments made by Ms. Harper and Ms. Ricci display in the w06B_Schedule_Revisions file. When View Side by Side is active, *synchronous scrolling*—both documents scroll simultaneously—is turned on by default.

Figure 6.44
w06B_Schedule_Revisions document

View Side by Side button—your view may differ

Synchronous Scrolling button—your view may differ

Comments

Your Lastname_Firstname_ 6B_Events_Schedule document

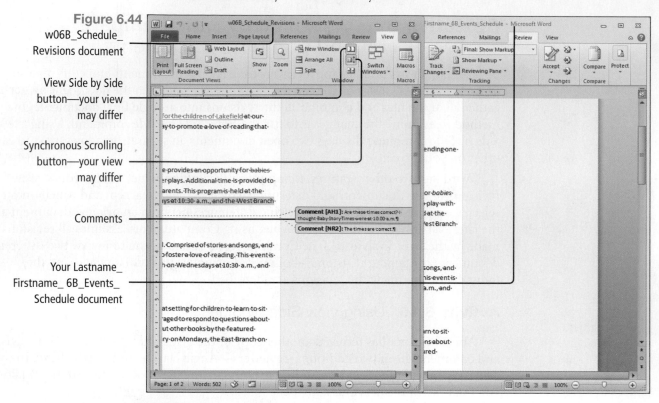

4 Close [X] the **w06B_Schedule_Revisions** document. Notice your **Lastname_Firstname_6B_Events_Schedule** document displays in full screen view.

5 Display **Backstage** view, and then **Close** your **Lastname_Firstname_6B_Events_Schedule** without closing Word.

Activity 6.17 | Combining Documents

In this activity, you will combine the document containing revisions and comments by Angie Harper and Natalia Ricci with your finalized version of the events schedule. Then, you will accept or reject the additional revisions to create a final document ready for distribution to the public.

1 On the **Review tab**, in the **Compare group**, click the **Compare** button. From the displayed list, click **Combine** to display the **Combine Documents** dialog box.

When using the Combine feature, it is not necessary to have an open document.

> **Another Way**
>
> To the right of the **Original document** box, click the **Browse** button.

2 In the **Combine Documents** dialog box, click the **Original document arrow**, and then click **Browse**. In the **Open** dialog box, navigate to your student files, select the file **w06B_Schedule_Revisions**, and then click **Open**.

Recall that this file includes revisions and comments from two additional reviewers. *Original document* usually refers to a document without revisions or, in this case, the document that you have not yet reviewed.

3 Under **Original document**, in the **Label unmarked changes with** box, delete the existing text, and then type your first and last names.

4 Click the **Revised document arrow**, and then click **Browse**. Navigate to your **Word Chapter 6** folder, select **Lastname_Firstname_6B_Events_Schedule**, and then click **Open**.

Revised document refers to the latest version of the document—in this case, the document where you accepted and rejected changes.

5 Under **Revised document**, in the **Label unmarked changes with** box, if your name does not display, delete the existing text, and then type your first and last names.

6 In the **Combine Documents** dialog box, click the **More** button, and then under **Show changes in**, be sure the **New document** option button is selected. Compare your screen with Figure 6.45.

The More button expands the dialog box to display additional settings. By selecting the New Document option, all changes in both files display in a new document.

Figure 6.45

Combine Documents dialog box

Original document selected

Revised document selected

New document selected

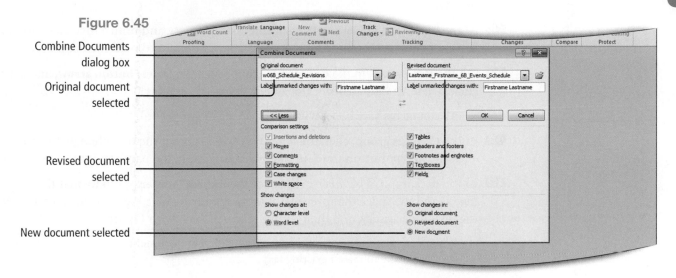

7 In the **Combine Documents** dialog box, click the **Less** button, and then click **OK**. Compare your screen with Figure 6.46.

The Tri-Pane Review Panel displays with the combined document in the left pane, the original document in the top right pane, and the revised document in the bottom right pane. The Reviewing Pane displays to the left of your screen, indicating all accepted changes in your Lastname_Firstname_6B_Events_Schedule file with your user name.

Figure 6.46

Reviewing Pane

New combined document

Original document

Revised document

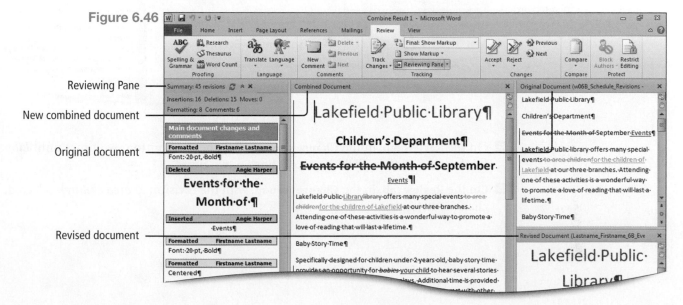

8 If necessary, click to place the insertion point at the beginning of the **Combined Document**. **Save** the document in your **Word Chapter 6** folder as **Lastname_Firstname_6B_Schedule_Combined**

9 On the **Insert tab**, in the **Header & Footer group**, click the **Footer** button, and then click **Edit Footer**. Delete any existing text, and then use **Quick Parts** to insert the file name in the footer. At the right end of the Ribbon, click the **Close Header and Footer** button.

10 At the top of the **Reviewing Pane**, locate the summary and notice that there are six comments in the combined document. Take a moment to read each comment.

11 On the **Review tab**, in the **Comments group**, click the **Delete button arrow**, and then click **Delete All Comments in Document**. Press Ctrl + Home.

All comments have been reviewed and are no longer needed.

12 In the **Changes group**, click the **Accept** button to accept the first change. Continue to click the **Accept** button until, in the third paragraph, the paragraph mark is selected.

13 In the paragraph *September Events*, use the **Format Painter** 🖌 to format the text *Events* and the space that precedes it to match the formatting of *September*. Deselect the text, if necessary, and then compare your screen with Figure 6.47.

When new changes are accepted from two different documents, you may need to modify the formatting to match existing text.

Figure 6.47

Formatted text

14 On the **Review tab**, in the **Changes group**, click the **Next** button two times until *Library* is selected, and then click the **Accept** button two times.

15 On the **Review tab**, in the **Changes group**, with the revision *to area children* selected, click the **Reject** button two times.

16 In the **Changes group**, click the **Accept button arrow**, and then click **Accept All Changes in Document**. In the **Reviewing Pane**, notice that no further revisions or comments remain. On the right of your screen, **Close** ⊠ the two panes—the original and revised documents. **Close** ⊠ the Reviewing Pane.

> Because all remaining revisions in the document are accepted, there is no longer a need to view the original or revised documents.

17 In the **Tracking group**, click the **Track Changes button arrow**, and then click **Change User Name**. If you made changes to the user name, delete your name and initials and type the name and initials that displayed originally. Click **OK** to close the dialog box.

> When sharing a computer with others, if you have made any changes, it is good practice to restore the settings when you are finished.

18 Press [Ctrl] + [Home]. On the **Page Layout tab**, in the **Page Background group**, click the **Page Color** button, and then click **Fill Effects**. In the **Fill Effects** dialog box, click the **Texture** tab, and then scroll to the bottom of the displayed textures. In the next to last row, click the first texture—**Blue tissue paper**. Click **OK**.

> The page background is added to improve the final appearance of the document. Because you have been assigned the task of preparing the final document for distribution, it is appropriate to make this formatting change.

Note | Printing Page Backgrounds

Page backgrounds do not display in Print Preview and do not print by default.

---

19 From **Backstage** view, display the **Document Information Panel**. In the **Author** box, delete any existing text, and then type your first and last names. In the **Subject** box, type your course name and section number, and in the **Keywords** box, type **events schedule, reviewed, combined Close** ⊠ the Document Information Panel.

20 Press [Ctrl] + [F2] to display the **Print Preview** in **Backstage** view. Examine the **Print Preview**, make any necessary adjustments, and then **Save** 🔲 your document. Print both documents or submit electronically as directed by your instructor. **Exit** Word.

More Knowledge | Printing Page Backgrounds

To print the background color or fill effect of a document, display the Word Options dialog box, select Display, and then under Printing Options, select the Print background colors and images check box. Click OK.

End **You have completed Project 6B** ————————————————

Content-Based Assessments

Summary

You created text box, graphic, and Quick Table building blocks and reused them in a document. Then you created and applied a theme template to enhance the appearance of the final document. You also used comments and edited and combined documents by use the Track Changes feature in Word.

Key Terms

Matching

Match each term in the second column with its correct definition in the first column by writing the letter of the term on the blank line in front of the correct definition.

_____ 1.   Reusable pieces of content or other documents parts.

_____ 2.   A movable, resizable container for text or graphics.

_____ 3.   A stored, user-defined set of colors, fonts, and effects.

_____ 4.   The owner, or creator, of the original document.

_____ 5.   A note that an author or reviewer adds to a document.

_____ 6.   Changes made to a document.

_____ 7.   The space to the left or right of a document where comments and formatting changes display in balloons.

_____ 8.   The outline shape in which a comment or formatting change displays.

_____ 9.   Identifies the person who makes comments and changes in a document.

_____ 10.   A feature that makes a record of the revisions made to a document.

_____ 11.   A separate scrollable window that displays all of the changes and comments that currently display in a document.

_____ 12.   A Track Changes view that displays the document with all proposed changes included and comments hidden.

_____ 13.   A Track Changes view that hides the tracked changes and shows the original, unchanged document with comments hidden.

A Author

B Balloon

C Building blocks

D Combine

E Comment

F Compare

G Final

H Markup area

I Original

J Reviewing Pane

K Revisions

L Text box

M Theme template

N Track Changes

O User name

_____ 14. A Track Changes feature that enables you to review differences between an original document and the latest version of the document.

_____ 15. A Track Changes feature that allows you to review two different documents containing revisions, both based on an original document.

Multiple Choice

Circle the correct answer.

1. You can view all available building blocks in the:
   A. Quick Tables gallery
   B. Building Blocks Organizer
   C. Quick Parts gallery

2. All of the reusable content pieces including building blocks, properties, and fields are:
   A. Quick Tables
   B. Quick Parts
   C. Text boxes

3. A predefined combination of colors, fonts, and effects that can be applied as a single selection is a:
   A. Quick Part
   B. theme
   C. style

4. In Word, an individual who marks changes in another person's document is referred to as:
   A. a reviewer
   B. an editor
   C. an author

5. The formatting Word uses to denote a document's revisions visually is called:
   A. markup
   B. balloons
   C. comments

6. When a line of text contains revisions, the left margin displays a:
   A. vertical change bar
   B. horizontal change bar
   C. balloon

7. When a reviewer makes a comment, the beginning of the comment displays:
   A. the reviewer's name
   B. the reviewer's initials
   C. the date of the comment

8. The view in which all revisions and comments are visible is:
   A. Combine
   B. Final: Show All
   C. Final: Show Markup

9. To display two documents next to each other in separate windows use the:
   A. Combine setting
   B. View Side by Side setting
   C. Two Pages view

10. To cause two displayed documents to scroll simultaneously, turn on:
    A. Track Changes
    B. synchronous viewing
    C. synchronous scrolling

Content-Based Assessments

Skills Review | Project **6C** Literacy Program

In the following Skills Review project, you will create and save building blocks and create a theme to be used in a flyer seeking volunteers for Lakefield Public Library's Adult Literacy Program. Your completed documents will look similar to Figure 6.48.

Project Files

For Project 6C, you will need the following files:

> Two new blank Word documents
> w06C_Literacy_Information

You will save your files as:

> Lastname_Firstname_6C_Literacy_Blocks
> Lastname_Firstname_6C_Literacy_Theme—not shown in figure
> Lastname_Firstname_6C_Literacy_Program

Project Results

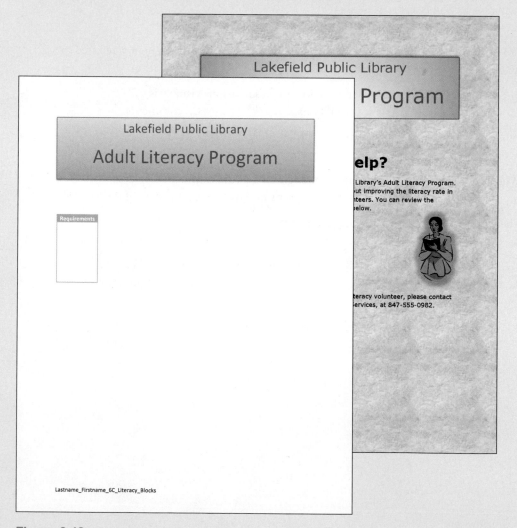

Figure 6.48

(Project 6C Literacy Program continues on the next page)

Skills Review | Project **6C** Literacy Program (continued)

1 **Start** Word to display a new blank document. If necessary, display the ruler and formatting marks. From **Backstage** view, display the **Save As** dialog box, navigate to your **Word Chapter 6** folder, and **Save** the document as **Lastname_Firstname_6C_Literacy_Blocks** Insert the file name in the footer.

a. On the **Insert tab**, in the **Text group**, click the **Text Box** button, and then locate and click **Simple Text Box**. On the **Format tab**, in the **Shape Styles group**, click the **More** button. In the fourth row, click the fifth style—**Subtle Effect – Purple, Accent 4**. If the **Size group** is visible, change the **Shape Width** to **6.5"**. Otherwise, to the right of the **Arrange group**, click the **Size** button, and then change the **Shape Width** to **6.5"**.

b. Replace the placeholder text by typing **Lakefield Public Library** Press Enter, and then type **Adult Literacy Program** Select both lines of text, change the **Font Color** to **Purple, Accent 4**, and then apply **Center**. Set the **Font Size** of the first line of text to **24**. Set the **Font Size** of the second line of text to **36**.

c. Click the outside edge of the text box to select it. On the **Insert tab**, in the **Text group**, click the **Text Box** button, and then click **Save Selection to Text Box Gallery**. As the **Name**, type **Literacy Heading** As the **Description**, type **Use as the heading for all literacy documents** Click **OK**.

2 Click outside the text box to deselect it, and then point slightly under the lower left corner of the text box to display the **click and type pointer** at approximately **2.5 inches on the vertical ruler**. Double-click to insert three blank paragraphs under the text box. With the insertion point in the third blank paragraph, on the **Insert tab**, in the **Tables group**, click the **Table** button, point to **Quick Tables**, scroll down, and then click **Tabular List**.

a. Select the text *ITEM*, and then type **Requirements** Press Tab, right-click, and then click **Delete Cells**. In the displayed **Delete Cells** dialog box, select the **Delete entire column** option button. Click **OK**. Select the text in all the remaining cells of the table, and then press Del.

b. Point slightly outside of the upper left corner of the table, and then click the **table move handle** to select the entire table. On the **Insert tab**, in the **Tables group**, click the **Table** button. Point to **Quick Tables**, and then at the bottom, click **Save Selection**

to Quick Tables Gallery. As the **Name**, type **Job Information** As the **Description**, type **Use for listing job requirements** Click **OK**.

c. With the table selected, move your pointer up to the left end of the horizontal ruler, and then point to the first **Move Table Column** marker. Drag the **Move Table Column** marker slightly to the right until the vertical dotted line aligns with the left edge of the text box, and then release the left mouse button.

d. From **Backstage** view, display the **Document Information Panel**, and type your first and last names as the **Author**. In the **Subject** box, type your course name and section number, and in the **Keywords** box, type **literacy, building blocks Close** the **Document Information Panel**. Click **Save**. Display **Backstage** view and **Close** the document but leave Word open.

3 Press Ctrl + N to display a new blank document.

a. On the **Page Layout tab**, in the **Themes group**, click the **Theme Colors** button, and then click **Concourse**. Click the **Theme Fonts** button, and then click **Aspect**. Click the **Theme Effects** button, and then click **Verve**. Click the **Themes** button, and then click **Save Current Theme**.

b. Navigate to your **Word Chapter 6** folder, and save the theme as **Lastname_Firstname_6C_Literacy_Theme** Display **Backstage** view and **Close** the document, without saving changes, but leave Word open.

4 Press Ctrl + N. Save the document in your **Word Chapter 6** folder as **Lastname_Firstname_6C_Literacy_Program** Insert the file name in the footer, and display rulers and formatting marks, if necessary.

a. On the **Page Layout tab**, in the **Themes group**, click the **Themes** button, and then click **Browse for Themes**. Navigate to your **Word Chapter 6** folder, select your **Lastname_Firstname_6C_Literacy_Theme**, and then click **Open**. In the **Page Background group**, click the **Page Color** button, and then click **Fill Effects**. In the **Fill Effects** dialog box, click the **Texture tab**, and then in the fourth row, click the fourth texture—**Stationery**. Click **OK**.

b. On the **Insert tab**, in the **Text group**, click the **Text Box** button. Scroll to the bottom of the list, and then under **General**, click your **Literacy Heading** building block. Click outside of the text box to deselect it, and

(Project 6C Literacy Program continues on the next page)

Content-Based Assessments

then point slightly under the lower left corner of the text box to display the ⌶ pointer at approximately **2.5 inches on the vertical ruler**. Double-click to insert three blank paragraphs under the text box.

c. On the **Insert tab**, in the **Text group**, click the **Object button arrow**, and then click **Text from File**. Navigate to your student files, click **w06C_Literacy_Information**, and then click **Insert**. At the end of the paragraph that ends *in the table below*, press Enter two times.

5 On the **Insert tab**, in the **Tables group**, click the **Table** button, point to **Quick Tables**, scroll toward the bottom of the list, and then under **General**, click **Job Information**.

a. On the **Design tab**, in the **Table Styles group**, click the **More** button, and then under **Built-In**, in the second row, click the fifth style—**Light List - Accent 4**.

b. Point slightly outside of the upper left corner of the table, and then click the **table move handle** ⊞ to select the entire table. Move your pointer to the left end of the horizontal ruler, and then point to the first **Move Table Column** marker. Drag the **Move Table Column** marker slightly to the right until the vertical dotted line aligns with the left edge of the text box, and then release the left mouse button.

c. Position the insertion point in the second row of the table. Type the following text in the table, pressing Tab after each line:

Possess a high school diploma or GED.
Pass a background check.
Be 21 years of age or older.
Attend all training sessions.
Tutor a minimum of two hours a week.

d. Select the last three empty rows of the table. On the **Layout tab**, in the **Rows & Columns group**, click the **Delete** button, and then click **Delete Rows**.

6 Position the insertion point in the blank paragraph below the table, if necessary. On **the Insert tab**, in the

Illustrations group, click the **Clip Art** button. In the **Clip Art** task pane, search for **reading** Be sure **All media file types** displays and the **Include Office.com content** box is selected, and then click **Go**. Locate the graphic shown in Figure 6.48, and then click to insert it—or select a similar graphic. **Close** the **Clip Art** task pane. On the **Format tab**, change the **Shape Height** to **1.8"**.

a. With the picture selected, on the **Format tab**, in the **Picture Styles group**, click the **Picture Effects** button, point to **Glow**, and then in the fourth row, click the fourth effect—**Blue, 18 pt glow, Accent color 4**. In the **Arrange group**, click the **Wrap Text** button, and then click **In Front of Text**. Drag to position the graphic at the right margin, spaced evenly between the two paragraphs of text, as shown in Figure 6.48.

b. Delete the blank paragraph at the end of the document, and then press Ctrl + Home. From **Backstage** view, display the **Document Information Panel**. In the **Author** box, type your first and last names. In the **Subject** box, type your course name and section number, and in the **Keywords** box, type **literacy program, volunteers Close** the **Document Information Panel**.

c. On the **Insert tab**, in the **Text group**, click the **Quick Parts** button, and then click **Building Blocks Organizer**. In the **Building Blocks Organizer** dialog box, in the upper left corner, click **Name** to sort the building blocks alphabetically by name. Locate your building block **Job Information**, click to select it, click the **Delete** button, and then click **Yes** to confirm the deletion. Using the same technique, scroll to locate your building block **Literacy Heading**, and then **Delete** it. **Close** the dialog box.

7 Print your two documents—you cannot print a theme—or submit all three files electronically as directed by your instructor. **Exit** Word. In the dialog box regarding changes to building blocks, click **Save** to accept the changes.

End **You have completed Project 6C**

Content-Based Assessments

Apply 6B skills from these Objectives:

- **4** Use Comments in a Document
- **5** Track Changes in a Document
- **6** View Side by Side, Compare, and Combine Documents

Skills Review | Project **6D** User Guide

In the following Skills Review project, you will edit a user guide for Lakefield Public Library by creating and deleting comments, inserting text, applying formatting, and accepting changes made by others. Your completed documents will look similar to Figure 6.49.

Project Files

For Project 6D, you will need the following files:

  w06D_User_Guide
  w06D_Reviewed_Guide

You will save your documents as:

  Lastname_Firstname_6D_User_Guide
  Lastname_Firstname_6D_Combined_Guide

Project Results

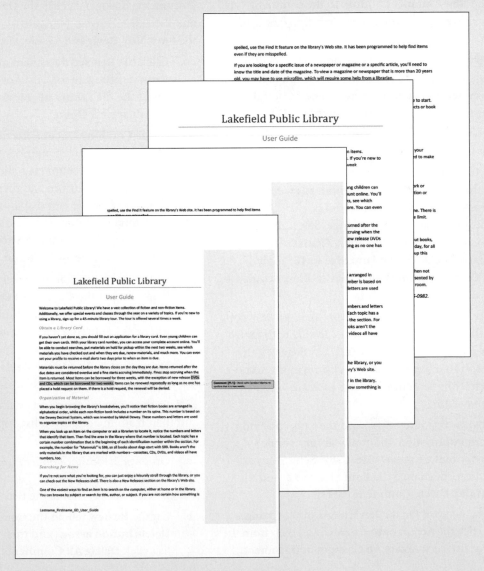

Figure 6.49

(Project 6D User Guide continues on the next page)

Content-Based Assessments

Skills Review | Project 6D User Guide (continued)

1 **Start** Word. Navigate to your student files and open the file **w06D_User_Guide**. **Save** the document in your **Word Chapter 6** folder as **Lastname_Firstname_6D_User_Guide** Insert the file name in the footer.

a. On the **Review tab**, in the **Tracking group**, click the **Track Changes button arrow**. From the list, click **Change User Name**. Under **Personalize your copy of Microsoft Office**, on a piece of paper, make a note of the **User name** and **Initials**. In the **User name** box, type your own first and last name, and then in the **Initials** box, type your initials, if necessary. Click **OK**.

b. In the paragraph beginning *Materials must be*, select the text *DVDs and CDs, which can be borrowed for two weeks.* On the **Review tab**, in the **Comments group**, click the **New Comment** button. In the comment, type **Check with Angie Harper to confirm that it is two weeks.**

c. Press ⌃ Ctrl + ⌂ Home. Click to position the insertion point in the text for **Comment [BH1]**, and then in the **Comments group**, click the **Delete** button. Using the same technique, delete **Comment [CM1]**.

d. Locate your comment, and then replace *Angie Harper* with **Caroline Marina**

2 In the **Tracking group**, click the **Display for Review arrow**, and then, if necessary, click **Final: Show Markup**. To enable tracking, in the **Tracking group**, click the **Track Changes** button so that it glows orange. Select the first paragraph—the title—and then apply **Center**. Select the second paragraph, change the **Font Size** to **18**, apply **Center**, and then change the **Font Color** to **Blue, Accent 1—** in the fifth column, the first color.

a. In the paragraph that begins *When you begin browsing*, in the third line, replace the text *Melville* with **Melvil** and then delete **Comment [BH2]**. On **Page 2**, in the paragraph that begins *The branches of*, in the second line, delete the sentence *We have many comfortable desks and chairs.*

b. Press ⌃ Ctrl + End. Press Enter, and then type **To find out more information about any library services, please contact us at 847-555-0982.** Select the text you just typed, change the **Font Size** to **12**, and then apply **Italic**. Delete **Comment [BH2]**.

c. Press ⌃ Ctrl + ⌂ Home. On the **Review tab**, in the **Changes group**, click the **Accept button arrow**, and then from the displayed list, click **Accept All Changes in Document**.

d. In the **Tracking group**, click the **Track Changes button arrow**, and then click **Change User Name**. If you made changes to the user name, delete your name and initials and type those that displayed originally. Click **OK**. Click the **Track Changes** button to turn off the **Track Changes** feature.

e. Display the **Document Information Panel**. Type your first and last names as the **Author**. In the **Subject** box, type your course name and section number, and in the **Keywords** box, type **user guide, edited** **Save** your document. Display **Backstage** view, and then **Close** the document but leave Word open.

3 On the **Review tab**, in the **Compare group**, click the **Compare** button, and then click **Combine**. In the **Combine Documents** dialog box, click the **Original document arrow**, and then click **Browse**. Navigate to your student files, select the file **w06D_Reviewed_Guide**, and then click **Open**.

a. Click the **Revised document arrow**, and then click **Browse**. Navigate to your **Word Chapter 6** folder, select the file **Lastname_Firstname_6D_User_Guide**, and then click **Open**.

b. In the **Combine Documents** dialog box, click the **More** button, and then under **Show changes in**, select the **New document** option button, if necessary. Click the **Less** button, and then click **OK**. If only the **Combined Document** displays, on the **Review tab**, in the **Compare group**, click the **Compare** button. From the displayed list, point to **Show Source Documents**, and then click **Show Both**.

c. If necessary, position the insertion point at the beginning of the **Combined Document**. Click **Save**, and then save the document in your **Word Chapter 6** folder as **Lastname_Firstname_6D_Combined_Guide** At the right of your screen, close the **Original Document Pane** and the **Revised Document Pane**. At the left of your screen, close the **Reviewing Pane**.

4 In the **Changes group**, click the **Accept button arrow**, and then from the displayed list, click **Accept All Changes in Document**.

a. On **Page 2**, locate *Comment [AH4]*. In the document, select the two sentences that begin *Be aware*, and end *wireless device.* **Delete** the two sentences.

b. On the **Review tab**, in the **Comments group**, click the **Delete button arrow**, and then from the displayed list, click **Delete All Comments in Document**.

(Project 6D User Guide continues on the next page)

Content-Based Assessments

Skills Review | Project **6D** User Guide (continued)

5 Right-click in the footer area, and then click **Edit Footer**. Right-click the existing text, and then from the shortcut menu, click **Update Field**. **Close** the footer area.

a. Press Ctrl + Home. Display the **Document Information Panel**. In the **Author** box, delete any existing text, and type your first and last names. In the **Subject** box, type your course name and section number, and in the **Keywords** box, type **user guide, reviewed, combined Close** the **Document Information Panel**.

b. **Save** your document.

6 Print both documents or submit them electronically as directed by your instructor. **Exit** Word.

End You have completed Project 6D

Content-Based Assessments

Apply **6A** skills from these Objectives:

1. Create Building Blocks
2. Create and Save a Theme Template
3. Create a Document by Using Building Blocks

Mastering Word | Project **6E** Seminar Agenda

In the following Mastering Word project, you will create and save building blocks and create a theme for an agenda for Lakefield Public Library's seminar on Public Libraries and the Internet. Your completed documents will look similar to Figure 6.50.

Project Files

For Project 6E, you will need the following files:

New blank Word document
w06E_Seminar_Agenda

You will save your files as:

Lastname_Firstname_6E_Seminar_Blocks
Lastname_Firstname_6E_Seminar_Theme—not shown in figure
Lastname_Firstname_6E_Seminar_Agenda

Project Results

Public Libraries and the Internet

Public Libraries and the Internet

...Employees

...12 at the Main library. All branches of the
...the sessions. As you know, there have
...at we remain informed on the latest
...e schedule below indicates the topics that
...etta Herman if you can attend this exciting

Time	Topic	Location	Speaker

...ocation	Speaker
...ommunity Room	
...omputer Lab A	Anthony Grant
...erenity Room	Alice DeLong
...ommunity Room	
...omputer Lab A	Josh Friedman
...ommunity Room	Irene McCarthy

6E_Seminar_Blocks_solution

Figure 6.50

(Project 6E Seminar Agenda continues on the next page)

Content-Based Assessments

1 **Start** Word; display rulers and formatting marks. Display the **Save As** dialog box, navigate to your **Word Chapter 6** folder, and save the document as **Lastname_Firstname_6E_Seminar_Blocks** Insert the file name in the footer.

2 **Insert** a **Simple Text Box**, set the **Shape Height** to **0.7"**, set the **Width** to **6.5"**, and then apply the shape style **Subtle Effect - Blue, Accent 1**—in the fourth row, the second style. If necessary, move the text box so that it is centered horizontally in the document. As the text, type **Public Libraries and the Internet** and then format the text with **Font Size 28** and **Bold** and **Center**. Select and then save the text box in the **Text Box** gallery with the name **Internet Seminar** and the **Description Use in all Internet Seminar documents**

3 Insert two or three blank paragraphs under the text box, and then from the **Quick Tables** gallery, click **Double Table**. **Delete** the text *The Greek Alphabet*. Change *Letter name* to **Time** and then press Tab. Change *Uppercase* to **Topic** Change *Lowercase* to **Location** Change *Letter name* to **Speaker Delete** the remaining columns, and then delete the remaining text. Apply the table style **Light Grid – Accent 1**. Select the entire table, and then align the left edge of the table with the left edge of the text box. Save the selected table in the **Quick Tables** gallery with the name **Seminar Schedule** and the **Description Use to display schedules for seminars**

4 Display the **Document Information Panel**, type your first and last names as the **Author**, your course name and section number as the **Subject**, and in the **Keywords** box, type **seminar, building blocks Save** and then **Close** the document, but leave Word open.

5 Create a new blank document. Change the **Theme Colors** to **Flow**, and then change the **Theme Effects** to **Clarity**. **Save** the custom theme to your **Word Chapter 6** folder as **Lastname_Firstname_6E_Seminar_Theme** From

Backstage view, **Close** the document without saving changes, but leave Word open.

6 Open the file **w06E_Seminar_Agenda**, save it in your **Word Chapter 6** folder as **Lastname_Firstname_6E_Seminar_Agenda** and then insert the file name in the footer. Apply your custom theme—**Lastname_Firstname_6E_Seminar_Theme**. In the first blank paragraph, from the **Text Box** gallery, insert your **Internet Seminar** text box. On the **Format tab**, in the **Arrange group**, change the text wrapping to **In Line with Text**.

7 Select the text *Spring Seminar for Employees*, apply the **Title** style, and then apply **Center**. On the **Page Layout tab**, in the **Paragraph group**, set the **Spacing Before** to **48 pt**. To the text *AGENDA*, apply the **Heading 1** style, apply **Center**, and then set the **Spacing After** to **12 pt**. Position the insertion point in the blank paragraph following *AGENDA*, and then from the **Quick Tables** gallery, insert your **Seminar Schedule** table. Create the table using the text shown in Table 1 below, deleting empty rows as necessary.

8 Select the table, right-click, point to **AutoFit**, and then click **AutoFit to Contents**. Right-click, point to **AutoFit**, and then click **AutoFit to Window**. Press Ctrl + Home.

9 Display the **Document Information Panel**. Type your name as the **Author** and your course name and section number as the **Subject**. In the **Keywords** box, type **seminar, agenda Close** the **Document Information Panel**. Click **Save**.

10 Display the **Building Blocks Organizer** dialog box, and then delete your building blocks **Internet Seminar** and **Seminar Schedule**. In the **Building Blocks Organizer** dialog box, click the **Close** button.

11 Print your two documents—you cannot print a theme—or submit all three files electronically as directed by your instructor. **Exit** Word; in the dialog box regarding changes to building blocks, click **Save** to accept the changes.

Table 1

Time	Topic	Location	Speaker
8 a.m. – 9 a.m.	Continental Breakfast	Community Room	
9 a.m. – 10 a.m.	Innovative Internet Librarians	Computer Lab A	Anthony Grant
10 a.m. – Noon	Privacy versus Technology	Serenity Room	Alice DeLong
Noon – 1 p.m.	Lunch	Community Room	
1 p.m. – 3 p.m.	Virtual Reference Desks	Computer Lab A	Josh Friedman
3 p.m. – 5 p.m.	Fair Use in the Digital Age	Community Room	Irene McCarthy

(Return to Step 7)

End You have completed Project 6E

Content-Based Assessments

Apply **6B** skills from these Objectives:

4. Use Comments in a Document
5. Track Changes in a Document
6. View Side by Side, Compare, and Combine Documents

Mastering Word | Project **6F** Library Classes

In the following Mastering Word project, you will edit a user guide for Lakefield Public Library by creating and deleting comments, inserting text, applying formatting, and accepting changes made by others. Your completed documents will look similar to Figure 6.51.

Project Files

For Project 6F, you will need the following files:

> w06F_Library_Classes
> w06F_Classes_Reviewed

You will save your documents as:

> Lastname_Firstname_6F_Library_Classes
> Lastname_Firstname_6F_Classes_Combined

Project Results

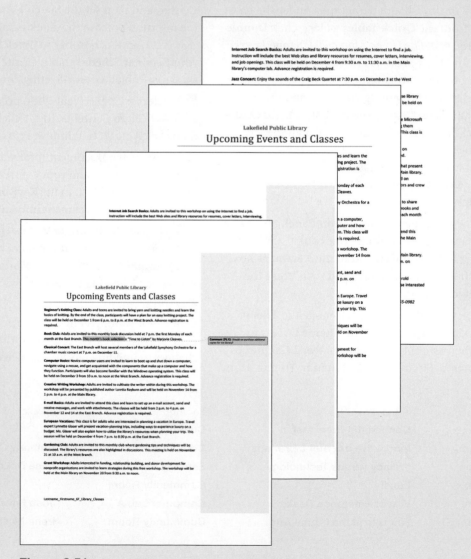

Figure 6.51

(Project 6F Library Classes continues on the next page)

Content-Based Assessments

1 **Start** Word, and then open the file **w06F_Library_Classes**. **Save** the document in your **Word Chapter 6** folder as **Lastname_Firstname_6F_Library_Classes** Insert the file name in the footer. On the **Review tab**, in the **Tracking group**, click the **Track Changes button arrow**, and then click **Change User Name**. Under **Personalize your copy of Microsoft Office**, type your name in the **User name** box, and then type your initials in the **Initials** box, if necessary.

2 In the fourth paragraph, select the text *This month's book selection*. Insert a **New Comment**, and then type **Should we purchase additional copies for the library?** In the markup area, delete **Comment [AG2]** and **Comment [CM2]**.

3 In the **Tracking group**, change the **Display for Review box** to **Final: Show Markup**, and then turn on **Track Changes**. Change the first paragraph to **Heading 1** style, and then apply **Center**. Change the second paragraph to **Title** style, and then apply **Center**. Position the insertion point to the left of the paragraph that begins *Internet*, and then press [Ctrl] + [Enter]. Locate the paragraph that begins *Microsoft Word*. **Delete** the text *101*, and then press [Ctrl] + [End]. Press [Enter], and then type **To register for a class or to obtain more information, contact Abigail Gardner at 847-555-0982.** Select the sentence you just typed, and then apply **Italic** and **Center**.

4 Press [Ctrl] + [Home], and then **Accept All Changes in Document**. Click the **Track Changes button arrow**, and then click **Change User Name**. Delete your name in the **User Name** box, and then delete your initials in the **Initials** box, if necessary. Turn off **Track Changes**. Display the **Document Information Panel**, type your first

and last names as the **Author**, and your course name and section number as the **Subject**. In the **Keywords** box, type **library classes, edited** **Close** the **Document Information Panel**. **Save** your document, and then from **Backstage** view, **Close** the document but leave Word open.

5 Display the **Combine Documents** dialog box. For the **Original document**, from your student data files, select the file **w06F_Classes_Reviewed**. For the **Revised document**, from your **Word Chapter 6** folder, select the file **Lastname_Firstname_6F_Library_Classes**. Click the **More** button, and then select the **New document** option button. Click the **Less** button, and then click **OK**. If a Microsoft Word dialog box displays, click Yes to continue with the comparison.

6 **Save** the document in your **Word Chapter 6** folder as **Lastname_Firstname_6F_Classes_Combined** Then, if displayed, **Close** the two document panes on the right side of your screen, and then **Close** the Reviewing Pane. Click the **Accept button arrow**, and then click **Accept All Changes in Document**. Delete the comment that contains your initials.

7 Double-click in the footer area, right-click the file name field, and then click **Update Field**. **Close** the footer area. Press [Ctrl] + [Home]. Display the **Document Information Panel**, type your name as **Author** and your course name and section number as the **Subject**. In the **Keywords** box, type **library classes, reviewed, combined** **Close** the **Document Information Panel**. **Save** your document.

8 Print both documents or submit electronically as directed by your instructor. **Exit** Word.

End **You have completed Project 6F** ——————————

Content-Based Assessments

Apply **6A** and **6B** skills from these Objectives:

1. Create Building Blocks
2. Create and Save a Theme Template
3. Create a Document by Using Building Blocks
4. Use Comments in a Document
5. Track Changes in a Document
6. View Side by Side, Compare, and Combine Documents

Mastering Word | Project **6G** Web Site Flyer

In the following Mastering Word project, you will create a document to announce the launch of Lakefield Public Library's new Web site by creating and inserting building blocks, deleting comments, inserting text, applying formatting, and accepting changes made by others. Your completed documents will look similar to Figure 6.52.

Project Files

For Project 6G, you will need the following files:

New blank Word document
w06G_Website_Flyer

You will save your documents as:

Lastname_Firstname_6G_Website_Block
Lastname_Firstname_6G_Website_Theme—not shown in figure
Lastname_Firstname_6G_Website_Flyer

Project Results

Figure 6.52

(Project 6G Web Site Flyer continues on the next page)

Content-Based Assessments

Mastering Word | Project 6G Web Site Flyer (continued)

1 **Start** Word and be sure rulers and formatting marks display. Display the **Save As** dialog box and save the new blank document to your **Word Chapter 6** folder as **Lastname_Firstname_6G_Website_Block** Insert the file name in the footer.

2 From the **Quick Tables** gallery, click **Tabular List**. In the first cell, select *ITEM*, and then type **Location** In the second cell, type **Day** On the **Layout tab**, in the **Rows & Columns group**, click the **Insert Right** button to create a third column. In the first cell of the third column, type **Time** Delete all remaining text in the table, and then apply the **Medium Shading 1 – Accent 3** table style. Select the entire table, and then save it in the **Quick Tables** gallery with the name **Training Schedule** and the **Description Use to display schedules for training**

3 Press Ctrl + Home. Display the **Document Information Panel**, type your name as the **Author** and your course name and section number as the **Subject**. In the **Keywords** box, type **IT Department, building block Close** the **Document Information Panel**, and then **Save** your changes. From **Backstage** view, **Close** the document but leave Word open.

4 Create a new blank document. Change the **Theme Colors** to **Austin**, and then save the custom theme to your **Word Chapter 6** folder as **Lastname_Firstname_6G_Website_Theme** From **Backstage** view, **Close** the document, without saving changes, but leave Word open.

5 Open the file **w06G_Website_Flyer**, and then save it in your **Word Chapter 6** folder as **Lastname_Firstname_6G_Website_Flyer** Insert the file name in the footer. Apply your custom theme—**Lastname_Firstname_6G_Website_Theme**.

6 Select the first two paragraphs of the document, and then format the text with **Font Size 28**, **Bold** and **Center**, and **Font Color Orange, Accent 6, Darker 25%**. Press Ctrl + End, and then **Insert** the **Training Schedule** Quick Table. Beginning in the first cell of the second row, type the following text in the table.

Item	Location	Day
Main library	Wednesday	2 p.m.
East Branch	Thursday	9 a.m.
West Branch	Friday	3 p.m.

7 Select all empty rows, and then click **Delete Rows**. **Center** the table horizontally in the document. Next, **Accept All Changes in Document**. Change the **Page Color** to the **Parchment Texture Fill Effect**.

8 Press Ctrl + Home. Display the **Document Information Panel**, type your name as the **Author** and your course name and section number as the **Subject**. In the **Keywords** box, type **Website flyer, reviewed Close** the **Document Information Panel**. **Save** your document, and then **Close** Word—do not save changes to building blocks.

9 Print both documents—you cannot print a theme—or submit all three files electronically as directed by your instructor. **Exit** Word.

End **You have completed Project 6G**

Content-Based Assessments

Apply a combination of
the **6A** and **6B** skills.

GO! Fix It | Project **6H** Internship Memo

Project Files

For Project 6H, you will need the following file:

> w06H_Internship_Memo

You will save your files as:

> Lastname_Firstname_6H_Internship_Theme
> Lastname_Firstname_6H_Internship_Memo

In this project you will edit a memo from Benedetta Herman, Director of Operations at Lakefield Public Library, to Greta Briggs, IT Director. Navigate to your student files, open the file **w06H_Internship_Memo**, and then save the file in your **Word Chapter 6** folder as **Lastname_Firstname_6H_Internship_Memo**

To complete the project, you must revise the file by changing the theme, inserting a building block, formatting text, and using various Track Changes features. Correct the following:

- The **Theme Colors** should be changed to **Metro**, and the current theme saved in your **Word Chapter 6** folder as **Lastname_Firstname_6H_Internship_Theme**
- The **Title** style should be applied to the first paragraph of text.
- A **Simple Text Box** should be inserted at the top of the document, and formatted **In Line with Text**, with **Shape Width** of **6.5"** and **Subtle Effect – Green, Accent 1** shape style applied. Insert the text **Lakefield Public Library Internship Program** displayed on two lines with **Font Size** of **26**, and apply **Center**.
- The **User Name** and **Initials** should be changed to reflect your own name.
- In the second paragraph of text, a comment should be inserted to check the correct title for Greta Briggs.
- Following the **Date** heading, type the current date.
- In the last paragraph, the day should be changed to **Tuesday**
- All changes in the documents should be accepted.
- A footer should be inserted that includes the file name; document properties should include the keywords **memo, internship**

Save your document, and then print the document—you cannot print a theme—or submit both files electronically as directed by your instructor.

End **You have completed Project 6H** —————————————

Content-Based Assessments

Apply a combination of the 6A and 6B skills.

GO! Make It | Project 6I Request Form

Project Files

For Project 6I, you will need the following files:

w06I_Request_Form
w06I_Library_Logo

You will save your document as:

Lastname_Firstname_6I_Request_Form

From your student files, open the file **w06I_Request_Form**, and create the document shown in Figure 6.53. The Theme Colors is set to Foundry, and Theme Fonts is set to Office Classic. Apply appropriate styles. From your student files, insert the picture **w06I_Library_Logo**. Use building blocks for the table—Matrix style—and the text box—Simple Text Box. Add document properties that include your name and the keywords **loan form, interlibrary** Save the file in your **Word Chapter 6** folder as **Lastname_Firstname_6I_Request_Form** Add the file name to the footer, and then print your document or submit electronically as directed by your instructor. Your completed document will look similar to Figure 6.53.

Project Results

Figure 6.53

Interlibrary Loan Request

Books and AV Materials

Lakefield Public Library

Date: _____
Last Name: _____
First Name: _____
Library Card Number: _____
Phone Number: _____ E-mail address: _____

Title Requested: _____
Author: _____
Other Information: _____

Please circle the appropriate format.			
Book			
Music	CD	Cassette	MP3
Audio Book	CD	Cassette	MP3
Movie	DVD	VHS	
Other			

(column headers: Unabridged, Large Print)

Interlibrary loans are processed immediately and may take 1-4 weeks to arrive. We cannot guarantee availability. A $5.00 fee will be charged for any items not picked up within 48 hours of notification.

Lastname_Firstname_6I_Request_Form

End You have completed Project 6I

Content-Based Assessments

GO! Solve It | Project **6J** Library Rules

Project Files

For Project 6J, you will need the following files:

New blank Word document
w06J_Library_Rules

You will save your documents as:

Lastname_Firstname_6J_Rules_Blocks
Lastname_Firstname_6J_Library_Rules

Display a new blank document and save it to your **Word Chapter 6** folder as **Lastname_Firstname_6J_Rules_Blocks** Insert a graphic related to a library and save it as a building block. Save a text box as a building block that includes the text **Library Rules** Insert the file name in the footer and add appropriate document properties.

From your student files, open the document **w06J_Library_Rules**. Accept all changes. Save the file to your **Word Chapter 6** folder as **Lastname_Firstname_6J_Library_Rules** Modify the theme and format the text to improve readability. Insert the building blocks you created. Adjust the building blocks and text to create an attractive, one-page document. Insert the file name in a footer and add appropriate document properties. Print both documents or submit electronically as directed by your instructor.

	Performance Level		
	Exemplary: You consistently applied the relevant skills	**Proficient:** You sometimes, but not always, applied the relevant skills	**Developing:** You rarely or never applied the relevant skills
Create a graphic building block	An appropriate graphic is saved as a building block.	A graphic is saved as a building block, but is not related to the topic.	No graphic is saved as a building block.
Create a text box building block	A text box containing the correct information is saved as a building block.	A text box is saved as a building block but contains incorrect information.	No text box is saved as a building block.
Accept changes	All changes are accepted.	Some changes are accepted but others are not.	No changes are accepted.
Modify theme and format text	The theme is modified and the text is formatted attractively.	The theme is not modified or the text is not formatted attractively.	The theme is not modified and the text is not formatted.
Insert building blocks	Both building blocks are inserted and positioned appropriately.	One building block is not inserted or is positioned inappropriately.	Both building blocks are not inserted or are positioned inappropriately.

Performance Element

End You have completed Project 6J

Content-Based Assessments

Apply a combination of the **6A** and **6B** skills.

GO! Solve It | Project **6K** Employee Newsletter

Project Files

For Project 6K, you will need the following file:

w06K_Newsletter_Items

You will save your documents as:

Lastname_Firstname_6K_Newsletter_Blocks
Lastname_Firstname_6K_Employee_Newsletter

Display a new blank document and save it to your **Word Chapter 6** folder as **Lastname_Firstname_6K_Newsletter_Blocks** Insert a graphic related to a library and save it as a building block. Save a text box as a building block that includes the text **Lakefield Public Library** Select and format a Quick Table to be used to display the name and department of new employees, and then save it as a building block. Insert the file name in the footer and add appropriate document properties.

Display a new blank document and save it to your **Word Chapter 6** folder as **Lastname_Firstname_6K_Employee_Newsletter** Create a newsletter, using your text box as a heading. Add an appropriate title and comment. Change to a two-column format, and then insert the text from student file **w06K_Newsletter_Items**. Insert the graphic and Quick Table building blocks, adding fictitious data to the table. Adjust paragraph and text formats to display attractively in a one-page document. Insert the file name in the footer, and add appropriate document properties. Print both documents or submit electronically as directed by your instructor.

		Performance Level	
	Exemplary: You consistently applied the relevant skills	**Proficient:** You sometimes, but not always, applied the relevant skills	**Developing:** You rarely or never applied the relevant skills
Create building blocks	All three building blocks are saved with appropriate content.	At least one building block is not saved or contains inappropriate content.	No building blocks are saved.
Change to two-column format	Below the title, the document is formatted in two columns.	The entire document is formatted in two columns.	The document is not formatted in two columns.
Insert title and comment	A title is inserted and formatted appropriately, and a comment is inserted.	A title is inserted but is not formatted appropriately or a comment is not inserted.	Neither a title nor a comment is inserted.
Insert building blocks	All building blocks are inserted and formatted appropriately.	At least one building block is not inserted or is formatted inappropriately.	No building blocks are inserted.
Enter data in table	Appropriate and sufficient data is entered in the table.	Inappropriate or insufficient data is entered in the table.	No data is entered in the table.

Performance Element (vertical label)

End You have completed Project 6K

Outcomes-Based Assessments

Rubric

The following outcomes-based assessments are *open-ended assessments*. That is, there is no specific correct result; your result will depend on your approach to the information provided. Make *professional quality* your goal. Use the following scoring rubric to guide you in *how* to approach the problem and then to evaluate *how well* your approach solves the problem.

The criteria—Software Mastery, Content, Format and Layout, and Process—represent the knowledge and skills you have gained that you can apply to solving the problem. The levels of performance—Professional Quality, Approaching Professional Quality, or Needs Quality Improvement—help you and your instructor evaluate your result.

	Your completed project is of Professional Quality if you:	Your completed project is Approaching Professional Quality if you:	Your completed project Needs Quality Improvements if you:
1-Software Mastery	Choose and apply the most appropriate skills, tools, and features and identify efficient methods to solve the problem.	Choose and apply some appropriate skills, tools, and features, but not in the most efficient manner.	Choose inappropriate skills, tools, or features, or are inefficient in solving the problem.
2-Content	Construct a solution that is clear and well organized, contains content that is accurate, appropriate to the audience and purpose, and is complete. Provide a solution that contains no errors in spelling, grammar, or style.	Construct a solution in which some components are unclear, poorly organized, inconsistent, or incomplete. Misjudge the needs of the audience. Have some errors in spelling, grammar, or style, but the errors do not detract from comprehension.	Construct a solution that is unclear, incomplete, or poorly organized; contains some inaccurate or inappropriate content; and contains many errors in spelling, grammar, or style. Do not solve the problem.
3-Format and Layout	Format and arrange all elements to communicate information and ideas, clarify function, illustrate relationships, and indicate relative importance.	Apply appropriate format and layout features to some elements, but not others. Overuse features, causing minor distraction.	Apply format and layout that does not communicate information or ideas clearly. Do not use format and layout features to clarify function, illustrate relationships, or indicate relative importance. Use available features excessively, causing distraction.
4-Process	Use an organized approach that integrates planning, development, self-assessment, revision, and reflection.	Demonstrate an organized approach in some areas, but not others; or, use an insufficient process of organization throughout.	Do not use an organized approach to solve the problem.

Outcomes-Based Assessments

Apply a combination of the 6A and 6B skills.

GO! Think | Project **6L** Fundraising Flyer

Project Files

For Project 6L, you will need the following file:

New blank Word document

You will save your documents as:

Lastname_Firstname_6L_Fundraising_Blocks
Lastname_Firstname_6L_Fundraising_Flyer

The Lakefield Public Library is conducting a fundraising campaign with a goal of $100,000 needed to upgrade the computer lab at the Main library and fund library programs. Donations can be sent to 1000 Oak Avenue, Lakefield, IL 60206. Benedetta Herman, Director of Operations, is chairing the fundraising committee and can be reached at 847-555-0982. Donor levels include:

Type of Recognition	Amount of Gift
Bronze Book Club	$100 or more
Silver Book Club	$500 or more
Gold Book Club	$1,000 or more

Create a document that includes a text box with the name and address of the library and an appropriate clip art image. Save both objects as building blocks. Save the document as **Lastname_Firstname_6L_Fundraising_Blocks** Create a flyer explaining the campaign and how donors will be acknowledged. Customize the theme, add appropriate text, and insert your building blocks. Include a Quick Table to display the recognition types. Format the flyer in a professional manner. Save the file as **Lastname_Firstname_6L_Fundraising_Flyer** For both documents, insert the file name in the footer and add document properties. Submit both documents as directed.

End You have completed Project 6L

Apply a combination of the 6A and 6B skills.

GO! Think | Project **6M** Reading Certificate

Project Files

For Project 6M, you will need the following file:

New blank Word document

You will save your documents as:

Lastname_Firstname_6M_Certificate_Blocks
Lastname_Firstname_6M_Reading_Certificate

The Lakefield Public Library conducts a children's summer reading program. Children are encouraged to read one book weekly over a 10-week period. Director of Programs and Youth Services Abigail Gardner keeps a record of books read by registered children. At the end of summer, every child who read at least ten books receives a certificate of achievement.

Create a document that includes an appropriate clip art image and a Quick Table. Edit the table to include places to record ten book titles and the dates read. Save the graphic and Quick Table as building blocks. Save the document as **Lastname_Firstname_6M_Certificate_Blocks** Create the award certificate. Add text appropriate for a certificate, including places to insert a name, date awarded, and signature of the library official. Insert your building blocks. Format the certificate in a professional manner. Insert a comment related to the certificate's design. Save the file as **Lastname_Firstname_6M_Reading_Certificate** For both documents, insert the file name in the footer, and add document properties. Print both documents or submit electronically as directed.

End You have completed Project 6M

Outcomes-Based Assessments

You and GO! | Project **6N** Personal Calendar

Project Files

For Project 6N, you will need the following file:

New blank Word document

You will save your documents as:

Lastname_Firstname_6N_Calendar_Block
Lastname_Firstname_6N_Personal_Calendar

In a new document, insert a Quick Table formatted as a calendar. Delete all the dates, and change the design or layout features to suit your taste. Save the table as a building block. Save the document as **Lastname_Firstname_6N_Calendar Block** Insert the file name in the footer and add appropriate document properties. In a new document, insert your Quick Table building block, change the month to the current month, and then insert the appropriate dates. For specific dates, enter scheduled events. These activities should include your current classes and any observed holidays. Add several comments related to particular events. Using the formatting skills you have practiced, format the document in a manner that is professional and easy to read. Save the file as **Lastname_Firstname_6N_Personal_Calendar** Insert the file name in the footer, and add appropriate document properties. Print both documents or submit electronically as directed by your instructor.

End **You have completed Project 6N** ————————————————

Business Running Case

Razvan CHIRNOAGA/Shutterstock

Front Range Action Sports is one of the country's largest retailers of sports gear and outdoor recreation merchandise. The company has large retail stores in Colorado, Washington, Oregon, California, and New Mexico, in addition to a growing online business. Major merchandise categories include fishing, camping, rock climbing, winter sports, action sports, water sports, team sports, racquet sports, fitness, golf, apparel, and footwear.

In this project, you will apply skills you practiced from the Objectives in Chapters 4–6. You will edit and create documents that relate to a new Front Range Action Sports retail store that is opening in Portland, Oregon. The first three documents are a flyer, a Web page, and a blog that announce the opening of the Portland store. The fourth document contains building blocks that are inserted in the final document—a memo to all media outlets announcing the new Portland store opening. Your completed documents will look similar to Figure 2.1.

Project Files

For Project BRC2, you will need the following files:

New blank Word document
New blog post—in Word
wBRC2_Store_Information
wBRC2_Web_Information
wBRC2_Portland_Memo

You will save your documents as:

Lastname_Firstname_BRC2_Portland_Flyer
Lastname_Firstname_BRC2_Portland_Webpage
Lastname_Firstname_BRC2_Portland_Blog
Lastname_Firstname_BRC2_Building_Blocks
Lastname_Firstname_BRC2_Portland_Memo
Lastname_Firstname_BRC2_Memo_Theme—not shown in figure

Project Results

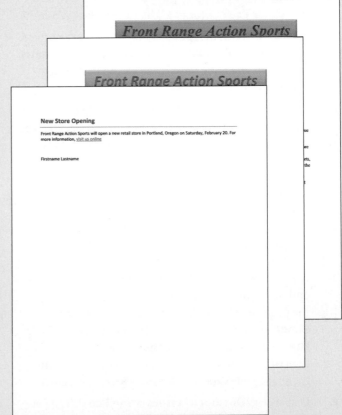

Figure 2.1

Business Running Case

Front Range Action Sports

1 **Start** Word. From your student files, open **wBRC2_Store_Information**. If necessary, in the location where you are storing your projects, create a new folder named **Front Range Action Sports** or navigate to this folder if you have already created it. **Save** the document as **Lastname_Firstname_BRC2_Portland_Flyer** and then insert the file name in the footer.

a. At the beginning of the document, insert a new paragraph, type **Front Range Action Sports** and then on a new line, type **New Store Opening in Portland** Select the first paragraph, and apply the **Title** style; select the second paragraph, and then apply the **Heading 1** style. **Center** both paragraphs. Change the **Theme** to **Trek**.

b. In the third paragraph, select the text *Front Range Action Sports*. Apply **Bold** and **Italic**, and then change the **Font Color** to **Orange, Accent 1, Darker 50%**. Save the selected text as a **Quick Style** with the name **FRAS** Apply the **FRAS** style to the remaining three occurrences of the company name.

c. Change the **Paragraph Spacing** style to **Tight**, and then change the **Page Color** to **Light Yellow, Background 2**.

d. Position the insertion point at the end of the document, and then type **The chart below indicates those states where we currently have retail stores or plan to open new stores.**

e. On a new line, insert a chart that uses the **Stacked Bar** style. In cell **B1**, type **Existing** and then in cell **C1**, type **Planned** Beginning in cell **A2**, type the following data:

California	2	3
Colorado	4	0
Nevada	0	1
Oregon	1	2
Washington	2	1

f. Resize the data range to include only **A1** through **C6**, and then **Close** Excel. Insert a **Chart Title** that uses the position **Above Chart**, and then type **Front Range Action Sports Retail Stores** Insert a **Primary Horizontal Axis Title** with **Title Below Axis**, and then type **Number of Stores** Format the chart area with the shape style **Colored Outline – Brown, Accent 2**.

g. Display the **Document Information Panel**, add your name, course information, and the **Keywords flyer, Portland store Save** your document.

2 With your **Lastname_Firstname_BRC2_Portland_Flyer** document open, display the **Save As** dialog box. Change **Save as type** to **Web Page**, change the title to **Portland Store Opening** and then save the document to your **Front Range Action Sports** folder as **Lastname_Firstname_BRC2_Portland_Webpage** In **Print Layout** view, update the footer. Display the document properties, and in the **Keywords** box, delete any existing text, and type **Web page, Portland store** If necessary, switch to **Web Layout** view.

a. In the third paragraph, select the first letter, and then insert a **Drop Cap** with **Lines to drop** set to **2**.

b. In the paragraph that begins *For more information*, select the text *www.fr-actionsports.com*, and then insert a **Hyperlink** with the text **Front Range Action Sports** for the **ScreenTip**.

c. After the fifth paragraph, which ends with the text *enthusiast*, insert a blank line. Type **To celebrate the opening of our Portland store, on February 20, we are offering the following discounts to all of our customers:** and then press [Enter].

d. From your student files, open the document **wBRC2_Web_Information**, select the last five paragraphs of the document, and then **Copy** the selection to the **Office Clipboard**. In your **Lastname_Firstname_BRC2_Portland_Webpage** file, in the blank line, paste the selection from the Clipboard. Select the inserted paragraphs, and then **Sort** in ascending order.

e. **Save** your document, and then **Close** any open documents.

3 Create a new **Blog post**. If necessary, in the displayed message box, click **Register Later**. Save the document to your **Front Range Action Sports** folder as **Lastname_Firstname_BRC2_Portland_Blog**

a. In the **Enter Post Title Here** field, type **New Store Opening** In the body text area, type **Front Range Action Sports will open a new retail store in Portland, Oregon on Saturday, February 20. For more information, visit us online.** Press [Enter] two times, and then type your first and last names.

b. Select the text *visit us online*, and insert a hyperlink to **www.fr-actionsports.com**

c. Display the **Document Information Panel**, add your name, course information, and the **Keywords blog, Portland store Save** and **Close** your document.

(Business Running Case: Front Range Action Sports continues on the next page)

Business Running Case

Front Range Action Sports (continued)

4 Create a new, blank document, and save it to your **Front Range Action Sports** folder as **Lastname_Firstname_BRC2_Building_Blocks** Insert the file name in the footer.

a. Insert a **Text Box** in the style **Simple Text Box**. Change the text wrapping to **In Line with Text**. Change the **Shape Width** to **6.0"** and the **Shape Height** to **0.8"**. Change the shape style to **Intense Effect – Olive Green, Accent 3**. In the text box, type **Front Range Action Sports** Change the **Font Size** to **36**, and then apply **Bold**, **Italic**, and **Center**. Apply the text effect **Gradient Fill – Orange, Accent 6, Inner Shadow**. Save the text box to the **Text Box** gallery with the name **Company Heading**

b. In the document, below the text box, insert a **Quick Table** in the **Tabular List** style. In the first row, in the first cell, change the text to **ITEMS** and then in the second cell, change the text to **DISCOUNT Delete** all remaining text in the table. Save the table to the **Quick Tables** gallery with the name **Discount Table**

c. Display the **Document Information Panel,** add your name, course information, and the **Keywords building blocks, Portland store Save** your changes, and from **Backstage** view, **Close** your document without closing Word.

5 Open the file **wBRC2_Portland_Memo**. Save it to your **Front Range Action Sports** folder as **Lastname_Firstname_BRC2_Portland_Memo** Insert the file name in the footer.

a. Accept all changes in the document, and then **Delete** the comment.

b. Change the **Theme Colors** to **Apex**, and then change the **Theme Fonts** to **Office Classic**. Save the current theme to your **Front Range Action Sports** folder as **Lastname_Firstname_BRC2_Memo_Theme**

c. At the beginning of the document, insert the **Company Heading** building block. If necessary, change text wrapping to **In Line with Text**. If necessary, position the insertion point to the left of *TO:*, and then press Enter.

6 In the paragraph that begins *To celebrate*, immediately to the left of *discounts*, type **the following** and then at the end of the sentence, replace the period with a colon. Press Enter.

a. Insert the **Quick Table** you created—**Discount Table**. Starting in the second row, type the following:

Backpacks	30%
Binoculars	25%
Footwear	20%
GPS Units	10%
Tents	15%

b. **Delete** any empty rows in the table. **Center** the data in the second column, and then **Center** the table horizontally on the page.

c. In the paragraph that begins *The company already*, locate and then select the text *attire*. Using the **Thesaurus**, replace the selected text with an appropriate synonym.

d. Press Ctrl + Home. Display the **Find and Replace** dialog box. In the **Find what** box, type **Front Range Sports** In the **Replace with** box, type **Front Range Action Sports** Display the **Replace Font** dialog box. Select **Bold Italic** and then change the **Font color** to **Lavender, Accent 6, Darker 25%**. Replace all three occurrences.

e. Display the **Document Information Panel**, add your name, course information, and the **Keywords memo, Portland store**

7 **Save** your document, **Delete** your two building blocks from the **Building Blocks Organizer,** and then **Close** Word. In the **Word** message box, **Save** the changes to building blocks.

8 Print all five documents—you cannot print the theme file—or submit electronically as directed by your instructor.

End **You have completed Business Running Case 2** ────────

Business Running Case 2: Includes Objectives from Word Chapters 4–6

Using Advanced Table Features

OUTCOMES

At the end of this chapter you will be able to:

PROJECT 7A
Use advanced table features such as custom table styles, sort, and properties.

OBJECTIVES

Mastering these objectives will enable you to:

1. Create and Apply a Custom Table Style (p. 403)
2. Format Cells (p. 407)
3. Use Advanced Table Features (p. 409)
4. Modify Table Properties (p. 416)

PROJECT 7B
Create a custom table that includes a nested table and an Excel spreadsheet.

5. Draw a Freeform Table (p. 420)
6. Use Nested Tables (p. 428)
7. Insert an Excel Spreadsheet (p. 430)

Natalia Barsukova/Shutterstock

In This Chapter

Recall that tables provide a convenient way to organize text. You have already practiced inserting a table by using the Table command on the Insert tab, but there are several other ways to create tables. For example, you can draw your own table, convert existing text into a table format, or insert Excel spreadsheets. You can also perform calculations on the data in a table.

Formatting a table makes data easier to read and provides a professional appearance. You will format tables by customizing table styles, merging and splitting cells, and changing the way text displays within the cells.

The projects in this chapter relate to **Rubanne Specialties**, a Montreal-based manufacturer of quality leather and fabric accessories for men and women. Products include wallets, belts, handbags, key chains, backpacks, business cases, laptop sleeves, and travel bags. The company distributes its products to department and specialty stores in the United States and Canada. It also has a Web site from which over 60 percent of its products are sold. The company pays shipping for both delivery and returns, and bases its operating philosophy on exceptional customer service.

Project 7A Product Summary

myitlab
Project 7A Training

In Activities 7.01 through 7.11, you will create, modify, and format tables containing new product information to produce a document that will be distributed to the Rubanne Specialties sales team. Rubanne Specialties is introducing new products for the fall season. Connor Fereday, Marketing Vice President, has asked you to create a document that summarizes the new product lines. Your completed document will look similar to Figure 7.1.

Project Files

For Project 7A, you will need the following file:

w07A_Product_Summary

You will save your document as:

Lastname_Firstname_7A_Product_Summary

Project Results

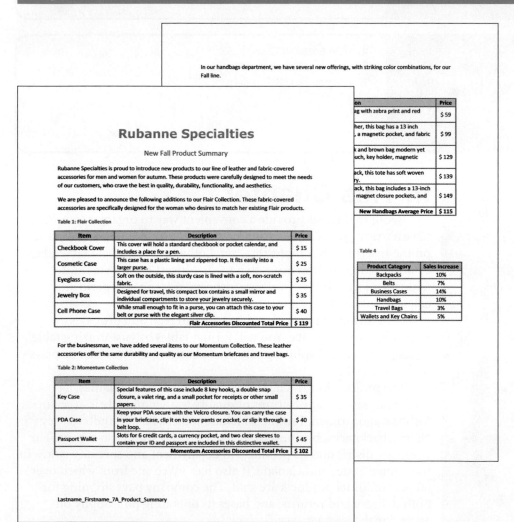

Figure 7.1
Project 7A Product Summary

Objective 1 | Create and Apply a Custom Table Style

Recall that a *style* is a combination of formatting commands—such as font size, shading, and text emphasis—that can be saved with a name and stored as a set. You can create a *table style* and apply it repeatedly to give your tables a consistent format. A table style can include formatting for the entire table and specific table elements, such as rows and columns.

Activity 7.01 | Creating a Table Style

When you create a table style, you can apply formats, such as borders, to the entire table and add special formats to individual parts of the table, such as bold emphasis and shading to specific cells. Creating a table style saves time when formatting multiple tables and provides a uniform appearance.

1 **Start** Word. From your student files, locate and open the file **w07A_Product_Summary**. If necessary, display the rulers and formatting marks. If any words are flagged as spelling or grammar errors, right-click, and then click **Ignore All**.

2 Display the **Save As** dialog box, and then navigate to the location where you are saving your files for this chapter. Create a new folder named **Word Chapter 7** and then using your own name, save the document as **Lastname_Firstname_7A_Product_Summary** Using **Quick Parts**, insert the file name in the footer.

3 Select the first paragraph—the company name *Rubanne Specialties*. On the Mini toolbar, change the **Font** to **Verdana**, change the **Font Size** to **22**, and apply **Bold** [B] and **Center** [≡]. Change the **Font Color** [A▾] to **Orange, Accent 6, Darker 25%**—in the last column, the fifth color.

4 Select the second paragraph that begins *New Fall*. On the Mini toolbar, change the **Font Size** to **14**, click **Center** [≡], and then change the **Font Color** [A▾] to **Orange, Accent 6, Darker 50%**—in the last column, the sixth color. Deselect the text. Compare your screen with Figure 7.2.

Figure 7.2

Formatted text ——

5 On the **Home tab**, in the **Styles group**, click the **Dialog Box Launcher** button [▣] to display the **Styles** window.

6 At the bottom of the **Styles** window, click the **New Style** button [⊞]. In the **Create New Style from Formatting** dialog box, under **Properties**, in the **Name** box, type **Rubanne Specialties** and then click the **Style type arrow**, and click **Table**.

A sample table displays in the preview area. You can create a new style to apply a set of formats to a table by using the Create New Style from Formatting dialog box.

7 Under **Formatting**, click the **Line Weight arrow**, and then click **1½ pt**. Click the **Border Color arrow**, and then under **Theme Colors**, in the last column, click the sixth color— **Orange, Accent 6, Darker 50%**. Click the **Border button arrow**, and then click **All Borders**. Compare your screen with Figure 7.3.

Notice that under *Formatting*, in the *Apply formatting to* box, the formatting will be applied to the whole table. By default, notice at the bottom of the dialog box that this style is available only in this document.

Figure 7.3

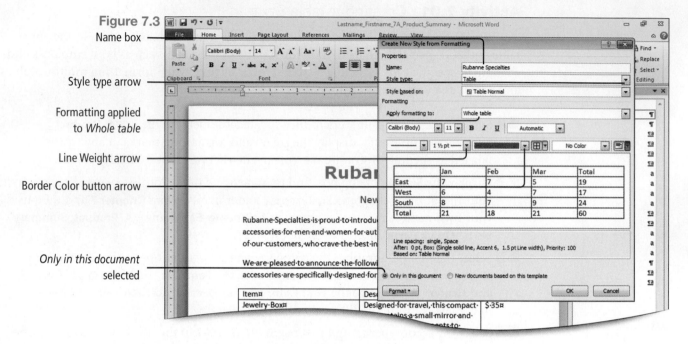

Name box

Style type arrow

Formatting applied to *Whole table*

Line Weight arrow

Border Color button arrow

Only in this document selected

8 Click **OK** to close the dialog box, and then **Close** ⊠ the **Styles** window. **Save** 🖫 your changes.

Activity 7.02 | Applying and Modifying a Table Style

You can apply a table style to an existing table. Additionally, you can modify an existing style or make formatting changes after a style has been applied to a table.

1 Scroll as necessary to display the first table in the document, and then click in the top left cell containing the text *Item*.

You can apply a table style when the insertion point is positioned anywhere within a table.

2 On the **Design tab**, in the **Table Styles group**, point to the first style on the left. Notice the displayed ScreenTip—*Rubanne Specialties*.

Alert! | Where Is the Style?

If the *Rubanne Specialties* style is not displayed, in the Table Styles group, click the More button, and then in the Table Styles gallery, select the style.

---

3 Click the **Rubanne Specialties** style to apply the table style to the table. Compare your screen with Figure 7.4.

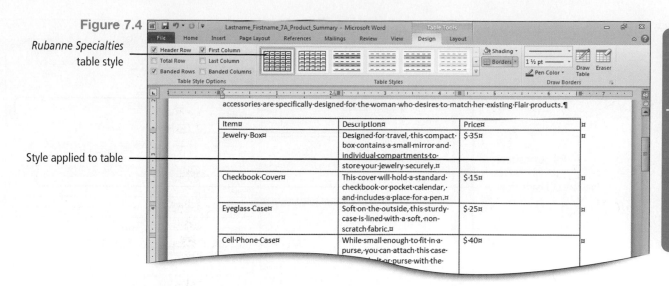

Figure 7.4

Rubanne Specialties table style

Style applied to table

4 Scroll as necessary, and then click to position the insertion point anywhere in the second table of the document—the table is split, displaying across two pages. On the **Design tab**, in the **Table Styles group**, click the first style on the left—**Rubanne Specialties**.

5 On the **Design tab**, in the **Table Styles group**, right-click the **Rubanne Specialties** style. A shortcut menu displays several options for working with styles as described in Figure 7.5.

Table Style Options

Style Option	Description
Apply (and Clear Formatting)	Table style applied; text formatting reverts to Normal style
Apply and Maintain Formatting	Table style applied, including text formatting
New Table Style	Option to create a new, custom table style
Modify Table Style	Option to edit the table style
Delete Table Style	Removes the style from the Table Styles gallery
Set as Default	Style is used as the default for all tables created in the document
Add Gallery to Quick Access Toolbar	Table Styles gallery is added to the Quick Access Toolbar

Figure 7.5

6 On the shortcut menu, click **Modify Table Style**. In the **Modify Style** dialog box, under **Formatting**, click the **Apply formatting to arrow**, and then click **Header row**.

You can apply formatting to specific table elements. In the *Rubanne Specialties* style, you want to change formats that only apply to the *header row*—the first row of a table containing column titles.

7 Click **Bold** B, and then click the **Fill Color arrow**. Under **Theme Colors**, in the last column, click the fourth color—**Orange, Accent 6, Lighter 40%**. Compare your screen with Figure 7.6.

Figure 7.6

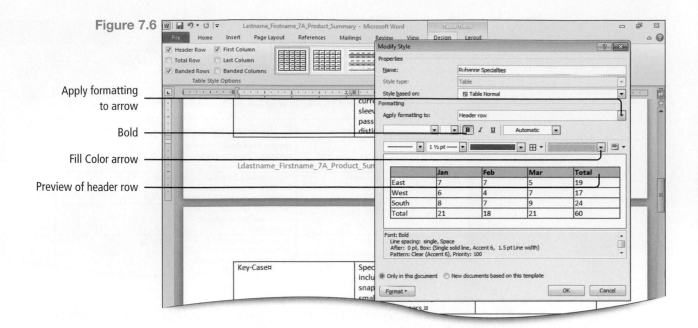

Apply formatting to arrow

Bold

Fill Color arrow

Preview of header row

8 Click **OK** to close the dialog box, and then press [Ctrl] + [Home]. On the **View tab**, in the **Zoom group**, click the **Two Pages** button. Compare your screen with Figure 7.7.

The additional formatting has been applied to the header rows in the first and second tables.

Figure 7.7

Header rows formatted

9 On the **View tab**, in the **Zoom group**, click the **100%** button, and then **Save** your changes.

More Knowledge | Repeating Header Rows

When a table is large enough to cause part of the table to display on a second page, the header row of the table can be repeated on the second page. With the insertion point in the header row, on the Layout tab, in the Table group, click the Properties button. In the Table Properties dialog box, click the Row tab, and then under Options, click *Repeat as header row at the top of each page*.

Objective 2 | Format Cells

Special formatting features that are unavailable for use with paragraph text are available in tables. For example, you can combine or divide cells and adjust the positioning of text.

Activity 7.03 | Merging and Splitting Cells

You can *merge* or *split* cells to change the structure of a table. Recall that merging is the process of combining two or more adjacent cells into one cell so that the text spans across multiple columns or rows. Splitting divides a selected cell into multiple cells with a specified number of rows and columns. In this activity, you will split cells to add column titles to a header row.

1 Locate the third table of your document, and then in the single cell in the first row, click to position the insertion point to the right of the text *New Handbags*.

2 On the **Layout tab**, in the **Table group**, if necessary, click the **View Gridlines** button to turn it on.

3 On the **Layout tab**, in the **Merge group**, click the **Split Cells** button. In the **Split Cells** dialog box, click the **Number of columns up spin arrow** to **3**. If necessary, click the **Number of rows down spin arrow** to **1**, and then compare your screen with Figure 7.8.

Because you want this header row to match the header rows in the other two product tables, you will split the cell into multiple cells and add column titles.

Figure 7.8

Split cells dialog box

Number of columns

Number of rows

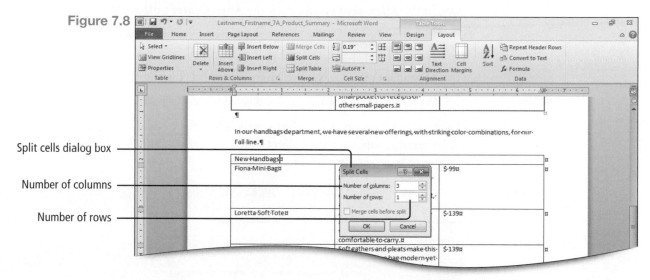

4 Click **OK** to close the dialog box. Notice that the selected cell has been split into three cells.

When splitting a cell that contains text, the text is automatically moved to the top left cell created by the division. When you change the structure of a table, some formatting features may be removed.

5 In the first cell of the header row, select the existing text *New Handbags*, and then type **Item** Press ⎡Tab⎤ to move to the second cell of the header row, and then type **Description** Press ⎡Tab⎤, and then in the last cell of the header row, type **Price** On the **Design tab**, in the **Table Styles group**, click the first style—**Rubanne Specialties**. Save 🖫 your changes, and then compare your screen with Figure 7.9.

Figure 7.9

Rubanne Specialties style applied

Header row

Activity 7.04 | Positioning Text within Cells

You can align text horizontally—left, center, or right—and vertically—top, center, or bottom—within cells. The default setting is to align text at the top left of a cell. Changing cell alignments creates a table with a professional appearance.

1 Locate the first table in your document, and then select the **header row**. On the **Layout tab**, in the **Alignment group**, click the **Align Center** button.

All text in the header row is centered horizontally and vertically within the cell.

2 Select all the cells below the header row in the first and second columns, and then in the **Alignment group**, click the **Align Center Left** button.

The selected text is left aligned and centered vertically within the cells.

3 In the third column, select all the cells below the header row, and then in the **Alignment group**, click the **Align Center** button. Deselect the text, and then compare your screen with Figure 7.10.

Figure 7.10

Align Center Left button

Align Center button

Text center left aligned

Text center aligned

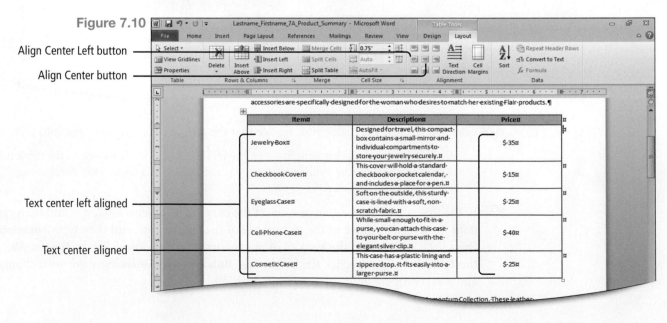

4 Using the technique you just practiced, format the **header row** in the second and third tables in the document to match the formatting of the header row in the first table— **Align Center** 🔲. In the second and third tables, **Align Center Left** 🔲 the first and second columns below the header row, and then **Align Center** 🔲 the text in the third column below the header row. Deselect the text, and then **Save** 🔲 your changes.

Objective 3 | Use Advanced Table Features

Word tables have some capabilities similar to those in an Excel spreadsheet—for example, sorting data and performing simple calculations. Additionally, you can convert existing text to a table format and resize tables in several ways.

Activity 7.05 | Sorting Tables by Category

In this activity, you will sort the data in the three product tables by price and item to make it easier for the sales team to reference specific items.

1 Scroll to display the entire contents of the first table, and then position the insertion point anywhere in the table.

Recall that data in a table can be sorted in ascending—from the smallest to the largest number or from A to Z order—or descending order—from the largest to the smallest number or from Z to A order. Regardless of the columns that are selected in the sort, all cells in each row are moved to keep the data intact.

2 On the **Layout tab**, in the **Data group**, click the **Sort** button.

The Sort dialog box allows you to sort text alphabetically, by number, or by date. The Sort feature can be applied to entire tables, selected data within tables, paragraphs, or body text that is separated by characters, such as tabs or commas. You can sort information using a maximum of three columns.

3 In the **Sort** dialog box, click the **Sort by arrow**, and then click **Price**. Compare your screen with Figure 7.11.

You are sorting the data in the table by the product's price. When a table has a header row, Word displays each column's header text in the *Sort by* list. By default, the Header row option is selected at the bottom left of the Sort dialog box. If a table does not have a header row, select the No header row option button. Without a header row, the sort options for a table will display as *Column 1*, *Column 2*, and so on. Because the Price column contains numbers, the Type box displays *Number*. When working in tables, the Using box displays the default *Paragraph*.

Figure 7.11

Ascending selected

Type set to *Number*

Sort by set to *Price*

Using set to *Paragraphs*

Header row selected

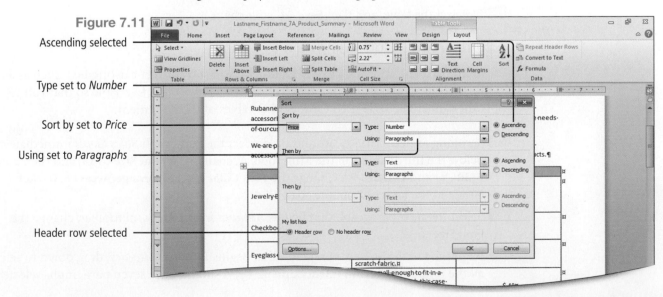

4 Under **Then by**, click the **Then by arrow**, and then click **Item**. Notice that the **Type** box displays *Text*.

> It is important to designate the columns in the order that you want them sorted. Word will first sort the data by price in ascending order. If two or more items have the same price, Word will arrange those items in alphabetical order.

5 Click **OK** to close the dialog box and notice that the two items with the same price of **$ 25** are listed in alphabetical order. Deselect the table, and then compare your screen with Figure 7.12.

Figure 7.12

Prices in ascending order

Items with same price in alphabetical order

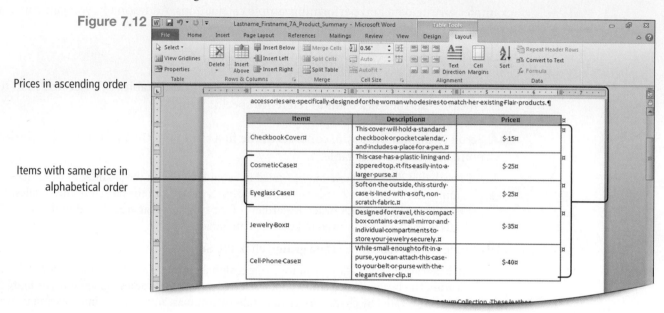

6 Click to position the insertion point anywhere in the second table of the document. On the **Layout tab**, click the **Sort** button.

> The Sort by box displays *Price*, and the Then by box displays *Item*. In the Sort dialog box, Word retains the last sort options used in a document.

7 Click **OK**, and notice that the table is sorted similarly to the first table.

8 Click to position the insertion point anywhere in the third table of the document. On the **Layout tab**, click the **Sort** button, and then click **OK**. Notice that the table is sorted in the same manner as the previous tables.

9 Deselect the table, and then **Save** 💾 your changes.

Activity 7.06 | Converting Text to a Table

To improve the appearance of a document, you can convert existing text, such as a list of information, to a table. In this activity, you will convert text to a table so that you can apply the same table style used for the other tables of the document.

1 Scrolling as necessary, locate and then select the paragraph *Sales Goals* immediately below the third table. On the Mini toolbar, change the **Font Size** to **14**, and then apply **Bold** B and **Center** ≡. Change the **Font Color** A to **Orange, Accent 6, Darker 50%**—in the last column, the sixth color.

2 Select the next paragraph that begins *Autumn is*. On the Mini toolbar, change the **Font Size** to **12**.

3 Beginning with the next paragraph that begins *Product Category*, drag down to select all the remaining text in the document—you should have seven paragraphs selected.

4 On the **Insert tab**, in the **Tables group**, click the **Table** button, and then click **Convert Text to Table** to display the **Convert Text to Table** dialog box. Compare your screen with Figure 7.13.

> Word uses characters such as tabs, commas, or hyphens to determine the number of columns. The selected text consists of seven paragraphs—or rows—with each paragraph containing a single tab. By default, Word uses the tab formatting mark to separate each paragraph into two parts—forming the two columns of the table. Under the *Separate text at* section, you can define the character Word uses to separate the text into columns. You can also change the number of columns or rows, based on the text you are converting.

Figure 7.13

Number of columns

Number of rows

Tabs selected

5 Click **OK** to close the dialog box. Notice that Word creates a table that contains two columns and seven rows. Notice that the table is split, displaying across two pages. **Save** 💾 your changes.

Activity 7.07 | Resizing Tables

Word provides several methods for resizing a table. The **AutoFit** command automatically adjusts column widths or the width of the entire table. **AutoFit Contents** resizes the column widths to accommodate the maximum field size. You can change a row height or column width by dragging a border, or designating specific width and height settings. To improve the overall appearance of the document, you will modify column widths.

1 In the first table in the document, point to the top border of the first column—*Item*—and when the ⬇ pointer displays, click to select the entire column. On the **Layout tab**, in the **Cell Size group**, click the **Width down spin arrow** to **1.5"**. Select the second column in the table—*Description*—and in the **Cell Size group**, click the **Width up spin arrow** to **4.5"**. Select the last column in the table—*Price*—and in the **Cell Size group**, click the **Width down spin arrow** to **0.5"**. Deselect the column, and then compare your screen with Figure 7.14.

Figure 7.14

Table column widths resized

2 In the second and third tables of the document, using the technique you just practiced, change the **Width** of the first column to **1.5"**, the **Width** of the second column to **4.5"**, and the **Width** of the third column to **0.5"**.

All product tables now have the same structure—the first, second, and third column widths in all tables are identical.

3 Click to position your insertion point anywhere in the last table of the document. On the **Layout tab**, in the **Cell Size group**, click the **AutoFit** button, and then click **AutoFit Contents**. Compare your screen with Figure 7.15.

AutoFit Contents resizes a table by changing the column widths to fit the existing data. In this table, the widths of both columns were decreased.

Figure 7.15

Table resized to fit data

4 Select the **header row**, and then on the **Layout tab**, in the **Alignment group**, click the **Align Center** button. Select the remaining cells in the second column, and then click **Align Center**.

5 Click to position the insertion point anywhere in the table, and then on the **Design tab**, in the **Table Styles group**, click the first style—**Rubanne Specialties**. **Save** your changes.

Activity 7.08 | Using Formulas in Tables

To perform simple calculations, you can insert a *formula* in a table. A formula is a mathematical expression that contains *functions*, operators, constants, and properties, and returns a value to a cell. A function is a predefined formula that performs calculations by using specific values in a particular order. Word includes a limited number of built-in functions—for example, SUM and AVERAGE.

Another Way

Position the insertion point to the right of the row border, and then press Enter.

1 In the first table, click to position the insertion point in the first cell of the last row. On the **Layout tab**, in the **Rows & Columns group**, click the **Insert Below** button.

2 Select the first two cells in the new row, and then on the **Layout tab**, in the **Merge group**, click the **Merge Cells** button. In the merged cell, type **Flair Accessories Total Price** Select the text, and then on the Mini toolbar, apply **Bold** B. On the **Layout tab**, in the **Alignment group**, click the **Align Center Right** button ▤. Press Tab to move to the last cell in the table. Compare your screen with Figure 7.16.

Figure 7.16

Item¤	Description¤	Price¤
Checkbook·Cover¤	This·cover·will·hold·a·standard·checkbook·or·pocket·calendar,·and·includes·a·place·for·a·pen.¤	$·15¤
Cosmetic·Case¤	This·case·has·a·plastic·lining·and·zippered·top.·It·fits·easily·into·a·larger·purse.¤	$·25¤
Eyeglass·Case¤	Soft·on·the·outside,·this·sturdy·case·is·lined·with·a·soft,·non-scratch·fabric.¤	$·25¤
Jewelry·Box¤	Designed·for·travel,·this·compact·box·contains·a·small·mirror·and·individual·compartments·to·store·your·jewelry·securely.¤	$·35¤
Cell·Phone·Case¤	While·small·enough·to·fit·in·a·purse,·you·can·attach·this·case·to·your·belt·or·purse·with·the·elegant·silver·clip.¤	$·40¤
	Flair·Accessories·Total·Price¤	|¤

Merged cell ⟶

Text center right aligned ⟶

¶

For·the·businessman,·we·have·added·several·items·to·our·Momentum·Collection.·These·leather·accessories·offer·the·same·durability·and·quality·as·our·Momentum·briefcases·and·travel·bags.¶

| | Description¤ | Price¤ |

3 On the **Layout tab**, in the **Data group**, click the **Formula** button. In the displayed **Formula** dialog box, under **Number format**, click the **Number format arrow**, and then click **#,##0**. Click to position the insertion point to the left of the displayed text, and then type **$** Compare your screen with Figure 7.17.

The Formula dialog box contains the default formula =SUM(ABOVE). All formulas begin with an equal sign =. This formula includes the SUM function and calculates the total of the numbers in all of the cells above the current cell—up to the first empty cell or a cell that contains text—and places the result in the current cell.

In the Formula dialog box, you can specify a special number format—in this case, a whole number preceded by a dollar sign. You can use the Paste function box to specify another built-in function—such as AVERAGE, PRODUCT, MIN or the minimum value in a list, or MAX or maximum value in a list.

Figure 7.17

Formula dialog box ⟶

Current formula ⟶

Number format box ⟶

Paste function box ⟶

4 Click **OK** to close the dialog box. Notice that *$140*—the sum of the prices for the Flair accessories—displays in the active cell.

> A formula is a type of *field*—a placeholder for data. The displayed number is a formula field representing the value calculated by the formula.

5 Select the inserted text, and then on the Mini toolbar, apply **Bold** B .

6 In the second table, click to position the insertion point in the first cell of the last row. On the **Layout tab**, in the **Rows & Columns group**, click the **Insert Below** button. In the new row, select the first two cells, right-click, and then from the shortcut menu, click **Merge Cells**. In the merged cell, type **Momentum Accessories Total Price** and then apply **Bold** B and **Align Center Right** . Press Tab .

7 On the **Layout tab**, in the **Data group**, click the **Formula** button. In the **Formula** dialog box, under **Number format**, click the **Number format arrow**, and then click **#,##0**. Position the insertion point to the left of the displayed text, and then type **$** Click **OK**. Notice that *$120*—the sum of the prices for the Momentum accessories—displays in the active cell.

8 Select the inserted text, and then on the Mini toolbar, apply **Bold** B .

9 Below the second table, click to position the insertion point to the left of the paragraph that begins *In our handbags department*, and then press Ctrl + Enter to insert a page break.

10 In the third table of the document, using the technique you practiced, insert a new row at the bottom of the table. In the new row, select the first two cells, and then using any technique you practiced, **Merge Cells**. In the merged cell, type **New Handbags Average Price** and then apply **Align Center Right** and **Bold** B .

11 Press Tab to position the insertion point in the last cell of the table, and then display the **Formula** dialog box. In the **Formula** box, delete the existing text, and then type **=** Under **Paste function**, click the **Paste function arrow**, and then click **AVERAGE**. In the **Formula** box, notice that *=AVERAGE* displays, followed by *()*. Click to position the insertion point between the left and right parentheses, if necessary, and then type **ABOVE**

> You can use the Paste function box to specify a function to be used in a formula. By typing *ABOVE*, the calculation includes all of the values listed above the current cell in the table. You are using the AVERAGE function to display the average price of the new handbags.

12 In the **Formula** dialog box, under **Number format**, click the **Number format arrow**, and then click **#,##0**. Click to position the insertion point to the left of the displayed text, and then type **$** Compare your screen with Figure 7.18.

Figure 7.18

Formula

Number format

13 Click **OK** to close the **Format** dialog box, and notice that *$117*—the average price of the five handbags—displays in the active cell. Select the inserted text, and then apply **Bold** B . **Save** your changes.

Activity 7.09 | Updating Formula Fields in Tables

If a value is changed in a table, it is necessary to manually update the field containing the formula. Additionally, you can edit an existing formula in a table.

1 In the first table, in the last row, click to position the insertion point to the left of *Total*, type **Discounted** and then press [Spacebar]. Press [Tab], right-click the selection, and then on the shortcut menu, click **Edit Field**. In the displayed **Field** dialog box, under **Field properties**, click the **Formula** button.

2 In the displayed **Formula** dialog box, in the **Formula** box, click to position the insertion point to the right of the displayed formula =*SUM(ABOVE)*, if necessary, and then type *.85 Compare your screen with Figure 7.19.

> Formulas are not restricted to the built-in functions. You can also create your own. Customers purchasing the entire accessories collection receive a 15 percent discount. The modified formula reflects this discounted price. The total price is multiplied by 85 percent (.85), representing 100 percent minus the 15 percent discount.

Figure 7.19

Current formula

3 Click **OK**, and notice that a new, lower value—*$119*—displays in the active cell.

4 In the second table, in the last row, click to position the insertion point to the left of *Total*, type **Discounted** and then press [Spacebar]. Press [Tab], right-click the selection, and then on the shortcut menu, click **Edit Field**. In the displayed **Field** dialog box, under **Field properties**, click the **Formula** button.

5 In the displayed **Formula** dialog box, in the **Formula** box, click to position the insertion point to the right of the displayed formula =*SUM(ABOVE)*, if necessary, and then type *.85 Click **OK**. Notice that *$102*—the discounted total for the Momentum accessories—displays in the active cell.

6 In the third table, in the last column, under the **header row**, click in the third cell, select only the number *139* and then type **129**

> Unlike Excel, when you change a value that is used in a formula, the resulting calculation is not automatically updated.

7 Select the text in the bottom right cell of the table. Right-click the selection, and on the shortcut menu, click **Update Field**. Notice that the value *$115* displays in the active cell.

> Recall the displayed value represents a formula field. If a number used in the calculation is changed, you must use the Update Field command to recalculate the value.

8 **Save** 🔲 your changes.

Note | Summing Rows

The default formula is =SUM(ABOVE), assuming the cell above the selected cell contains a number. If there is a number in the cell to the left of the selected cell and no number in the cell above, the default is =SUM(LEFT). To sum the entire range, be sure to avoid leaving a cell empty within a range. If there is no value, then enter a 0.

Activity 7.10 | Adding Captions to Tables

Captions are titles that can be added to Word objects, and Word numbers them sequentially as they are added to the document. You can add a caption to each table in a document to make it easier to refer to specific tables in the body text.

1 Click to position the insertion point anywhere in the first table. On the **References tab**, in the **Captions group**, click the **Insert Caption** button.

2 In the **Caption** dialog box, in the **Caption** box, if necessary, click to the right of *Table 1*, type **:** press Spacebar, and then type **Flair Collection** If necessary, under **Options**, click the **Position arrow**, and then click **Above selected item**. Compare your screen with Figure 7.20.

Because the object selected is a table, the default caption starts with *Table 1*. Word automatically numbers objects sequentially. If the selected object is not a table, you can change the object type by clicking the Label arrow in the Caption dialog box.

Figure 7.20

Caption

Label box

Position of caption

3 Click **OK** to close the **Caption** dialog box. Notice that the caption displays above the table.

4 Using the technique you just practiced, add captions to the second and third tables. For the second table caption, insert the caption **Table 2: Momentum Collection** above the table, and then for the third table, insert the caption **Table 3: New Handbags** above the third table.

5 **Save** 🖫 your changes.

Objective 4 | Modify Table Properties

Tables, like all other Word objects, have properties that can be altered. For example, you can change how text wraps around tables and define cell spacing. Modifying table properties can improve the overall appearance of your document.

Activity 7.11 | Wrapping Text Around Tables

If you have a long document with several tables and body text, you can apply text wrapping to have the text flow around the table. This can create a shorter document and improve the overall appearance of the document.

1 In the last table of the document, point to the upper left corner of the table until the Layout Selector ⊞ displays. Drag the table until the top border is at approximately **4.5 inches on the vertical ruler** and the right border is at approximately **6.5 inches on the horizontal ruler**. Compare your screen with Figure 7.21. If your table position does not match the figure, click the Undo button ↺ and begin again.

Figure 7.21

Top border aligns at approximately 4.5" on vertical ruler

Right border aligns at approximately 6.5" on horizontal ruler

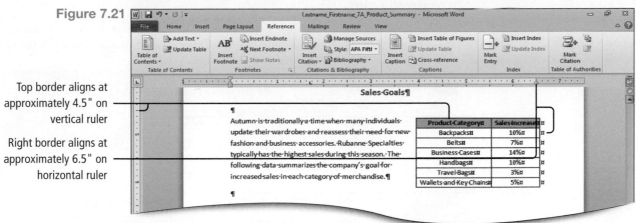

2 Click to position the insertion point anywhere in the table. On the **Layout tab**, in the **Table group**, click the **Properties** button. In the **Table Properties** dialog box, under **Text wrapping**, if necessary, click **Around**, and then click the **Positioning** button. In the **Table Positioning** dialog box, under **Distance from surrounding text**, click the **Left up spin arrow** to **0.5"**. If necessary, under **Options**, select both check boxes. Compare your screen with Figure 7.22.

> You can define how close existing text displays in relation to the top, bottom, left, or right of a table. By changing the Left box value to 0.5, the text will display one-half inch from the left border of the table.

Figure 7.22

Table Properties dialog box

Table Positioning dialog box

Left box

3 Click **OK** two times to close the dialog boxes.

4 With the insertion point in the table, on the **References tab**, in the **Captions group**, click the **Insert Caption** button. In the **Caption** dialog box, with *Table 4* displayed in the **Caption** box and *Above selected item* displayed in the **Position** box, click **OK** to close the dialog box and insert the caption at the left margin.

5 Select the caption. On the Mini toolbar, change the **Font Size** to **10**, and then change the **Font Color** [A▾] to **Orange, Accent 6, Darker 50%**—in the last column, the sixth color. At the left end of the horizontal ruler, if necessary, click the **Tab Alignment** button to display the **Left tab** button [⌐]. To set a left tab stop, click at **4.0 inches on the horizontal ruler**. Click to the left of the caption, and then press [Tab]. Compare your screen with Figure 7.23.

> You can format a caption, just as you would format body text. You will format the caption so that it displays above the table and coordinates with the color scheme of the table.

Figure 7.23

Tab stop —

Left tab button —

Tab formatting mark —

Formatted caption —

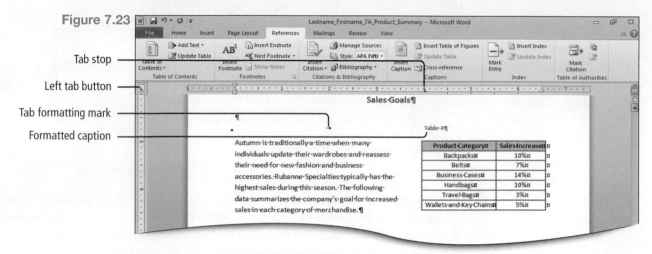

6 In the last sentence of the document, select the text *The following data*, and then type **Table 4**

> Adding a caption to a table enables you to refer to the table in the body text.

7 Select the caption, and on the **Home tab**, in the **Styles group**, click the **More** button [▾] , and then in the **Styles** gallery, click **Save Selection as a New Quick Style**.

8 In the **Create New Style from Formatting** dialog box, in the **Name** box, type **Table Caption** and then click **OK**.

9 Press [Ctrl] + [Home]. Select the first table caption, and then on the **Home tab**, in the **Styles group**, click the **Table Caption** style. In the same manner, apply the **Table Caption** style to the remaining two captions in the document.

10 Press [Ctrl] + [Home], and then display the **Document Information Panel**. In the **Author** box, delete any existing text, and then type your first and last names. In the **Subject** box, type your course name and section number, and in the **Keywords** box, type **product summary, tables Close** [✕] the Document Information Panel.

11 Examine the **Print Preview**, and make any necessary adjustments. **Save** [💾] your document. Print your document or submit electronically as directed by your instructor. **Exit** Word.

End **You have completed Project 7A** ——————————————————————

Project 7B Expense Form

Project 7B Training

Project Activities

In Activities 7.12 through 7.20, you will create an expense form by drawing a table, use nested tables to display expense codes, and insert an Excel spreadsheet. Adrianna Ramos, Chief Financial Officer for Rubanne Specialties, has asked you to design an expense reimbursement form to be used by the company's sales representatives. Your completed document will look similar to Figure 7.24.

Project Files

For Project 7B, you will need the following files:

New blank Word document
w07B_Logo

You will save your document as:

Lastname_Firstname_7B_Expense_Form

Project Results

Rubanne Specialties
Expense Reimbursement Form

Employee Name		Date of Report	
ID Number	Department	Position	

RS Attach any supporting receipts

Date	Purpose and Description	Code	Amount
		Total	

Employee Signature:

Type of Expense	Code
Food	F
Lodging	L
Mileage	M
Registration	R
Tools	T

To calculate the amount of your mileage reimbursement, double-click the spreadsheet below. Enter the trip name and number of miles, and then press Enter.

Trip	Miles	Amount
Example	247	123.50
		0.00
		0.00

Lastname_Firstname_7B_Expense_Form

Figure 7.24
Project 7B Expense Form

Objective 5 | Draw a Freeform Table

When a table is inserted into a Word document, the result is a table structure that consists of rows and columns of a uniform size. Sometimes you need to modify the table structure to create rows and columns of varying sizes, such as on a purchase order or employee expense form. Word provides tools that work like an electronic pencil and eraser to draw the table objects. After the table is drawn, you can use the features on the Design and Layout tabs to refine the table format.

Activity 7.12 | Drawing a Freeform Table

1 If you did not **Exit** Word at the end of the previous project, do so now. **Start** Word, and if necessary, open a new blank document. Save the document in your **Word Chapter 7** folder as **Lastname_Firstname_7B_Expense_Form** Using **Quick Parts**, insert the file name in the footer. If necessary, display the rulers and formatting marks.

> Restarting Word is necessary to reset the Draw Table settings to the defaults.

2 On the **Home tab**, in the **Styles group**, click the second style—**No Spacing**. Type **Rubanne Specialties** Press [Enter], type **Expense Reimbursement Form** and then press [Enter].

3 Select the first paragraph. On the Mini toolbar, change the **Font Size** to **26**, apply **Bold** [B] and **Center** [≡], and change the **Font Color** [A⁻] to **Orange, Accent 6, Darker 50%**—in the last column, the sixth color. Deselect the text. If *Rubanne* is marked as a spelling error, right-click, and then click **Ignore All**.

4 Select the second paragraph. On the Mini toolbar, change the **Font Size** to **14**, apply **Bold** [B] and **Center** [≡], and then change the **Font Color** [A⁻], to **Orange, Accent 6, Darker 25%**—in the last column, the fifth color.

5 In the third paragraph, click to position the insertion point. On the **Insert tab**, in the **Tables group**, click the **Table** button, and then click **Draw Table** to display the **Draw** pointer [✎]. Notice that faint dotted lines display on both the horizontal and vertical rulers that indicate the position of the Draw pointer. Compare your screen with Figure 7.25.

> It is a good idea to view the rulers while drawing a table. This enables you to make more precise measurements.

Figure 7.25

Visual guide on horizontal ruler

Draw pointer

Visual guide on vertical ruler

6 Position the [✎] pointer at the left margin and at approximately **0.75 inch on the vertical ruler**. Click and drag down and to the right until the guides are at approximately **6.5 inches on the horizontal ruler** and at approximately **6 inches on the vertical ruler**. Release the mouse button. If you are dissatisfied with the result, click Undo [↶] and begin again. Compare your screen with Figure 7.26.

> When drawing a table, always begin with the outside border of the table. Begin at the top left corner and drag the Draw pointer down and to the right. After the table is drawn, the Draw pointer continues to display, the Design tab is active, and in the Draw Borders group, the Draw Table button is turned on.

Figure 7.26

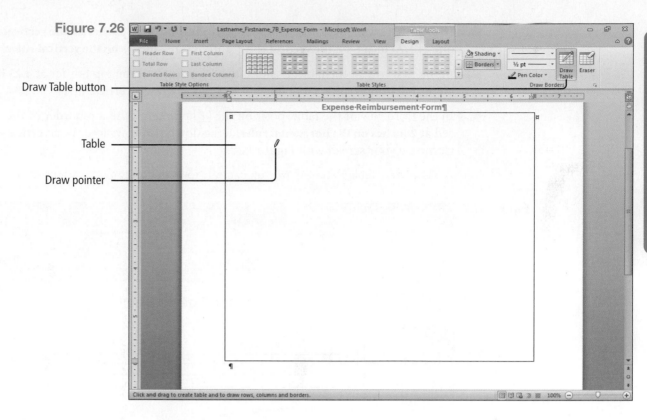

Draw Table button

Table

Draw pointer

7 Save 💾 your changes.

Activity 7.13 | Adding and Removing Columns and Rows

You can draw horizontal and vertical lines inside the table to create cells of various sizes. Your table requires a section for entering employee information and another section for listing expenses incurred. Each section requires cells that vary in size.

1 Position the tip of the ✏ pointer on the top border of the table at **0.5 inch on the horizontal ruler**. Drag down, and when you see the dotted vertical line extending to the bottom table border, release the mouse button.

By drawing a vertical dividing line, you have created an inside border forming two columns in the table.

2 Position the ✏ pointer on the left border of the table at **1.25 inches on the vertical ruler**. Drag to the right, and when you see the line extending to the right table border, release the mouse button to create the first row of the table. Compare your screen with Figure 7.27.

By drawing a horizontal line, you have created an inside border forming two rows in the table.

Figure 7.27

Inside column border

Inside row border

3 Draw three more horizontal lines—one beginning at **1.5 inches on the vertical ruler**, one at **1.75 inches on the vertical ruler**, and one at **2 inches on the vertical ruler**.

4 In the first row of the table, position the ✏ pointer at the top border at **4.25 inches on the horizontal ruler**. Drag down four rows to draw a vertical line.

5 In the third row of the table, position the ✏ pointer at the top border of the second cell at **2 inches on the horizontal ruler**. Drag down two rows to draw a vertical line. Compare your screen with Figure 7.28.

The Draw Table feature allows you to create rows and columns of various sizes.

Figure 7.28

New row and column borders

6 On the **Design tab**, in the **Draw Borders group**, click the **Eraser** button. Notice that the pointer displays as a small eraser ⌫.

7 In the first cell of the table, position the ⌫ pointer on the bottom cell border, and click. Notice that the line is removed.

8 In the newly merged cell, position the ⌫ pointer on the bottom cell border, and then click to remove the line. Position the ⌫ pointer on the bottom cell border, and click to remove the line, and then compare your screen with Figure 7.29.

Figure 7.29

Eraser button

One cell

Eraser pointer

9 On the **Design tab**, in the **Draw Borders group**, click the **Draw Table** button. In the last row of the table, in the first cell, position the ✏ pointer at the left border of the cell at **2.5 inches on the vertical ruler**. Drag across to draw a horizontal line extending to the right border of the table.

10 On the **Design tab**, in the **Draw Borders group**, click the **Draw Table** button to turn it off. Click in the last table cell. On the **Layout tab**, in the **Merge group**, click the **Split Cells** button. In the **Split Cells** dialog box, click the **Number of columns down spin arrow** to **1**, and then click the **Number of rows up spin arrow** to **9**. Click **OK**. Click in the paragraph immediately above the table. Compare your screen with Figure 7.30.

You can use Draw Table to create new rows, but sometimes it is faster to use Split Cells.

Figure 7.30

Nine rows created ——

11 Click anywhere in the table. On the **Design tab**, in the **Draw Borders group**, click the **Draw Table** button. In the sixth row of the table—the top row of the rows you just inserted—position the pointer at the top border of the row at **1.25 inches on the horizontal ruler**. Drag down to draw a vertical line extending to the bottom border of the table.

12 In the same row, draw two more vertical lines—one beginning at **5 inches on the horizontal ruler** and one beginning at **5.5 inches on the horizontal ruler**. On the **Design tab**, in the **Draw Borders group**, click the **Draw Table** button to turn it off. **Save** your changes, and then compare your screen with Figure 7.31.

Figure 7.31

New column borders ——

> **More Knowledge** | Deleting Table Elements
>
> You can delete cells, columns, rows, or an entire table. Click anywhere in the cell, column, row, or table that you wish to delete. On the Layout tab, in the Rows & Columns group, click the Delete button, and then click the appropriate button—Delete Rows, Delete Columns, Delete Table, or Delete Cells. If deleting cells, the Delete Cells dialog box will display allowing you to select how adjacent cells should be moved.

Activity 7.14 | Inserting Text and Graphics

You can insert text and objects, such as pictures and WordArt, into table cells.

1 In the first row of the table, position the insertion point in the second cell, and then type **Employee Name** Press Tab, and type **Date of Report**

2 Press Tab five times to move to the second cell in the third row of the table, and type **ID Number** Press Tab, type **Department** press Tab, and then type **Position**

3 In the sixth row, position the insertion point in the second cell, and then type **Date** Press Tab, and then type **Purpose and Description** Press Tab, type **Code** press Tab, and then type **Amount**

4 Select the first six rows of the table, and then on the **Layout tab**, in the **Alignment group**, click the **Align Center Left** button.

5 In the first row, select the text *Employee Name*, and on the Mini toolbar, apply **Bold** B. Using the same technique, apply **Bold** B to all the remaining text in the table, being careful not to apply Bold to empty cells. Compare your screen with Figure 7.32.

Figure 7.32

Text inserted and formatted

6 In the first column, position your insertion point in the second cell. On the **Insert tab**, in the **Illustrations group**, click the **Picture** button. Navigate to the location where the student data files are stored, locate the file **w07B_Logo**, and then click **Insert**. Notice that the picture—the company logo—is inserted in the cell.

The size of the graphic causes the column width and row height to be modified.

7 With the graphic selected, on the **Format tab**, in the **Size group**, click the **Width down spin arrow** to **0.5"**. Compare your screen with Figure 7.33.

Reducing the size of the image also reduces the row height and column width.

Figure 7.33

Width box

Picture inserted

---

8 In the second column, in the fifth row, click in the second cell, and then type **Attach any supporting receipts**

9 In the last row of the table, select the second, third, and fourth cells. On the **Layout tab**, in the **Merge group**, click the **Merge Cells** button. In the **Alignment group**, click the **Align Center Right** button ▤.

10 Click in the merged cell, and then type **Total** Select the text, and apply **Bold** **B**.

11 Click in the same cell to deselect the text, and then on the **Layout tab**, in the **Rows & Columns group**, click the **Insert Below** button to add a new row to the table.

12 In the last row of the table, with all the cells selected, on the **Layout tab**, in the **Merge group**, click the **Merge Cells** button. In the **Cell Size group**, click the **Height up spin arrow** to **0.4"**, and then in the **Alignment group**, click the **Align Center Left** button ▤.

13 With the insertion point in the last row of the table, type **Employee Signature:** Select the text, and on the Mini toolbar, apply **Bold** **B**. Deselect the text, **Save** ▤ your changes, and then compare your screen with Figure 7.34.

Figure 7.34

New row inserted
with cells merged

Text inserted
and formatted

Activity 7.15 | Changing Text Direction

Word tables include a feature that enables you to change the text direction. This is effective for column titles that do not fit at the top of narrow columns or for row headings that cover multiple rows.

1 Click to position the insertion point in the first cell of the table. On the **Layout tab**, in the **Alignment group**, click the **Text Direction** button two times. Notice that the insertion point displays horizontally in the cell.

> The Text Direction button can be used to change the positioning of text within a cell. The appearance of the Text Direction button changes to indicate the direction of the text within the currently selected cell.

2 Type **Employee Information** On the **Layout tab**, in the **Alignment group**, click the **Align Center** button [≣]. Select the text, and on the Mini toolbar, apply **Bold** [B]. Deselect the text, and then compare your screen with Figure 7.35.

Figure 7.35

Text Direction button

Text inserted and formatted

3 In the first column, click to position the insertion point in the third cell. On the **Layout tab**, in the **Alignment group**, click the **Text Direction** button two times. Notice that the insertion point displays horizontally in the cell.

4 Type **Expenses** On the **Layout tab**, in the **Alignment group**, click the **Align Center** button [≣]. Select the text, and then on the Mini toolbar, change the **Font Size** to **20** and apply **Bold** [B]. **Save** [💾] your changes.

Activity 7.16 | Distributing Rows and Columns

When you draw a freeform table, you may have rows that you want to be exactly the same height or columns that you want to be the same width. The **Distribute Columns** command adjusts the width of the selected columns so that they are equal. Similarly, the **Distribute Rows** command causes the height of the selected rows to be equal.

1 In the first four rows of the table, select all of the cells to the right of the first column. On the **Layout tab**, in the **Cell Size group**, click the **Distribute Rows** button [田]. Deselect the cells, and then compare your screen with Figure 7.36.

> The four rows you selected are now equal in height.

Figure 7.36

Distribute Rows button

Row height modified

2 Save [icon] your changes.

Activity 7.17 | Formatting a Table

Table cells can be formatted to enhance the appearance of a table. You will add shading to cells and modify the borders of the table.

1 In the first row, select the second and third cells. On the **Design tab**, in the **Table Styles group**, click the **Shading button arrow**, and then under **Theme Colors**, in the last column, click the third color—**Orange, Accent 6, Lighter 60%**.

2 In the third row, select the second, third, and fourth cells, and then in the **Table Styles group**, click the **Shading** button—not the Shading button arrow. In the sixth row, select cells two through five, and in the **Table Styles group**, click the **Shading** button. Deselect the cells, and then compare your screen with Figure 7.37.

The Shading button retains the color that was last selected. By clicking the Shading button, the current color is applied to the selected cells.

Figure 7.37

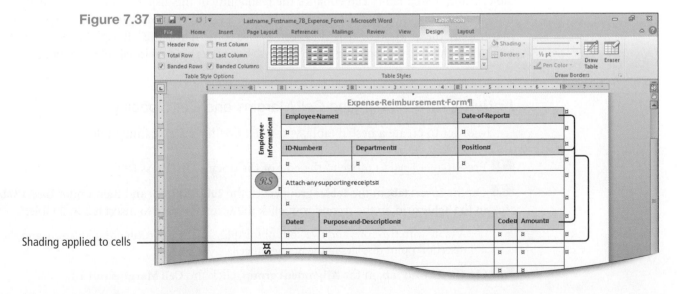

Shading applied to cells

3 In the first column, position the insertion point in the second cell, being careful not to select the graphic. On the **Design tab**, in the **Table Styles group**, click the **Borders button arrow**, and then click **Left Border**. Click the **Borders button arrow**, and then click **Right Border**. Notice that the borders of the cell no longer display; instead they are replaced by the dashed lines as shown in Figure 7.38.

> *Gridlines* are nonprinting cell borders that can be used as a guide for viewing table cells. They are useful when positioning content in a table when you are not using a table border. Removing borders can improve the appearance of certain content—for example, the graphic in this table.

Figure 7.38

Gridlines

4 Press [Tab]. In the **Table Styles group**, click the **Borders button arrow**, and then click **Right Border**.

5 On the **Layout tab**, in the **Table group**, click the **View Gridlines** button to turn it off. **Save** 💾 your changes.

> Hiding the gridlines allows you to see how a table will display in print.

Objective 6 | Use Nested Tables

A *nested table* is a table within a table. You can insert a table in any cell of an existing table. Using nested tables can enhance the readability of the displayed data. You can also improve the appearance of data within tables by changing *cell margins* and *cell spacing*. Cell margins are the amount of space between a cell's content and the left, right, top, and bottom borders of the cell. Cell spacing is the distance between the individual cells of a table.

Activity 7.18 | Changing Cell Margins and Cell Spacing

In order to create a nested table, you must first have an existing table.

1 Press [Ctrl] + [End] to move to the end of the document. Press [Enter].

2 On the **Insert tab**, in the **Tables group**, click the **Table** button, and then under **Insert Table**, in the **Table** grid, in the second row, click the second square to insert a 2 × 2 table.

> A table with two rows and two columns displays at the insertion point location, and the insertion point displays in the upper left cell.

3 On the **Layout tab**, in the **Alignment group**, click the **Cell Margins** button.

> The Table Options dialog box allows you to set the cell margins and cell spacing for a table.

4 In the **Table Options** dialog box, under **Default cell margins**, click the **Top up spin arrow** to **0.1"**. Using the same technique, change the **Bottom**, **Left**, and **Right** cell margins to **0.1"**.

Contents of each cell within the table will be displayed 0.1" from each cell border.

5 Under **Default cell spacing**, click to select the **Allow spacing between cells** check box, and then click the **Allow spacing between cells up spin arrow** to **0.05"**. Compare your screen with Figure 7.39.

All cells in the table will be separated by 0.05" of space.

Figure 7.39

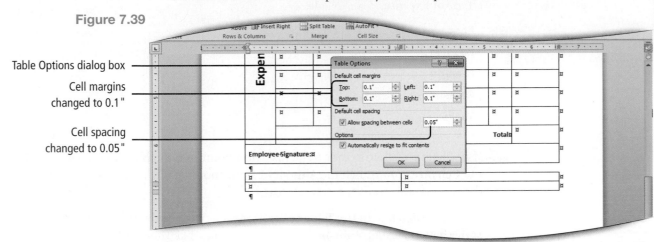

Table Options dialog box

Cell margins changed to 0.1"

Cell spacing changed to 0.05"

6 Click **OK**. In the table, select the two cells in the first column, and then on the **Layout tab**, in the **Merge group**, click the **Merge Cells** button. Compare your screen with Figure 7.40.

Figure 7.40

Cell spacing

Merged cell

Cells in second column

7 Point slightly outside of the upper left corner of the table to display the **Layout Selector** . With the pointer, click the **Layout Selector** to select the entire table.

8 On the **Design tab**, in the **Table Styles group**, click the **Borders button arrow**, and then click **No Border**. On the **Layout tab**, in the **Table group**, click the **View Gridlines** button to turn it on. **Save** your changes.

Activity 7.19 | Inserting a Nested Table

In this activity, you will create a nested table to display the codes that are used on the expense form.

1 Click to position the insertion point in the first cell of the table, and then on the **Insert tab**, in the **Tables group**, click the **Table** button. In the **Table** grid, in the sixth row, click the second square to insert a 2 × 6 table. Notice that a table containing two columns and six rows is created—or nested—within the first cell of the table.

2 In the first cell of the nested table, type **Type of Expense** Press `Tab`, and then type **Code**

3 In the same manner, enter the following data in the remaining cells of the table:

Type of Expense	Code
Food	F
Lodging	L
Mileage	M
Registration	R
Tools	T

4 If necessary, click to position the insertion point in the table. On the **Layout tab**, in the **Cell Size group**, click the **AutoFit** button, and then click **AutoFit Contents** to resize the nested table to fit the existing text.

5 On the **Design tab**, in the **Table Styles group**, click the **More** button ⮟. In the **Table Styles** gallery, under **Built-In**, in the last column, click the second style—**Light List – Accent 6**. Compare your screen with Figure 7.41. **Save** 💾 your changes.

Figure 7.41

Nested table with formatting applied

Objective 7 | Insert an Excel Spreadsheet

You can insert an Excel spreadsheet in a document to provide a table that performs calculations.

Activity 7.20 | Inserting an Excel Spreadsheet

In this activity, you will insert an Excel spreadsheet to assist employees with calculating mileage reimbursements.

1 In the second column in the original table, position the insertion point in the top cell. Type **To calculate the amount of your mileage reimbursement, double-click the spreadsheet below. Enter the trip name and number of miles, and then press Enter.**

2 Click to position the insertion point in the remaining blank cell. On the **Insert tab**, in the **Tables group**, click the **Table** button, and then click **Excel Spreadsheet**. Notice that an Excel spreadsheet displays and the table displays on **Page 2** in the document.

> **Alert! | Why Doesn't My Excel Spreadsheet Display?**
>
> If a message box displays telling you that Word has encountered a problem and asking if you want to continue, click Yes. If you see a new, large Excel window that covers your Word document, simply continue with Step 3.

3 In cell **A1**, type **Trip** and then press Tab. In cell **B1**, type **Miles** and then press Tab. In cell **C1**, type **Amount** Compare your screen with Figure 7.42.

Figure 7.42

Excel spreadsheet

Cell A1

Row 1 with text inserted

4 Click in cell **A2**, type **Example** and then press Tab. In cell **B2**, type **247** and then press Tab. In cell **C2,** type **=B2*0.5**

The formula is based on a mileage reimbursement rate of 50 cents per mile.

5 Press Enter, and notice that the value *123.5* displays in cell **C2**.

Calculations can be performed in the spreadsheet with the full capability of Excel. In Excel, all formulas are preceded by the = symbol. In this case, the formula prompts the program to multiply the number in cell B2 by 0.50, the company's mileage reimbursement rate. The calculated value displays in cell C2.

6 Click in cell **C2**, and then on the **Home tab**, in the **Number group**, click the **Increase Decimal** button.

7 With cell C2 selected, in the lower right corner of the cell, point to the fill handle—the small black square—until the + pointer displays, as shown in Figure 7.43.

Figure 7.43

Increase Decimal button

Cell C2

Fill handle pointer

8 With the ⊞ pointer displayed, drag down to cell **C8**. Notice that the number *0.00* displays in cells **C3** through **C8**.

> Dragging the fill handle copies the formula in C2 to the cells below. Excel changes the cell references in the formula to match the row number—for example, in cell C3 the formula is copied as =B3*0.5. Because you haven't entered any data in rows 3 through 8, the Amount column displays a value of 0 for those rows. You copied the formula so that the person using the form can calculate the reimbursement amount for several trips without having to delete any data in the spreadsheet.

9 Select cells **A1 through C1**. On the **Home tab**, in the **Styles group**, click the **Cell Styles** button. In the **Cell Styles** gallery, under **Themed Cell Styles**, in the last column, click the fourth style—**Accent6**.

10 On the right edge of the spreadsheet, point to the middle sizing handle until the ↔ pointer displays. Compare your screen with Figure 7.44

Figure 7.44

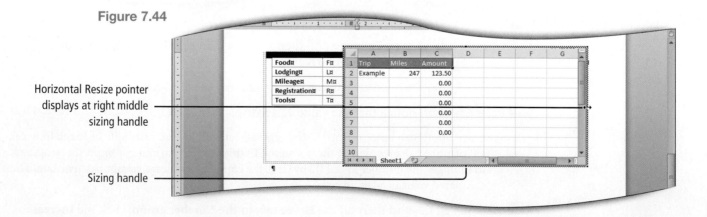

Horizontal Resize pointer displays at right middle sizing handle

Sizing handle

11 Drag to the left until only **columns A, B, and C** display. If necessary, on the right side of the spreadsheet, drag the middle sizing handle to fully display columns A, B, and C.

12 At the bottom of the spreadsheet, point to the middle sizing handle until the ⟂ pointer displays. Drag upward until only **rows 1 through 4** display. If necessary, at the bottom of the spreadsheet, drag the middle sizing handle up or down to fully display rows 1 through 4. Compare your screen with Figure 7.45.

Figure 7.45

Columns A to C

Rows 1 to 4

13 To close the Excel spreadsheet, click in a blank area of the document. Click in a blank area of the cell containing the Excel table, and then on the **Layout tab**, in the **Alignment group**, click the **Align Center** button ▤. In the **Table group**, click the **View Gridlines** button to turn it off.

14 Display the **Document Information Panel**. In the **Author** box, delete any existing text, and then type your first and last names. In the **Subject** box, type your course name and section number, and in the **Keywords** box, type **expense form, nested tables** **Close** ✕ the Document Information Panel.

15 **Save** ▤ your changes. Print your document, or submit electronically, as directed by your instructor. **Exit** Word.

End **You have completed Project 7B**

Content-Based Assessments

Summary

Word has advanced tools that enable you to present table data efficiently and attractively—such as changing alignment within cells, merging and splitting cells, sorting data, and changing text direction. Creating a table style standardizes the appearance of multiple tables. The Draw Table command gives you the flexibility to form rows and columns of varying size and format. Inserting an Excel spreadsheet allows for you to include complex calculations within the document.

Key Terms

Matching

Match each term in the second column with its correct definition in the first column by writing the letter of the term on the blank line in front of the correct definition.

_____ 1. A combination of formatting commands that can be saved with a name and stored as a set.

_____ 2. A style that includes formatting for the entire table and specific table elements.

_____ 3. The first row of a table containing column titles.

_____ 4. A feature that combines two or more adjacent cells into one cell.

_____ 5. A feature that divides a cell into multiple cells.

_____ 6. A feature that automatically adjusts table or column widths.

_____ 7. A mathematical expression that contains functions, operators, and constants.

_____ 8. A predefined formula that performs calculations using specific values.

_____ 9. A title that is added to a Word object and numbered sequentially.

_____ 10. A feature that resizes selected columns so that they are equal in width.

_____ 11. A feature that resizes selected rows so that they are equal in height.

_____ 12. Nonprinting lines that indicate cell borders.

_____ 13. A table inserted within a cell of another table.

_____ 14. The amount of space between a cell's content and the cell's borders.

_____ 15. The distance between the individual cells in a table.

A AutoFit

B Caption

C Cell margins

D Cell spacing

E Distribute Columns

F Distribute Rows

G Formula

H Function

I Gridlines

J Header row

K Merge

L Nested table

M Split

N Style

O Table style

Content-Based Assessments

Multiple Choice

Circle the correct answer.

1. What option do you select to edit an existing table style?
   A. Apply (and Clear Formatting)
   B. Apply and Maintain Formatting
   C. Modify Table Style

2. When splitting a cell that contains text, the text is moved to the:
   A. top left cell
   B. bottom right cell
   C. top right cell

3. In a table, you can define specific data to be sorted using a maximum of:
   A. three columns
   B. two columns
   C. one column

4. What command changes text separated by commas to a table format?
   A. Modify Table Style
   B. Convert Paragraph Text
   C. Convert Text to Table

5. To automatically resize the column width to accommodate existing text, select:
   A. AutoFit Contents
   B. AutoFit Text
   C. AutoFit Window

6. In Word, one of the built-in functions is:
   A. AVERAGE
   B. AVG
   C. TOTAL

7. A formula used in a Word table always begins with:
   A. a built-in function
   B. a left parenthesis
   C. an equal sign

8. A placeholder for data, such as a value calculated by a formula, is a:
   A. cell
   B. field
   C. table

9. What feature can you use to merge cells by removing specific borders from a table?
   A. Draw Table
   B. Eraser
   C. No Borders

10. In Excel, to copy a formula to adjacent cells use the:
    A. Copy handle
    B. Fill handle
    C. Resizing handle

Content-Based Assessments

Skills Review | Project **7C** Sales Conference

In the following Skills Review project, you will format tables and insert formulas to create a memo regarding a conference for sales managers at Rubanne Specialties. Your completed document will look similar to Figure 7.46.

Project Files

For Project 7C, you will need the following file:

w07C_Sales_Conference

You will save your file as:

Lastname_Firstname_7C_Sales_Conference

Project Results

Throughout the conference, we will be honoring many of you for the efforts you've made to secure new clients and maintain existing relationships. Several of you will also have the opportunity to share specific success stories from the past year that will inspire us all.

Rubanne Specialties

TO: All Sales Managers

FROM: Connor Fereday, Marketing Vice President

DATE: March 3

RE: Annual Sales Conference

This past year was highly successful for Rubanne Specialties. In preparation for the annual sales conference to be held March 20 at our corporate headquarters in Montreal, I would like to review our accomplishments during the past year.

After conducting extensive customer research and launching our extensive line of new products, we expanded our customer base to include leisure and adventure travelers, as well as fashion-savvy men and women.

We have had a huge increase in online sales due to a more attractive user-friendly Web site and new online marketing tactics. Rubanne Specialties products are being sold in forty additional retail stores in Canada and the United States, as noted in the tables below. We owe this success to the diligence of our extraordinary sales team.

Table 1: New Canadian Stores

Province	# of Stores
Nova Scotia	1
British Columbia	2
Quebec	3
Ontario	6
Total Stores	12

Table 2: New US Stores

State	# of Stores
New Hampshire	1
Michigan	2
Virginia	3
New York	6
Florida	7
California	9
Total Stores	28

...3 lists the topics and speakers for the ...ence. If you have not yet made your ...tion, please contact me at ...ay@rubannespecialties.com. I look ...d to seeing you at the conference on ...20.

Lastname_Firstname_7C_Sales_Conference

Figure 7.46

(Project 7C Sales Conference continues on the next page)

Content-Based Assessments

1 **Start** Word. Navigate to your student files and open the file **w07C_Sales_Conference**. **Save** the document in your **Word Chapter 7** folder as **Lastname_Firstname_7C_Sales_Conference** Using **Quick Parts**, insert the file name in the footer, and display the rulers and formatting marks. If any words are flagged as spelling errors, **Ignore All**.

a. Select the first paragraph, and then apply the **Title** style. For each of the next four paragraphs, select the heading—including the colon—and apply **Bold**.

b. On the **Home tab**, in the **Styles group**, click the **Dialog Box Launcher** to display the **Styles** window. At the bottom of the **Styles** window, click the **New Style** button. In the **Create New Style from Formatting** dialog box, under **Properties**, in the **Name** box, type **Sales Conference** click the **Style type arrow**, and then click **Table**.

c. Under **Formatting**, click the **Line Weight arrow**, and then click **2 ¼ pt**. Click the **Border Color arrow**, and then click **Blue, Accent 1**—in the fifth column, the first color. Click the **Border button arrow**, and then click **All Borders**.

d. Under **Formatting**, click the **Apply formatting to arrow**, and then click **Header row**. Click the **Fill Color arrow**, and then click **Blue, Accent 1, Lighter 60%**—in the fifth column, the third color. Click **OK**. **Close** the **Styles** window.

2 In the first table in the document, click in the first cell. On the **Design tab**, in the **Table Styles group**, click the **Sales Conference** table style. In a similar manner, click in the first cell in the second table of the document, and then apply the **Sales Conference** table style.

a. On the **Design tab**, in the **Table Style group**, right-click the **Sales Conference** table style, and then click **Modify Table Style**. Click the **Apply formatting to arrow**, and then click **Header row**. Apply **Bold**, and then click **OK**.

b. In the first table, position the insertion point to the right of *Province*. On the **Layout tab**, in the **Merge group**, click the **Split Cells** button, and then click **OK**. In the first row, click in the second cell, and type **# of Stores**

c. Select the header row, and then on the **Layout tab**, in the **Alignment group**, click the **Align Center** button. In the first column, select all cells below the header

row, and then click the **Align Center Left** button. In the second column, select all cells below the header row, and then click the **Align Center** button.

d. In the second table, position the insertion point to the right of *State*. On the **Layout tab**, in the **Merge group**, click the **Split Cells** button, and then click **OK**. In the first row, click in the second cell, and type **# of Stores**

e. Select the header row, and then on the **Layout tab**, in the **Alignment group**, click the **Align Center** button. In the first column, select all cells below the header row, and then click the **Align Center Left** button. In the second column, select all cells below the header row, and then click the **Align Center** button.

3 Click anywhere in the first table, and then on the **Layout tab**, in the **Data group**, click the **Sort** button. Click the **Sort by arrow**, click **# of Stores**, and then click **OK**. Click anywhere in the second table, and then in the **Data group**, click the **Sort** button. In the **Sort** dialog box, click the **Sort by arrow**, click **# of Stores**, if necessary, and then click **OK**.

4 Near the top of the **Page 2**, locate and then select the paragraph *Conference Information*. On the Mini toolbar, change the **Font Size** to **14**, apply **Bold** and **Center**, and then change the **Font Color** to **Blue, Accent 1, Darker 25%**—in the fifth column, the fifth color.

a. Locate the paragraph that begins *Topic*, and then drag to select all the remaining text in the document—a total of six paragraphs selected.

b. On the **Insert tab**, in the **Tables group**, click the **Table** button, and then click **Convert Text to Table**. Click **OK** to close the dialog box.

5 Click to position your insertion point anywhere in the table you inserted. On the **Design tab**, in the **Table Styles group**, click the **Sales Conference** table style.

a. On the **Layout tab**, in the **Cell Size group**, click the **AutoFit** button, and then click **AutoFit Contents**.

b. Select the **header row**, and then in the **Alignment group**, click the **Align Center** button. Select the remaining cells in the table, and then click the **Align Center Left** button.

6 In the first table, click to position the insertion point in the first cell of the last row. On the **Layout tab**, in the **Cell Size group**, click the **AutoFit** button, and then click

(Project 7C Sales Conference continues on the next page)

AutoFit Contents. In the **Rows & Columns group**, click the **Insert Below** button.

a. In the first cell of the last row, type **Total Stores** Select the text, and apply **Bold**. In the **Alignment group**, click the **Align Center Right** button. Press `Tab`, and then in the **Data group**, click the **Formula** button.

b. In the **Formula** dialog box, with *=SUM(ABOVE)* displayed, click the **Number format arrow**, and then click **0**. Click **OK**. Select the inserted text, and apply **Bold**.

7 In the second table, click to position the insertion point in the first cell of the last row. On the **Layout tab**, in the **Cell Size group**, click the **AutoFit** button, and then click **AutoFit Contents**. In the **Rows & Columns group**, click the **Insert Below** button.

a. In the first cell of the last row, type **Total Stores** Select the text, and apply **Bold**. In the **Alignment group**, click the **Align Center Right** button. Press `Tab`, and then in the **Data group**, click the **Formula** button.

b. In the **Formula** dialog box, with *=SUM(ABOVE)* displayed, click the **Number format arrow**, and then click **0**. Click **OK**. Select the inserted text, and apply **Bold**.

c. In the first table, in the second column, click in the fifth cell. Select *5*, and then type **6** In the last cell of the table, select *11*, right-click the selection, and then click **Update Field**.

d. In the second table, in the second column, click in the sixth cell. Select *8*, and then type **7** In the last cell of the table, select *29*, right-click the selection, and then click **Update Field**.

8 Click to position the insertion point anywhere in the first table. On the **References tab**, in the **Captions group**, click the **Insert Caption** button. In the **Caption** dialog box, with the insertion point to the right of *Table 1*, type **:** press `Spacebar`, and then type **New Canadian Stores** If necessary, under **Options**, click the **Position arrow**, and then click **Above selected item**. Click **OK**.

a. Click to position the insertion point anywhere in the second table. In the **Captions group**, click the **Insert**

Caption button. In the **Caption** dialog box, with the insertion point to the right of *Table 2*, type **:** press `Spacebar`, and then type **New US Stores** If necessary, under **Options**, click the **Position arrow**, and then click **Above selected item**. Click **OK**.

b. Click to position the insertion point anywhere in the last table. On the **Layout tab**, in the **Table group**, click the **Properties** button. In the **Table Properties** dialog box, if necessary, under **Text wrapping**, click **Around**, and then click the **Positioning** button.

c. In the **Table Positioning** dialog box, under **Distance from surrounding text**, click the **Right up spin arrow** to **0.5"**. Click **OK** two times to close the dialog boxes. Display the **Layout Selector**, and drag the table up until the top border is even with the first line of the last paragraph.

d. Click anywhere in the table. On the **References tab**, in the **Captions group**, click the **Insert Caption** button. In the **Caption** dialog box, with *Table 3* displayed, click **OK**. In the last paragraph of the document, select the text *Listed below are*, and then type **Table 3 lists**

9 Click to position the insertion point anywhere in the first table. On the **Layout tab**, in the **Table group**, click the **Properties** button. In the **Table Properties** dialog box, under **Alignment**, click the **Center** button, and then click **OK**. Click to position the insertion point anywhere in the second table. In the **Table group**, click the **Properties** button. In the **Table Properties** dialog box, under **Alignment**, click the **Center** button, and then click **OK**. Select the captions for *Table 1* and *Table 2*, and then apply **Center**.

10 Press `Ctrl` + `Home`, and then display the **Document Information Panel**. In the **Author** box, delete any existing text, and then type your first and last names. In the **Subject** box, type your course name and section number, and in the **Keywords** box, type **sales conference Close** the Document Information Panel. **Save** your document.

11 Print your document or submit electronically as directed by your instructor. **Exit** Word.

End You have completed Project 7C ─────────────

Content-Based Assessments

Apply 7B skills from these Objectives:

5 Draw a Freeform Table

6 Use Nested Tables

7 Insert an Excel Spreadsheet

Skills Review | Project **7D** Registration Form

In the following Skills Review project, you will create a registration form for the employee charity golf tournament sponsored by Rubanne Specialties. Your completed document will look similar to Figure 7.47.

Project Files

For Project 7D, you will need the following file:

w07D_Registration_Form

You will save your document as:

Lastname_Firstname_7D_Registration_Form

Project Results

Figure 7.47

(Project 7D Registration Form continues on the next page)

Content-Based Assessments

1 **Start** Word. Navigate to your student files and open the file **w07D_Registration_Form**. **Save** the document in your **Word Chapter 7** folder as **Lastname_Firstname_7D_Registration_Form** Using **Quick Parts**, insert the file name in the footer, and display the rulers and formatting marks. If any words are flagged as spelling errors, **Ignore All**.

a. Select the first two paragraphs. Change the **Font Size** to **26**, apply **Bold** and **Center**, and change the **Font Color** to **Olive Green, Accent 3, Darker 50%**. Select the fourth paragraph—*Registration Form*. Change the **Font Size** to **16**, apply **Bold** and **Center**, and change the **Font Color** to **Olive Green, Accent 3, Darker 50%**.

2 Click to position the insertion point in the fifth paragraph, which is blank. On the **Insert tab**, in the **Tables group**, click the **Table** button, and then click **Draw Table**.

a. Position the ✏ pointer at the left margin and at approximately **3.25 inches on the vertical ruler**. Drag down and to the right until the guides are at approximately **6.5 inches on the horizontal ruler** and at **8 inches on the vertical ruler**. Release the mouse button. If necessary, on the **Design tab**, in the **Draw Borders group**, change the **Line Weight** to **½ pt** and the **Pen Color to Automatic**.

b. With the insertion point in the table, on the **Home tab**, in the **Styles group**, click the **No Spacing** style, and then change the **Font Size** to **12**.

c. On the **Design tab**, in the **Draw Borders group**, click the **Draw Table** button. Position the ✏ pointer on the left border of the table at approximately **3.5 inches on the vertical ruler**, and then drag to the right table border. In a similar manner, draw horizontal lines at approximately **4 inches**, **4.75 inches**, and **7.5 inches on the vertical ruler**.

d. Position the ✏ pointer on the top border of the table at approximately **0.5 inch on the horizontal ruler**, and drag down three rows. Position the ✏ pointer on the top border at approximately **3.25 inches on the horizontal ruler**, and drag down to the bottom of the table. Click the **Draw Table** button to turn it off.

e. On the **Design tab**, in the **Draw Borders group**, click the **Eraser** button. In the first cell of the table, position the 🧽 pointer on the bottom cell border and click. In the newly merged cell, position the 🧽 pointer on

the bottom cell border and click. In the fourth row, in the first cell, position the 🧽 pointer on the right cell border and click. Click the **Eraser** button to turn it off.

3 Starting in the second column, select the first three rows of the table. On the **Layout tab**, in the **Cell Size group**, click the **Distribute Rows** button. Click in the fourth row. On the **Design tab**, in the **Table Styles group**, click the **Borders button arrow**, and then click **Left Border**. Click the **Borders button arrow**, and then click **Right Border**. Select the last row, click the **Borders button arrow**, and then click **No Border**. If necessary, on the **Layout tab**, in the **Table group**, click the **View Gridlines** button to display the gridlines.

a. In the first row of the table, in the second cell, type **Name:** Press Tab, and then type **Department:** In the second row, in the cell below *Name*, type **Phone:** Press Tab, and then type **E-mail:** In the third row, in the cell below *Phone*, type **Home Address:** Select the text in the three rows, and then on the **Layout tab**, in the **Alignment group**, click the **Align Center Left** button.

b. In the third row of the table, select the second and third cells, and then on the **Layout tab**, in the **Merge group**, click the **Merge Cells** button. Position the insertion point in the first cell of the table, and then on the **Layout tab**, in the **Alignment group**, click the **Text Direction** button two times. Type **Employee Information** In the **Alignment group**, click the **Align Center** button, and then apply **Bold**.

c. In the last row of the table, click in the first cell, and then in the **Alignment group**, click the **Align Center Right** button. Type **Amount Enclosed:** press Tab, and then type **$** In the **Alignment group**, click the **Align Center Left** button. In the last row, select both cells, and then apply **Bold**.

4 Click to position the insertion point in the fourth row of the table. On the **Insert tab**, in the **Tables group**, click the **Table** button, and then under **Insert Table**, in the **Table** grid, in the second row, click the second square to insert a 2×2 table.

a. On the **Layout tab**, in the **Alignment group**, click the **Cell Margins** button. In the **Table Options** dialog box, under **Default cell margins**, change the **Top** and **Bottom** margins to **0.01"**, change the **Left** and **Right** margins to **0.5"**.

(Project 7D Registration Form continues on the next page)

Content-Based Assessments

b. Under **Default cell spacing**, click to select the **Allow spacing between cells** check box, and then change the cell spacing to **0.1"**. Click **OK**.

c. In the nested table, select the two cells in the first column, and then on the **Layout tab**, in the **Merge group**, click the **Merge Cells** button. Select the nested table. On the **Design tab**, in the **Table Styles group**, click the **Borders button arrow**, and then click **No Border**.

5 Click to position the insertion point in the first cell of the nested table. On the **Insert tab**, in the **Illustrations group**, click the **Clip Art** button. In the displayed **Clip Art** pane, in the **Search for** box, type **golf** and then press Enter. In the **Clip Art** pane, click the image shown in Figure 7.47, or select a similar graphic. **Close** the **Clip Art** pane.

a. Click in the top right cell of the nested table, and then type **Use the Excel spreadsheet below to calculate the total amount due.** Click to position the insertion point in the bottom right cell. On the **Insert tab**, in the **Tables group**, click the **Table** button, and then click **Excel Spreadsheet**. If a message displays asking if you want to continue, click **Yes**.

b. Click to position the insertion point in cell **A1**, if necessary, and then type **Day** Press Tab, and then in cell **B1**, type **Item** Press Tab, and then in cell **C1**, type **Charge** Press Tab, and then in cell **D1**, type **Your Cost** Type the following text in the appropriate cells under the headings you typed:

Day	Item	Charge	Your Cost
	Entry Fee	$150	
Friday	Breakfast	$10	
Friday	Lunch	$20	
Saturday	Breakfast	$10	
Saturday	Lunch	$20	
	Total		

c. Click in cell **C7**, type **=SUM(C2:C6)** and then press Tab. In cell **D7**, type **=SUM(D2:D6)** and then press Enter. Select cells **A1 through D7**. On the **Home tab**, in the **Styles group**, click the **Cell Styles** button. In the **Cell Styles** gallery, under **Themed Cell Styles**, click **Accent3**.

d. On the right edge of the spreadsheet, point to the middle sizing handle, and drag to the left until only **columns A through D** display. At the bottom of the spreadsheet, point to the middle sizing handle, and drag upward until only **rows 1 through 7** display. To close the Excel spreadsheet, click in a blank area of the table. On the **Layout tab**, in the **Table group**, click the **View Gridlines** button to turn it off.

6 Press Ctrl + Home, and then display the **Document Information Panel**. In the **Author** box, type your first and last names. In the **Subject** box, type your course name and section number, and in the **Keywords** box, type **registration form, golf tournament Close** the Document Information Panel. **Save** your document. Print your document or submit electronically as directed by your instructor. Click the **File tab**, and then click **Exit** to exit Word.

End **You have completed Project 7D**

Content-Based Assessments

Mastering Word | Project **7E** Travel Bags

In the following Mastering Word project, you will create a memo to all Rubanne Specialties sales managers announcing the Illumina Collection of travel bags. Your completed document will look similar to Figure 7.48.

Project Files

For Project 7E, you will need the following file:

w07E_Travel_Bags

You will save your document as:

Lastname_Firstname_7E_Travel_Bags

Project Results

Memo

TO:	All Sales Managers
FROM:	Connor Fereday, Marketing Vice President
DATE:	September 20
RE:	Illumina Collection

Rubanne Specialties is proud to add the Illumina Collection to our travel bag line of leather and fabric accessories for men and women. Designed for the active traveler, these products were carefully crafted to meet the needs of our customers, who crave the best in quality, durability, functionality, and aesthetics. Please familiarize yourself with these items as they will be available for distribution to stores next month.

Table 1: Illumina Collection

Day Pack	This is a comfortable, roomy yet lightweight bag that can hold a wallet, sunglasses, camera, maps, and a guide book.	$ 59
Laptop Case	A classic style, this case includes a pocket ideal for storing a PDA, cell phone, cables, cords, and more. The sturdy frame holds your laptop securely. The shoulder strap has a shoulder pad to make carrying more comfortable.	$ 79
Tote Bag	This soft yet durable leather bag is perfect for shopping trips. It also includes a pocket for travel documents and other papers.	$ 79
Messenger Bag	This casual day bag carries all the essentials and includes many pockets to keep it all organized. The material is soft yet durable. The shoulder strap has a shoulder pad to make carrying more comfortable.	$ 99
Large Backpack	This backpack safely stores a laptop computer while providing plenty of extra room for electronic accessories, a change of clothes, personal items, and more. The backpack straps have been developed to be supportive and comfortable.	$ 129
Rolling Garment Bag	This bag includes individual shoe pockets, a hook for hanging garments, and foam padding to protect clothes and minimize wrinkling. It is ideal for a short trip.	$ 349
	Average Price	**$ 132**

Lastname_Firstname_7E_Travel_Bags

Figure 7.48

(Project 7E Travel Bags continues on the next page)

Content-Based Assessments

1 **Start** Word. Navigate to your student files, and open the file **w07E_Travel_Bags**. Save the document in your **Word Chapter 7** folder as **Lastname_Firstname_7E_Travel_Bags** Insert the file name in the footer, and display the rulers and formatting marks. **Ignore All** names flagged as spelling errors.

2 Select the first paragraph and apply the **Title** style. For each of the next four paragraphs, select the heading—including the colon—and apply **Bold**.

3 Display the **Styles** window, and then click the **New Style** button. In the **Create New Style from Formatting** dialog box, for the **Name**, type **Illumina Collection** Change the **Style type** to **Table**. Change the **Line Weight** to **2 ¼ pt**. Change the **Border Color** to **Dark Blue, Text 2, Lighter 40%**. Apply the border style to **All Borders**, and then click **OK**. **Close** the **Styles** window.

4 Locate the paragraph that begins *Rolling Garment Bag*, drag to select the remaining six paragraphs of the document, and then **Convert Text to Table**. With the insertion point anywhere in the table, **Sort** the table by **Column 3** in **Ascending** order. Apply the **Illumina Collection** table style. Select the first two columns of the table, and change the alignment to **Align Center Left**. Select the third column, and change the alignment to **Align Center**. Resize the table to **AutoFit Contents**. In the

second column, select all six cells, and then change the **Width** to **4.5"**.

5 Position the insertion point in the last row of the table, and then click **Insert Below**. Select the first and second cells in the bottom row, and then **Merge Cells**. Change the alignment to **Align Center Right**, type **Average Price** and then apply **Bold**. In the last cell of the table, click **Formula**, change the **Formula** to **=AVERAGE(ABOVE)** change the **Number format** to **#,##0**, and then to the left of the number format, type **$** Click **OK**. Select the displayed value, and apply **Bold**.

6 Display the **Table Properties** dialog box, and then change the table alignment to **Center**.

7 Click **Insert Caption**, and then modify the text as necessary to display as *Table 1: Illumina Collection*. Select the caption, and then change the **Font Size** to **12**.

8 Press [Ctrl] + [Home]. Display the **Document Information Panel**, type your name as **Author**, and your course name and section number as the **Subject**. In the **Keywords** box, type **travel bags, Illumina Close** the Document Information Panel, and then **Save** your document.

9 Print your document or submit electronically as directed by your instructor. **Exit** Word.

End **You have completed Project 7E** ——————————————

Content-Based Assessments

Mastering Word | Project **7F** Buyer Program

In the following Mastering Word project, you will create a flyer explaining the Frequent Buyer program to Rubanne Specialties customers. Your completed document will look similar to Figure 7.49.

Project Files

For Project 7F, you will need the following file:

w07F_Buyer_Program

You will save your document as:

Lastname_Firstname_7F_Buyer_Program

Project Results

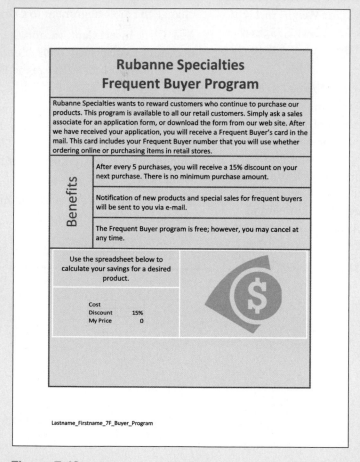

Figure 7.49

(Project 7F Buyer Program continues on the next page)

Content-Based Assessments

Mastering Word | Project 7F Buyer Program (continued)

1 **Start** Word. Navigate to your student files, and open the file **w07F_Buyer_Program**. **Save** the document in your **Word Chapter 7** folder as **Lastname_Firstname_7F_Buyer_Program** Using **Quick Parts**, insert the file name in the footer, and display rulers and formatting marks.

2 Select the entire document, change the style to **No Spacing**, change the **Font Size** to **14**, and then **Convert Text to Table**. Select the first cell, and change the **Width** to **1"**. Select the second cell, and change the **Width** to **5.5"**. Display the **Create New Style from Formatting** dialog box and create a new style named **Buyer Program** Set the **Style type** to **Table**, set the **Line Weight** to **2 ¼ pt**, set the **Border Color** to **Olive Green, Accent 3, Darker 50%**, and apply to **All Borders**. Apply the **Buyer Program** table style to the table.

3 On the **Layout tab**, in the **Rows & Columns group**, click **Insert Above**. Click anywhere in the second row, and then click **Insert Below**. In the last row, change the **Height** to **4.8"**. In the first row, change the **Height** to **1.2"**.

4 Click the **Draw Table** button. Begin at the left border of the table and at **5.5 inches on the vertical ruler**, and draw a horizontal line extending to the right border of the table. Begin at the right border of the first column and at **4.5 inches on the vertical ruler**, and draw a horizontal line extending to the right table border. In a similar manner, draw a horizontal line positioned at **5 inches on the vertical ruler**. In the first row, use the **Eraser** to remove the border between the two cells. In a similar manner, use the **Eraser** to remove the inside border in the second and sixth rows. Turn off the **Eraser**.

5 In the first row of the table, type **Rubanne Specialties** press Enter, and then type **Frequent Buyer Program** Select the text, change the **Font Size** to **28 pt**, apply **Bold** and **Center**, and then change the **Font Color** to **Olive Green, Accent 3, Darker 50%**. Click **Align Center**.

6 In the third row, select the first cell and three cells to the right of it, and then change the **Height** to **0.75"**. Click in the first cell of the third row, click **Align Center**, and then click **Text Direction** two times. Type **Benefits** Select

the text, and change the **Font Size** to **28 pt**, and the **Font Color** to **Olive Green, Accent 3, Darker 50%**.

7 In the second row, select the last sentence that begins *The Frequent*, and drag to move the text to the second cell in the fifth row. In a similar manner, move the sentence that begins *Notification* to the fourth row, and then move the two sentences beginning with *After* and ending with *amount* to the third row. Select all three cells to the right of *Benefits*, and then click **Align Center Left**. Remove any unnecessary spaces that display at the end of the paragraphs in **rows 2 through 5**.

8 In the last row of the table, insert a nested table that contains two rows and two columns. Select the entire nested table, and apply **No Border**. Change all **Cell Margins** to **0.1"**, change **Default cell spacing** to **0.3"**, and then click **Align Center**. Select the second column, and then **Merge Cells**. In the first cell of the first column, type **Use the spreadsheet below to calculate your savings for a desired product**. In the second cell of the first column, insert an **Excel Spreadsheet**—if necessary, click Yes to continue. In cell **A1**, type **Cost** in cell **A2**, type **Discount** and then in cell **A3**, type **My Price** In cell **B2**, type **15%** and then in cell **B3**, type **=B1*.85** Press Enter. Resize the spreadsheet to display only **columns A and B** and **rows 1 through 3**, and then click in a blank area of the document. In the second column, click to position the insertion point, display the **Clip Art** pane, search for **money** and then insert the image shown in Figure 7.49 or a similar graphic. **Close** the **Clip Art** pane.

9 Select the entire main table, and then change the **Shading** to **Olive Green, Accent 3, Lighter 60%**.

10 Press Ctrl + Home. Display the **Document Information Panel**, type your name as **Author** and your course name and section number as the **Subject**. In the **Keywords** box, type **frequent buyer program Close** the **Document Information Panel**, and then **Save** your document. Print your document or submit electronically as directed by your instructor. **Exit** Word.

End **You have completed Project 7F**

Content-Based Assessments

- **1** Create and Apply a Custom Table Style
- **2** Format Cells
- **3** Use Advanced Table Features
- **4** Modify Table Properties
- **5** Draw a Freeform Table
- **6** Use Nested Tables
- **7** Insert an Excel Spreadsheet

Mastering Word | Project **7G** Holiday Special

In the following Mastering Word project, you will create a flyer that provides descriptions of new products available for holiday shopping at Rubanne Specialties. Your completed document will look similar to Figure 7.50.

Project Files

For Project 7G, you will need the following file:

w07G_Holiday_Special

You will save your document as:

Lastname_Firstname_7G_Holiday_Special

Project Results

New Products for the Businesswoman

Just in time for the holiday shopping season, Rubanne Specialties is pleased to add three computer bags to our Mainline Collection designed for the professional woman. These bags offer the same durability and quality as our other business bags but with an extra dose of style and sophistication for today's fashionable woman.

Item	Description	Price
Compact Bag	Special features include a pocket for items such as tickets and other travel information, and the most comfortable shoulder strap on the market. The computer sleeve has extra padding for the ultimate protection.	$ 149
Streamlined Tote	Available in a choice of five colors, the front pocket provides ample storage for tickets and other documents, metal feet protect the bag from dirty surfaces, extra padding in the computer sleeve stores your laptop securely, and the removable pouch can hold personal items.	$ 199
Large Tote	Similar to our other computer totes, this item has plenty of extra room for notebooks, pens, presentation information, personal items, and electronic accessories.	$ 209
	Average Price	$ 186

As a sales incentive during December, these items will be available at a 25% discount.

Retail Price	
Discount	25%
Sale Price	0

Lastname_Firstname_7G_Holiday_Special

Figure 7.50

(Project 7G Holiday Special continues on the next page)

Content-Based Assessments

Mastering Word | Project **7G** Holiday Special (continued)

1 **Start** Word, and then open the file **w07G_Holiday_Special**. Save the document in your **Word Chapter 7** folder as **Lastname_Firstname_7G_Holiday_Special** Insert the file name in the footer, and display rulers and formatting marks.

2 Select the first paragraph. Change the **Font Size** to **20**, apply **Bold** and **Center**, and then change the **Text Effects** to **Fill – Red, Accent 2, Double Outline – Accent 2**. Select the second paragraph, and then change the **Font Size** to **12**. Select the remaining three paragraphs of the document, change the **Font Size** to **14**, and then with the text still selected, **Convert Text to Table**.

3 Display the **Styles** window, and then click the **New Style** button. Display the **Create New Style from Formatting** dialog box and create a new style named **Holiday** Set the **Style type** to **Table**. Set the **Line Weight** to **2 ¼ pt**, and then set the **Border Color** to **Red, Accent 2, Darker 25%** and apply to **All Borders**. Apply the **Holiday** style to the entire table.

4 Select the first column, and change the column **Width** to **1.2"**. Change the second column **Width** to **4.5"**, and the third column **Width** to **0.7"**. Position the insertion point anywhere the first row, and click **Insert Above**. In the first cell of the table, type **Item** press `Tab`, type **Description** press `Tab`, and then type **Price** Select the header row, apply **Bold**, and then click **Align Center**. Change the row **Height** of rows 2, 3, and 4 to **1.5**, **1.8**, and **1.4**, respectively.

5 In the first column, select the cells below the header row. Apply **Bold**, click **Align Center**, and then click **Text Direction** two times. In the second column, select all cells below the header row, and then click **Align Center Left**. In the last column, select all cells below the header row, and click **Align Center**.

6 Position the insertion point in the last row of the table, and then click **Insert Below**. In the last row, change the **Height** to **0.4"**. Select the first and second cells, and then **Merge Cells**. Click **Align Center Right**, and then click **Text Direction**. Type **Average Price** and then apply **Bold**. In the last cell of the table, insert this **Formula: =AVERAGE(ABOVE)** Change the **Number format** to **#,##0**, to the left of the number format, type **$** and then click **OK**. Select the displayed text, and then apply **Bold**.

7 In the last row, click **Insert Below**. Select both cells in the last row, and then **Merge Cells**. Insert a table containing one row and two columns. Select both cells, and then apply **No Border**. Change all **Cell Margins** to **0.1"**, and then set **Allow spacing between cells** to **0.2"**. Click **Align Center**.

8 In the first cell of the nested table, type **As a sales incentive during December, these items will be available at a 25% discount.** In the second cell of the nested table, insert an **Excel Spreadsheet**. If necessary, click Yes to continue. In cell **A1**, type **Retail Price** in cell **A2**, type **Discount** and in cell **A3**, type **Sale Price** In cell **B2**, type **25%** and in cell **B3**, type **=B1*.75** Press `Enter`. Resize the spreadsheet to display only columns A and B and rows 1 through 3, and then click in a blank area of the document.

9 Press `Ctrl` + `Home`. Display the **Document Information Panel**, type your name as **Author** and your course name and section number as the **Subject**. In the **Keywords** box, type **holiday special, Mainline Close** the **Document Information Panel**. **Save** your document. Print the document or submit electronically as directed by your instructor, and then **Exit** Word.

End **You have completed Project 7G**

Content-Based Assessments

GO! Fix It | Project 7H Safety Program

Project Files

For Project 7H, you will need the following file:

w07H_Safety_Program

You will save your document as:

Lastname_Firstname_7H_Safety_Program

In this project you will edit a memo from Roslyn Godfrey, President of Rubanne Specialties, to all production supervisors. Navigate to your student files, open the file **w07H_Safety_Program**, and then save the file in your **Word Chapter 7** folder as **Lastname_Firstname_7H_Safety_Program**

To complete the project, you must revise the file by creating and sorting a table, modifying a table style, and formatting tables and text. Correct the following:

- The Title style should be applied to the first paragraph, and the four memo headings should be bold.

- The four paragraphs that reference dates should be converted to a table and then the table should be sorted in ascending order by date.

- A header row should be inserted in the second table. Merge the cells, and then type **Session Topics**

- The cell containing the text *General Information* should be merged with the three empty cells below. The text direction should be changed so that the text displays in an upward manner. In a similar manner, the cells containing *Environmental Issues* and *Avoiding Accidents* should be merged with empty cells below and the text direction modified.

- The table style should be modified to the Light List – Accent 1 table style and by changing the header row fill color to Dark Blue – Text 2. Apply the modified **Light List - Accent 1** table style to both tables.

- Table properties and cell alignments should be modified to create an attractive, one-page document.

- A footer should be inserted that includes the file name, and document properties should include the keywords **safety program, memo**

Save your document, and then print the document or submit electronically as directed by your instructor.

End **You have completed Project 7H** ————————————————

Content-Based Assessments

Apply a combination of the **7A** and **7B** skills.

GO! Make It | Project 7I Product Flyer

Project Files

For Project 7I, you will need the following file:

New blank Word document

You will save your document as:

Lastname_Firstname_7I_Product_Flyer

Open a new blank document and create the document shown in Figure 7.51. Draw the outside border of a table that measures **6.5** inches in width and **8** inches in height. Draw rows and columns. Remove appropriate borders. Format cells, borders, and text using the **Orange, Accent 6** color scheme. If necessary, substitute another image. Add document properties that include the keywords **home page, prototype** Save the file in your **Word Chapter 7** folder as **Lastname_Firstname_7I_Product_Flyer** and then print your document or submit electronically as directed by your instructor.

Project Results

Figure 7.51

End You have completed Project 7I

Content-Based Assessments

Apply a combination of
the **7A** and **7B** skills.

GO! Solve It | Project **7J** Planning Committee

Project Files

For Project 7J, you will need the following file:

w07J_Trade_Show

You will save your document as:

Lastname_Firstname_7J_Planning_Committee

From your student files, open the document **w07J_Trade_Show**. Save the file to your **Word Chapter 7** folder as **Lastname_Firstname_7J_Planning_Committee** Create a table style and apply it to the tables. In the second table, create a formula to display the total amount. Modify table and cell properties to create a professional appearance. Insert appropriate captions above the tables, and then replace existing paragraph text to reference the table names. At the end of the document, insert an Excel spreadsheet. Include the names of three products and their prices, and a bottom line that displays the total price. Format the two title lines and paragraph headings in the document, and make any other formatting changes to create an attractive two-page document. Insert the file name in the footer and add appropriate document properties. Print the document or submit electronically as directed by your instructor.

	Performance Level		
	Exemplary: You consistently applied the relevant skills	**Proficient:** You sometimes, but not always, applied the relevant skills	**Developing:** You rarely or never applied the relevant skills
Create and apply a table style	A new table style is created and applied to the tables.	A table style is applied to the tables, but it is a built-in style—not new.	No table style is applied to the tables.
Create a formula	The total amount is calculated using a formula and displays in a new row.	The total amount displays in a new row, but a formula is not used.	The total amount does not display in a new row.
Modify table and cell properties	The table and cell properties are modified appropriately.	At least one table or cell property is not modified appropriately.	No changes are made to table and cell properties.
Insert captions and replace text	Captions are inserted and related paragraph text is replaced.	Captions are inserted, but related paragraph text is not replaced.	No captions are inserted.
Insert Excel spreadsheet	An Excel spreadsheet is inserted and data is entered correctly.	An Excel spreadsheet is inserted, but not all data is entered correctly.	An Excel spreadsheet is not inserted.

Performance Element

End You have completed Project 7J

Content-Based Assessments

Apply a combination of the **7A** and **7B** skills.

GO! Solve It | Project **7K** Wallet Collection

Project Files

For Project 7K, you will need the following file:

w07K_Wallet_Collection

You will save your document as:

Lastname_Firstname_7K_Wallet_Collection

Open the file **w07K_Wallet_Collection** and save it to your **Word Chapter 7** folder as **Lastname_Firstname_7K_Wallet_Collection** Using the information for the specific wallets, convert the text to a table. Insert a header row, add appropriate column headings, and then sort the table by price and item name. Create a formula to display the average price of the items. Create and apply a table style. Adjust paragraph, text, table, and cell formats to display attractively in a one-page document. Insert the file name in the footer and add appropriate document properties. Print your document or submit electronically as directed by your instructor.

Performance Element	Performance Level		
	Exemplary: You consistently applied the relevant skills	**Proficient:** You sometimes, but not always, applied the relevant skills	**Developing:** You rarely or never applied the relevant skills
Convert text to table	All appropriate text is displayed in a table.	At least one item of text is not displayed in a table.	No text is displayed in a table.
Sort the table	The data in the table is sorted by both price and item name.	The data in the table is sorted only by price or item name.	The data in the table is not sorted.
Create a formula	The average price is calculated using a formula and displays in a new row.	The average price displays in a new row, but a formula is not used.	The average price does not display in a new row.
Create and apply a table style	A new table style is created and applied to the table.	A table style is applied to the table, but it is a built-in style—not new.	No table style is applied to the table.
Format the document	All items in the document are formatted appropriately.	At least one item in the document is not formatted appropriately.	No items in the document are formatted.

End You have completed Project 7K ———————

Outcomes-Based Assessments

Rubric

The following outcomes-based assessments are *open-ended assessments*. That is, there is no specific correct result; your result will depend on your approach to the information provided. Make *Professional Quality* your goal. Use the following scoring rubric to guide you in *how* to approach the problem and then to evaluate *how well* your approach solves the problem.

The *criteria*—Software Mastery, Content, Format and Layout, and Process—represent the knowledge and skills you have gained that you can apply to solving the problem. The *levels of performance*—Professional Quality, Approaching Professional Quality, or Needs Quality Improvements—help you and your instructor evaluate your result.

	Your completed project is of Professional Quality if you:	Your completed project is Approaching Professional Quality if you:	Your completed project Needs Quality Improvements if you:
1-Software Mastery	Choose and apply the most appropriate skills, tools, and features and identify efficient methods to solve the problem.	Choose and apply some appropriate skills, tools, and features, but not in the most efficient manner.	Choose inappropriate skills, tools, or features, or are inefficient in solving the problem.
2-Content	Construct a solution that is clear and well organized, contains content that is accurate, appropriate to the audience and purpose, and is complete. Provide a solution that contains no errors in spelling, grammar, or style.	Construct a solution in which some components are unclear, poorly organized, inconsistent, or incomplete. Misjudge the needs of the audience. Have some errors in spelling, grammar, or style, but the errors do not detract from comprehension.	Construct a solution that is unclear, incomplete, or poorly organized; contains some inaccurate or inappropriate content; and contains many errors in spelling, grammar, or style. Do not solve the problem.
3-Format and Layout	Format and arrange all elements to communicate information and ideas, clarify function, illustrate relationships, and indicate relative importance.	Apply appropriate format and layout features to some elements, but not others. Overuse features, causing minor distraction.	Apply format and layout that does not communicate information or ideas clearly. Do not use format and layout features to clarify function, illustrate relationships, or indicate relative importance. Use available features excessively, causing distraction.
4-Process	Use an organized approach that integrates planning, development, self-assessment, revision, and reflection.	Demonstrate an organized approach in some areas, but not others; or, use an insufficient process of organization throughout.	Do not use an organized approach to solve the problem.

Outcomes-Based Assessments

Apply a combination of the **7A** and **7B** skills.

GO! Think | Project **7L** Company Picnic

Project Files

For Project 7L, you will need the following file:

New blank Word document

You will save your document as:

Lastname_Firstname_7L_Company_Picnic

Every year, Rubanne Specialties holds a picnic for employees and their families. This year the picnic will be held on June 16 from 10 a.m. to 4 p.m. at Regents Park in Montreal. Lunch and snacks are provided. There will be music and an assortment of games for young and old. In addition, other park activities are available for a fee—such as pony rides and miniature golf.

Using this information, create a flyer to distribute to employees as an e-mail attachment. Create a document that explains the picnic and lists the schedule of events in a table format. Insert a second table that lists fees for specific activities. Use a formula to provide the total cost for these events. Create a table style and apply it to both tables. Format the flyer, including table and cell properties, so that it is attractive and easy to read. Save the file as **Lastname_Firstname_7L_ Company_Picnic** Insert the file name in the footer and add appropriate document properties. Print the document or submit as directed by your instructor.

End You have completed Project 7L ———————————————

Apply a combination of the **7A** and **7B** skills.

GO! Think | Project **7M** Employee Newsletter

Project Files

For Project 7M, you will need the following file:

New blank Word document

You will save your document as:

Lastname_Firstname_7M_Employee_Newsletter

Connor Fereday, Marketing Vice President, sends a one-page monthly newsletter to all employees in the Sales Department at Rubanne Specialties. Articles include descriptions and prices of new products, employee birthdays, information about the outstanding employee of the month, and other pertinent information. Employees receive a 35 percent discount on any new product.

Using this information, design a new format for the newsletter. Create a document that contains a freeform table. Cells should include a newsletter heading, article headings, and space for article text. Using a nested table, insert an appropriate graphic and an Excel spreadsheet that employees can use to calculate the discounted prices of new products. Applying the skills you have practiced, format the table in a manner that is professional and easy to read. Save the file as **Lastname_Firstname_7M_Employee_Newsletter** Insert the file name in the footer and add appropriate document properties. Print your document or submit electronically as directed by your instructor.

End You have completed Project 7M ———————————————

Outcomes-Based Assessments

You and GO! | Project **7N** Personal Budget

Project Files

For Project 7N, you will need the following file:

New blank Word document

You will save your document as:

Lastname_Firstname_7N_Personal_Budget

In a new document, create a three-column table including a header row. In the first column, list a minimum of six categories of expenses you have—such as food, clothing, and tuition. The second column should include your estimated expenses for one month. The third column should display actual expenses. The last row of the table should include formulas to calculate totals for the second and third columns. Using the formatting skills you have practiced, format the document in a manner that is professional and easy to read. Save the file as **Lastname_Firstname_7N_Personal_Budget** Insert the file name in the footer, and add appropriate document properties. Print the document or submit electronically as directed by your instructor.

End You have completed Project 7N ——————————————

Creating Mass Mailings

OUTCOMES

At the end of this chapter you will be able to:

PROJECT 8A
Filter records and create envelopes.

1. Merge a Data Source and a Main Document (p. 457)
2. Create Envelopes (p. 466)

PROJECT 8B
Create and modify a data source and create a directory.

3. Edit and Sort a Data Source (p. 472)
4. Match Fields and Apply Rules (p. 478)
5. Create a Data Source and a Directory (p. 482)

OBJECTIVES

Mastering these objectives will enable you to:

R. Gino Santa Maria/Shutterstock

In This Chapter

Mail merge provides a time-saving and convenient way to produce mass mailings. You can create personalized documents, such as customized letters and envelopes. You can construct your own table of data or use an existing file. You can sort and filter the data to specify what information will be used. For example, you might want to send individual letters to customers who live in a particular state or who purchased a particular cruise.

You can also use a data source with mail merge to generate a directory—for example, a list of all company employees and their office phone extensions. In this chapter, you will use data sources with mail merge to create letters, envelopes, postcards, and a directory.

The projects in this chapter relate to **Agua Azul Caribbean Cruises**, which specializes in exciting cruises in the Caribbean. With its tropical beauty and cultural diversity, the Caribbean region offers lush jungles, freshwater caves, miles of white sand beaches, ancient ruins, and charming cities. Ships are innovative and include rock climbing walls and extensive spa facilities. A variety of accommodations are available on each ship to meet the needs and budgets of a wide array of travelers. The gourmet food and entertainment are rated as exceptional by all.

Project 8A Customer Letters

Project 8A Training

Project Activities

In Activities 8.01 through 8.07, you will create a customized form letter and envelope for Agua Azul Caribbean Cruises so that the company can send a personalized letter to a targeted group of customers. The company is launching a new rewards program for its valued customers and is creating a document to send to all customers who previously booked multiple cruises. Your completed documents will look similar to Figure 8.1.

Project Files

For Project 8A, you will need the following files:

> Two new blank Word documents
> w08A_Customers

You will save your files as:

> Lastname_Firstname_8A_Customers—not shown in figure
> Lastname_Firstname_8A_Letters_Main
> Lastname_Firstname_8A_Letters_Merged
> Lastname_Firstname_8A_Envelopes_Main
> Lastname_Firstname_8A_Envelopes_Merged

Project Results

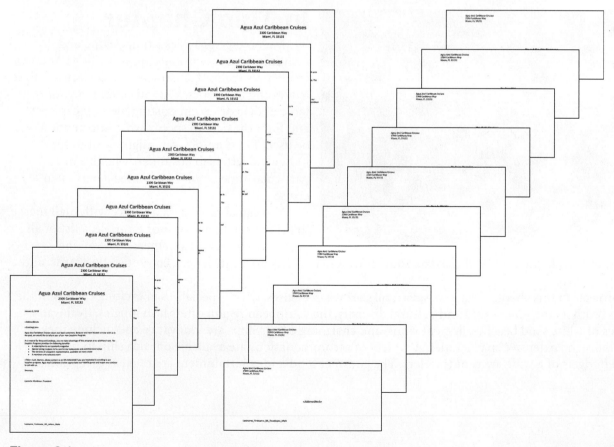

Figure 8.1
Project 8A Customer Letters

Objective 1 | Merge a Data Source and a Main Document

Recall that **mail merge** is a Word feature that joins a **data source** with a **main document** to create a customized document, such as mailing labels. The data source, containing categories of information such as names and addresses, can be stored in a variety of formats—a Word table, an Excel worksheet, an Access table or query, an Outlook contact list, or any text file that has text separated by **delimiters**. Delimiters are characters, such as commas and tabs, used to separate text into groups. Placeholders for the custom information from the data source are inserted in the main document. You can use mail merge to create personalized letters, envelopes, labels, or directories.

Activity 8.01 | Using an Excel Spreadsheet as a Data Source

Previously you used a Word table as a data source to create mailing labels. Excel worksheets can also be used as a data source. In this activity, you will examine an Excel worksheet containing information that will be used to create personalized letters to loyal customers explaining the Sapphire Program.

1 **Start** Excel. Click the **File tab** to display **Backstage** view. Click **Open**, and then from your student files, locate and open the file **w08A_Customers**. Compare your screen with Figure 8.2. Take a moment to study the data that includes names and addresses for current and potential customers.

Row 1 of the worksheet contains headers describing each field—column of data. The name of the worksheet—*Customer Information*—displays on the tab at the bottom of the worksheet. It is important to know the name of the worksheet you are using as a data source because an Excel file may contain several worksheets.

Figure 8.2

2 Click the **File tab** to display **Backstage** view. Click **Save As** to display the **Save As** dialog box. Navigate to the location where you are saving your files for this chapter, and then create a new folder named **Word Chapter 8** Using your own name, save the file to your **Word Chapter 8** folder as **Lastname_Firstname_8A_Customers**

3 **Close** ☒ Excel.

When performing a mail merge, it is not necessary to have a data source file—in this case, the Excel file—open.

Activity 8.02 | Using the Mailings Tab Commands to Begin Mail Merge

The Mailings tab contains commands for features that are inaccessible when using the Mail Merge wizard—for example, creating rules using fields and automatically checking for errors. In this activity, you will use the commands on the Mailings tab to define the main document and data source that will be used to create the letter to customers.

1 **Start** Word and display a new document. Using your own name, save the document to your **Word Chapter 8** folder as **Lastname_Firstname_8A_Letters_Main** If necessary, display the rulers and formatting marks.

2 On the **Mailings tab**, in the **Start Mail Merge group**, click the **Start Mail Merge** button, and from the displayed list, click **Letters**.

3 On the **Mailings tab**, in the **Start Mail Merge group**, click the **Select Recipients** button, and from the displayed list, click **Use Existing List**.

4 In the **Select Data Source** dialog box, navigate to your **Word Chapter 8** folder, locate and select the file **Lastname_Firstname_8A_Customers**, and then click **Open**.

5 In the **Select Table** dialog box, under **Name**, select **'Customer Information$'**, if necessary. At the bottom left of the dialog box, select the **First row of data contains column headers** check box, if necessary. Compare your screen with Figure 8.3.

Recall you are using the Excel worksheet named Customer Information as your data source. The worksheet contains column headers in row 1.

Figure 8.3

Select Table dialog box

Customer Information$ worksheet

First row of data contains column headers selected

6 Click **OK**. Leave Word open for the next activity.

Although visually nothing appears to happen, when you designate a data source, the file—in this case, the Excel file—is linked to the main document based on the current locations of both files.

> **More Knowledge** | Using Outlook as a Data Source
>
> You can use an Outlook Contacts list as a data source. To use the Contacts list, on the Mailings tab, in the Start Mail Merge group, click Select Recipients. Then, from the displayed list, click Select from Outlook Contacts. In the Choose Profile dialog box, select the folder where your Outlook Contacts list is stored, and then click OK.

Activity 8.03 | Filtering Records

A data source is comprised of *fields*, categories—or columns—of data, and *records*. A record is a row of information that contains the data for one entity—for example, information about one customer. When using a data source, you can *filter* the data source. A filter is a set of criteria applied to fields to display specific records—for example, information only for customers that live in a particular state. Because the Sapphire Program is available only to individuals who have previously toured with Agua Azul Caribbean Cruises, you will filter the data source to display only existing customers.

1 On the **Mailings tab**, in the **Start Mail Merge group**, click the **Edit Recipient List** button. In the **Mail Merge Recipients** dialog box, under **Refine recipient list**, click **Filter**.

2 In the **Filter and Sort** dialog box, on the **Filter Records tab**, click the **Field arrow**, and then scroll as necessary and click **Booked Cruise**. Click the **Comparison arrow**, and then click **Equal to**, if necessary. In the **Compare to** box, type **Yes** and then compare your screen with Figure 8.4.

> The data source will be filtered to display only those records where the Booked Cruise field is equal to Yes.

Figure 8.4

Field name
Comparison criteria
Compare to text

3 Click **OK**. In the **Mail Merge Recipients** dialog box, scroll horizontally and vertically as necessary, and notice that only nine records with *Yes* in the Booked Cruise field display.

4 Click **OK** to close the **Mail Merge Recipients** dialog box. Leave Word open for the next activity.

Activity 8.04 | Inserting Merge Fields

You are creating a *form letter*—a letter with standardized wording that can be sent to many different people. Each letter can be customized by inserting *merge fields*—placeholders that represent specific information in the data source. In this activity, you will type the letter and insert appropriate merge fields.

1 With the insertion point positioned at the beginning of the document, on the **Home tab**, in the **Styles group**, click the **No Spacing** style.

> Recall that Word, by default, has formatting associated with the Normal template, such as Before and After paragraph spacing. By choosing No Spacing, this spacing is removed.

2 Type **Agua Azul Caribbean Cruises** and then press Enter. Type **2300 Caribbean Way** Press Enter, type **Miami, FL 33132** and then press Enter.

3 Select the first line of text, and on the Mini toolbar, change the **Font Size** to **28** and apply **Center** ☰. On the **Home tab**, in the **Font group**, click the **Text Effects** button A⁻, and then in the third row, click the fourth style—**Gradient Fill – Blue, Accent 1**.

4 Select the second and third paragraphs, and then on the Mini toolbar, change the **Font Size** to **16** and apply **Center** ☰.

5 Position the insertion point in the blank paragraph, and then press Enter two times. Type **January 3, 2016** and then press Enter four times. Compare your screen with Figure 8.5.

> Because you are using a letter style as a main document, you created a letterhead for Agua Azul Caribbean Cruises and included the date of the letter.

Figure 8.5

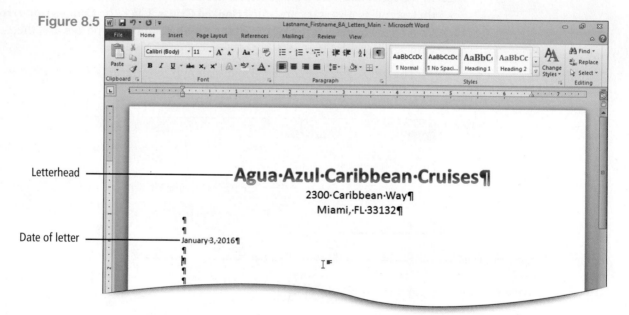

Letterhead

Date of letter

6 On the **Mailings tab**, in the **Write & Insert Fields group**, click the **Address Block** button. In the **Insert Address Block** dialog box, take a moment to examine the various settings associated with this dialog box, and then click **OK**. In the document, notice that the **Address Block merge field** is inserted.

> A standard feature of a business letter is the *inside address*—the name and address of the recipient of the letter. The *Address Block* is a predefined merge field that includes the recipient's name, street address, city, state, and postal code. The Insert Address Block dialog box provides options for changing the way the inside address displays. You are inserting the Address Block merge field as a placeholder for the inside address. Each merge field in a main document is surrounded by *chevrons*—characters used to distinguish where data will be populated.

7 Press `Enter` two times, and then in the **Write & Insert Fields group**, click the **Greeting Line** button. In the **Insert Greeting Line** dialog box, under **Greeting line format**, in the box on the right—the **Punctuation** box, click the **Punctuation arrow**, and then from the displayed list, click **:** (the colon). Compare your screen with Figure 8.6.

> Another standard feature of a business letter is the *salutation*—or greeting line. The *Greeting Line* is a predefined merge field that includes an introductory word, such as *Dear*, and the recipient's name. When using a business letter format, a colon usually follows the salutation. The Insert Greeting Line dialog box allows you to choose how the salutation displays. You can also select text to display if the data source name fields are empty for any recipient.

Figure 8.6

Colon displays at end of greeting line text

Greeting line text that displays if data source fields are blank

Address block surrounded by chevrons

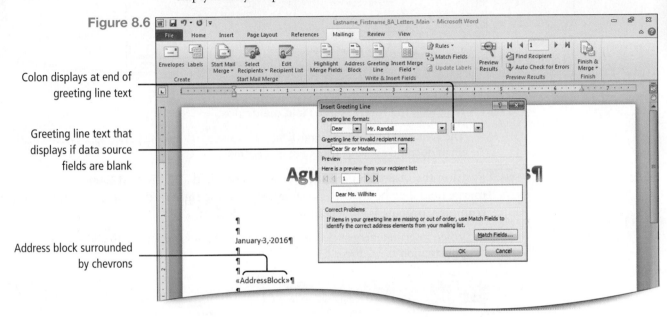

8 Click **OK**, and notice that the **Greeting Line merge field** is inserted in the document.

> The Greeting Line merge field is used as a placeholder for the salutation.

9 Press `Enter` two times, and then type the following:

> **Agua Azul Caribbean Cruises values our loyal customers. Because you have booked a cruise with us in the past, we would like to inform you of our new Sapphire Program.**

10 Press `Enter` two times, and type the following:

> **As a reward for frequent bookings, you can take advantage of this program at no additional cost. The Sapphire Program provides the following benefits:**

11 Press `Enter`, and then type the following text, pressing `Enter` after each line:

> **A subscription to our quarterly magazine**
>
> **Special savings coupons to be used in our restaurants and entertainment areas**
>
> **The services of a Sapphire representative, available on every cruise**
>
> **A members-only onboard event**

12 Select the four lines of text you just typed, and then on the **Home tab**, in the **Paragraph group**, click the **Bullets** button.

13 Position the insertion point in the blank line below the bulleted text, and then press `Enter`. On the **Mailings tab**, in the **Write & Insert Fields group**, click the **Insert Merge Field** button.

14 In the **Insert Merge Field** dialog box, under **Fields**, click **Title**, and then click **Insert**. Click the **Last Name** field, click **Insert**, and then compare your screen with Figure 8.7.

Figure 8.7

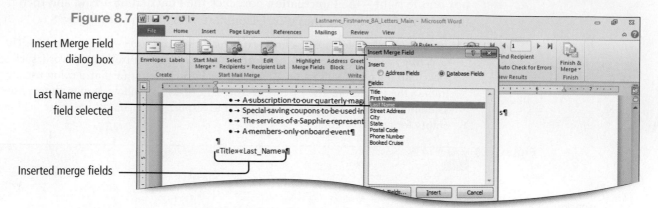

Insert Merge Field dialog box

Last Name merge field selected

Inserted merge fields

15 Close ☒ the **Insert Merge Field** dialog box.

The Title and Last Name merge fields are inserted within the paragraph. When creating a main document, merge fields can be inserted.

16 Position the insertion point between the **Title** field and the **Last Name** field—one merge field may be shaded. Press ⌴Spacebar⌴. To the right of the **Last Name** field, type a comma. Compare your screen with Figure 8.8.

When inserting merge fields as part of a sentence, it is important to add spaces or punctuation as required.

Figure 8.8

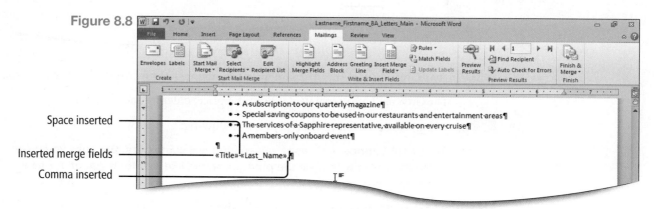

Space inserted

Inserted merge fields

Comma inserted

17 Press ⌴Spacebar⌴, and then type the following:

please contact us at 305-555-0333 if you are interested in enrolling in our Sapphire Program. Agua Azul Caribbean Cruises appreciates our faithful guests and hopes you continue to sail with us.

18 Press ⌴Enter⌴ two times, and then type **Sincerely,**

A ***complimentary closing***—such as *Sincerely* or *Yours truly*—is a phrase used to end a business letter. The complimentary closing is always followed by a comma.

19 Press Enter four times, and then type **Lynnette Waldman, President** Compare your screen with Figure 8.9.

> Extra line spacing is created between the complimentary closing and the signature line to allow for a handwritten signature by the writer of the letter.

Figure 8.9

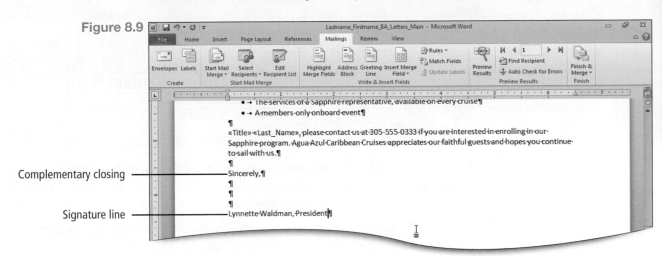

Complementary closing

Signature line

20 **Save** 💾 your changes.

Activity 8.05 | Previewing Merged Data

After the merge fields are added to the form letter, you can preview the letters one at a time. Before you complete the merge process, it is a good idea to scan the letters to check for spelling, punctuation, and spacing errors. If you find an error, correct it in the main document before completing the merge.

1 Press Ctrl + Home. On the **Mailings tab**, in the **Preview Results group**, click the **Preview Results** button. Notice that the merge fields are replaced with specific information from the data source. Compare your screen with Figure 8.10.

> Previewing the merged results allows you to see how each record will display in the letter. By default, the displayed information—in this case, the customer information—is from record 1, as indicated in the Go to Record box.

Figure 8.10

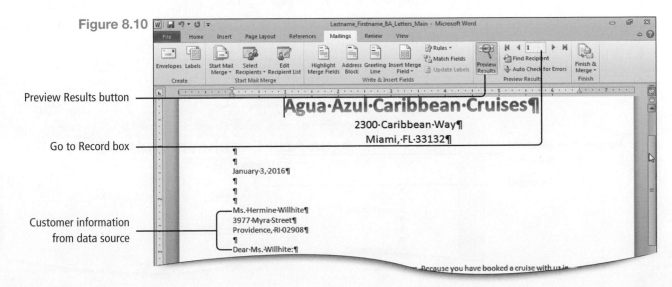

Preview Results button

Go to Record box

Customer information from data source

2 On the **Mailings tab**, in the **Preview Results group**, click the **Next Record** button ▶ two times. In the **Go to Record** box, notice that record **3** displays, as shown in Figure 8.11.

You can use the navigation buttons to preview how other letters will display after the merge.

Figure 8.11
First Record button
Previous Record button
Record 3 displays
Next Record button
Last Record button

3 On the **Mailings tab**, in the **Preview Results group**, click the **Last Record** button ⏭. In the **Go to Record** box, notice that record **9** displays and the record's information from the data source displays in the inside address, salutation, and last paragraph of the letter.

4 On the **Mailings tab**, in the **Preview Results group**, click the **First Record** button ⏮. In the **Go to Record** box, notice that record **1** displays.

5 On the **Mailings tab**, in the **Preview Results group**, click the **Preview Results** button to turn off the preview and display the merge fields display in the letter once again.

6 If *Azul* is flagged as a spelling error in the first occurrence, right-click, and then click **Ignore All**. **Save** 💾 your changes.

After previewing the document, it is good practice to correct any spelling or grammar errors.

Activity 8.06 | Merging to a New Document

Recall that your form letter is the main document containing the merge fields. You can print the letters directly from the main document or merge all of the letters into one document that you can edit. You will finish the merge process by merging the data source and the main document to a new, single document that contains the individual letters. This new document will no longer be connected to the data source.

1 On the **Mailings tab**, in the **Finish group**, click the **Finish & Merge** button, and then from the displayed list, click **Edit Individual Documents**. The **Merge to New Document** dialog box displays, as shown in Figure 8.12.

Although *All* is selected by default, you can use the Merge to New Document dialog box to specify which records you wish to merge to a new document.

Figure 8.12
Merge to New Document dialog box
All selected

2 In the **Merge to New Document** dialog box, click **OK**.

> A new merged document displays with *Letters1 – Microsoft Word* in the title bar.

3 Scroll to examine the document. Notice that the document consists of nine individual letters.

> You can edit individual letters in a merged document, if necessary.

4 Press Ctrl + Home, and then scroll to the bottom of **Page 1**. Compare your screen with Figure 8.13.

> The Status Bar indicates there are nine pages—the individual letters. Each page, or letter, is separated by a Next Page section break.

Figure 8.13

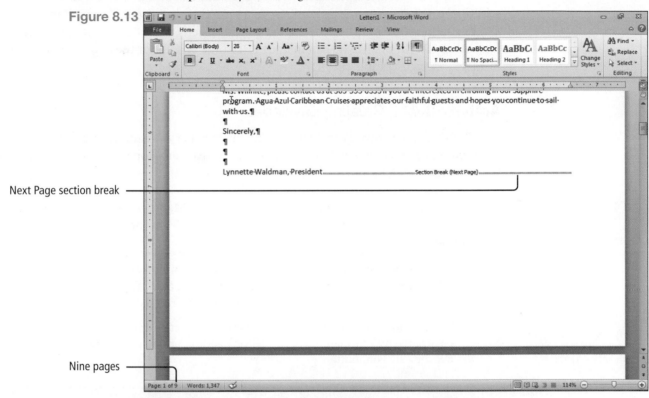

Next Page section break

Nine pages

5 From **Backstage** view, display the **Save As** dialog box, navigate to your **Word Chapter 8** folder, and then save the document as **Lastname_Firstname_8A_Letters_Merged** Scroll to the bottom of **Page 1**, right-click in the footer area, click **Edit Footer**, and then using **Quick Parts**, insert the file name. **Close** the footer area.

6 From **Backstage** view, display the **Document Information Panel**. In the **Author** box, delete any text, and then type your first and last names. In the **Subject** box, type your course name and section number, and in the **Keywords** box, type **customer letters, merged Close** ☒ the Document Information Panel.

7 **Save** 🖫 your changes, and then **Close** ☒ the document.

8 In the displayed document—the main document—scroll to the bottom of the page, and then using **Quick Parts**, insert the file name in the footer.

9 From **Backstage** view, display the **Document Information Panel**. In the **Author** box, delete any existing text, and then type your first and last names. In the **Subject** box, type your course name and section number, and in the **Keywords** box, type **customer letters, main Close** ☒ the Document Information Panel.

10 **Save** 🖫 your document. From **Backstage** view, **Close** the document but leave Word open.

Objective 2 | Create Envelopes

Word provides two options for creating envelopes. You can create a single envelope by selecting a recipient's name and address in an existing document. The mail merge process allows you to create multiple envelopes. You can specify the envelope size and text formatting. Additionally you can include electronic postage, if the appropriate software is installed on your computer.

Activity 8.07 | Creating Envelopes

The same data source can be used with any number of main documents of different types. In this activity, you will use mail merge to create envelopes for the form letters using the same filtered data source.

1 Press Ctrl + N to open a new document. On the **Mailings tab**, in the **Start Mail Merge group**, click the **Start Mail Merge** button, and then from the displayed list, click **Envelopes**.

2 In the **Envelope Options** dialog box, on the **Envelope Options tab**, under **Envelope size**, click the **Envelope size arrow**, if necessary, and then from the displayed list, click **Size 10 (4 1/8 x 9 1/2 in)**. Compare your screen with Figure 8.14.

The Envelope Options dialog box allows you to select an envelope size. You can also change the font formatting for the delivery address and return address by clicking the appropriate Font button.

Figure 8.14

Envelope Options tab

Envelope size box

Font buttons

3 Click **OK**. From **Backstage** view, display the **Save As** dialog box, navigate to your **Word Chapter 8** folder and then save the document as **Lastname_Firstname_8A_ Envelopes_Main**

4 On the **Mailings tab**, in the **Start Mail Merge group**, click the **Select Recipients** button, and then from the displayed list, click **Use Existing List**.

5 In the **Select Data Source** dialog box, navigate to your **Word Chapter 8** folder, select the file **Lastname_Firstname_8A_Customers**, and then click **Open**.

6 In the **Select Table** dialog box, select **'Customer Information$'**, if necessary. At the bottom left of the dialog box, select the **First row of data contains column headers** check box, if necessary. Click **OK**.

7 On the **Mailings tab**, in the **Start Mail Merge group**, click the **Edit Recipient List** button. In the **Mail Merge Recipients** dialog box, under **Refine recipient list**, click **Filter**.

8 In the **Filter and Sort** dialog box, on the **Filter Records tab**, click the **Field arrow**, and then scroll as necessary and click **Booked Cruise**. Click the **Comparison arrow**, and then click **Equal to**, if necessary. In the **Compare to** box, type **Yes** Compare your screen with Figure 8.15.

> The data source will be filtered to display only those records where the Booked Cruise field is equal to Yes.

Figure 8.15

Field name

Comparison criteria

Compare to text

9 Click **OK** two times to close the dialog boxes.

10 If necessary, press `Ctrl` + `Home`. If a return address displays, delete the existing text. Type the following return address, pressing `Enter` after the first and second lines. Compare your screen with Figure 8.16.

> **Agua Azul Caribbean Cruises**
>
> **2300 Caribbean Way**
>
> **Miami, FL 33132**

Figure 8.16

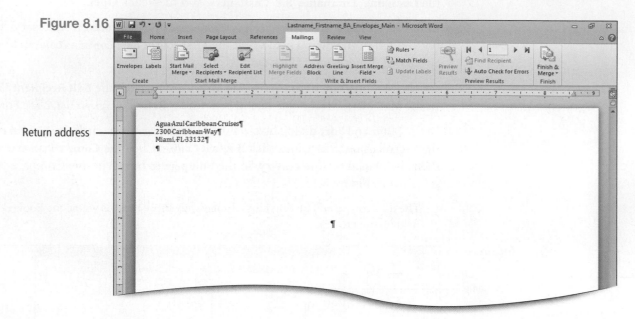

Return address

11 If *Azul* is flagged as a spelling error, right-click, and then click **Ignore All**.

12 In the center of the document, position the insertion point to the left of the paragraph mark. Notice that a rectangular box comprised of dashed lines displays to indicate the position of the delivery address.

13 On the **Mailings tab**, in the **Write & Insert Fields group**, click the **Address Block** button. In the **Insert Address Block** dialog box, click **OK** to insert the Address Block merge field in the document.

14 On the **Mailings tab**, in the **Preview Results group**, click the **Preview Results** button. Notice that the Address Block merge field is replaced with the name and address for record 1 in the data source. Compare your screen with Figure 8.17.

Figure 8.17

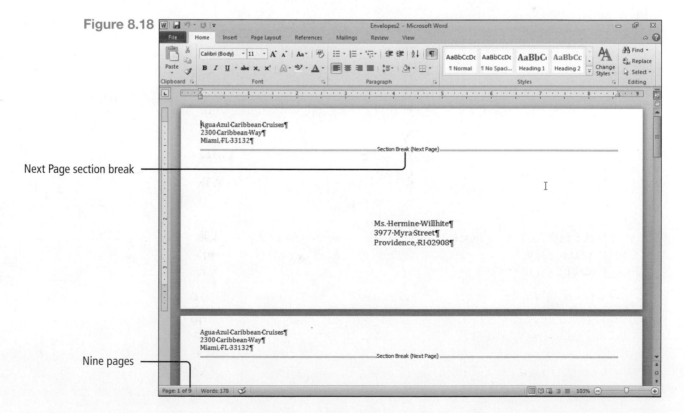

Preview Results button

Record 1

Name and address for record 1

Dashed line indicates position of delivery address

15 On the **Mailings tab**, in the **Preview Results group**, click the **Preview Results** button to turn off the preview.

16 On the **Mailings tab**, in the **Finish group**, click the **Finish & Merge** button, and then from the displayed list, click **Edit Individual Documents**. In the **Merge to New Document** dialog box, click **OK**. If necessary, press Ctrl + Home to move to the top of the document, and then compare your screen with Figure 8.18.

> Notice that the document contains nine pages—consisting of individual envelopes—separated by next page section breaks. Because the delivery address is in a text box, Word positions the section breaks below the return address.

Figure 8.18

Next Page section break

Nine pages

17 From **Backstage** view, display the **Save As** dialog box, navigate to your **Word Chapter 8** folder, and save the document as **Lastname_Firstname_8A_Envelopes_Merged** Right-click in the footer area, click **Edit Footer**, and then using **Quick Parts**, insert the file name. From **Backstage** view, display the **Document Information Panel**. In the **Author** box, type your first and last names. In the **Subject** box, type your course name and section number, and in the **Keywords** box, type **customer envelopes, merged Close** [X] the Document Information Panel. **Save** [🖫] your document, and then **Close** [x] the document.

18 In the main document, right-click in the footer area, click **Edit Footer**, and then using **Quick Parts**, insert the file name. From **Backstage** view, display the **Document Information Panel**. In the **Author** box, type your first and last names. In the **Subject** box, type your course name and section number, and in the **Keywords** box, type **customer envelopes, main Close** [X] the Document Information Panel. **Save** [🖫] your document.

19 Print your four documents—it is not necessary to print the data source—or submit all five files electronically as directed by your instructor. **Exit** Word.

More Knowledge | Printing an Envelope from Selected Data

To print a single envelope from selected data, in any document, select the name and address you want to use. On the Mailings tab, in the Create group, click the Envelopes button. On the Envelopes tab of the Envelopes and Labels dialog box, you can edit the return address or delivery address and make other changes, and then click Print.

End **You have completed Project 8A** ——————————

Project 8B Cruise Postcards

Project Activities

In Activities 8.08 through 8.17, you will use mail merge to create postcards for Agua Azul Caribbean Cruises, which is offering a special cruise to loyal customers. Paolo Alvarez, Cruise Consultant, has asked you to create postcards to advertise the cruise. You will also create a contact list for customers who are going on the cruise. Your completed files will look similar to Figure 8.19.

Project Files

For Project 8B, you will need the following files:

Two new blank Word documents
w08B_Cruise_Clients
w08B_Cruise_Ship

You will save your files as:

Lastname_Firstname_8B_Cruise_Clients—not shown in figure
Lastname_Firstname_8B_Postcards_Main
Lastname_Firstname_8B_Postcards_Merged
Lastname_Firstname_8B_List_Main
Lastname_Firstname_8B_Cruise_Contacts—not shown in figure
Lastname_Firstname_8B_List_Merged

Project Results

Figure 8.19
Project 8B Cruise Postcards

Objective 3 | Edit and Sort a Data Source

During the merge process you can modify information in the data source and arrange the records in a particular order. For example, you may wish to add new records or display the records in alphabetical or numerical order based on a specific field.

Activity 8.08 | Editing a Data Source

Sherry Rech, Database Coordinator for Agua Azul Caribbean Cruises, has asked you to edit the customer data source—a table in an Access *database*. A database is an organized collection of facts about people, events, things, or ideas related to a particular topic or purpose. In this activity, you will select a postcard template from available label options. Then you will add two customer records and delete a customer record from the data source.

1 Right-click the **Start** button, and then click **Open Windows Explorer**. Navigate to your student files, locate and then open the Access file **w08B_Cruise_Clients**. In the **Read-only** Message Bar, click the **Save as** button, navigate to your **Word Chapter 8** folder, and then save the file as **Lastname_Firstname_8B_Cruise_Clients Close** ❌ any open windows.

2 **Start** Word and display a new blank document. If necessary, display the rulers and formatting marks. On the **Mailings tab**, in the **Start Mail Merge group**, click the **Start Mail Merge** button, and then click **Labels**.

3 In the **Label Options** dialog box, under **Label information**, click the **Label vendors arrow**, and then from the displayed list, click **Avery US Letter**. Under **Product number**, scroll as necessary, and then click **3263 Postcards**. Compare your screen with Figure 8.20.

A description of the selected label displays under Label information on the right side of the Label Options dialog box. In addition to labels, some product numbers are designated as business cards, name tags, or—in this case—postcards.

Figure 8.20

- Label information
- Label vendors box
- Product number box
- 3263 Postcards selected

> **Alert!** | **The Product Number Does Not Display.**
>
> If the Avery US Letter 3263 label option does not display, in the Label Options dialog box, click the New Label button to create a custom postcard template. Set the Top Margin and Side Margin to 0. Set the Label Height to 4.25 and the Label Width to 5.5. Set the Vertical Pitch and the Horizontal Pitch to 5.5. Set the Number Across and Number Down to 2. Set the Page Size to Letter Landscape (11×8.5).

4 In the **Label Options** dialog box, click **OK**. Verify that the gridlines—dashed blue lines—display in the document. If necessary, turn on the gridlines by clicking the **Layout tab**, and then in the **Table group**, clicking the **View Gridlines** button.

The postcard template is a table consisting of four cells.

5 From **Backstage** view, display the **Save As** dialog box, navigate to your **Word Chapter 8** folder, and then save the document as **Lastname_Firstname_8B_Postcards_Main**

6 On the **Mailings tab**, in the **Start Mail Merge group**, click the **Select Recipients** button, and then click **Use Existing List**. In the **Select Data Source** dialog box, navigate to your **Word Chapter 8** folder, select **Lastname_Firstname_8B_Cruise_Clients**, and then click **Open**. In the second, third, and fourth cells, notice that the **<<Next Record>> field** displays.

When you are using a label template, the <<Next Record>> field allows the contents of the first label to be propagated to the remaining cells of the table during the mail merge process.

7 On the **Mailings tab**, in the **Start Mail Merge group**, click the **Edit Recipient List** button. In the **Mail Merge Recipients** dialog box, under **Data Source**, click **Lastname_Firstname_8B_Cruise_Clients**, and then click the **Edit** button.

You can edit a data source during the merge process by changing existing data or by adding or deleting records.

8 In the **ID** field, scroll as necessary, and locate the cell containing 7. To the left of the cell in the ID field, click the row selector box—the small square to the left of the row. Compare your screen with Figure 8.21.

Clicking the row selector box selects an entire record. This is useful if you want to delete a record.

Figure 8.21

ID field

Record 7 selected

Row selector box

9 In the **Edit Data Source** dialog box, click the **Delete Entry** button. In the **Microsoft Office Word** dialog box, click **Yes** to confirm the deletion of the record.

10 In the **Edit Data Source** dialog box, click the **New Entry** button. Notice that a new record line displays below the last current record with ID *14*. Compare your screen with Figure 8.22.

The new record line enables you to add information for a new client to the data source.

Figure 8.22

New record line

Default *0* displays

11 In the new record line, in the **ID** field, position the insertion point to the right of **0**, if necessary. Type **15** and then press [Tab]. In the **ID** field, notice that *15* displays, without the default *0*.

It is not necessary to delete the default 0 when entering data in cells containing numbers. In this case, the ID, Postal_Code, and Cruises_Booked fields all contain numbers and will display with the default 0.

12 In the cell in the **Title** field, type **Dr.** and then press [Tab]. Using the technique you practiced, type the following text in the remaining cells of the row, pressing [Tab] after each entry.

First_Name	Last_Name	Street	City	State	Postal_Code	Cruises_Booked
Lucyna	**Borkowski**	**2696 Morningview Lane**	**Ottumwa**	**IA**	**52501**	**3**

The data for a new customer has been entered, and a new line displays to add a new record.

13 In the same manner, type the following text in the cells for record 16, pressing [Tab] after each entry, except the last entry.

ID	Title	First_Name	Last_Name	Street	City	State	Postal_Code	Cruises_Booked
16	**Mr.**	**Michael**	**Damjanac**	**4372 Nixon Avenue**	**Winchester**	**OH**	**45697**	**2**

14 Press Enter. Scroll to the left as necessary to display the **ID** field. Compare your screen with Figure 8.23.

Data for a second customer has been entered as a new record.

Figure 8.23

Two records entered

15 Click **OK**. In the **Microsoft Office Word** dialog box, click **Yes** to update your recipient list and save the changes to Lastname_Firstname_8B_Cruise_Clients. Leave the **Mail Merge Recipients** dialog box open for the next activity.

Activity 8.09 | Sorting a Data Source

You can sort a data source so records display in a particular order in the final merge. Because you are creating postcards, you will sort the postcards by the postal code to qualify as *bulk mail*. Bulk mail is a large mailing, sorted by ZIP code, that is eligible for reduced postage rates, available from the United States Postal Service.

1 In the **Mail Merge Recipients** dialog box, scroll to display the **Postal_Code** field. To the right of **Postal_Code**, click the **arrow**, and then from the displayed list, click **Sort Ascending**. Compare your screen with Figure 8.24.

By sorting the records, when the merge process is complete, the individual postcards will display in order by postal code.

Figure 8.24

Postal_Code heading

Postal codes in ascending order

2 Click **OK**, and then **Save** 💾 your changes.

Activity 8.10 | Using Nested Tables and Formatting the Main Document

In Word documents, recall you can create a *nested table*—a table inserted in a cell of an existing table. In this activity, you will create a nested table to simplify formatting the postcard, and then add text and merge fields.

1 Press Ctrl + Home. On the **Insert tab**, in the **Tables group**, click the **Table** button. Under **Insert Table**, click the cell in the first row and second column to create a 2 × 1 table. Compare your screen with Figure 8.25.

A table containing one row and two columns displays within the first cell of the original table. You create a nested table whenever you insert a table within an existing cell.

Figure 8.25

New, nested table

First cell of original table

2 With the insertion point in the first cell of the nested table, drag to the right to select both cells in the new nested table. On the **Design tab**, in the **Table Styles group**, click the **Borders button arrow**, and then from the displayed list, click **No Border**.

3 With the cells still selected, on the **Layout tab**, in the **Cell Size group**, change the **Table Row Height** 1.5" to **4.5"**. Compare your screen with Figure 8.26.

Figure 8.26

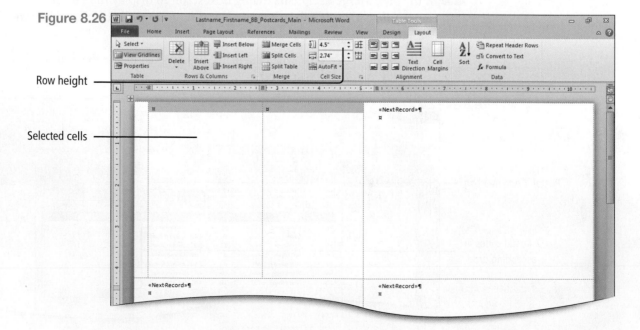

Row height

Selected cells

4 Position the insertion point in the second cell of the nested table. On the **Design tab**, in the **Draw Borders group**, click the **Line Style arrow** [▼], and then click the third line style. Click the **Line Weight arrow** [½ pt ▼], and then click **1 1/2 pt**. Click the **Pen Color button arrow**, and then under **Theme Colors**, in the ninth column, click the last color—**Aqua, Accent 5, Darker 50%**. In the **Table Styles group**, click the **Borders button arrow**, and then click **Left Border**.

5 Point to the left border of the second cell of the nested table, and then drag to the right until the border aligns at approximately **3 inches on the horizontal ruler**. Compare your screen with Figure 8.27.

> This border will visually separate the message from the delivery address in the completed postcards.

Figure 8.27

Border positioned at 3 inches

Formatted border

6 In the first cell of the nested table, click to position the insertion point. Type **Agua Azul Caribbean Cruises** and then press [Enter] three times. Select the text in the first paragraph. On the Mini toolbar, change the **Font Size** to **16**, apply **Bold** [B] and **Center** [≡], and then click the **Font Color** button [A ▼], and in the ninth column, click the fifth color—**Aqua, Accent 5, Darker 25%**. On the **Page Layout tab**, in the **Paragraph group**, change the **Spacing Before** to **18 pt**.

7 In the second paragraph, click to position the insertion point. On the **Insert tab**, in the **Illustrations group**, click the **Picture** button. From your student files, locate and insert **w08B_Cruise_Ship**. With the graphic selected, on the **Home tab**, in the **Paragraph group**, click the **Center** button [≡].

8 In the third paragraph, click to position the insertion point, and then type **Customer Appreciation Cruise** Select the text, and on the Mini toolbar, change the **Font Size** to **14**, apply **Bold** [B] and **Center** [≡], and then click the **Font Color** button [A ▼]. Deselect the text, and then compare your screen with Figure 8.28.

Figure 8.28

Picture inserted

Text inserted and formatted

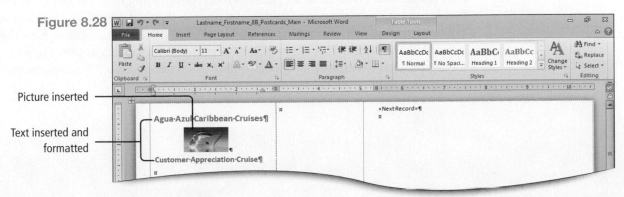

9 Position the insertion point in the last line of the cell—to the left of the end of the cell marker. On the **Insert tab**, in the **Text group**, click the **Object button arrow**, and then click **Text from File**. Navigate to your student files, select the file **w08B_Appreciation_Cruise**, and then click **Insert**.

10 Position the insertion point anywhere in the paragraph that begins *We are offering*. On the **Page Layout tab**, in the **Paragraph group**, click the **Spacing Before up spin arrow** to **12 pt**, and then click the **Spacing After up spin arrow** to **12 pt**.

11 Locate the paragraph that begins *Because you have booked*. Click to position the insertion point to the right of *booked*, and then press Spacebar. On the **Mailings tab**, in the **Write & Insert Fields group**, click the **Insert Merge Field button arrow**, and then click **Cruises_Booked**. Compare your screen with Figure 8.29.

The Cruises_Booked field contains the number of cruises previously booked by each customer. By inserting this merge field, you can personalize the postcards.

Figure 8.29

Inserted text

Cruises_Booked merge field

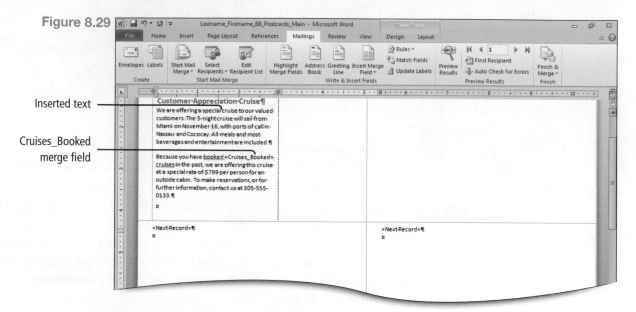

12 Save your changes.

Objective 4 | Match Fields and Apply Rules

Word enables you to use any data format—such as a Word table, an Excel worksheet, or an Access table—as a data source. However, the data source may not include the same field names that are used in the Address Block or Greeting Line merge fields. The **Match Fields** feature maps the predefined field names to the field names in your data source. You can apply **rules**—conditional Word fields—that allow you to determine how the merge process is completed. This allows you to personalize the final document in additional ways—for example, inserting a specific date in a letter based on the department field in a data source with employee information.

Activity 8.11 | Matching Fields to a Data Source

The Address Block and Greeting Line merge fields include specific field names—such as Last Name, Address 1, and Postal Code. Word enables you to match the fields in your data source with the fields used in the Address Block and Greeting Line dialog boxes. In this activity, you will use the Match Fields feature to map the Address Block fields to your data source fields to display the delivery address correctly.

1 In the nested table, click in the second cell to position the insertion point. On the **Mailings tab**, in the **Write & Insert Fields group**, click the **Address Block** button. Compare your screen with Figure 8.30.

In the Preview box, only the name, city, and state of the customer display.

Figure 8.30

Insert Address Block dialog box

Address preview

2 In the **Insert Address Block** dialog box, under **Correct Problems**, click the **Match Fields** button. In the **Match Fields** dialog box, click the **Address 1 arrow**, and then from the displayed list, click **Street**.

3 Click the **Postal Code arrow**, and then click **Postal_Code**. Compare your screen with Figure 8.31.

Word did not recognize the Street and Postal_Code fields in the data source, so it was necessary to associate them with the predefined Address 1 and Postal Code fields, respectively. When you are working with a data source, it is important to remember that *every* character is interpreted by Word. For example, the underscore in Postal_Code caused the field not to be recognized as the predefined Postal Code field.

Figure 8.31

Match Fields dialog box

Address 1 box

Postal Code box

4 Click **OK**, and in the **Microsoft Office Word** dialog box, when asked if you want to match this field to Unique Identifier, click **Yes**. Notice that the Preview box displays the complete mailing address.

5 Click **OK** to insert the Address Block merge field in the document.

6 If necessary, move the insertion point to the second cell of the nested table, and then on the **Layout tab**, in the **Alignment group**, click the **Align Center Left** button 📄. **Save** 💾 your changes.

Activity 8.12 | Applying Rules to a Merge

You can apply rules to add a decision-making element to the mail merge process. In this activity, you will add a rule that will place different cruise prices in the individual postcards, based on the number of cruises the customer has booked.

1 In the first cell of the nested table, in the last paragraph, select the text *$799*, being careful not to select the space formatting marks, and then press `Del`.

2 On the **Mailings tab**, in the **Write & Insert Fields group**, click the **Rules** button, and then click **If...Then...Else**.

3 In the **Insert Word Field: IF** dialog box, under **IF**, click the **Field name arrow**, scroll as necessary, and then click **Cruises_Booked**. Click the **Comparison arrow**, and then click **Greater than or equal**. In the **Compare to** box, type **3** In the **Insert this text** box, type **$549** In the **Otherwise insert this text** box, type **$699** Compare your screen with Figure 8.32.

> The If...Then...Else rule allows you to set a condition so that specific text is inserted if the condition is met, and different text is inserted if the condition is not satisfied. In this case, if the number of cruises booked is greater than or equal to 3, during the merge process, Word will insert the text $549. Otherwise, Word will insert the text $699.

Figure 8.32

Compare to box —
Comparison box —
Field name box —
Insert this text box —
Otherwise insert this text box —

4 Click **OK**, and notice that **$549** is inserted as the default value for the rule.

5 On the **Mailings tab**, in the **Write & Insert Fields group**, click the **Update Labels** button. In the **Preview Results group**, click the **Preview Results** button. Notice that the number of cruises booked, the text for the rule, and the mailing addresses display, with information for record 1 in the first cell. Compare your screen with Figure 8.33.

Figure 8.33

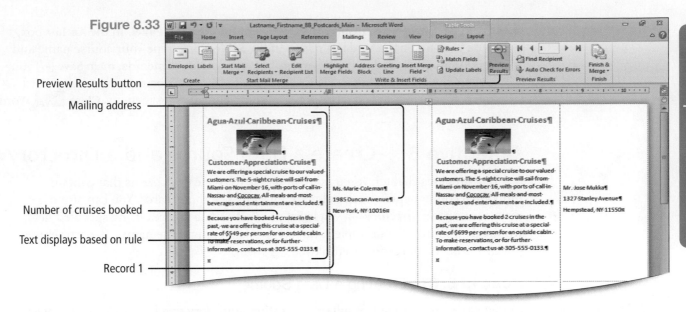

Preview Results button

Mailing address

Number of cruises booked

Text displays based on rule

Record 1

6 On the **Mailings tab**, in the **Preview Results group**, click the **Preview Results** button to turn off the preview.

7 In the **Finish group**, click the **Finish & Merge** button, and then click **Edit Individual Documents**. In the **Merge to New Document** dialog box, click **OK**. Compare your screen with Figure 8.34.

The new document contains the postcards with the merged data. Notice the rule text— cruise price—agrees with the number of cruises booked. By default, a blank page is included at the end of the document.

Figure 8.34

Number of cruises booked

Text displays based on rule

8 If any words are flagged as spelling errors, click **Ignore All**. From **Backstage** view, display the **Save As** dialog box, navigate to your **Word Chapter 8** folder, and then save the document as **Lastname_Firstname_8B_Postcards_Merged** Position the insertion point in the blank line at the top of **Page 5**. Press Enter two times, click the **Insert tab**, and then using **Quick Parts**, insert the file name.

9 From **Backstage** view, display the **Document Information Panel**. In the **Author** box, delete any text, and then type your first name and last name. In the **Subject** box, type your course name and section number, and in the **Keywords** box, type **cruise postcards, merged** Save your document, and then **Close** the document.

10 In the main document, position the insertion point in the blank line at the top of **Page 2**. Press Enter two times, click the **Insert tab**, and then using **Quick Parts**, insert the file name.

11 From **Backstage** view, display the **Document Information Panel**. In the **Author** box, type your first name and last name. In the **Subject** box, type your course name and section number, and in the **Keywords** box, type **cruise postcards, main Save** 🖫 your document. From **Backstage** view, click **Close** to close the document but leave Word open. If you need to take a break before completing the next activity, **Close** ❌ Word.

Objective 5 │ Create a Data Source and a Directory

In a previous chapter, you used mail merge to create documents that contain individual components—such as letters, envelopes, and postcards. You can also use mail merge to create a *directory*—a single list of selected data records using specified fields from a data source. For example, a directory might contain the names, departments, and phone numbers for company employees.

Activity 8.13 │ Creating a Data Source

Paola Alvarez, Cruise Consultant, is creating a directory that lists emergency contact information, which is recorded on paper forms, for customers on the Customer Appreciation Cruise. In this activity, you will create the data source as part of the mail merge process.

1 Press Ctrl + N to display a new document, or if necessary, **Start** Word. On the **Mailings tab**, in the **Start Mail Merge group**, click the **Start Mail Merge** button, and then click **Directory**.

2 From **Backstage** view, display the **Save As** dialog box, navigate to your **Word Chapter 8** folder, and **Save** the document as **Lastname_Firstname_8B_List_Main**

3 On the **Mailings tab**, in the **Start Mail Merge group**, click the **Select Recipients** button, and then from the displayed list, click **Type New List**. Compare your screen with Figure 8.35.

Because an electronic data source containing the necessary information does not exist, you need to create one. The New Address List dialog box allows you to customize the columns used in the data source.

Figure 8.35

New Address List dialog box

Customize Columns button

4 In the **New Address List** dialog box, click the **Customize Columns** button.

In your data source, you will customize the fields to include the customer's name, the name of the person to contact in case of an emergency, the contact's relationship to the customer, and the contact's phone number.

5 In the **Customize Address List** dialog box, under **Field Names**, click **Company Name**, and then click **Rename**. In the **Rename Field** dialog box, in the **To** box, type **Contact Name** and then click **OK**.

You can add new fields or rename existing fields. Solely for the purpose of this instruction you are renaming the *Company Name* field.

6 In the **Customize Address List** dialog box, click **Address Line 1**, and then click **Delete**. In the **Microsoft Office Word** dialog box, click **Yes** to confirm the deletion.

7 In the same manner, delete the following fields: **Address Line 2**, **City**, **State**, **ZIP Code**, **Country or Region**, **Work Phone**, and **E-mail Address**.

8 On the right side of the **Customize Address List** dialog box, click the **Add** button, and then in the **Add Field** dialog box, in the **Type a name for your field** box, type **Relationship** Click **OK**.

9 With **Relationship** selected, click the **Move Up** button, and then compare your screen with Figure 8.36.

Figure 8.36

Delete a field

Add a new field

Field names in data source

Rename a field

Move Up and Move Down buttons

10 Click **OK**. In the **New Address List** dialog box, click to position the insertion point in the **Title** field. Type the following data, pressing Tab after each entry except the last entry—208-555-7128.

Title	First Name	Last Name	Contact Name	Relationship	Home Phone
Mr.	Charles	Guernon	Mrs. Janet Deimler	daughter	410-555-7163
Mrs.	Bridget	Reinhard	Mr. Herman Reinhard	husband	218-555-2279
Mr.	Ernest	Zambrano	Mr. Tony Zambrano	son	310-555-8643
Mrs.	Nema	Eros	Ms. Maria Salva	sister	773-555-9244
Dr.	Ursula	Tezuka	Dr. Julius Tezuka	brother	208-555-7128

Recall that you can press Tab to move from cell to cell. Pressing Tab at the end of a row inserts a new record (row).

Alert! | I Have an Extra Record.

If you accidentally press Tab after that last entry, a new row will be inserted. To delete the new record, click the row selector box to select the row, click the Delete Entry button, and then click Yes to delete the entry.

---

11 In the **New Address List** dialog box, click **OK**. The **Save Address List** dialog box displays.

> When you create a new data source, it must be saved.

12 In the **Save Address List** dialog box, navigate to your **Word Chapter 8** folder, and then save the file as **Lastname_Firstname_8B_Cruise_Contacts** Notice that **Save as type** is set to **Microsoft Office Address Lists**.

> A data source that is created in Word is saved as an Access file with the .mdb file extension. It is not necessary to have Access installed on your computer to create data source files in Word.

Activity 8.14 | Creating the Main Document

In this activity, you will create the main document by inserting designated merge fields and setting tabs to align the content in those fields.

1 If necessary, press Ctrl + Home. At the left end of the horizontal ruler, if necessary, click the **Tab Alignment** button to display the **Left Tab** button ⌊. To set a left tab stop, click at approximately **2.25 inches on the horizontal ruler**. To set two additional left tab stops, click at approximately **4 inches** and then at **5.25 inches on the horizontal ruler**.

2 On the **Mailings tab**, in the **Write & Insert Fields group**, click the **Insert Merge Field** button. In the displayed **Insert Merge Field** dialog box, under **Fields**, click **Title**, and then click the **Insert** button.

3 Using the same technique, insert the **First Name**, **Last Name**, **Contact Name**, **Relationship**, and **Home Phone** fields. **Close** ❎ the **Insert Merge Field** dialog box, and then compare your screen with Figure 8.37.

> All of the merge fields from the data source are inserted on the first line of the document. Recall that each merge field in the main document is surrounded by chevrons. When the directory is created, all the information for one record—a customer—will display on a single line.

Figure 8.37

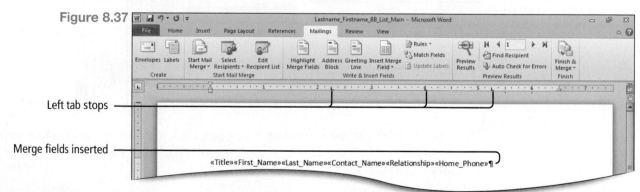

Left tab stops

Merge fields inserted

«Title»«First_Name»«Last_Name»«Contact_Name»«Relationship»«Home_Phone»¶

4 Position the insertion point between the **Title** field and the **First_Name** field. Press Spacebar. Use the same technique to insert a space between the **First_Name** and **Last_Name** fields.

> It is necessary to add spacing between merge fields in the same manner that you do with text.

5 Position the insertion point between the **Last_Name** field and **Contact_Name** field. Press Tab—because of the length of the field names, the tab formatting mark may not display. Using the same technique, insert a tab formatting mark between the **Contact_Name** and **Relationship** fields and between the **Relationship** and **Home_Phone** fields.

> The tabs will allow the data in each field to display in columns, creating a professional appearance.

6 Position the insertion point to the right of the **Home_Phone** field, press `Enter`. Compare your screen with Figure 8.38, and then **Save** 🖫 your changes.

By adding a new paragraph to the document, when the data is merged, each record will display on a new line.

Figure 8.38

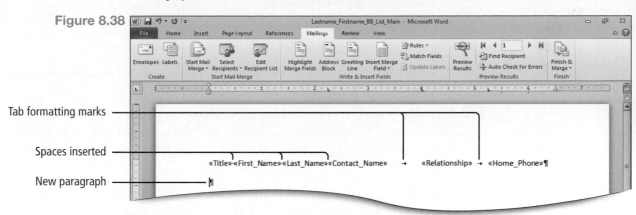

Tab formatting marks

Spaces inserted

«Title»·«First_Name»·«Last_Name»·«Contact_Name»   →   «Relationship» → «Home_Phone»¶

New paragraph

Activity 8.15 | Merging Files to Create a Directory

When completing the merge process for a directory, all of the data represented by the merge fields is displayed in a single document.

1 On the **Mailings tab**, in the **Preview Results group**, click the **Preview Results** button.

Because you are creating a directory, only one record—the first record—displays.

2 To view the second record, in the **Preview Results group**, click the **Next Record** button ▶. In the same manner, view the other three records, and then click the **Preview Results** button.

3 On the **Mailings tab**, in the **Finish group**, click the **Finish & Merge** button, and then click **Edit Individual Documents**. In the **Merge to New Document** dialog box, click **OK**. Compare your screen with Figure 8.39.

Figure 8.39

Displayed data in a list format

Mr.·Charles·Guernon	Mrs.·Janet·Deimler	daughter	410-555-7163¶
Mrs.·Bridget·Reinhard	Mr.·Herman·Reinhard	husband	218-555-2279¶
Mr.·Ernest·Zambrano	Mr.·Tony·Sambrano	son	310-555-8643¶
Mrs.·Nema·Eros	Ms.·Maria·Salva	sister	773-555-9244¶
Dr.·Ursla·Tezuka	Dr.·Julius·Tezuka	brother	208-555-7128¶

Activity 8.16 | Editing a Directory

In the final merged directory, you can add additional elements, such as a title and headings to improve the appearance of the final document.

1 With the insertion point at the beginning of the document, press [Enter], and then press [↑].

2 Type the following text, pressing [Enter] after each line.

Agua Azul Caribbean Cruises

Customer Appreciation Cruise

Emergency Contact List

When creating a directory, a title and other specific elements must be added after the merge process is completed.

3 Select the first paragraph, and on the Mini toolbar, change the **Font Size** to **28** and apply **Center** ☰. With the text selected, on the **Home tab**, in the **Font group**, click the **Text Effects** button Ⓐ·, and in the third row, click the fourth effect—**Gradient Fill – Blue, Accent 1**.

4 Select the second and third paragraphs. On the Mini toolbar, change the **Font Size** to **16**, apply **Bold** Ⓑ and **Center** ☰, and then click the **Font Color button arrow** Ⓐ·, and in the ninth column, click the fifth color—**Aqua, Accent 5, Darker 25%**.

5 Position the insertion point in the blank paragraph immediately above the first customer record. Type **Customer** press [Tab], type **Contact** press [Tab], type **Relationship** press [Tab], and then type **Home Phone** Select the entire paragraph, and then on the Mini toolbar, apply **Bold** Ⓑ and **Underline** Ⓤ·. Deselect the text, and then compare your screen with Figure 8.40.

Figure 8.40

Text inserted and formatted

6 In your **Word Chapter 8** folder, save the document as **Lastname_Firstname_8B_List_Merged**

Activity 8.17 | Inserting a Watermark

A *watermark* is a text or graphic element that displays behind document text. You add a watermark to identify the status of a document or to create a visual impact. In this activity, you will add a watermark to indicate that the directory information is confidential.

1 On the **Page Layout tab**, in the **Page Background group**, click the **Watermark** button. In the **Watermark** gallery, under **Confidential**, click the first style—**CONFIDENTIAL 1**. Notice that the word *CONFIDENTIAL* displays in the background of the document. Compare your screen with Figure 8.41.

Inserting the Confidential watermark helps ensure the privacy of customers when the document is distributed.

Figure 8.41

Confidential watermark

2 Using **Quick Parts**, insert the file name in the footer. Display the **Document Information Panel**. In the **Author** box, type your name. In the **Subject** box, type your course name and section number, and in the **Keywords** box, type **contact list, merged Save** 🖫 your document, and then **Close** ✕ the document.

3 In the displayed document—the main document—use **Quick Parts** to insert the file name in the footer. Display the **Document Information Panel**. In the **Author** box, type your name. In the **Subject** box, type your course name and section number, and in the **Keywords** box, type **contact list, main Save** 🖫 your document.

4 Print the four Word documents—it is not necessary to print the data sources—or submit all six files electronically as directed by your instructor, and then **Exit** Word.

End **You have completed Project 8B** ———————————————

Content-Based Assessments

Summary

In this chapter you used mail merge to customize documents. You created a main document and joined it with a data source—an Excel spreadsheet or an Access database. In order to display specific information in the merged document, you inserted merge fields, sorted the data source, applied filters, and created rules.

Key Terms

Matching

Match each term in the second column with its correct definition in the first column by writing the letter of the term on the blank line in front of the correct definition.

_____ 1. A file containing variable text that is merged with a main document to create a customized document.

_____ 2. In a mail merge, the document that contains the text or formatting that remains constant.

_____ 3. A category or column of information in a data source.

_____ 4. A row of information in a data source.

_____ 5. A set of criteria applied to fields in a data source to display specific records.

_____ 6. A letter with standardized wording that can be sent to many different people.

_____ 7. In a mail merge, a placeholder that represents specific information in a data source.

_____ 8. In a letter, the name and address of the recipient.

_____ 9. A predefined merge field that includes the recipient's name and address.

_____ 10. The greeting line of a letter.

_____ 11. A phrase that is used to end a business letter.

_____ 12. A large mailing, sorted by ZIP code, that is eligible for reduced postage rates.

_____ 13. A Word feature that maps predefined field names to the field names in a data source.

_____ 14. A conditional Word field that allows you to determine how the merge process is completed.

_____ 15. A single list of records using specified fields from a data source.

A Address Block

B Bulk mail

C Complimentary closing

D Data source

E Directory

F Field

G Filter

H Form letter

I Inside address

J Main document

K Match Fields

L Merge fields

M Record

N Rule

O Salutation

Content-Based Assessments

Multiple Choice

Circle the correct answer.

1. A Word feature that joins a data source and a main document to create a customized document is:
   A. Combine Documents   B. Data Merge   C. Mail merge

2. Characters that are used to separate text into groups are referred to as:
   A. delimiters   B. formatting marks   C. wildcards

3. Characters that surround a merge field to distinguish where data will be populated in the mail merge are:
   A. carets   B. chevrons   C. merge characters

4. The predefined merge field that includes an introductory word and the recipient's name is the:
   A. Greeting line   B. Merged greeting   C. Salutation

5. When Preview Results is turned on, you can view:
   A. only the first record   B. only the last record   C. all records

6. An organized collection of facts related to a particular topic or purpose is called a:
   A. database   B. data source   C. spreadsheet

7. When using a label template, what field displays in the table cells—except the first—to allow data to be propagated during a mail merge?
   A. <<Next Label>>   B. <<Next Record>>   C. <<Merged Record>>

8. A table inserted in a cell of an existing table is called a:
   A. nested table   B. split table   C. stacked table

9. An address list created during the mail merge process is saved as:
   A. a Word file   B. an Excel file   C. an Access file

10. A text or graphic element that displays behind document text is a:
    A. background object   B. watermark   C. wrapped object

Content-Based Assessments

Apply **8A** skills from these Objectives:

■ 1 Merge a Data Source and a Main Document

■ 2 Create Envelopes

Skills Review | Project **8C** Eastern Cruise

In the following Skills Review project, you will create a form letter, customized for current customers, that announces a new cruise offered by Agua Azul Caribbean Cruises. You will also create envelopes to accompany the letters. Your completed documents will look similar to Figure 8.42.

Project Files

For Project 8C, you will need the following files:

> New blank Word document
> w08C_Eastern_Letter
> w08C_Eastern_Customers

You will save your files as:

> Lastname_Firstname_8C_Eastern_Customers—not shown in figure
> Lastname_Firstname_8C_Eastern_Main
> Lastname_Firstname_8C_Eastern_Merged
> Lastname_Firstname_8C_EasternEnv_Main
> Lastname_Firstname_8C_EasternEnv_Merged

Project Results

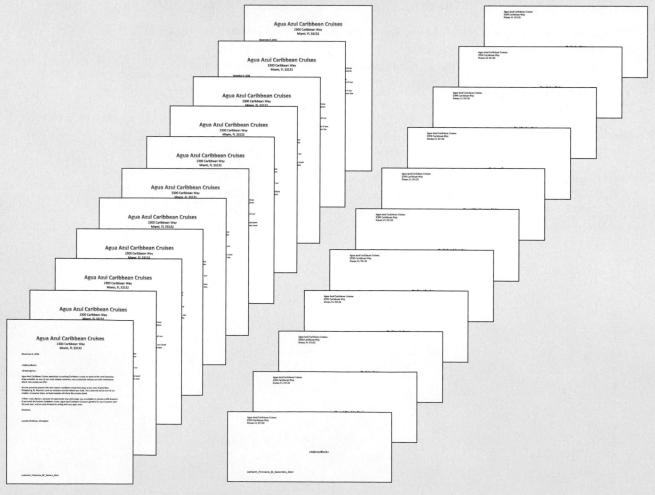

Figure 8.42

(Project 8C Eastern Cruise continues on the next page)

Content-Based Assessments

Skills Review | Project **8C** Eastern Cruise (continued)

1 **Start** Excel. Click the **File tab** to display **Backstage** view. Click **Open**, and then from your student files, locate and open the file **w08C_Eastern_Customers**. From **Backstage** view, click **Save As**, navigate to your **Word Chapter 8** folder, and then save the file as **Lastname_Firstname_8C_Eastern_Customers Close** Excel.

a. **Start** Word. Navigate to your student files, open the file **w08C_Eastern_Letter**, and then save the document to your **Word Chapter 8** folder as **Lastname_Firstname_8C_Eastern_Main** If necessary, display the rulers and formatting marks. For any words flagged as a spelling error, click **Ignore All**.

b. On the **Mailings tab**, in the **Start Mail Merge group**, click the **Start Mail Merge** button, and from the displayed list, click **Letters**. In the **Start Mail Merge group**, click the **Select Recipients** button, and from the displayed list, click **Use Existing List**. In the **Select Data Source** dialog box, navigate to your **Word Chapter 8** folder, select the file **Lastname_Firstname_8C_Eastern_Customers**, and then click **Open**.

c. In the **Select Table** dialog box, select '**Cruise Customers$**', if necessary, and then select the **First row of data contains column headers** check box, if necessary. Click **OK**. On the **Mailings tab**, in the **Start Mail Merge group**, click the **Edit Recipient List** button. In the **Mail Merge Recipients** dialog box, under **Refine recipient list**, click **Filter**. In the **Filter and Sort** dialog box, on the **Filter Records** tab, click the **Field arrow**, and then scroll as necessary and click **Repeat Customer**. Click the **Comparison arrow**, and then click **Equal to**, if necessary. In the **Compare to** box, type **Yes** Click **OK** two times to close the dialog boxes.

d. Select the first paragraph, change the **Font Size** to **28**, and then apply **Center**. On the **Home tab**, in the **Font group**, change the **Text Effects** to **Gradient Fill – Blue, Accent 1**—in the third row, the fourth effect. Select the second and third paragraphs, change the **Font Size** to **16**, and then apply **Center**.

e. In the blank paragraph following the date, click to position the insertion point, and then press [Enter] three times. On the **Mailings tab**, in the **Write & Insert Fields group**, click the **Address Block** button. In the **Insert Address Block** dialog box, click **OK**. Press [Enter] two times, and then in the **Write & Insert**

Fields group, click the **Greeting Line** button. In the **Insert Greeting Line** dialog box, under **Greeting line format**, in the box on the right—the **Punctuation** box, click the **Punctuation arrow**, and then from the displayed list, click **:** (the colon). Click **OK**, and then press [Enter].

2 Position the insertion point to the left of the paragraph that begins *Because*. Select the word *Because*, and then press [Del]. On the **Mailings tab**, in the **Write & Insert Fields group**, click the **Insert Merge Field** button. In the **Insert Merge Field** dialog box, under **Fields**, click **Title**, and then click **Insert**. Click the **Last Name** field, click **Insert**, and then **Close** the **Insert Merge Field** dialog box.

a. Click to position the insertion point between the **Title** field and the **Last_Name** field, and then press [Spacebar]. Click to position the insertion point to the right of the **Last_Name** field, and then type **, because** Press [Spacebar] and then **Save** your changes. On the **Mailings tab**, in the **Finish group**, click the **Finish & Merge** button, and then click **Edit Individual Documents**. In the **Merge to New Document** dialog box, click **OK**.

b. Press [Ctrl] + [Home], if necessary. Navigate to your **Word Chapter 8** folder, and then save the document as **Lastname_Firstname_8C_Eastern_Merged** Scroll to the bottom of **Page 1**, right-click in the footer area, click **Edit Footer**, and then using **Quick Parts**, insert the file name. **Close** the footer area.

c. Display the **Document Information Panel**, and in the **Author** box, type your first and last names. In the **Subject** box, type your course name and section number, and in the **Keywords** box, type **eastern cruise letters, merged Close** the Document Information Panel. **Save** your changes, and then **Close** the document.

3 In the displayed document, scroll to the bottom of the page, right-click in the footer area, click **Edit Footer**, and then using **Quick Parts**, insert the file name. **Close** the footer area. Display the **Document Information Panel**, and in the **Author** box, type your first and last names. In the **Subject** box, type your course name and section number, and in the **Keywords** box, type **eastern cruise letters, main Close** the Document Information Panel. **Save** your document, display **Backstage** view, and then click **Close** to close the document, but leave Word open.

(Project 8C Eastern Cruise continues on the next page)

Content-Based Assessments

4 Press Ctrl + N to open a new document. On the **Mailings tab**, in the **Start Mail Merge group**, click the **Start Mail Merge** button, and then click **Envelopes**. In the **Envelope Options** dialog box, on the **Envelope Options tab**, under **Envelope size**, click **Size 10 (4 1/8 × 9 1/2 in)**. Click **OK**. Navigate to your **Word Chapter 8** folder, and then save the document as **Lastname_Firstname_8C_EasternEnv_Main**

a. On the **Mailings tab**, in the **Start Mail Merge group**, click the **Select Recipients** button, and from the displayed list, click **Use Existing List**. In the **Select Data Source** dialog box, navigate to your **Word Chapter 8** folder, locate and select the file **Lastname_Firstname_8C_Eastern_Customers**, and then click **Open**. In the **Select Table** dialog box, select **'Cruise Customers$'**, if necessary, and then select the **First row of data contains column headers** check box, if necessary. Click **OK**.

b. On the **Mailings tab**, in the **Start Mail Merge group**, click the **Edit Recipient List** button. In the **Mail Merge Recipients** dialog box, under **Refine recipient list**, click **Filter**. In the **Filter and Sort** dialog box, on the **Filter Records tab**, click the **Field arrow**, and then scroll as necessary and click **Repeat Customer**. Click the **Comparison arrow**, and then click **Equal to**, if necessary. In the **Compare to** box, type **Yes** Click **OK** two times to close the dialog boxes.

c. Type the following return address, pressing Enter after the first and second lines.

Agua Azul Caribbean Cruises

2300 Caribbean Way

Miami, FL 33132

d. If *Azul* is flagged as a spelling error, right-click, and then click **Ignore All**. In the center of the document, position the insertion point to the left of the paragraph mark. On the **Mailings tab**, in the **Write & Insert Fields group**, click the **Address Block** button. In the **Insert Address Block** dialog box, click **OK**. On the **Mailings tab**, in the **Finish group**, click the **Finish & Merge** button, and then click **Edit Individual Documents**. In the **Merge to New Document** dialog box, click **OK**.

5 Navigate to your **Word Chapter 8** folder, and save the document as **Lastname_Firstname_8C_EasternEnv_Merged** Right-click in the footer area, click **Edit Footer**, and then using **Quick Parts**, insert the file name. **Close** the footer area. Display the **Document Information Panel**, and in the **Author** box, type your first and last names. In the **Subject** box, type your course name and section number, and in the **Keywords** box, type **customer envelopes, merged Close** the Document Information Panel. **Save** your document, and then **Close** the document.

6 In the main document, right-click in the footer area, click **Edit Footer**, and then using **Quick Parts**, insert the file name. **Close** the footer area. Display the **Document Information Panel**, and in the **Author** box, type your first and last names. In the **Subject** box, type your course name and section number, and in the **Keywords** box, type **customer envelopes, main Close** the Document Information Panel. **Save** your document.

7 Print your four documents—it is not necessary to print the data source—or submit all five files electronically as directed by your instructor. **Exit** Word.

End You have completed Project 8C

Apply **8B** skills from these Objectives:

▣ Edit and Sort a Data Source

④ Match Fields and Apply Rules

⑤ Create a Data Source and a Directory

Skills Review | Project **8D** Name Tags

In the following Skills Review project, you will use mail merge to create name tags for customers taking the Western Caribbean cruise by selecting a label option, editing records, and sorting the data source. You will create a new data source and match fields to create a list of Western Caribbean cruise employees and their addresses. Your completed documents will look similar to Figure 8.43.

Project Files

For Project 8D, you will need the following files:

Two new blank Word documents
w08D_Cruise_Customers

You will save your files as:

Lastname_Firstname_8D_Cruise_Customers—not shown in figure
Lastname_Firstname_8D_NameTags_Main
Lastname_Firstname_8D_NameTags_Merged
Lastname_Firstname_8D_Western_Employees—not shown in figure
Lastname_Firstname_8D_Employee_List

Project Results

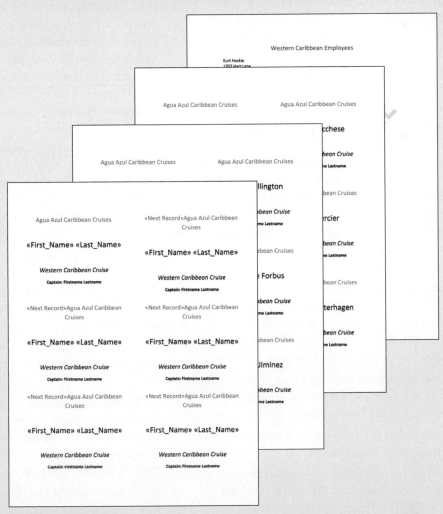

Figure 8.43

(Project 8D Name Tags continues on the next page)

1 **Start** Windows Explorer, navigate to your student files, and locate the Access file **w08D_Cruise_Customers. Copy** the file to your **Word Chapter 8** folder, right-click the file, and then **Rename** the file as **Lastname_Firstname_ 8D_Cruise_Customers Close** any open windows. **Start** Word. If necessary, display the rulers and formatting marks.

a. On the **Mailings tab**, in the **Start Mail Merge group**, click the **Start Mail Merge** button, and then click **Labels**. In the **Labels Options** dialog box, under **Label information**, click the **Label vendors arrow** and select **Avery US Letter**, and then in the **Product number** box, scroll as necessary and click **5392 Name Badges Insert Refills**. Click **Yes**. To display gridlines, click the **Layout tab**, and then in the **Table group**, click the **View Gridlines** button. Navigate to your **Word Chapter 8** folder, and then save the document as **Lastname_Firstname_8D_NameTags_Main**

b. On the **Mailings tab**, in the **Start Mail Merge group**, click the **Select Recipients** button, and then click **Use Existing List**. In the **Select Data Source** dialog box, navigate to your **Word Chapter 8** folder, select **Lastname_Firstname_8D_Cruise_Customers**, and then click **Open**.

c. On the **Mailings tab**, in the **Start Mail Merge group**, click the **Edit Recipient List** button. In the **Mail Merge Recipients** dialog box, at the bottom left under **Data Source**, click **Lastname_Firstname_8D_Cruise_ Customers**, and then click the **Edit** button. In the **Edit Data Source** dialog box, click the **New Entry** button. In the new record line, in the **First_Name** field, type **Lawrence** and then press Tab. In the **Last_Name** field, type **Forbus** and then press Tab. In the **Country** field, type **USA** and then press Tab.

d. In the new line, in the **First_Name** field, type **Melissa** and then press Tab. In the **Last_Name** field, type **Baker** and then press Tab. In the **Country** field, type **CANADA** Click **OK**. In the **Microsoft Office Word** dialog box, click **Yes** to update your recipient list.

e. In the **Mail Merge Recipients** dialog box, immediately to the right of **Last_Name**, click the **arrow**, and then click **Sort Ascending**. Click **OK**.

2 Select the entire table, and then on the **Layout tab**, in the **Alignment group**, click **Align Center**.

a. In the first cell of the table, click to position the insertion point. Type **Agua Azul Caribbean Cruises** and then press Enter two times. Select the text you just

typed, change the **Font Size** to **16**, and then change the **Font Color** to **Aqua, Accent 5, Darker 25%**.

b. In the third paragraph, click to position the insertion point. On the **Mailings tab**, in the **Write & Insert Fields group**, click the **Insert Merge Field button arrow**, and then click **First_Name**. Press Spacebar, click the **Insert Merge Field button arrow**, and then click **Last_Name**. Press Enter three times. Select the merge fields you just inserted, and then change the **Font Size** to **20**.

c. In the fifth paragraph, click to position the insertion point, and then type **Western Caribbean Cruise** Select the text, change the **Font Size** to **16**, and then apply **Italic**. In the sixth paragraph, type **Captain:** press Spacebar, and then using your own name, type your first and last names. Select the text you just typed, and then apply **Bold**.

d. On the **Mailings tab**, in the **Write & Insert Fields group**, click the **Update Labels** button. In the **Finish group**, click the **Finish & Merge** button, and then click **Edit Individual Documents**. In the **Merge to New Document** dialog box, click **OK**. Navigate to your **Word Chapter 8** folder, and then save the document as **Lastname_Firstname_8D_NameTags_Merged** Display the **Document Information Panel**, and in the **Author** box, type your first and last names. In the **Subject** box, type your course name and section number, and in the **Keywords** box, type **name tags, merged Close** the Document Information Panel. **Save** your document, and then **Close** the document.

3 In the main document, display the **Document Information Panel**. In the **Author** box, type your first and last names. In the **Subject** box, type your course name and section number, and in the **Keywords** box, type **name tags, main Close** the Document Information Panel. **Save** your document. **Close** the document, but leave Word open.

4 Press Ctrl + N to display a new document. On the **Home tab**, in the **Styles group**, change the style to **No Spacing**.

a. On the **Mailings tab**, in the **Start Mail Merge group**, click the **Start Mail Merge** button, and then click **Directory**. On the **Mailings tab**, in the **Start Mail Merge group**, click the **Select Recipients** button, and then click **Type New List**.

b. In the **New Address List** dialog box, click the **Customize Columns** button. In the **Customize**

(Project 8D Name Tags continues on the next page)

Content-Based Assessments

Skills Review | Project **8D** Name Tags (continued)

Address List dialog box, under **Field Names**, click the **State** field, and then click **Rename**. In the **Rename Field** dialog box, in the **To** box, type **State/Province** and then click **OK**. In the **Customize Address List** dialog box, under **Field Names**, click **Title**, click the **Delete** button, and then click **OK** to confirm the deletion. In a similar manner, delete the **Company Name**, **Address Line 2**, **Home Phone**, **Work Phone**, and **E-mail Address** fields. Click **OK**.

c. In the **New Address List** dialog box, under **First Name**, position the insertion point in the first cell, if necessary. Type the data shown in **Table 1**, pressing Tab after each entry except the last entry—CANADA.

d. In the **New Address List** dialog box, click **OK**. In the **Save Address List** dialog box, navigate to your **Word Chapter 8** folder. Save the file as **Lastname_Firstname_8D_Western_Employees** On the **Mailings tab**, in the **Write & Insert Fields group**, click the **Address Block** button. In the **Insert Address Block** dialog box, under **Correct Problems**, click the **Match Fields** button. In the **Match Fields** dialog box, click the **State arrow**, and then from the displayed list, click **State/Province**. Click **OK** two times to close the dialog boxes.

e. Position the insertion point to the right of the *Address Block* merge field, if necessary, and then press Enter two times. On the **Mailings tab**, in the **Finish group**, click the **Finish & Merge** button, and

then click **Edit Individual Documents**. In the **Merge to New Document** dialog box, click **OK**.

5 With the insertion point at the beginning of the document, press Enter two times. In the first paragraph, type **Western Caribbean Employees** Select the paragraph, change the **Font Size** to **16**, apply **Center**, and then change the **Font Color** to **Dark Blue, Text 2**—in the fourth column, the first color.

a. On the **Page Layout tab**, in the **Page Background group**, click the **Watermark** button. In the **Confidential** gallery, click **CONFIDENTIAL 1**.

b. Press Ctrl + Home. Navigate to your **Word Chapter 8** folder, and save the document as **Lastname_Firstname_8D_Employee_List** Right-click in the footer area, click **Edit Footer**, and then using **Quick Parts**, insert the file name in the footer. **Close** the footer area.

c. Display the **Document Information Panel**, and in the **Author** box, type your first and last names. In the **Subject** box, type your course name and section number, and in the **Keywords** box, type **employee list, addresses Close** the Document Information Panel. **Save** your document, and then **Close** the document. **Exit** Word without saving the main document.

6 Print your three documents—it is not necessary to print the data sources—or submit all five files electronically as directed by your instructor.

Table 1

First Name	Last Name	Address Line 1	City	State/ Province	ZIP Code	Country or Region
Kurt	Hoskie	1707 Hart Lane	Calgary	AB	TOH 1AO	CANADA
Ryan	Graves	691 Kidd Avenue	Berne	NY	12059	USA
Katy	Reese	2304 Rose Court	Sugar Land	TX	77478	USA
Paul	Rogers	1157 Zappia Drive	Dallas	TX	75247	USA
Jill	Brandt	4938 Linden Street	Montreal	QC	H3Z 2YZ	CANADA

(Return to Step 4c)

End **You have completed Project 8D**

Content-Based Assessments

Apply **8A** skills from these Objectives:

- ◼ Merge a Data Source and a Main Document
- ◼ Create Envelopes

Mastering Word | Project **8E** Hospitality Team

In the following Mastering Word project, you will use mail merge to filter a data source and customize a form letter to employees that have been selected for the hospitality team for the Caribbean Calypso cruise. Your completed documents will look similar to Figure 8.44.

Project Files

For Project 8E, you will need the following files:

> New blank Word document
> w08E_Hospitality_Team
> w08E_Hospitality_Letter

You will save your files as:

> Lastname_Firstname_8E_Hospitality_Team—not shown in figure
> Lastname_Firstname_8E_Hospitality_Main
> Lastname_Firstname_8E_Hospitality_Merged
> Lastname_Firstname_8E_HospitalityEnv_Main
> Lastname_Firstname_8E_HospitalityEnv_Merged

Project Results

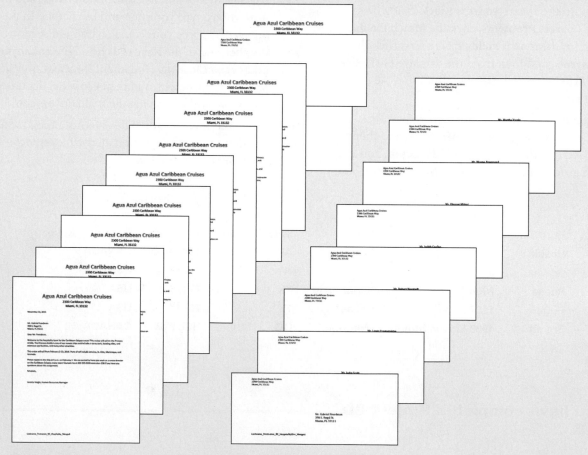

Figure 8.44

(Project 8E Hospitality Team continues on the next page)

Content-Based Assessments

Mastering Word | Project **8E** Hospitality Team (continued)

1 **Start** Excel. Navigate to your student files, and open the file **w08E_Hospitality_Team**. **Save** the file to your **Word Chapter 8** folder as **Lastname_Firstname 8E_Hospitality_Team Exit** Excel.

2 **Start** Word. Navigate to your student files, and open the file **w08E_Hospitality_Letter**. **Save** the document to your **Word Chapter 8** folder as **Lastname_Firstname_8E_Hospitality_Main** If necessary, display the rulers and formatting marks.

3 **Start Mail Merge**, and select **Letters**. From your **Word Chapter 8** folder, select the file **Lastname_Firstname_8E_Hospitality_Team**, and then select **'Employee Information$'** as the data source. **Filter** the data source so that the **Job Title** field is **Not equal to lounge manager**

4 Select the first paragraph, change the **Font Size** to **28**, apply **Center**, and then change the **Text Effects** to **Gradient Fill – Blue, Accent 1**. Select the second and third paragraphs, change the **Font Size** to **16**, and then apply **Center**.

5 Position the insertion point in the blank paragraph following the date, press [Enter] three times, and then insert the **Address Block** merge field. Press [Enter] two times, insert the **Greeting Line** merge field, and then press [Enter]. Locate the paragraph that begins *Please report*, and then in the second sentence, position the insertion point to the left of *on*. Type **work as a** and then press [Spacebar]. Insert the **Job_Title** merge field, and then press [Spacebar].

6 Finish the merge to **Edit Individual Documents**. **Save** the document in your **Word Chapter 8** folder as **Lastname_Firstname_8E_Hospitality_Merged** and then insert the file name in the footer. Display the **Document Information Panel**, type your name as the **Author**, and your course name and section number as the **Subject**. In the **Keywords** box, type **hospitality letter, merged Save** your changes, and then **Close** the document.

7 In the main document, insert the file name in the footer. Display the **Document Information Panel**, type your name as the **Author**, and your course name and section number as the **Subject**. In the **Keywords** box, type **hospitality letter, main Save** your document, and then **Close** the document, but leave Word open.

8 In a new document, **Start Mail Merge**, select **Envelopes**, and then select **Size 10 (4 1/8 × 9 1/2 in)**. **Save** the document to your **Word Chapter 8** folder as **Lastname_Firstname_8E_HospitalityEnv_Main** From your **Word Chapter 8** folder, select the file **Lastname_Firstname_8E_Hospitality_Team**, and then select **'Employee Information$'** as the data source. **Filter** the data source so that the **Job Title** field is **Not equal to lounge manager** In the center of the document, insert the **Address Block** merge field. Press [Ctrl] + [Home], and then using three lines, type the return address:

    Agua Azul Caribbean Cruises

    2300 Caribbean Way

    Miami, FL 33132

9 Finish the merge to **Edit Individual Documents**. **Save** the document to your **Word Chapter 8** folder as **Lastname_Firstname_8E_HospitalityEnv_Merged** and then insert the file name in the footer. Display the **Document Information Panel**, type your name as the **Author**, and your course name and section number as the **Subject**. In the **Keywords** box, type **hospitality envelope, merged Save** your changes, and then **Close** the document.

10 In the main document, insert the file name in the footer. Display the **Document Information Panel**, type your name as the **Author**, and your course name and section number as the **Subject**. In the **Keywords** box, type **hospitality envelope, main Save** your document.

11 Print all four documents—it is not necessary to print the data source—or submit all five files electronically as directed by your instructor. **Close** Word.

End **You have completed Project 8E**

Apply **8B** skills from these Objectives:

▪ Edit and Sort a Data Source

▪ Match Fields and Apply Rules

▪ Create a Data Source and a Directory

Mastering Word | Project **8F** Cruise Ships

In the following Mastering Word project, you will use mail merge and sort a data source to create jewel case labels for DVDs containing information about Agua Azul's cruises and ships. Additionally, you will create a directory listing customer information. Your completed documents will look similar to Figure 8.45.

Project Files

For Project 8F, you will need the following files:

New blank Word document
w08F_Ships_Data

You will save your files as:

Lastname_Firstname_8F_Ships_Data—not shown in figure
Lastname_Firstname_8F_Ships_Main
Lastname_Firstname_8F_Ships_Merged
Lastname_Firstname_8F_Eastern_Data—not shown in figure
Lastname_Firstname_8F_Cruise_Roster

Project Results

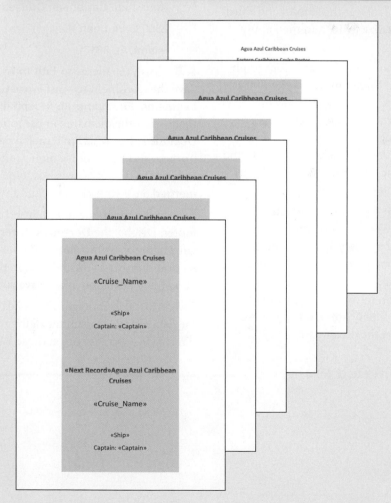

Figure 8.45

(Project 8F Cruise Ships continues on the next page)

Content-Based Assessments

Mastering Word | Project **8F** Cruise Ships (continued)

1 From your student files, locate the Access file **w08F_Ships_Data. Copy** the file to your **Word Chapter 8** folder, and **Rename** the file as **Lastname_Firstname_8F_Ships_Data Close** any open windows.

2 **Start** Word, **Start Mail Merge**, and select **Labels**. Change the **Label vendors** to **Avery US Letter**, and then change the **Product number** to **8955 Jewel Case Inserts**. **Save** the document to your **Word Chapter 8** folder as **Lastname_Firstname_8F_Ships_Main** Select the file **Lastname_Firstname_8F_Ships_Data** as the data source. Edit the data source—in the **Captain** field, replace *Brian Picard* with your first and last names. Sort the data source to display the **Cruise_Name** field in ascending order.

3 Select the entire table. Change the alignment to **Align Center**, and then change the **Shading** to **Dark Blue, Text 2, Lighter 80%**—in the fourth column, the second color. In the first cell, type **Agua Azul Caribbean Cruises** and then press Enter two times. Insert the **Cruise_Name** merge field, and then press Enter three times. Insert the **Ship** merge field, and then press Enter. Type **Captain:** press Spacebar and then insert the **Captain** merge field.

4 Select the first paragraph, change the **Font Size** to **22**, and change the **Text Effects** to **Gradient Fill – Blue, Accent 1**. Select the third paragraph, change the **Font Size** to **24**, and change the **Font Color** to **Dark Blue, Text 2**—in the fourth column, the first color. Select the fourth, blank paragraph, and then apply **Bold**. Select the sixth and seventh paragraphs, change the **Font Size** to **20**, and change the **Font Color** to **Dark Blue, Text 2**.

5 Position the insertion point in the paragraph below the *Cruise_Name* merge field. Create an **If...Then...Else** rule so that if the **Days** field is **Greater than 7** then the text **Extended Tour** is inserted. **Update Labels**, and then finish the merge to **Edit Individual Documents**. **Save** the document to your **Word Chapter 8** folder as **Lastname_Firstname_8F_Ships_Merged** For the **Document Properties**, type your name as the **Author**, and your course name and section number as the **Subject**. In the **Keywords** box, type **cruises, merged Save** your document, and then **Close** the document.

6 In the main document, from **Backstage** view, display the **Advanced Properties** dialog box. Type your name as the **Author**, and your course name and section number as the **Subject**. In the **Keywords** box, type **cruises, main Save** your document, and then **Close** the document but leave Word open.

7 In a new document, **Start Mail Merge**, and then select **Directory**. To **Select Recipients, Type New List.**

Display the **Customize Address List** dialog box, **Move Up** the **City** and **State** field names to display directly below **Last Name**. Beginning with **Company Name**, delete all remaining field names.

8 In the **New Address List** dialog box, under **Title**, position the insertion point in the first cell, and then type the following data in the appropriate cells:

Title	First Name	Last Name	City	State
Mr. and Mrs.	Jacqui	Epps	Marietta	GA
Mr.	Walter	Perry	Conyers	SC
Mrs.	Kelley	Bondurant	Centerville	VA
Mr. and Mrs.	Taylor	Dunham	Lima	OH
Ms.	Jessica	Flynn	Smyrna	MD

9 In the **Save Address List** dialog box, navigate to your **Word Chapter 8** folder, and save the file as **Lastname_Firstname_8F_Eastern_Data** as the data source. Sort the data source to display the **Last Name** field in ascending order.

10 On the horizontal ruler, set left tabs at approximately the **2.5-inch mark** and the **3.5-inch mark**. Insert the **Title** merge field, press Spacebar, insert the **First Name** merge field, press Spacebar, and then insert the **Last Name** merge field. Press Tab, insert the **City** merge field, press Tab, insert the **State** merge field, and then press Enter. Finish the merge to **Edit Individual Documents**.

11 With the insertion point at the beginning of the document, press Enter. In the first paragraph, type **Agua Azul Caribbean Cruises** Press Enter, and then type **Eastern Caribbean Cruise Roster** Press Enter two times, type **Name** press Tab, type **City** press Tab and then type **State** Select the first two paragraphs, change the **Font Size** to **16**, apply **Bold** and **Center**, and then change the **Font Color** to **Aqua, Accent 5, Darker 25%**. Select the fourth paragraph, and then apply **Bold** and **Underline**.

12 **Save** the document to your **Word Chapter 8** folder as **Lastname_Firstname_8F_Cruise_Roster** and then insert the file name in the footer. Display the **Document Information Panel**. Type your name as the **Author**, and your course name and section number as the **Subject**. In the **Keywords** box, type **customers, roster Save** your document, and then **Close** the document. **Close** Word without saving the main document.

13 Print your three documents—it is not necessary to print the data sources—or submit all five files electronically as directed by your instructor.

End **You have completed Project 8F**

Apply **8A** and **8B** skills
from these Objectives:

Apply **8A** and **8B** skills
from these Objectives:

1. Merge a Data
   Source and a Main
   Document
2. Create Envelopes
3. Edit and Sort a Data
   Source
4. Match Fields and
   Apply Rules
5. Create a Data
   Source and a
   Directory

Mastering Word | Project **8G** Entertainers

In the following Mastering Word project, you will create a letter to solicit entertainers for next year's Agua Azul cruises. You will filter the data source, match fields, and insert merge fields to modify the form letter. Your completed documents will look similar to Figure 8.46.

Project Files

For Project 8G, you will need the following files:

> New blank Word document
> w08G_Entertainers
> w08G_Entertainers_Letter

You will save your files as:

> Lastname_Firstname_8G_Entertainers—not shown in figure
> Lastname_Firstname_8G_Entertainers_Main
> Lastname_Firstname_8G_Entertainers_Merged
> Lastname_Firstname_8G_EntertainersEnv_Main
> Lastname_Firstname_8G_EntertainersEnv_Merged
> Lastname_Firstname_8G_Entertainers_Directory

Project Results

Figure 8.46

(Project 8G Entertainers continues on the next page)

Content-Based Assessments

Mastering Word | Project 8G Entertainers (continued)

1 **Start** Excel. Navigate to your student files, and open the file **w08G_Entertainers**. **Save** the file to your **Word Chapter 8** folder as **Lastname_Firstname_8G_Entertainers Close** Excel. **Start** Word. Navigate to your student files, and open the file **w08G_Entertainers_Letter**. **Save** the document to your **Word Chapter 8** folder as **Lastname_Firstname_8G_Entertainers_Main** If necessary, display the rulers and formatting marks.

2 **Start Mail Merge**, and select **Letters**. From your **Word Chapter 8** folder, select the file **Lastname_Firstname_8G_Entertainers**, and then select **'Entertainer Information$'** as the data source. **Edit** the data source by changing the **Postal Code** for *Cynthia Teets* to **33101**

3 Select the first paragraph, change the **Font Size** to **28**, apply **Center**, and then change the **Text Effects** to **Gradient Fill – Blue, Accent 1**. Select the second and third paragraphs, change the **Font Size** to **16**, and apply **Center**.

4 Position the insertion point in the blank paragraph following the date, and press [Enter] three times. Insert the **Address Block** merge field, matching the field **Street** with the **Address 1** field. Press [Enter] two times, insert the **Greeting Line** merge field, and then press [Enter]. Locate the paragraph that begins *Because you have*, and then position the insertion point to the right of *past*, before the comma. Press [Spacebar], type **as a** and then press [Spacebar]. Insert the **Talent** merge field.

5 Finish the merge to **Edit Individual Documents**. **Save** the document in your **Word Chapter 8** folder as **Lastname_Firstname_8G_Entertainers_Merged** and then insert the file name in the footer. In the **Document Information Panel**, type your name and your course name and section number. For the **Keywords**, type **entertainers letter, merged Save** and then **Close** the document.

6 In the main document, insert the file name in the footer. In the **Document Information Panel**, type your name and your course name and section number. For the **Keywords**, type **entertainers letter, main Save** and then **Close** the document, but leave Word open.

7 In a new document, **Start Mail Merge**, select **Envelopes**, and then select **Size 10 (4 1/8 × 9 1/2 in)**. **Save** the document to your **Word Chapter 8** folder as **Lastname_Firstname_8G_EntertainersEnv_Main** From your **Word Chapter 8** folder, select the file **Lastname_Firstname_8G_Entertainers** as the data source. In the center of the document, insert the **Address Block** merge field, matching the field **Street** with the **Address 1** field. Press [Ctrl] + [Home], and then using three lines, type the return address:

Agua Azul Caribbean Cruises

2300 Caribbean Way

Miami, FL 33132

8 Finish the merge to **Edit Individual Documents**. **Save** the document to your **Word Chapter 8** folder as **Lastname_Firstname_8G_EntertainersEnv_Merged** and then insert the file name in the footer. In the **Document Information Panel**, type your name and your course name and section number. For the **Keywords**, type **entertainers envelope, merged Save** and then **Close** the document.

9 In the main document, insert the file name in the footer. In the **Document Information Panel**, type your name and your course name and section number. For the **Keywords**, type **entertainers envelope, main Save** your document. **Close** the document without closing Word.

10 Press [Ctrl] + [N] to display a new document. **Start Mail Merge**, and select **Directory**. Select the file **Lastname_Firstname_8G_Entertainers** as the data source. Sort the data source to display the **Talent** field in ascending order.

11 On the horizontal ruler, set left tabs at the **3-inch mark** and the **5-inch mark**. Insert the **First_Name** merge field, press [Spacebar], and then insert the **Last_Name** merge field. Press [Tab], insert the **Home_Phone** merge field, press [Tab], and then insert the **Talent** merge field. Press [Enter]. Finish the merge to **Edit Individual Documents**.

12 Press [Ctrl] + [Home], press [Enter], and then press [↑]. Type **Agua Azul Caribbean Cruises** Press [Enter], type **Available Entertainers** and then press [Enter]. Type **Name** press [Tab], type **Home Phone** press [Tab], and then type **Talent** Select the first two paragraphs, change the **Font Size** to **16**, apply **Bold** and **Center**, and then change the **Font Color** to **Aqua, Accent 5, Darker 25%**. Select the third paragraph, and apply **Bold** and **Underline**.

13 **Save** the document to your **Word Chapter 8** folder as **Lastname_Firstname_8G_Entertainers_Directory** and then insert the file name in the footer. In the **Document Information Panel**, type your name and your course name and section number. For the **Keywords**, type **entertainers directory, merged Save** and then **Close** the document. **Exit** Word without saving the main document.

14 Print all five documents—it is not necessary to print the data source—or submit all six files electronically as directed by your instructor.

End **You have completed Project 8G**

GO! Fix It | Project **8H** Marketing Plan

Project Files

For Project 8H, you will need the following files:

> w08H_Employees_Data
> w08H_Marketing_Memo

You will save your files as:

> Lastname_Firstname_8H_Employees_Data
> Lastname_Firstname_8H_Memo_Merged
> Lastname_Firstname_8H_Memo_Main

In this project, you will edit a memo from Janelle Leighton, Vice President of Marketing at Agua Azul Caribbean Cruises, to all employees in the marketing department. Navigate to your student files, copy the file **w08H_Employees_Data** to your **Word Chapter 8** folder, and then rename the file as **Lastname_Firstname_8H_Employees_Data** From your student files, open the file **w08H_Marketing_Memo**. Begin the mail merge process for letters.

To complete the project, you must correct the following:

- Glenn Ruel, Marketing Assistant, and Zack Dierson, Graphic Designer, should be added to the **Lastname_Firstname_8H_Employees_Data** data source. They are both in the marketing department.

- The data source should be sorted by last name and filtered to display only employees in the marketing department.

- The memo headings should be formatted in a professional manner and the First Name, Last Name, and Title merge fields should be inserted following the TO: heading. Appropriate punctuation and spacing should be inserted.

- At the beginning of the last paragraph, the First Name merge field should be inserted, adding appropriate punctuation and spacing to create a complete sentence.

- Merge to edit individual documents, and then save the merged document in your **Word Chapter 8** folder as **Lastname_Firstname_8H_Memo_Merged** Insert the file name in the footer and add document properties that include the keywords **marketing memo, merged**

- Save the main document in your **Word Chapter 8** folder as **Lastname_Firstname_8H_Memo_Main** Insert the file name in the footer and add document properties that include the keywords **marketing memo, main**

Print both documents or submit all three files electronically as directed by your instructor.

End **You have completed Project 8H** ——————————————————

Content-Based Assessments

Apply a combination of the **8A** and **8B** skills.

GO! Make It | Project 8I Business Cards

Project Files

For Project 8I, you will need the following files:

New blank Word document
w08I_Card_Data

You will save your files as:

Lastname_Firstname_8I_Card_Data—not shown in figure
Lastname_Firstname_8I_Business_Cards

Save the file **w08I_Card_Data** to your **Word Chapter 8** folder as **Lastname_Firstname_8I_Card_Data** Using mail merge, select label option **Avery US Letter**, product number **28877 Clean Edge Business Cards**, and then create the document shown in Figure 8.47. Use **Lastname_Firstname_8I_Card_Data** as the data source. Edit the data source, by replacing the name in the first record. Change the name Kate to your first name, and then change the name Alcevedo to your last name. Filter the data source as necessary to display only those records shown in Figure 8.47. If necessary, substitute another graphic. All text is in the Calibri font. Employee names are 18 pt, the department name and phone number are 12 pt, and the company information is in 11 pt. Save the merged document in your **Word Chapter 8** folder as **Lastname_Firstname_8I_Business_Cards** Add document properties that include the keywords **business cards, sales** and then print your document or submit both files electronically as directed by your instructor.

Project Results

Figure 8.47

End You have completed Project 8I

Content-Based Assessments

Apply a combination of the **8A** and **8B** skills.

GO! Solve It | Project **8J** Planning Session

Project Files

For Project 8J, you will need the following files:

> w08J_Planning_Data
> w08J_Planning_Memo

You will save your files as:

> Lastname_Firstname_8J_Planning_Data
> Lastname_Firstname_8J_Planning_Main
> Lastname_Firstname_8J_Planning_Merged

From your student files, locate the file **w08J_Planning_Data**, copy it to your **Word Chapter 8** folder, and rename as **Lastname_Firstname_8J_Planning_Data** From your student files, open **w08J_Planning_Memo** and save it to your **Word Chapter 8** folder as **Lastname_Firstname_8J_Planning_Main** To begin the mail merge process, select Letters. Edit the **Lastname_Firstname_8J_Planning_Data** data source to include Suzi Rutkowski, an executive assistant in the Administration department. Sort the data source by last name and filter to display only employees in Administration.

Insert name and job title merge fields in the memo heading and format the memo appropriately. Create a rule for the job title field so that if it matches Chief Financial Officer, text is entered below the last document paragraph reminding Cristina to bring pertinent financial records to the meeting. Insert a watermark. Finish the merge, and save the merged document in your **Word Chapter 8** folder as **Lastname_Firstname_8J_Planning_Merged** Insert the file name in the footer and add appropriate document properties. Save the main document. Insert the file name in the footer and add appropriate document properties. Print both documents or submit all three files electronically as directed by your instructor.

Performance Element	Exemplary: You consistently applied the relevant skills	Proficient: You sometimes, but not always, applied the relevant skills	Developing: You rarely or never applied the relevant skills
Edit the data source	All information is added to the data source.	At least one item is not added to the data source.	No items are added to the data source.
Sort the data source	The data source is sorted appropriately.	The data source is sorted using an incorrect field.	The data source is not sorted.
Filter the data source	The data source is filtered appropriately.	The data source is filtered using an incorrect field.	The data source is not filtered.
Insert merge fields and format the memo	All items are inserted and merged appropriately.	At least one item is not inserted or is not formatted appropriately.	No items are inserted or formatted appropriately.
Create a rule	A rule is created and text displays correctly.	A rule is not created or text does not display correctly.	No rule is created and no text displays.

End **You have completed Project 8J**

Content-Based Assessments

Apply a combination of the **8A** and **8B** skills.

GO! Solve It | Project **8K** Shipping Information

Project Files

For Project 8K, you will need the following files:

Two new blank Word documents
w08K_Shipping_Information

You will save your files as:

Lastname_Firstname_8K_Shipping_Information
Lastname_Firstname_8K_Shipping_Main
Lastname_Firstname_8K_Shipping_Merged
Lastname_Firstname_8K_Calypso_Directory

From your student files, copy the file **w08K_Shipping_Information** to your **Word Chapter 8** folder and rename it as **Lastname_Firstname_8K_Shipping_Information** Using mail merge, select a label option for a mailing label with a height of 1.5″ and a width of 4″. Save the document to your **Word Chapter 8** folder as **Lastname_Firstname_8K_Shipping_Main** Use **Lastname_Firstname_8K_Shipping_Information** as the data source, sort the data by Postal Code and apply a filter to display only individuals on the Calypso cruise. Include the Address Block merge field—match fields as necessary—and the Cruise merge field and any related text on the label. Format the document. Save the merged document as **Lastname_Firstname_8K_Shipping_Merged** Save the main document. Create a directory that includes the name, city, state, and phone numbers for all individuals on the Calypso cruise. Add appropriate text and format the document to create a professional appearance. Save the merged directory as **Lastname_Firstname_8K_Calypso_Directory** Insert the file name in the footer. For all saved files, add appropriate document properties. Print your three documents or submit all four files electronically as directed.

	Performance Level		
Performance Element	**Exemplary:** You consistently applied the relevant skills	**Proficient:** You sometimes, but not always, applied the relevant skills	**Developing:** You rarely or never applied the relevant skills
Select a mailing label	A mailing label template is used and the labels are the correct size.	A mailing label template is used, but the labels are not the correct size.	No label template is used.
Sort and filter the data source	The data source is sorted and filtered.	The data source is not sorted or it is not filtered.	The data source is neither sorted nor filtered.
Match fields in the Address Block	All fields are matched and display correctly in the Address Block.	Some fields are not matched and do not display in the Address Block.	No fields are matched.
Insert text and merge fields in labels	Text and merge fields are inserted and formatted appropriately.	At least one item is not inserted or is not formatted appropriately.	No items are inserted or formatted appropriately.
Create a directory	All text and merge fields are inserted and formatted appropriately.	At least one item is not inserted or is not formatted appropriately.	No items are inserted or formatted appropriately.

End **You have completed Project 8K**

Outcomes-Based Assessments

Rubric

The following outcomes-based assessments are *open-ended assessments*. That is, there is no specific correct result; your result will depend on your approach to the information provided. Make *Professional Quality* your goal. Use the following scoring rubric to guide you in *how* to approach the problem and then to evaluate *how well* your approach solves the problem.

The *criteria*—Software Mastery, Content, Format and Layout, and Process—represent the knowledge and skills you have gained that you can apply to solving the problem. The *levels of performance*—Professional Quality, Approaching Professional Quality, or Needs Quality Improvements—help you and your instructor evaluate your result.

	Your completed project is of Professional Quality if you:	Your completed project is Approaching Professional Quality if you:	Your completed project Needs Quality Improvements if you:
1-Software Mastery	Choose and apply the most appropriate skills, tools, and features and identify efficient methods to solve the problem.	Choose and apply some appropriate skills, tools, and features, but not in the most efficient manner.	Choose inappropriate skills, tools, or features, or are inefficient in solving the problem.
2-Content	Construct a solution that is clear and well organized, contains content that is accurate, appropriate to the audience and purpose, and is complete. Provide a solution that contains no errors in spelling, grammar, or style.	Construct a solution in which some components are unclear, poorly organized, inconsistent, or incomplete. Misjudge the needs of the audience. Have some errors in spelling, grammar, or style, but the errors do not detract from comprehension.	Construct a solution that is unclear, incomplete, or poorly organized; contains some inaccurate or inappropriate content; and contains many errors in spelling, grammar, or style. Do not solve the problem.
3-Format and Layout	Format and arrange all elements to communicate information and ideas, clarify function, illustrate relationships, and indicate relative importance.	Apply appropriate format and layout features to some elements, but not others. Overuse features, causing minor distraction.	Apply format and layout that does not communicate information or ideas clearly. Do not use format and layout features to clarify function, illustrate relationships, or indicate relative importance. Use available features excessively, causing distraction.
4-Process	Use an organized approach that integrates planning, development, self-assessment, revision, and reflection.	Demonstrate an organized approach in some areas, but not others; or, use an insufficient process of organization throughout.	Do not use an organized approach to solve the problem.

Outcomes-Based Assessments

Apply a combination of the 8A and 8B skills.

GO! Think | Project 8L Health Insurance

Project Files

For Project 8L, you will need the following file:

New blank Word document

You will save your documents as:

Lastname_Firstname_8L_Insurance_Main
Lastname_Firstname_8L_Insurance_Data
Lastname_Firstname_8L_Insurance_Merged

Agua Azul Caribbean Cruises is changing to a new health insurance provider—MediReady—at the beginning of the year. MediReady offers more coverage at a lower rate and a variety of plans for employees. Loretta Voight, Human Resources Manager, is conducting information sessions for employees during November in Conference Room D at 10 a.m. The Administrative department will meet on November 1; all other departments will meet on November 3. The enrollment period begins November 10 and ends November 30.

Create a memo to department managers, from Ms. Voight, informing them of the new provider and the scheduled time for the department's information session. Save the main document as **Lastname_Firstname_8L_Insurance_Main** Create a data source that includes the name of each department and department manager; you should include at least five departments, including the Administrative department. Save the data source as **Lastname_Firstname_8L_ Insurance_Data** Insert appropriate merge fields in the memo, and create a rule to display the date of the session based on department. Format the memo in a professional manner. Save the merged document as **Lastname_Firstname_8L_Insurance_Merged** For each document you save, insert the file name in the footer and add appropriate document properties. Print your documents or submit all three files electronically as directed by your instructor.

 You have completed Project 8L ——————————————————

Outcomes-Based Assessments

Apply a combination of the **8A** and **8B** skills.

GO! Think | Project **8M** Training Sessions

Project Files

For Project 8M, you will need the following file:

New blank Word document

You will save your documents as:

Lastname_Firstname_8M_Training_Main
Lastname_Firstname_8M_Training_Data
Lastname_Firstname_8M_Training_Merged
Lastname_Firstname_8M_Training_Directory

Agua Azul Caribbean Cruises is conducting two training seminars for its employees:

Session	Session Code	Date
Communication Skills	CS	March 7
Team Building	TB	April 4

Using mail merge, select a label option for name tags. Save the main document as **Lastname_Firstname_8M_Training_Main** Create a data source that includes employee names and session codes for the session they are attending; include at least six names for each session. Use your own name as one of the employees attending the Team Building session. Save the data source as **Lastname_Firstname_8M_Training_Data** Sort the data source to display session codes in ascending order. Include appropriate information in the name tag, and apply a rule that will display the name of the session, instead of the code. Save the merged document as **Lastname_ Firstname_8M_Training_Merged** and add appropriate document properties. Save the main document and add appropriate document properties. Using mail merge, create a directory to display the list of everyone attending the team building session. Save the merged directory as **Lastname_Firstname_8M_Training_Directory** Add appropriate text, including the date of the session. Insert the file name in the footer and add appropriate document properties. Print your three documents or submit all four files electronically as directed by your instructor.

End You have completed Project 8M ——————————

Outcomes-Based Assessments

Apply a combination of the **8A** and **8B** skills.

You and GO! | Project **8N** Graduation Invitation

Project Files

For Project 8N, you will need the following files:

Two new blank Word documents

You will save your files as:

Lastname_Firstname_8N_Invitation_Main
Lastname_Firstname_8N_Invitation_Data
Lastname_Firstname_8N_Invitation_Merged
Lastname_Firstname_8N_Envelopes_Main
Lastname_Firstname_8N_Envelopes_Merged

Using mail merge, create a form letter and corresponding envelopes that can be sent to family and friends regarding your college graduation. Save the main document as **Lastname_Firstname_8N_Invitation_Main** Create a new data source including names and addresses for at least ten people. Save the data source as **Lastname_Firstname_8N_Invitation_Data** Type the letter, and insert appropriate merge fields. Using the formatting skills you have practiced, format the document in a manner that is professional and easy to read. Save the merged letter as **Lastname_Firstname_8N_Invitiation_Merged** Insert the file name in the footer, and add appropriate document properties. Save the main document, insert the file name in the footer, and add appropriate document properties. Using mail merge, create an envelope. Save the document as **Lastname_Firstname_8N_Envelopes_Main** Use the file **Lastname_Firstname_8N_Invitation_ Data** as the data source. Insert appropriate text and merge fields. Save the merged document as **Lastname_Firstname_8N_Envelopes_Merged** Insert the file name in the footer and add appropriate document properties. Save the main document, insert the file name in the footer and add appropriate document properties. Print all four documents or submit all five files electronically as directed by your instructor.

End **You have completed Project 8N** ————————————————

Creating Standardized Forms and Managing Documents

OUTCOMES

At the end of this chapter you will be able to:

PROJECT 9A
Create and protect a customized form that uses content controls.

OBJECTIVES

Mastering these objectives will enable you to:

1. Create a Customized Form (p. 513)
2. Modify and Protect a Form (p. 523)
3. Use a Template to Complete a Form (p. 527)

PROJECT 9B
Format illustrations, insert signature lines, and add protection to documents.

4. Customize the Ribbon (p. 531)
5. Format Pictures and Text Boxes (p. 534)
6. Add a Digital Signature to a Document (p. 540)
7. Prepare a Document for Distribution (p. 542)

grafica/Shutterstock

In This Chapter

A form is a structured document that includes fields, such as check boxes, that assist the user with entering information. A form can be saved as a template, protected from unauthorized changes, and then made available to others for completion in Word.

To improve productivity and use advanced graphic features to enhance the appearance of a document, you can customize the Ribbon. Also, you can prepare documents that require a signature so that an individual can digitally sign a Word document. Removing document properties and personal information prepares a document for distribution.

The projects in this chapter relate to **Laurales Herbs and Spices**. After ten years as an Executive Chef, Laura Morales started her own business, which offers quality products for cooking, eating, and entertaining in retail stores and online. In addition to herbs and spices, there is a wide variety of condiments, confections, jams, sauces, oils, and vinegars. Later this year, Laura will add a line of tools, cookbooks, and gift baskets. The company name is a combination of Laura's first and last names, and also the name of an order of plants related to cinnamon.

Project 9A Survey Form

myitlab
Project 9A Training

Project Activities

In Activities 9.01 through 9.10, you will create a form that will be used to measure customer satisfaction. John Tillman, Marketing Vice President, wants to get feedback from customers regarding the quality of products and services offered by Laurales Herbs and Spices. You will customize the form and save it as a template so that it can be completed by individual users. To test the form prior to distribution, you will enter customer information in the survey form. Your completed documents will look similar to Figure 9.1.

Project Files

For Project 9A, you will need the following files:

> w09A_Customer_Survey
> New blank Word document

You will save your documents as:

> Lastname_Firstname_9A_Survey_Template
> Lastname_Firstname_9A_Survey_Completed

Project Results

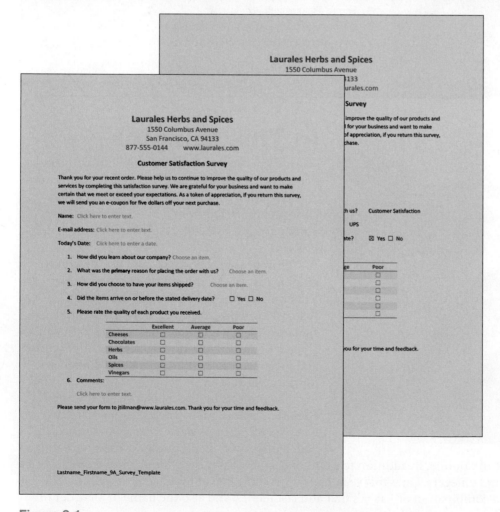

Figure 9.1
Project 9A Survey Form

Objective 1 | Create a Customized Form

A *form* is a structured document that has *static text*—descriptive text such as headings and labels—and reserved spaces, or *content controls*, for information to be entered by the user. A content control is a data entry field in a form in which a particular type of information, such as a name or date, is supplied by the user. For example, you can create a survey form that provides a place for the user to enter text or choose a specific entry from a list. You can also protect the form to restrict changes made by a user.

Activity 9.01 | Saving the Form as a Template

A form is usually stored as a *template* so that it can be used repeatedly without changing the original document. A template is a predefined structure that contains basic document settings, such as fonts, margins, and available styles. A document template can also store elements such as building blocks and content controls. Recall Microsoft Office provides built-in templates; however, in this activity, you will create your own document template.

1 **Start** Word. From **Backstage** view, click **Save As**. In the **Save As** dialog box, navigate to the location where you are saving the files for this chapter, and then create a new folder named **Word Chapter 9** Click the **Save as type arrow**, and then click **Word Template**. Using your own name for the file name, type **Lastname_Firstname_9A_Survey_Template** and then compare your screen with Figure 9.2.

> Because you will submit your file to your instructor, and others do not require access to it, you will save the template in your Word Chapter 9 folder instead of the default Templates folder. Document templates are saved with a .dotx file extension.

Figure 9.2

Word Template file type

2 Click **Save**. If necessary, display the rulers and formatting marks.

Activity 9.02 | Displaying the Developer Tab

Content controls are inserted in forms that will be filled in electronically. Content controls are accessed from the Developer tab; and by default, the Developer tab does not display on the Ribbon.

1 Below the **Backstage tabs**, click **Options**. In the **Word Options** dialog box, click **Customize Ribbon**. Take a moment to review the **Main Tabs** list that displays on the right side of the dialog box.

2 In the **Main Tabs** list, locate and then click to select the **Developer** check box. Compare your screen with Figure 9.3.

Main tabs that display on the Ribbon are indicated with a checkmark.

Figure 9.3

Developer tab selected

Main Tabs list

3 Click **OK** to close the **Word Options** dialog box. On the Ribbon, locate the **Developer tab** that now displays. Click the **Developer tab**, and then compare your screen with Figure 9.4.

The Developer tab enables you to extend the capabilities of Word. For example, a form can be created and then integrated with other applications to read the information that users enter into the form. Content control commands are located in the Controls group.

Figure 9.4

Developer tab

Controls group

4 On the **Insert tab**, in the **Text group**, click the **Object button arrow**, and then click **Text from File**. In the **Insert File** dialog box, navigate to your student files, click **w09A_Customer_Survey**, and then click **Insert**. If any words are flagged as a spelling error, click **Ignore All**.

The displayed text is the static text in the document that cannot be modified when the form is filled in by a user.

5 Select the first three paragraphs of the document, and then on the **Home tab**, in the **Styles group**, click the **No Spacing** style.

6 Select the first paragraph of the document. On the Mini toolbar, change the **Font Size** to **18**. Apply **Bold** B, and then click **Center** ≡. Click the **Font Color button arrow** A▾, and then in the sixth column, click the fifth color—**Red, Accent 2, Darker 25%**.

7 Select the next three paragraphs. On the Mini toolbar, change the **Font Size** to **14**, click **Center** ≡, and then click the **Font Color** button A▾.

8 Select the fifth paragraph. On the Mini toolbar, change the **Font Size** to **14**. Apply **Bold** B, and then click **Center** ≡. Click the **Font Color button arrow** A▾, and then in the sixth column, click the last color—**Red, Accent 2, Darker 50%**. **Save** 🖫 your changes.

Activity 9.03 │ Inserting a Plain Text Content Control

The ***Plain Text content control*** adds a field to the form that enables the user to insert ***unformatted text***—plain text—in the document. You will add several plain text content controls to the form so that the user can provide personal information and comments.

1 Locate the paragraph with the text *Name*, and then scroll as necessary so that the paragraph displays near the top of your screen. Click to position the insertion point to the right of the colon after *Name*, and then press Tab.

2 Click the **Developer tab**, and then in the **Controls group**, click the **Design Mode** button so that it glows orange.

> Turning on ***Design Mode*** enables you to work with content controls that are inserted in a document.

3 In the **Controls group**, click the **Plain Text Content Control** button Aa. At the insertion point, notice that a field with the default text *Click here to enter text.* displays. Compare your screen with Figure 9.5.

> The default text is used as a placeholder so that the person filling in the form knows what to do.

Figure 9.5

Plain Text Content
Control button

Design Mode button

Plain Text content control

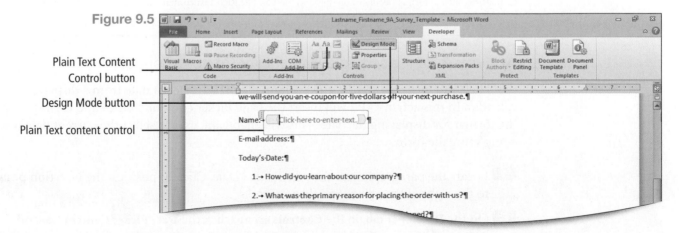

4 Locate the paragraph with the text *E-mail address*. Click to position the insertion point to the right of the colon, press Tab, and then in the **Controls group**, click the **Plain Text Content Control** button Aa.

5 Press Ctrl + End to move to the end of the document. If necessary, delete the blank paragraph at the end of the document, and then click to position the insertion point in the blank paragraph above the last paragraph.

6 Press Tab two times, and then in the **Controls group**, click the **Plain Text Content Control** button Aa . Click anywhere in the document to deselect the Plain Text content control, and then compare your screen with Figure 9.6.

Figure 9.6

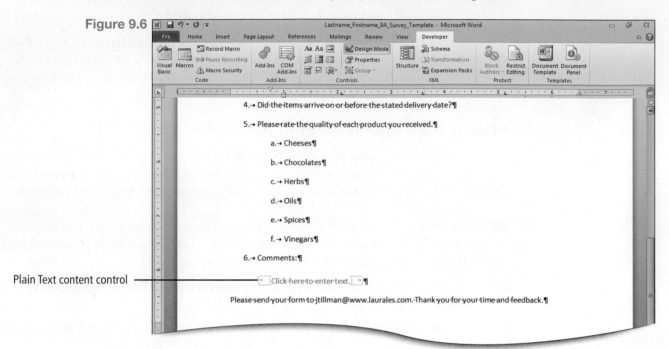

Plain Text content control ——————

7 **Save** 💾 your changes.

More Knowledge | Inserting a Rich Text Content Control

The Controls group includes a *Rich Text content control* that allows the user to add text with most types of formatting, such as formats available on the Mini toolbar. The Rich Text content control also allows the insertion of tables and graphics.

Activity 9.04 | Inserting a Date Picker Content Control

The *Date Picker content control* allows the user to select a date from a displayed calendar. In this activity, you will insert the Date Picker content control and then specify the format for displaying the date. This will enable the user to select the current date when completing the form.

1 Locate the paragraph with the text *Today's Date*. Click to position the insertion point to the right of the colon, and then press Tab.

2 On the **Developer tab**, in the **Controls group**, click the **Date Picker Content Control** button 📅 . Notice that the default text *Click here to enter a date.* displays in the content control.

3 With the Date Picker content control selected, in the **Controls group**, click the **Properties** button. In the **Content Control Properties** dialog box, under **Date Picker Properties**, in the **Display the date like this** box, click the third style—your date will differ. Compare your screen with Figure 9.7.

The Content Control Properties dialog box is used to modify settings for a content control—in this case, the date format. The date selected by a user will display in the format you specify.

Figure 9.7

Properties button

Date Picker Content Control button

Content Control Properties dialog box

Date format—your date will vary

Date Picker content control

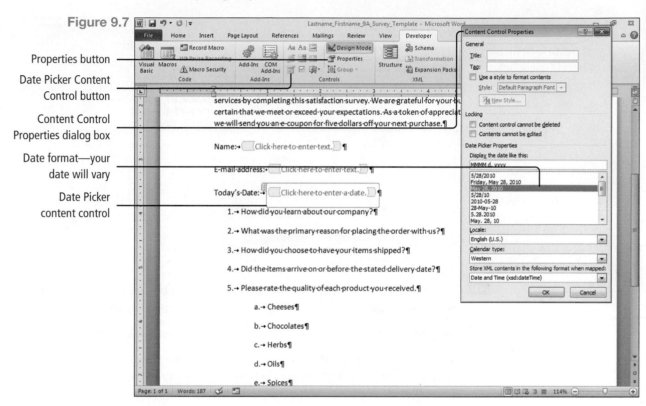

4 Click **OK** to close the **Content Control Properties** dialog box, and then **Save** your changes.

Activity 9.05 | Inserting a Drop-Down List Content Control

The **Drop-Down List content control** allows the user to select a specific item from a list, created by the designer of the form. By providing a list, you limit the choices for the user and ensure acceptable responses. You will use the Drop-Down List content control to solicit information regarding company awareness and shipping options.

1 Locate the paragraph that begins *1. How did you learn*. Click to position the insertion point to the right of the question mark, and then press Tab.

2 In the **Controls group**, click the **Drop-Down List Content Control** button .With the Drop-Down List content control selected, in the **Controls group**, click the **Properties** button.

3 In the **Content Control Properties** dialog box, under **Drop-Down List Properties**, click the **Add** button. In the **Add Choice** dialog box, in the **Display Name** box, type **Internet** Notice that as you type, the text in the **Value** box changes to match what you typed in the Display Name box. Compare your screen with Figure 9.8.

The Add button enables you to specify the items that will be included on the Drop-Down List content control. Each item in the list is identified by a name and a value. The display name is the text that will display to users when they view the list.

Figure 9.8

Drop-Down List Content Control button

Display Name of item

Value of item

Drop-Down List content control

4 Click **OK**. In the **Content Control Properties** dialog box, click the **Add** button. In the **Add Choice** dialog box, in the **Display Name** box, type **Magazine** and then click **OK**.

5 Using the technique you just practiced, **Add** the choices **Television** and **Friend**

6 In the **Content Control Properties** dialog box, under **Drop-Down List Properties**, click **Friend**, and then click the **Move Up** button three times. Compare your screen with Figure 9.9.

It is helpful for the user if the items in the list are in alphabetical order. You can use the Move Up and Move Down buttons to modify the order of the displayed items.

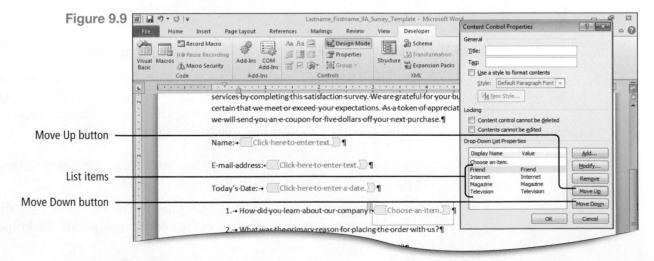

Figure 9.9

Move Up button

List items

Move Down button

7 Click **OK**, and then on the **Developer tab**, in the **Controls group**, click the **Design Mode** button to turn off Design Mode. In the inserted **Drop-Down List content control**, click the **Drop-Down List arrow**, and then compare your screen with Figure 9.10.

The listed items are the various ways that a customer might have learned about the company. When Design Mode is turned off, you can view the document as it will be seen by the person filling in the form. The text *Choose an item.* always displays by default.

Figure 9.10

Drop-Down List arrow

List items

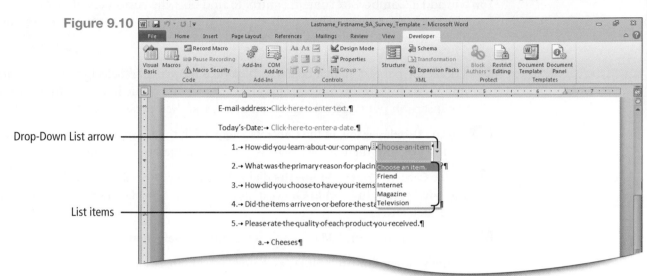

8 Click in an empty area of the document to deselect the Drop-Down List content control. On the **Developer tab**, in the **Controls group**, click the **Design Mode** button to turn on Design Mode.

9 Locate the paragraph that begins *3. How did you choose*. Click to position the insertion point to the right of the question mark, and then press Tab.

10 In the **Controls group**, click the **Drop-Down List Content Control** button , and then in the **Controls group**, click the **Properties** button.

11 In the **Content Control Properties** dialog box, click the **Add** button. Using the technique you practiced, in the **Add Choice** dialog box, in the **Display Name** box, add the three terms **FedEx UPS** and **USPS** and then compare your screen with Figure 9.11.

The three items in the list represent the shipping providers used by Laurales Herbs and Spices.

Figure 9.11

List items

12 In the **Content Control Properties** dialog box, click **OK**, and then **Save** 🔲 your changes.

Activity 9.06 | Inserting a Combo Box Content Control

A **Combo Box content control**, which is similar to a Drop-Down List content control, allows the user to select from an existing list, but also allows the user to enter new text. You will add a Combo Box content control to find out why customers place orders with Laurales Herbs and Spices. The Combo Box will allow the customer to enter a reason that is different from the listed items.

1 Locate the paragraph that begins *2. What was the primary*. Select the word **primary**, and then on the Mini toolbar, apply **Bold** B . On the same line, click to position the insertion point after the question mark, and then press Tab .

2 On the **Developer tab**, in the **Controls group**, click the **Combo Box Content Control** button 🔳, and then in the **Controls group**, click the **Properties** button.

3 In the **Content Control Properties** dialog box, under **Drop-Down List Properties**, click the **Add** button. In the **Add Choice** dialog box, in the **Display Name** box, type **Price** and then click **OK**.

4 In a similar manner, **Add** the choices **Quality** and **Selection**

5 In the **Content Control Properties** dialog box, under **Drop-Down List Properties**, click the default text *Choose an item.*, and then click the **Modify** button.

6 In the **Modify Choice** dialog box, in the **Display Name** box, position the insertion point to the left of the period, press Spacebar , and then type **or type another reason.** Click **OK**. Compare your screen with Figure 9.12.

> Recall that a Combo Box content control allows the user to insert new text. In this case, you want to provide the customer with the option to enter a reason—that is not already listed—for choosing Laurales Herbs and Spices.

Figure 9.12

Combo Box Content Control button

Combo Box content control

Combo Box items

7 In the **Content Control Properties** dialog box, click **OK**, and then **Save** 🔲 your changes.

Activity 9.07 | Inserting a Check Box Content Control

A *Check Box content control* is a field that allows the user to select—or not select—a specific option. In this activity, you will add several check boxes to the form.

1 Locate the paragraph that begins *4. Did the items arrive.* Click to position the insertion point to the right of the question mark, and then press Tab.

2 On the **Developer tab**, in the **Controls group**, click the **Check Box Content Control** button ☑. Click to position the insertion point to the right of the inserted check box, and then press End. Press Spacebar two times, and then type **Yes**

3 With the insertion point to the right of *Yes*, press Tab, and then in the **Controls group**, click the **Check Box Content Control** button ☑. Click to position the insertion point to the right of the check box, and then press End. Press Spacebar two times, type **No** Compare your screen with Figure 9.13.

A check box can be selected or deselected when the person using the form clicks the field.

Figure 9.13

Check Box Content Control button

Check Box content control

4 Select the six numbered paragraphs—which are formatted with lowercase letters—beginning with *a. Cheeses* and ending with *f. Vinegars*. On the **Home tab**, click the **Numbering** button to turn off the numbered format. On the **Insert tab**, in the **Tables group**, click the **Table** button, and then click **Convert Text to Table**.

5 In the **Convert Text to Table** dialog box, under **Separate text at**, be sure the **Paragraphs** option button is selected. Click **OK**, and then compare your screen with Figure 9.14.

Recall that a table can be used to display information in an organized manner.

Figure 9.14

Text converted to table format

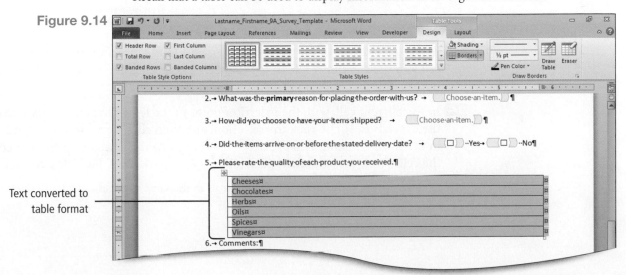

6 In the first cell of the table, click to position the insertion point to the right of *Cheeses*. On the **Layout tab**, in the **Rows & Columns group**, click the **Insert Right** button three times to insert three additional table columns.

7 Click to position the insertion point anywhere in the first row of the table, and then on the **Layout tab**, in the **Rows & Columns group**, click the **Insert Above** button to insert a new row at the top of the table.

8 In the first row of the table, click to position the insertion point in the second cell. Type **Excellent** press Tab, type **Average** press Tab, and then type **Poor**

9 On the **Design tab**, in the **Table Styles group**, click the **More** button ⏷. From the **Table Styles** gallery, under **Built-In**, in the first row, click the third style—**Light Shading – Accent 2**.

10 On the **Layout tab**, in the **Table group**, click the **View Gridlines** button, if necessary, to display gridlines.

11 Click the **Table Move Handle** ⊞ to select the entire table. On the **Layout tab**, in the **Cell Size group**, change the **Height** to **0.2"**. In the **Cell Size group**, in the **Width** box, type **1** and then press Enter.

12 On the **Layout tab**, in the **Table group**, click the **Properties** button. In the **Table Properties** dialog box, on the **Table tab**, under **Alignment**, click **Center**. Click **OK**, deselect the table, and then compare your screen with Figure 9.15.

Figure 9.15

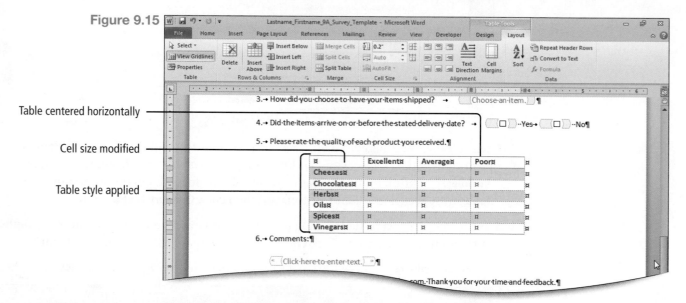

Table centered horizontally

Cell size modified

Table style applied

13 In the second row of the table, click to position the insertion point in the second cell. On the **Developer tab**, in the **Controls group**, click the **Check Box Content Control** button ☑.

14 In the current cell, with the insertion point to the left of the check box, drag to select the check box. Right-click the selection, and then click **Copy**. In the second row, click in the third cell, and then press Ctrl + V to paste the Check Box content control in the cell. Press Tab, and then press Ctrl + V to paste the Check Box content control.

You can copy and paste content controls in the same manner as text and graphics.

15 In a similar manner, paste the Check Box content control in the remaining empty cells of the table.

16 Select the second, third, and fourth columns of the table. On the **Layout tab**, in the **Alignment group**, click the **Align Center** button 🔲. Press Ctrl + End, and then compare your screen with Figure 9.16. **Save** 🔲 your changes.

Figure 9.16

Align Center applied to columns

Check Box content control

More Knowledge | **Inserting Other Controls**

The Picture content control allows the user to insert an image—for example, a photo for identification. Use the Building Block Gallery content control to insert a building block in a content control—allowing the user to add specific text.

Objective 2 | Modify and Protect a Form

You can manage the information provided by the person filling in the form by modifying the properties of content controls. In addition, when a form is distributed, you can protect it so that the static text and content controls cannot be edited or removed by the user.

Activity 9.08 | Setting Content Control Properties

You can designate the characteristics of a content control by modifying its properties—for example, assign a style in a Plain Text content control.

1 Locate the paragraph *Name*, and then in the same paragraph, click the **Plain Text content control** to select it.

2 On the **Developer tab**, in the **Controls group**, click the **Properties** button.

3 In the **Content Control Properties** dialog box, under **General**, click to select the **Use a style to format contents** check box. Click the **Style arrow**, and then click **Strong**. Compare your screen with Figure 9.17.

Styles can be used with content controls in the same manner as other text in the document. In addition to the displayed styles, you can create a new style. When the customer types his name, the text will be formatted with the Strong style.

Figure 9.17

Use a style to format contents check box

Strong style selected

Plain Text content control selected

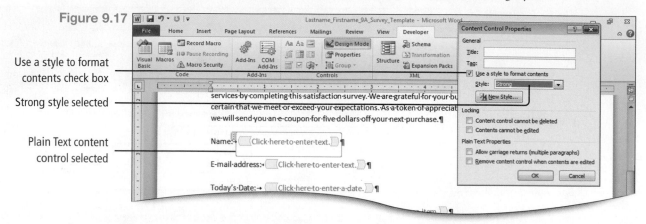

4 Click **OK**. Locate the paragraph that begins *E-mail address*, and then in the same paragraph, click the **Plain Text content control** to select it.

5 In the **Controls group**, click the **Properties** button. In the **Content Control Properties** dialog box, under **General**, click to select the **Use a style to format contents** check box. Click the **Style arrow**, click **Strong**, and then click **OK**.

The customer's e-mail address will be formatted with the Strong style.

6 Press **Ctrl** + **End**, and then above the last paragraph of the document, click the **Plain Text content control** to select it.

7 In the **Controls group**, click the **Properties** button. In the **Content Control Properties** dialog box, under **General**, click to select the **Use a style to format contents** check box. Click the **Style arrow**, click **Quote**, and then click **OK**.

The customer's comments will be formatted with the Quote style.

8 Press **Ctrl** + **Home**. On the **Page Layout tab**, in the **Page Background group**, click the **Page Color** button, and then under **Theme Colors**, in the sixth column, click the second color—**Red, Accent 2, Lighter 80%**. Compare your screen with Figure 9.18, and then **Save** your changes.

Figure 9.18

Page color applied

Activity 9.09 | Protecting a Document

Individuals using a form should be able to enter data in the content controls only—without editing other text or modifying any formats in the document. You can protect a form to restrict its use to allow the user to enter data in the control fields only. In this activity, you will apply restrictions and add a password to safeguard the form.

1 On the **Developer tab**, in the **Controls group**, click the **Design Mode** button to turn off Design Mode.

> When you finish designing a form, you must turn off Design Mode before it can be restricted and distributed for use.

2 On the **Developer tab**, in the **Protect group**, click the **Restrict Editing** button to display the **Restrict Formatting and Editing** task pane.

> By restricting the formatting and editing, you can control the changes that a user makes in a document.

3 In the **Restrict Formatting and Editing** task pane, under **2. Editing restrictions**, click to select the **Allow only this type of editing in the document** check box.

4 Click the **Allow only this type of editing in the document arrow**, and then click **Filling in forms**. Compare your screen with Figure 9.19.

> This option restricts the use of the document so that a user can only fill in the content controls in the document.

Figure 9.19

Restrict Formatting and Editing task pane

Filling in forms selected

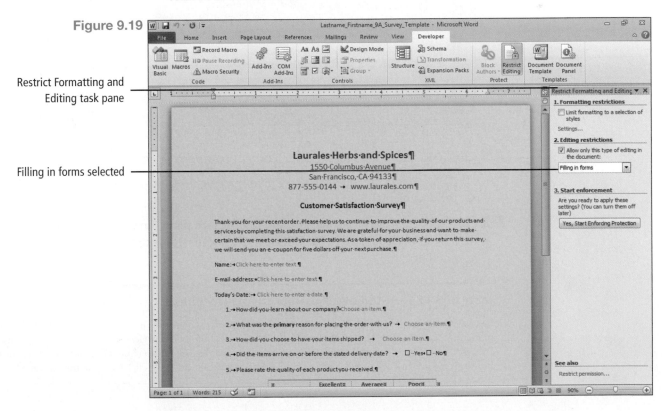

5 In the **Restrict Formatting and Editing** task pane, under **3. Start enforcement**, click the **Yes, Start Enforcing Protection** button.

> Before you begin enforcing protection, you should always confirm that all elements of the document display correctly.

6 In the **Start Enforcing Protection** dialog box, in the **Enter new password (optional)** box, type **survey33** Notice that as you type the characters are replaced with bullets.

A *password* is a code that is used to gain access to a file—in this case, the customer survey document.

7 In the **Reenter password to confirm** box, type **survey33** and then compare your screen with Figure 9.20.

Figure 9.20

Password entered, replaced by bullets

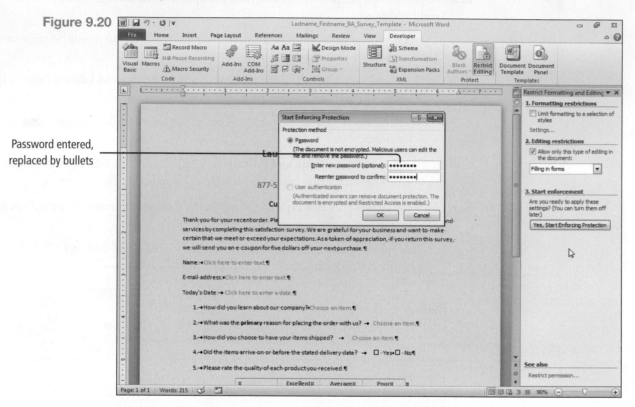

8 Click **OK**, and notice that the first content control is selected.

By restricting the editing to filling in forms, only the content controls are accessible in the document.

9 **Close** ⊠ the **Restrict Formatting and Editing** task pane. **Save** 🖫 your changes, and then from **Backstage** view, click **Close** to close your document. Leave **Word** open for the next activity.

More Knowledge | Adding a Password to Any Document

You can add a password to any document to prevent unauthorized persons from making changes. At the bottom of the Save As dialog box, click Tools, and then click General Options. In the General Options dialog box, in the Password to open or Password to modify box, type a password. Click OK to close the General Options dialog box. In the Confirm Password dialog box, type the password again, and then click OK. Save the document.

Objective 3 | Use a Template to Complete a Form

After the form is protected, it can be distributed to others by sending it as an e-mail attachment. The user can complete the form in Word.

Activity 9.10 | Filling in the Form

In this activity, you will complete the customer satisfaction survey.

1 From **Backstage** view, click the **New tab**. Under **Available Templates**, click **New from existing**. Navigate to your **Word Chapter 9** folder, click the file **Lastname_Firstname_ 9A_Survey_Template**, and then click the **Create New** button. Notice that the customer satisfaction survey form displays, as shown in Figure 9.21.

Because you are using the template to create a new document, the form displays with the default file name *Document1*—your number may vary. The first content control is selected because the form has been restricted.

Figure 9.21

Document1—your number may vary

Content control selected

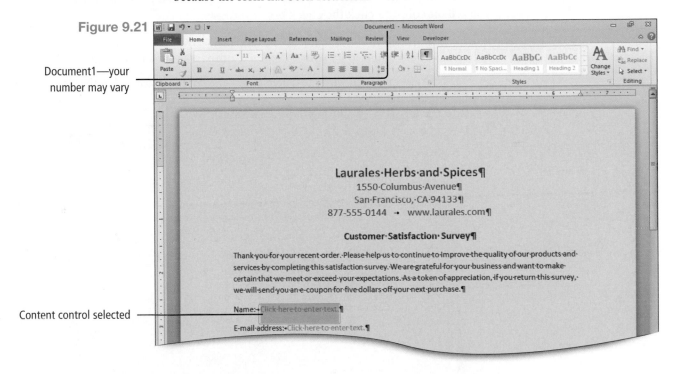

2 From **Backstage** view, click **Save As**, and then navigate to your **Word Chapter 9** folder. Using your own name, type the file name **Lastname_Firstname_9A_Survey_Completed** and then click **Save**.

3 In the **Plain Text content control** following *Name*, using your own name, type **Firstname Lastname**

Your name is formatted with the Strong style—the style you selected in the Content Control Properties dialog box.

4 Press (Tab), and then in the **Plain Text content control** following *E-mail address*, substituting your own last name, type **Lastname@laurales.com**

Because the form is protected—only filling in information is allowed—you can move from one content control to the next by pressing (Tab).

5 Press (Tab), click the **Date Picker content control arrow** to display the calendar, and then at the bottom of the calendar, click the **Today** button.

The date displays with the format you selected in the Content Control Properties dialog box. In the Date Picker content control, you can navigate through the displayed calendar to select any date.

6 Press Tab. To the right of the paragraph that begins with *1*, click the **Drop-Down List content control arrow**, and then click **Internet**.

7 Press Tab. To the right of the paragraph that begins with *2*, click the **Combo Box content control arrow**, click **Choose an item or type another reason.** and then type **Customer Satisfaction**

> Recall that you modified the default text to display *Choose an item or type another reason.* The user of the form can type a response that differs from the listed items.

8 Press Tab. To the right of the paragraph that begins *3*, click the **Drop-Down List content control arrow**, and then click **UPS**.

9 Locate the paragraph that begins *4*, and then click the **Check Box content control** to the left of **Yes**.

10 In the table, in the **Cheeses** row, in the **Average** column, click the check box. In the **Herbs** row, in the **Excellent** column, click the check box. In the **Spices** row, in the **Excellent** column, click the check box.

11 Below the paragraph that begins *6. Comments*, click the **Plain Text content control**, and then type **I am eager to try your vinegars.** Compare your screen with Figure 9.22.

> The text is formatted with the Quote style—the style you selected in the Content Control Properties dialog box.

Figure 9.22

Completed form—your date will differ

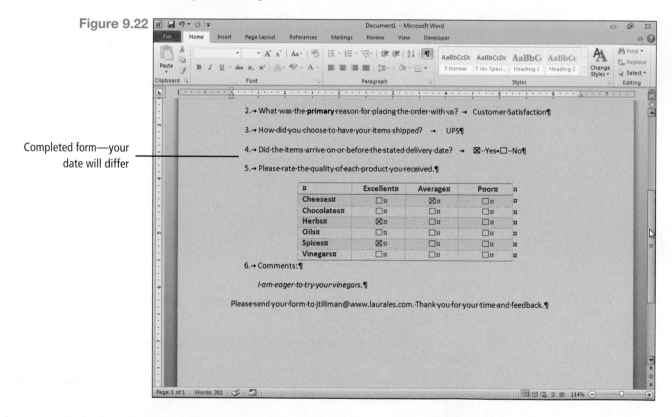

12 Press Ctrl + Home. In the **Document Information Panel**, in the **Author** box, type your first and last names. In the **Subject** box, type your course name and section number, and then in the **Keywords** box, type **customer survey, completed Close** ☒ the Document Information Panel. **Save** 🖫 your changes, and then from **Backstage** view, **Close** the document.

13 From **Backstage** view, click **Open**, and then open the file **Lastname_Firstname_9A_ Survey_Template**.

14 On the **Developer tab**, in the **Protect group**, click the **Restrict Editing** button to display the **Restrict Formatting and Editing** task pane. At the bottom of the **Restrict Formatting and Editing** task pane, click the **Stop Protection** button. In the **Unprotect Document** dialog box, in the **Password** box, type **survey33** Click **OK**.

> Recall the form is protected with a password. You must know the password to unprotect the document.

15 **Close** ☒ the **Restrict Formatting and Editing** task pane, and then using **Quick Parts**, insert the file name in the footer.

16 Display **Backstage** view. With the **Info** section selected, on the right side of the window, click **Properties**, and then click **Show Document Panel**. In the **Document Information Panel**, in the **Author** box, type your first and last names. In the **Subject** box, type your course name and section number, and then in the **Keywords** box, type **customer survey, template Close** ☒ the **Document Information Panel**.

17 From **Backstage** view, click **Options**. In the **Word Options** dialog box, click **Customize Ribbon**. In the **Main Tabs** list, locate and then click the check box to the left of **Developer** to remove the check mark. Click **OK**, and notice that the Developer tab no longer displays on the Ribbon.

18 **Save** 🖫 your changes, and then print both files or submit electronically as directed by your instructor. **Exit** Word.

End You have completed Project 9A

Project 9B Moving Agreement

myitlab
Project 9B Training

Project Activities

In Activities 9.11 through 9.18, you will create a document pertaining to an upcoming office move. Laurales Herbs and Spices is relocating its administrative offices. To help ensure that no items are lost or damaged, Ryan Koch, who is in charge of the move, has asked each employee to sign an agreement indicating that everything has been properly packed, labeled, and is ready to be moved. The completed document is to be returned through interoffice mail. You will customize the Ribbon to increase your efficiency in creating the agreement. You will also use a combination of graphic elements to create a company heading on the document and insert a signature line. Your completed document will look similar to Figure 9.23.

Project Files

For Project 9B, you will need the following files:

w09B_Spices
w09B_Moving_Agreement

You will save your document as:

Lastname_Firstname_9B_Moving_Agreement

Project Results

Figure 9.23
Project 9B Moving Agreement

Objective 4 | Customize the Ribbon

The Ribbon contains groups of commands on various tabs that are organized in a logical way. You can personalize Word and improve your efficiency by adding frequently used commands to an existing tab or by creating a new custom tab.

Activity 9.11 | Creating a Custom Tab

1 **Start** Word. Display **Backstage** view, and then below the **Backstage tabs**, click **Options**.

2 In the **Word Options** dialog box, click **Customize Ribbon**, and then compare your screen with Figure 9.24.

The Word Options dialog box displays a list of popular commands on the left and main tabs on the right. Under Main Tabs, the checkmarks to the left of tab names indicate tabs that are currently available on the Ribbon. You can expand or collapse the view of tabs and groups by clicking ⊞ or ⊟, respectively. By default, Home is selected and expanded to display the groups on the Home tab.

Figure 9.24

Popular Commands

Customize Ribbon

Main Tabs

Home expanded to display groups

3 In the **Word Options** dialog box, below the **Main Tabs** list, with **Home** selected, click the **New Tab** button, and then compare your screen with Figure 9.25.

In the Main Tabs list, New Tab (Custom) displays in expanded view with New Group (Custom) indented and selected.

Figure 9.25

New Tab (Custom)

New Group (Custom)

New Tab button

4 Click **New Tab (Custom)** to select it, and then at the bottom right of the **Word Options** dialog box, click the **Rename** button. In the **Rename** dialog box, in the **Display name** box, type your initials, and then click **OK**.

5 Click **New Group (Custom)** to select it, and then at the bottom right of the **Word Options** dialog box, click the **Rename** button. In the **Rename** dialog box, in the **Display name** box, type **Common Tasks** and then click **OK**. Leave the **Word Options** dialog box open for the next activity.

Activity 9.12 | Adding Commands to a Tab

Commands are usually arranged within groups on a tab. You can add any command directly to a tab, but it is good practice to add related commands to a group.

1 In the **Word Options** dialog box, near the top, locate the **Choose commands from** box, and notice that **Popular Commands** displays.

2 In the scroll box under **Popular Commands**, scroll as necessary to click **Print Preview and Print**, and then click the **Add** button. In the **Main Tabs** list, notice that **Print Preview and Print** now displays below the **Common Tasks (Custom)** group you created. Compare your screen with Figure 9.26.

Figure 9.26

Popular Commands selected

Common Tasks (Custom) group

Your Initials (Custom) tab

Print Preview and Print

Add button

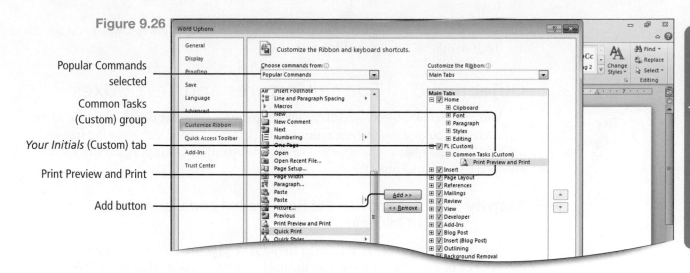

3 In the **Word Options** dialog box, click the **Choose commands from arrow**, and then click **All Commands**.

The Choose commands from box allows you to select a different group of available commands.

4 Under **All Commands**, scroll as necessary to click **Edit Footer**, and then click the **Add** button. In the **Main Tabs** list, notice that in the **Common Tasks (Custom)** group, **Edit Footer** displays below **Print Preview and Print**.

5 Click the **Choose commands from arrow**, and then click **File Tab**.

6 In the **File Tab** list, click **Close**, and then click the **Add** button.

This command enables you to close a document without displaying Backstage view.

7 In the **Main Tabs** list, with **Close** selected, to the right of the **Main Tabs** list, click the **Move Up** button ▲ two times. Click **Edit Footer**, click the **Move Up** button ▲, and then compare your screen with Figure 9.27.

The commands are displayed in alphabetical order. You can use the Move Up and Move Down buttons to arrange tabs, groups, and commands in any order.

Figure 9.27

Move Up button

Commands arranged alphabetically

Move Down button

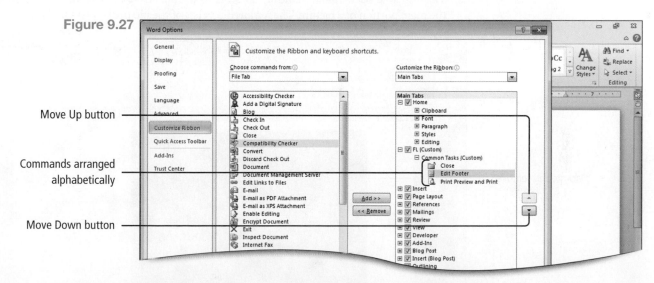

8 Click **OK** to close the **Word Options** dialog box, and notice that your custom tab with your initials displays to the right of the **Home tab** on the Ribbon.

9 Click the *your initials* **tab**. Notice that the **Common Tasks group** displays on the left and includes the three commands you added.

Objective 5 | Format Pictures and Text Boxes

You can format objects—such as clip art, pictures, and text boxes—in a variety of ways. Making color adjustments, removing backgrounds, and changing the size and orientation can enhance the appearance of an illustration. Multiple graphics can be grouped to form one object.

Activity 9.13 | Removing the Background and Correcting Colors in a Picture

Just as you customized the Ribbon to improve productivity, you can improve the appearance of a picture by removing the background and adjusting the colors.

1 Display **Backstage** view, and then from your student files, locate and open the file **w09B_Moving_Agreement**.

2 From **Backstage** view, display the **Save As** dialog box, navigate to your **Word Chapter 9** folder, and then save the document as **Lastname_Firstname_9B_Moving_Agreement** If necessary, display the rulers and formatting marks.

3 On the *your initials* **tab**, in the **Common Tasks group**, click the **Edit Footer** button, and then using **Quick Parts**, insert the file name in the footer. **Close** the footer area.

4 Press Ctrl + Home. On the **Insert tab**, in the **Illustrations group**, click the **Picture** button. In the **Insert Picture** dialog box, navigate to your student files, select the file **w09B_Spices**, and then click **Insert**.

5 On the **Format tab**, in the **Arrange group**, click the **Wrap Text** button, and then click **Top and Bottom**.

6 On the **Format tab**, in the **Adjust group**, click the **Remove Background** button. Compare your screen with Figure 9.28.

> The displayed Background Removal tab contains commands to remove the color surrounding the main portion of a picture. The removed portion of the picture displays in dark pink.

Figure 9.28

Background Removal tab

Background removed

7 On the **Background Removal tab**, in the **Close group**, click the **Keep Changes** button.

8 If necessary, select the graphic, and then on the **Format tab**, in the **Adjust group**, click the **Corrections** button. In the displayed **Corrections** gallery, point to several options and notice how the colors change in the picture.

9 In the **Corrections** gallery, under **Brightness and Contrast**, in the fourth row, click the fourth option—**Brightness: +20% Contrast: +20%**. Notice that the picture is brighter and more distinct.

> *Brightness* is the light to dark ratio of an image. Increasing the value creates a brighter image. *Contrast* is the difference in colors in a graphic. Increasing the contrast value creates more distinct colors in the graphic. In this case, to improve the appearance of the picture, you are changing the brightness and contrast.

10 Save 🔲 your changes.

Activity 9.14 | Cropping, Rotating, and Aligning Pictures

In this activity, you will *crop* a picture to focus the attention on a particular portion of the picture. Cropping is the process of removing any unwanted parts from the edges of a picture. You will also rotate the picture and create a mirror image.

1 With the picture selected, on the **Format tab**, in the **Picture Styles group**, click the **Picture Border button arrow**, and then in the last column, click the fifth color—**Orange, Accent 6, Darker 25%**.

> Because the picture is selected, the border color may not display on all edges.

2 On the **Format tab**, in the **Size group**, click the **Crop** button, which causes black crop handles to display around the image.

3 On the left border of the graphic, point to the middle crop handle. When the 🔡 pointer displays, drag to the right to approximately **0.5 inch on the horizontal ruler**. Compare your screen with Figure 9.29.

> The cropped portions of a picture are not deleted, just hidden. You can redisplay cropped portions of an image by using the crop handles.

Figure 9.29

Cropped picture

Crop handle

4 Using the same technique, on the top border, drag the middle crop handle down to approximately **0.5 inch on the vertical ruler**. In a similar manner, crop the right border to display at approximately **4.5 inches on the horizontal ruler**, and then crop the bottom border to display at approximately **4 inches on the vertical ruler**.

5 In the **Size group**, click the **Crop button arrow**, click **Crop to Shape**, and then under **Basic Shapes**, click the first shape—**Oval**.

In addition to cropping the edges of a graphic, you can also display the graphic within a shape.

6 In the **Size group**, change the **Shape Height** to **1"**, and then compare your screen with Figure 9.30.

Figure 9.30

Height changed to 1 inch—your screen may differ

Shape Width—your screen may differ

Oval shape applied

7 In the **Arrange group**, click the **Rotate** button, and then click **More Rotation Options**.

8 In the **Layout** dialog box, on the **Size tab**, under **Rotate**, click the **Rotation up spin arrow** to **10°**. Compare your screen with Figure 9.31.

To specify an exact degree of rotation for an image, use the Layout dialog box.

Figure 9.31

Layout dialog box

Rotation box

> **More Knowledge | Rotating an Image**
>
> If a precise angle is not required, point to the green rotate handle on the selected image, and when the ⟳ pointer displays, drag to rotate an image.

9 Click **OK**, right-click the picture, and then from the shortcut menu, click **Copy**. Click in a blank area of the document, and then press Ctrl + V.

The copied image is pasted on top of the original image.

10 Point to the selected copied image, and when the ⛺ pointer displays, drag to the right until the top right corner of the image is aligned at approximately **6 inches on the horizontal ruler**. With the image selected, on the **Format tab**, in the **Arrange group**, click the **Rotate** button 🔄, and then click **Flip Horizontal**. Compare your screen with Figure 9.32.

> *Flipping* a graphic reverses the direction of a graphic either vertically or horizontally.

Figure 9.32

Image pasted and flipped horizontally

11 With the image on the right selected, press and hold down Ctrl, click the image on the left, and then release Ctrl. With both images selected, in the **Arrange group**, click the **Align** button 🔲, and then click **Align Top**. Deselect the images, and then compare your screen with Figure 9.33.

> Use the Align feature to position objects in a consistent manner. You can align—line up the top, bottom, sides, or middle—of multiple graphic elements. In this case, you are ensuring that the top points of both images are aligned.

Figure 9.33

Top points of images aligned

12 **Save** 💾 your changes.

More Knowledge | Resetting Graphics

If you make changes to a picture and then decide those changes are unnecessary, on the Format tab, in the Adjust group, click the Reset Picture button. All formatting changes will be cleared, and the image will display in its original format.

Activity 9.15 | Stacking and Grouping Objects

You will insert two additional objects—a text box and *WordArt*—in the document. WordArt is a feature that applies combinations of decorative formatting to text, including shadows, reflections, and 3-D effects, as well as changing the line and fill color of the text. When multiple objects are inserted in a document, they are automatically *stacked*—placed in individual layers. You can modify the stacking order to allow the objects to overlap. Additionally, you can group individual objects to form a single object—in this case, the company heading.

1 In the blank paragraph below the images, click to position the insertion point. On the **Insert tab**, in the **Text group**, click the **Text Box** button, and then click **Draw Text Box**. Notice that the ✛ pointer displays.

2 Position the ✛ pointer at approximately **0.5 inch on the horizontal ruler** and **0.5 inch on the vertical ruler**, and then drag to approximately the **6-inch mark on the horizontal ruler** and the **1-inch mark on the vertical ruler**. Notice that the images are partially covered by the text box.

3 With the text box selected, on the **Format tab**, in the **Size group**, click the **Size** button, if necessary, and then change the **Shape Height** 1.5" to **0.9"** and the **Shape Width** 1.37" to **5.5"**. Compare your screen with Figure 9.34, and then, if necessary, move your text box so that it matches the location shown in the figure.

> Adding the text box to the document creates a third layer. The original image and the second pasted image represent the other two layers. When you add a visual object to a document, by default that object becomes the top layer in the stacking order.

Figure 9.34

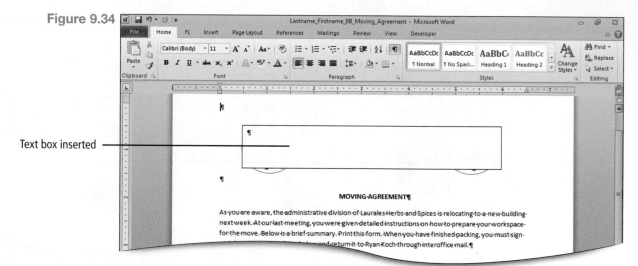

Text box inserted

4 With the insertion point positioned in the text box, on the **Home tab**, in the **Styles group**, click the **No Spacing** style. Press Enter, and then type **1550 Columbia Avenue** Press Enter, and then type **San Francisco, CA 94133** Press Enter, type **877-555-0144** press Tab, and then type **www.laurales.com** If www.laurales.com displays as a hyperlink, point to the text, right-click, and then from the shortcut menu, click **Remove Hyperlink**.

5 Select the three paragraphs of text. On the Mini toolbar, click **Center** ≡, and then change the **Font Color** to **Orange, Accent 6, Darker 50%**—in the last column, the last color.

6 On the **Format tab**, in the **Shape Styles group**, click the **Shape Outline button arrow** ✎, and then click **No Outline**.

The outline for the text box changes to a dashed blue line.

7 In the **Arrange group**, click the **Send Backward button arrow**, and then click **Send to Back**. Compare your screen with Figure 9.35. If necessary, adjust your images to display as shown in Figure 9.35.

The Send to Back command causes the text box to become the bottom layer in the stacking order. This allows the two images to display completely.

Figure 9.35

Send Backward button arrow

No Outline applied to text box

Images display completely

Formatted text

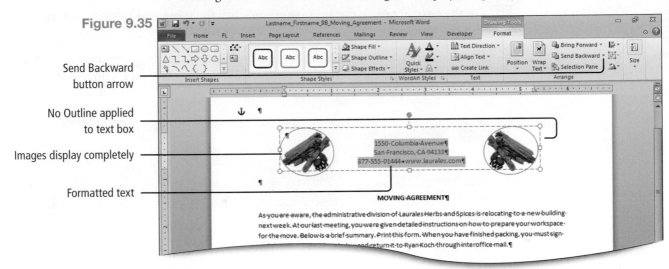

8 Click on the border of the text box to display a solid blue line and sizing handles. With the text box selected, hold down Ctrl. On the left side of the document, below the text box, click the image to select it. Continue to hold down Ctrl, and then on the right side of the document, below the text box, click the other image. Release Ctrl, and notice that all three graphics are selected. Compare your screen with Figure 9.36.

Pressing Ctrl allows you to select several graphics at the same time.

Figure 9.36

All three graphics selected

9 With all three graphics selected, on the **Drawing Tools Format tab**, in the **Arrange group**, click the **Group** button 🔲, and then click **Group**. Notice that only sizing handles for the entire grouped object display and the object moves into the text area of the document.

Grouping is the process of combining multiple elements into a single object. You can move or resize the entire group, ensuring that the individual elements remain together in the same position and stacking order.

10 On the **Drawing Tools Format tab**, in the **Arrange group**, click the **Wrap Text** button, and then click **Top and Bottom**. Deselect the grouped object, and then **Save** 💾 your changes.

11 Press Ctrl + Home. On the **Insert tab**, in the **Text group**, click the **WordArt** button, and then in the displayed **WordArt** gallery, in the fourth row, click the second style— **Gradient Fill, Orange, Accent 6, Inner Shadow**.

12 With the placeholder text selected, type **Laurales Herbs and Spices** Select the text, and then on the Mini toolbar, change the **Font Size** to **22**. If *Laurales* is flagged as a spelling error, click **Ignore All**.

13 On the **Format tab**, in the **Arrange group**, click the **Wrap Text** button, and then click **Top and Bottom**.

14 Point to the border of the **WordArt** text box, and when the ⬚ pointer displays, drag the **WordArt** text box so that it is centered above the grouped graphic as shown in Figure 9.37.

Figure 9.37

WordArt text box centered

15 With the **WordArt** text box selected, click the border to display a solid blue outline. Press and hold down Shift, point to the grouped graphic, and when the ⬚ pointer displays, click the grouped graphic. With both objects selected, on the **Drawing Tools Format tab**, in the **Arrange group**, click the **Group** button 🔳, and then click **Group**. **Save** 💾 your changes.

More Knowledge | Compressing Graphics

If you plan to transmit a document electronically, you can compress the graphic—reduce the file size. On the Picture Tools Format tab, in the Adjust group, click the Compress Pictures button to compress an image to a smaller size.

Objective 6 | Add a Digital Signature to a Document

When a document is sent electronically, the recipient must be able to confirm the source of the file. With a paper document, a signature and notarization are legal tools used to identify the validity of the signature and file source. When a document is transmitted electronically, a ***digital signature*** can be applied. A digital signature is an electronic stamp that is added to a document to verify the document's authenticity. To use a digital signature, you must create a ***digital certificate***. A digital certificate, or ***digital ID***, is a file that contains information about a person and is used to electronically sign a document. A digital signature is based on the digital identification and verifies that the document is valid and has not been changed since the signature was added.

Activity 9.16 | Adding a Signature Line to a Document

A *signature line* is an element added to a document that specifies who should sign the document. In this activity, you will add a signature line, indicating that an employee signature is required to confirm that items are ready to be moved.

1 Locate the paragraph that begins *Remove all items*. Click to position the insertion point at the beginning of the paragraph, and then select the next five paragraphs, ending with the text *return to Ryan Koch*. On the Mini toolbar, change the **Font Size** to **16**, and then change the **Font Color** to **Orange, Accent 6, Darker 50%**—in the last column, the last color. On the **Home tab**, in the **Paragraph group**, click the **Numbering** button. Deselect the text, and then compare your screen with Figure 9.38.

Figure 9.38

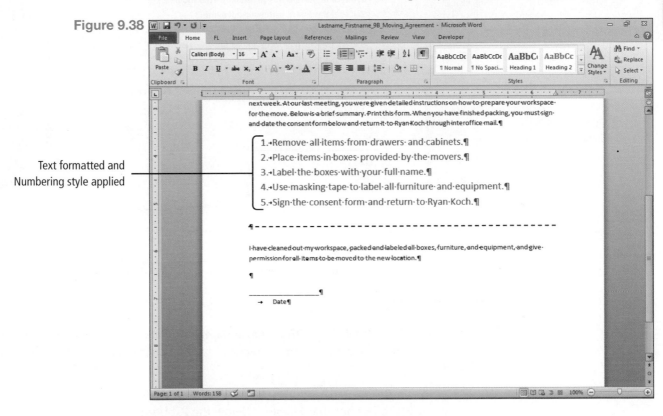

Text formatted and Numbering style applied

2 Below the paragraph that begins *I have cleaned*, click to position the insertion point in the empty paragraph. On the **Insert tab**, in the **Text group**, click the **Signature Line button arrow**, and then click **Microsoft Office Signature Line**. In the **Microsoft Office Word** dialog box, click **OK**.

3 In the **Signature Setup** dialog box, in the **Suggested signer** box, type **Employee Name** In the **Suggested signer's title** box, type **Administration**

4 Click **OK** to insert the signature line in the document. Compare your screen with Figure 9.39.

The signer can sign a hard copy—a printed copy—or sign the document electronically by inserting an image of a signature or by using a *stylus*—a pen-like device—with a *tablet PC*—a computer with a monitor that allows you to write on the screen.

Figure 9.39

Signature line inserted

More Knowledge | Inserting a Digital ID

You can also sign a document electronically by inserting a digital ID. Digital IDs can be purchased from a certification authority.

---

5 On the *your initials* **tab**, in the **Common Tasks group**, click the **Print Preview and Print** button. Return to your document, correct any spelling errors, and then **Save** 🔲 your document.

Alert! | What Is the Banner that Displays Below the Ribbon?

If you open a file that contains a signature line, but the document has not been digitally signed, a banner displays below the Ribbon stating the document needs to be signed. For purposes of this instruction, you can ignore the banner.

Objective 7 | Prepare a Document for Distribution

Before a document is distributed to others, it should be inspected to make sure it does not contain personal information or *metadata*—descriptive data about document properties. In addition, the document should be identified as being in final form.

Activity 9.17 | Inspecting a Document

In this activity, you will remove all personal information from your document.

1 Press [Ctrl] + [Home]. Display **Backstage** view, and then, if necessary, click **Info**. In the **Prepare for Sharing** section, click the **Check for Issues** button, and then click **Inspect Document**.

2 In the **Document Inspector** dialog box, be sure all six check boxes are selected, and then click the **Inspect** button. Notice that the results of the inspection display in the **Document Inspector** dialog box. Compare your screen with Figure 9.40.

The document is inspected for many types of data including comments and revisions, document properties and personal information, custom XML data, and hidden text.

Figure 9.40

Inspection results

3 To the right of **Document Properties and Personal Information**, click the **Remove All** button.

This will remove all personal information found in the document properties.

4 To the right of **Custom XML Data**, click the **Remove All** button to remove this information.

Personal information was also found in the footer, but you will not remove this because it is needed to identify your document to your instructor.

5 In the **Document Inspector** dialog box, click **Close**.

Activity 9.18 | Restricting Editing

After all changes have been made, a document can be identified as a final version—making it a *read-only file*. A read-only file can be viewed but not changed.

1 From **Backstage** view, display the **Document Information Panel**. In the **Author** box, type your first and last names. In the **Subject** box, type your course name and section number, and in the **Keywords** box, type **moving agreement, graphics Close** ☒ the **Document Information Panel**.

> Although you removed the document properties in the previous activity, as a part of this instruction, you will include the properties to identify your document to your instructor.

2 Display **Backstage** view, and then with the **Info** tab selected, in the **Permissions** section, click the **Protect Document** button, and then click **Restrict Editing**.

3 In the **Restrict Formatting and Editing** task pane, under **2. Editing restrictions**, click to select the **Allow only this type of editing in the document** check box. Compare your screen with Figure 9.41.

> The Allow only this type of editing in the document box displays No changes (Read only). The viewer will be able to read the document, but not make any changes. The Exceptions (optional) box indicates that this restriction will apply to everyone that views the document.

Figure 9.41

Restrict Formatting and Editing task pane

Allow only this type of editing in the document check box

4 In the **Restrict Formatting and Editing** task pane, under **3. Start enforcement**, click the **Yes, Start Enforcing Protection** button. In the **Start Enforcing Protection** dialog box, click **OK**.

> Although you can further protect the document by assigning a password, for purposes of this instruction it is not necessary.

5 **Close** ☒ the **Restrict Formatting and Editing** task pane, and then **Save** 🔲 your changes.

6 On the *your initials* tab, in the **Common Tasks group**, click the **Close** button to close your document.

7 Display **Backstage** view, click **Recent**, and then click the first document— **Lastname_Firstname_9B_Moving_Agreement**. Notice that the Message Bar— *Signatures*—displays below the Ribbon.

> The Message Bar is a reminder that the document needs to be signed. Clicking the View Signatures button will allow the user to digitally sign the document with a digital ID. Because you do not have a digital ID, this message can be ignored.

8 Print your document or submit electronically as directed by your instructor.

9 On the *your initials* **tab**, in the **Common Tasks group**, click the **Close** button to close your document.

10 Display **Backstage** view, and then click **Options**. In the **Word Options** dialog box, click **Customize Ribbon**. In the **Main Tabs** list, right-click *your initials* **(Custom)**, and then from the shortcut menu, click **Remove**. Click **OK** to close the dialog box, and notice that your custom tab no longer displays on the Ribbon.

11 **Exit** Word. In the displayed **Microsoft Word** message box, click **Don't Save**.

12 Print your document or submit electronically as directed by your instructor.

End **You have completed Project 9B** ————————————————————

Content-Based Assessments

Summary

You created a custom form and saved it as a template. By inserting content controls and protecting the form, users are able to enter data without modifying the structure or format of the form. Additionally, you modified objects to create a letterhead, and inserted a signature line so that a document can be signed electronically.

Key Terms

Matching

Match each term in the second column with its correct definition in the first column by writing the letter of the term on the blank line in front of the correct definition.

_____ 1. A data entry field where particular information is supplied by the user.

_____ 2. A content control that enables the user to enter unformatted text.

_____ 3. A content control that enables the user to enter text and apply formatting.

_____ 4. A content control that allows the user to select a specific item from a list.

_____ 5. A content control that that allows the user to select an item from a list or enter new text.

_____ 6. A code that is used to gain access to a file.

_____ 7. The light to dark ratio of an image.

_____ 8. The difference in colors in a graphic.

_____ 9. The process of removing unwanted parts from the edges of a picture.

_____ 10. The process of reversing the direction of an object either vertically or horizontally.

_____ 11. The process of placing objects in individual layers of the document.

_____ 12. The process of combining multiple elements into a single object.

_____ 13. An electronic stamp that verifies a document's authenticity.

_____ 14. Descriptive data about document properties.

_____ 15. A file that can be viewed but not changed.

A Brightness

B Combo Box

C Content control

D Contrast

E Cropping

F Digital signature

G Drop-Down List

H Flipping

I Grouping

J Metadata

K Password

L Plain Text

M Read-only

N Rich Text

O Stacking

Content-Based Assessments

Multiple Choice

Circle the correct answer.

1. A structured document that has reserved spaces for information to be entered by the user is a:
   A. form   **B.** table   **C.** template

2. In a form, descriptive text, such as labels and headings, is referred to as:
   A. fixed text   **B.** plain text   **C.** static text

3. A predefined document that contains basic settings such as font, margins, and styles is a:
   A. form   **B.** table   **C.** template

4. Plain text refers to:
   A. restricted text   **B.** unformatted text   **C.** uniform text

5. A feature that enables you to work with content controls that are inserted in a document is:
   A. Design Mode   **B.** Protect Mode   **C.** Restrict Editing

6. What content control allows the user to select a date?
   A. Calendar   **B.** Date Picker   **C.** Drop-Down List

7. A user can either select or deselect an option in a:
   A. check box   **B.** combo box   **C.** drop-down list

8. In a document, the element that specifies who should sign the document is the:
   A. digital certificate   **B.** digital ID   **C.** signature line

9. A computer with a monitor that allows you to write on the screen is a:
   A. laptop   **B.** notebook   **C.** tablet PC

10. The Word feature that checks for hidden text and metadata is the:
    A. Document Inspector   **B.** Restrict Editing   **C.** Style Inspector

Content-Based Assessments

Apply **9A** skills from these Objectives:

- **1** Create a Customized Form
- **2** Modify and Protect a Form
- **3** Use a Template to Complete a Form

Skills Review | Project **9C** Meeting Reservation

In the following Skills Review, you will add content controls to create a form for reserving space for meetings at Laurales Herbs and Spices. After the form is protected and saved as a template, you will fill in the form. Your completed documents will look similar to Figure 9.42.

Project Files

For Project 9C, you will need the following file:

w09C_Meeting_Reservation

You will save your documents as:

Lastname_Firstname_9C_Meeting_Reservation
Lastname_Firstname_9C_Reservation_Completed

Project Results

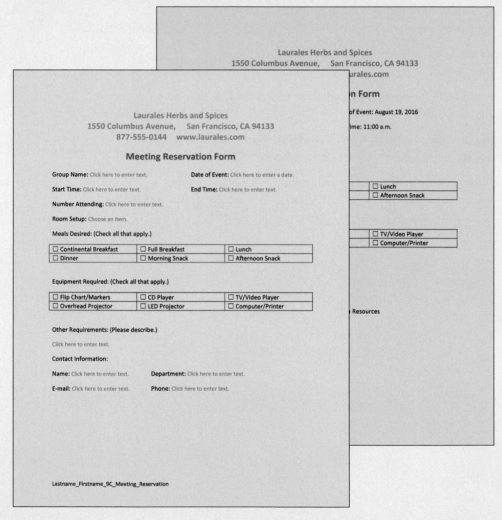

Figure 9.42

(Project 9C Meeting Reservation continues on the next page)

Content-Based Assessments

Skills Review | Project 9C Meeting Reservation (continued)

1 **Start** Word. From **Backstage** view, click **Save As**. In the **Save As** dialog box, navigate to your **Word Chapter 9** folder. Click the **Save As type arrow**, and then click **Word Template**. Using your own name, save the document as **Lastname_Firstname_9C_Meeting_Reservation** and then click **Save**. If necessary, display the rulers and formatting marks.

a. From **Backstage** view, below the **Backstage tabs**, click **Options**. On the left side of the **Word Options** dialog box, click **Customize Ribbon**.

b. In the **Main Tabs** list, locate and then click to select the **Developer** check box. Click **OK** to close the **Word Options** dialog box.

c. On the **Insert tab**, in the **Text group**, click the **Object button arrow**, and then click **Text from File**. In the **Insert File** dialog box, navigate to your student files, click **w09C_Meeting_Reservation**, and then click **Insert**. If *Laurales* is flagged as a spelling error, click **Ignore All**.

d. Select the first three paragraphs. On the Mini toolbar, change the **Font Size** to **16**, apply **Bold**, and then click **Center**. Change the **Font Color** to **Olive Green, Accent 3, Darker 25%**—in the seventh column, the fifth color.

e. Select the paragraph that begins *Meeting*. Change the **Font Size** to **18**, apply **Bold**, and then click **Center**. Change the **Font Color** to **Olive Green, Accent 3, Darker 50%**—in the seventh column, the last color.

2 Locate the text *Group Name*. Position the insertion point to the right of the colon, and then press Spacebar.

a. On the **Developer tab**, in the **Controls group**, click the **Design Mode** button to turn on Design Mode.

b. In the **Controls group**, click the **Plain Text Content Control** button.

c. In a similar manner, click to the right of the colon for each of the following terms—*Start Time*, *End Time*, and *Number Attending*—press Spacebar, and then insert a **Plain Text Content Control**.

d. Locate the text *Date of Event*. Position the insertion point to the right of the colon, press Spacebar, and then in the **Controls group**, click the **Date Picker Content Control** button.

e. With the **Date Picker content control** selected, in the **Controls group**, click the **Properties** button. In the **Content Control Properties** dialog box, under **Date**

Picker Properties, in the **Display the date like this** box, click the third style—October 9, 2016—your date will differ. Click **OK**.

3 Locate the text *Room Setup*. Position the insertion point to the right of the colon, press Spacebar, and then in the **Controls group**, click the **Drop-Down List Content Control** button.

a. With the **Drop-Down List content control** selected, in the **Controls group**, click the **Properties** button. In the **Content Control Properties** dialog box, under **Drop-Down List Properties**, click the **Add** button. In the **Add Choice** dialog box, in the **Display Name** box, type **Banquet** Click **OK**.

b. Using the same technique, add the following choices to the **Drop-Down List content control**:

Classroom

Hollow Square

U-Shape

c. Click **OK** two times to close the dialog boxes. Select the two paragraphs that begin *Continental* and *Dinner*. On the **Insert tab**, in the **Tables group**, click the **Table** button, and then click **Convert Text to Table**. In the **Convert Text to Table** dialog box, click **OK**.

d. In the table, click to position the insertion point to the left of *Continental*. On the **Developer tab**, in the **Controls group**, click the **Check Box Content Control** button. Select the check box, right-click, and then from the shortcut menu, click **Copy**. Position the insertion point to the left of *Full Breakfast*, and then press Ctrl + V.

e. In a similar manner, insert a **Check Box Content Control** to the left of each of the remaining items in the table. For all items with a check box, be sure there is a space between the check box and the text.

4 Select the two paragraphs that begin *Flip Chart* and *Overhead Projector*. On the **Insert tab**, in the **Tables group**, click the **Table** button, and then click **Convert Text to Table**. Click **OK**.

a. Using the technique you just practiced, insert a **Check Box Content Control** to the left of all the items in the table.

b. Click to position the insertion point in the blank paragraph above *Contact Information*. In the **Controls group**, click the **Plain Text Content Control** button.

(Project 9C Meeting Reservation continues on the next page)

c. Below *Contact Information*, locate the text *Name*. Click to position the insertion point to the right of the colon, and then press [Spacebar].

d. In the **Controls group**, click the **Plain Text Content Control** button.

e. In a similar manner, to the right of the colon for each of the following items—*Department*, *E-mail*, and *Phone*—press [Spacebar], and then insert a **Plain Text Content Control**.

5 Press [Ctrl] + [Home]. On the **Developer tab**, in the **Controls group**, click the **Design Mode** button to turn off **Design Mode**.

a. On the **Page Layout tab**, in the **Page Background group**, click the **Page Color** button, and then in the seventh column, click the third color—**Olive Green, Accent 3, Lighter 60%**.

b. On the **Developer tab**, in the **Protect group**, click the **Restrict Editing** button.

c. In the **Restrict Formatting and Editing** task pane, under **2. Editing restrictions**, click to select the **Allow only this type of editing in the document** check box. Click the **Allow only this type of editing in the document arrow**, and then click **Filling in forms**.

d. In the **Restrict Formatting and Editing** task pane, under **3. Start enforcement**, click the **Yes, Start Enforcing Protection** button.

e. In the **Start Enforcing Protection** dialog box, click **OK**. **Close** the **Restrict Formatting and Editing** task pane, and then **Save** your changes. From **Backstage** view, click **Close** to close your document.

6 From **Backstage** view, click **New**. Under **Available Templates**, click **New from existing**. Navigate to your **Word Chapter 9** folder, click the file **Lastname_Firstname_9C_Meeting_Reservation**, and then click the **Create New** button. From **Backstage** view, click **Save As**, and then navigate to your **Word Chapter 9** folder. Using your own name, type the file name **Lastname_Firstname_9C_Reservation_Completed** and then click **Save**.

a. In the content control following *Group Name*, type **Planning Committee** Press [Tab], click the **Date Picker content control arrow**, and then click **Today**. Continue filling in the form using the following information.

Start Time	**9:00 a.m.**
End Time	**11:00 a.m.**
Number Attending	**10**
Room Setup	**U-Shape**
Meals Desired	**Morning Snack**
Equipment Required	**Flip Chart/Markers**
Other Requirements	**Legal pads and pens for each person.**
Name	Use your first and last names
Department	**Human Resources**
E-mail	*YourLastname*@laurales.com
Phone	**555-0145**

b. Display the **Document Information Panel**. In the **Author** box, type your first and last names. In the **Subject** box, type your course name and section number, and in the **Keywords** box, type **meeting reservation, completed Close** the **Document Information Panel**. **Save** your changes, and then from **Backstage** view, **Close** the document.

c. From **Backstage** view, click **Open**. Navigate to your **Word Chapter 9** folder, and then open the file **Lastname_Firstname_9C_Meeting_Reservation**.

d. On the **Developer tab**, in the **Protect group**, click the **Restrict Editing** button. At the bottom of the **Restrict Formatting and Editing** task pane, click the **Stop Protection** button. **Close** the **Restrict Formatting and Editing** task pane. Press [Ctrl] + [End], and then using **Quick Parts**, insert the file name in the footer.

e. Display the **Document Information Panel**. In the **Author** box, type your first and last names. In the **Subject** box, type your course name and section number, and in the **Keywords** box, type **meeting reservation, template Close** the **Document Information Panel**, and then **Save** your changes.

7 From **Backstage** view, click **Options**. In the **Word Options** dialog box, click **Customize Ribbon**. In the **Main Tabs** list, locate and then click to deselect the **Developer** check box. Click **OK**, and notice that the Developer tab no longer displays on the Ribbon.

8 Print both documents or submit electronically as directed by your instructor. **Exit** Word.

End You have completed Project 9C ———————

Content-Based Assessments

Apply 9B skills from these Objectives:

- **4** Customize the Ribbon
- **5** Format Pictures and Text Boxes
- **6** Add a Digital Signature to a Document
- **7** Prepare a Document for Distribution

Skills Review | Project **9D** Privacy Policy

In the following Skills Review, you will finalize a document that explains the privacy policy of Laurales Herbs and Spices. This will require creating a grouped object, inserting a signature line, and formatting the document. Your completed document will look similar to Figure 9.43.

Project Files

For Project 9D, you will need the following files:

> w09D_Privacy
> w09D_Security
> w09D_Privacy_Policy

You will save your document as:

> Lastname_Firstname_9D_Privacy_Policy

Project Results

Laurales Herbs and Spices Privacy Policy

Laurales Herbs and Spices believes in protecting the privacy of our online visitors. This policy applies only to our Web site and to e-mails you may send us; it does not apply to telephone calls you make to us or postal mail you may send.

Information We Collect

In certain locations on our Web site we may request that you provide personal information—for example, when filling in order forms or registering for our monthly newsletter. We may request your name, e-mail address, mailing address, and telephone number. Only information we believe we need to fulfill our obligation to you will be marked *required*. You may choose not to provide particular information; however, this may result in not being able to utilize all of our Web site's services.

We may also collect certain non-personal information which cannot be used to identify or contact you. This technical information may include your IP address, the type of browser your system uses, and the Web sites you visit before and after the Laurales Herbs and Spices site.

How Collected Information Is Used

The personal information we gather will usually be in response to a service you are requesting. We will use that information to fulfill your online orders, enter you in a contest, provide information you requested, and compile data you have provided in surveys and polls. We combine the non-personal information we gather to better understand the demographics of our users and determine how our site is being used. This data allows us to refine our Web site content and improve our product offerings.

If you send us e-mail or fill out an online form, we may use your personal information to contact you with a response to a question or concern. We may also keep information for future data compilation. We do not share your personal information with any non-affiliated third party without your consent. We may, however, disclose the statistical data gathered through non-personal information with our third-party affiliates.

Any questions you may have regarding our Privacy Policy should be directed to privacy@laurales.com.

X _____

Laura Morales
President

Lastname_Firstname_9D_Privacy_Policy

Figure 9.43

(Project 9D Privacy Policy continues on the next page)

1 **Start** Word. Display **Backstage** view, and then click **Options**. In the **Word Options** dialog box, click **Customize Ribbon**.

a. Below the **Main Tabs** list, with **Home** selected, click the **New Tab** button. Click **New Tab (Custom)**, and then click the **Rename** button. In the **Rename** dialog box, in the **Display name** box, type your initials, and then click **OK**.

b. Click **New Group (Custom)**, and then click the **Rename** button. In the **Rename** dialog box, in the **Display name** box, type **Frequent Tasks** and then click **OK**.

c. With **Frequent Tasks (Custom)** selected, in the **Word Options** dialog box, click the **Choose commands from arrow**, and then click **All Commands**. Under **All Commands**, scroll as necessary to click **Edit Footer**, and then click the **Add** button. Click **OK** to close the **Word Options** dialog box.

2 Display **Backstage** view, click **Save As**, navigate to your **Word Chapter 9** folder, and then save the document as **Lastname_Firstname_9D_Privacy_Policy** If necessary, display the rulers and formatting marks.

a. On the *your initials* tab, in the **Frequent Tasks group**, click the **Edit Footer** button, and then using **Quick Parts**, insert the file name in the footer. **Close** the footer area.

b. On the **Insert tab**, in the **Illustrations group**, click the **Picture** button. In the **Insert Picture** dialog box, navigate to your student files, select the file **w09D_Security**, and then click **Insert**.

c. On the **Format tab**, in the **Arrange group**, click the **Wrap Text** button, and then click **Square**. In the **Adjust group**, click the **Corrections** button. In the **Corrections** gallery, under **Brightness and Contrast**, in the third row, click the fourth option—**Brightness: +20% Contrast: 0% (Normal)**.

d. In the **Picture Styles group**, click the **Picture Effects** button, point to **Soft Edges**, and then click **10 Point**.

e. In the **Size group**, change the **Shape Width** to **2.7"**. Click to the right of the picture to deselect it.

3 On the **Insert tab**, in the **Illustrations group**, click the **Picture** button. In the **Insert Picture** dialog box, navigate to your student files, select the file **w09D_Privacy**, and then click **Insert**. In the **Size group**, change the

Shape Width to **2"**. In the **Arrange group**, click the **Wrap Text** button, and then click **In Front of Text**.

a. In the **Size group**, click the **Crop** button. On the left border, drag the middle crop handle 🖼 to the right to approximately **3.25 inches on the horizontal ruler** until the border is slightly to the left of the text *Privacy*.

b. Using the same technique, drag the top middle crop handle down approximately **0.5 inch** until the border is slightly above the text.

c. In a similar manner, crop the right and bottom edges by approximately **0.5 inch**. In the **Size group**, click the **Crop** button to turn it off.

d. In the **Arrange group**, click the **Rotate** button, and then click **More Rotation Options**. In the **Layout** dialog box, on the **Size tab**, under **Rotate**, click the **Rotation down spin arrow**, and change to **-65**. Click **OK**.

4 Drag the picture to the left and position it as shown in Figure 9.43. If necessary, in the **Arrange group**, click the **Rotate** button, click **More Rotation Options**, and then change the **Rotation** box so that the privacy picture is rotated as shown in Figure 9.43.

a. With the privacy picture selected, press and hold Ctrl, and then click the security picture. Release Ctrl. With both images selected, on the **Format tab**, in the **Arrange group**, click the **Group** button, and then click **Group**.

b. On the **Drawing Tools Format tab**, in the **Arrange group**, click the **Wrap Text** button, and then click **Square**. Click to deselect the group.

c. On the **Insert tab**, in the **Text group**, click the **Object button arrow**, and then click **Text from File**. Navigate to your student files, select the file **w09D_Privacy_Policy**, and then click **Insert**. If any words are flagged as spelling or grammar errors, click **Ignore All**.

d. Select the first paragraph. Change the **Font Size** to **20**, apply **Bold**, and then click **Center**. Select the second paragraph, and then change the **Font Size** to **12**.

e. Select the paragraph *Information We Collect*, change the **Font Size** to **14**, and apply **Bold**. Select the paragraph that begins *How Collected*, change the **Font Size** to **14**, and then apply **Bold**.

(Project 9D Privacy Policy continues on the next page)

Content-Based Assessments

Skills Review | Project **9D** Privacy Policy (continued)

5 At the bottom of your document, click to select the grouped picture. Drag the picture up to the right of the second, third, and fourth paragraphs as shown in Figure 9.43.

a. Press ⌃Ctrl + End. On the **Insert tab**, in the **Text group**, click the **Signature Line button arrow**, and then click **Microsoft Office Signature Line**. In the **Microsoft Office Word** dialog box, click **OK**.

b. In the **Signature Setup** dialog box, in the **Suggested signer** box, type **Laura Morales** In the **Suggested signer's title** box, type **President** and then click **OK**.

c. **Save** your changes.

6 Press ⌃Ctrl + Home. Display **Backstage** view, and then, if necessary, click **Info**. In the **Prepare for Sharing** section, click the **Check for Issues** button, and then click **Inspect Document**.

a. In the **Document Inspector** dialog box, be sure all six check boxes are selected, and then click the **Inspect** button.

b. To the right of **Document Properties and Personal Information**, click the **Remove All** button.

c. In the **Document Inspector** dialog box, click **Close**.

7 From **Backstage** view, display the **Document Information Panel**. In the **Author** box, type your first and last names. In the **Subject** box, type your course

name and section number, and in the **Keywords** box, type **privacy policy, grouped object Close** the Document Information Panel.

a. Display **Backstage** view. With the **Info** section selected, in the **Permissions** section, click the **Protect Document** button, and then click **Restrict Editing**.

b. In the **Restrict Formatting and Editing** task pane, under **2. Editing Restrictions**, click to select the **Allow only this type of editing in the document** check box.

c. Under **3. Start enforcement**, click the **Yes, Start Enforcing Protection** button. In the **Start Enforcing Protection** dialog box, click **OK**. **Close** the **Restrict Formatting and Editing** task pane.

d. **Save** your changes.

8 Print your document or submit electronically as directed by your instructor. Display **Backstage** view, and then click **Close** to close your document without closing Word.

a. Display **Backstage** view, and then click **Options**. In the **Word Options** dialog box, click **Customize Ribbon**. In the **Main Tabs** list, right-click *your initials* (**Custom**), and then from the shortcut menu, click **Remove**. Click **OK**, and then **Exit** Word.

End **You have completed Project 9D** ⎯⎯⎯⎯⎯⎯⎯⎯⎯⎯⎯⎯⎯

Content-Based Assessments

Apply **9A** skills from these Objectives:

1. Create a Customized Form
2. Modify and Protect a Form
3. Use a Template to Complete a Form

Mastering Word | Project **9E** Ergonomic Study

In the following Mastering Word project, you will create a form for the IT Department at Laurales Herbs and Spices. The department plans to survey employees regarding health issues related to their workstations. You will insert content controls, restrict editing, and save the document as a template. Using the template, you will fill in the form. Your completed documents will look similar to Figure 9.44.

Project Files

For Project 9E, you will need the following file:

w09E_Ergonomic_Study

You will save your documents as:

Lastname_Firstname_9E_Ergonomic_Study
Lastname_Firstname_9E_Study_Completed

Project Results

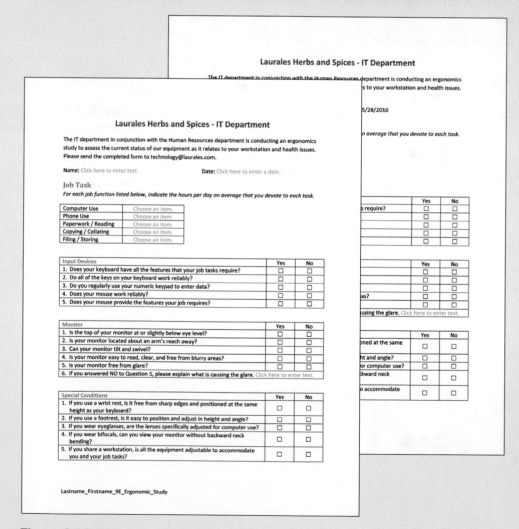

Figure 9.44

(Project 9E Ergonomic Study continues on the next page)

Content-Based Assessments

Mastering Word | Project **9E** Ergonomic Study (continued)

1 **Start** Word. Navigate to your student files, and then open the document **w09E_Ergonomic_Study**.In your **Word Chapter 9** folder, save the document as a **Word Template** using the name **Lastname_Firstname_9E_Ergonomic_Study** If necessary, display the rulers and formatting marks. On the Ribbon, display the **Developer tab**. If any words are flagged as a spelling error, **Ignore All**.

2 Select the first paragraph. Change the **Font Size** to **16**, apply **Bold** and **Center**, and then change the **Font Color** to **Dark Blue, Text 2**. Select the paragraph *Job Task*, and then on the **Home tab**, in the **Styles group**, click the **Heading 2** style. Select the paragraph that begins *For each*, and then apply **Italic**. In the second, third, and fourth tables, select the text in the first cell, apply **Bold**, and then change the **Font Color** to **Dark Blue, Text 2, Lighter 40%**.

3 Turn on **Design Mode**. In the document, locate the text *Name*, position the insertion point to the right of the colon, press Spacebar, and then insert a **Plain Text Content Control**. Locate the text *Date*, position the insertion point to the right of the colon, press Spacebar, and then insert a **Date Picker Content Control**.

4 In the first table, in the first row, click in the second cell, and then insert a **Drop-Down List Content Control**. Display the **Content Control Properties** dialog box, and then click the **Add** button. In the **Add Choice** dialog box, in the **Display Name** box, type **1** In a similar manner, add the numbers **2** through **8** to the list. **Copy** the content control to the remaining empty cells in the first table. Select the second column, and then **Align Center**.

5 In the second table, position the insertion point in the first empty cell below *Yes*, and then insert a **Check Box Content Control**. **Copy** the content control to the remaining empty cells in all three tables. For the second, third, and fourth tables, select the second and third columns, and then **Align Center**.

6 In the third table, in the last row, position the insertion point in the first cell. On the **Layout tab**, in the **Rows & Columns group**, click the **Insert Below** button. With all three cells selected, click the **Merge Cells** button. In the **Alignment group**, click the **Align Center Left** button.

7 Click in the merged cell, and then type **6. If you answered NO to Question 5, please explain what is causing the glare.** Press Spacebar, and then insert a **Plain Text Content Control**.

8 Press Ctrl + Home, and then turn off **Design Mode**. Display the **Restrict Formatting and Editing** task pane, and then under **2. Editing restrictions**, click to select the **Allow only this type of editing in the document** check box. Click the **Allow only this type of editing in the document arrow**, and then click **Filling in forms**. Under **3. Start enforcement**, click the **Yes, Start Enforcing Protection** button. In the **Start Enforcing Protection** dialog box, click **OK**. **Close** the **Restrict Formatting and Editing** task pane.

9 Display the **Document Information Panel**. In the **Author** box, type your first and last names. In the **Subject** box, type your course name and section number, and in the **Keywords** box, type **ergonomic study, template Close** the **Document Information Panel**, and then **Save** your changes. From **Backstage** view, **Close** your document without closing Word.

10 From **Backstage** view, click **New**, and then click **New from existing**. Navigate to your **Word Chapter 9** folder, click **Lastname_Firstname_9E_Ergonomic_Study**, and then click the **Create New** button. **Save** the file to your **Word Chapter 9** folder as **Lastname_Firstname_9E_Study_Completed**

11 In the content control following *Name*, using your own name, type **Firstname Lastname** Press Tab, click the **Date Picker content control arrow**, and then click the **Today** button. Press Tab. To the right of *Computer Use*, click the **Drop-Down List content control arrow**, and then click **5**.

12 Display the **Document Information Panel**. In the **Author** box, type your first and last names. In the **Subject** box, type your course name and section number, and in the **Keywords** box, type **ergonomic study, completed Close** the **Document Information Panel**, and then **Save** your changes. From **Backstage** view, **Close** your document.

13 From **Backstage** view, open the file **Lastname_Firstname_9E_Ergonomic_Study**. Display the **Restrict Formatting and Editing** task pane, and then click the **Stop Protection** button. Insert the file name in the footer, and then **Save** your changes.

14 In the **Word Options** dialog box, turn off the display of the **Developer tab**.

15 Print your documents or submit electronically as directed by your instructor. **Exit** Word.

 You have completed Project 9E ————————————

Apply **9B** skills from these Objectives:

- ▣ Customize the Ribbon
- ▣ Format Pictures and Text Boxes
- ▣ Add a Digital Signature to a Document
- ▣ Prepare a Document for Distribution

Mastering Word | Project **9F** Staffing Needs

In the following Mastering Word project, you will create a memo from Craig Westrich, Director of Human Resources, explaining staffing needs for next year at Laurales Herbs and Spices. The document will require you to group objects to create a letterhead, insert a signature line, and mark the document as final. Your completed document will look similar to Figure 9.45.

Project Files

For Project 9F, you will need the following files:

w09F_Staff
w09F_Staffing_Needs

You will save your document as:

Lastname_Firstname_9F_Staffing_Needs

Project Results

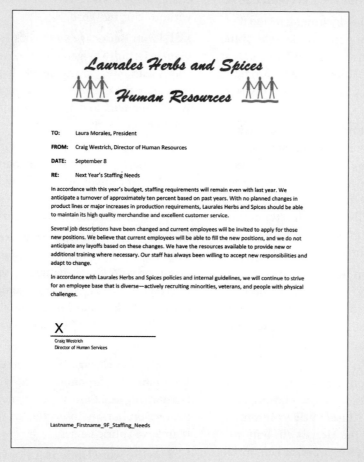

Figure 9.45

(Project 9F Staffing Needs continues on the next page)

Mastering Word | Project **9F** Staffing Needs (continued)

1 **Start** Word. Navigate to your **Word Chapter 9** folder, and save the document as **Lastname_Firstname_9F_ Staffing_Needs** Insert the file name in the footer. If necessary, display the rulers and formatting marks.

2 Insert a **Simple Text Box**, and then change the **Shape Width** to **6.5"**. Change **Wrap Text** to **In Front of Text**, and then set the shape outline to **No Outline**.

3 In the text box, type **Laurales Herbs and Spices** Press Enter, and then type **Human Resources** Select both paragraphs, change the **Font** to **Brush Script MT**, and then change the **Font Size** to **36**. Apply **Bold**, click **Center**, and then change the **Font Color** to **Dark Blue, Text 2**— in the fourth column, the first color. Deselect the text box.

4 Display the **Insert Picture** dialog box, navigate to your student files, and then **Insert** the file **w09F_Staff**. Set **Wrap Text** to **In Front of Text**, and then change the **Shape Width** to **1"**. Position the picture so that it displays to the left of *Human Resources* as shown in Figure 9.45. **Copy** the picture, click in a blank area of the document, and then press Ctrl + V. Position the picture to the right of *Human Resources*. Select both pictures, and then click **Align Top**.

5 Select both pictures and the text box, and then **Group** the items. Change **Wrap Text** to **In Line with Text**. Press Enter to position the insertion point below the graphic.

6 From your student files, insert **Text from File** using the file **w09F_Staffing_Needs**. If any names are flagged as spelling errors, click **Ignore All**.

7 Press Ctrl + End, and then insert a **Microsoft Office Signature Line**. For the **Suggested signer**, type **Craig Westrich** For the **Suggested signer's title**, type **Director of Human Resources Save** your changes.

8 Press Ctrl + Home. Display the **Document Inspector** dialog box, and with all check boxes selected, **Inspect** the document. To the right of **Document Properties and Personal Information**, click the **Remove All** button, and then **Close** the **Document Inspector** dialog box.

9 In the **Document Information Panel**, in the **Author** box, type your first and last names. In the **Subject** box, type your course name and section number, and in the **Keywords** box, type **staffing needs, memo Close** the **Document Information Panel**.

10 Display the **Restrict Formatting and Editing** task pane. Under **2. Editing restrictions**, click the **Allow only this type of editing in the document** check box, and then click the **Yes, Start Enforcing Protection** button. **Save** your changes.

11 Print your document or submit electronically as directed by your instructor. **Exit** Word. When prompted regarding content on the Clipboard, click **No**.

End **You have completed Project 9F** ——————————————————

Content-Based Assessments

Apply **9A** and **9B** skills from these Objectives:

1. Create a Customized Form
2. Modify and Protect a Form
3. Use a Template to Complete a Form
4. Customize the Ribbon
5. Format Pictures and Text Boxes
6. Add a Digital Signature to a Document
7. Prepare a Document for Distribution

Mastering Word | Project **9G** Seminar Evaluation

In the following Mastering Word project, you will create a custom form that will be used by employees to evaluate training seminars at Laurales Herbs and Spices. As part of the document, you will format and group objects to create a heading. Your completed document will look similar to Figure 9.46.

Project Files

For Project 9G, you will need the following files:

> w09G_Seminar_Evaluation
> w09G_Training_Room
> w09G_Training_Seminar

You will save your document as:

> Lastname_Firstname_9G_Seminar_Evaluation

Project Results

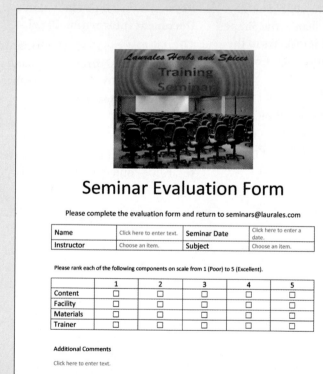

Figure 9.46

(Project 9G Seminar Evaluation continues on the next page)

Content-Based Assessments

Mastering Word | Project **9G** Seminar Evaluation (continued)

1 **Start** Word. From your student files, navigate to your **Word Chapter 9** folder, and open the file **w09G_Seminar_Evaluation**. In your **Word Chapter 9** folder, save the document as a **Word Template** using the name **Lastname_Firstname_9G_Seminar_Evaluation** Insert the file name in the footer. If necessary, display rulers and formatting marks. Display the **Developer tab**.

2 Press Ctrl + Home. From your student files, **Insert** the picture **w09G_Training_Room**. Change **Wrap Text** to **Square**. Deselect the picture, and then from your student files, **Insert** the picture **w09G_Training_Seminar**. **Crop** the picture so the edges are close to the text—approximately **1"** from the left, **1.5"** from the right, **1"** from the top, and **1.75"** from the bottom.

3 Change **Wrap Text** to **In Front of Text**. Drag the Training Seminar picture up so that the top left corner is aligned with the top left corner of the Training Room picture. With the Training Seminar picture selected, drag the right middle sizing handle to the right until the right border of the picture is aligned with the right border of the Training Room picture as shown in Figure 9.46.

4 Group the two pictures, and then change **Wrap Text** to **In Line with Text**. With the grouped object selected, change the **Shape Height** to **3"** and the **Shape Width** to **3.5"**. Select the grouped object, including the paragraph mark next to it, and then **Center** the grouped object.

5 Position the insertion point in the empty paragraph immediately below the grouped object. Type **Seminar Evaluation Form** and then press Enter. Select the text you just typed, and then change the **Font Size** to **36** and apply **Center**.

6 Position the insertion point in the empty paragraph above the first table, and then type **Please complete the evaluation form and return to seminars@laurales.com.** Change the **Font Size** to **14** and apply **Center**. If necessary, remove the hyperlink. Position the insertion point in the empty paragraph above the second table, and then type **Please rank each of the following components on a scale from 1 (Poor) to 5 (Excellent).**

7 Turn on **Design Mode**. In the first table, in the cell to the right of *Name*, insert a **Plain Text Content Control**. In the cell to the right of *Seminar Date*, insert a **Date Picker Content Control**, and then change the format to **M/d/yy**. In the cell following *Instructor*, insert a **Drop-Down List Content Control**, and then add the following names:

Alvin Barnes

Charles Corbin

Susan Parrish

8 In the last cell of the table, insert a **Drop-Down List Content Control**, and then add the following topics:

Customer Service

Employee Benefits

Microsoft Office

Safety Issues

9 In the second table, insert a **Check Box Content Control** in each of the empty cells. Press Ctrl + End, and then insert a **Plain Text Content Control**. Turn off **Design Mode**, and then **Save** your changes.

10 From **Backstage** view, display the **Document Information Panel**. In the **Author** box, type your first and last names. In the **Subject** box, type your course name and section number, and in the **Keywords** box, type **seminar evaluation, form Close** the **Document Information Panel**.

11 Press Ctrl + Home. Display the **Restrict Formatting and Editing** task pane. Under **2. Editing restrictions**, click the **Allow only this type of editing in the document** check box. Click the **Allow only this type of editing in the document arrow**, and then click **Filling in forms**. Under **3. Start enforcement**, click the **Yes, Start Enforcing Protection** button. In the **Start Enforcing Protection** dialog box, click **OK**. **Close** the **Restrict Formatting and Editing** task pane.

12 From the **Word Options** dialog box, turn off the display of the **Developer tab**, and then **Save** your changes.

13 Print your document or submit electronically as directed by your instructor. **Exit** Word.

End You have completed Project 9G

Content-Based Assessments

Apply a combination of
the **9A** and **9B** skills.

GO! Fix It | Project **9H** Complaint Form

Project Files

For Project 9H, you will need the following files:

> w09H_Complaint_Form
> w09H_Logo

You will save your document as:

> Lastname_Firstname_9H_Complaint_Form

From your student files, locate and open the file **w09H_Complaint_Form**. Save the file as a Word template in your **Word Chapter 9** folder as **Lastname_Firstname_9H_Complaint_Form** This document requires additional formatting and changes in content. Read and examine the document, and then make modifications to complete the document and improve the appearance.
Changes that should be made include:

- The text **Laurales Herbs and Spices** should be inserted in a text box, the Font Size changed to 24, and the Fill – Red, Accent 2, Double Outline – Accent 2 text effect applied.

- The picture **w09H_Logo**, located in your student files, should be inserted at the beginning of the document, and changed to a width of 1.5".

- The picture and text box should be formatted and grouped to form a single object. The single object should be centered at the top of the document.

- A Plain Text content control should be inserted to the right of the following paragraphs: *Name, Address, Phone Number, E-mail Address, Order Number,* and *Comments.*

- A Drop-Down List content control should be inserted to the right of the paragraph *Best Time to Call,* and then the three items Morning, Afternoon, and Evening added to the list.

- A Date Picker content control should be inserted to the right of the *Order Date* paragraph and formatted as MM, dd, yyyy.

- A Drop-Down List content control should be inserted to the right of the paragraph *Items Purchased,* and then the five items Accessories, Books, Herbs, Pamphlets, and Spices added to the list.

- A Combo Box content control should be inserted to the right of the paragraph *Type of Issue,* and then the four items Defective Merchandise, Item Missing from Shipment, Returns, and Shipping added to the list.

- The document should be restricted to filling in the form.

Insert the file name in the footer, and then display the Document Information Panel. In the Author box, type your first and last names. In the Subject box, type your course name and section number, and in the Keywords box, type **complaint form, template** Save your changes, and print the document or submit electronically as directed by your instructor.

End **You have completed Project 9H** ———————

Content-Based Assessments

Apply a combination of the **9A** and **9B** skills.

GO! Make It | Project 9I Phone Request

Project Files

For Project 9I, you will need the following files:

New blank Word document
w09I_Phone

You will save your document as:

Lastname_Firstname_9I_Phone_Request

Open a new blank document, and save it to your **Word Chapter 9** folder as **Lastname_Firstname_9I_Phone_Request** Use the skills you practiced in this chapter to create the document shown in Figure 9.47. The picture **w09I_Phone** is located in your student files. The font is Calibri. Insert WordArt and a text box and group them with the picture—cropped to shape—to form one object. Enter appropriate content controls. For the Combo Box content control, add these four terms: **Friend Internet Magazine ad** and **Radio ad** Insert the file name in the footer. In the Document Information Panel, add your name, course information, and the keywords **phone request, form** Save your document and print or submit electronically as directed by your instructor.

Project Results

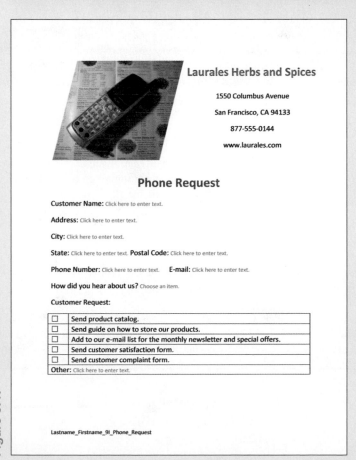

Figure 9.47

End You have completed Project 9I

Content-Based Assessments

GO! Solve It | Project 9J Accident Report

Project Files

For Project 9J, you will need the following files:

New blank Word document
w09J_Accident_Data

You will save your document as:

Lastname_Firstname_9J_Accident_Report

Laurales Herbs and Spices tracks all work-related accidents that result in minor or major injury. All supervisors are trained in the procedures to follow in the case of an accident—assessing the injury, giving first aid, and if necessary referring the patient to another facility. Design a report form that includes appropriate text and content controls for the required information. The user should be able to select the department and medical facility from a list. Using at least three objects, group them to create a company letterhead. The bottom of the report should include a signature line for the supervisor. The required information can be found in the student file **w09J_Accident_Data**. Save your document as a Word template with the file name **Lastname_Firstname_9J_Accident_Report** Insert the file name in the footer and add appropriate document properties. Restrict editing to filling in forms. Print your document or submit electronically as directed by your instructor.

	Performance Level		
	Exemplary: You consistently applied the relevant skills	**Proficient:** You sometimes, but not always, applied the relevant skills	**Developing:** You rarely or never applied the relevant skills
Insert and format text	All required information is included and formatted appropriately.	Some information is missing or not formatted appropriately.	No specific information is included.
Insert content controls	Appropriate content controls are used and required items are added.	Some content controls are inappropriate or some required items are missing.	No content controls are inserted.
Insert and group objects	Objects are inserted and grouped.	Objects are inserted but not grouped.	No objects are inserted.
Insert signature line	A signature line is inserted with a proper title.	A signature line is inserted but the title is missing.	No signature line is inserted.
Save as template and restrict editing	The document is saved as a template and restricted to filling in forms.	The document is not saved as a template or not restricted to filling in forms.	The document is not saved as a template and the form is not restricted.

Performance Element (vertical label)

End You have completed Project 9J ——————

Content-Based Assessments

Apply a combination of the **9A** and **9B** skills.

GO! Solve It | Project **9K** Staff Promotion

Project Files

For Project 9K, you will need the following files:

> New blank Word document
> w09K_Promotion_Data

You will save your document as:

> Lastname_Firstname_9K_Staff_Promotion

Laura Morales, President of Laurales Herbs and Spices, needs to fill the position of Executive Assistant. She would like to promote an individual from within the company. She has identified ten candidates; however, she wants the department managers to identify the strengths and weaknesses of the individuals. Create a memorandum from Ms. Morales to department managers, including the current date and an appropriate subject line. In the body of the memo, design a form that includes appropriate content controls to select the name of the individual being evaluated and rate the candidate on a variety of skills using a five-point scale ranging from Poor to Excellent. Information regarding candidates' names and required skills can be found in the student file **w09K_Promotion_Data**. Save the document as a Word template with the file name **Lastname_Firstname_9K_Staff_Promotion** Insert the file name in the footer and add appropriate document properties. Restrict editing to filling in the form. Print your document or submit electronically as directed by your instructor.

Performance Element		Performance Level		
		Exemplary: You consistently applied the relevant skills	**Proficient:** You sometimes, but not always, applied the relevant skills	**Developing:** You rarely or never applied the relevant skills
	Insert and format text	All required information is included and the document is formatted as a memo.	Some information is missing or the document is not formatted as a memo.	No specific information is included and the document is not formatted as a memo.
	Insert content controls	Appropriate content controls are used and required items are added.	Some content controls are inappropriate or some required items are missing.	No content controls are inserted.
	Insert 5-point rating scale	The scale allows for 5 ratings and displays appropriately with skills and content controls.	The scale does not contain 5 ratings or does not display appropriately with skills and content controls.	There is no scale.
	Save as template and restrict editing	The document is saved as a template and is restricted to filling in forms.	The document is not saved as a template or is not restricted to filling in forms.	The document is not saved as a template and the form is not restricted.

End You have completed Project 9K

Outcomes-Based Assessments

Rubric

The following outcomes-based assessments are *open-ended assessments*. That is, there is no specific correct result; your result will depend on your approach to the information provided. Make *Professional Quality* your goal. Use the following scoring rubric to guide you in *how* to approach the problem and then to evaluate *how well* your approach solves the problem.

The *criteria*—Software Mastery, Content, Format and Layout, and Process—represent the knowledge and skills you have gained that you can apply to solving the problem. The *levels of performance*—Professional Quality, Approaching Professional Quality, or Needs Quality Improvements—help you and your instructor evaluate your result.

	Your completed project is of Professional Quality if you:	Your completed project is Approaching Professional Quality if you:	Your completed project Needs Quality Improvements if you:
1-Software Mastery	Choose and apply the most appropriate skills, tools, and features and identify efficient methods to solve the problem.	Choose and apply some appropriate skills, tools, and features, but not in the most efficient manner.	Choose inappropriate skills, tools, or features, or are inefficient in solving the problem.
2-Content	Construct a solution that is clear and well organized, contains content that is accurate, appropriate to the audience and purpose, and is complete. Provide a solution that contains no errors in spelling, grammar, or style.	Construct a solution in which some components are unclear, poorly organized, inconsistent, or incomplete. Misjudge the needs of the audience. Have some errors in spelling, grammar, or style, but the errors do not detract from comprehension.	Construct a solution that is unclear, incomplete, or poorly organized; contains some inaccurate or inappropriate content; and contains many errors in spelling, grammar, or style. Do not solve the problem.
3-Format and Layout	Format and arrange all elements to communicate information and ideas, clarify function, illustrate relationships, and indicate relative importance.	Apply appropriate format and layout features to some elements, but not others. Overuse features, causing minor distraction.	Apply format and layout that does not communicate information or ideas clearly. Do not use format and layout features to clarify function, illustrate relationships, or indicate relative importance. Use available features excessively, causing distraction.
4-Process	Use an organized approach that integrates planning, development, self-assessment, revision, and reflection.	Demonstrate an organized approach in some areas, but not others; or, use an insufficient process of organization throughout.	Do not use an organized approach to solve the problem.

Outcomes-Based Assessments

Apply a combination of the **9A** and **9B** skills.

GO! Think | Project **9L** Computer Equipment

Project Files

For Project 9L, you will need the following files:

Two new blank Word documents

You will save your documents as:

Lastname_Firstname_9L_Computer_Equipment
Lastname_Firstname_9L_Computer_Request

Every three years, the IT department of Laurales Herbs and Spices updates computer equipment and software for the administrative staff. Employees may choose either a desktop or laptop computer. Other options include, but are not limited to, a choice of printers or a scanner. In conjunction with the new computer rollout, the IT department wants to prioritize training needs by asking employees to select a topic—File Management, Microsoft Office, or Web Site Development—that would be most helpful to them.

Create a questionnaire that can be sent to the administrative staff. Include appropriate text and content controls for the employee's name, the current date, and types of computer equipment and training. Restrict editing the document to filling in forms. Save the document as a Word template with the file name **Lastname_Firstname_9L_Computer_Equipment** Using the template, create a new document and complete the form, using your name as the employee. Save the document as **Lastname_Firstname_9L_Computer_Request** Add appropriate document properties, and mark the document as final. In your template, insert the file name in the footer and add appropriate document properties. Print both documents or submit electronically as directed by your instructor.

 You have completed Project 9L _____

Apply a combination of the **9A** and **9B** skills.

GO! Think | Project **9M** Vacation Compensation

Project Files

For Project 9M, you will need the following file:

New blank Word document

You will save your document as:

Lastname_Firstname_9M_Vacation_Compensation

Laurales Herbs and Spices provides an option for employees to be paid for vacation days instead of taking time off. If an employee selects compensation, the vacation days are forfeited. Approval of the employee's immediate supervisor is required. The compensation option is available only in the current fiscal year and does not apply to previous or subsequent years. Create a form with appropriate text and content controls for employee information. Using several objects, group them to create a company letterhead. Include a signature line for the employee and the immediate supervisor. Save the document as a template with the file name **Lastname_Firstname_9M_Vacation_Compensation** Insert the file name in the footer and add appropriate document properties. Print the document or submit electronically as directed by your instructor.

 You have completed Project 9M _____

Outcomes-Based Assessments

You and GO! | Project **9N** Cover Page

Project Files

For Project 9N, you will need the following file:

New blank Word document

You will save your document as:

Lastname_Firstname_9N_Cover_Page

Create a cover page template that you can use for your assignments, such as research papers. The document should include your name and appropriate content controls to select a date, select a subject or course name, and type an assignment title. Add appropriate static text, format the document in an attractive manner, and check for spelling errors. Save the document as a Word template with the file name **Lastname_Firstname_9N_Cover_Page** Insert the file name in the footer. Add appropriate properties including the keywords **cover sheet, personal** Restrict the document to allow only filling in the form. Print your document or submit electronically as directed by your instructor.

End **You have completed Project 9N** ——————————————————————

Business Running Case

Razvan CHIRNOAGA/Shutterstock

Front Range Action Sports is one of the country's largest retailers of sports gear and outdoor recreation merchandise. The company has large retail stores in Colorado, Washington, Oregon, California, and New Mexico, in addition to a growing online business. Major merchandise categories include fishing, camping, rock climbing, winter sports, action sports, water sports, team sports, racquet sports, fitness, golf, apparel, and footwear.

In this project, you will apply skills you practiced from the Objectives in Chapters 7–9. You will edit and create documents that relate to a strategy meeting for employees in the Front Range Action Sports sales department. The documents include a data source containing employee contact information, a memo that has been personalized using mail merge, an employee directory, and a customer survey form. Your completed documents will look similar to Figure 3.1.

Project Files

For Project BRC3, you will need the following files:

New blank Word document
wBRC3_Employee_Information
wBRC3_Employee_Memo
wBRC3_Logo_Memo
wBRC3_Customer_Survey
wBRC3_Parasailing

You will save your documents as:

Lastname_Firstname_BRC3_Employee_ Information
Lastname_Firstname_BRC3_Memo_Main
Lastname_Firstname_BRC3_Memo_Merged
Lastname_Firstname_BRC3_Employee_Directory
Lastname_Firstname_BRC3_Customer_Survey

Project Results

Figure 3.1

Business Running Case

Front Range Action Sports

1 **Start** Word. From your student files, open **wBRC3_ Employee_Information**. If necessary, in the location where you are storing your projects, create a new folder named **Front Range Action Sports** or navigate to this folder if you have already created it. **Save** the document as **Lastname_Firstname_BRC3_Employee_Information** and then insert the file name in the footer.

a. Select all paragraphs in the document, and then **Convert Text to Table**. Insert a new row above the first row of the table. In the first cell of the table, type **Employee_First** press [Tab], type **Employee_Last** press [Tab], type **Department** press [Tab], and then type **Phone**

b. Display the **Create New Style from Formatting** dialog box, and create a new **Table** style with the name **Employees** Change the **Line Weight** to ½ pt, and the **Border Color** to **Red, Accent 2, Darker 25%**—in the sixth column, the fifth color. Change the border to display **All Borders**. Apply the **Employee** table style to the table.

c. Modify the **Employee** table style by setting **Apply formatting to** the **Header row**. Apply **Bold**, and then change the **Fill Color** to **Red, Accent 2, Lighter 60%**—in the sixth column, the third color.

d. Click anywhere in the table, and then resize the table to **AutoFit Contents**. **Sort** the table by **Employee_ Last** in ascending order, and then by **Employee_First** in ascending order.

e. Display the **Document Information Panel**, add your name, course information, and the **Keywords employee information, data source Save** your changes, and then **Close** your document without closing Word.

2 From your student files, open the document **wBRC3_ Employee_Memo**, and then save the document to your **Front Range Action Sports** folder as **Lastname_ Firstname_BRC3_Memo_Main** If any words are flagged as spelling errors, click **Ignore All**.

a. In the blank paragraph immediately above the last paragraph of the document, click to position the insertion point. Insert a table containing two columns and one row. With the entire table selected, change all **Cell Margins** to **0.1"**, change **Allow spacing between cells** to **0.3"**, and then change **Borders** to **No Border**. Change the **Alignment** to **Align Center**.

b. In the first cell of the table, insert an **Microsoft Excel Worksheet**. If a Microsoft message box displays, click Yes. In cell **A1**, type **Item** in cell **B1**, type **Price** in cell **A7**, type **Total** and then in cell **B7**, type **=SUM(B2:B6)** Press [Enter], and then resize the spreadsheet to display only columns A and B and rows 1 through 7. Select cells **A1** and **B1**, and then on the **Home tab**, in the **Cell Styles** gallery, apply the **Accent3** style. Click in a blank area of the document to close the spreadsheet.

c. In the second cell of the table, insert an **Microsoft Excel Worksheet**. If a Microsoft message box displays, click Yes. In cell **A1**, type **Item** in cell **B1**, type **Price** in cell **A7**, type **Total** and then in cell **B7**, type **=SUM(B2:B6)** Press [Enter], and then resize the spreadsheet to display only columns A and B and rows 1 through 7. Select cells **A1** and **B1**, and then in the **Cell Styles** gallery, apply the **Accent3** style. Click in a blank area of the document to close the spreadsheet.

d. Click to select the first Excel table, and then click **Insert Caption**. Following the text *Figure 1*, type **:** **Best Selling Items** Change the **Position** to **Above selected item**, if necessary. In a similar manner, above the second Excel table, click **Insert Caption**. Following the text *Figure 2*, type **:** **Worst Selling Items** For both captions, change the **Font Color** to **Olive Green, Accent 3, Darker 50%**—in the seventh column, the last color. Press [Ctrl] + [Home], and then **Save** your changes without closing the document.

3 From your student files, open the document **wBRC3_ Logo_Memo**. **Copy** the image of the arrow to the Clipboard, and then **Close** the document. In your **Lastname_Firstname_BRC3_Memo_Main** document, click the **Paste** button three times.

a. Move the images so that the three arrows display above the paragraph *MEMO*, with the left edge of each graphic aligned at approximately **0 inch**, **1 inch**, and **2 inches on the horizontal ruler**, respectively. Select all three images, align the top of the images, if necessary, and then **Group** the images.

b. Beginning at approximately **3 inches on the horizontal ruler** and **0 inches on the vertical ruler**, draw a **Simple Text Box** that extends to approximately **6.5 inches on the horizontal ruler** and **0.5 inch on the vertical ruler**. Change the **Shape Fill** to **Olive Green, Accent 3**—in the seventh column, the first color—and then change the **Shape Outline** to **Olive Green, Accent 3, Darker 50%**—in the seventh column, the last color.

(Business Running Case: Front Range Action Sports continues on the next page)

Business Running Case

Front Range Action Sports (continued)

c. In the text box, type **Front Range Action Sports** Change the **Font Size** to **20**, apply **Center**, and then change the **Text Effects** to **Gradient Fill – Orange, Accent 6, Inner Shadow**—in the fourth row, the second effect.

d. Select the text box and the grouped graphic, apply **Align Middle**, and then **Group** the two objects. If necessary move the grouped object so that it is positioned above *MEMO* as shown in Figure 3.1. **Save** your changes.

4 With **Lastname_Firstname_BRC3_Memo_Main** open, click **Start Mail Merge**, and then click **Letters**. Select the **Lastname_Firstname_BRC3_Employee_ Information** file you created as the data source. **Edit** the data source for **Record 5** by changing **Phone** to **555-2365 Filter** the data source to display only individuals in the **Sales** department.

a. In the paragraph that begins *TO*, delete the text **Sales Representatives**. To the right of the tab formatting mark, insert the merge fields **Employee_First** and **Employee_Last**. Insert a space between the two merge fields.

b. Click **Finish & Merge**, and then click **Edit Individual Documents**, merging all records to a new document. **Save** the document to your **Front Range Action Sports** folder with the file name **Lastname_ Firstname_BRC3_Memo_Merged** Insert the file name in the footer. Display the **Document Information Panel**, add your name, course information, and the **Keywords strategy memo, merged Save** your changes, and then **Close** the document.

c. In the **Lastname_Firstname_BRC3_Memo_Main** document, insert the file name in the footer. Display the **Document Information Panel**, add your name, course information, and the **Keywords strategy memo, main Save** your changes, and then from **Backstage** view, **Close** your document without closing Word. In the Microsoft message box, click **Yes** to save changes to the data source **Lastname_Firstname_ BRC3_Employee_Information**.

5 Display a new document. Click **Start Mail Merge**, and then click **Directory**. Click **Select Recipients**, click **Use Existing List**, and then open the **Lastname_Firstname_ BRC3_Employee_Information** document you created. **Sort** the recipient list by **Department**, then by **Employee_**

Last, and then by **Employee_First**. Set left tab stops at **3 inches** and **4 inches**. Insert the merge field **Employee_ First**, press Spacebar, insert **Employee_Last**, press Tab, insert **Phone**, press Tab, insert **Department**, and then press Enter.

a. Merge all records to a new document. At the top of the new, merged document, insert a new paragraph. Position the insertion point in the blank paragraph, type **Employee Name** press Tab, type **Phone** press Tab, and then type **Department** Select the paragraph, apply **Bold** and **Underline**, and then change the **Font Color** to **Olive Green, Accent 3, Darker 50%**—in the seventh column, the last color. Insert a watermark— **CONFIDENTIAL 2**.

b. **Save** the document to your **Front Range Action Sports** folder with the file name **Lastname_Firstname_ BRC3_Employee_Directory** Insert the file name in the footer. Display the **Document Information Panel**, add your name, course information, and the **Keywords employee directory, merged Save** your changes, and then **Close** the document. In the document containing the merge fields, **Close** the document without saving changes.

6 Open the file **wBRC3_Customer_Survey**. Save it to your **Front Range Action Sports** folder as a **Word Template** with the file name **Lastname_Firstname_BRC3_ Customer_Survey** Insert the file name in the footer.

a. From your student files, insert the picture **wBRC3_ Parasailing**. Change the **Shape Height** to **1.6"**, and then change **Wrap Text** to **Tight**. Position the picture so that the top edge is aligned with the first paragraph and the right edge is aligned with the right margin.

b. Click the **Corrections** button, and then click **Brightness: -20% Contrast: +40%**—in the fifth row, the second option. Change the **Glow** picture effect to **Blue, 11 pt glow, Accent color 1**—in the third row, the first option.

7 In the first cell of the table, click **Table Eraser**, and then erase the right border. In a similar manner, in the first cell in the sixth through ninth rows, erase the right border.

a. Turn on the **Draw Table** command. In the second cell of the second row, point to the top border. With the pointer at approximately **7 inches on the horizontal ruler**, drag down to draw a line extending to the bottom border of the fifth row. Turn off the **Draw Table** command.

(Business Running Case: Front Range Action Sports continues on the next page)

Business Running Case 3: Includes Objectives from Word Chapters 7-9

Business Running Case

Front Range Action Sports (continued)

b. In the second through fifth rows, select the second and third columns, and then click **Distribute Columns**. Apply the table style **Medium Grid 1 – Accent 3**—in the eighth row, the fourth option. Select the entire table, apply **Align Center Left**, and then click **Distribute Rows**.

c. If necessary, display the Developer tab. Turn on **Design Mode**. In the first row of the table, position the insertion point after the question mark, press Spacebar, and then insert a **Drop-Down List** content control. Add the choice **Very satisfied** to the list. In a similar manner, add the choices **Somewhat satisfied** and **Unsatisfied** to the list.

d. In the second row, in the second cell, insert a **Check Box** content control, press → two times, press Spacebar, and then type **Yes** Press Tab, insert a **Check Box** content control, press → two times, press

Spacebar, and then type **No** Apply **Bold** to *Yes* and *No*. In a similar manner, in the third, fourth, and fifth rows, insert **Check Box** content controls and the appropriate **Yes** and **No** text with **Bold** applied.

e. In rows six through nine, following the existing text in each row, press Spacebar, insert a **Plain Text** content control, and then change the **Properties** to the **Strong** style. Turn off **Design Mode**.

f. Press Ctrl + Home. Display the **Document Information Panel**, add your name, course information, and the **Keywords customer survey, content controls** and then close the Document Information Panel. **Restrict Editing** to **Filling in forms**, and then **Save** your changes.

8 Print or submit all five documents as directed by your instructor. **Exit** Word.

End **You have completed Business Running Case 3** ————————————

Working with Long Documents

Travis Houston/Shutterstock

In This Chapter

When several people work on a document, keeping track of the different versions can be difficult. In this chapter, you will create a master document and subdocuments from a multipage file to allow parts of the document to be edited while maintaining the integrity of the complete document. The navigation features in Word allow you to view and edit the final master document. Additionally, you will create navigational and reference aids for a long document, including a table of contents, a table of figures, and an index. Defining the flow of text on the pages of the document will improve readability.

The projects in this chapter relate to the **City of Golden Grove**, a growing community located between Los Angeles and San Diego, about 20 miles from the Pacific shore. Just 10 years ago the population was under 100,000; today it has grown to almost 300,000. Community leaders have always focused on quality of life and economic development in decisions on housing, open space, education, and infrastructure, making the city a model for other communities its size around the United States. The city provides many recreational and cultural opportunities with a large park system and thriving arts community.

Project 10A Spring Schedule

myitlab
Project 10A Training

Project Activities

In Activities 10.01 through 10.10, you will create a master document with four subdocuments. The finished document will be a description of the spring activities offered by the City of Golden Grove. Your completed documents will look similar to Figure 10.1.

Project Files

For Project 10A, you will need the following files:

w10A_Spring_Schedule
w10A_Teens

You will save your documents as:

Lastname_Firstname_10A_Spring_Schedule
Lastname_Firstname_10A_Teens

Project Results

Figure 10.1
Project 10A Spring Schedule

Objective 1 | Create a Master Document and Subdocuments

You can organize a long document into sections—a ***master document*** and ***subdocuments***, to make it easier to work with different parts of the document. A master document is a Word document that serves as a container for the different parts of a document. A subdocument is a section of the document that is linked to the master document. Changes made in the subdocument are reflected in the master document. Using subdocuments enables the individuals collaborating on a project to edit the various sections of the document without altering the entire long document. Each individual can work on a specific section, and then the sections can be integrated into the final document.

Using a master document allows you to maintain consistent formatting and styles across all of the subdocuments even though different people are working on the sections. ***Outline view*** displays the overall organization, or hierarchy, of parts of a document, including headings, subheadings, and subordinate text.

Activity 10.01 | Creating a Master Document from an Existing Document

1 **Start** Word. From your student files, locate and open the file **w10A_Spring_Schedule**. From **Backstage** view, display the **Save As** dialog box, navigate to the location where you are saving your files for this chapter, and create a folder named **Word Chapter 10** Open the **Word Chapter 10** folder, and then create a folder named **Project 10A Save** the document to your **Project 10A** folder as **Lastname_Firstname_10A_Spring_Schedule** Using **Quick Parts**, insert the file name in the footer. If necessary, display the rulers and formatting marks.

2 Press Ctrl + Home. On the **Page Layout tab**, in the **Themes group**, click the **Themes** button, and then from the **Themes** gallery, click **Module**. Click the **Home tab**, and then compare your screen with Figure 10.2.

> Recall that changing the theme affects the default fonts, colors, and styles. In this case, the Corbel font is applied to ***body text***—text that does not have a style applied—and some Quick Styles change to a gold color scheme.

Figure 10.2

Font in Module theme

Styles in Module theme

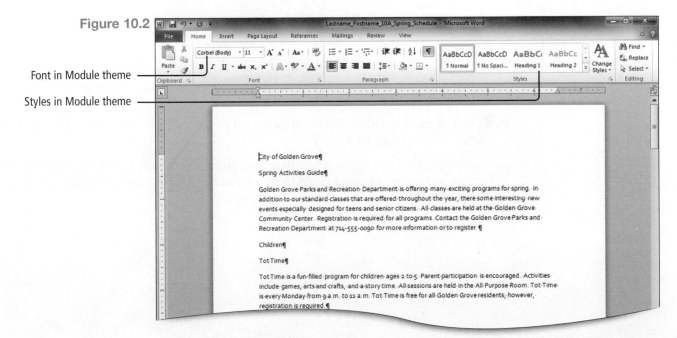

3 Select the first paragraph of the document. On the Mini toolbar, change the **Font Size** to **28**, and then click **Center** ≡. With the text selected, on the **Home tab**, in the **Font group**, click the **Text Effects** button A⁻, and then in the **Text Effects** gallery, in the third row, select the fourth effect—**Gradient Fill - Gold, Accent 1**.

4 Select the second paragraph. On the Mini toolbar, change the **Font Size** to **36**, apply **Bold** B and **Center** ≡, and then click the **Font Color button arrow** A⁻ and change the color to **Gold, Accent 1, Darker 25%**—in the fifth column, the fifth color. Select the third paragraph, and then on the Mini toolbar, change the **Font Size** to **12**.

5 Select the fourth paragraph *Children*. On the **Home tab**, in the **Styles group**, click the third style—**Heading 1**. In a similar manner, apply the **Heading 1** style to the paragraphs *Adults*, *Families*, *Senior Citizens*, and *Ballroom Dancing*. Deselect the text.

6 On the **View tab**, in the **Document Views group**, click the **Outline** button, and then press Ctrl + Home. Compare your screen with Figure 10.3.

Outline view makes it easy to view the different levels in a document. The paragraphs formatted with the Heading 1 style are designated as Level 1 headings and display with a gray bullet containing a plus sign—indicating that subordinate levels display below those paragraphs. All other paragraphs are indented and display with a smaller gray bullet to indicate body text. Outline view does not display paragraph alignments—in this case, the first two paragraphs do not display as centered.

Figure 10.3

Outlining tab

Body text

Level 1 heading

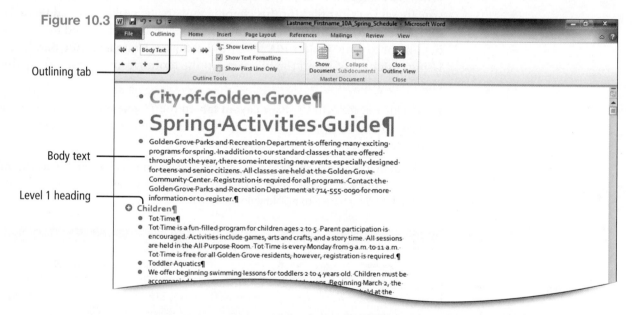

7 Click to place the insertion point to the left of the paragraph *Children*. Compare your screen with Figure 10.4.

On the Outlining tab, in the Outline Tools group, the Outline Level box displays Level 1, indicating the paragraphs formatted with Heading 1 are the top-level paragraphs in the document.

Figure 10.4

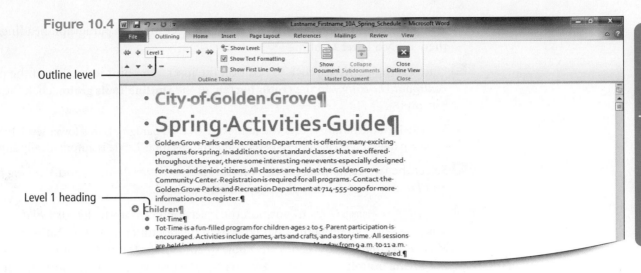

Outline level

Level 1 heading

8 Immediately below the paragraph *Children*, click to position the insertion point to the left of the paragraph *Tot Time*. On the **Outlining tab**, in the **Outline Tools group**, click the **Outline Level arrow** ⌷Body Text ⌷, and then click **Level 2**. Notice that a gray bullet containing a plus sign displays to the left of *Tot Time* and the text formatting is changed.

> You can set levels for specific paragraphs by using Outline view. The *Tot Time* paragraph is now assigned a Level 2 heading and the Heading 2 style is automatically applied.

9 Click to position the insertion point to the left of the paragraph *Toddler Aquatics*. On the **Outlining tab**, in the **Outline Tools group**, click the **Promote** button ⌷. Notice that this paragraph displays as a *Level 2* paragraph—the same level and format as the *Tot Time* paragraph. Compare your screen with Figure 10.5.

> The Promote button allows you to move a selected paragraph to a higher level.

Figure 10.5

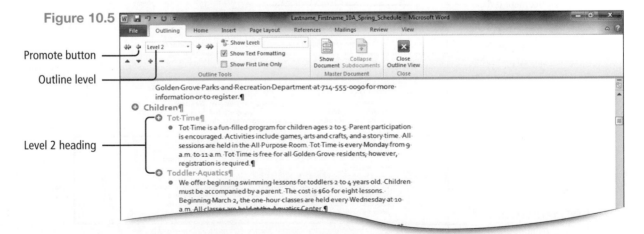

Promote button

Outline level

Level 2 heading

10 Using the same technique, **Promote** ⌷ the paragraphs *Ballet for Preschoolers*, *Tap Dance*, and *Beginning Karate*.

11 Under *Adults*, select the paragraph *Self Defense*. Press and hold down ⌷Ctrl⌷, and then select the paragraphs *Losing Weight Healthfully* and *Gardening for the Novice*. With the three paragraph headings selected, on the **Outlining tab**, in the **Outline Tools group**, click the **Outline Level arrow** ⌷Body Text ⌷, and then click **Level 2**.

12 Using the same technique, under *Families*, select the four paragraph headings, and then apply a **Level 2** outline level.

13 Under *Senior Citizens*, click to position the insertion point to the left of the paragraph *Ballroom Dancing*. On the **Outlining tab**, in the **Outline Tools group**, click the **Demote** button ⇥.

> The Demote button allows you to move a selected paragraph to a lower level. In this case, the paragraph is changed to Level 2, and the Heading 2 style is automatically applied.

14 Select the two remaining paragraph headings—*Water Aerobics* and *Walking for Fun and Fitness*—and then apply a **Level 2** outline level.

15 Press [Ctrl] + [Home]. Click to position the insertion point to the left of *Children*. Drag down to select all remaining paragraphs in the document. On the **Outlining tab**, in the **Master Document group**, click the **Show Document** button to turn it on, and then click the **Create** button. Press [Ctrl] + [End], scroll as necessary, and then compare your screen with Figure 10.6.

> The first heading level in the selection determines where each subdocument is created. In this instance, the Level 1 headings of the document are used to create subdocuments. If the selected text begins with a Level 2 heading, a subdocument is created at each Level 2 heading. A light gray border displays around each subdocument, and a subdocument icon displays to the left of the first line of each new subdocument. All of the text that was not selected remains as body text within the master document.

> ***Continuous section breaks*** define the beginning and end of each subdocument. Recall that a ***section break*** is a mark that stores the section formatting information, such as the margins, page orientation, headers and footers, and sequence of page numbers. A continuous section break indicates that the section will begin on the same page of the document.

Figure 10.6

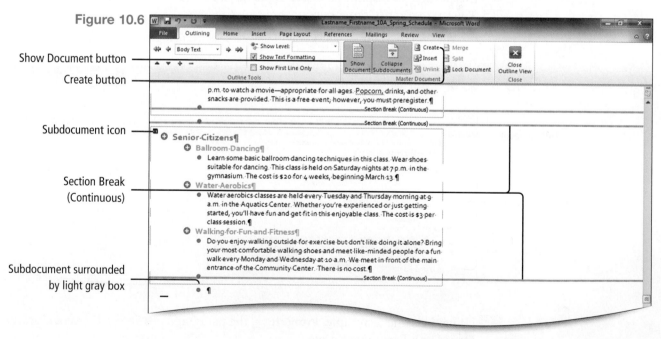

Show Document button
Create button
Subdocument icon
Section Break (Continuous)
Subdocument surrounded by light gray box

16 **Save** 🖫 your changes.

Activity 10.02 | Collapsing and Rearranging Subdocuments

When a master document is created, the subdocuments display in expanded form—all text in the document is visible. You can collapse one or more subdocuments to hide a portion of the text. Collapsing all subdocuments is useful if you want to change the position of a subdocument in the master document.

1 On the **Outlining tab**, in the **Master Document group**, click the **Collapse Subdocuments** button. Compare your screen with Figure 10.7.

The subdocuments are collapsed and display as hyperlinks. Each subdocument is saved as a separate document in the same location as the master document—in this case, your Word Chapter 10 folder. The file name of the subdocument is created automatically by using the heading text of the subdocument. All files for a master document and its subdocuments are usually stored in the same folder.

When the master document is collapsed, the Lock icon displays next to the links for all subdocuments. When a subdocument is locked, no one else can make changes to it.

Figure 10.7

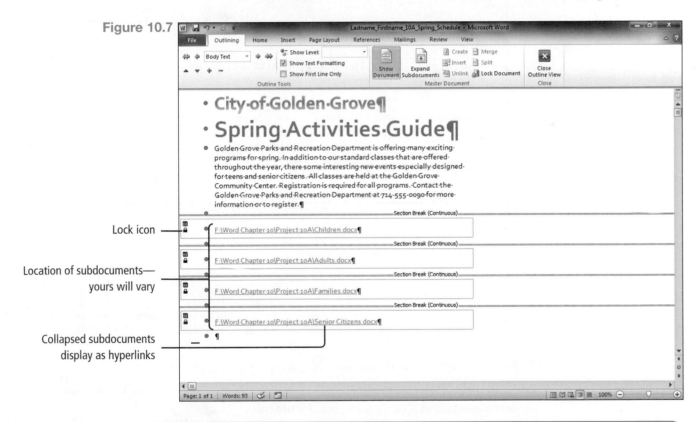

Lock icon

Location of subdocuments— yours will vary

Collapsed subdocuments display as hyperlinks

More Knowledge | Locking a Subdocument

If you want to lock a specific subdocument, position the insertion point in the subdocument, and then on the Outlining tab, in the Master Document group, click the Lock Document button.

2 Point to the **Word Chapter 10\Project 10A\Children.docx** hyperlink, press and hold down Ctrl, and then click to open the link—in this case, the *Children* subdocument. Notice that the subdocument displays in a new window.

3 **Close** ❎ the **Children** document.

Because you opened the Children subdocument by clicking the hyperlink, the color of the hyperlink changes in the master document.

4 To the left of the *Children* subdocument, click the **Subdocument** icon 🗐.

5 Drag down until the *Children* **Subdocument** icon displays above the **Section Break (Continuous)** that begins the *Families* subdocument. When a thick gray line indicates the location shown in Figure 10.8, release the mouse button.

Figure 10.8

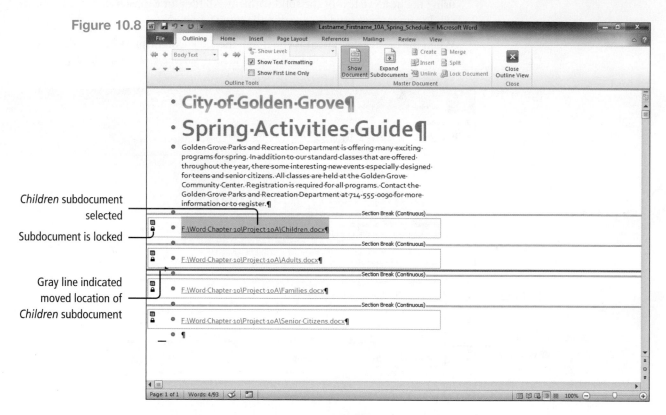

Children subdocument selected

Subdocument is locked

Gray line indicated moved location of Children subdocument

6 Deselect the text, and then **Save** 💾 your changes.

More Knowledge | Rearranging Subdocuments

If you want to move multiple subdocuments that are located adjacent to each other, select the first subdocument, hold down Shift, and then select the last subdocument. You can then move the group to a new location. In addition, you can select nonadjacent subdocuments by holding down the Ctrl key as you select the documents. All of the selected documents can then be relocated.

Activity 10.03 | Inserting an Existing File as a Subdocument

Any existing document can be inserted as a subdocument in a master document. It is necessary to expand the subdocuments when inserting a new document.

1 On the **Outlining tab**, in the **Master Document group**, click the **Expand Subdocuments** button. From your student files, locate and open the file **w10A_Teens**.

> The first paragraph is formatted with the Heading 1 style, and the four paragraph headings are formatted with the Heading 2 style.

2 From **Backstage** view, display the **Save As** dialog box, navigate to your **Project 10A** folder, and then compare your screen with Figure 10.9.

> The four subdocuments that were saved when you created the master document display in your Project 10A folder along with your master document.

Figure 10.9

Subdocuments

Master document

3 **Save** the file in your **Project 10A** folder as **Lastname_Firstname_10A_Teens** Display the **Document Information Panel**, and then in the **Author** box, type your first and last names. In the **Subject** box, type your course name and section number, and in the **Keywords** box, type **subdocument, teens Close** ☒ the **Document Information Panel**. **Save** ▣ your changes, and then **Close** ☒ the *Teens* document.

4 Press Ctrl + End to move to the end of the **Lastname_Firstname_10A_Spring_Schedule** document. On the **Outlining tab**, in the **Master Document group**, click the **Show Document** button to turn it on, if necessary, and then click the **Insert** button. In the **Insert Subdocument** dialog box, navigate to your **Project 10A** folder, select **Lastname_ Firstname_10A_Teens**, and then click **Open**.

> An existing document is now inserted as a subdocument. Because Heading 1 and Heading 2 styles were applied in the *Teens* document, the respective levels are maintained in the subdocument.

5 **Save** 🖫 your changes, and then compare your screen with Figure 10.10.

Figure 10.10

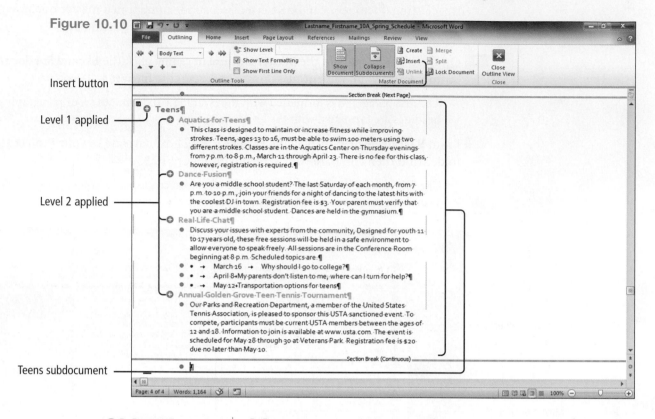

Insert button

Level 1 applied

Level 2 applied

Teens subdocument

Objective 2 │ Manage a Master Document and Subdocuments

The main reason to work with a master document is to allow different people to edit subdocuments without affecting the master document. There are two ways to edit a subdocument—by editing the master document or by editing the subdocument.

Activity 10.04 │ Editing a Master Document and Subdocuments

1 In the master document, under *Teens*, locate the paragraph under *Dance Fusion*. Change the registration fee from *$3* to **$4**

Changes to a subdocument can be made in the master document.

2 From **Backstage** view, navigate to your **Project 10A** folder, and then open the document named **Lastname_Firstname_10A_Teens**. Notice that the change you made to the cost for *Dance Fusion* displays as *$4* in this subdocument.

When changes are made to the master document, they are also reflected in the subdocument.

3 In the *Lastname_Firstname_10A_Teens* document, locate the paragraph below *Real Life Chat*. In the second sentence, change the ages from *11 to 17* to **13 to 16** Compare your screen with Figure 10.11.

Figure 10.11

Lastname_Firstname_
10A_Teens document

Registration fee changed

Ages changed

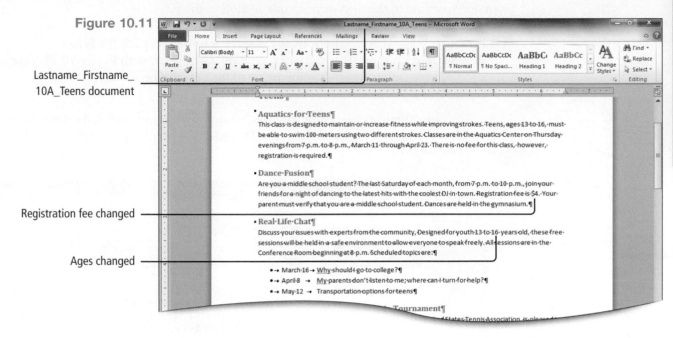

4 **Save** 🔲 your changes, and then **Close** ❎ the **Lastname_Firstname_10A_Teens** document.

5 In the displayed **Lastname_Firstname_10A_Spring_Schedule** document, under *Teens*, locate the paragraph below *Real Life Chat*, and notice that the change has been made for ages *13 to 16*.

6 On the **Outlining tab**, in the **Close group**, click the **Close Outline View** button. **Save** 🔲 your changes.

Objective 3 | Navigate and Inspect the Master Document

After all subdocuments have been edited, it is important to view the master document and, if necessary, make any final revisions. Word provides many features for examining a document—such as browsing the document by pages or locating a specific item. In a long document, these features allow you to navigate quickly to the sections you wish to review.

Activity 10.05 | Using the Select Browse Object Feature

The Select Browse Object button is located at the bottom of the vertical scroll bar and can be used to navigate through a document by type of object. For example, you can move from one footnote to the next or from one section to the next.

1 Press Ctrl + Home. At the bottom of the vertical scroll bar, click the **Select Browse Object** button, and then compare your screen with Figure 10.12. Take a moment to point to each button and read the description for each button in Figure 10.13.

The Select Browse Object menu displays. When you point to a button, the name of the button displays at the top of the menu. The order of the buttons may differ on your computer.

Figure 10.12

Select Browse Object button

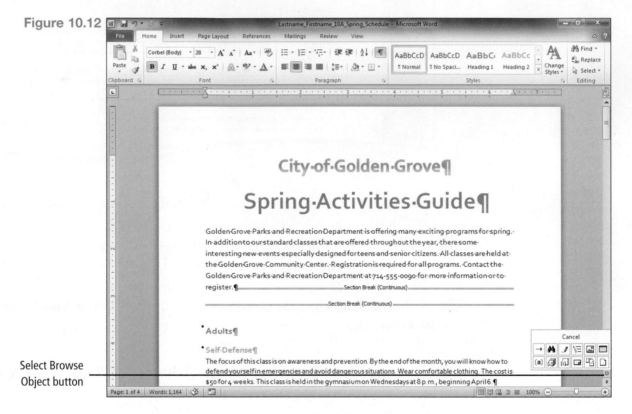

Buttons on the Select Browse Object Menu

Button Name	Button	Description
Go To	→	Moves to the next occurrence of an object as defined in the Go To tab of the Find and Replace dialog box.
Find	🔭	Moves to the next word or phrase that has been typed in the Find and Replace dialog box.
Browse by Edits	✐	Moves between edits that have been made to the document using the Track Changes command.
Browse by Heading	☰	Moves between Heading styles that have been applied to the document.
Browse by Graphic	🖼	Moves between graphic objects that have been inserted in the document.
Browse by Table	▦	Moves between tables in the document.
Browse by Field	{a}	Moves between objects in the document that have been defined as fields.
Browse by Endnote	🗐	Moves from one endnote to the next.
Browse by Footnote	🗐	Moves from one footnote to the next.
Browse by Comment	🗔	Moves between comments that have been inserted in the document.
Browse by Section	🗗	Moves from one section to the next.
Browse by Page	▯	Moves page by page in your document.

Figure 10.13

2 On the **Select Browse Object** menu, click the **Browse by Page** button ▯. Notice that the insertion point moves to the top of **Page 2**.

Browse by Page is the most common way to browse a document and is the default setting for the Select Browse Object button.

3 Directly below the **Select Browse Object** button, point to the ⊻ button. Notice that *Next Page* displays as the ScreenTip.

Because you selected the Browse by Page button on the Select Browse Object menu, the Next Page button is set to move to the next page in the document.

> **Note** | ScreenTip for the Next Button
>
> The ScreenTip for the ⊻ button changes based on the selected Browse Object.

4 Click the **Next Page** button ⊻ two times. Notice that the insertion point moves to the top of **Page 4**.

5 Directly above the **Select Browse Object** button, point to the ⊼ button, and notice that *Previous Page* displays as the ScreenTip. Compare your screen with Figure 10.14.

Because you selected the Browse by Page button on the Select Browse Object menu, the Previous Page button is set to move to the previous page in the document.

Figure 10.14

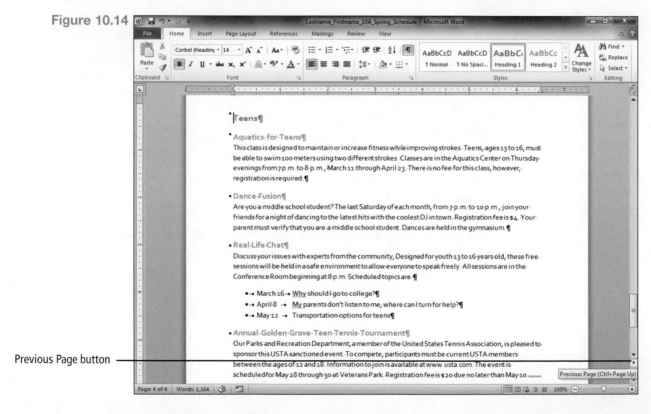

Previous Page button

6 Click the **Previous Page** button ⊼. Notice that the insertion point moves to the top of **Page 3**.

7 Click the **Select Browse Object** button ⊙, and then click the **Browse by Heading** button ☷. Notice that the insertion point moves to the *Popcorn and a Movie* heading—the second heading on **Page 3**.

8 Click the **Next Heading** button ⊤. Notice that the insertion point moves to the next heading—*Senior Citizens*.

> When you select a button in the Select Browse Object menu, the Previous button and Next button functions change accordingly.

9 Click the **Select Browse Object** button ⊙, and then click the **Browse by Page** button ⬜.

> The Select Browse Object button retains the method of browsing that was last selected. Changing to Browse by Page function returns the Select Browse Object button to the most common method for browsing a document.

Activity 10.06 | Using the Navigation Pane to View a Document

1 Press Ctrl + Home. On the **View tab**, in the **Show group**, click to select the **Navigation Pane** check box. Notice that the **Navigation Pane** displays to the left of your document. Click the second tab—the **Browse the pages in your document tab**. Compare your screen with Figure 10.15.

> The *Navigation Pane* contains three tabs that allow you to browse your document by headings, by pages, or by using the results of a search. The Navigation Pane displays *thumbnails*—graphical representations of pages—for all the pages in your document. The current page—where the insertion point is located—displays and is selected in the Navigation Pane.

Figure 10.15

Navigation Pane—your screen may differ

Browse the pages in your document tab

Thumbnails of document pages

2 In the **Navigation Pane**, click the icon for page **3**. Notice that the top of **Page 3** displays.

3 In the **Navigation Pane**, click the first tab—the **Browse the headings in your document tab**. Compare your screen with Figure 10.16.

> Because the *Browse the headings in your document* tab is active, the individual headings in your document display.

Figure 10.16

Browse the headings in your document tab

Headings in document

4 In the **Navigation Pane**, under **Children**, click the heading **Beginning Karate**. Notice that the *Beginning Karate* heading displays at the top of your screen.

More Knowledge | Rearranging the Content in a Document

You can drag and drop a tab in the Browse Headings list to move a heading or subheading and all related paragraphs to a new location in the document.

Activity 10.07 | Creating Bookmarks

A ***bookmark*** identifies the exact location of text, a table, or other object that you name for future reference. You can use bookmarks to locate specific parts of a document quickly.

Another Way

You can use the Browse by Object, and the Next Heading and Previous Heading buttons, to navigate to a heading paragraph.

1 In the **Navigation Pane**, click the heading **Adults**. Select the text for the heading *Adults*, being careful not to select the paragraph mark.

2 On the **Insert tab**, in the **Links group**, click the **Bookmark** button.

3 In the **Bookmark** dialog box, in the **Bookmark name** box, type **Adults** Compare your screen with Figure 10.17.

Figure 10.17

Bookmark button

Bookmark dialog box

Bookmark name box

4 Click the **Add** button.

5 In the **Navigation Pane**, click the heading **Children**. Select the text for the heading *Children*, being careful not to select the paragraph mark. In the **Links group**, click the **Bookmark** button. In the **Bookmark** dialog box, in the **Bookmark name** box, type **Children** and then click **Add**.

6 In a similar manner, insert a bookmark for the *Families* heading, using the name **Families**

> When bookmarks are added to a document, by default they display in alphabetical order by name.

7 Select the text *Senior Citizens*. In the **Links group**, click the **Bookmark** button. In the **Bookmark** dialog box, in the **Bookmark name** box, type **Senior_Citizens** and then click **Add**.

> Spaces are not allowed in bookmarks, so you inserted an underscore between the two words in a bookmark name.

8 In a similar manner, insert a bookmark for the *Teens* heading, using the **Bookmark name Teens**.

9 Press Ctrl + Home, and then **Close** ✕ the **Navigation Pane**.

10 On the **Home tab**, in the **Editing group**, click the **Find button arrow**, and then click **Go To**. In the **Find and Replace** dialog box, in the **Go to what** box, scroll as necessary and then click **Bookmark**. Click the **Enter bookmark name arrow**, and then compare your screen with Figure 10.18.

> All five bookmarks display in alphabetical order.

Figure 10.18

Find and Replace dialog box

Go to what box

Enter bookmark name box

11 From the displayed list, click **Children**, and then click the **Go To** button. **Close** the **Find and Replace** dialog box.

The section of the document that begins with the bookmark *Children* displays.

12 **Save** 🖫 your changes.

Activity 10.08 | Creating Cross-References

A ***cross-reference*** is a text link to an item that displays in another location in the document, such as a heading, a caption of a figure, or a footnote. Cross-references function as internal hyperlinks that enable you to move quickly to specific locations in a document.

1 Press Ctrl + Home. In the third paragraph, in the second sentence, select the text *teens*, being careful not to select any spaces.

> When creating a cross-reference, either select text or place the insertion point where you want the cross-reference to display in your document. In this case, you want the cross-reference to display instead of the word *teens*.

Another Way

On the References tab, in the Captions group, click the Cross-reference button.

2 On the **Insert tab**, in the **Links group**, click the **Cross-reference** button.

3 In the **Cross-reference** dialog box, click the **Reference type arrow**, and then click **Bookmark**. If necessary, click the **Insert reference to arrow** to display **Bookmark text**, and then select the **Insert as hyperlink** check box.

4 Under **For which bookmark**, click **Teens**, and then compare your screen with Figure 10.19.

Figure 10.19

Cross-reference dialog box

Reference type box

Insert as hyperlink check box

Insert reference to box

5 In the **Cross-reference** dialog box, click **Insert**, and then click **Close**.

> The text you selected when you created the bookmark replaces the existing text in the paragraph and matches the formatting of the replaced word, except for font size.

6 Click anywhere in the text *Teens*. Notice that it displays as a gray box representing a field—a cross-reference. Double-click to select the entire field *Teens*. On the Mini toolbar, apply **B**.

7 In the same sentence, select the text *senior citizens*. On the **Insert tab**, in the **Links group**, click the **Cross-reference** button.

8 In the **Cross-reference** dialog box, click the **Reference type arrow**, and then if necessary click **Bookmark**. Be sure the **Insert reference to** box displays **Bookmark text**, and the **Insert as hyperlink** check box is selected. Under **For which bookmark**, click **Senior_ Citizens**. Click **Insert**, and then click **Close**.

The formatting of the inserted bookmark text matches the rest of the paragraph, except the underscore is replaced with a space.

9 Select the *Senior Citizens* cross-reference text. On the Mini toolbar, apply $\boxed{B}$ and then deselect the text.

10 With your $\boxed{I}$ pointer displayed, point to the **Teens** cross-reference. Compare your screen with Figure 10.20.

A ScreenTip displays indicating how to activate the hyperlink.

Figure 10.20

ScreenTip

Teens cross-reference

11 Hold down $\boxed{\text{Ctrl}}$, and when the $\boxed{\text{🖑}}$ pointer displays, click **Teens**.

The Teens section of the document displays at the bookmark location.

12 Press $\boxed{\text{Ctrl}}$ + $\boxed{\text{Home}}$. **Save** $\boxed{\text{🖫}}$ your changes.

Activity 10.09 | Reviewing Word Count and Readability Statistics

The ***word count*** of a document indicates the number of pages, words, and characters in a document. If the document will be distributed to a group of people, you may want to determine the ease of readability based on the average number of syllables per word and words per sentence by viewing the ***readability statistics***. Readability Statistics is a Spelling and Grammar tool that analyzes a document and determines the reading level of the text.

1 On the **Review tab**, in the **Proofing group**, click the **Word Count** button. Compare your screen with Figure 10.21.

The Word Count dialog box indicates how many words, paragraphs, pages, and characters are contained in the document. In addition, the word count displays on the status bar in Word.

Figure 10.21

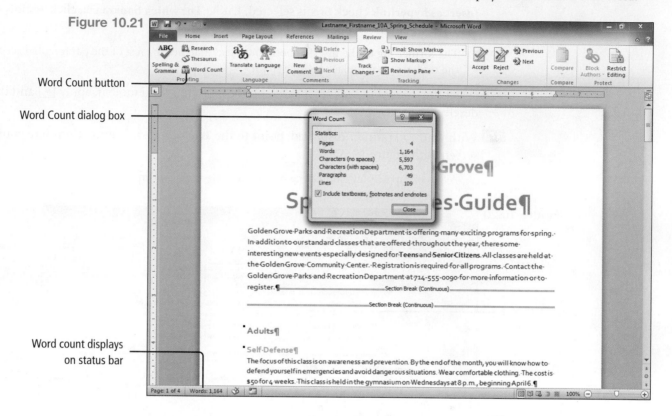

Word Count button

Word Count dialog box

Word count displays on status bar

2 Click **Close** to close the **Word Count** dialog box.

3 From **Backstage** view, click **Options**. In the **Word Options** dialog box, click **Proofing**. Under **When correcting spelling and grammar in Word**, select the **Show readability statistics** check box to turn on the display of readability statistics. Click **OK**.

4 On the **Review tab**, in the **Proofing group**, click the **Spelling & Grammar** button.

You must complete a spelling and grammar check in order to review the readability statistics.

5 In the **Spelling and Grammar** dialog box, click **Ignore Once** for all found errors. In the **Microsoft Word** dialog box, click **OK**. Compare your screen with Figure 10.22.

The Readability Statistics dialog box displays three readability ratings. The first rating is the percentage of passive sentences in the document. The Flesch Reading Ease score is based on a 100-point scale—the higher the score, the easier it is for the reader to understand the document. The Flesch-Kincaid Grade Level score displays the reading level based upon U.S. grade levels. For example, 9.0 indicates the document can be comprehended by a student reading at a ninth grade level.

Figure 10.22

Readability Statistics dialog box

Spelling & Grammar button

Readability ratings

6 Click **OK** to close the **Readability Statistics** dialog box. From **Backstage** view, click **Options**. In the **Word Options** dialog box, click **Proofing**. Under **When correcting spelling and grammar in Word**, click to deselect the **Show readability statistics** check box to turn off the display of readability statistics. Click **OK**.

Activity 10.10 | Finalizing a Master Document

To prepare a master document for distribution, you should remove the links to the subdocuments.

1 If necessary, press Ctrl + Home. On the **View tab**, in the **Document Views group**, click the **Outline** button. On the **Outlining tab**, in the **Master Document group**, click the **Show Document** button to turn it on. If necessary, click the **Expand Subdocuments** button. If a Microsoft Word dialog box displays, click OK to save changes to the master document.

2 Scroll so that the *Adults* paragraph displays near the top of your screen. To the left of the paragraph *Adults*, click the **Subdocument** icon 🔳 to select the entire *Adults* subdocument. Compare your screen with Figure 10.23.

Figure 10.23

Subdocument icon

Subdocument selected

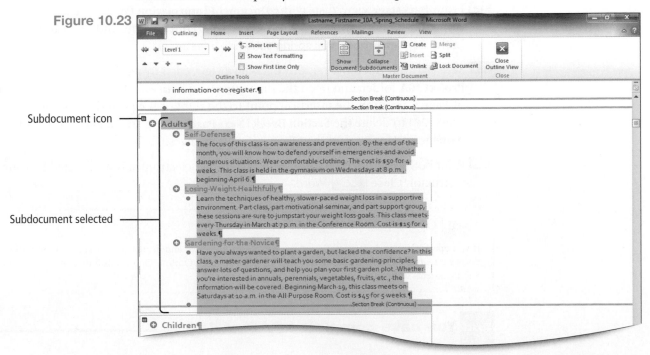

3 With the *Adults* subdocument selected, in the **Master Document group**, click the **Unlink** button.

The Adults paragraph and all subordinate paragraphs are no longer linked to a subdocument. The Subdocument icon and gray border surrounding the text no longer display.

4 To the left of the paragraph *Children*, click the **Subdocument** icon 🖹 to select the entire *Children* subdocument. In the **Master Document group**, click the **Unlink** button.

5 In a similar manner, **Unlink** the subdocuments *Families*, *Senior Citizens*, and *Teens*.

6 Above the paragraph *Adults*, click to position the insertion point to the right of the first bullet for **Section Break (Continuous)**. Compare your screen with Figure 10.24.

Figure 10.24

Section Break
(Continuous)

7 Press Del to remove the **Section Break (Continuous)**. In a similar manner, delete all instances of **Section Break (Continuous)** and **Section Break (Next Page)**.

The section breaks are no longer needed because the subdocuments are no longer defined.

8 On the **Outlining tab**, in the **Close group**, click the **Close Outline View** button. Position the insertion point to the left of the paragraph *Children*, and then press Ctrl + Enter.

9 In the third paragraph, in the second sentence, position the insertion point to the left of *some*, type **are** and then press Spacebar. Proofread and, if necessary, correct any other errors.

10 From **Backstage** view, display the **Document Information Panel**. In the **Author** box, type your name. In the **Subject** box, type your course name and section number, and in the **Keywords** box, type **spring schedule, master**

11 **Save** 🖫 your document. From **Backstage** view, click **Open**, navigate to your **Project 10A** folder, and open the file **Lastname_Firstname_10A_Teens**. At the bottom of **Page 1**, position the insertion point to the right of the period in the last paragraph. Press Del to delete the **Section Break (Next Page)**. Using **Quick Parts**, insert the file name in the footer, and then **Save** 🖫 your changes.

12 Print both your documents or submit your files electronically as directed by your instructor. **Close** ❌ Word.

Alert! | Opening a Master Document

If you open a master document, the subdocuments are collapsed and display as hyperlinks. To view the entire document, on the View tab, in the Document Views group, click Outline. On the Outlining tab, click the Expand Subdocuments button.

End **You have completed Project 10A** ──────────

Project 10B Reference Guide

Project 10B Training

Project Activities

In Activities 10.11 through 10.20, you will add an index, a table of contents, and a table of figures to a document that describes the City of Golden Grove. Your completed document will look similar to Figure 10.25.

Project Files

For Project 10B, you will need the following file:

w10B_Reference_Guide

You will save your document as:

Lastname_Firstname_10B_Reference_Guide

Project Results

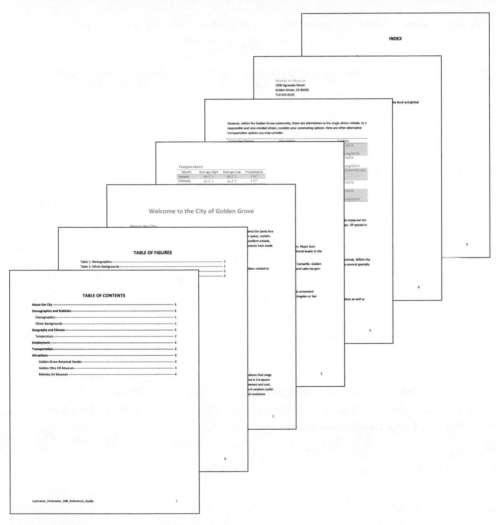

Figure 10.25
Project 10B Reference Guide

Word | Chapter 10

Objective 4 | Create an Index

An *index* is a compilation of topics, names, and terms accompanied by page numbers that displays at the end of a document. Each entry indicates where the *index entry* can be found. An index entry is a word or phrase that will be included in the index. To create an entry, you mark the words you want to include in the index as an index entry.

Activity 10.11 | Formatting the Document

1 **Start** Word. From your student files, open the file **w10B_Reference_Guide**. Save the file in your **Word Chapter 10** folder as **Lastname_Firstname_10B_Reference_Guide** If necessary, display the rulers and formatting marks. **Ignore All** spelling errors.

2 Scroll to the bottom of **Page 1**, right-click in the footer area, and then click **Edit Footer**. Using **Quick Parts**, insert the file name in the footer. With the footer area displayed, be sure the insertion point is to the right of the file name, and then press `Tab` two times. On the **Design tab**, in the **Header & Footer group**, click the **Page Number** button, click **Current Position** to display the **Page Number** gallery, and then compare your screen with Figure 10.26.

> The page numbers in the document are used as a reference in the index. The Page Number gallery provides built-in formats for inserting page numbers.

Figure 10.26

Current Position selected

Page Number gallery

3 In the **Page Number** gallery, under **Simple**, click the first style—**Plain Number**. Notice that the page number *1* is inserted in the footer at the right margin. In the **Close group**, click the **Close Header and Footer** button.

4 On the **Page Layout tab**, in the **Themes group**, click the **Theme Colors** button ![icon], and then click **Trek**.

5 Select the first paragraph. On the Mini toolbar, change the **Font Size** to **22**, apply **Bold** ![B] and **Center** ![icon], and then change the **Font Color** ![A] to **Orange, Accent 1**—in the fifth column, the first color.

6 Select the second paragraph. On the **Home tab**, in the **Styles group**, click the **Heading 1** style. In a similar manner, apply the **Heading 1** style to the paragraphs *Demographics and Statistics*, *Geography and Climate*, *Employment*, *Transportation*, and *Attractions*.

7 On **Page 1**, select the paragraph *Demographics*, and then in the **Styles group**, click the **Heading 2** style. In a similar manner, apply the **Heading 2** style to the paragraphs *Ethnic Backgrounds* and *Temperature*.

8 On **Page 3**, select the paragraph *Golden Grove Botanical Garden*. On the Mini toolbar, apply **Bold** ![B], and then click the **Font Color** button ![A]. In a similar manner, for the paragraphs *Golden Olive Oil Museum* and *Melesky Art Museum*, apply **Bold** ![B], and then click the **Font Color** button ![A].

9 Press (Ctrl) + (Home). Locate the first table in the document—under *Demographics*. Click to position the insertion point anywhere in the table. On the **Design tab**, in the **Table Style Options group**, click to deselect the **Header Row** check box. In the **Table Styles group**, click the third style—**Light Shading - Accent 1**. Apply the same formatting to the *Ethnic Backgrounds* table.

10 On **Page 2**, click to position the insertion point in the *Temperature* table. On the **Design tab**, in the **Table Styles group**, click **Light Shading - Accent 1**. Scroll to the bottom of **Page 2**, and then apply the same formatting to the table in the *Transportation* section. **Save** ![icon] your changes.

Activity 10.12 | Marking Index Entries

1 Press (Ctrl) + (Home). In the third paragraph, select the text *Santa Ana Mountains*.

When creating an index, you must first identify which terms will be used for index entries—in this case the selected text *Santa Ana Mountains* will be used as an index entry.

2 On the **References tab**, in the **Index group**, click the **Mark Entry** button to display the **Mark Index Entry** dialog box. Compare your screen with Figure 10.27, and then take a moment to read the description of the dialog box features in the table shown in Figure 10.28.

Santa Ana Mountains displays in the Main entry box. When text is selected, by default it displays in the Main entry box.

Figure 10.27

Mark Index Entry dialog box

Main entry box

Mark Index Entry Dialog Box Features	
Feature	**Description**
Main entry	The word, phrases, or selected text that will be used to identify the index entry.
Subentry	A more specific term that refers to the main entry. For example, the index entry *Transportation* could have subentries for *Automobiles*, *Buses*, and *Trains*.
Cross-reference	An entry that refers the reader to another topic that provides more information. For example, the main entry *England* might be listed in the index as *See United Kingdom*.
Current page	The index entry is marked with the current page number.
Page range	The index entry is marked with a range of page numbers.
Page number format	These options control how the page number will display in the index.
Mark	Marks only the selected text.
Mark All	Marks all occurrences of the selected text in the document.

Figure 10.28

3 In the **Mark Index Entry** dialog box, click the **Mark All** button, and then click **Close**. Notice that the marked index entry displays to the right of the selected text. Compare your screen with Figure 10.29.

> After you mark text as an index entry, Word inserts an ***index entry field***, to the right of the selected text. An index entry field is code containing the identifier **XE**, and the term to be used in the index. The code is formatted as ***hidden text***—nonprinting text. Because you clicked the Mark All button, the occurrence of *Santa Ana Mountains* at the bottom of Page 1 is also marked.

Figure 10.29

Index entry field —

4 On **Page 1**, select the paragraph *Demographics and Statistics*. On the **References tab**, in the **Index group**, click the **Mark Entry** button. In the **Mark Index Entry** dialog box, with *Demographics and Statistics* displayed in the **Main entry** box, click the **Mark** button, but do not close the **Mark Index Entry** dialog box.

> The text *Demographics and Statistics* is marked as an entry for the index.

5 Click in the document, and then select the paragraph *Geography and Climate*. If necessary, point to the **Mark Index Entry** dialog box to display the 🔲 pointer, and then drag the **Mark Index Entry** dialog box to the side of your screen. With the paragraph still selected, click in the **Main entry** box, and notice that *Geography and Climate* displays. Click the **Mark** button.

6 In a similar manner, **Mark** entries for the paragraphs *Employment*, *Transportation*, and *Attractions*.

7 Below *Attractions*, locate the text *Golden Grove Botanical Garden*, and then position the insertion point to the right of *Garden*. In the **Mark Index Entry** dialog box, double-click in the **Main entry** box, and then type **Attractions** In the **Subentry** box, type **Golden Grove Botanical Garden** Click the **Mark** button, and then compare your screen with Figure 10.30.

> The text *Golden Grove Botanical Garden* is added as an index entry—as a subentry under *Attractions*. The index entry field displays the main entry text, a colon, and the subentry text.

Figure 10.30

Main entry
Index entry field
Subentry

8 Position the insertion point to the right of the text *Golden Olive Oil Museum*. In the **Main entry** box, type **Attractions** In the **Subentry** box, type **Golden Olive Oil Museum** Click the **Mark** button.

9 With the **Mark Index Entry** dialog box still open, position the insertion point to the right of the text *Melesky Art Museum*. In the **Main Entry** box, type **Attractions** In the **Subentry** box, type **Melesky Art Museum** Click the **Mark** button, and then click the **Close** button.

10 Save 💾 your changes.

Activity 10.13 | Inserting an Index

After text or phrases have been marked as index entries, the next step is to insert the index. Generally an index is inserted on a separate page at the end of a document.

1 Press (Ctrl) + (End), and then press (Ctrl) + (Enter) to insert a manual page break.

2 With the insertion point at the top of the new page, type **INDEX** and then press (Enter) two times.

3 Select the *INDEX* paragraph you just typed. On the Mini toolbar, change the **Font Size** to **16**, and then apply **Bold** B and **Center** ☰.

4 Click to position the insertion point in the last paragraph of the document. On the **References tab**, in the **Index group**, click the **Insert Index** button to display the **Index** dialog box.

5 In the **Index** dialog box, on the **Index** tab, click the **Formats arrow**, and then from the list, click **Classic**. Compare your screen with Figure 10.31.

The Index dialog box allows you to select from predefined index formats and preview the selection. You can also modify an existing format or create your own.

Figure 10.31

Index dialog box

Print Preview

Formats arrow

6 Click **OK**, and then compare your screen with Figure 10.32.

The index is inserted in a two-column format. Word distributes the text evenly between the two columns.

Figure 10.32

Subentries

Main entry

Index

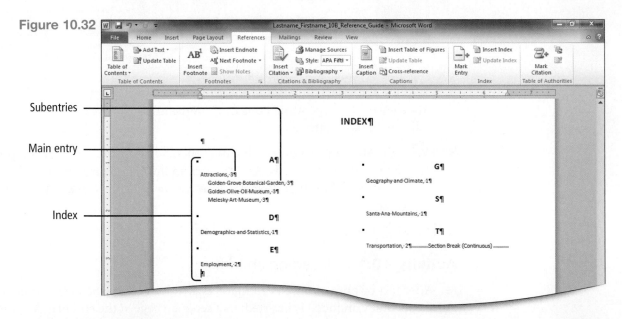

7 **Save** your changes.

Activity 10.14 | Updating an Index

After an index has been inserted into a document, the index can be updated if you want to include additional words in the index or if the page numbers in the document change.

1 Scroll to the top of **Page 2**, and position the insertion point to the right of *Temperature*.

2 On the **References tab**, in the **Index group**, click the **Mark Entry** button. In the **Mark Index Entry** dialog box, in the **Main entry** box, type **Geography and Climate** In the **Subentry** box, type **Temperature** Click the **Mark** button, and then click the **Close** button.

3 Press Ctrl + End. Position the insertion point anywhere in the index entries, and notice that under the *Geography and Climate* main entry, the newly marked subentry—*Temperature*—does not display in the existing index.

Because the index is a field, it displays as shaded text.

> **Another Way**
>
> Right-click the Index field, and then from the shortcut menu, click Update Field or press F9.

4 On the **References tab**, in the **Index group**, click the **Update Index** button. Compare your screen with Figure 10.33.

The index is updated to include the additional entry *Temperature*.

Figure 10.33

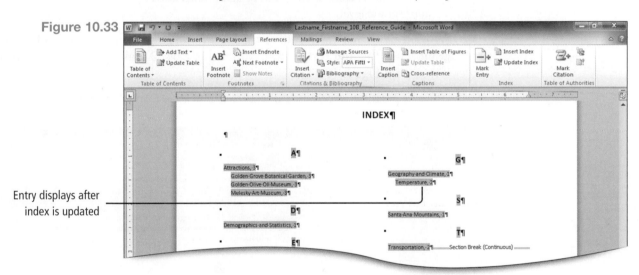

Entry displays after index is updated

5 **Save** 🖫 your changes.

More Knowledge | Creating a Concordance File

If a document contains words that are frequently used as index entries, the words can be saved as a ***concordance file***. A concordance file is a Word document that contains a two-column table that is used to mark words that will be used as index entries. In the first column of the table, you type the words you want to index as main entries. In the second column, you type the main entry and subentries. You can mark all entries by going to the References tab and then clicking the Insert Index button. In the Index dialog box, click the Mark All button.

Objective 5 | Create a Table of Contents

A *table of contents* is a list of a document's headings and subheadings, marked with the page numbers on which those headings and subheadings occur. Many times a table of contents will be abbreviated and referred to as a *TOC*. The TOC is a useful way to navigate a long document because clicking the heading or subheading in the TOC moves you to the page of the heading or subheading you clicked. In most instances, a table of contents displays at the beginning of a document.

Activity 10.15 | Assigning Heading Levels

1 Press `Ctrl` + `Home`. At the beginning of **Page 1**, select the second paragraph—*About the City*.

2 On the **References tab**, in the **Table of Contents group**, click the **Add Text** button. Notice that *Level 1* is selected.

> The Add Text button is used to identify the entries that will be included in the table of contents. Each entry in the TOC is identified by a heading level—Level 1 being the highest. When text is formatted with a heading style, Word matches the heading style number with the corresponding level number and automatically adds it to the TOC. In this case, Level 1 is selected because the text is formatted with the Heading 1 style. You can change the level for selected text or add unformatted text to the TOC by assigning the appropriate level.

3 Above the first table, select the paragraph *Demographics*. In the **Table of Contents group**, click the **Add Text** button. Notice that *Level 2* is already selected. Compare your screen with Figure 10.34.

> Level 2 is selected because the text *Demographics* is formatted with the Heading 2 style.

Figure 10.34

Add Text button

Level 2 selected

Selected paragraph

4 On **Page 3**, select the paragraph *Golden Grove Botanical Garden*. In the **Table of Contents group**, click the **Add Text** button, and then click **Level 3**. In a similar manner, assign **Level 3** to the paragraphs *Golden Olive Oil Museum* and *Melesky Art Museum*.

> Because these paragraphs were not formatted with a Heading style, you must assign a level for the terms to display in the TOC. By assigning Level 3, Word applies the Heading 3 style to the paragraphs.

5 Press `Ctrl` + `Home`, and then **Save** 💾 your changes.

Activity 10.16 | Creating a Table of Contents

A table of contents can be customized to include formatting. Any formatting added to the TOC will not affect the rest of the document. It is a good idea to format the TOC to make it stand out from the rest of the document.

1 With the insertion point at the beginning of the document, on the **Page Layout tab**, in the **Page Setup group**, click the **Breaks** button, and then under **Section Breaks**, click **Next Page**.

A table of contents is typically displayed as a separate, first page of a document.

2 Press [Ctrl] + [Home] to move to the beginning of the document. On the **Home tab**, in the **Styles group**, click the **Normal** style.

3 Type **TABLE OF CONTENTS** and then press [Enter] two times.

4 Select the paragraph you just typed. On the Mini toolbar, change the **Font Size** to **16**, and then apply **Bold** [B] and **Center** [≡].

5 On **Page 1**, click to position the insertion point in the last paragraph on the page—to the left of the section break. On the **References tab**, in the **Table of Contents group**, click the **Table of Contents** button. Notice that the **Table of Contents** gallery displays. Compare your screen with Figure 10.35.

You can either use a Quick Style to insert a table of contents or create your own TOC style by selecting Insert Table of Contents.

Figure 10.35

Table of Contents button

Quick Styles

Insert Table of Contents

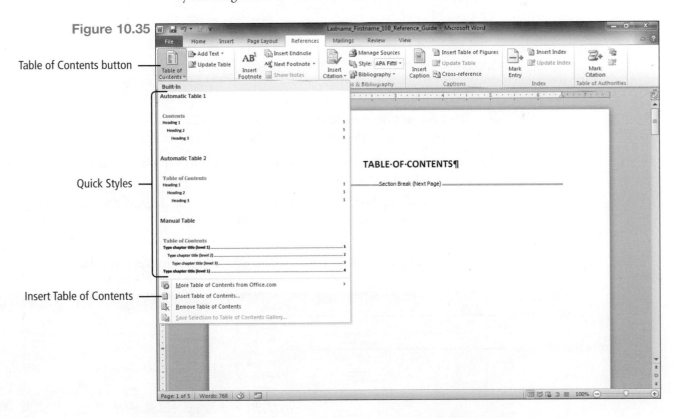

6 From the **Table of Contents** gallery, click **Insert Table of Contents**.

7 In the **Table of Contents** dialog box, under **Web Preview**, select the **Use hyperlinks instead of page numbers** check box, if necessary. Notice that the **Print Preview** box displays the TOC format with Heading 2 and Heading 3 indented. Compare your screen with Figure 10.36.

A hyperlink will enable a reader of a document to click a page number in the TOC and move to that part of the document. The Show levels box displays *3*—representing the three heading levels assigned to specific text in the document. By using the Formats arrow, you can select a formatting style for the TOC. The Options button allows you to indicate the heading levels to be used in the TOC. The Modify button allows you to change the formatting of the TOC—for example, fonts, paragraphs, and tabs.

Figure 10.36

Table of Contents dialog box

Print Preview

Use hyperlinks instead of page numbers selected

Formats arrow

Three levels display

8 In the **Table of Contents** dialog box, click the **Modify** button. In the displayed **Style** dialog box, under **Styles**, if necessary, click to select **TOC 1**.

Under Preview, the current format for Heading Level 1 displays along with a description of the specific format elements.

9 In the **Style** dialog box, click the **Modify** button. In the displayed **Modify Style** dialog box, under **Formatting**, click the **Bold** button ⬚B⬚. Compare your screen with Figure 10.37.

All text assigned Heading Level 1 will have bold formatting applied in the TOC.

Figure 10.37

TOC1 selected

Modify Style dialog box

Bold selected

10 Click **OK** two times. On the left side of the **Table of Contents** dialog box, click the **Tab leader arrow**, and then from the displayed list, click the second line style—a dashed line.

> A **tab leader** is a dotted, dashed, or solid line used to connect related information and improve the readability of a line.

11 Click **OK**. Compare your screen with Figure 10.38.

> All document headings display with the related page number. If a document is edited and page numbers change, you can update the TOC to reflect the changes.

Figure 10.38

Tab leader

Headings

Page numbers

12 Point to the *Attractions* entry in the table of contents to display the ScreenTip, which indicates the entry is a hyperlink. Press and hold [Ctrl] and click the **Attractions** entry.

> The insertion point moves to Page 4, where the related text begins, and is positioned to the left of the *Attractions* heading.

13 Save 💾 your changes.

More Knowledge | Creating a Table of Authorities

You can create a **table of authorities**—a list of legal references—by using the features on the References tab. To create a table of authorities, on the References tab, in the Table of Authorities group, click the Mark Citation button to mark legal citations, and then click the Insert Table of Authorities button to insert the table.

Objective 6 | Create a Table of Figures

A *table of figures* is a list of the figure captions in a document. In most instances, a table of figures displays at the beginning of a document, on a separate page following the table of contents.

Activity 10.17 | Creating a Table of Figures

In this activity, you will add captions to the four tables in the document, and then create the table of figures.

1 On **Page 2**, click anywhere in the first table—below the heading *Demographics*. On the **References tab**, in the **Captions group**, click the **Insert Caption** button.

2 In the displayed **Caption** dialog box, in the **Caption** box, with the insertion point to the right of *Table 1*, type a colon, press [Spacebar], and then type **Demographics** Click the **Position arrow**, and then click **Below selected item**. Compare your screen with Figure 10.39.

Figure 10.39

Caption dialog box
Caption added
Position selected

3 Click **OK**. Notice that the caption displays below the table.

Recall that a caption is a title that is added to a Word object and numbered sequentially.

4 Click anywhere in the second table on **Page 2**. In the **Captions group**, click the **Insert Caption** button.

5 In the **Caption** dialog box, under **Caption**, with the insertion point to the right of *Table 2*, type a colon, press [Spacebar], and then type **Ethnic Backgrounds** Notice that the **Position** box displays *Below selected item*. Click **OK**.

6 In a similar manner, below the third table in the document, insert the caption **Table 3: Temperature** and then, below the fourth table, insert the caption **Table 4: Transportation**

7 Press [Ctrl] + [Home]. Click to position the insertion point in the last paragraph of **Page 1**—to the left of the section break. Press [Ctrl] + [Enter] to insert a manual page break. Notice that the insertion point moves to the first paragraph on the new, second page.

8 Type **TABLE OF FIGURES** and then press Enter two times. Select the paragraph you just typed. On the Mini toolbar, change the **Font Size** to **16**, and then apply **Bold** [B] and **Center** [≡].

9 Click to position the insertion point in the blank paragraph above the section break. On the **References tab**, in the **Captions group**, click the **Insert Table of Figures** button. In the **Table of Figures** dialog box, click the **Tab leader arrow**, and then click the second line style—the dashed line.

> The Table of Figures dialog box is similar to the Table of Contents dialog box and provides many of the same options.

10 Click **OK** to insert the table of figures. Compare your screen with Figure 10.40.

> The captions and their respective page numbers display, separated by the dashed line tab leader.

Figure 10.40

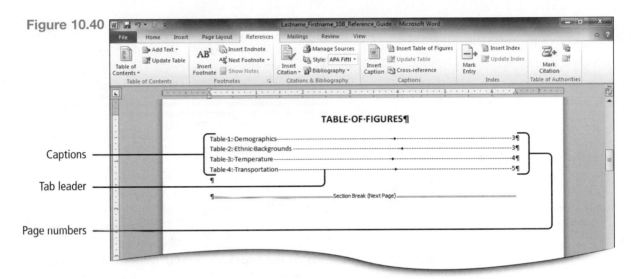

Captions

Tab leader

Page numbers

11 Point to the *Temperature* entry in the table of figures to display a ScreenTip, which indicates the entry is a hyperlink. Press and hold Ctrl, and then click the **Temperature** entry.

> The insertion point moves to Page 4, and is positioned to the left of the *Table 3: Temperature* caption.

12 Save [💾] your changes.

Objective 7 | Control the Flow and Formatting of Pages and Text

Recall that page breaks and section breaks allow you to control how text, tables, page numbers, and other objects display in your document. It is important that text flows smoothly and page numbers display properly. The process of arranging and numbering the pages in a document is called **pagination**.

Activity 10.18 | Hiding White Space and Applying Hyphenation

In Print Layout view, to maximize your view of the document, you can hide the white spaces at the top and bottom of each page, and the gray space between the pages. By utilizing Word's **hyphenation** feature you can control how words are split between two lines, resulting in a less ragged edge at the right margin. Applying the hyphenation feature improves the flow of text within paragraphs.

1 Scroll up to display the bottom of **Page 3** and the top of **Page 4**. Position the pointer between the pages until it changes to the **Double-click to hide white space** pointer, and then double-click. Notice the white space, including the footer, at the top and bottom of the pages and the gray space between the pages no longer displays. Compare your screen with Figure 10.41.

> You must be in Print Layout view to use the Hide White Space feature.

Figure 10.41

Hidden white space

2 On the **Page Layout tab**, in the **Page Setup group**, click the **Hyphenation** button, and then compare your screen with Figure 10.42.

> *None* is selected because the hyphenation feature is turned off by default. Selecting *Automatic* will cause Word to automatically hyphenate the entire document. If you modify the document, as you work Word will change the hyphenation as necessary. Selecting *Manual* allows you to decide how specific words should be hyphenated. You can select *Hyphenation Options* to modify hyphenation settings for either automatic or manual hyphenation.

Figure 10.42

Hyphenation button

Hyphenation list

3 On the displayed list, click **Automatic**, and then on the **Home tab**, hide the formatting marks.

> To view how hyphenation will be applied in the final document, it is useful to hide the formatting marks for the Mark Entry references.

4 Scroll to **Page 3**, and then in the paragraph below the *About the City* heading, in the second line, notice *containing* is hyphenated—your screen may differ.

> **Alert** | **Different Words Are Hyphenated**
>
> Depending upon the width of your screen, word wrapping may cause your text to display differently. The hyphenated word may display on a different line, or the word may display without any hyphenation.

5 Scroll to **Page 4**, and then in the two paragraphs below the *Employment* heading, notice *businesses* and *generation* are hyphenated—your screen may differ.

6 Scroll to display the bottom of **Page 3** and the top of **Page 4**. Point to the gray border separating the two pages, and then when the **Double-click to hide white space** pointer ⊞ displays, double-click. Notice the white space at the top and bottom of the page and the gray space between the pages displays.

7 **Save** 🖫 your changes.

Activity 10.19 | Keeping Paragraphs Together on a Page

There are times when it may enhance the readability and appeal of text to keep paragraphs together on the same page. For example, a bulleted list may be separated and displayed on two pages, but you may want to keep the entire list together on a single page.

1 Scroll until the bottom of **Page 4** and the top of **Page 5** are visible. Notice that the table is split across two pages.

> To edit split text, you should hide formatting marks and always work from the beginning to the end of the document.

2 At the bottom of **Page 4**, above the table, select the paragraph that begins *However,* and then continue the selection to include the entire table including the caption.

3 On the **Home tab**, in the **Paragraph group**, click ⬜ to display the **Paragraph** dialog box.

4 In the **Paragraph** dialog box, click the **Line and Page Breaks** tab, and then under **Pagination**, click the **Keep with next** check box so that it displays with a check mark. Compare your screen with Figure 10.43, and then take a moment to study the table in Figure 10.44.

> In this case, Word will keep the entire selection—the paragraph and the table—together on the same page.

> The *Keep with next* command causes two elements, such as paragraphs, to display together on the same page. For example, this could be used to keep a heading together with the paragraph of text that follows it.

Figure 10.43

Paragraph dialog box

Keep with next selected

Line and Page Breaks tab

Pagination Commands

Widow/Orphan control	Prevents a paragraph from splitting to display a single line at the top—widow—or bottom—orphan—of a page.
Keep with next	Causes two elements, such as paragraphs, to display together on the same page. For example, a heading will display on the same page as the paragraph of text that follows it.
Keep lines together	Prevents a page break from occurring within a paragraph.
Page break before	Forces a page break to occur before a paragraph.

Figure 10.44

5 Click **OK**. Deselect the text, and notice that the paragraph that begins *However* is at the top of **Page 5**, above the table.

> The last sentence of the paragraph refers to the information in the table. Keeping the paragraph and table together on the same page improves the readability.

6 Display formatting marks, and then **Save** 💾 your changes.

> Because Mark Entry formatting marks are displayed in some paragraphs, the hyphenation of the document changes when formatting marks are displayed.

7 At the bottom of **Page 5**, click to position the insertion point to the left of the paragraph *Melesky Art Museum*. Select this paragraph and the next four paragraphs.

> All five paragraphs provide information regarding the museum so it makes sense to keep them on the same page.

8 On the **Home tab**, in the **Paragraph group**, click 🔲 to display the **Paragraph** dialog box. In the **Paragraph** dialog box, with the **Line and Page Breaks** tab displayed, under **Pagination**, select the **Keep with next** check box, and then click **OK**.

9 **Save** 💾 your changes.

Activity 10.20 | Modifying Page Numbers

When a document contains introductory information, such as a cover page or TOC, those pages are frequently assigned a different page numbering format. In this activity, you will modify the page numbering for the document and then update the TOC, table of figures, and index to reflect the changes you made.

1 Press (Ctrl) + (Home), and then scroll to the bottom of **Page 1**. Right-click in the footer area, and then click **Edit Footer**.

2 In the footer, select the page number *1*. On the **Design tab**, in the **Header & Footer group**, click the **Page Number** button, and then click **Format Page Numbers**.

> You can use the Page Number Format dialog box to modify page number styles.

3 In the **Page Number Format** dialog box, click the **Number Format arrow**, and then click the fifth numbering style—**i, ii, iii**. Compare your screen with Figure 10.45.

Figure 10.45

Page Number Format dialog box

Number format

4 Click **OK**, and notice that the page number changes to *i*.

5 Scroll to the bottom of **Page 3**. Notice that the page number retains the original numbering style—*3*. Click to position the insertion point anywhere in the footer area.

At the top left of the footer area, the *Footer - Section 2* tab displays. Page 3 begins Section 2. When you created the TOC page, you inserted a Next Page section break. The TOC and table of figures are in Section 1 of the document. At the top right of the footer area, the *Same as Previous* tab displays.

6 On the **Design tab**, in the **Navigation group**, click the **Link to Previous** button to turn it off. Notice that the **Same as Previous** tab no longer displays at the top right of the footer area on **Page 3**. Compare your screen with Figure 10.46.

By clicking the Link to Previous button, the footer for Section 2—the rest of the document—is no longer linked to the footer for Section 1—the first two pages. The Section 2 footer can be modified without affecting the Section 1 footer.

Figure 10.46

Link to Previous button

Footer - Section 2 tab

Page number 3

Same as Previous no longer displays

7 In the footer, select the page number *3*. On the **Design tab**, in the **Header & Footer group**, click the **Page Number** button, and then click **Format Page Numbers**. In the **Page Number Format** dialog box, under **Page numbering**, click the **Start at** option button, and then compare your screen with Figure 10.47.

The Start at option button allows you to select the first page number that should display in a new section of a document. By default, the number *1* displays in the Start at box.

Figure 10.47

Number format

Start at option button selected

8 Click **OK**. Notice that the page number *1* displays in the footer on the third page of the document. In the **Close group**, click the **Close Header and Footer** button.

Another Way

On the References tab, in the Table of Contents group, click the Update Table button.

9 Press Ctrl + Home. Click to position the insertion point in the TOC, right-click, and then click **Update Field**. In the **Update Table of Contents** dialog box, with the **Update page numbers only** option button selected, click **OK** to update the page numbers in the TOC. Click in the blank paragraph below the TOC, and then compare your screen with Figure 10.48.

Because you inserted breaks and changed page numbering styles, it is necessary to update the page numbers for the TOC, table of figures, and the index.

Figure 10.48

Page numbers updated ——

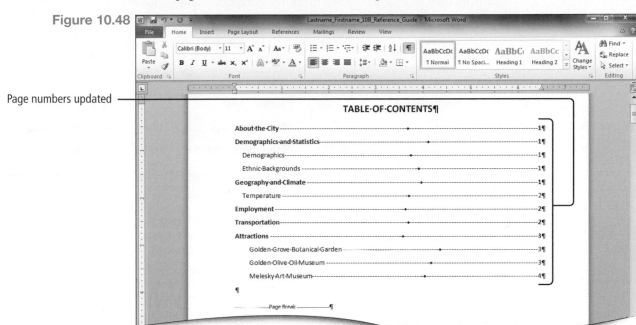

10 On the second page of the document—**page ii**—click to position the insertion point in the table of figures. Right-click, and then click **Update Field**. In the **Update Table of Figures** dialog box, with the **Update page numbers only** option button selected, click **OK**.

Another Way

On the References tab, in the Captions group, click the Update Table button.

11 Press Ctrl + End. Click to position the insertion point in the index, right-click, and then click **Update Field**.

When updating an index, changes are made automatically.

12 Press Ctrl + Home, and then display the **Document Information Panel**. In the **Author** box, type your first and last names. In the **Subject** box, type your course name, and section number, and in the **Keywords** box, type **reference guide, toc, index** Close ×️ the **Document Information Panel**.

13 Save 🖫 your changes. Print your document or submit electronically as directed by your instructor. **Close** Word.

More Knowledge | Inserting a Cover Page

A cover page is the first page of a complex document that provides introductory information. To insert a cover page, on the Insert tab, in the Pages group, click the Cover Page button. In the Cover Page gallery, click the style you want to use. In the inserted page, click in the text boxes to enter specific information.

End **You have completed Project 10B** ————————

Content-Based Assessments

Summary

When a document is created or edited by several people, one efficient way of assembling or editing the document is to create a master document that is divided into subdocuments. Subdocuments can be edited independently of the master document. In a long document, you can create several types of references. An index indicates where in the document specific words or phrases can be located. A table of contents helps readers navigate directly to specific topics. A table of figures allows readers to go directly to graphic elements, such as tables, in a document. You can apply hyphenation and insert section breaks to modify formats such as page numbers. Finally, the document can be analyzed to view the readability statistics of the document.

Key Terms

Body text.........................573	Hyphenation 606	Outline view 573	Table of figures..............604
Bookmark 586	Index 594	Pagination 605	Thumbnails 585
Concordance file 599	Index entry 594	Readability statistics 589	Word count 589
Continuous section break 576	Index entry field 596	Section break 576	XE.....................................596
	Keep with next 608	Subdocument 573	
Cross-reference 588	Master document..........573	Table of authorities 603	
Hidden text 596	Navigation Pane 585	Table of contents (TOC)..600	

Matching

Match each term in the second column with its correct definition in the first column by writing the letter of the term on the blank line in front of the correct definition.

_____ 1. A document that serves as a container for the different parts of a document.

_____ 2. A section of a document that is linked to the master document.

_____ 3. A view that displays the overall organization of the document's parts including headings, subheadings, and subordinate text.

_____ 4. Text that does not have a heading style applied.

_____ 5. A mark that stores the formatting information for a section of a document.

_____ 6. A text link to an item that displays in another location in the document.

_____ 7. A Word feature that indicates the number of pages, words, and characters in a document.

_____ 8. A Spelling and Grammar tool that analyzes a document and determines the reading level of the text.

_____ 9. A word or phrase that is listed in the index.

_____ 10. The code that identifies an index entry.

_____ 11. Nonprinting text.

_____ 12. A list of a document's headings and subheadings, marked with page numbers where they occur.

_____ 13. A list of legal references.

_____ 14. The process of arranging and numbering the pages in a document.

_____ 15. A Word tool that controls how words are split between two lines.

A Body text

B Cross-reference

C Hidden text

D Hyphenation

E Index entry

F Master document

G Outline

H Pagination

I Readability statistics

J Section break

K Subdocument

L Table of authorities

M Table of contents

N Word count

O XE

Content-Based Assessments

Multiple Choice

Circle the correct answer.

1. In Outline view, to move a paragraph to a higher level, click the:
   A. Demote button
   B. Expand button
   C. Promote button

2. A type of section break that marks the beginning and end of subdocuments is called:
   A. column
   B. continuous
   C. page

3. A link that identifies the exact location of text, a table, or other object is a:
   A. bookmark
   B. caption
   C. footnote

4. The window that allows you to browse a document by headings, by pages, or by using the results of a search is the:
   A. Find and Replace dialog box
   B. Navigation Pane
   C. Research Pane

5. A compilation of topics, names, and terms accompanied by page numbers that displays at the end of a document is the:
   A. bibliography
   B. index
   C. TOC

6. The code inserted to the right of a term that includes the identifier *XE* is an:
   A. index
   B. index entry
   C. index entry field

7. A Word document that contains a two-column table that is used to mark words as index entries is a:
   A. concordance file
   B. citations file
   C. table of authorities

8. TOC is the abbreviation for a:
   A. Table of credentials
   B. Table of citations
   C. Table of contents

9. A Table of figures is a list of:
   A. captions
   B. index entries
   C. tables

10. A command that causes two paragraphs to display together on the same page is:
    A. Keep with next
    B. Keep with previous
    C. Keep together

Content-Based Assessments

Apply **10A** skills from these Objectives:

1. Create a Master Document and Subdocuments
2. Manage a Master Document and Subdocuments
3. Navigate and Inspect the Master Document

Skills Review | Project **10C** Summer Calendar

In the following Skills Review, you will create a master document and subdocuments for events happening during the summer in the City of Golden Grove. Your completed documents will look similar to Figure 10.49.

Project Files

For Project 10C, you will need the following files:

w10C_Summer_Calendar
w10C_Shakespeare_Festival

You will save your documents as:

Lastname_Firstname_10C_Summer_Calendar
Lastname_Firstname_10C_Shakespeare_Festival

Project Results

Figure 10.49

(Project 10C Summer Calendar continues on the next page)

Content-Based Assessments

Skills Review | Project 10C Summer Calendar (continued)

1 **Start** Word. From your student files, locate and open the file **w10C_Summer_Calendar**. Display the **Save As** dialog box, navigate to your **Word Chapter 10** folder, and then create a folder named **Project 10C** Save the document to your **Project 10C** folder as **Lastname_Firstname_10C_Summer_Calendar** Using **Quick Parts**, insert the file name in the footer. If necessary, display the rulers and formatting marks.

   a. Press Ctrl + Home. On the **Page Layout tab**, in the **Themes group**, click the **Themes** button, and then click **Composite**.

   b. Select the first paragraph. On the Mini toolbar, change the **Font Size** to **28**, and then click **Center**. With the text selected, on the **Home tab**, in the **Font group**, click the **Text Effects** button, and then in the **Text Effects** gallery, in the third row, select the fourth effect—**Gradient Fill - Lime, Accent 1**. Select the second paragraph. On the Mini toolbar, change the **Font Size** to **36**, apply **Bold** and **Center**, and then change the **Font Color** to **Lime, Accent 1, Darker 25%**—in the fifth column, the fifth color.

   c. Select the fourth paragraph *Golden Grove Half-Marathon and Marathon*. On the **Home tab**, in the **Styles group**, click the third style—**Heading 1**. In a similar manner, apply the **Heading 1** style to the paragraphs *Farmer's Market* and *Golden Grove Music Festival*. Deselect the text.

   d. Press Ctrl + Home, and then on the **View tab**, in the **Document Views group**, click the **Outline** button to switch to Outline view. Click to position the insertion point to the left of *Golden Grove Half-Marathon and Marathon*. Drag down to select all remaining paragraphs in the document.

   e. On the **Outlining tab**, in the **Master Document group**, click the **Show Document** button to turn it on, and then click the **Create** button. Scroll down to the bottom of the document and notice the inserted section breaks. Press Ctrl + Home.

   f. On the **Outlining tab**, in the **Master Document group**, click the **Collapse Subdocuments** button. In the **Microsoft Word** dialog box, click **OK** if necessary. Locate the *Golden Grove Half-Marathon and Marathon* subdocument, and then to the left of the subdocument, click the **Subdocument** icon. Drag down until the **Subdocument** icon is above the *Section Break (Continuous)* for the *Golden Grove Music*

Festival subdocument. Deselect the text, and then **Save** your changes. On the **Outlining tab**, in the **Master Document group**, click the **Expand Subdocuments** button.

2 From your student files, locate and open the file **w10C_Shakespeare_Festival**.

   a. From **Backstage** view, display the **Save As** dialog box. Save the file in your **Project 10C** folder as **Lastname_Firstname_10C_Shakespeare_Festival** From **Backstage** view, display the **Document Information Panel**. In the **Author** box, type your first and last names. In the **Subject** box, type your course name and section number, and in the **Keywords** box, type **subdocument, Shakespeare** Close the **Document Information Panel**. **Save** your changes, and then **Close** the *Shakespeare Festival* document.

   b. In the master document, press Ctrl + End to move to the end of the document. In the **Master Document group**, click the **Insert** button. In the **Insert Subdocument** dialog box, navigate to your **Project 10C** folder, select **Lastname_Firstname_10C_Shakespeare_Festival**, and then click **Open**.

   c. In the master document, under *Summer Shakespeare Festival*, in the second bulleted item, change the month from *July* to **August**

   d. On the **Outlining tab**, in the **Close group**, click the **Close Outline View** button. **Save** your changes.

3 Press Ctrl + Home. At the bottom of the scroll bar, click the **Select Browse Object** button, and then click the **Browse by Heading** button. Notice that the insertion point moves to the heading *Farmer's Market*.

   a. Click the **Next Heading** button. Notice that the insertion point moves to the heading *Golden Grove Half-Marathon and Marathon*.

   b. Click the **Select Browse Object** button, and then click the **Browse by Page** button. Notice that the insertion point moves to the top of **Page 2**.

   c. Press Ctrl + Home. On the **View tab**, in the **Show group**, click to select the **Navigation Pane** check box. If necessary, in the **Navigation Pane**, click the first tab—**Browse the headings in your document**.

   d. In the **Navigation Pane**, click the **Golden Grove Music Festival** heading. In the document, select the text *Golden Grove Music Festival*, being careful not to select the paragraph mark.

(Project 10C Summer Calendar continues on the next page)

Content-Based Assessments

e. On the **Insert tab**, in the **Links group**, click the **Bookmark** button. In the **Bookmark** dialog box, in the **Bookmark name** box, type **Golden_Grove_Music_Festival** and then click the **Add** button.

f. **Close** the **Navigation Pane**.

4 Press Ctrl + Home. On the **Home tab**, in the **Editing group**, click the **Find button arrow**, and then click **Go To**. In the **Find and Replace** dialog box, in the **Go to what** box, click **Bookmark**.

a. Under the **Enter bookmark name** box, which displays *Golden_Grove_Music_Festival*, click the **Go To** button. **Close** the **Find and Replace** dialog box.

b. Press Ctrl + Home. In the third paragraph, in the second sentence, select the text *Music Festival*, being careful not to select the space to the left or the period on the right.

c. On the **Insert tab**, in the **Links group**, click the **Cross-reference** button.

d. In the **Cross-reference** dialog box, click the **Reference type arrow**, and then click **Bookmark**. If necessary, click the **Insert reference to arrow** to display **Bookmark text**, and select the **Insert as hyperlink** check box.

e. Under **For which bookmark**, with *Golden_Grove_Music_Festival* selected, click **Insert**, and then click **Close**.

5 Move your I pointer over the **Golden Grove Music Festival** cross-reference. Hold down Ctrl, and when the pointer displays, click **Golden Grove Music Festival**.

a. Press Ctrl + Home. From **Backstage** view, click **Options**. In the **Word Options** dialog box, click **Proofing**. Under **When correcting spelling and grammar in Word**, select the **Show readability statistics** check box to turn on the display of readability statistics. Click **OK**.

b. On the **Review tab**, in the **Proofing group**, click the **Spelling & Grammar** button. In the **Microsoft Word** dialog box, click **OK**.

c. Click **OK** to close the **Readability Statistics** dialog box. From **Backstage** view, click **Options**. In the

Word Options dialog box, click **Proofing**. Under **When correcting spelling and grammar in Word**, select the **Show readability statistics** check box to turn off the display of readability statistics. Click **OK**.

6 Press Ctrl + Home. On the **View tab**, in the **Document Views group**, click **Outline**. If necessary, on the **Outlining tab**, in the **Master Document group**, click the **Show Document** button.

a. To the left of the paragraph *Farmer's Market*, click the **Subdocument** icon to select the entire *Farmer's Market* subdocument. In the **Master Document group**, click the **Unlink** button.

b. In a similar manner, **Unlink** the subdocuments *Golden Grove Half-Marathon and Marathon, Golden Grove Music Festival*, and *Summer Shakespeare Festival*.

c. Above the paragraph *Farmer's Market*, click to position the insertion point to the right of the first bullet for **Section Break (Continuous)**, and then press Del.

d. In a similar manner, delete all instances of **Section Break (Continuous)** and **Section Break (Next Page)** that display.

e. On the **Outlining tab**, in the **Close group**, click the **Close Outline View** button.

f. **Save** your changes.

7 Display the **Document Information Panel**. In the **Author** box, type your name. In the **Subject** box, type your course name and section number, and in the **Keywords** box, type **summer calendar, master Close** the **Document Information Panel**.

a. **Save** your document. From **Backstage** view, click **Open**, navigate to your **Project 10C** folder, and open the file **Lastname_Firstname_10C_Shakespeare_Festival**. Press Del to delete the **Section Break (Next Page)**. Right-click in the footer area, and then click **Edit Footer**. Using **Quick Parts**, insert the file name in the footer, and then **Save** your changes.

8 Print both of your documents or submit your files electronically as directed by your instructor. **Close** Word.

End You have completed Project 10C —————

Apply 10B skills from these Objectives:

4 Create an Index

5 Create a Table of Contents

6 Create a Table of Figures

7 Control the Flow and Formatting of Pages and Text

Skills Review | Project **10D** Job Descriptions

In the following Skills Review, you will add an index, a table of contents, and a table of figures to the listing of job descriptions for the City of Golden Grove. Your completed document will look similar to Figure 10.50.

Project Files

For Project 10D, you will need the following file:

w10D_Job_Descriptions

You will save your document as:

Lastname_Firstname_10D_Job_Descriptions

Project Results

Figure 10.50

(Project 10D Job Descriptions continues on the next page)

Content-Based Assessments

Skills Review | Project **10D** Job Descriptions (continued)

1 **Start** Word. From your student files, open the file **w10D_Job_Descriptions**. Save the file in your **Word Chapter 10** folder as **Lastname_Firstname_10D_Job_Descriptions** If necessary, display the rulers and formatting marks. If any words are flagged as spelling errors, right-click the first occurrence of each, and then click **Ignore All**.

a. Scroll to the bottom of **Page 1**, right-click in the footer area, and then click **Edit Footer**. Using **Quick Parts**, insert the file name in the footer. With the footer area displayed, be sure the insertion point is to the right of the file name, and then press Tab two times. On the **Design tab**, in the **Header & Footer group**, click the **Page Number** button, and then click **Current Position**. In the **Page Number** gallery, under **Simple**, click **Plain Number**. In the **Close group**, click the **Close Header and Footer** button.

b. On the **Page Layout tab**, in the **Themes group**, click the **Theme Colors** button, and then click **Aspect**.

c. Select the first paragraph. Change the **Font Size** to **22**, apply **Bold** and **Center**, and then change the **Font Color** to **Orange, Accent 1**—in the fifth column, the first color.

d. Select the second paragraph. On the **Home tab**, in the **Styles group**, click the **Heading 1** style.

e. On **Page 1**, select the paragraph *Accounting Specialist*, and then in the **Styles group**, click the **Heading 2** style. In a similar manner, apply the **Heading 2** style to the paragraphs *Data Entry Specialist* and *Records Specialist*.

f. Press Ctrl + Home. Locate the first table in the document—under *Accounting Specialist*. Click to position the insertion point anywhere in the table. On the **Design tab**, in the **Table Style Options group**, click to deselect the **Header Row** check box. In the **Table Styles group**, click the **More** button, and then under **Built-in**, click the second style—**Light Shading - Accent 1**. In a similar manner, deselect the **Header Row** check box and apply the **Light Shading – Accent 1** style to the remaining two tables.

g. Press Ctrl + Home, and then **Save** your changes.

2 In the fourth paragraph, select the text *Application Tips*. On the **References tab**, in the **Index group**, click the **Mark Entry** button. In the **Mark Index Entry** dialog box, click the **Mark** button.

a. Click in the document, and then select the paragraph *Accounting Specialist*. If necessary, point

to the **Mark Index Entry** dialog box to display the pointer, and then drag the **Mark Index Entry** dialog box to the side of your screen. With the paragraph selected, click in the **Main entry** box, and notice that *Accounting Specialist* displays. Click the **Mark** button.

b. Without closing the **Mark Index Entry** dialog box, in a similar manner, **Mark** entries for *Data Entry Specialist* and *Records Specialist*.

c. On **Page 1**, position the insertion point to the right of *Job Description*. In the **Mark Index Entry** dialog box, click in the **Main entry** box, and then type **Accounting Specialist** In the **Subentry** box, type **Job Description** Click the **Mark** button. On **Page 2**, position the insertion point to the right of *Qualifications*. In the **Main entry** box, type **Accounting Specialist** in the **Subentry** box, type **Qualifications** and then click the **Mark** button. On **Page 2**, position the insertion point to the right of *Career Advancement*. In the **Main entry** box, type **Accounting Specialist** in the **Subentry** box, type **Career Advancement** and then click the **Mark** button.

d. Using the technique you just practiced, under the paragraph heading *Data Entry Specialist*, mark *Job Description*, *Qualifications*, and *Career Advancement* as subentries for the main entry **Data Entry Specialist**

e. In a similar manner, under the paragraph heading *Records Specialist*, mark subentries for *Job Description*, *Qualifications*, and *Career Advancement* as subentries for the main entry **Records Specialist**

f. **Close** the **Mark Entry** dialog box, and then **Save** your changes.

3 Press Ctrl + End, and then press Ctrl + Enter to insert a manual page break. With the insertion point at the top of the new page, type **INDEX** and then press Enter. Select the text *INDEX*, including the paragraph mark, change the **Font Size** to **16**, sand then apply **Bold** and **Center**.

a. Click to position the insertion point in the last paragraph of the document. On the **References tab**, in the **Index group**, click the **Insert Index** button to display the **Index** dialog box.

b. In the **Index** dialog box, on the **Index** tab, click the **Formats arrow**, and then from the list, click **Formal**. Click **OK**.

(Project 10D Job Descriptions continues on the next page)

Content-Based Assessments

c. On **Page 1**, select the first paragraph with italic formatting—*Application Tips*. On the **References tab**, in the **Table of Contents group**, click the **Add Text** button, and then click **Level 3**. In a similar manner, assign **Level 3** to the remaining nine italicized paragraph headings. Press Ctrl + Home, and then **Save** your changes.

4 With the insertion point at the beginning of the document, on the **Page Layout tab**, in the **Page Setup group**, click the **Breaks** button, and then under **Section Breaks**, click **Next Page**. Press Ctrl + Home to move to the beginning of the document. On the **Home tab**, in the **Styles group**, click the **Normal** style.

a. Type **TABLE OF CONTENTS** and then press Enter. Select the text you just typed, including the paragraph mark, change the **Font Size** to **16**, and then apply **Bold** and **Center**.

b. Click to position the insertion point in the last paragraph on the page—to the left of the section break. On the **References tab**, in the **Table of Contents group**, click the **Table of Contents** button. From the **Table of Contents** gallery, click **Insert Table of Contents**. In the **Table of Contents** dialog box, if necessary, select the **Use hyperlinks instead of page numbers** check box. Under **General**, click the **Formats arrow**, and then click **Formal**. Click **OK**, and then **Save** your changes.

5 On **Page 2**, below the heading *Accounting Specialist*, click anywhere in the first table. On the **References tab**, in the **Captions group**, click the **Insert Caption** button.

a. In the **Caption** dialog box, in the **Caption** box, with the insertion point to the right of *Table 1*, type a colon, press Spacebar, and then type **Accounting Specialist** Click the **Position arrow**, and then click **Below selected item**. Click **OK**.

b. On **Page 3**, click anywhere in the table. In the **Captions group**, click the **Insert Caption** button. In the **Caption** dialog box, in the **Caption** box, with the insertion point to the right of *Table 2*, type a colon, press Spacebar, and then type **Data Entry Specialist** Click **OK**.

c. In a similar manner, insert the caption **Table 3: Records Specialist** below the third table in the document. Click **OK**.

6 Press Ctrl + Home. Click to position the insertion point in the last paragraph of the page—to the left of the

section break. Press Ctrl + Enter to insert a manual page break.

a. Type **TABLE OF FIGURES** and then press Enter. Select the text you just typed, change the **Font Size** to **16**, and then apply **Bold** and **Center**.

b. Click to position the insertion point in the last paragraph on **Page 2**—to the left of the section break. On the **References tab**, in the **Captions group**, click the **Insert Table of Figures** button.

c. In the **Table of Figures** dialog box, under **General**, click the **Formats arrow**, and then click **Formal**. Click **OK**, and then **Save** your changes.

d. On the **Page Layout tab**, in the **Page Setup group**, click the **Hyphenation** button, and then from the displayed list, click **Automatic**.

7 Press Ctrl + Home, and then scroll to the bottom of **Page 1**. Right-click in the footer area, and then click **Edit Footer**. In the footer, select the page number.

a. On the **Design tab**, in the **Header & Footer group**, click the **Page Number** button, and then click **Format Page Numbers**.

b. In the **Page Number Format** dialog box, click the **Number Format arrow**, and then click the fifth numbering style—**i, ii, iii**. Click **OK**.

c. On **Page 3**, click to position the insertion point anywhere in the footer area. On the **Design tab**, in the **Navigation group**, click the **Link to Previous** button to turn it off.

d. In the footer, select the page number 3. On the **Design tab**, in the **Header & Footer group**, click the **Page Number** button, and then click **Format Page Numbers**. In the **Page Number Format** dialog box, under **Page numbering**, click the **Start at** option button. With *1* displayed in the **Start at** box, click **OK**. In the **Close group**, click the **Close Header and Footer** button.

8 Click to position the insertion point in the TOC, right-click, and then click **Update Field**. In the **Update Table of Contents** dialog box, with the **Update page numbers only** option button selected, click **OK**.

a. On **Page 2**, click to position the insertion point in the table of figures. Right-click, and then click **Update Field**. In the **Update Table of Figures** dialog box, with the **Update page numbers only** option button selected, click **OK**.

(Project 10D Job Descriptions continues on the next page)

Content-Based Assessments

b. Press [Ctrl] + [End]. Click to position the insertion point in the index, right-click, and then click **Update Field**.

c. Press [Ctrl] + [Home]. Display the **Document Information Panel**. In the **Author** box, type your first and last names. In the **Subject** box, type your course name, and section number, and in the **Keywords** box, type **jobs, TOC, index Close** the **Document Information Panel**. **Save** your changes.

9 Print your document or submit electronically as directed by your instructor. **Close** Word.

End **You have completed Project 10D** _____

Content-Based Assessments

Apply **10A** skills from these Objectives:

1. Create a Master Document and Subdocuments
2. Manage a Master Document and Subdocuments
3. Navigate and Inspect the Master Document

Mastering Word | Project **10E** Council Topics

In the following Mastering Word project, you will create a master document and subdocuments for a document that summarizes topics to be discussed at the February meeting of the Golden Grove City Council. Your completed documents will look similar to Figure 10.51.

Project Files

For Project 10E, you will need the following files:

w10E_Council_Topics
w10E_Agenda_Item

You will save your documents as:

Lastname_Firstname_10E_Council_Topics
Lastname_Firstname_10E_Agenda_Item

Project Results

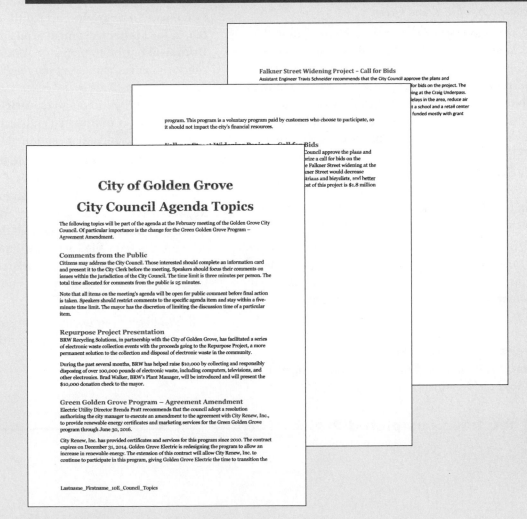

Figure 10.51

(Project 10E Council Topics continues on the next page)

Content-Based Assessments

Mastering Word | Project 10E Council Topics (continued)

1 **Start** Word. From your student files, locate and open the file **w10E_Council_Topics**. Navigate to your **Word Chapter 10** folder, and create a folder named **Project 10E** Save the file in your **Project 10E** folder as **Lastname_Firstname_10E_Council_Topics** Using **Quick Parts**, insert the file name in the footer. If necessary, display the rulers and formatting marks.

2 Press Ctrl + Home. Apply the **Civic** theme. Select the first paragraph of the document, change the **Font Size** to **28**, apply **Center**, and then change the **Text Effects** to **Gradient Fill - Red, Accent 1**. Select the second paragraph, change the **Font Size** to **28**, apply **Bold** and **Center**, and then change the **Font Color** to **Red, Accent 1, Darker 25%**. Apply the **Heading 1** style to the paragraphs that begin *Repurpose, Comments,* and *Green.*

3 Change to **Outline** view. Select the paragraph that begins *Repurpose,* and then select all the remaining paragraphs in the document. On the **Outlining tab**, in the **Master Document group**, click the **Show Document** button to turn it on, and then click the **Create** button. In the **Master Document group**, click the **Collapse Subdocuments** button, and then move the *Repurpose Project Presentation* subdocument directly above the *Section Break (Continuous)* for the *Green Golden Grove Program* subdocument. Deselect the text, and then in the **Master Document group**, click the **Expand Subdocuments** button. **Save** your changes.

4 From your student files, locate and open the file **w10E_Agenda_Item**. Save the file in your **Project 10E** folder as **Lastname_Firstname_10E_Agenda_Item** In the **Document Information Panel**, in the **Author** box, type your first and last names. In the **Subject** box, type your course name and section number, and in the **Keywords** box type **subdocument, falkner street** Close the **Document Information Panel**. **Save** your changes, and then **Close** the document.

5 Press Ctrl + End. **Insert** the **Lastname_Firstname_10E_Agenda_Item** document you created. In the master document, under *Falkner Street Widening Project,* in the last sentence, change the cost from *$1.6* to **$1.8** Click the **Close Outline View** button, and then **Save** your changes.

6 Press Ctrl + Home. Select the entire heading that begins *Green Golden Grove Program,* being careful not to select the paragraph mark. Display the **Bookmark** dialog box, and for the **Bookmark name**, type **Agreement_Amendment** Click the **Add** button. In the third paragraph, select the text *Green Golden Grove Program.* **Insert** a cross-reference that is linked to the *Agreement_Amendment* bookmark.

7 Press Ctrl + Home. On the **View tab**, in the **Document Views group**, click **Outline**. On the **Outlining tab**, in the **Master Document group**, click the **Show Document** button to turn it on. **Unlink** the subdocuments *Comments from the Public, Repurpose Project Presentation, Green Golden Grove Program,* and *Falkner Street Widening Project.* **Delete** all instances of **Section Break (Continuous)** and **Section Break (Next Page)** from the document, and then **Close Outline View.**

8 In the **Document Information Panel**, in the **Author** box, type your first and last names. In the **Subject** box, type your course name and section number, and in the **Keywords** box type **council topics, master** Close the **Document Information Panel**, and then **Save** your changes. **Open** the file **Lastname_Firstname_10E_Agenda_Item**. **Delete** the **Section Break (Next Page)**. Insert the file name in the footer, and then **Save** your changes.

9 Print both your documents or submit your files electronically as directed by your instructor. **Close** Word.

End **You have completed Project 10E** ——————————————

Content-Based Assessments

Apply 10B skills from these Objectives:

- 4 Create an Index
- 5 Create a Table of Contents
- 6 Create a Table of Figures
- 7 Control the Flow and Formatting of Pages and Text

Mastering Word | Project **10F** Business FAQ

In the following Mastering Word project, you will add an index, a table of contents, and a table of figures to a document containing frequently asked questions and answers related to doing business with the City of Golden Grove. Your completed document will look similar to Figure 10.52.

Project Files

For Project 10F, you will need the following file:

> w10F_Business_FAQ

You will save your document as:

> Lastname_Firstname_10F_Business_FAQ

Project Results

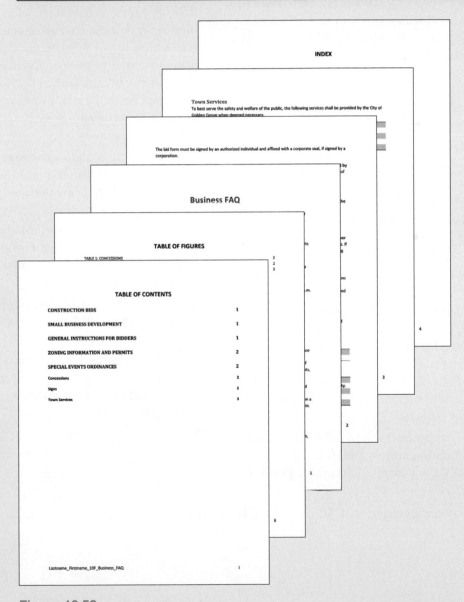

Figure 10.52

(Project 10F Business FAQ continues on the next page)

Content-Based Assessments

1 **Start** Word. From your student files, open the file **w10F_Business_FAQ**. Save the file in your **Word Chapter 10** folder as **Lastname_Firstname_10F_Business_FAQ** If necessary, display the rulers and formatting marks. If any words are flagged as spelling errors, right-click the first occurrence of each, and click **Ignore All**. Using **Quick Parts**, insert the file name in the footer, and then press Tab two times. Click the **Page Number** button, click **Current Position**, and then click **Plain Number**. **Close** the footer.

2 Change the **Theme Colors** to **Hardcover**. Select the first paragraph, change the **Font Size** to **22**, apply **Bold** and **Center**, and then change the **Font Color** to **Dark Red, Accent 1**. Apply the **Heading 1** style to the paragraph headings that begin *Construction*, *Small Business*, *General Instructions*, *Zoning*, and *Special Events*. Apply the **Heading 2** style to the paragraphs *Concessions*, *Signs*, and *Town Services*. For each table apply the **Light Shading – Accent 1** table style without using a **Header Row**.

3 For each *Heading 1* paragraph, use the **Mark Entry** dialog box to **Mark** the text as a **Main entry** for the index. For each *Heading 2* paragraph—*Concessions*, *Signs*, and *Town Services*—type the paragraph text as a **Subentry** for the **Main entry Special Events Ordinances**

4 At the end of the document, press Ctrl + Enter, type **INDEX** and then press Enter two times. Select the *INDEX* paragraph you just typed, change the **Font Size** to **16**, and then apply **Bold** and **Center**. In the last paragraph of the document, insert an index with the **Classic** format.

5 Press Ctrl + Home, and then insert a **Next Page** section break. Press Ctrl + Home, and then apply the **Normal** style. Type **TABLE OF CONTENTS** and then press Enter. Select the text you typed, change the **Font Size** to **16**, and then apply **Bold** and **Center**. In the last paragraph on the page, insert a table of contents with the **Classic** format. **Save** your changes.

6 Click anywhere in the first table in the document. Click the **Insert Caption** button, and then change the **Caption** to **Table 1: Concessions** Change the **Position** to

Below selected item. In a similar manner, for the second and third tables, change the captions to **Table 2: Signs** and **Table 3: Town Services**

7 Press Ctrl + Home. Click to position the insertion point in the last paragraph of the page—to the left of the section break. Press Ctrl + Enter, type **TABLE OF FIGURES** and then press Enter. Select the text you typed, change the **Font Size** to **16**, and then apply **Bold** and **Center**. In the last paragraph on the page, insert a table of figures with the **Classic** format. **Save** your changes.

8 Press Ctrl + Home. Change the **Hyphenation** to **Automatic**.

9 On **Page 1**, in the footer, select the page number, and then in the **Page Number Format** dialog box, change the **Format** to **i, ii, iii**. Click **OK**. On the third page of the document, click to position the insertion point in the footer area. Click the **Link to Previous** button to unlink the footer. Select the page number, and then in the **Page Number Format** dialog box, change the **Page numbering** to **Start at** the number **1**.

10 Click to position the insertion point in the TOC, and then display the **Update Table of Contents** dialog box. With the **Update page numbers only** option button selected, click **OK**.

11 On **Page 2**, click to position the insertion point in the table of figures, and then display the **Update Table of Figures** dialog box. With the **Update page numbers only** option button selected, click **OK**.

12 Press Ctrl + End. Click to position the insertion point in the index, right-click, and then click **Update Field**.

13 Press Ctrl + Home. Display the **Document Information Panel**. In the **Author** box type your first and last names. In the **Subject** box type your course name and section number, and in the **Keywords** box type **business FAQ, TOC, index Save** your changes.

14 Print your document or submit electronically as directed by your instructor. **Close** Word.

 You have completed Project 10F _____

Content-Based Assessments

Apply **10A** and **10B** skills from these Objectives:

1. Create a Master Document and Subdocuments
2. Manage a Master Document and Subdocuments
3. Navigate and Inspect the Master Document
4. Create an Index
5. Create a Table of Contents
6. Create a Table of Figures
7. Control the Flow and Formatting of Pages and Text

Mastering Word | Project **10G** Chamber Programs

In the following Mastering Word project, you will create a master document and subdocuments related to the programs offered by Golden Grove's Chamber of Commerce. The final document will include an index, table of contents, and table of figures. Your completed documents will look similar to Figure 10.53.

Project Files

For Project 10G, you will need the following files:

w10G_Chamber_Programs
w10G_Ambassadors_Club

You will save your documents as:

Lastname_Firstname_10G_Chamber_Programs
Lastname_Firstname_10G_Ambassadors_Club

Project Results

Figure 10.53

(Project 10G Chamber Programs continues on the next page)

Content-Based Assessments

Mastering Word | Project 10G Chamber Programs (continued)

1 **Start** Word. From your student files, locate and open the file **w10G_Chamber_Programs**. Navigate to your **Word Chapter 10** folder, and then create a folder named **Project 10G Save** the document in your **Project 10G** folder as **Lastname_Firstname_10G_Chamber_Programs** In the footer, using **Quick Parts**, insert the file name, and then press `Tab` two times. Click the **Page Number** button, click **Current Position**, and then click **Plain Number**. **Close** the footer.

2 Change the **Theme Colors** to **Equity**. Select the first two paragraphs, change the **Font Size** to **24**, apply **Bold** and **Center**, and then change the **Font Color** to **Orange, Accent 1, Darker 25%**. Apply the **Heading 1** style to the paragraphs *Networking, Special Events, Workshops and Seminars,* and *Other Chamber Services.* Apply the **Heading 2** style to the paragraphs that begin *Morning, Lunches, Ribbon, Business Training, New Member, Industrial, Government,* and *Recycling.* For each table, apply the **Light Shading – Accent 1** without using a **Header Row**.

3 Change to **Outline** view. Beginning with the paragraph *Networking,* select all remaining text in the document. On the **Outlining tab**, click the **Show Document** button, and then click the **Create** button. From your student files, open the file **w10G_Ambassadors_Club**. Save the file in your **Project 10G** folder as **Lastname_Firstname_10G_Ambassasors_Club** In the **Document Information Panel**, type your name in the **Author** box, type your course name and section number in the **Subject** box, and then in the **Keywords** box, type **subdocument, ambassadors club Save** your changes, and then **Close** the document.

4 In the master document, press `Ctrl` + `End`, and then **Insert** the **Lastname_Firstname_10G_Ambassadors_Club** file as a subdocument. In the *Ambassadors Club* subdocument, change the word *various* to **numerous Save** your changes. **Unlink** all subdocuments, and then remove all instances of **Section Break (Continuous)** and **Section Break (Next Page)**. **Close Outline View**.

5 For each *Heading 1* and *Heading 2* paragraph, use the **Mark Entry** dialog box to **Mark** the text as a **Main entry** or **Subentry** for the index as appropriate. At the end of the document, press `Ctrl` + `Enter`, type **INDEX** and then press `Enter` two times. Select the text you typed, change the **Font Size** to **16**, and then apply **Bold** and **Center**. In the last paragraph, insert an index with the **Formal** format.

6 Press `Ctrl` + `Home`, and then insert a **Next Page** section break. Press `Ctrl` + `Home`, and then apply the

Normal style. Type **TABLE OF CONTENTS** and then press `Enter` two times. Select the text you typed, change the **Font Size** to **16**, and then apply **Bold** and **Center**. In the last paragraph on the page, insert a table of contents with the **Formal** format. **Save** your changes.

7 For each table, click the **Insert Caption** button, and then change the **Position** to display **Above selected item**. Change the captions to display as follows:

> **Table 1: Appliances**
>
> **Table 2: Glass and Aluminum**
>
> **Table 3: Old Tires**
>
> **Table 4: Scrap Metal**

Press `Ctrl` + `Home`. Click to position the insertion point in the last paragraph of the page—to the left of the section break. Press `Ctrl` + `Enter`, type **TABLE OF FIGURES** and then press `Enter`. Select the text you typed, change the **Font Size** to **16**, and then apply **Bold** and **Center**. In the last paragraph on the page, insert a table of figures with the **Formal** format. **Save** your changes.

8 Change the **Hyphenation** to **Automatic**.

9 Press `Ctrl` + `Home`. In the footer, select the page number, and then in the **Page Number Format** dialog box, change the **Format** to **i, ii, iii**. Click **OK**. On **Page 3**, click to position the insertion point in the footer area. Click the **Link to Previous** button to unlink the footer. Select the page number, and then in the **Page Number Format** dialog box, change the **Page numbering** to **Start at** the number **1**.

10 Click to position the insertion point in the TOC, and then display the **Update Table of Contents** dialog box. With the **Update page numbers only** option button selected, click **OK**. On **Page 2**, click to position the insertion point in the table of figures, and then display the **Update Table of Figures** dialog box. With the **Update page numbers only** option button selected, click **OK**. Press `Ctrl` + `End`. Right-click the index, and then click **Update Field**. Press `Ctrl` + `Home`.

11 Display the **Document Information Panel**. In the **Author** box, type your first and last names. In the **Subject** box, type your course name, and section number, and in the **Keywords** box, type **chamber programs, TOC, index Save** your changes. **Open** the **Lastname_Firstname_10G_Ambassadors Club** document, insert the file name in the footer, and then **Save** your changes.

12 Print both documents or submit electronically as directed by your instructor. **Close** Word.

End **You have completed Project 10G**

Content-Based Assessments

Apply a combination of the 10A and 10B skills.

GO! Fix It | Project **10H** Boards Summary

Project Files

For Project 10H, you will need the following files:

> w10H_Boards_Summary
> w10H_Contact_Information

You will save your document as:

> Lastname_Firstname_10H_Boards_Summary

In this project you will create a document that describes the various boards, commissions, and committees that function under the direction of Golden Grove's City Council. Navigate to your student files, open the file **w10H_Boards_Summary**. Navigate to your **Word Chapter 10** folder and create a folder named **Project 10H** Save the file to your **Project 10H** folder as **Lastname_Firstname_10H_Boards_Summary**

To complete the project, you must correct the following:

- The file name and page number should be inserted in the footer. The first two paragraphs should be formatted appropriately for a document title. The Heading 1 style should be applied to all bold, paragraph headings.

- A master document should be created using the paragraphs formatted with the Heading 1 style as the beginning of each subdocument. From your student files, the file **w10H_Contact_Information** should be inserted as a subdocument at the end of the document. The subdocuments should be unlinked and any unnecessary section breaks deleted.

- Captions, with appropriate text, should be inserted above each of the two tables.

- Using the Formal style, a table of contents should be created and formatted as a new, first page of the document, and then a table of figures should be created and formatted as a new, second page. Each paragraph heading should be marked as an index entry. An index should be created and formatted, using the Formal style, as a separate page at the end of the document.

- A bookmark should be created for the paragraph heading text *Contact Information*. Below the two title paragraphs of the document, in the paragraph that begins *The City Council*, a cross-reference should be created for the text *Contact Information*.

- The document should be automatically hyphenated and pagination modified so that the page numbers for the first two pages display in a different numbering format, and body text pages start at 1.

- Appropriate paragraphs should be kept together on a page and then the table of contents, table of figures, and index should be updated.

- Document properties should include the keywords **boards, commissions, committees**

Print the document or submit electronically as directed by your instructor.

End You have completed Project 10H —————————————————

Content-Based Assessments

Apply a combination of
the **10A** and **10B** skills.

GO! Make It | Project 10I Internship Program

Save the file **w10I_Internship_Program** to your **Word Chapter 10** folder as **Lastname_Firstname_10I_Internship_Program** Apply the Opulent theme and appropriate heading styles. Use the Classic format to create the table of contents and index as shown in Figure 10.54. Mark appropriate entries for the index. Modify the page numbers so that the TOC displays with *i*, and the remaining pages are numbered in a 1, 2, 3 style. Print your document or submit electronically as directed by your instructor.

Project Files

For Project 10I, you will need the following file:

w10I_Internship_Program

You will save your document as:

Lastname_Firstname_10I_Internship_Program—only the first and last pages are shown

Project Results

Table of Contents

SELECTION PROCESS 1

INTERN SCHOLARSHIP PROGRAM 1

SUMMER INTERNSHIP PROGRAMS 1

AVAILABLE INTERNSHIP POSITIONS 2

Engineering Intern 2

Marketing Intern 2

Cultural Affairs Intern 2

Visual Graphics Intern 2

Financial Intern 2

City Health Intern 2

Information Technology Intern 3

Human Resources Intern 3

International Tourism Intern 3

Bilingual International Business Intern 3

Urban Affairs Intern 3

Index

A

Available Internship Positions, 2
  Bilingual International Business Intern, 3
  City Health Intern, 3
  Cultural Affairs Intern, 2
  Engineering Intern, 2
  Financial Intern, 2
  Human Resources Intern, 3
  Information Technology Intern, 3
  International Tourism Intern, 3
  Marketing Intern, 2

Urban Affairs Intern, 4
Visual Graphics Intern, 2

I

Intern Scholarship Program, 1

S

Selection Process, 1
Summer Internship Programs, 1

Lastname_Firstname_10I_Internship_Program   i

Lastname_Firstname_10I_Internship_Program   4

Figure 10.54

End You have completed Project 10I

628   **Word** | Chapter 10: Working with Long Documents

Content-Based Assessments

Apply a combination of the **10A** and **10B** skills.

GO! Solve It | Project **10J** Health Department

Project Files

For Project 10J, you will need the following files:

> w10J_Police_Department
> w10J_Health_Department

You will save your documents as:

> Lastname_Firstname_10J_Police_Department
> Lastname_Firstname_10J_Health_Department

In your **Word Chapter 10** folder, create a folder named **Project 10J** From your student files, copy the file **w10J_Police_Department** to your **Project 10J** folder and rename it as **Lastname_Firstname_10J_Police_Department** Open the file **w10J_Health_Department** and save it to your **Project 10J** folder as **Lastname_Firstname_10J_Health_Department** Format the title paragraph and apply appropriate styles to the paragraph headings and the subheadings listing the contact information. Create a master document containing three subdocuments. Move subdocuments as necessary so that the paragraph headings display in alphabetical order. Insert the file **Lastname_Firstname_10J_Police_Department** as a subdocument. In the subdocument, change the number of civilian employees to **695** Unlink all subdocuments. In the second paragraph, create a cross-reference that links to the police department paragraph heading. For both files saved with your name, format the documents to create a professional appearance, insert the file name in the footer, and add appropriate document properties. Print both documents or submit electronically as directed by your instructor.

	Performance Level		
	Exemplary: You consistently applied the relevant skills	Proficient: You sometimes, but not always, applied the relevant skills	Developing: You rarely or never applied the relevant skills
Apply styles	All styles are applied correctly.	At least one style is not applied properly.	No styles are applied properly.
Insert and alphabetize subdocuments	A subdocument is inserted and all text displays correctly.	A subdocument is not inserted or text does not display correctly.	A subdocument is not inserted and text does not display correctly.
Modify text in subdocument	Text is modified in subdocument and displays in master document.	Text is modified in subdocument but does not display in master document.	Text is not modified.
Create a cross-reference	A cross-reference is created correctly.	A cross-reference is created but linked incorrectly.	A cross-reference is not created.
Format attractively and appropriately	Formatting is attractive and appropriate.	The document has inadequate or no formatting.	Inadequate or no formatting.

Performance Element

End **You have completed Project 10J** ⸻⸻⸻⸻

Content-Based Assessments

GO! Solve It | Project **10K** Volunteer Program

Project Files

For Project 10K, you will need the following file:

> w10K_Volunteer_Program

You will save your document as:

> Lastname_Firstname_10K_Volunteer_Program

Open the file **w10K_Volunteer_Program** and save it to your **Word Chapter 10** folder as **Lastname_Firstname_10K_Volunteer_Program** Using fields, insert the file name and page number in the footer. Format the title paragraphs and apply styles to paragraph headings. Format the tables attractively and insert captions. Create a table of contents and table of figures on separate pages. Create an index that displays main headings and specific names for departments and organizations. Hyphenate and paginate the document. Modify the page number format for the first two pages. Add appropriate document properties. Print your document or submit electronically as directed by your instructor.

		Performance Level		
		Exemplary: You consistently applied the relevant skills	**Proficient:** You sometimes, but not always, applied the relevant skills	**Developing:** You rarely or never applied the relevant skills
Performance Element	**Format tables and insert captions**	All tables are formatted attractively and appropriate captions are inserted.	At least one table is not formatted or an appropriate caption is not inserted.	No tables are formatted and no captions are inserted.
	Create table of contents and table of figures	The table of contents and table of figures are created correctly.	The table of contents or table of figures is not created correctly.	The table of contents and table of figures are not created.
	Create index	The index is created and includes appropriate entries.	The index is created but some entries are missing.	The index is not created.
	Hyphenate and paginate	The document is hyphenated and paginated appropriately.	The document is not hyphenated or is not paginated appropriately.	The document is not hyphenated and is not paginated appropriately.
	Insert and format page numbers	Page numbers are inserted in the footer and formatted correctly.	Page numbers are inserted in the footer but not formatted correctly.	Page numbers are not inserted in the footer.

End You have completed Project 10K

Outcomes-Based Assessments

Rubric

The following outcomes-based assessments are *open-ended assessments*. That is, there is no specific correct result; your result will depend on your approach to the information provided. Make *Professional Quality* your goal. Use the following scoring rubric to guide you in *how* to approach the problem and then to evaluate *how well* your approach solves the problem.

The *criteria*—Software Mastery, Content, Format and Layout, and Process—represent the knowledge and skills you have gained that you can apply to solving the problem. The *levels of performance*—Professional Quality, Approaching Professional Quality, or Needs Quality Improvements—help you and your instructor evaluate your result.

	Your completed project is of Professional Quality if you:	Your completed project is Approaching Professional Quality if you:	Your completed project Needs Quality Improvements if you:
1-Software Mastery	Choose and apply the most appropriate skills, tools, and features and identify efficient methods to solve the problem.	Choose and apply some appropriate skills, tools, and features, but not in the most efficient manner.	Choose inappropriate skills, tools, or features, or are inefficient in solving the problem.
2-Content	Construct a solution that is clear and well organized, contains content that is accurate, appropriate to the audience and purpose, and is complete. Provide a solution that contains no errors in spelling, grammar, or style.	Construct a solution in which some components are unclear, poorly organized, inconsistent, or incomplete. Misjudge the needs of the audience. Have some errors in spelling, grammar, or style, but the errors do not detract from comprehension.	Construct a solution that is unclear, incomplete, or poorly organized; contains some inaccurate or inappropriate content; and contains many errors in spelling, grammar, or style. Do not solve the problem.
3-Format and Layout	Format and arrange all elements to communicate information and ideas, clarify function, illustrate relationships, and indicate relative importance.	Apply appropriate format and layout features to some elements, but not others. Overuse features, causing minor distraction.	Apply format and layout that does not communicate information or ideas clearly. Do not use format and layout features to clarify function, illustrate relationships, or indicate relative importance. Use available features excessively, causing distraction.
4-Process	Use an organized approach that integrates planning, development, self-assessment, revision, and reflection.	Demonstrate an organized approach in some areas, but not others; or, use an insufficient process of organization throughout.	Do not use an organized approach to solve the problem.

Outcomes-Based Assessments

Apply a combination of the **10A** and **10B** skills.

GO! Think | Project **10L** Technology Plan

Project Files

For Project 10L, you will need the following files:

    Two new blank Word documents

You will save your documents as:

    Lastname_Firstname_10L_Technology_Plan
    Lastname_Firstname_10L_Maintenance

The City of Golden Grove is developing a new technology plan. Search the Internet for information related to technology plans for government. Save a new document as **Lastname_Firstname_10L_Technology_Plan** Using the data you find, in your own words, create a report—including headings and subheadings—that explains the steps required to develop a plan. These steps should include the following topics: a vision statement, the goals, a needs assessment, design and purchase, and implementation. Note: You are defining what each step means; you are not entering specific technology data. Create a master document with subdocuments for each step. Save a second, new document as **Lastname_Firstname_10L_Maintenance** Create information defining maintenance—the final step in a technology plan. Insert this file as a subdocument in the master document. Unlink the subdocuments. Insert at least one bookmark and related cross-reference. Format both documents in a professional manner. For each document, insert the file name in the footer and add appropriate document properties. Print both documents or submit electronically as directed by your instructor.

 You have completed Project 10L ——————————————

Apply a combination of the **10A** and **10B** skills.

GO! Think | Project **10M** City Parks

Project Files

For Project 10M, you will need the following file:

    New blank Word document

You will save your document as:

    Lastname_Firstname_10M_City_Parks

To meet the needs of its residents, the City of Golden Grove maintains an excellent park system. Search the Internet for descriptions of twelve city parks—including the size, opening and closing times, and features. Save a new document as **Lastname_Firstname_10M_City_Parks** Insert the file name and page number in the footer using fields. Create a summary of the parks, using fictitious names. Include a descriptive paragraph for each park. Create a table that lists the opening and closing schedule for each park. Insert a second table that lists park fees—listed by park—for specific amenities, such as swimming or fishing. Create a table of contents, table of figures, and index. Format the document to create a professional appearance including hyphenation and proper pagination. Add appropriate document properties. Print your document or submit electronically as directed by your instructor.

 You have completed Project 10M ——————————————

Outcomes-Based Assessments

Apply a combination of the **10A** and **10B** skills.

You and GO! | Project **10N** Personal Journal

Project Files

For Project 10N, you will need the following file:

New blank Word document

You will save your document as:

Lastname_Firstname_10N_Personal_Journal

    In this project, you will create a document that can be used as a journal to record entries about different areas of your life. Save the document as **Lastname_Firstname_10N_Personal_Journal** Insert the file name and page number in the footer. Add your name, your course name and section number, and the keywords **journal, TOC, index** to the document properties.

    Add a minimum of four headings for selected facets of your life—such as school, family, friends, and hobbies. Include a minimum of three subheadings where appropriate. Insert at least one specific comment below each heading or subheading. Include a date for each comment. Display each main topic on a new page. Format each of the headings and subheadings to be used in a TOC. Insert a TOC at the beginning of the document. Mark each heading and subheading as an index entry. Insert an index at the end of the document. Format the page numbers so that the TOC page has a numbering style different from the rest of the document. Check for spelling errors. Print your file, or submit electronically, as directed by your instructor.

End You have completed Project 10N ───────────────────────

Embedding and Linking Objects and Using Macros

OUTCOMES
At the end of this chapter you will be able to:

OBJECTIVES
Mastering these objectives will enable you to:

PROJECT 11A
Embed and link objects.

1. Embed Objects in a Word Document (p. 637)
2. Link Objects to a Word Document (p. 644)

PROJECT 11B
Create, edit, and run macros.

3. Create Macros (p. 651)
4. Use Macros (p. 660)
5. Write a Procedure in VBA (p. 664)

javarman/Shutterstock

In This Chapter

In this chapter, you will add objects to an existing document from files created with other Office applications. Because Microsoft Office 2010 is an integrated program suite, you can make use of the features of other programs within your Word document. Using Word features and the Visual Basic Editor, you will also create macros. A macro allows you to improve your efficiency by performing a series of tasks in a single action.

The projects in this chapter relate to **The Minneapolis-St. Paul Job Fair**. Each year the organization holds a number of targeted job fairs. In addition, the annual Minneapolis-St. Paul Job Fair event draws over 200 employers in more than 40 industries and registers more than 8,000 candidates. Candidate registration is free; employers pay a nominal fee to display and present at the fair. Candidate resumes and employer postings are managed by a computerized state-of-the-art database system, allowing participants quick and accurate access to job data and candidate qualifications.

Project 11A Survey Memo

Project Activities

In Activities 11.01 through 11.05, you will insert various objects—Excel charts, an Access table, a PowerPoint presentation, and a Word document—in a memo that discusses a publicity plan for the annual Minneapolis-St. Paul Job Fair. Related files are based on survey responses from employers and job seekers. Your completed documents will look similar to Figure 11.1.

Project Files

For Project 11A, you will need the following files:

w11A_Survey_Memo
w11A_Fair_Growth
w11A_Fair_Participants
w11A_Publicity_Strategy
w11A_Survey_Results
w11A_Participant_Survey

You will save your files as:

Lastname_Firstname_11A_Survey_Memo
Lastname_Firstname_11A_Survey_Results
Lastname_Firstname_11A_Participant_Survey

Project Results

Figure 11.1
Project 11A Survey Memo

Objective 1 | Embed Objects in a Word Document

All Microsoft Office programs support *OLE*, which stands for *Object Linking and Embedding*. OLE is a program-integration technology for sharing information between Office programs. An *object* such as a table, chart, file, or other form of information created in one Office program—the *source file*—can be inserted in a file created with a different Office program—the *destination file*. *Embedding* is the process of inserting information from a source file, using a format that you specify, into a destination file. An *embedded object* maintains the structure of the original application, but is not connected to the source file.

Activity 11.01 | Using Paste Special to Embed an Excel Chart

When working with numerical data and creating charts, it makes sense to use Excel. Embedding an Excel chart in a Word document allows the reader to review the data in a visual format without viewing an entire spreadsheet.

1 **Start** Word. From your student files, locate and open the file **w11A_Survey_Memo**. From **Backstage** view, display the **Save As** dialog box, navigate to the location where you are saving your files for this chapter, and create a new folder named **Word Chapter 11** Save the document as **Lastname_Firstname_11A_Survey_Memo** Using **Quick Parts**, insert the file name in the footer. If necessary, display the rulers and formatting marks.

2 On the Windows taskbar, click the **Start** button 🌐, and then locate and click **Microsoft Excel 2010**. In Excel, click the **File tab** to display **Backstage** view, and then click **Open**. From your student files, locate and open the file **w11A_Fair_Growth**. Compare your screen with Figure 11.2.

Figure 11.2

Fair Growth Excel file

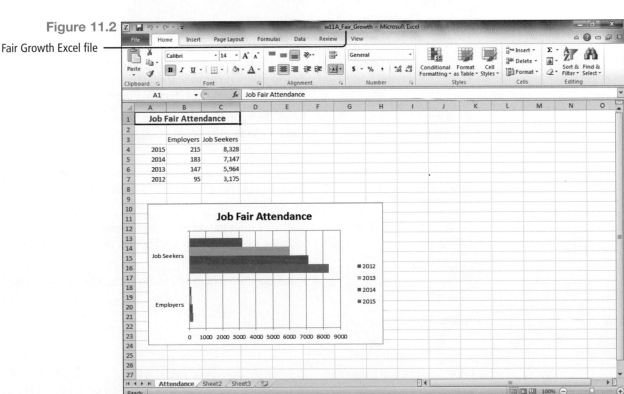

3 Right-click on a border of the *Job Fair Attendance* chart, and then from the shortcut menu, click **Copy** to copy the Excel chart to the Windows Clipboard.

4 On the Windows taskbar, click the **Word** button to make the *Lastname_Firstname_11A_Survey_Memo* document active. Immediately below the horizontal line, locate the paragraph that begins *The Minneapolis*. Click to position the insertion point at the end of the paragraph, and then press [Enter].

5 On the **Home tab**, in the **Clipboard group**, click the **Paste button arrow** to display the **Paste Options** gallery. Compare your screen with Figure 11.3.

> There are different ways to paste an Excel chart into a Word document. The displayed options vary according to the type of object you are pasting in the document.

Figure 11.3

Paste Option button ———

Paste Options ———

6 In the **Paste Options** gallery, point to each of the buttons, and then read the **ScreenTip**. Take a moment to study the table shown in Figure 11.4, which describes the various pasting options.

Paste Options

Command Name	Description
Use Destination Theme & Embed Workbook	Pastes the information applying formatting based on the destination file's theme and enables you to edit the object using Word's features without changing the source file.
Keep Source Formatting & Embed Workbook	Pastes the information using the formatting in the source file and enables you to edit the object using Word's features without changing the source file.
Use Destination Theme & Link Data	Pastes the information applying formatting based on the destination file's theme and links the data so that any editing uses the features of—and changes—the source file.
Keep Source Formatting & Link Data	Pastes the information using the formatting of the source file and links the data so that any editing uses the features of—and changes—the source file.
Picture	Pastes the information as a picture object in the document.

Figure 11.4

7 In the **Paste Options** gallery, click the **Keep Source Formatting & Embed Workbook** button .

The Excel chart displays in the Word document.

8 Click in a blank area of the chart. On the **Layout tab**, in the **Labels group**, click the **Data Labels** button, and then click **Outside End**. On the **Format tab**, in the **Size group**, click the **Shape Height spin box down arrow** to **2.1"**.

When you embed an Excel chart using the *Keep Source Formatting & Embed Workbook* paste option, you can use the Chart Tools contextual tabs in Word to edit the chart.

9 Right-click a border of the chart, and then on the Mini toolbar, click **Center** . Compare your screen with Figure 11.5.

Figure 11.5

Chart Tools contextual tabs

Chart centered
Data Labels inserted

10 At the bottom right corner of the chart, click to the left of the paragraph mark to deselect the chart. **Save** your changes.

11 On the Windows taskbar, click the **Excel** button to make the *w11A_Fair_Growth* file active.

Because you embedded the chart, the changes you made in your Word document are not reflected in the Excel workbook—the source file.

12 **Close** Excel without saving changes.

Activity 11.02 | Using Paste Special to Embed an Access Table

Recall that Access is a database application. You can copy an Access table, or query, and paste it in a Word document in a tabular format. The embedded table can be modified in Word without opening or changing the Access file.

1 On the Windows taskbar, click the **Start** button 🔵, and then locate and click **Microsoft Access 2010**. In Access, from your student files, locate and open the file **w11A_Fair_Participants**. In the *Security Warning* Message Bar displayed immediately below the Ribbon, click the **Enable Content** button.

Although the Access 2010 files display *(Access 2007)* in the title bar, the files are Access 2010 files.

Alert! | What If I Don't Have Access?

If you don't have Microsoft Access installed on your computer, consult your instructor.

---

2 On the left side of the Access window, under **Tables**, double-click the table **Major_Participants**. Compare your screen with Figure 11.6.

Figure 11.6

w11A_Fair_Participants Access file

Major_Participants table

3 Press Ctrl + A to select the entire table. On the **Home tab**, in the **Clipboard group**, click the **Copy** button. **Close** Access.

4 In your Word document, with the insertion point immediately to the right of the chart, press Enter. On the **Home tab**, in the **Clipboard group**, click the **Paste button arrow** to display the **Paste Options** gallery. Point to each of the three buttons and read the **ScreenTip**.

Recall that the displayed buttons will vary depending on the type of object you are pasting—in this case, an Access table.

5 In the **Paste Options** gallery, click **Paste Special**. In the displayed **Paste Special** dialog box, under **As**, click each option and then under **Result**, for each option, read the description of how the Access data will be pasted in the document.

The Paste Special feature enables the user to insert data from the Access table in various formats.

6 In the **Paste Special** dialog box, under **As**, click **Formatted Text (RTF)**. Compare your screen with Figure 11.7.

> Selecting the Formatted Text (RTF) option will insert the data in a table format. By default, the Paste option button is selected.

Figure 11.7

Paste Special dialog box

Paste option button selected

As box

Result description

7 In the **Paste Special** dialog box, click **OK**.

8 In the table, click in the first cell—*Company*. On the **Design tab**, in the **Table Styles group**, click the **More** button ⬇. In the **Table Styles** gallery, under **Built-In**, in the second row, select the third table style—**Light List – Accent 2**.

> The Access table is embedded into the Word document. Because the data was inserted in a tabular format, you can use the Table Tools contextual tabs in Word to modify the table.

9 On the **Layout tab**, in the **Data group**, click the **Sort** button. In the **Sort** dialog box, be sure *Company* displays in the **Sort by** box. Under **My list has**, be sure the **Header row** option button is selected, and then click **OK**.

> The table is sorted to display company names in ascending order. By embedding the table, you can edit the data in Word, without changing the original Access file. Additionally, if changes are made to the Access file, they will not be reflected in the Word document.

10 On the **Layout tab**, in the **Table group**, click the **Properties** button. In the **Table Properties** dialog box, on the **Table tab**, under **Alignment**, click **Center**, and then click **OK**. Deselect the table, and then compare your screen with Figure 11.8.

Figure 11.8

Table Style applied and table centered

Company names in ascending order

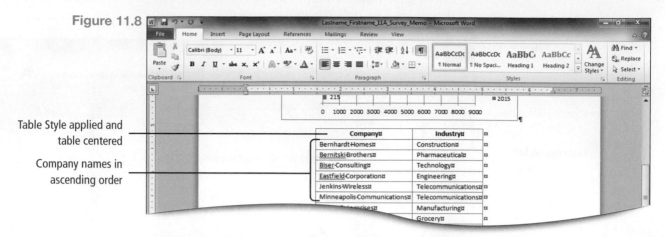

11 In the table, **Ignore All** spelling errors, and then **Save** 💾 your changes.

Activity 11.03 | Embedding a PowerPoint File

1 On the Windows taskbar, click the **Start** button 🔵, and then locate and click **Microsoft PowerPoint 2010**. If necessary, Maximize 🔲 the PowerPoint window.

> PowerPoint is used to create slide show presentations. You can embed an entire PowerPoint presentation within a Word document.

2 From **Backstage** view, open the file **w11A_Publicity_Strategy**. Compare your screen with Figure 11.9.

> A PowerPoint presentation contains individual slides that may include text, graphic elements, and other objects. This file contains six slides and is formatted with the *Urban* theme.

Figure 11.9

File opened in PowerPoint

Slide 1

Number of slides

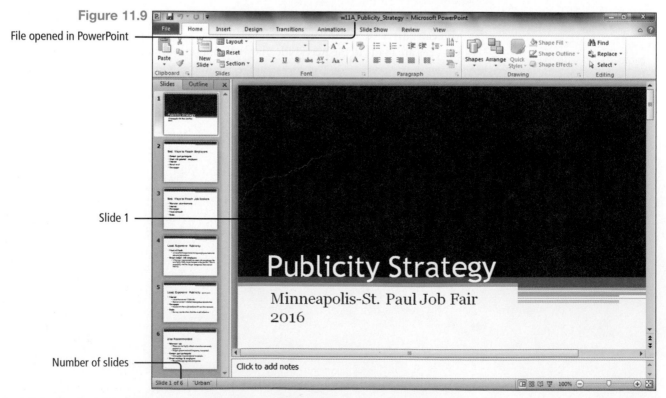

3 **Close** ![close button] **PowerPoint.**

It is good practice to view a file before embedding it to be sure that the file contains the correct information.

4 In your Word document, locate the paragraph that begins *Based on the results*. Position the insertion point at the end of the paragraph, and then press [Enter]. On the **Insert tab**, in the **Text group**, click the **Object** button.

The displayed Object dialog box enables you to choose what type of object to insert in the document. By default, the Create New tab displays—allowing you to create a new object in a variety of formats.

5 In the **Object** dialog box, click the **Create from File** tab. Click **Browse**, navigate to your student files, click **w11A_Publicity_Strategy**, and then click **Insert**. Compare your screen with Figure 11.10.

The Create from File tab allows you to embed an existing object—in this case, a PowerPoint file. The file name displays in the File name box.

Figure 11.10

Object dialog box ——

File to be embedded ——

6 Click **OK**. Notice that the first slide of the PowerPoint presentation displays in the Word document.

7 Double-click the PowerPoint object, and then compare your screen with Figure 11.11.

The PowerPoint presentation opens in Slide Show view and displays the first slide.

Figure 11.11

First slide displays in
Slide Show view ——

Another Way

Press ⬇ to advance to
the next slide.

8 Click the mouse button to advance to the next slide. In the same manner, view the remaining slides in the presentation. Notice that after the last click, you return to the Word document.

9 In the Word document, right-click the PowerPoint object. From the displayed shortcut menu, point to **Presentation Object**, and then click **Edit** to switch to Edit mode.

> Although you remain in Word, the Ribbon changes to PowerPoint features. You can modify the embedded presentation without changing the original source file.

10 On the Ribbon, click the **Design tab**. In the **Themes group**, click the **More** button ⬇. Under **Built-in**, click **Newsprint**. Compare your screen with Figure 11.12.

> In the same manner as Word, themes can be changed in PowerPoint presentations.

Figure 11.12

Design tab

Newsprint theme applied

Themes group

Your view may
differ—rulers
may display

11 In the Word document, click outside the PowerPoint object to exit Edit mode. Click the slide to select the object, and then on the **Home tab**, in the **Paragraph group**, click **Center** ≡ .

12 Press Ctrl + Home. **Save** 💾 your changes.

Objective 2 | Link Objects to a Word Document

You can modify embedded objects without changing the source files. If you want to make changes to an object in a document and have those changes reflected in the original file, then *linking*, rather than embedding, the object is what you want to do. Linking is the process of inserting information from a source file into a destination file while maintaining a connection between the two.

Activity 11.04 | Linking to an Excel File

A *linked object* is an object that maintains a direct connection to the source file. Linked data is stored in the source file—for example, an Excel workbook; the linked data is not stored in the destination file—in this case, a Word document.

1 From the **Start** menu 🔵, locate and then open **Microsoft Excel 2010**. In Excel, locate and open the file **w11A_Survey_Results**. Click the **File tab** to display **Backstage** view, and then click **Save As**. Save the file to your **Word Chapter 11** folder as **Lastname_Firstname_11A_Survey_Results** Compare your screen with Figure 11.13.

Figure 11.13

File opened in Excel ———

2 On the **Insert tab**, in the **Text group**, click the **Header & Footer** button. Scroll to the bottom of **Page 1**, and then click **Click to add footer**. With the insertion point in the footer, on the **Design tab**, in the **Header & Footer Elements group**, click the **File Name** button. Compare your screen with Figure 11.14.

The default text *&[File]* displays.

Figure 11.14

Footer displays in Excel ———

3 Click in any blank cell to deselect the footer. Notice that the file name displays in the footer. **Save** 🖫 your changes, and then **Close** ⊠ Excel.

4 In your Word document, at the bottom of **Page 1**, click to position the insertion point to the left of the paragraph that begins *I have analyzed*, and then press [Ctrl] + [Enter] to insert a page break. At the top of **Page 2**, click to position the insertion point at the end of the first paragraph, and then press [Enter].

5 On the **Insert tab**, in the **Text group**, click the **Object** button. In the displayed **Object** dialog box, click the **Create from File** tab, which allows you to create a link to existing objects.

6 Click **Browse**, navigate to your **Word Chapter 11** folder, and then click **Lastname_Firstname_11A_Survey_Results**. Click **Insert**.

7 On the right side of the **Object** dialog box, select the **Link to file** check box, and then select the **Display as icon** check box. Compare your screen with Figure 11.15.

A link will be established between the Word document and the Excel spreadsheet. When linking a file, you can choose to have the entire file display in your document or simply choose to display an icon representing the linked file. In this case, by selecting the *Display as icon* check box, your linked file will display as an icon in the Word document.

Figure 11.15

Create from File tab
File name box
Link to file check box
Display as icon check box

8 In the **Object** dialog box, click the **Change Icon** button. In the **Change Icon** dialog box, in the **Icon** box, select the first icon. In the **Caption box**, select the existing text, and then type **Survey Results** Compare your screen with Figure 11.16.

Figure 11.16

Change Icon dialog box
Selected icon
Caption box

9 Click **OK** two times.

> An Excel file icon with the modified caption displays in the document. Changing the caption does not change the file name of the linked file.

Another Way

Alternatively, right-click the icon, from the shortcut menu point to Linked Worksheet Object, and then click Open Link.

10 Above *Survey Results,* double-click the icon.

> Double-clicking the object icon causes the linked object—in this case, the Lastname_Firstname_11A_Survey_Results file—to open within Word.

11 Click in cell **B4**—that contains the value *34%*. Type **41** and then press Enter. Notice that the chart displays the revised *Job Seekers* value for *Internet.* Compare your screen with Figure 11.17.

Figure 11.17
Excel file open—
your view may differ

Edited data in cell B4

Edited Internet value
displays in chart

12 **Save** your changes, and then **Close** Excel. In your Word document, **Save** your changes.

Note | Opening a Document Containing a Linked File

If you close a Word document that contains one or more linked files, when you reopen the document a Microsoft Word message box will display. The message will prompt you to update the document with data from a linked file. Click Yes to maintain the link and update the information. Additionally, a link will not remain intact if the linked file is moved to a new location.

Activity 11.05 | Linking to Another Word Document

When linking objects in Word, you are not limited to using different Office application files. You can also link one Word document to another Word document.

1 In Word, from your student files, locate and open the file **w11A_Participant_Survey**. From **Backstage** view, save the file to your **Word Chapter 11** folder as **Lastname_Firstname_11A_Participant_Survey** Using **Quick Parts**, insert the file name in the footer. **Close** the footer area.

2 **Save** ![save icon] your changes. From **Backstage** view, **Close** the **Lastname_Firstname_ 11A_Participant_Survey** document.

3 In your **Lastname_Firstname_11A_Survey_Memo** document, if necessary, click to position the insertion point to the right of the *Survey Results* icon. Press [Tab].

4 On the **Insert tab**, in the **Text group**, click the **Object** button. In the displayed **Object** dialog box, click the **Create from File** tab. Click **Browse**, navigate to your **Word Chapter 11** folder, and then click **Lastname_Firstname_11A_Participant_Survey**. Click **Insert**.

5 On the right side of the **Object** dialog box, select the **Link to file** check box, and then select the **Display as icon** check box. In the **Object** dialog box, click the **Change Icon** button. In the **Change Icon** dialog box, in the **Caption box**, select the text, and then type **Participant Survey** Click **OK**. Compare your screen with Figure 11.18.

Figure 11.18

Object dialog box

File to be linked

Word icon with caption

6 Click **OK** to close the **Object** dialog box, and then compare your screen with Figure 11.19.

Figure 11.19

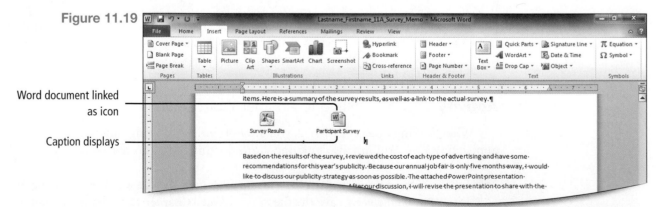

Word document linked as icon

Caption displays

7 Above *Participant Survey*, double-click the icon, and notice that the linked Word file displays.

When linking an object, it is good practice to verify that the link is working.

8 In the **Lastname_Firstname_11A_Participant_Survey** document, in the first paragraph, click to position the insertion point to the left of *Fair*, type **Job** and then press [Spacebar].

9 **Save** 🖫 your changes. **Close** ⊠ the **Lastname_Firstname_11A_Participant_Survey** document but leave Word open.

10 Select the paragraph containing the two linked files, and then on the Mini toolbar, click **Center** ≣.

More Knowledge | Editing a Linked File

You can edit a linked file by directly opening the file and making changes. If the document containing the link is open, right-click the link, and then click Update Link. If the document containing the link is closed, you will be prompted to update the data the next time you open the document.

---

11 Press [Ctrl] + [Home]. In the **Document Information Panel**, in the **Author** box, type your first and last names, and then in the **Subject** box, type your course name and section number. In the **Keywords** box, type **survey memo, linked and embedded objects Close** ⊠ the **Document Information Panel**.

12 **Save** 🖫 your changes. Print all three files—the two Word documents and the Excel *Survey Results* file—or submit electronically as directed by your instructor. **Close** ⊠ Word.

End **You have completed Project 11A** ——————————————

Project 11B Fair Flyer

Project Activities

In Activities 11.06 through 11.16, you will assist Emily Kentros, Employer Coordinator for Minneapolis-St. Paul Job Fair, in automating Word tasks by creating macros that will be executed with a single click or keyboard shortcut. These actions include inserting a specific footer, adding a formatted heading, inserting the current date and time in a header, adjusting indentation in a bulleted list, and placing quotation marks around selected text. Your completed documents will look similar to Figure 11.20.

Project Files

For Project 11B, you will need the following files:

w11B_Fair_Flyer
w11B_Fair_Memo

You will save your documents as:

Lastname_Firstname_11B_Fair_Flyer
Lastname_Firstname_11B_Fair_Memo
Lastname_Firstname_11B_Screen_Captures

Project Results

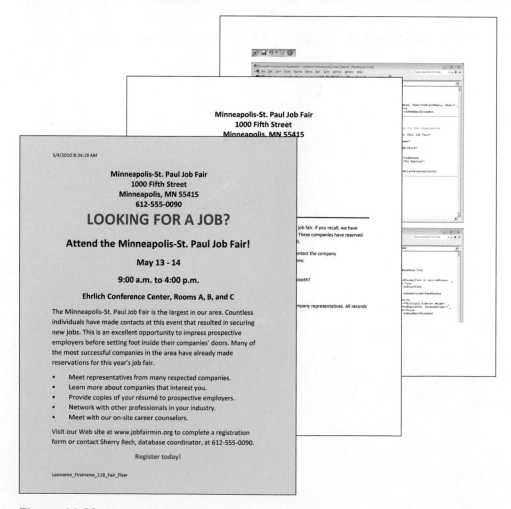

Figure 11.20
Project 11B Fair Flyer

Objective 3 | Create Macros

A *macro* is set of commands and instructions that can be grouped as a single command to accomplish a task automatically. When using Word, all macros are created in a programming language called *Visual Basic for Applications*, or *VBA*. You can use a macro to save time when performing routine editing and formatting, to combine several repetitive steps into one step, to make an option in a dialog box more accessible, or to automate a complex series of tasks. For example, you could create a macro that performs the steps to produce a customized header. The header could then be inserted into multiple documents without having to re-create the formatting steps for each document.

Activity 11.06 | Saving a Macro-Enabled Document

When you create, save, and use macros in a document, you must save the document as a Word Macro-Enabled Template (.dotm) or as a Word Macro-Enabled Document (.docm). Saving a document as either a Word document (.docx) or Word Template (.dotx) will cause any macros to be removed.

1 **Start** Word. If necessary, display the rulers and formatting marks. Locate and open the file **w11B_Fair_Flyer**. From **Backstage** view, display the **Save As** dialog box, and then navigate to your **Word Chapter 11** folder.

2 In the lower portion of the dialog box, click the **Save as type arrow**, and then from the displayed list, click **Word Macro-Enabled Document**.

3 In the **File name** box, using your own name, type **Lastname_Firstname_11B_Fair_Flyer** and then compare your screen with Figure 11.21.

Figure 11.21

Word Chapter 11 folder

File name box

Save as type arrow

4 Click **Save**.

By saving your file as a macro-enabled document, new macros and changes to existing macros are automatically saved.

Activity 11.07 | Changing Macro Security Settings

When you create your own macros, you can trust the source. However, macros written by others may pose a potential security risk. Because a macro is written in programming language, files can be erased or damaged by inserting unauthorized code. This unauthorized code is called a ***macro virus***. To protect systems from this type of virus, organizations commonly set their security programs to disable macros automatically or block any e-mail attachment that contains a macro. Because the staff of Minneapolis-St. Paul Job Fair uses macros to automate some of their tasks, you will adjust the security level in Word to allow macros to run.

1 From **Backstage** view, click the **Options** button. In the displayed **Word Options** dialog box, on the left side, click **Customize Ribbon**.

Main tabs that display on the Ribbon are indicated with a checkmark.

2 In the **Main Tabs** list, locate and then click to select the **Developer** check box. Compare your screen with Figure 11.22.

The Developer tab extends the capabilities of Word—including commands for inserting content controls and creating macros.

Figure 11.22

Word Options dialog box

Main Tabs list

Customize Ribbon selected

Developer tab selected

3 Click **OK** to close the Word options dialog box. On the Ribbon, notice that the **Developer tab** displays.

4 On the **Developer tab**, in the **Code group**, click the **Macro Security** button. Compare your screen with Figure 11.23, and then take a few moments to study the table in Figure 11.24 to examine macro security settings.

> Macro Settings display in the Trust Center dialog box. Your selected option may differ.

Figure 11.23

Trust Center dialog box

Macro Settings—your selected option may differ

Macro Security Settings

Macro Security Settings	Description of Security Settings
Disable all macros without notification	Macros will not run in a document, and no notification message will display.
Disable all macros with notification	Macros will not run in a document, but a notification message will display with an option to run macros.
Disable all macros except digitally signed macros	Macros that have a valid digital signature and have been confirmed by Microsoft will be allowed to run.
Enable all macros	All macros will run. This option is a high security risk.

Figure 11.24

5 In the **Trust Center** dialog box, under **Macro Settings**, click to select the **Disable all macros with notification** option button.

> By selecting this macro setting, opening a document that has a macro attached will cause a security warning to display and give you the option to disable the macro.

6 Click **OK** to close the **Trust Center** dialog box, and then **Save** 🔲 your changes.

Activity 11.08 | Recording a Keyboard-Activated Macro

The process of creating a macro is called *recording* a macro. Before you record a macro, the first thing you should do is plan the exact steps you will perform; and it is a good idea to write down those steps. For example, if you want to apply bold formatting and a specific Text Effect style during the recording of a macro, review the steps required to achieve this formatting before you begin recording the macro. You then can record the macro by completing all of the steps. In this activity, you will create a macro that will insert the file name in the footer.

1 Right-click in the footer area, and then click **Edit Footer**.

2 On the **Developer tab**, in the **Code group**, click the **Record Macro** button.

3 In the displayed **Record Macro** dialog box, in the **Macro name** box, type **Footer**

> Each macro must be given a unique name. It is a good idea to name the macro with a descriptive name to help you recall the function of the macro. If you reuse a name, the new macro will replace the original macro. Macro names cannot contain spaces; however, you can use underscores to improve readability.

4 Under **Store macro in**, if necessary, click the Store macro in arrow, and then click *All Documents (Normal.dotm)*.

> By default, the macro will be saved in the Normal macro-enabled template so that it can be used in other documents.

5 In the **Description** box, click to position the insertion point, and then type **Inserts the file name in a footer** Compare your screen with Figure 11.25.

Figure 11.25

Record Macro dialog box
Macro name
Button icon
Store macro in box
Macro description
Keyboard icon

6 Under **Assign macro to**, click the **Keyboard** icon.

> You can assign a button or a shortcut key to a macro. By clicking the *Keyboard* icon, you can assign a shortcut key that, when pressed, will cause the macro to run, or be executed.

7 In the displayed **Customize Keyboard** dialog box, with the insertion point in the **Press new shortcut key** box, press and hold ⌈Alt⌋, and then press ⌈F⌋.

> *Alt+F* displays in the *Press new shortcut key* box. If the shortcut key you choose is already in use, you should select another combination so that the original shortcut is not replaced. If the combination of keys is already in use, it will display next to *Currently assigned to*.

8 Near the bottom of the dialog box, click the **Assign** button. Compare your screen with Figure 11.26.

Alt+F displays in the *Current keys* box. This keyboard sequence is assigned to the macro that is selected in the *Commands* box—your *Footer* macro. The macro name displays as *Normal.NewMacros.Footer* to indicate that the macro is user-created and stored in the Normal template.

Figure 11.26

Commands box

Press new shortcut key box

Current keys box

9 Near the bottom of the **Customize Keyboard** dialog box, click the **Close** button. Point anywhere in the document, and notice that the pointer changes to a 🔲 pointer. Compare your screen with Figure 11.27.

The 🔲 pointer indicates that you are now in Recording mode. Any actions that you make will be recorded as part of the macro until you turn off the recording of the macro. It is important to take your time as you perform each action so that extra steps are not recorded as part of the macro.

Figure 11.27

Pointer

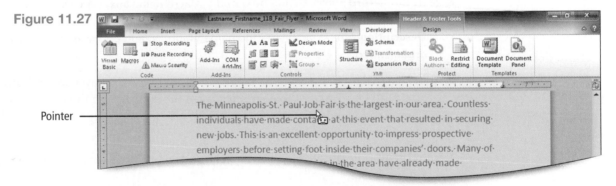

10 With the insertion point in the footer, on the **Design tab**, in the **Insert group**, click the **Quick Parts** button. From the displayed list, click **Field**. In the **Field** dialog box, under **Field names**, scroll and then click **FileName**. Click **OK**. On the **Design tab**, in the **Close group**, click the **Close Header and Footer** button.

11 On the **Developer tab**, in the **Code group**, click the **Stop Recording** button.

All of the actions you performed in Steps 10 and 11 are recorded as part of the *Footer* macro. The same actions can be repeated by pressing [Alt] + [F].

12 To test your macro, right-click in the footer area, and then click **Edit Footer**. Select the existing text, and then press ⌦. Press ⌥ + Ⓕ.

The macro runs—inserting the file name in the footer, and then closing the footer area.

Alert! | What If My Macro Doesn't Work?

If your macro doesn't work properly, on the Developer tab, in the Code group, click the Macros button. In the Macros dialog box, click the name of your macro, and then click Delete. Close the dialog box, and then record the macro again.

---

13 Save 🖫 your changes.

More Knowledge | Pausing While Recording a Macro

When recording a macro, you can temporarily suspend the recording if you need to perform other actions, and then resume the recording. To pause the recording, in the Code group, click the Pause Recording button. When you are ready to continue, click the Resume Recorder button.

Activity 11.09 | Recording a Button-Activated Macro

You can assign a macro to a command button that displays on the Quick Access Toolbar or on the Ribbon. In this activity, you will create a macro to insert a heading and assign it to a button.

1 Press Ⓒⓣⓡⓛ + Ⓗⓞⓜⓔ. Press Ⓔⓝⓣⓔⓡ, and then press ⬆ to position the insertion point in the first paragraph.

2 On the **Developer tab**, in the **Code group**, click the **Record Macro** button.

3 In the **Record Macro** dialog box, in the **Macro name box**, type **Heading** In the **Store macro in** box, be certain that *All Documents (Normal.dotm)* displays. In the **Description** box, type **Inserts the name, address, and phone number for the organization**

4 Under **Assign macro to**, click the **Button** icon. In the displayed **Word Options** dialog box, with **Quick Access Toolbar** selected in the left pane, in the right pane, under **Choose commands from**, click *Normal.NewMacros.Heading*—the name Word uses for your *Heading* macro.

5 In the middle of the dialog box, click the **Add** button. Compare your screen with Figure 11.28.

Figure 11.28

Word Options dialog box

Heading macro

Quick Access Toolbar selected

Add button

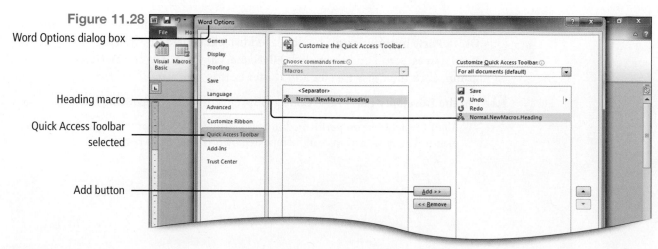

6 On the right side of the **Word Options** dialog box, click to select *Normal.NewMacros.Heading*. Below the list of commands, click the **Modify** button.

7 In the **Modify Button** dialog box, under **Symbol**, in the first row, click the third symbol—a blue circle containing a white *i*. In the **Display name** box, notice that the macro name displays. Compare your screen with Figure 11.29.

Figure 11.29

Modify Button dialog box

Symbol selected

8 Click **OK**. In the list of Quick Access Toolbar commands, notice that the selected symbol displays to the left of *Normal.NewMacro.Heading*. Click **OK** to close the **Word Options** dialog box. Notice that the 🔲 pointer displays in the document and the *Heading* button you created displays on the Quick Access Toolbar.

9 Type the following text, pressing [Enter] after each of the first three lines.

Minneapolis Job Fair

1000 Fifth Street

Minneapolis, MN 55415

612-555-0090

10 With the insertion point to the right of the phone number, press [Ctrl] + [Shift] + [Home] to select all four lines.

> When you are recording a macro, you must use the keyboard to select text; you cannot drag.

11 With all four lines selected, on the **Home tab**, change the style to **No Spacing**, change the **Font Size** to **18**, click **Bold** [B], and then click **Center** [≡].

12 On the **Developer tab**, in the **Code group**, click the **Stop Recording** button. Compare your screen with Figure 11.30.

All of the text you typed and formatted is saved as part of the macro.

Figure 11.30

Inserted heading

13 Press Ctrl + Home, and then **Save** 💾 your changes.

Activity 11.10 │ Creating a Macro That Runs Automatically

You can create a macro that runs automatically based on the occurrence of a specific event—for example, when you open a Word document or exit Word. In this activity, you will create a macro to insert the date and time in the header when you close a document.

1 On the **Developer tab**, in the **Code group**, click the **Record Macro** button.

2 In the **Record Macro** dialog box, in the **Macro name** box, type **AutoClose** Click the **Store macro in arrow**, and then click **Lastname_Firstname_11B_Fair_Flyer (document)**. Compare your screen with Figure 11.31, and then take a few moments to study the table in Figure 11.32 to examine the categories of automatic macros.

AutoClose is a reserved word understood by Microsoft Word. When the term is used as a macro name, the macro will automatically run when the document is closed. Therefore, you do not need to assign a keystroke or button to the macro.

Figure 11.31

Record Macro dialog box

Macro name box

Store macro in arrow

Automatic Macros	
Macro Name	**Description of Automatic Macros**
AutoExec	Runs when Word starts.
AutoOpen	Runs each time a document is opened.
AutoNew	Runs each time a new document is created.
AutoClose	Runs each time a document is closed.
AutoExit	Runs whenever you exit Word.

Figure 11.32

> **Alert! | Should the Macro Be Saved in the Normal Template?**
>
> Be careful to save this macro in your document, rather than in the Normal.dotm template. If you save the macro in the Normal.dotm template on your computer, the macro will run every time any document is closed.

3 Click **OK** to start recording.

4 On the **Insert tab**, in the **Header & Footer group**, click the **Header** button, and then from the displayed list, click **Edit Header**.

5 Press Ctrl + A, and then press Del.

Any existing text is selected, and then deleted. Because this macro will insert the current date and time whenever the document is closed, you want any existing content to be deleted.

6 On the **Design tab**, in the **Insert group**, click the **Date & Time** button.

7 In the **Date and Time** dialog box, from the displayed list, click the thirteenth format—with the date and time displayed in seconds. Compare your screen with Figure 11.33.

Figure 11.33

Date and Time dialog box

Selected date and time format (your date and time will differ)

8 Click **OK** to close the **Date and Time** dialog box. On the **Design tab**, in the **Close group**, click the **Close Header and Footer** button.

9 Click the **Developer tab**. In the **Code group**, click the **Stop Recording** button.

10 Save 🔲 your changes. From **Backstage** view, click **Close** to close your document without exiting Word. Compare your screen with Figure 11.34.

When you close your document, the *AutoClose* macro runs—inserting the current date and time in the header. Because this change is made while closing the document, a Microsoft Word message box displays prompting you to save your changes.

Figure 11.34

Date and time inserted in header (your date and time will differ)

Microsoft Word message box

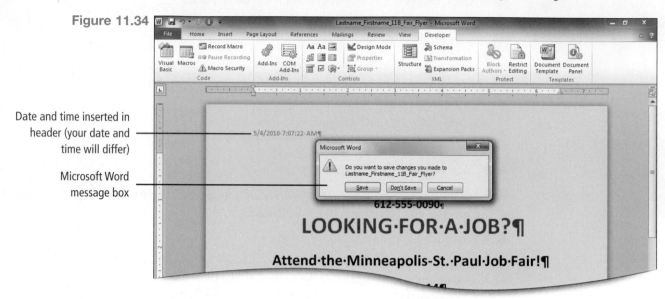

11 In the **Microsoft Word** message box, click **Save** to save your changes and close the document.

Objective 4 | Use Macros

After a macro has been recorded, it can be reused so that you can work more efficiently.

Activity 11.11 | Running a Macro

1 Click the **File tab**, and then open the file **w11B_Fair_Memo**. Display the **Save As** dialog box, and then navigate to your **Word Chapter 11** folder. In the lower portion of the dialog box, click the **Save as type arrow**, and then from the displayed list, click **Word Macro-Enabled Document**.

2 In the **File name** box, using your own name, type **Lastname_Firstname_11B_Fair_Memo** and then click **Save**. If any words are flagged as spelling errors, right-click the word, and then click Ignore All.

3 With the insertion point at the beginning of your document, on the **Quick Access Toolbar**, click the button assigned to your **Heading** macro—the blue circle containing a white *i*. Click anywhere in the document to cancel the selection, and then compare your screen with Figure 11.35.

> The Heading macro is executed, and the heading information is inserted in your document. Recall that although you created the *Heading* macro in your *11B_Fair_Flyer* document, the macro was saved in the Normal template, allowing it to be available to other documents.

Figure 11.35

Heading inserted in document

4 At the bottom of the page, in the footer area, right-click, and then click **Edit Footer**.

5 Press [Alt] + [F]. If necessary, scroll to the bottom of the page to view the footer.

> The *Footer* macro runs—inserting the file name in the footer and then closing the footer area.

6 Press [Ctrl] + [Home], and then **Save** 🖫 your changes.

Activity 11.12 │ Editing a Macro in the Visual Basic Editor

One way to edit macros is by using the ***Visual Basic Editor***, or ***VBE***. The Visual Basic Editor enables you to view the programming code for existing macros. You can use the Visual Basic Editor either to edit a macro or to create a new macro.

1 Locate the first paragraph of the document, and notice that it contains the text *Minneapolis Job Fair*.

> Recall that the name of the organization is Minneapolis-St. Paul Job Fair.

2 On the **Developer tab**, in the **Code group**, click the **Macros** button. In the **Macros** dialog box, click the **Heading** macro, and then click the **Edit** button. If necessary, maximize the *Normal-NewMacros (Code)* pane. Compare your screen with Figure 11.36.

> The Visual Basic Editor displays the code associated with the *Footer* and *Heading* macros. A macro ***procedure***—a block of programming code that performs one or more tasks—begins with the term *Sub* and ends with the term *End Sub*. The name following the word *Sub* indicates the name of the procedure. The description that you typed when you created the *Heading* macro displays as a ***comment***. A comment is a line of text that is used solely for documentation—for example, the name of the individual who wrote the macro or the purpose of the macro. A comment is preceded by a single quotation mark, displays in green text, and is skipped when the macro runs.

Figure 11.36

Visual Basic Editor ———

Heading macro code,
typed text displays
in quotes

Alert! | Why Does My Visual Basic Editor Display Differently?

Depending upon how the Visual Basic Editor was last used, different panes may be displayed. For purposes of this instruction, the only panes that are required are the Project pane on the left and the Code pane on the right.

---

3 In the pane on the right, locate the text *Minneapolis Job Fair*. Click to position the insertion point to the right of *Minneapolis*, and then type **-St. Paul**

> You are editing the macro so that when it runs, the correct name of the organization displays.

4 Near the top of the window, on the toolbar, click the **Save Normal** button 🖫 to save changes to your macro code.

Another Way

Alternatively, at the top right of the Visual Basic Editor window, click the Close button.

5 On the menu bar, click **File**, and then from the displayed list, click **Close and Return to Microsoft Word**.

6 In the **Lastname_Firstname_11B_Fair_Memo** document, delete the heading text—the first four paragraphs—leaving one blank paragraph above the word *MEMO*. On the **Quick Access Toolbar**, click the button assigned to your **Heading** macro, and then compare your screen with Figure 11.37.

The edited text displays in the heading.

Figure 11.37

Edited text in macro displays

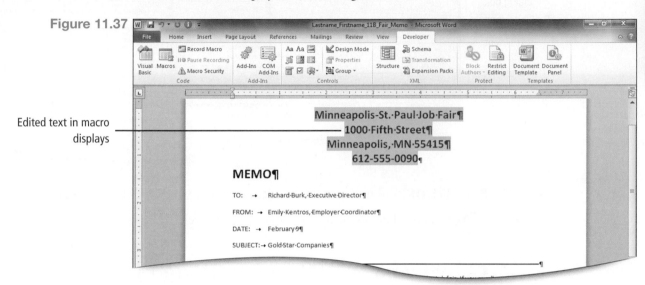

7 Click anywhere in the document to cancel the selection, and then **Save** your changes.

Activity 11.13 | Using a Built-in Word Macro

Word has many macros that are already built-in and available in each document. In this activity, you will use a macro that will allow you to adjust the size of the indents for a bulleted list.

1 In the document, locate and select the four bulleted paragraphs.

2 On the **Developer tab**, in the **Code group**, click the **Macros** button. In the **Macros** dialog box, click the **Macros in arrow**, and then click **Word commands**. Under **Macro name**, scroll as necessary, and then from the displayed list, click **AdjustListIndents**. Note: Macro names are in alphabetical order.

A list of available Word commands (macros) displays. The Description area explains what a selected command will do. The *AdjustListIndents* command allows you to modify the indenting of a bulleted or numbered list.

3 In the **Macros** dialog box, click the **Run** button. In the **Adjust Line Indents** dialog box, click the **Bullet position spin box up arrow** to **0.4"**. Click the **Text indent spin box up arrow** to **0.6"**. Compare your screen with Figure 11.38.

Figure 11.38

4 Click **OK**, and notice that the indentation of the bulleted list has changed.

5 Click anywhere in the document to cancel the selection, and then **Save** 🖫 your changes.

Objective 5 | Write a Procedure in VBA

You can use the Visual Basic Editor to write code in the Visual Basic for Applications language. To write effective procedures, you should take a formal course in VBA programming. However, you can learn the basic elements of a VBA code for a macro by entering a prewritten program.

Activity 11.14 | Writing a Procedure in VBA to Apply Quotation Marks

In this activity, you will write a procedure to apply quotation marks to selected text.

1 On the **Developer tab**, in the **Code group**, click the **Visual Basic** button. If necessary, Maximize 🔲 the Normal-NewMacros (Code) window.

The code for the *Footer* and *Heading* macros displays.

2 In the **Heading** macro, position the insertion point to the right of *End Sub*, and then press [Enter]. Using your own first and last names, type the following text, pressing [Enter] after each line—except the last line. Compare your screen with Figure 11.39.

Sub Quotes()

'

'Quotes Macro

'Macro created by Firstname Lastname

'

Quote\$ = Chr\$ (34)

Selection.InsertBefore Quote\$

Selection.InsertAfter Quote\$

> The first line indicates that the following section of code is named *Quotes*. The name of the macro is followed by two parentheses with no space between them. When you type the *Sub* statement, an *End Sub* statement is added automatically.
>
> The next four lines, formatted with a green font color, begin with a single quotation mark, indicating that these are comments.
>
> The remaining four lines you typed are the actual instructions that determine what actions will be performed when the macro is executed.

Figure 11.39

3 At the top of the **Microsoft Visual Basic for Applications** window, click **File**, and then from the displayed list, click **Close and Return to Word**.

4 In the paragraph immediately below the horizontal line, select the text *Gold Star*.

5 On the **Developer tab**, in the **Code group**, click the **Macros** button. In the **Macros** dialog box, click the **Macros in arrow**, and then click **All active templates and documents**. In the list of macro names, click **Quotes**. Compare your screen with Figure 11.40.

Figure 11.40

Macros dialog box

Quotes

Macros in box

6 In the **Macros** dialog box, click the **Run** button. Notice that quotation marks are inserted before and after the selected text.

Alert! | Did You Receive an Error Message?

Any typing error in the program code will cause a compilation error that prevents the macro from running properly. When this occurs, the Visual Basic Editor will open, and the line with the error will be highlighted. The usual cause of error is misspelling. For example, if you type *InsertBefore* as *Insert Before*, the program will not work. Also, if you type *End Sub* at the end of a macro, and the program has already inserted this command, the program will display a compile error. You can correct your mistake in the editor, save your changes, and then close the editor.

---

7 Click anywhere in the document to cancel the selection, and then **Save** 🖫 your changes.

Activity 11.15 │ Creating Screen Captures

There are several ways to capture images of your screen. In a Word document, you can use the *Screenshot Tool*. This feature allows you to capture an image of any open window and automatically paste the image into the active Word document. In this activity, you will capture images of your macro codes and the Quick Access Toolbar.

1 On the **Developer tab**, in the **Code group**, click the **Visual Basic** button.

The Visual Basic code associated with all three macros in the document displays.

2 On the Windows taskbar, point to the **Word** icon, and then click the **Lastname_Firstname_11B_Fair_Memo** document to make it active.

3 Press [Ctrl] + [N] to display a new document. Save the document in your **Word Chapter 11** folder as **Lastname_Firstname_11B_Screen_Captures** Right-click in the footer area, and then click **Edit Footer**. Press [Alt] + [F] to insert the file name in the footer.

4 On the **Insert tab**, in the **Illustrations group**, click the **Screenshot** button. Compare your screen with Figure 11.41.

> The Available Windows gallery displays thumbnails of all open windows that are not minimized. In this case, the *Lastname_Firstname_11B_Fair_Memo* and *Visual Basic Editor* display. The Screen Clipping option allows you to select only a portion of an open window for the screen capture.

Figure 11.41

Available Windows gallery

Lastname_Firstname_
11B_Fair_Memo

Visual Basic Editor

Screen Clipping option

5 In the **Available Windows** gallery, click **Screen Clipping**.

> The *Lastname_Firstname_11B_Fair_Memo* document displays in a faded view and the pointer changes to a ⊞ pointer.

6 Move the ⊞ pointer to the top left corner of your screen, and then press and hold the left mouse button and drag to select only the *Quick Access Toolbar*. Release the mouse button. Compare your screen with Figure 11.42.

> The image of the Quick Access Toolbar is pasted in your *Lastname_Firstname_11B_Screen_Captures* document.

Figure 11.42

Lastname_Firstname_11B_
Screen_Captures document

Image of Quick
Access Toolbar

7 Click to the right of the image, and then press [Enter]. On the **Insert tab**, in the **Illustrations group**, click the **Screenshot** button, and then in the **Available Windows** gallery, click the thumbnail of the **Visual Basic Editor** window.

> The image of the entire Visual Basic Editor window is pasted in your *Lastname_Firstname_11B_Screen_Captures* document.

8 Click to the right of the image, and then press [Enter]. **Save** 🖫 your changes.

9 On the Windows taskbar, point to the **Word** icon, right-click the **Visual Basic Editor** window, and then click **Close**. On the taskbar, point to the **Word** icon, and then click the **Lastname_Firstname_11B_Fair_Memo** document to make it active.

10 In the **Lastname_Firstname_11B_Fair_Memo** document, press Ctrl + Home. Display the **Document Information Panel**. In the **Author** box type, your first and last names, and then in the **Subject** box, type your course name and section number. In the **Keywords** box, type **job fair memo, with macros** Close ☒ the **Document Information Panel**. **Save** 🖫 your changes, and then **Close** ☒ the document.

11 With the **Lastname_Firstname_11B_Screen_Captures** document displayed, from **Backstage** view, open the file **Lastname_Firstname_11B_Fair_Flyer**. If necessary, on the Security Warning Message Bar, click Enable Content.

12 On the **Developer tab**, in the **Code group**, click the **Visual Basic** button.

13 In the **Visual Basic Editor**, on the left side of the screen, locate the **Project - Normal** pane. Position the pointer on the right side of the Project pane, until the ⊞ pointer displays. Drag to the right until the full name for the **Project (Lastname_Firstname_11B_Fair_Flyer)** folder displays. Under **Project (Lastname_Firstname_11B_Fair_Flyer)**, double-click the **Modules** folder, and then double-click **NewMacros**. Compare your screen with Figure 11.43.

> The code for the *AutoClose* macro displays. Because this macro is stored only in this document (project), this code displays separately from the other macro codes that are stored in the Normal template.

Figure 11.43

Project pane
Project (Lastname_Firstname_11B_Fair_Flyer)
Modules folder
NewMacros
AutoClose code

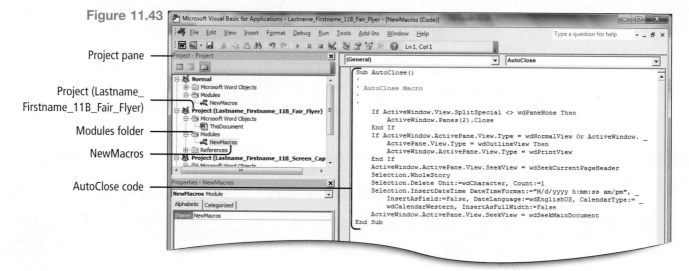

14 On the Windows taskbar, point to the **Word** icon, and then click the **Lastname_Firstname_11B_Screen_Captures** document to make it active.

15 On the **Insert tab**, in the **Illustrations group**, click the **Screenshot** button, and then in the **Available Windows** gallery, click the thumbnail of the **Visual Basic Editor**.

> The image of the entire Visual Basic Editor window is pasted in your *Lastname_Firstname_11B_Screen_Captures* document.

16 With the image selected, on the **Format tab**, in the **Size group**, click the **Crop** button. Point to the bottom center cropping handle, and drag upward until the bottom of the image is immediately below the last line of code—*End Sub*. Scroll as necessary, and deselect the image. Compare your screen with Figure 11.44.

> By cropping the image, it now displays at the bottom of Page 1.

Figure 11.44

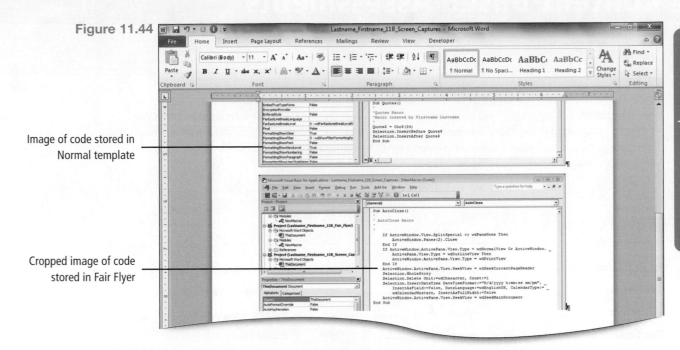

Image of code stored in Normal template

Cropped image of code stored in Fair Flyer

17 **Save** 🖫 your changes. **Close** ⊠ the document. **Close** ⊠ the Visual Basic Editor.

18 In the **Lastname_Firstname_11B_Fair_Flyer** document, delete the heading—the first four paragraphs, leaving one blank paragraph above the paragraph that begins *Looking*. On the **Quick Access Toolbar**, click the button for your **Heading** macro. Press Ctrl + Home.

19 Display the **Document Information Panel**. In the **Author** box type your first and last names, and then in the **Subject** box, type your course name and section number. In the **Keywords** box, type **job fair flyer, with macros Close** ⊠ the **Document Information Panel**. **Save** 🖫 your changes.

Activity 11.16 | Restoring Default Settings

Because you will not need the macros you created in the Normal template after completing this project, you will delete them and restore the default settings you changed.

1 On the **Developer tab**, in the **Code group**, click the **Macros** button. In the **Macros** dialog box, in the **Macros in** box, be sure **All active templates and documents** displays. Under **Macro name**, click **Footer**, and then click the **Delete** button. In the **Microsoft Word** message box, click **Yes**.

2 Using the same technique, **Delete** the **Heading** and **Quotes** macros.

You are not deleting the *AutoClose* macro because it is stored only in this document.

3 Display **Backstage** view, and then click **Options**. In the **Word Options** dialog box, click **Customize Ribbon**. Under **Main Tabs**, click to deselect the **Developer** check box.

4 On the left side of the **Word Options** dialog box, click **Quick Access Toolbar**. On the right side, under **Customize Quick Access Toolbar**, click **Normal.NewMacros.Heading**. In the middle, click the **Remove** button, and then click **OK**.

5 **Close** ⊠ Word. In the **Microsoft Word** message box, click **Save** to save your changes.

6 Print your three documents—the flyer, the memo, and the screen captures—or submit electronically as directed by your instructor.

End **You have completed Project 11B**

Content-Based Assessments

Summary

When using Word, you can insert objects—such as other Office application files—into a Word document either by linking to the object or embedding the object in the document. In addition, you can automate tasks when using Word by creating macros. You can record macros, use built-in macros, or type macro code. The Visual Basic Editor enables you to edit macros. You can work more efficiently in Word by using macros.

Key Terms

Matching

Match each term in the second column with its correct definition in the first column by writing the letter of the term on the blank line in front of the correct definition.

_____ 1. A program-integration technology for sharing information between Office programs.

_____ 2. A table, chart, graphic, file, or other form of information.

_____ 3. The file where an object is created.

_____ 4. The file where an object is embedded or linked.

_____ 5. An object that maintains the structure of the original application, but is not connected to the source file.

_____ 6. A command that enables the user to insert copied data in various ways.

_____ 7. An Office application used to create slide show presentations.

_____ 8. An object that maintains a direct connection to the source file.

_____ 9. A set of commands and instructions that can be grouped as a single command to accomplish a task automatically.

_____ 10. A programming language used to create macros.

_____ 11. A high security risk macro setting.

_____ 12. The process of creating a macro.

_____ 13. A macro that will automatically run when a file is closed.

_____ 14. A line of text in a macro procedure that is used solely for documentation.

_____ 15. A built-in macro code that allows you to modify the indenting of a bulleted or numbered list.

A AdjustListIndents

B AutoClose

C Comment

D Destination file

E Embedded object

F Enable all macros

G Linked object

H Macro

I Object

J OLE

K Paste Special

L PowerPoint

M Recording

N Source file

O VBA

Multiple Choice

Circle the correct answer.

1. The process of inserting information from a source file, using a format you specify, into a destination file is:

   A. copying   **B.** embedding   **C.** importing

2. What application is used to edit an Excel chart that is embedded in a Word document?

   A. Excel   **B.** OLE   **C.** Word

3. When you use the OLE feature to insert an object that maintains a connection to the source file, it is called:

   A. embedding   **B.** linking   **C.** pasting

4. The first step in creating a macro is:

   A. planning   **B.** practicing   **C.** recording

5. A macro-enabled document is saved with the file extension:

   A. .doc   **B.** .docm   **C.** .docx

6. A macro that causes files to be erased or damaged by inserting unauthorized code is a macro:

   A. virus   **B.** bug   **C.** programming error

7. Macro code can be viewed or edited in the:

   A. Visual Basic Application   **B.** Visual Basic Editor   **C.** Macro Editor

8. In VBA, all macro procedures begin with the word:

   A. Begin   **B.** Name   **C.** Sub

9. When viewing macro code, a comment line is indicated by:

   A. a single quotation mark   **B.** double quotation marks   **C.** parentheses

10. To automatically capture an image of an open window and paste the image in an active document, use:

   A. Paste Special   **B.** OLE   **C.** Screenshot Tool

Skills Review | Project **11C** Sponsorship Program

In the following Skills Review, you will use OLE to include objects and files from other Office applications in a memo to Richard Burk, Executive Director of Minneapolis-St. Paul Job Fair. The memo and related files explain the corporate sponsorship program. Your completed files will look similar to Figure 11.45.

Project Files

For Project 11C, you will need the following files:

w11C_Sponsorship_Memo   w11C_Top_Sponsors
w11C_Sponsors_Chart   w11C_Revenue
w11C_Sponsorship_Program   w11C_Agenda

You will save your files as:

Lastname_Firstname_11C_Sponsorship_Memo
Lastname_Firstname_11C_Revenue
Lastname_Firstname_11C_Agenda

Project Results

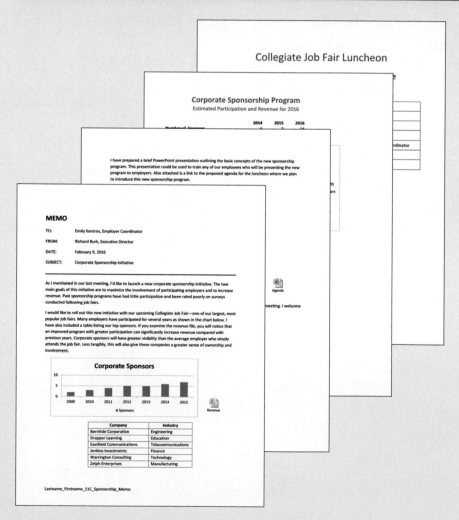

Figure 11.45

(Project 11C Sponsorship Program continues on the next page)

Content-Based Assessments

Skills Review | Project **11C** Sponsorship Program (continued)

1 **Start** Word. From your student files, locate and open the file **w11C_Sponsorship_Memo**. Save it to your **Word Chapter 11** folder as **Lastname_Firstname_11C_Sponsorship_Memo** Using **Quick Parts**, insert the file name in the footer.

a. On the Windows taskbar, click the **Start** button. Locate and then click **Microsoft Excel 2010**. In Excel, click the **File tab** to display **Backstage** view, and then click **Open**. From your student files, open the file **w11C_Sponsors_Chart**.

b. Right-click on a border of the chart, and then click **Copy**. On the Windows taskbar, click the **Word** button to make the **Lastname_Firstname_11C_Sponsorship_Memo** document active. In your Word document, locate the paragraph that begins *I would like*, click to position the insertion point at the end of the paragraph, and then press Enter.

c. On the **Home tab**, in the **Clipboard group**, click the **Paste button arrow**. From the **Paste Options** gallery, click the **Keep Source Formatting & Embed Workbook** button.

d. Click in a blank area of the chart. On the **Layout tab**, in the **Labels group**, click the **Legend** button, and then click **Show Legend at Bottom**.

e. On the **Format tab**, in the **Size group**, click the **Height spin box down arrow** to 2". Right-click on a border of the chart, and then on the Mini toolbar, click **Center**.

f. **Save** the changes in your Word document, and then **Close** Excel.

2 On the Windows taskbar, click the **Start** button. Locate and then click **Microsoft Access 2010**. From your student files, locate and open the file **w11C_Top_Sponsors**. In the **Security Warning** Message Bar, click the **Enable Content** button.

a. On the left side of the Access window, under **Tables**, double-click the **Top Sponsors** table. Press Ctrl + A to select the entire table, and then on the **Home tab**, in the **Clipboard group**, click the **Copy** button. **Close** Access.

b. In your Word document, with the insertion point to the right of the chart, press Enter. On the **Home tab**, in the **Clipboard group**, click the **Paste button arrow**.

c. In the **Paste Options** gallery, click **Paste Special**. In the **Paste Special** dialog box, under **As**, click **Formatted Text (RTF)**, and then click **OK**.

d. Click in the first cell of the table. On the **Design tab**, in the **Table Styles group**, click the **More** button. In the **Table Styles** gallery, under **Built-in**, in the second row, select the second table style—**Light List – Accent 1**.

e. On the **Layout tab**, in the **Data group**, click the **Sort** button. In the **Sort** dialog box, be sure *Company* displays in the **Sort by** box and the **Header row** option button is selected, and then click **OK**.

f. On the **Layout tab**, in the **Table group**, click the **Properties** button. In the **Table Properties** dialog box, on the **Table tab**, under **Alignment**, click **Center**, and then click **OK**. For each name in the table flagged as a spelling error, right-click, and then click **Ignore All**. **Save** your changes.

3 On **Page 2** of your Word document, click to position the insertion point at the end of the first paragraph, and then press Enter.

a. On the **Insert tab**, in the **Text group**, click the **Object** button.

b. In the **Object** dialog box, click the **Create from File tab**. Click **Browse**, navigate to your student files, click **w11C_Sponsorship_Program**, and then click **Insert**. Click **OK**.

c. Right-click the PowerPoint object, and then from the shortcut menu, point to **Presentation Object**, and then click **Edit**.

d. In the PowerPoint window, click the **Design tab**. In the **Themes group**, click the **More** button. Under **Built-in**, click **Angles**. Above the PowerPoint object, click anywhere to exit Edit mode.

e. Click the slide to select the object, and then on the **Home tab**, in the **Paragraph group**, click **Center**. Press Ctrl + Home, and then **Save** your changes.

4 On the Windows taskbar, click the **Start** button. Locate and then click **Microsoft Excel 2010**.

a. From **Backstage** view, locate and then open the file **w11C_Revenue**. Click the **File tab** to display **Backstage** view, and then click **Save As**. **Save** the file to your **Word Chapter 11** folder as **Lastname_Firstname_11C_Revenue**

(Project 11C Sponsorship Program continues on the next page)

Skills Review | Project **11C** Sponsorship Program (continued)

b. On the **Insert tab**, in the **Text group**, click the **Header & Footer** button. Scroll to the bottom of **Page 1**, and then click the text *Click to add footer*. With the insertion point in the footer box, click the **Design tab**, and then in the **Header & Footer Elements group**, click the **File Name** button. Click in any blank cell to deselect the footer.

c. **Save** your changes, and then **Close** Excel.

5 In your Word document, click to position the insertion point to the right of the chart. On the **Insert tab**, in the **Text group**, click the **Object** button.

a. In the **Object** dialog box, click the **Create from File** tab. Click **Browse**, navigate to your **Word Chapter 11** folder, and then click **Lastname_Firstname_11C_Revenue**. Click **Insert**.

b. On the right side of the **Object** dialog box, select the **Link to file** check box, and then select the **Display as icon** check box.

c. In the **Object** dialog box, click the **Change Icon** button, and then in the **Caption** box, delete the existing text, and then type **Revenue** Click **OK** two times.

d. Double-click the icon to open the Excel file. **Maximize** all open Excel windows.

e. Click in cell **D5**, which contains the value *12*. Type **14** and then press [Enter]. **Save** your changes, and then **Close** Excel.

f. Press [Ctrl] + [End]. **Save** the changes in your Word document.

6 In Word, from your student files, open the file **w11C_Agenda**. Display the **Save As** dialog box, and

then save the file to your **Word Chapter 11** folder as **Lastname_Firstname_11C_Agenda** Using **Quick Parts**, insert the file name in the footer.

a. **Save** your changes, and then from **Backstage** view, click **Close** to close the **Lastname_Firstname_11C_Agenda** document but leave Word open.

b. In your **Lastname_Firstname_11C_Sponsorship_Memo** document, on **Page 2**, click to position the insertion point to the right of the PowerPoint object. On the **Insert tab**, in the **Text group**, click the **Object** button. In the **Object** dialog box, click the **Create from File** tab. Click **Browse**, navigate to your **Word Chapter 11** folder, click **Lastname_Firstname_11C_Agenda**, and then click **Insert**.

c. On the right side of the **Object** dialog box, select the **Link to file** check box, and then select the **Display as icon** check box. Click the **Change Icon** button. In the **Caption** box, delete the existing text, and then type **Agenda** Click **OK** two times.

d. Double-click the **Agenda** icon. In the first paragraph, delete the text **Kick-Off**. **Save** your changes, and then **Close** the document.

e. Press [Ctrl] + [Home]. In the **Document Information Panel**, in the **Author** box, type your first and last names, and then in the **Subject** box, type your course name and section number. In the **Keywords** box, type **sponsorship, linked and embedded objects** **Close** the Document Information Panel. **Save** your changes.

7 Print all three files—your two Word documents and the Excel file—or submit electronically as directed by your instructor.

 You have completed Project 11C _____

Content-Based Assessments

Apply **11B** skills from these Objectives:

- ◧ Create Macros
- ◨ Use Macros
- ◩ Write a Procedure in VBA

Skills Review | Project **11D** Fair Schedule

In the following Skills Review, you will create macros to improve your efficiency in editing a letter and press release that explain the scheduled job fairs conducted by Minneapolis-St. Paul Job Fair. Your completed documents will look similar to Figure 11.46.

Project Files

For Project 11D, you will need the following files:

> w11D_Fair_Schedule
> w11D_Press_Release

You will save your documents as:

> Lastname_Firstname_11D_Fair_Schedule
> Lastname_Firstname_11D_Press_Release
> Lastname_Firstname_11D_Schedule_Code

Project Results

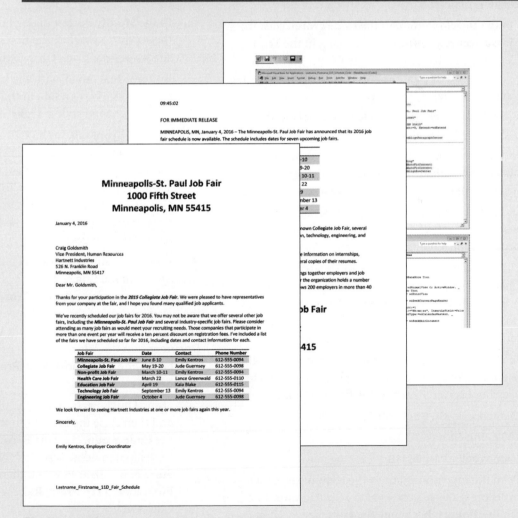

Figure 11.46

(Project 11D Fair Schedule continues on the next page)

1 **Start** Word. Locate and open the file **w11D_Fair_Schedule**. Display the **Save As** dialog box, and then navigate to your **Word Chapter 11** folder. In the lower portion of the dialog box, click the **Save as type arrow**, and then from the list, click **Word Macro-Enabled Document**. In the **File name** box, using your own name, type **Lastname_Firstname_11D_Fair_Schedule** and then click **Save**.

a. Using **Quick Parts**, insert the file name in the footer.

b. Display **Backstage** view, and then click the **Options** button. In the **Word Options** dialog box, on the left side, click **Customize Ribbon**.

c. In the **Main Tabs** list, locate and then click to select the **Developer** check box. Click **OK** to close the **Word Options** dialog box.

d. On the **Developer tab**, in the **Code group**, click the **Macro Security** button. If necessary, in the Trust Center dialog box, under Macro Settings, click to select **Disable all macros with notification**. Click **OK** to close the dialog box. **Save** your changes.

2 Press [Ctrl] + [Home]. On the **Developer tab**, in the **Code group**, click the **Record Macro** button.

a. In the **Record Macro** dialog box, in the **Macro name** box, type **Heading** Be sure the **Store macro in** box displays **All Documents (Normal.dotm)**.

b. In the **Description** box, click to position the insertion point, and then type **Inserts the organization's name and address**

c. Under **Assign macro to**, click **Keyboard**. In the **Customize Keyboard** dialog box, with the insertion point in the **Press new shortcut key** box, press and hold [Alt], and then press [H]. Click the **Assign** button, and then click the **Close** button.

d. In Recording mode, with the insertion point at the beginning of the document, type the following text, pressing [Enter] after each of the first two lines.

Minneapolis-St. Paul Job Fair

1000 Fifth Street

Minneapolis, MN 55418

e. With the insertion point to the right of the postal code, press [Ctrl] + [Shift] + [↑] to select all three lines. On the **Home tab**, change the **Font Size** to **22**, and then apply **Bold** and **Center**. On the **Developer tab**, in the **Code group**, click the **Stop Recording** button. **Save** your changes.

3 In the first cell of the table, click to position the insertion point. On the **Developer tab**, in the **Code group**, click the **Record Macro** button. In the **Record Macro** dialog box, in the **Macro name** box, type **Table_Style** Be sure the **Store macro in** box displays **All Documents (Normal.dotm)**.

a. Under **Assign macro to**, click the **Button** icon. In the **Word Options** dialog box, with **Quick Access Toolbar** selected in the left pane, in the right pane, under **Choose commands from**, click **Normal.NewMacros .Table_Style**. Click the **Add** button.

b. On the right side of the **Word Options** dialog box, click to select **Normal.NewMacros.Table_Style**. Below the list of commands, click the **Modify** button.

c. In the **Modify Button** dialog box, under **Symbol**, in the seventh row, click the first symbol—a box with shades of gray. Click **OK** two times.

d. In Recording mode, with the insertion point in the table, on the **Design tab**, in the **Table Styles group**, click the second style—**Light Shading**.

e. On the **Layout tab**, in the **Cell Size group**, click the **AutoFit** button, and then click **AutoFit Contents**. In the **Table group**, click the **Properties** button. In the **Table Properties** dialog box, under **Alignment**, click **Center**, and then click **OK**. On the **Developer tab**, in the **Code group**, click the **Stop Recording** button. **Save** your changes.

4 From your student files, open the file **w11D_Press_Release**. From **Backstage** view, display the **Save As** dialog box, and then navigate to your **Word Chapter 11** folder. In the lower portion of the dialog box, click the **Save as type arrow**, and then from the list, click **Word Macro-Enabled Document**. In the **File name** box, using your own name, type **Lastname_Firstname_11D_Press_Release** and then click **Save**.

a. Using **Quick Parts**, insert the file name in the footer, and then close the footer. On the **Developer tab**, in the **Code group**, click the **Record Macro** button. In the **Macro name** box, type **AutoClose** Click the **Store macro in arrow**, and then click **Lastname_Firstname_11D_Press_Release (document)**. Click **OK**.

b. On the **Insert tab**, in the **Header & Footer group**, click the **Header** button, and then from the displayed list, click **Edit Header**.

(Project 11D Fair Schedule continues on the next page)

c. Press Ctrl + A, and then press Del. On the **Design tab**, in the **Insert group**, click the **Date and Time** button. In the **Date and Time** dialog box, click the last option to display the time, and then click **OK**.

d. On the **Design tab**, in the **Close group**, click the **Close Header and Footer** button. On the **Developer tab**, in the **Code group**, click the **Stop Recording** button.

5 In the first cell of the table, click to position the insertion point. On the **Quick Access Toolbar**, click the button with shades of gray to run the *Table_Style* macro and format the table.

a. On the **Developer tab**, in the **Code group**, click the **Macros** button. In the **Macros** dialog box, select the **Heading** macro, and then click the **Edit** button.

b. In the **Heading** macro, locate the postal code **55418**. Position the insertion point to the right of *8*, press Backspace, and then type **5**

c. Near the top of the **Visual Basic Editor** window, click the **Save Normal** button to save your changes. On the menu bar, click **File**, and then click **Close and Return to Microsoft Word**.

d. Press Ctrl + End, and then press Alt + H to run the *Heading* macro. Deselect the text.

e. Select the text *For Immediate Release*. On the **Developer tab**, in the **Code group**, click the **Macros** button. In the **Macros** dialog box, click the **Macros in arrow**, and then click **Word commands**. Under **Macro name**, locate and click **AllCaps**, and then click **Run** to change the text to all uppercase letters. Press Ctrl + Home, and then **Save** your changes.

6 From the Windows taskbar, point to the **Word** icon, and then click your **Lastname_Firstname_11D_Fair_Schedule** document to make it active. Select the three heading paragraphs, being careful not to include the blank paragraph above the date. Press Del. Press Alt + H to run your edited *Heading* macro. **Save** your changes.

a. On the **Developer tab**, in the **Code group**, click the **Visual Basic** button. In the **Table_Style** macro, click to position the insertion point immediately below the line *End Sub*. Pressing Enter after each line, except the last line, and using your own first and last names, type the following text.

Sub Text_Format()

'Macro created by Firstname Lastname

Selection.Font.Bold = wdToggle

Selection.Font.Italic = wdToggle

b. At the top of the **Visual Basic Editor** window, click **File**, and then click **Close and Return to Word**. In the first paragraph below the *Greeting* line, select the text *2015 Collegiate Job Fair*. On the **Developer tab**, in the **Code group**, click the **Macros** button.

c. In the **Macros** dialog box, click the **Macros in arrow**, and then click **All active templates and documents**. Click **Text_Format**, and then click **Run** to apply bold and italic formatting to the selected text.

d. In the next paragraph, in a similar manner, select the text *Minneapolis-St. Paul Job Fair*, and then **Run** the **Text_Format** macro. Deselect the text, and then **Save** your changes.

e. In the **Document Information Panel**, in the **Author** box, type your first and last names, and then in the **Subject** box, type your course name and section number. In the **Keywords** box, type **schedule, macros Save** your changes, and then **Close** your **Lastname_Firstname_11D_Fair_Schedule** document.

f. On the **Developer tab**, in the **Code group**, click the **Visual Basic** button. On the Windows taskbar, point to the **Word** icon, and then click the **Lastname_Firstname_11D_Press_Release** document to make it active.

7 Press Ctrl + N to display a new document. **Save** the document to your **Word Chapter 11** folder as **Lastname_Firstname_11D_Schedule_Code** Using **Quick Parts**, insert the file name in the footer.

a. On the **Insert tab**, in the **Illustrations group**, click the **Screenshot** button. In the **Available Windows** gallery, click **Screen Clipping**. Move the + pointer to the top left corner of your screen, press and hold the left mouse button and drag to select only the **Quick Access Toolbar**. Release the mouse button to paste the selected image in your document.

b. Click to the right of the image, and then press Enter. On the **Insert tab**, in the **Illustrations group**, click the **Screenshot** button, and then in the **Available Windows** gallery, click the thumbnail of the **Visual Basic Editor** window. Click to the right of the image, and then press Enter. **Save** your changes.

(Project 11D Fair Schedule continues on the next page)

c. On the Windows taskbar, click the **Visual Basic Editor** window to make it active. On the left, locate **Project(Lastname_Firstname_11D_Press_Release)**. Immediately below the project, double-click the **Modules** folder, and then double-click **New Macros**.

d. On the Windows taskbar, make the **Lastname_Firstname_11D_Schedule_Code** document active. On the **Insert tab**, in the **Illustrations group**, click the **Screenshot** button, and then in the **Available Windows** gallery, click the thumbnail for **Visual Basic Editor**.

e. With the image selected, on the **Format tab**, in the **Size group**, click the **Crop** button. Point to the bottom center cropping handle, and then drag upward until the bottom of the image is immediately below **End Sub**.

8 Display the **Document Information Panel**, add appropriate document properties including the **Keywords** schedule, code **Save** your changes, and then **Close** your document. **Close** the Visual Basic Editor.

a. In **Lastname_Firstname_11D_Press_Release**, display the **Document Information Panel**, and add appropriate document properties including the **Keywords schedule, press release**.

b. On the **Developer tab**, in the **Code group**, click the **Macros** button. In the **Macros** dialog box, for each of the three macros—*Heading*, *Table_Style*, and *Text_Format*, select the macro, and then press Del. From **Backstage** view, display the **Word Options** dialog box, and then click **Quick Access Toolbar**. On the right side of the window, click **Normal .NewMacros.Table_Style**, click the **Remove** button, and then click **OK**. **Close** Word, and then click **Save** to save your changes.

9 Print your three documents or submit electronically as directed by your instructor.

End **You have completed Project 11D** ———————————

Content-Based Assessments

Apply **11A** skills from these Objectives:

1. Embed Objects in a Word Document
2. Link Objects to a Word Document

Mastering Word | Project **11E** Counseling Program

In the following Mastering Word project, you will use OLE to include objects and files from other Office applications in a memo to Richard Burk, Executive Director of the Minneapolis-St. Paul Job Fair. The memo and related files support a proposal to provide career counseling services at job fairs. Your completed documents will look similar to Figure 11.47.

Project Files

For Project 11E, you will need the following files:

w11E_Counseling_Memo   w11E_Career_Counseling
w11E_Counseling_Survey   w11E_Counselors
w11E_Scheduled_Fairs   w11E_Jobseeker_Survey

You will save your files as:

Lastname_Firstname_11E_Counseling_Memo
Lastname_Firstname_11E_Counselors
Lastname_Firstname_11E_Jobseeker_Survey

Project Results

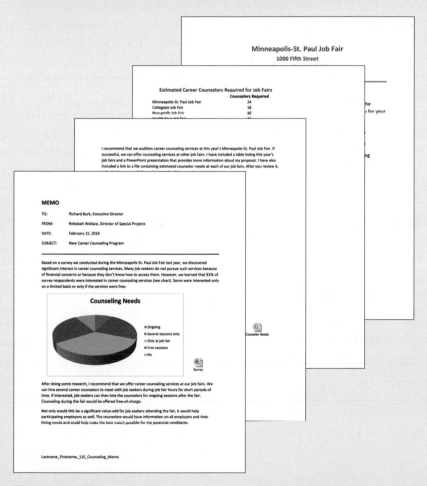

Figure 11.47

(Project 11E Counseling Program continues on the next page)

Mastering Word | Project **11E** Counseling Program (continued)

1 **Start** Word. Open the file **w11E_Counseling_Memo**, and then save it to your **Word Chapter 11** folder as **Lastname_Firstname_11E_Counseling_Memo** Using **Quick Parts**, insert the file name in the footer. From your student files, open the Excel file **w11E_Counseling_Survey**. **Copy** the chart. Make your Word document active, place the insertion point at the end of the paragraph that begins *Based on*, and then press Enter. From the **Paste Options** gallery, click the **Keep Source Formatting & Embed Workbook** button. **Center** the chart horizontally on the page. **Save** your changes, and then **Close** Excel.

2 Start **Access**, and then open the Access file **w11E_Scheduled_Fairs**. In the **Security Warning** Message Bar, click the **Enable Content** button. Open the **Job Fairs** table, and then **Copy** the entire table. **Close** Access without saving changes. In your Word document, press Ctrl + End, and then press Enter. Paste the table as **Formatted Text (RTF)**. Apply the **Light List – Accent 3** table style, and then **Center** the table in the document. **Save** your changes.

3 In the paragraph below the table, click to position the insertion point, and then press Enter. Display the **Object** dialog box, click the **Create from File** tab, locate and then **Insert** the PowerPoint file **w11E_Career_Counseling**. Right-click the PowerPoint object, and then from the shortcut menu, point to **Presentation Object** and click **Edit**. Change the **Built-in** theme to **Austin**. **Center** the presentation object in the document, and then **Save** your changes.

4 From your student files, open the **Excel** file **w11E_Counselors**. **Save** the file to your **Word Chapter 11** folder as **Lastname_Firstname_11E_Counselors** Insert the file name in the footer. **Close** Excel.

5 In your Word document, to the right of the chart, click to position the insertion point. **Insert** the

Lastname_Firstname_11E_Counselors file as a linked file displayed as an icon with the modified caption **Counselor Needs** Double-click the inserted icon, click in cell **B5**, and then type **10** Press Enter, **Save** your changes, and then **Close** Excel. **Save** the changes in your Word document.

6 From your student files, open the **Word** file **w11E_Jobseeker_Survey**. Save the file to your **Word Chapter 11** folder as **Lastname_Firstname_11E_Jobseeker_Survey** Insert the file name in the footer. In the **Document Information Panel**, in the **Author** box, type your first and last names, and then in the **Subject** box, type your course name and section number. In the **Keywords** box, type **survey, linked Save** your changes, and then **Close** the document.

7 In your **Lastname_Firstname_11E_Counseling_Memo** document, on **Page 1**, click to position the insertion point to the right of the chart. Insert the file **Lastname_Firstname_11E_Jobseeker_Survey** as a linked file displayed as an icon with the modified caption **Survey** Double-click the **Survey** icon. In the first paragraph, position the insertion point to the left of *Fair*, type **Job** and then press Spacebar. **Save** your changes, and then **Close** the *Survey* document.

8 At the bottom of **Page 1**, position the insertion point to the left of the last paragraph that begins *I recommend*, and then insert a **Page Break**. Press Ctrl + Home. In the **Document Information Panel**, in the **Author** box, type your first and last names, and then in the **Subject** box, type your course name and section number. In the **Keywords** box, type **counseling, linked and embedded objects Close** the Document Information Panel. **Save** your changes.

9 Print all three files—your two Word documents and the Excel file—or submit electronically as directed by your instructor.

End **You have completed Project 11E** ─────────────

Content-Based Assessments

Apply 11B skills from these Objectives:

- 3 Create Macros
- 4 Use Macros
- 5 Write a Procedure in VBA

Mastering Word | Project 11F Collegiate Fair

In the following Mastering Word project, you will create macros to assist you with editing documents that will be sent to employers who are registered for the Collegiate Fair conducted by Minneapolis-St. Paul Job Fair. Your completed documents will look similar to Figure 11.48.

Project Files

For Project 11F, you will need the following files:

New blank Word document
w11F_Collegiate_Fair
w11F_Recruiting_Tips

You will save your documents as:

Lastname_Firstname_11F_Collegiate_Fair
Lastname_Firstname_11F_Recruiting_Tips
Lastname_Firstname_11F_Collegiate_Code

Project Results

Figure 11.48

(Project 11F Collegiate Fair continues on the next page)

Content-Based Assessments

Mastering Word | Project 11F Collegiate Fair (continued)

1 **Start** Word. Locate and open the file **w11F_Collegiate_Fair**. Save the file to your **Word Chapter 11** folder as a **Word Macro-Enabled Document** with the file name **Lastname_Firstname_11F_Collegiate_Fair** Display the **Developer tab**, and then change your **Macro Security** setting to **Disable all macros with notification**.

2 Right-click in the footer area, and then click **Edit Footer**. Display the **Record Macro** dialog box, and then in the **Macro name** box, type **Footer** Be sure the **Store macro in** box displays **All Documents (Normal.dotm)**. For the **Description**, type Inserts the file name Assign the shortcut key Alt + F. In Recording mode, use **Quick Parts** to insert the **FileName**, click **Close Header and Footer**, and then click **Stop Recording**. **Save** your changes.

3 Display the **Record Macro** dialog box. In the **Record Macro** dialog box, in the **Macro name** box, type **Header** Be sure the **Store macro in** box displays **All Documents (Normal.dotm)**. Click the **Button** icon, and then in the **Word Options** dialog box, **Add** the **Normal.NewMacros .Header** to the **Quick Access Toolbar**. Click the **Modify** button, and then under **Symbol**, in the first row, click the third button—a blue circle containing a white *i*. In Recording mode, on the **Insert tab**, click the **Insert Header** button, and then click **Edit Header**. Press Ctrl + A, press Tab, type **Minneapolis-St. Paul** and then click **Close Header and Footer**. Click **Stop Recording**.

4 From your student files, open the file **w11F_Recruiting_Tips**. Save the file to your **Word Chapter 11** folder as a **Word Macro-Enabled Document** with the file name **Lastname_Firstname_11F_Recruiting_Tips** Right-click in the footer area, click **Edit Footer**, and then press Alt + F to insert the file name. Display the **Document Information Panel**. In the **Author** box, type your first and last names, and then in the **Subject** box, type your course name and section number. In the **Keywords** box, type **tips, macros**

5 Display the **Macros** dialog box, select the **Header** macro, and then click the **Edit** button. Position the insertion point to the right of *St. Paul*, press Spacebar, and then type **Job Fair** Click the **Save Normal** button, click **File**, and then click **Close and Return to Microsoft Word**. Press Ctrl + Home. On the **Quick Access Toolbar**, click the **Header** macro button. Select all the bulleted paragraphs, and then display the **Macros** dialog box. Click the **Macros in arrow**, and then click **Word commands**. Under **Macro**

name, locate and click **AdjustListIndents**, and then click **Run**. Change the **Bullet position** to **0.2"** and the **Text indent** to **0.4"**, and then click **OK**. **Save** your changes, and then **Close** the **Lastname_Firstname_11F_Recruiting_Tips** document.

6 In your **Lastname_Firstname_11F_Collegiate_Fair** document, on the Quick Access Toolbar, run the **Header** macro. **Save** your changes. Display the **Visual Basic Editor**. Display a new Word document. **Save** the document to your **Word Chapter 11** folder as **Lastname_Firstname_11F_Collegiate_Code** Right-click in the footer area, click **Edit Footer**, and then press Alt + F. Display the **Document Information Panel**. In the **Author** box, type your first and last names, and then in the **Subject** box, type your course name and section number. In the **Keywords** box, type **collegiate fair, code Save** your changes.

7 On the **Insert tab**, in the **Illustrations group**, click the **Screenshot** button. In the **Available Windows** gallery, click **Screen Clipping**. Move the + pointer to the top left corner of your screen, select only the **Quick Access Toolbar**, and then paste the selected image in your document. Click to the right of the image, and then press Enter. On the **Insert tab**, in the **Illustrations group**, click the **Screenshot** button, and then in the **Available Windows** gallery, click the thumbnail of the **Visual Basic Editor** window. Press Ctrl + Home. **Save** your changes, and then **Close** the **Lastname_Firstname_11G_Collegiate_Code** document. **Close** the Visual Basic Editor.

8 In the **Collegiate_Fair** document, display the **Document Information Panel**. In the **Author** box, type your first and last names, and then in the **Subject** box, type your course name and section number. In the **Keywords** box, type **fair agenda, macros**

9 Display the **Macros** dialog box, click the **Macros in arrow**, and then click **All active templates and documents**. **Delete** the **Header** and **Footer** macros. Display the **Word Options** dialog box, and then click **Quick Access Toolbar**. On the right side of the window, click **Normal.NewMacros.Header**, click the **Remove** button, and then click **OK**. **Save** your changes, and then **Close** Word.

10 Print your three documents or submit electronically as directed by your instructor.

 You have completed Project 11F

Content-Based Assessments

Apply 11A and 11B skills from these Objectives:

■1 Embed Objects in a Word Document

■2 Link Objects to a Word Document

■3 Create Macros

■4 Use Macros

■5 Write a Procedure in VBA

Mastering Word | Project 11G Catering

In the following Mastering Word project, you will use OLE to include objects in a letter to a caterer. Minneapolis-St. Paul Job Fair provides luncheons and snacks to the employers attending the job fairs. You will create macros that will be used to increase your efficiency in creating documents to explain the job fair needs to the caterer. Your completed documents will look similar to Figure 11.49.

Project Files

For Project 11G, you will need the following files:

New blank Word document
w11G_Catering_Letter
w11G_Catering_Needs
w11G_Catering_Budget

You will save your documents as:

Lastname_Firstname_11G_Catering_Letter
Lastname_Firstname_11G_Catering_Budget
Lastname_Firstname_11G_Catering_Code

Project Results

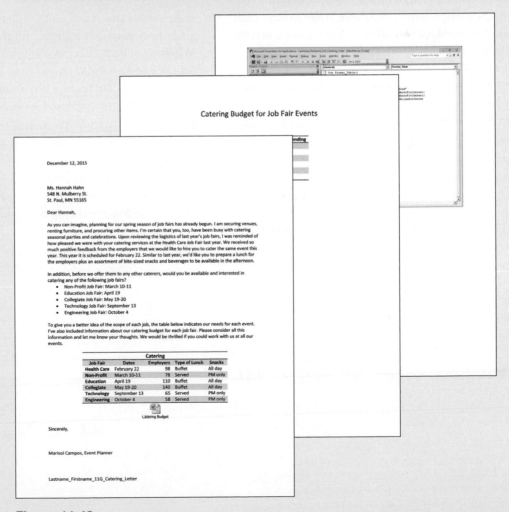

Figure 11.49

(Project 11G Catering continues on the next page)

Content-Based Assessments

1 **Start** Word. Open the file **w11G_Catering_Letter**, and then save it to your **Word Chapter 11** folder as a **Word Macro-Enabled Document** with the file name **Lastname_Firstname_11G_Catering_Letter** Using **Quick Parts**, insert the file name in the footer.

2 Open the Access file **w11F_Catering_Needs** and click the **Enable Content** button. Open and then **Copy** the entire **Catering** table. **Close** Access. In your Word document, position the insertion point at the end of the paragraph that begins *To give you*, and then press Enter two times. Paste the table as **HTML Format**.

3 In the first cell of the table, click to position the insertion point. Display the **Record Macro** dialog box, and then in the **Macro name** box, type **Format_Table** Be sure the **Store macro in** box displays **All Documents (Normal.dotm)**. For the **Description**, type **Formats the table** Assign the **shortcut key** Alt + T. **Close** the dialog box. In Recording mode, with the insertion point in the table, on the **Design tab**, in the **Table Styles group**, click the second style—**Light Shading**. On the **Layout tab**, in the **Cell Size group**, click the **AutoFit** button, and then click **AutoFit Contents**. In the **Table group**, click the **Properties** button. In the **Table Properties** dialog box, under **Alignment**, click **Center**, and then click **OK**. Click the **Stop Recording** button, and then **Save** your changes.

4 From your student files, open the file **w11G_Catering_Budget**. Save the file to your **Word Chapter 11** folder as a **Word Macro-Enabled Document** with the file name **Lastname_Firstname_11G_Catering_Budget** Using **Quick Parts**, insert the file name in the footer. Display the **Document Information Panel**. In the **Author** box, type your first and last names, and then in the **Subject** box, type your course name and section number. In the **Keywords** box, type **budget, macro** Position the insertion point in the first cell of the table, and then run the **Format_Table** macro. **Save** your changes, and then **Close** the document.

5 In **Lastname_Firstname_11G_Catering_Letter**, below the table, position the insertion point in the blank paragraph. **Insert** the **Lastname_Firstname_11G_Catering_Budget** file as a linked file displayed as an icon with the modified caption **Catering Budget Center** the icon. Double-click the icon, and then change the **Number Attending** the **Health Care** Job Fair to **100 Save** your changes, and then **Close** the **Lastname_Firstname_11G_Catering_Budget** document.

6 Press Ctrl + Home. Display the **Visual Basic Editor**. Display a new Word document. **Save** the document to your **Word Chapter 11** folder as **Lastname_Firstname_11G_Catering_Code** Using **Quick Parts**, insert the file name in the footer. Display the **Document Information Panel**. In the **Author** box, type your first and last names, and then in the **Subject** box, type your course name and section number. In the **Keywords** box, type **catering needs, code Save** your changes.

7 On the **Insert tab**, in the **Illustrations group**, click the **Screenshot** button, and then in the **Available Windows** gallery, click the thumbnail of the **Visual Basic Editor** window. Press Ctrl + Home. **Save** your changes, and then **Close** the **Lastname_Firstname_11G_Catering_Code** document. **Close** the Visual Basic Editor.

8 In the **Lastname_Firstname_11G_Catering_Letter** document, display the **Document Information Panel**. In the **Author** box, type your first and last names, and then in the **Subject** box, type your course name and section number. In the **Keywords** box, type **letter, linked, macro** Display the **Macros** dialog box, and then **Delete** the **Format_Table** macro.

9 Print your three documents or submit electronically as directed by your instructor.

End **You have completed Project 11G** —————————

Apply a combination of the **11A** and **11B** skills.

GO! Fix It | Project **11H** Employer Letter

Project Files

For Project 11H, you will need the following files:

> New blank Word document
> w11H_Employer_Letter
> w11H_Employer_Satisfaction

You will save your files as:

> Lastname_Firstname_11H_Employer_Letter
> Lastname_Firstname_11H_Employer_Code

In this project, you will create a letter from Emily Kentros, Employer Coordinator for Minneapolis-St. Paul Job Fair, to a local engineering company regarding upcoming job fairs. Navigate to your student files, open the file **w11H_Employer_Letter**, and then save it to your **Word Chapter 11** folder as a macro-enabled document with the file name **Lastname_Firstname_11H_Employer_Letter**

To complete the project, you must correct the following:

- The file name should be inserted in the footer and document properties added that include the keywords **employer letter, macros**

- A page break should be inserted before the paragraph that begins *I've also attached.*

- The chart in the student file **w11H_Employer_Satisfaction** should be embedded in the second blank paragraph on Page 2 of the document. Data labels should be added to the outside end of the data points, and the chart should be center aligned horizontally.

- The AdjustListIndents Word command (macro) should be run to change the bullet position to 0.1 and the text indent to 0.4.

- In the Visual Basic Editor, with NewMacros for the Normal template selected in the Project pane, the following macro code for a Quotes macro should be typed:

Sub Quotes()

'Quotes Macro created by Firstname Lastname

Selection.InsertBefore Chr$(147)

Selection.InsertAfter Chr$(148)

- By displaying the Macro dialog box, the Quotes macro should be applied to the text in each of the three bulleted paragraphs, excluding the name of the individual and company.

- A new document should be saved to your **Word Chapter 11** folder as **Lastname_Firstname_11H_Employer_Code** The image of your Quotes macro code should be pasted in this document.

- The file name should be inserted in the footer and document properties added that include the keywords **employer letter, macro code**

- Delete all macros that you created before submitting your files.

Print both documents or submit electronically as directed by your instructor.

 You have completed Project 11H ——————————————

Content-Based Assessments

Apply a combination
of the **11A** and **11B**
skills.

GO! Make It | Project 11I Engineering Fair

Project Files

For Project 11I, you will need the following files:

New blank Word document
w11I_Engineering_Fair
w11I_Engineering_Fields

You will save your files as:

Lastname_Firstname_11I_Engineering_Fair
Lastname_Firstname_11I_Engineering_Code

Save the file **w11I_Engineering_Fair** to your **Word Chapter 11** folder as a macro-enabled document with the file name **Lastname_Firstname_11I_Engineering_Fair** Embed the table from the file **w11I_Engineering_Fields**. Using the Olive Green color scheme, format the document as shown in Figure 11.50. Create an AutoClose macro that will insert the date and time. Save a new document as **Lastname_Firstname_11I_Engineering_Code** to insert an image of your macro code. Print both documents or submit electronically as directed by your instructor.

Project Results

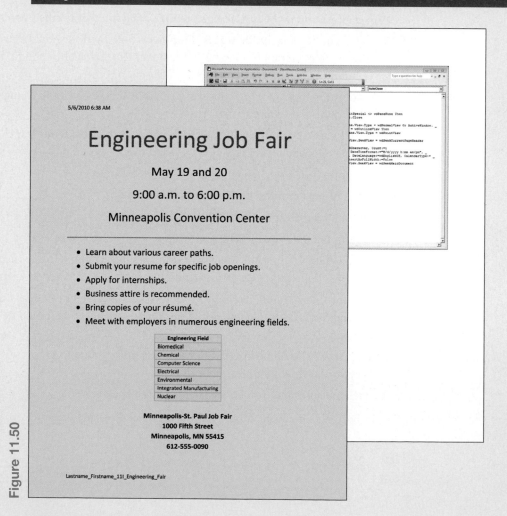

Figure 11.50

End You have completed Project 11I

Content-Based Assessments

Apply a combination of the **11A** and **11B** skills.

GO! Solve It | Project **11J** Job Support

Project Files

For Project 11J, you will need the following files:

New blank Word document
w11J_Survival_Guide
w11J_Job_Support
w11J_Career_Services

You will save your documents as:

Lastname_Firstname_11J_Survival_Guide
Lastname_Firstname_11J_Job_Support
Lastname_Firstname_11J_Support_Code

Open the file **w11J_Survival_Guide**, save it to your **Word Chapter 11** folder as a macro-enabled document with the file name **Lastname_Firstname_11J_Survival_Guide** and then close the document. Open the file **w11J_Job_Support** and save it to your **Word Chapter 11** folder as a macro-enabled document with the file name **Lastname_Firstname_11J_Job_Survival** Create a macro that inserts **Minneapolis-St. Paul Job Fair** in a header with center alignment. Assign a keyboard command to the macro. Insert a comment in the macro code that describes the keyboard command. Embed the file **w11J_Career_Services**, and then change the design to Angles. Link the file **Lastname_Firstname_11J_Survival_Guide** displayed as an icon. Open the linked file and run the macro. Save a new document in your **Word Chapter 11** folder as **Lastname_Firstname_11J_Support_Code** Insert your macro code as a screen capture. For all three documents, insert the file name in the footer and add appropriate document properties. Delete the macro you created, and then print all three documents or submit electronically as directed by your instructor.

	Performance Level		
	Exemplary: You consistently applied the relevant skills	**Proficient:** You sometimes, but not always, applied the relevant skills	**Developing:** You rarely or never applied the relevant skills
Save files	Files are saved with the appropriate name and file type.	Files are saved with the appropriate name but the wrong file type.	Files are saved with the wrong name and file type.
Create a macro	The macro is created and a comment inserted.	The macro is created but a comment is not inserted.	The macro is not created.
Embed and edit a file	The file is embedded and the design modified.	The file is embedded but the design is not modified.	The file is not embedded.
Link and edit a file	The file is linked and the header is modified.	The file is linked but the header is not modified.	The file is not linked.
Paste an image	The image is pasted correctly.	The image is pasted but is not in the correct document.	The image is not pasted.

(Performance Element)

End You have completed Project 11J

Content-Based Assessments

Apply a combination
of the **11A** and **11B**
skills.

GO! Solve It | Project **11K** Fair Attendance

Project Files

For Project 11K, you will need the following files:

New blank Word document
w11K_Attendance_Memo
w11K_Increased_Attendance
w11K_Attendance

You will save your documents as:

Lastname_Firstname_11K_Attendance_Memo
Lastname_Firstname_11K_Attendance
Lastname_Firstname_11K_Attendance_Code

Open the Excel file **w11K_Attendance** and save it to your **Word Chapter 11** folder as **Lastname_Firstname_11K_Attendance** Insert the file name in the footer. Open the file **w11K_Attendance_Memo** and save it to your **Word Chapter 11** folder as a macro-enabled document with the file name **Lastname_Firstname_11K_Attendance_Memo** Create a macro to insert the file name in the footer. Assign the macro to the Quick Access Toolbar as a button. Embed the **w11K_Increased_Attendance** PowerPoint file and link the **Lastname_Firstname_11K_Attendance** file as an icon at the appropriate places in the memo. In the Excel file, change the value for *2015 Attendance* to **8,732** Format the document to create a professional appearance. Create a new Word document and save it to your **Word Chapter 11** folder as **Lastname_Firstname_11K_Attendance_Code** Insert the file name in the footer. Paste images of the Quick Access Toolbar and macro code in the document. Add appropriate document properties in both Word documents. Delete the macros you created, and then print both Word documents and the Excel file or submit all three files as directed by your instructor.

Performance Element		Performance Level		
		Exemplary: You consistently applied the relevant skills	**Proficient:** You sometimes, but not always, applied the relevant skills	**Developing:** You rarely or never applied the relevant skills
	Create a macro	The macro is created and displays as a button on the Quick Access Toolbar.	The macro is created but does not display as a button on the Quick Access Toolbar.	A macro is not created.
	Embed a file	The file is embedded at an appropriate location.	The file is embedded but is at an inappropriate location.	The file is not embedded.
	Link and edit a file	The file is linked, displays as an icon, and is edited.	The file is linked but does not display as an icon or is not edited.	The file is not linked.
	Format document	Formatting is attractive and appropriate.	Adequate formatting but difficult to read or unattractive.	Either there is no formatting or it is inadequate.
	Paste images	Both images are pasted correctly.	Only one image is pasted correctly.	No images are pasted in the document.

End You have completed Project 11K

Outcomes-Based Assessments

Rubric

The following outcomes-based assessments are *open-ended assessments*. That is, there is no specific correct result; your result will depend on your approach to the information provided. Make *Professional Quality* your goal. Use the following scoring rubric to guide you in *how* to approach the problem and then to evaluate *how well* your approach solves the problem.

The *criteria*—Software Mastery, Content, Format and Layout, and Process—represent the knowledge and skills you have gained that you can apply to solving the problem. The *levels of performance*—Professional Quality, Approaching Professional Quality, or Needs Quality Improvements—help you and your instructor evaluate your result.

	Your completed project is of Professional Quality if you:	Your completed project is Approaching Professional Quality if you:	Your completed project Needs Quality Improvements if you:
1-Software Mastery	Choose and apply the most appropriate skills, tools, and features and identify efficient methods to solve the problem.	Choose and apply some appropriate skills, tools, and features, but not in the most efficient manner.	Choose inappropriate skills, tools, or features, or are inefficient in solving the problem.
2-Content	Construct a solution that is clear and well organized, contains content that is accurate, appropriate to the audience and purpose, and is complete. Provide a solution that contains no errors in spelling, grammar, or style.	Construct a solution in which some components are unclear, poorly organized, inconsistent, or incomplete. Misjudge the needs of the audience. Have some errors in spelling, grammar, or style, but the errors do not detract from comprehension.	Construct a solution that is unclear, incomplete, or poorly organized; contains some inaccurate or inappropriate content; and contains many errors in spelling, grammar, or style. Do not solve the problem.
3-Format and Layout	Format and arrange all elements to communicate information and ideas, clarify function, illustrate relationships, and indicate relative importance.	Apply appropriate format and layout features to some elements, but not others. Overuse features, causing minor distraction.	Apply format and layout that does not communicate information or ideas clearly. Do not use format and layout features to clarify function, illustrate relationships, or indicate relative importance. Use available features excessively, causing distraction.
4-Process	Use an organized approach that integrates planning, development, self-assessment, revision, and reflection.	Demonstrate an organized approach in some areas, but not others; or, use an insufficient process of organization throughout.	Do not use an organized approach to solve the problem.

Outcomes-Based Assessments

Apply a combination of the **11A** and **11B** skills.

GO! Think | Project **11L** Health Fair

Project Files

For Project 11L, you will need the following files:

Three new blank Word documents

You will save your documents as:

Lastname_Firstname_11L_Health_Flyer
Lastname_Firstname_11L_Health_Letter
Lastname_Firstname_11L_Health_Code

The Minneapolis-St. Paul Job Fair conducts a health care job fair every year. The organization is located at 1000 Fifth Street, Minneapolis, MN 55415. Search the Internet for the types of job opportunities that are available for health care careers. Save a new macro-enabled document as **Lastname_Firstname_11L_Health_Flyer** Create a flyer indicating the types of job recruiters that will be attending the fair. Use fictitious information for the date, time, and location. Create a macro for job fair contact information that will run in all documents. Create an AutoClose macro that will automatically insert the date and time in the header—only in this document. Format the document to create a professional appearance, insert the file name in the footer, and add appropriate document properties. Save a second, new macro-enabled document as **Lastname_Firstname_11L_Health_ Letter** Create a letter to be sent to the local college—use fictitious information—asking that copies of the flyer be made available to students. Run the job fair's contact information macro in a letterhead and use your own name in the signature line. Insert a link to your flyer, displaying it as an icon. Insert the file name in the footer and add appropriate document properties. Save a third blank document as **Lastname_Firstname_11L_Health_Code** Insert the contact information and AutoClose macro codes, insert the file name in the footer, and add appropriate document properties. Delete the macros you created, and then print all three documents or submit electronically as directed by your instructor.

End You have completed Project 11L ——————————

Outcomes-Based Assessments

Apply a combination of the **11A** and **11B** skills.

GO! Think | Project **11M** Jobseeker Tips

Project Files

For Project 11M, you will need the following files:

Three new blank Word documents

You will save your documents as:

Lastname_Firstname_11M_Jobseeker_Tips
Lastname_Firstname_11M_Tips_Memo
Lastname_Firstname_11M_Jobseeker_Code

The registration office of the Minneapolis-St. Paul Job Fair receives frequent inquiries from jobseekers regarding what they should bring, how they should dress, and other tips for success at job fairs. Search the Internet for information related to success at job fairs. Save a new macro-enabled document as **Lastname_Firstname_11M_Jobseeker_Tips** Using the data you find, in your own words, create a one-page document—including bulleted items—that would be useful for jobseekers. Create a macro that inserts that name of the organization and the phone number 612-555-0090 as formatted text in the header of any document. Insert an appropriate description of the macro as a comment. For the bulleted items, run the AdjustListIndents macro to adjust the bullet position and text indent. Save a second, new macro-enabled document as **Lastname_Firstname_11M_Tips_Memo** Create a memo from you to Joyce Spinoza, Registration Coordinator. Summarize the contents and explain how you gathered the information. Link your Jobseeker_Tips document, displaying it as an icon. Run the macro you created to insert the organization information in the header. Save a third blank document as **Lastname_Firstname_11M_Jobseeker_Code** Insert your macro code. For each document, inscrt the file name in the footer and add appropriate document properties. Delete the macro you created. Print all three documents or submit electronically as directed by your instructor.

End You have completed Project 11M —————————

Apply a combination
of the **11A** and **11B**
skills.

You and GO! | Project **11N** Personal Letterhead

Project Files

For Project 11N, you will need the following files:

> Two new blank Word documents

You will save your documents as:

> Lastname_Firstname_11N_Personal_Letterhead
> Lastname_Firstname_11N_Personal_Code

Create a document that contains a macro that inserts a letterhead with your contact information. In a blank document, record a macro that will insert your name, address, and phone number as formatted text in any document based on the Normal template. Name the macro appropriately and add an adequate description as a comment. Save the macro-enabled document as **Lastname_Firstname_11N_Personal_Letterhead** Insert the file name in the footer. Add your name, course name and section number, and the keywords **personal letterhead, macro** to the document properties. Save a new macro-enabled document as **Lastname_Firstname_11N_Personal_Code** Insert the file name in the footer and add appropriate document properties. Run your letterhead macro in this document. Insert your macro code in the document. Delete the macro you created. Save your changes, and then print both documents or submit electronically as directed by your instructor.

End You have completed Project 11N ——————————————

Integrating Word with PowerPoint and Modifying the Document Layout

OUTCOMES

At the end of this chapter you will be able to:

OBJECTIVES

Mastering these objectives will enable you to:

PROJECT 12A
Integrate Word with PowerPoint.

1. Integrate Word with PowerPoint (p. 695)
2. Modify a PowerPoint Presentation (p. 702)

PROJECT 12B
Modify the document layout and format graphic and text elements.

3. Modify the Document Layout (p. 710)
4. Format Graphic and Text Elements (p. 715)

Nikolay Okhitin/Shutterstock

In This Chapter

Microsoft Office 2010 is an integrated application suite. This integration enables you to use each application for its specified purpose, and then combine components for a final result. For example, you can create a table in Access, and then use that table to perform a mail merge in Word.

You can customize Word in a variety of ways—for example, change the paper size, apply advanced formatting features to text, and modify graphic and text elements—to create a professional-looking document that meets your exact specifications.

The projects in this chapter will relate to **Fascination Entertainment Group**, which operates 15 regional theme parks across the United States, Mexico, and Canada. Park types include traditional theme parks, water parks, and wildlife adventure parks. This year the company will launch three of its new "Imagination Parks" where attractions combine fun and the discovery of math and science information, and where teens and adults enjoy the free Friday night concerts. Fascination Entertainment Group also operates family-friendly resort hotels on many of their properties.

Project 12A Planning Presentation

myitlab
Project 12A Training

Project Activities

In Activities 12.01 through 12.05, you will prepare an outline in Word to be used as a foundation for a PowerPoint presentation. After creating the presentation, you will create a handout in Word that includes thumbnails of each slide and a place for notes. At the next marketing meeting, Katie Hecart, Marketing Vice President of Fascination Entertainment Group, would like to discuss the results of a survey of visitors to the company's animal parks. You will create the PowerPoint presentation and handouts for the meeting. Your completed files will look similar to Figure 12.1.

Project Files

For Project 12A, you will need the following files:

> A new blank PowerPoint presentation
> w12A_Planning_Outline
> w12A_Tiger
> w12A_Toucan

You will save your files as:

> Lastname_Firstname_12A_Planning_Outline
> Lastname_Firstname_12A_Planning_Presentation
> Lastname_Firstname_12A_Planning_Handout

Project Results

Figure 12.1
Project 12A Planning Presentation

Objective 1 | Integrate Word with PowerPoint

An *outline* provides a way to organize the contents of a document in a structured manner. Previously you used Outline view to create a master document and subdocuments. Outlines created in Word can also be used to create slides in PowerPoint. In Outline view, each paragraph is treated as a separate topic, or level, in the outline. Each topic is assigned either an *outline level* or is identified as body text. An outline level defines the position of the paragraph in relation to all topics in the document and is formatted with a corresponding heading style. You can assign up to nine levels in an outline.

Activity 12.01 | Creating an Outline in Outline View

In this activity, you will apply outline levels to existing paragraphs and move paragraphs in order to create an outline.

1 **Start** Word. From your student files, open the file **w12A_Planning_Outline**. Navigate to the location where you are saving your files for this chapter, and then create a new folder named **Word Chapter 12** Using your own name, save the document to your **Word Chapter 12** folder as **Lastname_Firstname_12A_Planning_Outline**

2 Insert the file name in the footer. If necessary, display rulers and formatting marks. If any words are flagged as spelling errors, click **Ignore All**.

> **Another Way**
>
> Click the Outline button on the Status bar.

3 On the **View tab**, in the **Document Views group**, click the **Outline** button.

> All paragraphs are preceded by an *outline symbol*—a small gray circle that identifies heading and body text paragraphs in an outline.

4 In the first paragraph, click the outline symbol to select the paragraph. On the **Outlining tab**, in the **Outline Tools group**, click the **Outline Level arrow** [Body Text ▾], and then click **Level 1**. Compare your screen with Figure 12.2.

> The paragraph is designated as Level 1 and is formatted with the Heading 1 style—not visible in Outline view. A *plus outline symbol* displays to the left of the paragraph indicating there are subordinate heading or body text paragraphs.

Figure 12.2

Outline level arrow

Plus outline symbol

Level 1 and Heading 1 style assigned

5 In the third paragraph, click the outline symbol to select the paragraph. On the **Outlining tab**, in the **Outline Tools group**, click the **Promote to Heading 1** button [⇤].

> The paragraph is designated as Level 1 and formatted with the Heading 1 style.

Another Way
Click the Print Layout button on the Status bar.

6 On the **Outlining tab**, in the **Close group**, click the **Close Outline View** button. Compare your screen with Figure 12.3.

The paragraphs designated as Level 1 display with the Heading 1 style. In Print Layout view, however, the outline symbols do not display.

Figure 12.3

Paragraphs display with Heading 1 style applied

7 On the **View tab**, in the **Document Views group**, click the **Outline** button. Using the technique you practiced, assign **Level 1** to the paragraphs *Survey Conducted*, *Most Highly Rated Areas*, *Areas Needing the Most Improvement*, *Planning for Change*, and *General Survey Results*. Compare your screen with Figure 12.4.

Figure 12.4

Level 1 and Heading 1 style applied

8 In the second paragraph, click the outline symbol, click the **Outline Level arrow** [Body Text ▾], and then click **Level 2**.

The paragraph is indented, designated as Level 2, and the Heading 2 style is applied. The **minus outline symbol** displays, indicating there are no subordinate heading or body text paragraphs. Paragraphs are indented based on the assigned outline level.

9 Below the paragraph *Our Goals*, select all three body text paragraphs. Click the **Outline Level arrow** `Body Text ▾`, and then click **Level 2**.

10 In a similar manner, below each of the remaining *Level 1* paragraphs, select the body text paragraphs, and then apply the **Level 2** outline level. Compare your screen with Figure 12.5.

Figure 12.5

Level 2 and Heading 2 style applied

11 Below the *Survey Conducted* heading, select the two paragraphs that begin *Scale range* and *Rating scale*. On the **Outlining tab**, in the **Outline Tools group**, click the **Demote** button `⇥`. Compare your screen with Figure 12.6.

> The Demote button assigns a paragraph to a lower level. In this case, the paragraphs are assigned a Level 3 outline level and the Heading 3 style is applied.

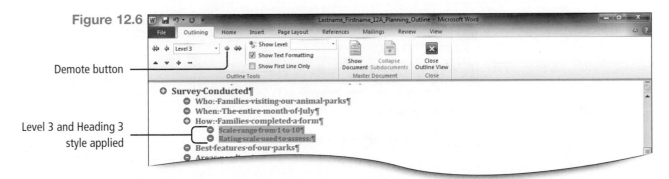

Figure 12.6

Demote button

Level 3 and Heading 3 style applied

12 Below the paragraph that begins *Rating scale*, select the next two paragraphs, and then click the **Demote** button `⇥` two times.

> The paragraphs are assigned a Level 4 outline level and the Heading 4 style is applied.

13 Below the paragraph *Staff*, select the next five paragraphs, and then click the **Demote** button `⇥`.

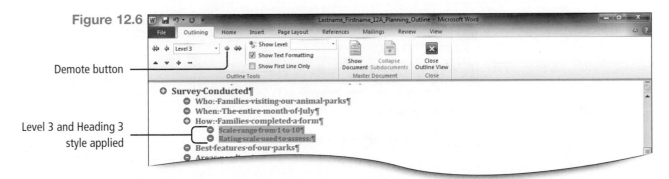

14 Select the paragraph *Park Maps*, and then in the **Outline Tools group**, click the **Promote** button. Compare your screen with Figure 12.7.

> The Promote button assigns a paragraph to a higher level. In this case, the *Park Maps* paragraph is assigned a Level 2 outline level.

Figure 12.7

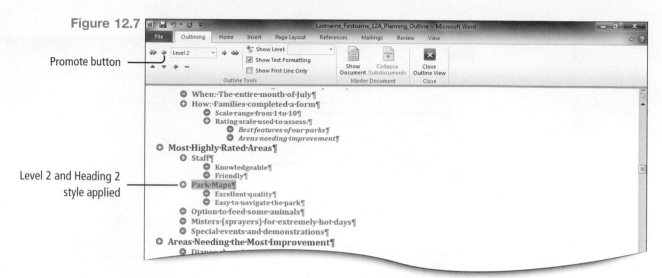

Promote button

Level 2 and Heading 2 style applied

15 To the paragraphs that begin *Install*, *Healthy*, *Research*, *Prioritize*, and *Determine*, assign a **Level 3** outline level. **Save** your changes.

Activity 12.02 | Collapsing and Expanding Outline Levels

1 Locate the paragraph *Survey Conducted*, and then double-click the plus outline symbol to collapse the level. Compare your screen with Figure 12.8.

> Collapsing an outline level hides all subordinate heading and body text paragraphs.

Figure 12.8

Collapsed paragraph

2 Select the paragraph *Most Highly Rated Areas*, press and hold Ctrl, and then select the remaining **Level 1** paragraphs in the document. With the paragraphs selected, in the **Outline Tools group**, click the **Collapse** button.

3 Select the paragraph *General Survey Results*, and then in the **Outline Tools group**, click the **Move Up** button ▲ three times. Compare your screen with Figure 12.9.

Moving a collapsed level allows you to easily organize the topics in an outline. When you move a collapsed paragraph, all subordinate heading and body text paragraphs are also moved.

Figure 12.9

Move Up button

Paragraph moved

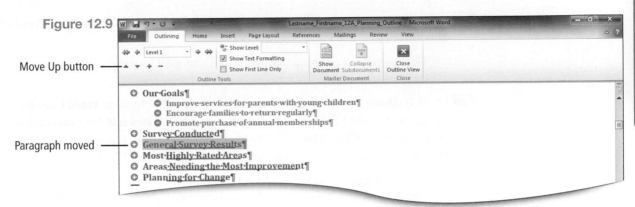

4 On the **Outlining tab**, in the **Close group**, click the **Close Outline View** button.

Although paragraphs were collapsed in Outline view, all text displays in Print Layout view—the current view.

5 On the **Page Layout tab**, in the **Themes group**, click the **Theme Colors** button ▣, and then in the displayed **Theme Colors** gallery, click **Equity**. Compare your screen with Figure 12.10.

Figure 12.10

Equity theme color applied

6 Display the **Document Information Panel**. In the **Author** box, type your first and last names. In the **Subject** box, type your course name and section number, and then in the **Keywords** box, type **planning presentation, outline** Close ✕ the Document Information Panel.

7 Save 🖫 your changes, and then **Exit** Word.

Activity 12.03 | Using a Word Outline to Create a PowerPoint Presentation

Because Microsoft Office is an integrated suite of programs, you can open a Word outline in PowerPoint to automatically create slides based on the level in the outline. The outline levels are used to determine the slide titles and bulleted items.

1 From the **Start** menu 🌐, locate and then click **Microsoft Office PowerPoint 2010**. **Maximize** 🔲 the **PowerPoint** window.

> The PowerPoint program may be located under All Programs or Microsoft Office or on the Start menu.

2 From **Backstage** view, click **Open**, and then navigate to your **Word Chapter 12** folder. At the bottom of the **Open** dialog box, click the **All PowerPoint Presentations arrow**, and then click **All Outlines**. Notice that your **Lastname_Firstname_12A_Planning_Outline** file displays. Compare your screen with Figure 12.11.

> By default, only existing PowerPoint files display in the Open dialog box. Because your outline is a Word document, it is necessary to change the setting to All Outlines.

Figure 12.11

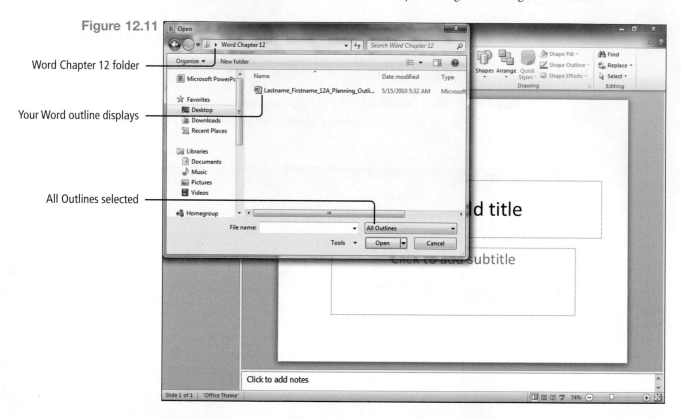

Word Chapter 12 folder

Your Word outline displays

All Outlines selected

3 Click to select **Lastname_Firstname_12A_Planning_Outline**, and then click **Open.** Select *Hecart*, right-click, and then click **Ignore All**. Compare your screen with Figure 12.12, and then take a moment to study the table in Figure 12.13.

> Seven slides are created based on the outline levels you created for the outline. Heading 1 style paragraphs display as the title for each slide. Subordinate paragraphs display as bulleted items.

Figure 12.12

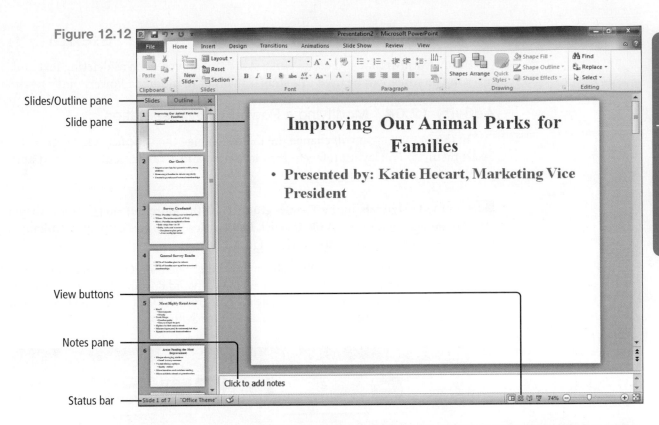

Slides/Outline pane

Slide pane

View buttons

Notes pane

Status bar

Microsoft PowerPoint Screen Elements

Screen Element	Description
Slide pane	Displays a large image of the active slide.
Slides/Outline pane	Displays either the presentation outline (Outline tab) or all of the slides in the presentation in the form of thumbnails (Slides tab).
Notes pane	Displays below the Slide pane and allows you to type notes regarding the active slide.
Status bar	A horizontal bar at the bottom of the presentation window that displays the current slide number, number of slides in a presentation, the applied theme, View buttons, Zoom slider, and Fit slide to current window button.
View buttons	A set of commands that controls the look of the presentation window.

Figure 12.13

More Knowledge | Using Body Text in an Outline

When you use a Word outline to create slides in PowerPoint, heading styles must be applied to all paragraphs. Body text paragraphs will not display in the slides.

---

4 From **Backstage** view, display the **Save As** dialog box, and then navigate to your **Word Chapter 12** folder. Using your own name, **Save** the file as **Lastname_Firstname_12A_ Planning_Presentation**

PowerPoint files are saved with the default file extension *.pptx*.

Objective 2 | Modify a PowerPoint Presentation

Many features that you use to edit a Word document, such as deleting text and inserting pictures, can be used in a similar manner to modify a PowerPoint presentation.

Activity 12.04 | Modifying a PowerPoint Presentation

In this activity, you will change the theme, change the slide *layout*, delete text, and insert pictures. The layout refers to the placement and arrangement of the text and graphic elements on a slide.

1 On the **Design tab**, in the **Themes group**, click the **More** button. In the displayed **All Themes** gallery, under **Built-In**, click **Equity**. Note: Themes display in alphabetical order. Compare your screen with Figure 12.14.

The themes available in Word also exist in other Microsoft Office applications. Recall that you changed the theme color to *Equity* in your Word document. The slides are formatted with the *Equity* theme to coordinate the background, bullet styles, and title with the existing text. The *Equity* theme displays on the Status bar.

Figure 12.14

Equity theme applied to all slides

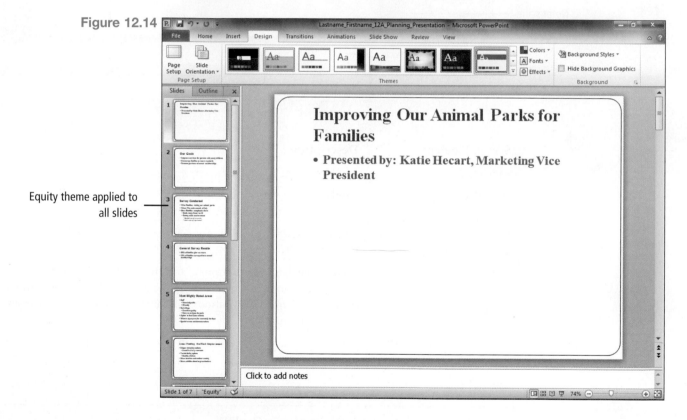

2 On the **Home tab**, in the **Slides group**, click the **Layout arrow** to display the **Slide Layout** gallery. Compare your screen with Figure 12.15.

> Ten slide arrangements display. By default, when you use a Word outline to create slides in PowerPoint, the Title and Text slide layout is applied to all slides.

Figure 12.15

Layout arrow

Slide Layout gallery

3 With **Slide 1** selected in the **Slide** pane, in the **Slide Layout** gallery, click the first option—**Title Slide**. Compare your screen with Figure 12.16.

> It is good practice to begin each presentation with a title slide. The title slide for the Equity theme displays the main title—the Heading 1 style—near the middle of the slide, and the subtitle—the Heading 2 style—displays below the main title.

Figure 12.16

Title Slide layout applied to Slide 1

Main title

Subtitle

4 On **Slide 1**, select the text *for Families*. Compare your screen with Figure 12.17.

Content placeholders are used to display all text on slides.

Figure 12.17

Selected text

Content placeholder

5 Press [Del]. On **Slide 1**, in the second content placeholder, position the insertion point to the left of *Katie*, and then press [Enter].

6 In the **Slides/Outline** pane, click the thumbnail for **Slide 4**. In the **Slide** pane, with **Slide 4** displayed, double-click the text *surveyed*, and then press [Del]. In a similar manner, display **Slide 6**, and then in the title, delete the text *the Most*.

7 **Save** [💾] your changes, and then compare your screen with Figure 12.18.

Figure 12.18

Title

8 In the **Slides/Outline** pane, click the thumbnail for **Slide 1**. On the **Insert tab**, in the **Images group**, click the **Picture** button.

9 In the **Insert Picture** dialog box, navigate to your student files for this chapter, click **w12A_Tiger**, and then click **Insert**.

10 If necessary, on the View tab, in the Show group, click to select the Ruler check box. On the **Format tab**, in the **Size group**, change the **Shape Height** to **2.5"**. Position the picture so that the bottom border displays at **approximately 3.5 inches on the vertical ruler** and the right border displays at **approximately 4.5 inches on the horizontal ruler**. Click in a blank area to deselect the picture, and then compare your screen with Figure 12.19.

Figure 12.19

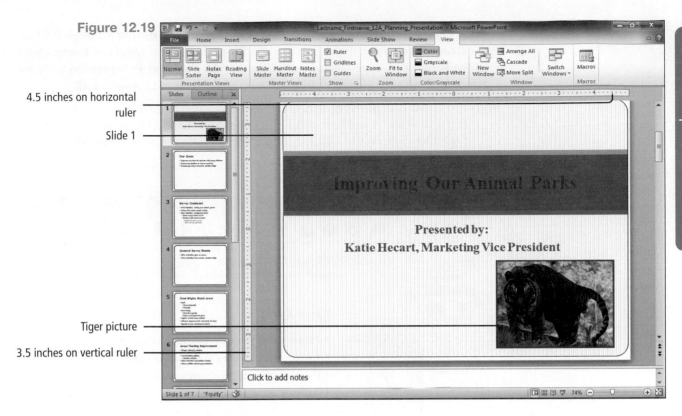

4.5 inches on horizontal ruler

Slide 1

Tiger picture

3.5 inches on vertical ruler

11 Using the same technique, navigate to your student files, and then **Insert** the **w12A_ Toucan** picture. Change the **Shape Height** to **2.5"**. Position the picture so that it displays in the approximate location shown in Figure 12.20. Deselect the picture, and then compare your screen with Figure 12.20.

Figure 12.20

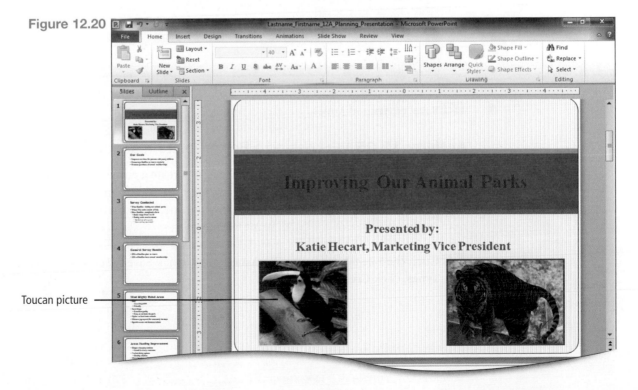

Toucan picture

12 Click the **Insert tab**, and then in the **Text group**, click the **Header & Footer** button. In the **Header and Footer** dialog box, on the **Slide** tab, click to select the **Footer** check box. In the **Footer** box, type **Lastname_Firstname_12A_Planning_Presentation** Click to select the **Don't show on title slide** check box, and then click **Apply to All**.

Unlike Word, PowerPoint does not provide the option to insert the file name using Quick Parts. The Header and Footer dialog box allows you to select the slides on which you want the footer to display. In this case, the footer will display on all slides except the title slide.

13 In the **Slides/Outline** pane, click **Slide 2**, and then compare your screen with Figure 12.21.

Figure 12.21

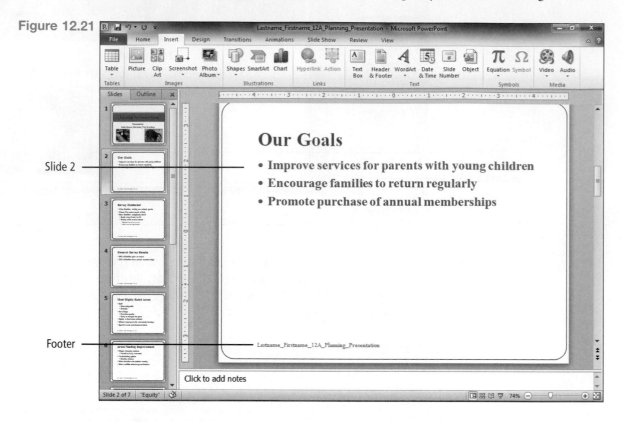

Slide 2

Footer

14 **Save** your changes.

Activity 12.05 | Publishing a PowerPoint Presentation in Word

Any PowerPoint presentation can be used to create a corresponding *handout* in Word. A handout is a document that is given to an audience to accompany a lecture. The handout may include thumbnails of slides, a text-only outline, and an area displaying the presenter's notes or blank lines for the participant to enter notes.

1 Click the **File tab** to display **Backstage** view. Click **Save & Send**, and then under **File Types**, click **Create Handouts**.

2 Under **Create Handouts in Microsoft Word**, click the **Create Handouts** button, and then compare your screen with Figure 12.22.

> The Send To Microsoft Word dialog box displays, allowing the user to select the PowerPoint elements to include in the handout.

Figure 12.22

Send to Microsoft Word dialog box

Handout options

3 In the displayed **Send To Microsoft Word** dialog box, under **Page layout in Microsoft Word**, click to select the **Blank lines next to slides** option button, and then click **OK**.

4 On the **Taskbar**, click the **Word** icon to display the newly created Word document, and then compare your screen with Figure 12.23. If necessary, on the Layout tab, in the Table group, click the View Gridlines button.

> The Word document contains three pages and includes a table with three columns and seven rows. The first column displays the number of each slide in a separate cell. The second column displays a thumbnail of each slide, and the third column displays blank lines in each cell.

Figure 12.23

Slide number

Slide thumbnail

Blank lines

5 From the **Backstage** view, display the **Save As** dialog box, navigate to your **Word Chapter 12** folder, and then using your own name, save the file as **Lastname_Firstname_12A_ Planning_Handout** Using **Quick Parts**, insert the file name in the footer.

6 In the first row of the table, in the third cell, select the first three lines, and then press [Del].

7 In a similar manner, in the third column, delete the first three lines from each of the remaining six cells.

8 On **Page 1**, point slightly outside of the upper left corner of the table to display the **Table Move Handle** 田. With the pointer displayed, click the **Table Move Handle** 田 to select the entire table. On the **Layout tab**, in the **Cell Size group**, change the **Height** to **1.8"**. Compare your screen with Figure 12.24.

The handout can be modified to suit your purposes. In this case, you have deleted blank lines and reduced the row height to create a two-page handout.

Figure 12.24

Cell height modified

Table selected

9 Press [Ctrl] + [Home]. Display the **Document Information Panel**. In the **Author** box, type your first and last names. In the **Subject** box, type your course name and section number, and then in the **Keywords** box, type **planning presentation, handout Close** ⊠ the Document Information Panel. **Save** 🔲 your changes, and then **Exit** Word.

10 In **PowerPoint**, with your PowerPoint presentation displayed, **Save** 🔲 your changes, and then **Exit** PowerPoint.

11 Print both Word documents or submit all three files electronically as directed by your instructor.

End **You have completed Project 12A** ——————————

Project 12B Park Brochure

Project Activities

In Activities 12.06 through 12.12, you will create a brochure for visitors to the theme parks operated by Fascination Entertainment Group. To customize the document, you will change the paper size, modify how text displays, and edit graphics. Your completed document will look similar to Figure 12.25.

Project Files

For Project 12B, you will need the following files:

> w12B_Park_Brochure
> w12B_Carousel
> w12B_Coaster
> w12B_Comments
> w12B_Brochure_Bullet

You will save your document as:

> Lastname_Firstname_12B_Park_Brochure

Project Results

Catering for Groups

We offer several venues in each park for your group event.

More Comments

My wife and I appreciated the large number of kiddie rides for our 4 preschoolers. A. Berman

OUR THEME PARKS

Rides

Each of our parks has a variety of rides to suit all ages—from our classic carousel with organ music and brass rings to our exhilarating roller coasters.

Here is a summary of our rides.

- Family Rides
- Kiddie Rides
- Roller Coasters
- Water Rides

There are plenty of benches for individuals choosing not to ride.

Some rides have height requirements.

Lastname_Firstname_12B_Park_Brochure

Entertainment

We offer award-winning shows at all of our parks. Our resident entertainers provide professional stage shows. In addition, you will always find strolling groups of musicians and comedians throughout the park.

Food

All of our parks are known for both the variety and quality of food served. There are several different options in each park. Enjoy a relaxed meal in one of our full-service, air-conditioned restaurants or the cafeteria.

If you are in a hurry or desire a snack, head to a food court. We offer tasty treats such as pizza, sandwiches, ice cream, and caramel corn.

Kosher, vegetarian, and reduced sugar options are available at all locations.

Theme Park FAQ

<u>When to Visit:</u>
Weekdays are ideal. Saturdays are usually our busiest day. To avoid standing in line to buy tickets, you can purchase them in advance.

<u>Weather Tips:</u>
When it is sunny, be sure to use sunscreen. If it rains, there is no need to leave. Wear a poncho, see a show, or go shopping. Sunscreen and ponchos are available for purchase in many of our stores.

<u>Guest Services:</u>
Visit our Guest Services office that is located immediately outside the entrance to the park. Our staff can assist you with the following services.

- Stroller rentals
- Child Finder Program
- Help for guests with disabilities
- Park maps

...n for all ages!

Figure 12.25
Project 12B Park Brochure

Objective 3 | Modify the Document Layout

Word provides many features to format and display text in an attractive manner, such as changing the spacing between characters and controlling the display of phrases where the individual components should not be split between two lines. Additionally, the paper size can be changed to produce the desired result—in this case, a small brochure.

Activity 12.06 | Changing Paper Size

1 **Start** Word. From your student files, open the file **w12B_Park_Brochure**. Save the document to your **Word Chapter 12** folder as **Lastname_Firstname_12B_Park_Brochure** Insert the file name in the footer, and then display rulers and formatting marks. If any words are flagged as spelling errors, click **Ignore All**.

2 On the **Page Layout tab**, in the **Page Setup group**, click the **Orientation** button, and then click **Landscape**.

3 In the **Page Setup group**, click the **Margins** button, and then click **Narrow**. In the **Page Setup group**, click the **Columns** button, and then click **Three**.

4 On **Page 1**, in the first column, position the insertion point to the left of the paragraph *Entertainment*. In the **Page Setup group**, click the **Breaks** button, and then under **Page Breaks**, click **Column**. At the bottom of the second column, position the insertion point to the left of the paragraph *Theme Park FAQ*. In the **Page Setup group**, click the **Breaks** button, and then under **Page Breaks**, click **Column**.

5 In the third column, position the insertion point to the left of the paragraph *Catering for Groups*, and then press [Ctrl] + [Enter]. Scroll up as necessary, and then notice that the column and page breaks display as shown in Figure 12.26.

Figure 12.26

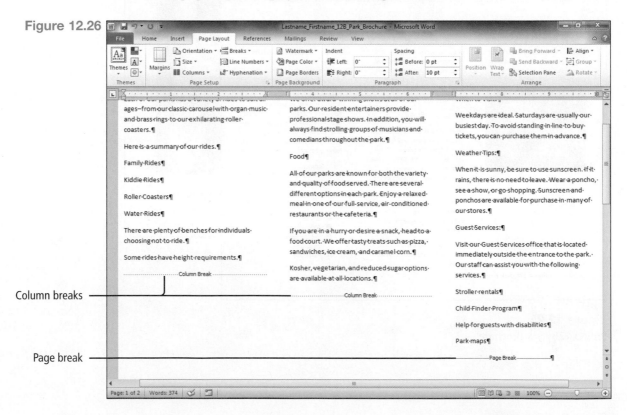

Column breaks

Page break

6 On **Page 2**, position the insertion point to the left of the paragraph *Fascination Entertainment Group*. In the **Page Setup group**, click the **Breaks** button, and then under **Page Breaks**, click **Column**. In the second column, position the insertion point in the last blank paragraph of the document, and then using the technique you practiced, insert a **Column** break.

Another Way

Click the dialog box launcher to display the Page Setup dialog box, and then click the Paper tab.

7 Press Ctrl + Home. In the **Page Setup group**, click the **Size** button, and then at the bottom of the displayed list, click **More Paper Sizes**.

8 In the **Page Setup** dialog box, with the **Paper** tab displayed, under **Paper size,** click the **Paper size arrow**, which displays *Letter*, scroll as necessary, and then click **Custom size**. Click the **Width spin box down arrow** to **9"**. Click the **Height spin box down arrow** to **7"**. Compare your screen with Figure 12.27.

> You can change the paper size to accommodate any type of document. In this case, the brochure requires a custom paper size.

Figure 12.27

Page size

Width

Height

9 Click **OK** to close the **Page Setup** dialog box. Note: Changing the paper size causes some text to move to a second and third page; you will adjust this in subsequent steps.

10 Save your changes.

Activity 12.07 | Changing Character Spacing

You will format the text in the brochure by changing font sizes and applying styles. You will also change the ***character spacing*** for selected text to improve the appearance or readability of a document. Character spacing is a Word feature that allows you to change the default spacing between characters. You can manually set spacing options or use ***kerning*** to have Word automatically modify space between characters in selected text. Kerning automatically adjusts the spacing between pairs of characters, with a specified minimum point size, so that words and letters display as equally spaced.

1 In the first column, select the first paragraph—*Rides*. On the Mini toolbar, change the **Font Size** to **14**, apply **Bold** B and **Center** ☰, click the **Font Color button arrow** A▾, and then in the eighth column, click the last color—**Purple, Accent 4, Darker 50%**.

2 With the paragraph *Rides* selected, on the **Home tab**, in the **Font group**, click the **dialog box launcher** .

3 In the **Font** dialog box, click the **Advanced** tab. Under **Character Spacing**, click the **Spacing arrow**, and then click **Expanded**. Click the **By spin box up arrow** to **1.2 pt**. Compare your screen with Figure 12.28, and then take a moment to study the character spacing options in Figure 12.29.

Word has several different features that allow you to modify the character spacing. By changing the spacing to Expanded by 1.2 pt, the space between the characters is increased slightly. A preview of the character spacing displays in the Font dialog box.

Figure 12.28

Character Spacing Options

Option	Description
Scale	Expands or compresses text horizontally as a percentage of the current size.
Spacing	Expands or compresses spacing between characters by a specified number of points.
Position	Raises or lowers the location of text in relation to the current vertical location.
Kerning for fonts	Automatically adjusts the spacing between pairs of characters, with a specified minimum point size, so that words and letters display as equally spaced.
By	Specifies the number of points that should be used to space characters.

Figure 12.29

4 Click **OK** to close the **Font** dialog box. In the **Clipboard group**, double-click the **Format Painter** button to turn it on. Select each of the following paragraphs to apply the same formatting you applied to *Rides*: *Entertainment*, *Food*, *Theme Park FAQ*, and *Catering for Groups*. In the **Clipboard group**, click the **Format Painter** button to turn it off. Press Ctrl + Home and then compare your screen with Figure 12.30.

Figure 12.30

Formatted paragraphs

5 On **Page 1**, in the first column, select the four paragraphs beginning with *Family Rides* and ending with *Water Rides*. In the **Paragraph group**, click the **Bullets** button.

6 On **Page 1**, in the third column, select the paragraph *When to Visit*, being sure to include the colon. On the Mini toolbar, apply **Bold** and **Underline**, click the **Font Color button arrow**, and then in the eighth column, click the fifth color—**Purple, Accent 4, Darker 25%**. In the **Paragraph group**, click the **Line and Paragraph Spacing** button, and then click **Remove Space After Paragraph**.

7 In the **Clipboard group**, double-click the **Format Painter** button, and then apply the formatting you applied to *When to Visit* to the paragraphs *Weather Tips*, *Guest Services*, *Food Options*, and *Bookings*. In the **Clipboard group**, click the **Format Painter** button to turn it off.

8 On **Page 1**, at the bottom of the third column, select the four paragraphs beginning with *Stroller rentals* and ending with *Park maps*. In the **Paragraph group**, click the **Bullets** button. Click to position the insertion point anywhere in the paragraph *Park maps*. In the **Paragraph group**, click the **Line and Paragraph Spacing** button, and then click **Remove Space After Paragraph**.

9 At the bottom of **Page 1**, in the first column, select the paragraph that begins *Some rides*. On the Mini toolbar, change the **Font Size** to **10**, and then apply **Italic**. Deselect the text, and then compare your screen with Figure 12.31. **Save** your changes.

Figure 12.31

Paragraph with italic format

Bulleted paragraphs

Formatted paragraphs

Activity 12.08 | Inserting Nonbreaking Hyphens and Nonbreaking Spaces

Recall that word wrap automatically moves text from the right edge of a paragraph to the beginning of the next line as is necessary to fit within the margins. You can insert a *nonbreaking hyphen* to prevent a hyphenated word or phrase—such as a phone number—from being displayed on separate lines. Similarly, you can insert a *nonbreaking space* to keep two or more words together so that both words will wrap even if only the second word would normally wrap to the next line. For example, inserting nonbreaking spaces in a date will keep the entire date—month, day, and year—on the same line.

Another Way

On the Insert tab, in the Symbols group, click the Symbol button, then click More Symbols. In the Symbols dialog box, click the Special Characters tab, click Nonbreaking Hyphen, and then click Insert.

1 On **Page 1**, in the second column, in the fourth paragraph, locate the phrase *air-conditioned*. Select the hyphen, and then press Ctrl + Shift + - to insert a nonbreaking hyphen. Notice that the entire term *air-conditioned* now displays on the same line. Compare your screen with Figure 12.32.

You can improve the readability of a document by inserting a nonbreaking hyphen.

Figure 12.32

Nonbreaking hyphen

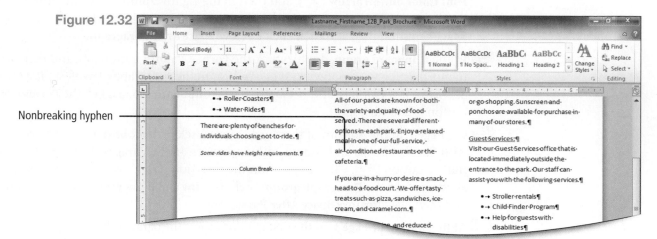

2 On **Page 2**, in the first column, in the fourth paragraph, locate the phrase *all–you-care-to-eat*. Select the hyphen between *all* and *you*, and then press Ctrl + Shift + - . In a similar manner, insert nonbreaking hyphens to replace each of the remaining three hyphens in the phrase.

If you have a hyphenated term that contains multiple hyphens, it is good practice to replace all hyphens with nonbreaking hyphens. If preceding text or other elements are modified, this will ensure that the text will display on a single line.

3 On **Page 2**, in the first column, in the last paragraph, locate the phone number. Using the technique you just practiced, replace the two hyphens with nonbreaking hyphens. Compare your screen with Figure 12.33.

Figure 12.33

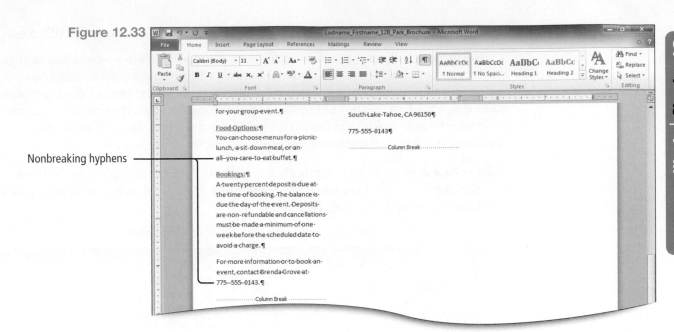

Nonbreaking hyphens

4 On **Page 1**, in the second column, in the fifth paragraph, locate the term *ice cream*. Select the space following *ice*, and then press Ctrl + Shift + Spacebar. Compare your screen with Figure 12.34.

> The term *ice cream* displays on one line. A small raised circle, the nonbreaking space formatting mark, displays between the two words.

Figure 12.34

Nonbreaking space

5 In the last line of the same paragraph, using the technique you just practiced, replace the space between *caramel* and *corn* with a nonbreaking space.

6 **Save** your changes.

Objective 4 | Format Graphic and Text Elements

Inserting and formatting graphics and text can enhance the appearance of a document. Word provides many features to modify graphic and text elements. You have used some of these features in previous projects. In this project, you will utilize additional features to modify text boxes, pictures, bullets, and text.

Activity 12.09 | Viewing Document Gridlines and Linking Text Boxes

Document gridlines—nonprinting horizontal and vertical lines—assist you in aligning graphics and other elements. Recall that text boxes are movable, resizable containers for text or graphics. Word includes a feature to link two or more text boxes. When text boxes are linked, if the first text box cannot hold all of the inserted text, the text automatically flows into the next, linked text box. In this activity, you will display gridlines to help position text boxes, link text boxes, and insert text from an existing file.

1 On **Page 2**, in the third column, click to position the insertion point in the blank paragraph. On the **View tab**, in the **Show group**, click to select the **Gridlines** check box. Compare your screen with Figure 12.35.

> The gridlines display only within the margins of the document.

Figure 12.35

Gridlines check box

View tab

Gridlines

2 On **Page 2**, in the first column, click to position the insertion point at the end of the last paragraph. On the **Insert tab**, in the **Text group**, click the **Text Box** button, and then click **Draw Text Box**. Using the gridlines, position the ➕ pointer at the left margin two gridlines below the last paragraph, drag to the right **18** squares, drag down **7** squares, and then release the mouse button. If necessary, resize the text box so that the right border aligns at approximately 2 inches on the horizontal ruler and the bottom border aligns at approximately 0.75 inch on the lower portion of the vertical ruler. Compare your screen with Figure 12.36.

Figure 12.36

Text box

3 Deselect the text box. On **Page 2**, in the second column, select the four paragraphs, and then on the Mini toolbar, apply **Bold** B and **Center** ☰. On the **Home tab**, in the **Paragraph group**, click the **Line and Paragraph Spacing** button ‡≡⁻, and then click **Remove Space After Paragraph**.

4 In the second column, position the insertion point to the left of the first paragraph, and then press Enter two times.

5 In the second column, position the insertion point in the first blank paragraph. On the **Insert tab**, in the **Text group**, click the **Text Box** button, and then click **Draw Text Box**. Using the gridlines and existing text as a guide, position the ⊞ pointer at the top margin one gridline to the left of *Fascination*. Drag to the right **18** squares until the border is one gridline to the right of *Group*, drag down until the bottom of the text box is aligned with the gridline located below the text *avoid a charge* (in the first column), and then release the mouse button. If necessary, resize the text box so that the right border aligns at approximately 2 inches on the horizontal ruler and the bottom border aligns at approximately 3.75 inches on the vertical ruler.

6 With the text box selected, on the **Format tab**, in the **Arrange group**, click the **Wrap Text** button, and then click **Top and Bottom**. Compare your screen with Figure 12.37.

> Top and Bottom text wrapping causes the four paragraphs of text and the two blank paragraphs above them to be moved below the text box.

Figure 12.37

Text box

Formatted paragraphs

7 At the bottom of the first column, click in the text box to select it. On the **Format tab**, in the **Text group**, click the **Create Link** button ⚭.

8 Move the pointer into a blank area of the document, and notice that the ⛾ pointer displays.

> The upright pitcher indicates that the first text box is ready to be linked to another text box.

9 Move your pointer into the text box in the second column, and notice that the 🍶 pointer displays. Compare your screen with Figure 12.38.

The pouring pitcher indicates that this second text box can be linked to the first text box.

Figure 12.38

Pointer displays as pouring pitcher

10 With the 🍶 pointer displayed, click in the second text box to create a link.

11 If necessary, click to position the insertion point in the first text box. On the **Insert tab**, in the **Text group**, click the **Object button arrow**, and then click **Text from File**. Navigate to the student files for this chapter, select the file **w12B_Comments**, and then click **Insert**. Compare your screen with Figure 12.39.

The first two paragraphs of text display in the first text box and the remaining text displays in the second text box.

Figure 12.39

Inserted text

12 In the first text box, select the first paragraph, and then on the Mini toolbar, apply **Bold** **B** and **Center** ≡ .

13 In the second text box, click to position the insertion point to the left of the first paragraph, press Enter, press ↑ , and then type **More Comments** Select the text you just typed, and then on the Mini toolbar, apply **Bold** **B** and **Center** ≡ .

14 On the **Format tab**, in the **Shape Styles group**, click the **More** button ⏷ . In the **Shape Styles** gallery, in the fourth row, click the fifth style—**Subtle Effect – Purple, Accent 4**. In a similar manner, apply the **Subtle Effect – Purple, Accent 4** shape style to the other text box. Compare your screen with Figure 12.40.

Figure 12.40

Formatted text boxes

15 On the **View tab**, in the **Show group**, click to deselect the **Gridlines** check box to hide the gridlines. **Save** 🖫 your changes.

Activity 12.10 | Modifying Text Effects

You can modify the built-in text effects in Word in a variety of ways—for example, by changing the weight and color of the outline and by altering the type of reflection.

1 On **Page 2**, position the insertion point at the top of the third column, and then type **OUR THEME PARKS**

2 Press Enter two times, and then type **Fun for all ages!** Select the paragraph you just typed, and then on the Mini toolbar, change the **Font Size** to **20**, and apply **Italic** **I** and **Center** ≡ .

3 On the **Home tab**, in the **Font group**, click the **Text Effects** button. In the **Text Effects** gallery, in the first row, click the third effect—**Fill – White, Drop Shadow**. With the text still selected, click the **Text Effect**s button, point to **Outline**, and then under **Theme Colors**, in the eighth column, click the fifth color—**Purple, Accent 4, Darker 25%**. In the **Font group**, click the **Font Color button arrow** ![A] , and then in the eighth column, click the fourth color—**Purple, Accent 4, Lighter 40%**. Deselect the text, and then compare your screen with Figure 12.41.

> The theme allows you to choose a consistent color scheme to create a professional-looking document.

Figure 12.41

Text Effects button

Formatted paragraph

4 In the third column, select the first paragraph. On the Mini toolbar, change the **Font Size** to **20**, and then apply **Bold** ![B] and **Center** ![≡]. On the **Home tab**, in the **Font group**, click the **Text Effects** button, and then in the fourth row, click the fifth effect—**Gradient Fill – Purple, Accent 4, Reflection**. Click the **Text Effects** button, point to **Glow**, and then under **Glow Variations**, in the third row, click the fourth option—**Purple, 11 pt glow, Accent color 4**. Deselect the text, and then compare your screen with Figure 12.42.

Figure 12.42

Paragraphs formatted with Text Effects

5 **Save** ![save] your changes.

Activity 12.11 | Applying Artistic Effects to Pictures

You can change the appearance of a picture by applying an ***artistic effect***—a filter that you apply to an image to create a special effect.

1 On **Page 1**, in the first column, position the insertion point at the end of the second paragraph, and then press Enter.

2 On the **Insert tab**, in the **Illustrations group**, click the **Picture** button. In the **Insert Picture** dialog box, navigate to your student files, select the file **w12B_Carousel**, and then click **Insert**.

3 On the **Format tab**, in the **Adjust group**, click the **Artistic Effects** button. Point to the various options.

> Live preview allows you to see how each option will modify the picture.

4 In the **Artistic Effects** gallery, in the fourth row, click the last option—**Plastic Wrap**. Compare your screen with Figure 12.43.

Figure 12.43

Artistic Effects button

Formatted picture

5 On **Page 2**, in the third column, position the insertion point in the second, blank paragraph. On the **Home tab**, in the **Paragraph group**, click **Center** ⬛.

6 On the **Insert tab**, in the **Illustrations group**, click the **Picture** button. In the **Insert Picture** dialog box, navigate to your student files, select the file **w12B_Coaster**, and then click **Insert**. Notice that the picture is inserted in the first column on **Page 3**. On the **Format tab**, in the **Size group**, click in the **Shape Height** box ⬛ 1.5" ▾, select the existing text, type **4.2** and then press Enter. Notice that the resized picture displays in the third column on **Page 2**.

7 In the **Adjust group**, click the **Artistic Effects** button, and then in the second row, click the fourth option—**Glow Diffused**.

8 On the **Format tab**, in the **Picture Styles group**, click the **More** button ▾, and then click the first option—**Simple Frame, White**. In the **Picture Styles group**, click the **Picture Border button arrow**, and then in the eighth column, click the first color—**Purple, Accent 4**. Compare your screen with Figure 12.44.

Figure 12.44

Picture Border button

Single Frame,
White picture style

Shape Height box

Formatted picture

9 Save 🖫 your changes.

Activity 12.12 | Using a Picture as a Bullet

In this activity, you will use a picture to replace the bullets in the document.

1 On **Page 1**, in the first column, select the four bulleted paragraphs. On the **Home tab**, in the **Paragraph group**, click the **Bullets button arrow** ⊞▾, and then click **Define New Bullet**.

2 In the **Define New Bullet** dialog box, under **Bullet character**, click the **Picture** button.

3 In the **Picture Bullet** dialog box, click the **Import** button.

4 In the **Add Clips to Organizer** dialog box, navigate to your student files, select **w12B_Brochure_Bullet**, and then click the **Add** button. Compare your screen with Figure 12.45.

> The picture—a combination of purple, red, and orange squares—displays in the Picture Bullet dialog box. The new bullet is stored in the Bullet Library of the Clip Organizer.

Figure 12.45

Picture Bullet dialog box

Picture added—your view may differ

5 If necessary, click the picture, and then click **OK**. Notice that the picture displays as a bullet in the Preview box.

6 Click **OK**, and notice that the picture displays as bullets for the four paragraphs.

7 On **Page 1**, in the third column, select the four bulleted paragraphs. In the **Paragraph group**, click the **Bullet arrow** ⊞▾, and then compare your screen with Figure 12.46.

> The new picture bullet displays under Recently Used Bullets, Bullet Library, and Document Bullets.

Figure 12.46

Picture bullet

8 Under **Recently Used Bullets**, click the new picture bullet to apply the bullet to the selected paragraphs. Deselect the paragraphs, and then compare your screen with Figure 12.47.

Figure 12.47

Picture bullet applied

9 Press Ctrl + Home, and then display the **Document Information Panel**. In the **Author** box, type your first and last names. In the **Subject** box, type your course name and section number, and then in the **Keywords** box, type **brochure, graphics Close** the Document Information Panel.

10 **Save** 💾 your changes. Print your document or submit electronically as directed by your instructor, and then **Exit** Word.

End You have completed Project 12B ———————————————

Content-Based Assessments

Summary

In this chapter, you created an outline in Word by assigning levels and then used the outline to create a PowerPoint presentation. The presentation was published in Word as a handout displaying the slides and blank lines for notes. You changed the paper size of a document and modified how text displays by changing character spacing, and creating nonbreaking hyphens and spaces. Finally, you enhanced the document by linking text boxes, applying text and artistic effects, and using a picture as a bullet.

Key Terms

.pptx.....................701	Kerning 711	Outline 695
Artistic effect 720	Layout 702	Outline level 695
Character spacing 711	Minus outline symbol....696	Outline symbol 695
Document gridlines 716	Nonbreaking hyphen 714	Plus outline symbol 695
Handout.........................706	Nonbreaking space 714	

Matching

Match each term in the second column with its correct definition in the first column by writing the letter of the term on the blank line in front of the correct definition.

_____ 1. A Word feature that allows you to organize the contents of a document in a structured manner.

_____ 2. A Word feature that defines the position of a paragraph in relation to all topics in a document and is formatted with a heading style.

_____ 3. A paragraph mark that indicates there are subordinate heading or body text paragraphs.

_____ 4. A paragraph mark that indicates there are no subordinate heading or body text paragraphs.

_____ 5. The action of assigning a paragraph to a lower level.

_____ 6. The action of assigning a paragraph to a higher level.

_____ 7. The action of hiding all subordinate heading and body text paragraphs.

_____ 8. The placement of the text and graphic elements on a slide.

_____ 9. This is normally the first slide in a presentation.

_____ 10. A document that is given to an audience to accompany a lecture.

_____ 11. A character spacing option that raises or lowers text in relation to the current vertical location.

_____ 12. A character spacing option that automatically adjusts the spacing between pairs of letters.

_____ 13. A formatting mark that prevents a hyphenated word or phrase from being displayed on two lines.

_____ 14. Nonprinting horizontal and vertical lines used to assist in aligning graphics and other elements.

_____ 15. A filter that is applied to an image to create a special effect.

A Artistic effect

B Collapse

C Demote

D Document gridlines

E Handout

F Kerning

G Layout

H Minus outline symbol

I Nonbreaking hyphen

J Outline

K Outline level

L Plus outline symbol

M Position

N Promote

O Title Slide

Content-Based Assessments

Multiple Choice

Circle the correct answer.

1. A paragraph that is not assigned an outline level is called:

   A. body text
   B. primary text
   C. unformatted text

2. In order to display all subordinate paragraphs, a paragraph assigned an outline level must be:

   A. collapsed
   B. expanded
   C. promoted

3. You can open a Word outline in PowerPoint because Microsoft Office is an:

   A. integrated program
   B. integrated suite
   C. interconnected program

4. What is the default PowerPoint 2010 file extension?

   A. .ppt
   B. .wpt
   C. .pptx

5. What is the Word feature that allows you to change the default spacing constraints between characters?

   A. character spacing
   B. character formatting
   C. text spacing

6. To expand or compress spacing between characters by a specific number of points, use the:

   A. Position option
   B. Scale option
   C. Spacing option

7. A formatting mark that keeps two words together so that both words will wrap even if only the second word would normally wrap to the next line is a:

   A. nonbreaking hyphen
   B. nonbreaking return
   C. nonbreaking space

8. In order to have text automatically flow from one text box to another, the text boxes must be:

   A. embedded
   B. linked
   C. merged

9. To maintain a consistent color scheme throughout a document, you should apply a:

   A. format
   B. style
   C. theme

10. When you use a picture to define a bullet, the image is stored in the:

    A. Clip Organizer
    B. Building Blocks Organizer
    C. Quick Parts gallery

Content-Based Assessments

1. Integrate Word with PowerPoint
2. Modify a PowerPoint Presentation

Skills Review | Project **12C** Park Changes

In the following Skills Review project, you will create an outline and then use it to create a PowerPoint presentation explaining proposed changes for Fascination Entertainment Group's water parks for the upcoming season. You will also create a handout for management based on the presentation. Your completed files will look similar to Figure 12.48.

Project Files

For Project 12C, you will need the following files:

> w12C_Changes_Outline
> w12C_Water_Park

You will save your files as:

> Lastname_Firstname_12C_Changes_Outline
> Lastname_Firstname_12C_Changes_Presentation
> Lastname_Firstname_12C_Changes_Handout

Project Results

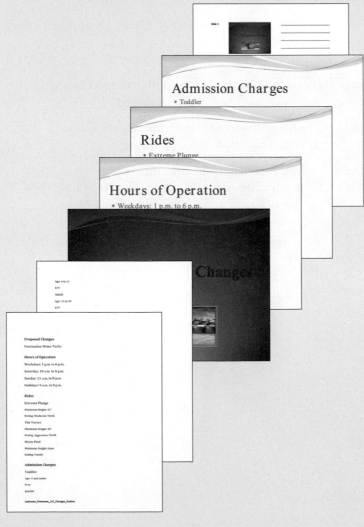

Figure 12.48

(Project 12C Park Changes continues on the next page)

Skills Review | Project 12C Park Changes (continued)

1 **Start** Word. From your student files, open the file **w12C_Changes_Outline**. Save it to your **Word Chapter 12** folder as **Lastname_Firstname_12C_Changes_Outline** Insert the file name in the footer.

 a. On the **View tab**, in the **Document Views group**, click the **Outline** button.

 b. Select the first paragraph. On the **Outlining tab**, in the **Outline Tools group**, click the **Outline Level arrow**, and then click **Level 1**.

 c. For each of the three remaining paragraphs formatted with bold, on the **Outlining tab**, in the **Outline Tools group**, click the **Promote to Heading 1** button.

 d. Select the second paragraph of the document, click the **Outline Level arrow**, and then click **Level 2**.

 e. Below the paragraph *Hours of Operation*, select all four paragraphs, click the **Outline level arrow**, and then click **Level 2**.

 f. In a similar manner, below each of the remaining *Level 1* paragraphs, select the body text paragraphs, and then assign the **Level 2** outline level.

2 Below the paragraph *Toddler*, select the two paragraphs *Age: 3 and under* and *Free*. On the **Outlining tab**, in the **Outline Tools group**, click the **Demote** button.

 a. Below the paragraph *Junior*, select the two paragraphs. On the **Outlining tab**, in the **Outline Tools group**, click the **Demote** button.

 b. In a similar manner, select the two paragraphs below the **Level 2** paragraphs *Adult*, *Senior*, *Extreme Plunge*, *The Vortex*, and *Wave Pool*, and then click the **Demote** button.

 c. Select the paragraphs *Hours of Operation*, *Admission Charges*, and *Rides*. In the **Outline Tools group**, click the **Collapse** button.

 d. Select the paragraph *Rides*, and then in the **Outline Tools group**, click the **Move Up** button. Select the three collapsed **Level 1** paragraphs, and then in the **Outline Tools group**, click the **Expand** button.

 e. On the **Outlining tab**, in the **Close group**, click the **Close Outline View** button.

3 Press Ctrl + Home. On the **Page Layout tab**, in the **Themes group**, click the **Theme Colors** button, and then in the **Theme Colors** gallery, click **Flow**.

 a. Display the **Document Information Panel**. In the **Author** box, type your first and last names. In the

(Project 12C Park Changes continues on the next page)

Subject box, type your course name and section number, and then in the **Keywords** box, type **park changes, outline** Close the Document Information Panel.

 b. **Save** your changes, and then **Exit** Word.

4 From the **Start** menu, locate then click **Microsoft Office PowerPoint 2010. Maximize** the PowerPoint window.

 a. In **Backstage** view, click **Open**, and then navigate to your **Word Chapter 12** folder. At the bottom of the **Open** dialog box, click the **All PowerPoint Presentations arrow**, and then click **All Outlines**. Click to select **Lastname_Firstname_12C_Changes_Outline**, and then click **Open**.

 b. From **Backstage** view, display the **Save As** dialog box, navigate to your **Word Chapter 12** folder, and then using your own name, save the file as **Lastname_Firstname_12C_Changes_Presentation**

 c. On the **Design tab**, in the **Themes group**, click the **More** button. In the **Themes** gallery, under **Built-In**, click **Flow**.

 d. On the **Home tab**, in the **Slides group**, click the **Layout** button to display the **Slide Layout** gallery.

 e. With **Slide 1** displayed in the **Slide pane**, in the **Slide Layout** gallery, click the first option—**Title Slide**.

5 On the **Insert tab**, in the **Images group**, click the **Picture** button.

 a. In the **Insert Picture** dialog box, navigate to your student files for this chapter, click **w12C_Water_Park**, and then click **Insert**.

 b. If necessary, on the View tab, in the Show group, click the Ruler check box to select it. Position the picture so that the top border of the picture displays at **approximately 1 inch on the lower portion on the vertical ruler** and the center of the picture aligns at **approximately 0 inch on the horizontal ruler**.

 c. Click the **Insert tab**, and then in the **Text group**, click the **Header & Footer** button.

 d. In the **Header and Footer** dialog box, on the **Slide tab**, click to select the **Footer** check box. In the **Footer** box, type **Lastname_Firstname_12C_Changes_Presentation** Click to select the **Don't show on title slide** check box, and then click **Apply to All**.

 e. **Save** your changes.

Content-Based Assessments

6 Click the **File tab** to display **Backstage** view. Click **Save & Send**, and then under **File Types**, click **Create Handouts**.

a. Under **Create Handouts in Microsoft Word**, click the **Create Handouts** button. In the **Send to Microsoft Word** dialog box, under **Page layout in Microsoft Word**, click to select the **Blank lines next to slides** option button. Click **OK**.

b. On the **Taskbar**, click the **Word** icon. If necessary, on the Layout tab, in the Table group, click to select the View Gridlines check box.

c. From **Backstage** view, display the **Save As** dialog box, navigate to your **Word Chapter 12** folder, and then using your own name, save the file as **Lastname_ Firstname_12C_Changes_Handout** Using **Quick Parts**, insert the file name in the footer.

d. In the first row of the table, in the third cell, select the first three lines, and then press **Del**. In a similar manner, in the third column, delete the first three lines from each of the remaining three cells.

e. Point slightly outside of the upper left corner of the table to display the **Table Move Handle**. Click the **Table Move Handle** to select the entire table. On the **Layout tab**, in the **Cell Size group**, change the **Shape Height** to **2.2"**.

f. Press **Ctrl** + **Home**, and then display the **Document Information Panel**. In the **Author** box, type your first and last names. In the **Subject** box, type your course name and section number, and then in the **Keywords** box, type **park changes, handout Close** the Document Information Panel.

g. **Save** your changes, and then **Exit** Word. In PowerPoint, **Save** your changes, and then **Exit** PowerPoint. Print both Word documents or submit all three files electronically as directed by your instructor.

End **You have completed Project 12C**

Content-Based Assessments

Apply **12B** skills from these Objectives:

3 Modify the Document Layout

4 Format Graphic and Text Elements

Skills Review | Project **12D** Resort Facilities

In the following Skills Review project, you will format a document, insert graphics, and link text boxes to create a brochure containing information about Fascination Entertainment Group's resorts. Your completed document will look similar to Figure 12.49.

Project Files

For Project 12D, you will need the following files:

w12D_Resort_Facilities
w12D_Resort_Reviews
w12D_Pool
w12D_Room
w12D_Towel
w12D_Resort_Bullet

You will save your document as:

Lastname_Firstname_12D_Resort_Facilities

Project Results

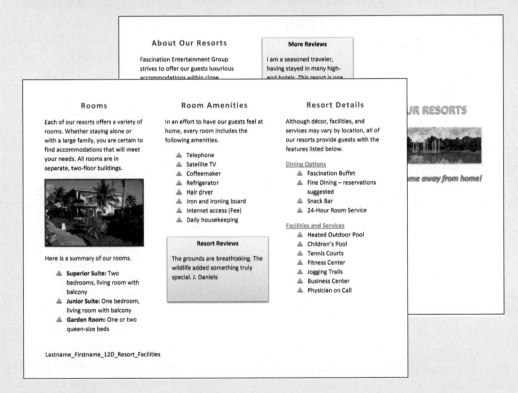

Figure 12.49

(Project 12D Resort Facilities continues on the next page)

Content-Based Assessments

Skills Review | Project **12D** Resort Facilities (continued)

1 **Start** Word. From your student files, open the file **w12D_Resort_Facilities**. Save the document to your **Word Chapter 12** folder as **Lastname_Firstname_12D_Resort_Facilities** Insert the file name in the footer.

a. On the **Page Layout tab**, in the **Page Setup group**, click the **Orientation** button, and then click **Landscape**. In the **Page Setup group**, click the **Margins** button, and then click **Narrow**. In the **Page Setup group**, click the **Columns** button, and then click **Three**.

b. On **Page 1**, in the first column, position the insertion point to the left of the paragraph *Room Amenities*. In the **Page Setup group**, click the **Breaks** button, and then under **Page Breaks**, click **Column**. In the second column, position the insertion point to the left of the paragraph *Resort Details*. Using the technique you just practiced, insert a **Column** break.

c. In the third column, to the left of the paragraph *About Our Resorts*, click to position the insertion point, and then press Ctrl + Enter.

d. On **Page 2**, position the insertion point to the left of the paragraph *Resorts Division*, and then using the technique you practiced, insert a **Column** break.

e. In the **Page Setup group**, click the **Size** button, and then at the bottom of the list, click **More Paper Sizes**. In the **Page Setup** dialog box, under **Paper size**, click the **Paper size arrow**, and then click **Custom size**. Click the **Width spin box down arrow** to 9". Click the **Height spin box down arrow** to 7". Click **OK**, and then **Save** your changes.

2 In the first column, select the *Rooms* paragraph. On the Mini toolbar, change the **Font Size** to 14, apply **Bold** and **Center**, click the **Font Color button arrow**, and then click **Olive Green, Accent 3, Darker 50%**—in the seventh column, the last color.

a. With the paragraph still selected, on the **Home tab**, in the **Font group**, click the **dialog box launcher**. In the **Font** dialog box, click the **Advanced** tab. Under **Character Spacing**, click the **Spacing arrow**, and then click **Expanded**. Click the **By spin box up arrow** to **1.2 pt**. Click **OK**.

b. In the **Clipboard group**, double-click the **Format Painter** button. Select each of the following paragraphs to apply the format: *Room Amenities*, *Resort Details*, and *About Our Resorts*. Click the **Format Painter** button to turn it off.

c. On **Page 1**, in the first column, select the last three paragraphs beginning with *Superior Suite*. In the **Paragraph group**, click the **Bullets** button.

d. On **Page 1**, in the third column, select the paragraph *Dining Options*. On the Mini toolbar, apply **Bold** and **Underline**, click the **Font Color button arrow**, and then click **Olive Green, Accent 3, Darker 25%**—in the seventh column, the fifth color.

e. In the **Paragraph group**, click the **Line and Paragraph Spacing** button, and then click **Remove Space After Paragraph**. In the **Clipboard group**, click the **Format Painter** button, and then in the third column, apply the format to the paragraph *Facilities and Services*.

f. In the second column, select the eight paragraphs beginning with *Telephone* and ending with *Daily housekeeping*, and then in the **Paragraph group**, click the **Bullets** button. In a similar manner, apply bullets to the four paragraphs below *Dining Options*, and the seven paragraphs below *Facilities and Services*.

g. On **Page 2**, in the first column, in the last paragraph, locate the phone number. Select the hyphen following *775*, and then press Ctrl + Shift + - to insert a non-breaking hyphen. In a similar manner, select the hyphen following *555*, and then insert a nonbreaking hyphen. **Save** your changes.

3 Press Ctrl + Home. On the **View tab**, in the **Show group**, click to select the **Gridlines** check box.

a. On the **Insert tab**, in the **Text group**, click the **Text Box** button, and then click **Draw Text Box**. In the second column, position the ⊞ pointer at the beginning of the column break formatting mark. Drag to the right until you are one gridline past the column break formatting mark, drag down **12** squares, and then release the mouse button. If necessary, resize the text box so that the right border aligns with the second gridline to the right of the 2-inch mark on the horizontal ruler and the bottom border aligns at approximately 1.5 inches on the lower portion of the vertical ruler.

b. On **Page 2**, in the second column, click to position the insertion point to the left of *Resorts Division*. On the **Insert tab**, in the **Text group**, click the **Text Box** button, and then click **Draw Text Box**. In the second column, position the ⊞ pointer at the top margin one line to the right of the beginning of the

(Project 12D Resort Facilities continues on the next page)

paragraph *Resorts*. Drag to the right **18** squares until the border is two squares to the right of *Group*, and then drag down until the bottom of the text box is aligned with the line below the text *Lodging* (in the first column). Release the mouse button. If necessary, resize the text box so that the right border aligns at approximately 2 inches on the horizontal ruler and the bottom border aligns at approximately 3.25 inches on the vertical ruler.

c. On the **Format tab**, in the **Arrange group**, click the **Wrap Text** button, and then click **Top and Bottom**. Scroll, if necessary, to display a portion of both text boxes simultaneously. On **Page 1**, in the second column, click the text box to select it. On the **Format tab**, in the **Text group**, click the **Create Link** button. On **Page 2**, point to the text box, and then click to create a link.

d. If necessary, on Page 1, click to position the insertion point in the text box. On the **Insert tab**, in the **Text group**, click the **Object button arrow**, and then click **Text from File**. From your student files, select the file **w12D_Resort_Reviews**, and then click **Insert**.

e. In the second text box, click to the left of the text *I am*, type **More Reviews** and then press Enter. Select the text you just typed, and on the Mini toolbar, apply **Bold** and **Center**.

f. With the second text box selected, on the **Format tab**, in the **Shape Styles group**, click the **More** button. In the **Shape Styles** gallery, in the fourth row, click the fourth style—**Subtle Effect – Olive Green, Accent 3**. In a similar manner, apply the shape style to the first text box.

g. On the **View tab**, in the **Show group**, click to deselect the **Gridlines** check box to hide the gridlines. **Save** your changes.

4 On **Page 2**, in the second column, select the five paragraphs below the text box. On the Mini toolbar, apply **Bold** and **Center**. On the **Home tab**, in the **Font group**, click the **Text Effects** button, and then in the fourth row, click the second text effect—**Gradient Fill – Orange, Accent 6, Inner Shadow**.

a. On **Page 2**, in the second column, position the insertion point at the end of the last paragraph, and then press Enter. On the **Page Layout tab**, in the **Page Setup group**, click the **Breaks** button. Under **Page Breaks**, click **Column**.

b. With the insertion point at the beginning of the third column, on the **Home tab**, in the **Styles group**, click the **Normal** style.

c. Type **OUR RESORTS** Press Enter two times, and then type **Your home away from home!**

d. Select the paragraph you just typed, and then on the Mini toolbar, change the **Font Size** to **14**, and apply **Italic** and **Center**. On the **Home tab**, in the **Font group**, click the **Text Effects** button. In the **Text Effects** gallery, in the first row, click the third effect—**Fill – White, Drop Shadow**. Click the **Text Effects** button, point to **Outline**, and then under **Theme Colors**, click **Olive Green, Accent 3, Darker 25%**—in the seventh column, the fifth color. In the **Font group**, click the **Font Color button arrow**, and then click **Olive Green, Accent 3, Lighter 40%**—in the seventh column, the fourth color.

e. Select the first paragraph in the column. On the Mini toolbar, change the **Font Size** to **20**, and then apply **Bold** and **Center**. On the **Home tab**, in the **Font group**, click the **Text Effects** button, and then click **Fill – Olive Green, Accent 3, Outline - Text 2**—in the first row, the last effect. **Save** your changes.

5 On **Page 1**, in the first column, position the insertion point at the end of the second paragraph, and then press Enter. On the **Insert tab**, in the **Illustrations group**, click the **Picture** button. In the **Insert Picture** dialog box, navigate to your student files, select the file **w12D_Room**, and then click **Insert**.

a. On the **Format tab**, in the **Adjust group**, click the **Artistic Effects** button. In the **Artistic Effects** gallery, in the fourth row, click the second option—**Texturizer**.

b. On **Page 2**, in the third column, click in the third, blank paragraph. On the **Insert tab**, in the **Illustrations group**, click the **Picture** button. In the **Insert Picture** dialog box, navigate to your student files, select the file **w12D_Pool**, and then click **Insert**.

c. On the **Format tab**, in the **Adjust group**, click the **Artistic Effects** button. In the **Artistic Effects** gallery, in the third row, click the second option—**Watercolor Sponge**.

d. Position the insertion point to the left of the paragraph *Our Resorts*, and then press Enter two times. **Save** your changes.

(Project 12D Resort Facilities continues on the next page)

Content-Based Assessments

6 On **Page 1**, in the first column, select the three bulleted paragraphs. On the **Home tab**, in the **Paragraph group**, click the **Bullets button arrow**, and then click **Define New Bullet**.

   a. In the **Define New Bullet** dialog box, under **Bullet character**, click the **Picture** button. In the **Picture Bullet** dialog box, click **Import**.

   b. In the **Add Clips to Organizer** dialog box, navigate to your student files, select **w12D_Resort_Bullet**, and then click the **Add** button. Click **OK** two times to close the dialog boxes.

   c. In the second column, select the bulleted list. In the **Paragraph group**, click the **Bullet arrow**. Under

Recently Used Bullets, click the *Resort Bullet*. In the same manner, apply the *Resort Bullet* to the two bulleted lists in the third column.

   d. Press Ctrl + Home. Display the **Document Information Panel**. In the **Author** box, type your first and last names. In the **Subject** box, type your course name and section number, and then in the **Keywords** box, type **facilities, graphics, reviews Close** the Document Information Panel.

   e. **Save** your changes.

7 Print your document or submit electronically as directed by your instructor. **Exit** Word.

End **You have completed Project 12D** ———————————————

Content-Based Assessments

Apply **12A** skills from these Objectives:

- **1** Integrate Word with PowerPoint
- **2** Modify a PowerPoint Presentation

Mastering Word | Project **12E** Summer Employment

In the following Mastering Word project, you will create an outline and then use it to create a PowerPoint presentation that can be shown to individuals interested in summer employment at a Fascination Entertainment Group theme park. You will also create a handout for individuals based on the presentation. Your completed files will look similar to Figure 12.50.

Project Files

For Project 12E, you will need the following files:

> w12E_Employment_Outline
> w12E_Vendor

You will save your files as:

> Lastname_Firstname_12E_Employment_Outline
> Lastname_Firstname_12E_Employment_Presentation
> Lastname_Firstname_12E_Employment_Handout

Project Results

Figure 12.50

(Project 12E Summer Employment continues on the next page)

Content-Based Assessments

Mastering Word | Project 12E Summer Employment (continued)

1 **Start** Word. Navigate to your student files, and open the file **w12E_Employment_Outline**. **Save** the document to your **Word Chapter 12** folder as **Lastname_Firstname_12E_Employment_Outline** Insert the file name in the footer.

2 In **Outline** view, assign **Level 1** to all paragraphs formatted with bold, and then assign **Level 2** to all remaining paragraphs. **Collapse** the paragraphs *Benefits* and *Available Positions*. **Move Up** the *Available Positions* paragraph and subtext so that it displays above *Benefits*. **Expand** all *Level 1* paragraphs.

3 In **Print Layout** view, display the **Theme Colors** gallery, and then click **Solstice**. Display the **Document Information Panel**. In the **Author** box, type your first and last names. In the **Subject** box, type your course name and section number, and then in the **Keywords** box, type **employment, outline Save** your changes, and then **Exit** Word.

4 **Start** PowerPoint. Display the **Open** dialog box, change the types of files to **All Outlines**, and then from your **Word Chapter 12** folder, open your **Lastname_Firstname_12E_Employment_Outline** file. **Save** the PowerPoint file to your **Word Chapter 12** folder as **Lastname_Firstname_12E_Employment_Presentation** Display the **Themes** gallery, and click **Solstice**. Display

the **Layout** gallery, and then apply the **Title Slide** layout to **Slide 1**.

5 On **Slide 1**, from your student files, locate and then **Insert** the **Picture** file **w12E_Vendor**. Move the picture so that the bottom right corner of the picture aligns with the bottom right corner of the slide, as shown in Figure 12.50. Display the **Header and Footer** dialog box. Select the **Footer** and **Don't show on title slide** check boxes, and then in the **Footer** box, type **Lastname_Firstname_12E_Presentation Save** your changes.

6 To create a handout, display the **Send To Microsoft Word** dialog box, and then select the **Blank lines next to slides** option button. Click **OK**.

7 In **Word**, save the document to your **Word Chapter 12** folder as **Lastname_Firstname_12E_Employment_Handout** Insert the file name in the footer. Display the **Document Information Panel**. In the **Author** box, type your first and last names. In the **Subject** box, type your course name and section number, and then in the **Keywords** box, type **employment, handout Save** your changes, and then **Exit** Word. In PowerPoint, **Save** your changes, and then **Exit** PowerPoint.

8 Print both Word documents or submit all three files electronically as directed by your instructor.

End **You have completed Project 12E** —————————————

Content-Based Assessments

Apply **12B** skills from
these Objectives:

- **3** Modify the
  Document Layout
- **4** Format Graphic and
  Text Elements

Mastering Word | Project **12F** First Aid

In the following Mastering Word project, you will format a document, insert graphics, and link text boxes to create a leaflet containing first aid information for Fascination Entertainment Group's employees. Your completed document will look similar to Figure 12.51.

Project Files

For Project 12F, you will need the following files:

> w12F_First_Aid
> w12F_Contact_Information
> w12F_Cabinet
> w12F_Medical_Bullet

You will save your document as:

> Lastname_Firstname_12F_First_Aid

Project Results

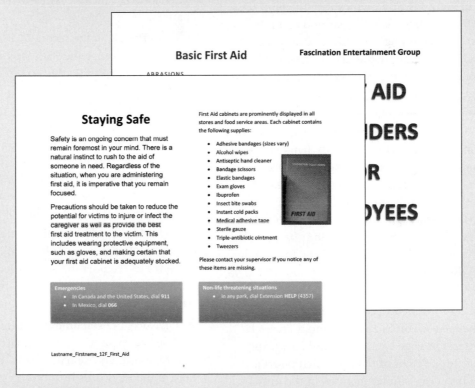

Figure 12.51

(Project 12F First Aid continues on the next page)

1 **Start** Word. From your student files, open the file **w12F_First_Aid**. Save the document to your **Word Chapter 12** folder as **Lastname_Firstname_12F_First_Aid** Insert the file name in the footer.

2 Change the **Orientation** to **Landscape**, and then change the **Columns** to **Two**. On **Page 1**, in the first column, position the insertion point to the left of the fourth paragraph, and then insert a **Column** break. In the second column, position the insertion point to the left of the paragraph *Basic First Aid*, and then press Ctrl + Enter. Display the **Page Setup** dialog box, change the **Paper Size** to **Custom size**, and then change the **Width** to **10"**. **Save** your changes.

3 Select the first paragraph—*Staying Safe*. Change the **Font Size** to **28**, and then apply **Bold** and **Center**. Select the next two paragraphs, and then change the **Font** to **Arial** and the **Font Size** to **14**. In the second column, select the 13 paragraphs beginning with *Adhesive* and ending with *Tweezers*, and then apply **Bullets**. In the second column, select all the text, and then change the **Font Size** to **12**. On **Page 2**, select the first paragraph. Change the **Font Size** to **26**, apply **Bold** and **Center**, and then change the **Font Color** to **Red, Accent 2, Darker 25%**.

4 Select the paragraph *ABRASIONS*. Change the **Font Size** to **14**, change the **Font Color** to **Red, Accent 2, Darker 25%**, and then set the **Spacing** to **Expanded** by **1.4 pt**. Double-click the **Format Painter**, and then apply the formatting to the paragraphs *SPRAINS* and *CHOKING*. Turn off the **Format Painter**. Select the four paragraphs below *ABRASIONS*, and then apply **Bullets**. In a similar manner, apply **Bullets** to the paragraphs below *SPRAINS* and *CHOKING*.

5 On **Page 2**, in the second column, select the first paragraph, change the **Font Size** to **18**, and then apply **Bold** and **Center**. On **Page 1**, in the second paragraph, select the space to the right of *first*, and then insert a nonbreaking space. In a similar manner, in the third paragraph, in the first sentence, select the space to the right of *first*, and then insert a nonbreaking space. **Save** your changes.

6 Display the document **Gridlines**. Display the **Text Box** gallery, and then click **Draw Text Box**. On **Page 1**, at the bottom of the column, begin at the left margin **4** gridlines below the last paragraph, drag down **9** squares, and then drag to the right until the border of the text box aligns with the end of the paragraph. In the second column, draw a text box, beginning **3** gridlines below the last paragraph, approximately the same size as the first text box, as shown in Figure 12.51. Position the insertion point in the first text box, click the **Create Link** button, and then create a link to the second text box. On the **Insert tab**, click the **Object button arrow**, and then click **Text from File**. From your student files, insert text from the file **w12F_Contact_Information**. Apply the **Moderate Effect – Olive Green, Accent 3** shape style to both text boxes. Turn off the display of **Gridlines**. **Save** your changes.

7 On **Page 2**, in the second column, select the last four paragraphs. Change the **Font Size** to **48**, and then apply **Center**. Change the **Text Effects** to **Fill – Red, Accent 2, Double Outline – Accent 2**. Change the **Font Color** to **Red, Accent 2, Darker 25%**. On **Page 1**, position the insertion point to the right of the first paragraph. From your student files, **Insert** the **Picture** file **w12F_Cabinet**. Change **Wrap Text** to **In Front of Text**, and then change the **Shape Height** to **2"**. Position the picture to the right of the bulleted list as shown in Figure 12.51. Display the **Artistic Effects** gallery, and then apply **Texturizer**.

8 On **Page 2**, select the first bulleted list, and then display the **Define New Bullet** dialog box. From your student files, **Import** the **w12F_Medical_Bullet**, and then apply it to the bulleted list. Apply the medical bullet to the remaining bulleted lists in the column.

9 Display the **Document Information Panel**. In the **Author** box, type your first and last names. In the **Subject** box, type your course name and section number, and then in the **Keywords** box, type **first aid, leaflet** Close the Document Information Panel. **Save** your changes.

10 Print your document or submit electronically as directed by your instructor. **Exit** Word.

End **You have completed Project 12F** ————————————

Content-Based Assessments

Apply **12A** and **12B** skills from these Objectives:

1. Integrate Word with PowerPoint
2. Modify a PowerPoint Presentation
3. Modify the Document Layout
4. Format Graphic and Text Elements

Mastering Word | Project **12G** Imagination Parks

In the following Mastering Word project, you will format an outline and then use it to create a PowerPoint presentation describing features of the new Imagination Parks operated by Fascination Entertainment Group. You will also edit a letter by inserting graphics and modifying text. The company plans to send these files as e-mail attachments to its newsletter subscribers. Your completed documents will look similar to Figure 12.52.

Project Files

For Project 12G, you will need the following files:

w12G_Imagination_Outline
w12G_Technology
w12G_Park_Letter
w12G_Imagination_Bullet

You will save your files as:

Lastname_Firstname_12G_Imagination_Outline
Lastname_Firstname_12G_Imagination_Presentation
Lastname_Firstname_12G_Park_Letter

Project Results

Figure 12.52

(Project 12G Imagination Parks continues on the next page)

Content-Based Assessments

Mastering Word | Project **12G** Imagination Parks (continued)

1 **Start** Word. Navigate to your student files, and open the file **w12G_Imagination_Outline**. **Save** the document to your **Word Chapter 12** folder as **Lastname_Firstname_12G_Imagination_Outline** Insert the file name in the footer.

2 In **Outline** view, assign **Level 1** to all paragraphs formatted with bold, and then assign **Level 2** to all remaining paragraphs. Switch to **Print Layout** view. Display the **Document Information Panel**. In the **Author** box, type your first and last names. In the **Subject** box, type your course name and section number, and then in the **Keywords** box, type **imagination, outline Save** your changes, and then **Exit** Word.

3 **Start** PowerPoint. Display the **Open** dialog box, change the types of files to **All Outlines**, and then from your **Word Chapter 12** folder, open your **Lastname_Firstname_12G_Imagination_Outline** file. **Save** the PowerPoint file to your **Word Chapter 12** folder as **Lastname_Firstname_12G_Imagination_Presentation** Display the **Themes** gallery, and then apply the **Composite** theme. Display the **Layout** gallery, and apply the **Title Slide** layout to **Slide 1**.

4 Display the **Insert Picture** dialog box, and then from your student files, locate and open the file **w12G_Technology**. Change the **Shape Height** to **3.2"**. Position the picture in the top left corner of **Slide 1**. Display the **Header and Footer** dialog box. Select the **Footer** and **Don't show on title slide** check boxes, and then for the **Footer**, type **Lastname_Firstname_12G_Imagination Save** your changes, and then **Exit** PowerPoint.

5 **Start** Word. From your student files, open the file **w12G_Park_Letter**. Save the document to your **Word**

Chapter 12 folder as **Lastname_Firstname_12G_Park_Letter** Insert the file name in the footer. If any words are flagged as spelling errors, click Ignore All. Select the first four paragraphs. Change the **Font Size** to **18**, and then apply **Bold** and **Center**. Select the first paragraph, and then change the **Spacing** to **Expanded** by **1.5 pt**.

6 Select the six paragraphs below the paragraph that begins *The featured exhibits*, change the **Font Size** to **14**, and then apply **Bullets**. In the paragraph that begins *Our parks*, locate the phone number, and then change both hyphens to nonbreaking hyphens. **Save** your changes.

7 Position the insertion point at the end of the paragraph that begins *The featured exhibit*. From your student files, **Insert** the **Picture** file named **w12G_Topiary**. Change **Wrap Text** to **In Front of Text**, and then change the **Shape Height** to **1.8"**. Position the picture to the right of the bulleted list, below the paragraph text *special events*. Display the **Artistic Effects** gallery, and then apply the effect **Paint Brush**.

8 Select the bulleted list, and then display the **Define New Bullet** dialog box. From your student files, **Import** the picture **w12G_Imagination_Bullet**, and then apply it to the bulleted list. Press [Ctrl] + [Home].

9 Display the **Document Information Panel**. In the **Author** box, type your first and last names. In the **Subject** box, type your course name and section number, and then in the **Keywords** box, type **letter, graphics, bullets Close** the Document Information Panel. **Save** your changes.

10 Print your two Word documents or submit all three files electronically as directed by your instructor. **Exit** Word.

 You have completed Project 12G _____

Content-Based Assessments

Apply a combination of the 12A and 12B skills.

GO! Fix It | Project 12H Grand Opening

Project Files

For Project 12H, you will need the following files:

> w12H_Grand_Opening
> w12H_Baskets
> w12H_Science
> w12H_Opening_Bullet

You will save your document as:

> Lastname_Firstname_12H_Grand_Opening

In this project, you will edit a memo from Katie Hecart, Vice President of Marketing at Fascination Entertainment Group, to all employees on the executive team regarding the grand opening of three new Imagination Parks. Navigate to your student files, open the file **w12H_Grand_Opening**, and then save it to your **Word Chapter 12** folder as **Lastname_Firstname_12H_Grand_Opening**

To complete the project, you must correct the following:

- The text effect Gradient Fill – Purple, Accent 4, Reflection should be applied to the first paragraph, and the character spacing should be expanded to 1.3 pt.

- In the paragraph that begins *The grand opening*, the text *May 5* should have a nonbreaking space.

- In the last paragraph of the document, the phone number should have nonbreaking hyphens.

- Bullets should be applied to the eight paragraphs listing general topics, the three paragraphs listing the types of visitors, and the three paragraphs listing contact information for coordinators.

- A new bullet should be defined using the file **w12H_Opening_Bullet** and applied to all bulleted lists.

- The file **w12H_Baskets** should be inserted to the right of the first bulleted list with the left edge aligned at approximately 4 inches on the horizontal ruler. Text wrapping should be changed to In Front of Text, the height should be changed to 1.8, and the Cement artistic effect should be applied.

- A page break should be inserted following the second bulleted list.

- The file **w12H_Science** should be inserted in the blank paragraph at the end of the document. The picture should be centered and the Glow Diffused artistic effect applied.

- The file name should be inserted in a footer, and document properties should include the keywords **memo, imagination opening**

Print the document or submit electronically as directed by your instructor.

End **You have completed Project 12H**

Content-Based Assessments

GO! Make It | Project **12I** Season Pass

Project Files

For Project 12I, you will need the following files:

> w12I_Pass_Outline
> w12I_Pass_Picture

You will save your document as:

> Lastname_Firstname_12I_Pass_Handout

Save the file **w12I_Pass_Outline** to your **Word Chapter 12** folder as **Lastname_Firstname_12I_Pass_Outline** Assign outline levels to display the heading and subheading paragraphs shown in Figure 12.53. Create a PowerPoint presentation from your outline and apply the Adjacency theme. From your student files, insert the picture **w12I_Pass_Picture**, and then position the picture as shown. Create a handout in Word from your PowerPoint presentation. Save the handout in your **Word Chapter 12** folder as **Lastname_Firstname_12I_Pass_Handout** Insert the file name in the footer and add document properties that include the keywords **season pass, handout** Print your handout or submit electronically as directed by your instructor.

Project Results

Figure 12.53

End You have completed Project 12I

Content-Based Assessments

Apply a combination of the **12A** and **12B** skills.

GO! Solve It | Project **12J** Employee Interviews

Project Files

For Project 12J, you will need the following files:

> w12J_Interview_Outline
> w12J_Application

You will save your files as:

> Lastname_Firstname_12J_Interview_Outline
> Lastname_Firstname_12J_Interview_Presentation
> Lastname_Firstname_12J_Interview_Handout

From your student files, open the file **w12J_Interview_Outline** and save it your **Word Chapter 12** folder as **Lastname_Firstname_12J_Interview_Outline** Complete the outline by applying appropriate levels to all paragraphs. Insert the file name in the footer and add appropriate document properties.

Create a PowerPoint presentation from the outline that can be used to inform Fascination Entertainment Group staff about the interview process. Save the presentation to your **Word Chapter 12** folder as **Lastname_Firstname_12J_Interview_Presentation** Insert the file **w12J_ Application** on the title slide and apply an appropriate theme. Insert the file name in the footer and add appropriate document properties. Create a one-page handout from the presentation that can be given to employees. Save the document to your **Word Chapter 12** folder as **Lastname_ Firstname_12J_Interview_Handout** Print both documents or submit all three files electronically as directed by your instructor.

Performance Element		Performance Level		
		Exemplary: You consistently applied the relevant skills	**Proficient:** You sometimes, but not always, applied the relevant skills	**Developing:** You rarely or never applied the relevant skills
	Create an outline	Paragraphs are assigned appropriate levels.	At least one paragraph is not assigned an appropriate level.	No levels are assigned to paragraphs.
	Create a presentation from an outline	The information displays appropriately on four slides.	Not all information displays or four slides are not created.	The presentation is not created.
	Change the layout and theme	The first slide is a title slide and a theme is applied.	The first slide is not a title slide or a theme is not applied.	The first slide is not a title slide and no theme is applied.
	Insert a picture	The picture is inserted and displays appropriately.	The picture is inserted but does not display appropriately.	No picture is inserted.
	Create a handout	A one-page handout is created.	A handout is created but displays on two pages.	No handout is created.

End You have completed Project 12J

Content-Based Assessments

GO! Solve It | Project **12K** Appreciation Day

Project Files

For Project 12K, you will need the following files:

w12K_Appreciation_Day
w12K_Teacher_Quotes
w12K_School_Bullet

You will save your document as:

Lastname_Firstname_12K_Appreciation_Day

From your student files, open the file **w12K_Appreciation_Day** and save it to your **Word Chapter 12** folder as **Lastname_Firstname_12K_Appreciation_Day** Change the page orientation to landscape and the paper size to a width of 7 inches and a height of 5 inches. Format the text so that the first five paragraphs display on the first page and the remaining text is on a second page. Format the document attractively and apply character spacing and text effects to the appropriate text. On the second page, create a bulleted list for the five paragraphs describing benefits. Use the file **w12K_School_Bullet** to define and apply a picture bullet to the list. Draw text boxes at the bottom of both pages. Link the text boxes and insert text from the file **w12K_Teacher_Quotes**. Apply a shape style to both text boxes. Insert the file name in the footer and add appropriate document properties. Print your document or submit electronically as directed by your instructor.

	Performance Level		
	Exemplary: You consistently applied the relevant skills	**Proficient:** You sometimes, but not always, applied the relevant skills	**Developing:** You rarely or never applied the relevant skills
Change orientation and paper size	Page orientation and paper size are changed correctly.	The page orientation is not changed or the paper size is not changed.	No changes were made to the document layout.
Format text including character spacing and text effects	Text is formatted attractively and character spacing and text effects are applied.	Text is formatted attractively but either no character spacing or no text effect is applied.	Text is formatted but character spacing and text effects are not applied.
Define bullet and apply to list	A bullet is defined and applied to appropriate paragraphs.	A bulleted list is created but a picture bullet is not defined or applied.	No bulleted list is created.
Insert and link text boxes	Text boxes are inserted appropriately and linked.	Text boxes are inserted but do not display appropriately or are not linked.	No text boxes are inserted.
Insert text in text boxes and apply shape style	Text is inserted and a shape style is applied to both text boxes.	Text is not inserted or a shape style is not applied to both text boxes.	No text is inserted and a shape style is not applied.

Performance Element

End You have completed Project 12K

Outcomes-Based Assessments

Rubric

The following outcomes-based assessments are *open-ended assessments*. That is, there is no specific correct result; your result will depend on your approach to the information provided. Make *Professional Quality* your goal. Use the following scoring rubric to guide you in *how* to approach the problem and then to evaluate *how well* your approach solves the problem.

The *criteria*—Software Mastery, Content, Format and Layout, and Process—represent the knowledge and skills you have gained that you can apply to solving the problem. The *levels of performance*—Professional Quality, Approaching Professional Quality, or Needs Quality Improvements—help you and your instructor evaluate your result.

	Your completed project is of Professional Quality if you:	Your completed project is Approaching Professional Quality if you:	Your completed project Needs Quality Improvements if you:
1-Software Mastery	Choose and apply the most appropriate skills, tools, and features and identify efficient methods to solve the problem.	Choose and apply some appropriate skills, tools, and features, but not in the most efficient manner.	Choose inappropriate skills, tools, or features, or are inefficient in solving the problem.
2-Content	Construct a solution that is clear and well organized, contains content that is accurate, appropriate to the audience and purpose, and is complete. Provide a solution that contains no errors in spelling, grammar, or style.	Construct a solution in which some components are unclear, poorly organized, inconsistent, or incomplete. Misjudge the needs of the audience. Have some errors in spelling, grammar, or style, but the errors do not detract from comprehension.	Construct a solution that is unclear, incomplete, or poorly organized; contains some inaccurate or inappropriate content; and contains many errors in spelling, grammar, or style. Do not solve the problem.
3-Format and Layout	Format and arrange all elements to communicate information and ideas, clarify function, illustrate relationships, and indicate relative importance.	Apply appropriate format and layout features to some elements, but not others. Overuse features, causing minor distraction.	Apply format and layout that does not communicate information or ideas clearly. Do not use format and layout features to clarify function, illustrate relationships, or indicate relative importance. Use available features excessively, causing distraction.
4-Process	Use an organized approach that integrates planning, development, self-assessment, revision, and reflection.	Demonstrate an organized approach in some areas, but not others; or, use an insufficient process of organization throughout.	Do not use an organized approach to solve the problem.

Outcomes-Based Assessments

Apply a combination of
the 12A and 12B skills.

GO! Think | Project **12L** Group Events

Project Files

For Project 12L, you will need the following file:

New blank Word document

You will save your files as:

Lastname_Firstname_12L_Group_Outline
Lastname_Firstname_12L_Group_Presentation
Lastname_Firstname_12L_Group_Handout

Fascination Entertainment Group offers special packages for a variety of groups. Types of groups include schools, family reunions, tour groups, service clubs, youth groups, and businesses. Benefits of a group program include reduced admission, catered meals, priority seating at shows, discounts at all concession stands, free parking, and the services of a park consultant.

Create an outline defining the group program. Save it as **Lastname_Firstname_12L_Group_ Outline** Create a PowerPoint presentation from your outline file. Include a picture and apply an appropriate theme. Save the presentation as **Lastname_Firstname_12L_Group_Presentation** Create a one-page handout in Word. Save the document as **Lastname_Firstname_12L_Group_ Handout** Insert the file name in the footer and add appropriate document properties to all three files. Print your documents or submit all three files electronically as directed by your instructor.

End You have completed Project 12L ———————————————

Apply a combination of
the 12A and 12B skills.

GO! Think | Project **12M** Employment Opportunities

Project Files

For Project 12M, you will need the following file:

New blank Word document

You will save your document as:

Lastname_Firstname_12M_Employment_Opportunities

Fascination Entertainment Group is creating a flyer to advertise employment opportunities. Jobs are available in the following areas: entertainment, finance, food services, event relations, landscaping, security, and in retail stores. Interested persons may include seniors, students, and individuals desiring full-time employment. Internships are available in some areas. Benefits of employment include free admission to parks, health plan, use of fitness center, and food discounts.

Save your document as **Lastname_Firstname_12M_Employment_Opportunites** Create a two-page document. The paper size should be changed to a height of 8 inches and a width of 6 inches. The document should include text that is formatted attractively. Include the following elements: character spacing, text effects, and at least one bulleted list with a defined picture bullet. (You can use a picture bullet from your student files.) Insert an appropriate picture and apply an artistic effect. Insert the file name in the footer and add appropriate document properties. Print your document or submit electronically as directed by your instructor.

End You have completed Project 12M ———————————————

Outcomes-Based Assessments

Apply a combination of the 12A and 12B skills.

You and GO! | Project **12N** Personal Highlights

Project Files

For Project 12N, you will need the following file:

New blank Word document

You will save your documents as:

Lastname_Firstname_12N_Highlights_Outline
Lastname_Firstname_12N_Highlights_Presentation
Lastname_Firstname_12N_Highlights_Handout

Create an outline listing significant events in your life. The events should relate to general topics, such as family, school, activities, and awards. The outline should include a minimum of three main levels with related sublevels. Save the document as **Lastname_Firstname_12N_ Highlights_Outline** Create a PowerPoint presentation from your outline file. Include a picture and apply an appropriate theme. Save the presentation as **Lastname_Firstname_12N_Highlights_ Presentation** Create a handout in Word. Save the document as **Lastname_Firstname_12N_ Highlights_Handout** Insert the file name in the footer and add appropriate document properties to all three files. Print your documents or submit all three files electronically as directed by your instructor.

 You have completed Project 12N ————————————————

Business Running Case

Razvan CHIRNOAGA/Shutterstock

Front Range Action Sports is one of the country's largest retailers of sports gear and outdoor recreation merchandise. The company has large retail stores in Colorado, Washington, Oregon, California, and New Mexico, in addition to a growing online business. Major merchandise categories include fishing, camping, rock climbing, winter sports, action sports, water sports, team sports, racquet sports, fitness, golf, apparel, and footwear. In this project, you will apply skills you practiced from the Objectives in Chapters 10–12. You will edit and create files that relate to the current services Front Range Action Sports provides and possible new products the company will sell. Your completed files will look similar to Figure 4.1.

Project Files

For Project BRC4, you will need the following files:

> New blank Word document
> wBRC4_Services_Report
> wBRC4_Fitness_Services
> wBRC4_Product_Outline
> wBRC4_Product_Memo
> wBRC4_Sales_Increases

You will save your documents as:

Lastname_Firstname_BRC4_Services_Report
Lastname_Firstname_BRC4_Fitness_Services
Lastname_Firstname_BRC4_Product_Outline
Lastname_Firstname_BRC4_Product_
   Presentation
Lastname_Firstname_BRC4_Product_Memo
Lastname_Firstname_BRC4_Product_Code
Lastname_Firstname_BRC4_Sales_Increases

Project Results

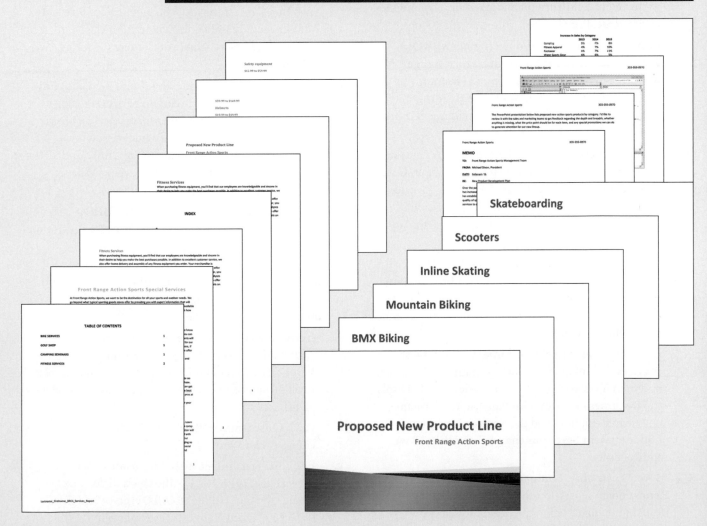

Figure 4.1

Business Running Case

Front Range Action Sports

1 **Start** Word. From your student files, open the file **wBRC4_Services_Report**. If necessary, in the location where you are storing your projects, create a new folder named **Front Range Action Sports** or navigate to this folder if you have already created it. **Save** the document as **Lastname_Firstname_BRC4_Services_Report** Using **Quick Parts**, insert the file name in the footer, press Tab two times, and then in the **Current Position**, insert a **Plain Number** page number. **Close** the footer.

a. Press Ctrl + Home. Apply the **Composite** theme. Select the first paragraph, change the **Font Size** to **20**, apply **Center**, and then change the **Text Effects** to **Gradient Fill – Lime, Accent 1**. Change the **Character Spacing** to **Expanded** by **1.3 pt**. Apply the **Heading 1** style to all paragraphs formatted with bold.

b. In **Outline** view, select the paragraph that begins *Bike Services*, and then select all the remaining paragraphs in the document. Turn on **Show Document**, and then click **Create**. Press Ctrl + End. **Save** your changes.

c. From your student files, open the file **wBRC4_Fitness_Services**. **Save** it to your **Front Range Action Sports** folder as **Lastname_Firstname_BRC4_Fitness_Services** Apply the **Heading 1** style to the first paragraph. **Save** your changes, and then **Close** the document.

d. With the insertion point at the end of your **Lastname_Firstname_BRC4_Services_Report** document, **Insert** your **Lastname_Firstname_BRC4_Fitness_Services** document as a subdocument. In the paragraph below *Fitness Services*, in the first sentence, change the word *wisest* to **best Save** your changes.

e. **Unlink** the four subdocuments, and then **Delete** all section breaks. Display the **Document Information Panel**, add your name, course information, and the **Keywords services, master Save** your changes, and then switch to **Print Layout** view.

f. Open your **Lastname_Firstname_BRC4_Fitness_Services** document, insert the file name in the footer, and then if necessary, delete the section break. Display the **Document Information Panel**, add your name, course information, and the **Keywords services, subdocument Save** your changes, and then **Close** the document.

2 In your **Lastname_Firstname_BRC4_Services_Report** document, select the paragraph heading *Camping Seminars* being careful not to select the

paragraph mark. **Insert** a **Bookmark** with the name **Camping** In the second paragraph of the document, select the text *Camping seminars*, and then **Insert** a **Cross-reference** that links to the **Camping** bookmark.

a. For each *Heading 1* paragraph, use the **Mark Index Entry** dialog box to **Mark** the text as a **Main entry** for an index. In the paragraph following *Golf Shop*, select the text *golf lessons*. **Mark golf lessons** as a **Subentry** for the **Main entry Golf Shop**

b. At the end of the document, insert a new page, type **INDEX** and then press Enter two times. Select *INDEX*, change the **Font Size** to **16**, and then apply **Bold** and **Center**. In the last paragraph of the document, insert an index with the **Classic** format.

c. Press Ctrl + Home, and then insert a **Next Page** section break. Press Ctrl + Home, and then click the **Normal** style. Type **TABLE OF CONTENTS** and then press Enter two times. Select the text, change the **Font Size** to **16**, and then apply **Bold** and **Center**. In the last paragraph on the page, insert a **Table of Contents** with the **Classic** format.

d. On **Page 1**, right-click the footer, and then click **Edit Footer**. Display the **Page Number Format** dialog box, and then change the **Number format** to **i, ii, iii**. On **Page 2**, in the footer, turn off **Link to Previous**. Change the **Page Numbering** to **Start at 1**. Update the table of contents and the index. **Save** your changes, and then **Close** the document, but leave Word open.

3 From your student files, open the file **wBRC4_Product_Outline**. **Save** it to your **Front Range Action Sports** folder as **Lastname_Firstname_BRC4_Product_Outline** Insert the file name in a footer. Display the **Document Information Panel**, add your name, course information, and the **Keywords products, outline levels**

a. In **Outline** view, **Promote** all paragraphs formatted with bold to **Level 1**. Assign the second paragraph to **Level 2**. For all remaining paragraphs, assign **Level 2** to all product descriptions, and then assign **Level 3** to all prices.

b. Click **Close Outline View**, and then **Save** your changes. **Exit** Word.

c. From the **Start** menu, open **Microsoft Office PowerPoint 2010**. Display the **Open** dialog box, change the types of files to **All Outlines**, and then from your **Front Range Action Sports** folder, open

(Business Running Case: Front Range Action Sports continues on the next page)

Business Running Case

Front Range Action Sports (continued)

your **Lastname_Firstname_BRC4_Product_Outline** document. Save the PowerPoint file to your Front Range Sports folder as **Lastname_Firstname_BRC4_ Product_Presentation**

d. Change the **Layout** of the first slide to **Title Slide**, and then change the **Theme** to **Concourse**. Display the **Header and Footer** dialog box, select the **Footer** check box, and then in the **Footer** box, type **Lastname_ Firstname_BRC4_PPT** Be sure a check mark displays in the **Don't Show on title slide** check box, and then click **Apply to All**.

e. Display the **Document Information Panel**, add your name, course information, and the **Keywords products, from outline Save** your changes, and then **Exit** PowerPoint.

4 **Start** Word. From your student files, open the file **wBRC4_Product_Memo**. **Save** it to your **Front Range Action Sports** folder as a **Word Macro-Enabled Document** with the file name **Lastname_Firstname_ BRC4_Product_Memo** Insert the file name in the footer.

a. Record a macro with the **Macro name Header** to insert company contact information in a header. For the **Description**, type **Inserts contact information** The macro should be available in **All Documents (Normal.dotm)**. Assign the **Keyboard** command [Alt] + [H].

b. In recording mode, position the insertion point in the header, press [Ctrl] + [A], and then press [Del]. Type **Front Range Action Sports** press [Tab] two times, and then type **303-555-0970 Close** the header, and then click **Stop Recording**.

c. Display the **Visual Basic Editor**. Open a new Word document. **Save** it to your **Front Range Action Sports** folder as a **Word Macro-Enabled Document** with the file name **Lastname_Firstname_BRC4_Product_ Code** Insert the file name in a footer. Display the **Document Information Panel**, add your name, course information, and the **Keywords header, macro code**

d. Click the **Screenshot** button, and then in the **Available Windows** gallery, click the thumbnail of the **Visual Basic Editor** window. In your **Lastname_Firstname_ BRC4_Product_Code** document, **Run** your **Header**

macro. **Save** your changes, and then **Close** the document. **Close** the Visual Basic Editor.

5 In your **Lastname_Firstname_BRC4_Product_Memo** document, press [Ctrl] + [End]. Display the **Object** dialog box. From your **Front Range Action Sports** folder, locate the file **Lastname_Firstname_BRC4_Product_ Presentation**, and then insert the file as an embedded object. Display the **Presentation Object** in **Edit** mode. Change the **Built-In** theme to **Austin**, and then from the **Header and Footer** dialog box, delete the footer text. **Center** the presentation object in your document, and then **Save** your changes.

a. **Start** Excel. From your student files, open the Excel file **wBRC4_Sales_Increases**. **Save** the file to your **Front Range Action Sports** folder with the file name **Lastname_Firstname_BRC4_Sales_Increases** Insert the file name in the **Footer** box. Display the **Document Information Panel**, add your name, course information, and the **Keywords sales, chart Save** your changes, and then **Close** Excel.

b. In your **Lastname_Firstname_BRC4_Product_Memo** document, position the insertion point at the end of the paragraph that begins *I have carefully*, and then press [Enter]. Insert the **Lastname_Firstname_BRC4_ Sales_Increases** file as a linked file displayed as an icon with the modified caption **Sales Increases**

c. In your Word document, double-click the icon to open the Excel file. In cell **C5**, type **7** and then press [Enter]. **Save** your changes, and then **Close** Excel.

d. **Center** the icon in the document, and then **Save** your changes.

6 Position the insertion point at the end of the paragraph that begins *Over the past*, and then press [Enter]. Insert the **Lastname_Firstname_BRC4_Services_Report** file as a linked file displayed as an icon with the modified caption **Services Report Center** the icon in the document.

a. Delete the **Header** macro.

b. Press [Ctrl] + [Home]. Display the **Document Information Panel**, add your name, course information, and the **Keywords services, report**

c. **Save** your changes and then **Exit** Word.

7 Print or submit all seven files as directed by your instructor.

End You have completed Business Running Case 4 ————————

Glossary

Address bar The bar at the top of a folder window with which you can navigate to a different folder or library, or go back to a previous one.

Address Block A predefined merge field that includes the recipient's name and address.

AdjustListIndents A command that allows you to modify the indenting of a bulleted or numbered list.

Alignment The placement of paragraph text relative to the left and right margins.

All Programs An area of the Start menu that displays all the available programs on your computer system.

American Psychological Association (APA) One of two commonly used style guides for formatting research papers.

Anchor The symbol that indicates to which paragraph an object is attached.

Application Another term for a program.

Area chart A chart type that shows trends over time.

Artistic effect A filter that is applied to an image to create a special effect.

Ascending The order of text sorted alphabetically from A to Z or numbers sorted from smallest to the largest.

Author The owner, or creator, of the original document.

AutoClose A macro that will automatically run when the document is closed.

AutoCorrect A feature that corrects common spelling errors as you type, for example, changing *teh* to *the*.

AutoFit A table feature that automatically adjusts column widths or the width of the entire table.

AutoFit Contents A table feature that resizes the column widths to accommodate the maximum field size.

AutoPlay A Windows feature that displays when you insert a CD, a DVD, or other removable device, and which lets you choose which program to use to start different kinds of media, such as music CDs, or CDs and DVDs containing photos.

Back and Forward buttons Buttons at the top of a folder window that work in conjunction with the address bar to change folders by going backward or forward one folder at a time.

Backstage tabs The area along the left side of Backstage view with tabs to display various pages of commands.

Backstage view A centralized space for file management tasks; for example, opening, saving, printing, publishing, or sharing a file. A navigation pane displays along the left side with tabs that group file-related tasks together.

Balloon The outline shape in which a comment or formatting change displays.

Bar chart A chart type that shows a comparison among related data.

Bar tab stop A vertical bar that displays at a tab stop.

Bibliography A list of cited works in a report or research paper also referred to as *Works Cited*, *Sources*, or *References*, depending upon the report style.

Blog A Web site that displays dated entries, short for *Web log*.

Blog post An individual article entered in a blog with a time and date stamp.

Body The text of a letter.

Body text Text that does not have a heading style applied.

Bookmark A link that identifies the exact location of text, a table, or other object.

Brightness The light to dark ratio of an image.

Browser Software that interprets HTML files, formats them into Web pages, and then displays them. Also referred to as *Web browser*.

Building blocks Reusable pieces of content or other document parts—for example, headers, footers, and page number formats—that are stored in galleries.

Building Blocks Organizer Provides a view of all available building blocks from all the different galleries in one location.

Bulk mail A large mailing, sorted by ZIP code, that is eligible for reduced postage rates, available from the United States Postal Service.

Bulleted list A list of items with each item introduced by a symbol such as a small circle or check mark, and which is useful when the items in the list can be displayed in any order.

Bullets Text symbols such as small circles or check marks that precede each item in a bulleted list.

Caption A title that is added to a Word object and numbered sequentially.

Cell The intersection of a column and a row.

Cell margins The amount of space between a cell's content and the left, right, top, and bottom borders of the cell.

Cell spacing The distance between the individual cells in a table.

Center alignment An arrangement of text in which the text is centered between the left and right margins.

Center tab stop A tab stop in which the text centers around the tab stop location.

Character spacing A Word feature that allows you to change the default spacing constraints between characters.

Character style A style, indicated by the symbol **a**, that contains formatting characteristics that you apply to text, such as font name, font size, font color, bold emphasis, and so on.

Chart A visual representation of numerical data.

Chart area The entire chart and all its elements.

Chart data range The group of cells surrounded by a blue border that Excel will use to create a chart.

Chart style The overall visual look of a chart in terms of its graphic effects, colors, and backgrounds.

Check Box content control A content control that allows the user to select, or not select, a specific option.

Chevrons Characters used to surround a merge field to distinguish where data will be populated in the mail merge.

Citation A note inserted into the text of a research paper that refers the reader to a source in the bibliography.

Click The action of pressing the left button on your mouse pointing device one time.

Click and type pointer The text select—I-beam—pointer with various attached shapes that indicate which formatting—left-aligned, centered, or right-aligned—will be applied when you double-click in a blank area of a document.

Clip art Predefined graphics included with Microsoft Office or downloaded from the Web.

Column break indicator A single dotted line with the text *Column Break* that indicates where a manual column break was inserted.

Column chart A chart type that shows a comparison among related data.

Combine A Track Changes feature that allows you to review two different documents containing revisions, both based on an original document.

Combo Box content control A content control that allows the user to select an item from a list or enter new text.

Command An instruction to a computer program that causes an action to be carried out.

Comment (1) A note that an author or reviewer adds to a document. (2) A line of text in a macro procedure that is used solely for documentation.

Common dialog boxes The set of dialog boxes that includes Open, Save, and Save As, which are provided by the Windows programming interface, and which display and operate in all of the Office programs in the same manner.

Compare A Track Changes feature that enables you to review differences between an original document and the latest version of the document.

Complimentary closing A phrase —such as *Sincerely* or *Yours truly* — that is used to end a business letter.

Compressed file A file that has been reduced in size and thus takes up less storage space and can be transferred to other computers quickly.

Concordance file A Word document that contains a two-column table that is used to mark words as index entries.

Content control (1) In a template, an area indicated by placeholder text that can be used to add text, pictures, dates, or lists. (2) A data entry field where the particular type of information is supplied by the user.

Context sensitive command A command associated with activities in which you are engaged.

Contextual tabs Tabs that are added to the Ribbon automatically when a specific object, such as a picture, is selected, and that contain commands relevant to the selected object.

Contiguous Items that are adjacent to one another.

Continuous section break A mark that defines the beginning and end of each subdocument.

Contrast The difference in colors in a graphic.

Copy A command that duplicates a selection and places it on the Clipboard.

Cropping The process of removing unwanted parts from the edges of a picture.

Cross-reference A text link to an item that appears in another location in the document, such as a heading, a caption, or a footnote.

Cut A command that removes a selection and places it on the Clipboard.

Data labels The part of a chart that displays the value represented by each data marker.

Data markers The shapes in a chart representing each of the cells that contain data.

Data points The cells that contain numerical data used in a chart.

Data range border The blue line that surrounds the cells that display in the chart.

Data series In a chart, related data points represented by a unique color.

Data source (Word) A list of variable information, such as names and addresses, that is merged with a main document to create customized form letters or labels.

Database An organized collection of facts about people, events, things, or ideas related to a particular topic or purpose.

Date line The first line in a business letter that contains the current date and that is positioned just below the letterhead if a letterhead is used.

Date Picker content control A content control that allows the user to select a date from a displayed calendar.

Decimal tab stop A tab stop in which the text aligns with the decimal point at the tab stop location.

Default The term that refers to the current selection or setting that is automatically used by a computer program unless you specify otherwise.

Delimiters Characters, such as commas and tabs, that are used to separate text into groups.

Descending The order of text sorted alphabetically from Z to A or numbers sorted from the largest to the smallest.

Deselect The action of canceling the selection of an object or block of text by clicking outside of the selection.

Design Mode A feature that enables the user to work with content controls that are inserted in a document.

Desktop In Windows, the opening screen that simulates your work area.

Destination file The file where an object is embedded or linked.

Details pane The area at the bottom of a folder window that displays the most common file properties.

Dialog box A small window that contains options for completing a task.

Dialog Box Launcher A small icon that displays to the right of some group names on the Ribbon, and which opens a related dialog box or task pane providing additional options and commands related to that group.

Digital certificate (Digital ID) A file that contains information about a person and is used to electronically sign a document.

Digital signature An electronic stamp that is added to a document to verify the document's authenticity.

Direct formatting The process of applying each format separately, for example, bold, then font size, then font color, and so on.

Directory A single list of records using specified fields from a data source.

Distribute Columns A feature that resizes selected columns so that they are equal in width.

Distribute Rows A feature that resizes selected rows so that they are equal in height.

Document gridlines Nonprinting horizontal and vertical lines used to assist in aligning graphics and other elements in a document.

Document properties Details about a file that describe or identify it, including the title, author name, subject, and keywords that identify the document's topic or contents; also known as *metadata*.

Dot leader A series of dots preceding a tab that guides the eye across the line.

Double-click The action of clicking the left mouse button two times in rapid succession.

Drag The action of holding down the left mouse button while moving your mouse.

Drag and drop The action of moving a selection by dragging it to a new location.

Drawing objects Graphic objects, such as shapes, diagrams, lines, or circles.

Drop cap A large capital letter at the beginning of a paragraph that formats text in a visually distinctive manner.

Drop-Down List content control A content control that allows the user to select a specific item from list.

Dropped The position of a drop cap when it is within the text of the paragraph.

Edit The actions of making changes to text or graphics in an Office file.

Ellipsis A set of three dots indicating incompleteness; when following a command name, indicates that a dialog box will display.

Embedded object An object that maintains the structure of the original application, but is not connected to the source file.

E-mail address link A hyperlink that opens a new message window so that an individual viewing a Web site can send an e-mail message.

Embedding The process of inserting an object, such as a chart, into a Word document so that it becomes part of the document.

Enclosures Additional documents included with a business letter.

Endnote In a research paper, a note placed at the end of a document or chapter.

Enhanced ScreenTip A ScreenTip that displays more descriptive text than a normal ScreenTip.

Extract To decompress, or pull out, files from a compressed form.

Field (Data Source) A category or column of data in a data source.

Field (Word) A placeholder that displays preset content, such as the current date, the file name, a page number, or other stored information.

Fields In a mail merge, the column headings in the data source.

File A collection of information stored on a computer under a single name, for example a Word document or a PowerPoint presentation.

File list In a folder window, the area on the right that displays the contents of the current folder or library.

Fill The inside color of an object.

Filter A set of criteria applied to fields in a data source to display specific records.

Final A Track Changes view that displays the document with all proposed changes included and comments hidden.

Final: Show Markup The default Track Changes view that displays the final document with all revisions and comments visible.

Flipping The process of reversing the direction of an object either vertically or horizontally.

Floating object A graphic that can be moved independently of the surrounding text characters.

Folder A container in which you store files.

Folder window In Windows, a window that displays the contents of the current folder, library, or device, and contains helpful parts so that you can navigate.

Font A set of characters with the same design and shape.

Font styles Formatting emphasis such as bold, italic, and underline.

Footer A reserved area for text or graphics that displays at the bottom of each page in a document.

Footnote In a research paper, a note placed at the bottom of the page.

Form A structured document that has static text and reserved spaces for information to be entered by the user.

Form letter A letter with standardized wording that can be sent to many different people.

Format Painter An Office feature that copies formatting from one selection of text to another.

Formatting The process of establishing the overall appearance of text, graphics, and pages in an Office file—for example, in a Word document.

Formatting marks Characters that display on the screen, but do not print, indicating where the Enter key, the Spacebar, and the Tab key were pressed; also called *nonprinting characters*.

Formula A mathematical expression that contains functions, operators, constants, and properties, and returns a value to a cell.

Function A predefined formula that performs calculations by using specific values in a particular order.

Gallery An Office feature that displays a list of potential results instead of just the command name.

Graphics Pictures, clip art images, charts, or drawing objects.

Greeting Line A predefined merge field that includes an introductory word, such as *Dear*, and the recipient's name.

Gridlines Non-printing lines that indicate cell borders.

Grouping The process of combining multiple elements into a single object.

Groups On the Office Ribbon, the sets of related commands that you might need for a specific type of task.

Handout A document that is given to an audience to accompany a lecture.

Hanging indent An indent style in which the first line of a paragraph extends to the left of the remaining lines, and that is commonly used for bibliographic entries.

Header A reserved area for text or graphics that displays at the top of each page in a document.

Header row The first row of a table containing column titles.

Hidden text Nonprinting text—for example, an index entry field.

Horizontal axis The axis that displays along the lower edge of a chart, also referred to as the *X-axis*.

HTML See Hypertext Markup Language (HTML).

Hyperlinks Text, buttons, pictures, or other objects that, when clicked, access other Web pages, other sections of the active page, or another file.

Hypertext Markup Language (HTML) The language used to format documents that can be opened using any Web browser.

Hyphenation A tool in Word that controls how words are split between two lines.

Icons Pictures that represent a program, a file, a folder, or some other object.

In margin The position of a drop cap when it is in the left margin of a paragraph.

Index A compilation of topics, names, and terms accompanied by page numbers that displays at the end of a document.

Index entry A word or phrase that is listed in the index.

Index entry field Code, formatted as hidden text and displaying to the right of an index entry, containing the identifier *XE* and term to be included in the index.

Info tab The tab in Backstage view that displays information about the current file.

Ink Revision marks made directly on a document by using a stylus on a Tablet PC.

Inline object An object or graphic inserted in a document that acts like a character in a sentence.

Insertion point A blinking vertical line that indicates where text or graphics will be inserted.

Inside address The name and address of the person receiving the letter; positioned below the date line.

Internal link A hyperlink that connects to another page in the same Web site.

Internet Explorer A Web browser developed by Microsoft.

Justified alignment An arrangement of text in which the text aligns evenly on both the left and right margins.

Keep lines together A formatting feature that prevents a single line from displaying by itself at the bottom of a page or at the top of a page.

Keep with next A formatting feature that keeps a heading with its first paragraph of text on the same page.

Kerning A character spacing option that automatically adjusts the spacing between pairs of characters, with a specified minimum point size, so that words and letters display as equally spaced.

Keyboard shortcut A combination of two or more keyboard keys, used to perform a task that would otherwise require a mouse.

KeyTips The letter that displays on a command in the Ribbon and that indicates the key you can press to activate the command when keyboard control of the Ribbon is activated.

Label control A control on a form or report that contains descriptive information, typically a field name.

Landscape orientation A page orientation in which the paper is wider than it is tall.

Layout The placement and arrangement of the text and graphic elements on a slide.

Leader characters Characters that form a solid, dotted, or dashed line that fills the space preceding a tab stop.

Left alignment An arrangement of text in which the text aligns at the left margin, leaving the right margin uneven.

Left tab stop A tab stop in which the text is left aligned at the tab stop and extends to the right.

Legend The part of a chart that identifies the colors assigned to each data series or category.

Letterhead The personal or company information that displays at the top of a letter.

Library In Windows, a collection of items, such as files and folders, assembled from various locations that might be on your computer, an external hard drive, removable media, or someone else's computer.

Line break indicator A small nonprinting bent arrow that displays where a manual line break was inserted.

Line chart A chart type that shows trends over time.

Line spacing The distance between lines of text in a paragraph.

Linked object An object that maintains a direct connection to the source file.

Linked style A style, indicated by the symbol ¶a, that behaves as either a character style or a paragraph style, depending on what you select.

Linking The process of inserting information from a source file into a destination file, while maintaining a connection between the two files.

List style A style that applies a format to a list.

Live Preview A technology that shows the result of applying an editing or formatting change as you point to possible results—*before* you actually apply it.

Location Any disk drive, folder, or other place in which you can store files and folders.

Macro A set of commands and instructions that can be grouped as a single command to accomplish a task automatically.

Macro virus A macro that causes files to be erased or damaged by inserting unauthorized code.

Mail merge A Microsoft Word feature that joins a main document and a data source to create customized letters or labels.

Main document In a mail merge, the document that contains the text or formatting that remains constant.

Manual column break An artificial end to a column to balance columns or to provide space for the insertion of other objects.

Manual line break The action of ending a line, before the normal end of the line, without creating a new paragraph.

Manual page break The action of forcing a page to end and placing subsequent text at the top of the next page.

Margins The space between the text and the top, bottom, left, and right edges of the paper.

Markup The formatting Word uses to denote a document's revisions visually.

Markup area The space to the right or left of a document where comments and formatting changes display in balloons.

Master document A Word document that serves as a container for the different parts of a document.

Match Field A Word feature that maps predefined field names to the field names in the data source.

Memo A written message sent to someone working in the same organization; also referred to as a *memorandum*.

Memorandum See *Memo*.

Merge A table feature that combines two or more adjacent cells into one cell, allowing text to span across multiple rows or columns.

Merge field In a mail merge, a placeholder that represents specific information in a data source.

Metadata Details about a file that describe or identify it, including the title, author name, subject, and keywords that identify the document's topic or contents; also known as *document properties*.

Microsoft Access A database program, with which you can collect, track, and report data.

Microsoft Communicator An Office program that brings together multiple modes of communication, including instant messaging, video conferencing, telephony, application sharing, and file transfer.

Microsoft Excel A spreadsheet program, with which you calculate and analyze numbers and create charts.

Microsoft InfoPath An Office program that enables you to create forms and gather data.

Microsoft Office 2010 A Microsoft suite of products that includes programs, servers, and services for individuals, small organizations, and large enterprises to perform specific tasks.

Microsoft OneNote An Office program with which you can manage notes that you make at meetings or in classes.

Microsoft Outlook An Office program with which you can manage e-mail and organizational activities.

Microsoft PowerPoint A presentation program, with which you can communicate information with high-impact graphics.

Microsoft Publisher An Office program with which you can create desktop publishing documents such as brochures.

Microsoft SharePoint Workspace An Office program that enables you to share information with others in a team environment.

Microsoft Word A word processing program, also referred to as an authoring program, with which you create and share documents by using its writing tools.

Mini toolbar A small toolbar containing frequently used formatting commands that displays as a result of selecting text or objects.

Minus outline symbol A formatting mark that indicates there are no subordinate heading or body text paragraphs.

Modern Language Association (MLA) One of two commonly used style guides for formatting research papers.

Multilevel list A list in which the items display in a visual hierarchical structure.

Nameplate The banner on the front page of a newsletter that identifies the publication; also referred to as a *banner*, *flag*, or *masthead*.

Navigate (Excel) The process of moving within a worksheet or workbook.

Navigation bar A series of text links across the top or bottom of a Web page that, when clicked, will link to another Web page on the same site.

Navigation pane (Windows) In a folder window, the area on the left in which you can navigate to, open, and display favorites, libraries, folders, saved searches, and an expandable list of drives.

Nested table A table inserted in a cell of an existing table.

New from existing The Word command that opens an existing document as a new unnamed document, so that you can use it as a starting point for a new document.

No Spacing style The Word style that inserts *no* extra space following a paragraph and uses single spacing.

Nonbreaking hyphen A formatting mark that prevents a hyphenated word or phrase from being displayed on two lines.

Nonbreaking space A formatting mark that keeps two words together so that both words will wrap even if only the second word would normally wrap to the next line.

Noncontiguous Items that are not adjacent to one another.

Nonprinting characters Characters that display on the screen, but do not print, indicating where the Enter key, the Spacebar, and the Tab key were pressed; also called *formatting marks*.

Normal Quick Style The default style in Word for new documents and which includes default styles and customizations that determine the basic look of a document; for example, it includes the Calibri font, 11 point font size, multiple line spacing at 1.15, and 10 pt. spacing after a paragraph.

Normal template The template that serves as a basis for all new Word documents.

Note In a research paper, information that expands on the topic, but that does not fit well in the document text.

Nudge The action of moving an object on the page in small precise increments.

Numbered list A list of items in which each item is introduced by a consecutive number to indicate definite steps, a sequence of actions, or chronological order.

Numerical data Numbers that represent facts.

Object A table, chart, graphic, file, or other form of information.

Object Linking and Embedding (OLE) A program-integration technology for sharing information between Office programs.

Office Clipboard A temporary storage area that holds text or graphics that you select and then cut or copy.

Open dialog box A dialog box from which you can navigate to, and then open on your screen, an existing file that was created in that same program.

Option button A round button that allows you to make one choice among two or more options.

Options dialog box A dialog box within each Office application where you can select program settings and other options and preferences.

Original A Track Changes view that hides the tracked changes and shows the original, unchanged document with comments hidden.

Original: Show Markup A Track Changes view that displays the original document with all revisions and comments visible.

Outline A Word feature that allows you to organize the contents of a document in a structured manner.

Outline level A Word feature that defines the position of a paragraph in relation to all topics in a document and is formatted with a corresponding heading style.

Outline symbol A small gray circle that identifies heading and body text paragraphs.

Outline view A document view that displays the overall organization of the document's parts including headings, subheadings, and subordinate text.

Page break indicator A dotted line with the text *Page Break* that indicates where a manual page break was inserted.

Pagination The process of arranging and numbering the pages in a document.

Paragraph style A style, indicated by the symbol ¶, that includes everything that a character style contains, plus all aspects of a paragraph's appearance; for example, text alignment, tab stops, line spacing, and borders.

Paragraph symbol The symbol ¶ that represents a paragraph.

Parenthetical citation In the MLA style, a citation that refers to items on the *Works Cited* page, and which is placed in parentheses; the citation includes the last name of the author or authors, and the page number in the referenced source.

Password A code that is used to gain access to a file.

Paste The action of placing text or objects that have been copied or moved from one location to another location.

Paste Options Icons that provide a Live Preview of the various options for changing the format of a pasted item with a single click.

PDF (Portable Document Format) file A file format that creates an image that preserves the look of your file, but that cannot be easily changed; a popular format for sending documents electronically, because the document will display on most computers.

Picture styles Frames, shapes, shadows, borders, and other special effects that can be added to an image to create an overall visual style for the image.

Pie chart A chart type that shows the proportion of parts to a whole.

Placeholder text Text in a content control that indicates the type of information to be entered in a specific location.

Plain Text content control A content control that enables the user to enter unformatted text.

Plus outline symbol A formatting mark that indicates there are subordinate heading or body text paragraphs.

Point The action of moving your mouse pointer over something on your screen.

Pointer Any symbol that displays on your screen in response to moving your mouse.

Points A measurement of the size of a font; there are 72 points in an inch, with 10-12 points being the most commonly used font size.

Portrait orientation A page orientation in which the paper is taller than it is wide.

.pptx The default file extension for a PowerPoint file.

Preview pane button In a folder window, the button on the toolbar with which you can display a preview of the contents of a file without opening it in a program.

Print Preview A view of a document as it will appear when you print it.

Procedure A block of programming code that performs one or more tasks.

Program A set of instructions that a computer uses to perform a specific task, such as word processing, accounting, or data management; also called an *application*.

Program-level control buttons In an Office program, the buttons on the right edge of the title bar that minimize, restore, or close the program.

Protected view A security feature in Office 2010 that protects your computer from malicious files by opening them in a restricted environment until you enable them; you might encounter this feature if you open a file from an e-mail or download files from the Internet.

Pt. The abbreviation for *point*; for example when referring to a font size.

Quick Access Toolbar In an Office program, the small row of buttons in the upper left corner of the screen from which you can perform frequently used commands.

Quick Commands The commands Save, Save As, Open, and Close that display at the top of the navigation pane in Backstage view.

Quick Parts All of the reusable pieces of content that are available to insert into a document, including building blocks, document properties, and fields.

Quick Styles Combinations of formatting options that work together and look attractive together.

Quick Tables Tables that are stored as building blocks.

Read-Only A property assigned to a file that prevents the file from being modified or deleted; it indicates that you cannot save any changes to the displayed document unless you first save it with a new name.

Read-only file A file that can be viewed but not changed.

Readability statistics A Spelling and Grammar tool that analyzes a document and determines the reading level of the text.

Record All of the categories of data pertaining to one person, place, thing, event, or idea, and which is formatted as a row in a database table.

Recording The process of creating a macro.

Reviewer An individual who reviews and marks changes on a document.

Reviewing Pane A separate scrollable window that displays all of the current changes and comments in a document.

Revisions Changes made to a document.

Ribbon The user interface in Office 2010 that groups the commands for performing related tasks on tabs across the upper portion of the program window.

Ribbon tabs The tabs on the Office Ribbon that display the names of the task-oriented groups of commands.

Rich Text A content control that enables the user to enter text and apply formatting.

Rich Text Format (RTF) A universal file format, using the *.rtf* file extension, that can be read by many word processing programs.

Right alignment An arrangement of text in which the text aligns at the right margin, leaving the left margin uneven.

Right tab stop A tab stop in which the text is right aligned at the tab stop and extends to the left.

Right-click The action of clicking the right mouse button one time.

RTF See Rich Text Format.

Rules Conditional Word fields that allow you to determine how the merge process is completed.

Salutation The greeting line of a letter, such as *Dear Sir*.

Sans serif A font design with no lines or extensions on the ends of characters.

Screenshot An image of an active window on your computer that you can paste into a document.

Screenshot Tool A Word feature that allows you to capture an image of any open window and automatically paste the image into the active Word document.

ScreenTip A small box that that displays useful information when you perform various mouse actions such as pointing to screen elements or dragging.

Scroll bar A vertical or horizontal bar in a window or a pane to assist in bringing an area into view, and which contains a scroll box and scroll arrows.

Scroll box The box in the vertical and horizontal scroll bars that can be dragged to reposition the contents of a window or pane on the screen.

Search box In a folder window, the box in which you can type a word or a phrase to look for an item in the current folder or library.

Section A portion of a document that can be formatted differently from the rest of the document.

Section break (1) A double dotted line that indicates the end of one section and the beginning of another section. (2) A mark that stores the formatting information for a section of a document.

Select To highlight, by dragging with your mouse, areas of text or data or graphics, so that the selection can be edited, formatted, copied, or moved.

Serif font A font design that includes small line extensions on the ends of the letters to guide the eye in reading from left to right.

Shapes Lines, arrows, stars, banners, ovals, rectangles, and other basic shapes with which you can illustrate an idea, a process, or a workflow.

Shortcut menu A menu that displays commands and options relevant to the selected text or object.

Signature line An element added to a document that specifies who should sign the document.

Single File Web Page A document saved using HTML and that opens using a Web browser.

Small caps A font effect, usually used in titles, that changes lowercase text into capital (uppercase) letters using a reduced font size.

SmartArt A designer-quality visual representation of your information that you can create by choosing from among many different layouts to effectively communicate your message or ideas.

Sort The action of ordering data, usually in alphabetical or numeric order.

Source file The file where an object is created.

Spin box A small box with an upward- and downward-pointing arrow that lets you move rapidly through a set of values by clicking.

Split A table feature that divides a selected cell into multiple cells with a specific number of rows and columns.

Split button A button divided into two parts and in which clicking the main part of the button performs a command and clicking the arrow opens a menu with choices.

Stacking The process of placing objects in individual layers of the document.

Start button The button on the Windows taskbar that displays the Start menu.

Start menu The Windows menu that provides a list of choices and is the main gateway to your computer's programs, folders, and settings.

Static text Descriptive text such as labels or headings.

Status bar The area along the lower edge of an Office program window that displays file information on the left and buttons to control how the window looks on the right.

Style A group of formatting commands, such as font, font size, font color, paragraph alignment, and line spacing that can be applied to a paragraph with one command.

Style guide A manual that contains standards for the design and writing of documents.

Style set A group of styles that are designed to work together.

Styles window A pane that displays a list of styles and contains tools to manage styles.

Stylus A pen-like device used for writing on an electronic document.

Subdocument A section of a document that is linked to the master document.

Subfolder A folder within a folder.

Subject line The optional line following the inside address in a business letter that states the purpose of the letter.

Subpoints Secondary-level information in a SmartArt graphic.

Synchronous scrolling The setting that causes two documents to scroll simultaneously.

Synonyms Words with the same or similar meaning.

Tab stop Specific locations on a line of text, marked on the Word ruler, to which you can move the insertion point by pressing the Tab key, and which is used to align and indent text.

Table (Word) An arrangement of information organized into rows and columns.

Table of authorities A list of legal references.

Table of contents (TOC) A list of a document's headings and subheadings, marked with the page numbers where the headings and subheadings occur.

Table of figures A list of figure captions in a document.

Table style A style that includes formatting for the entire table and specific table elements, such as rows and columns.

Tablet PC A computer with a monitor that allows you to write on the screen.

Tabs On the Office Ribbon, the name of each activity area in the Office Ribbon.

Tags Custom file properties that you create to help find and organize your own files.

Task pane A window within a Microsoft Office application in which you can enter options for completing a command.

Template An existing document that you use as a starting point for a new document; it opens a copy of itself, unnamed, and then you use the structure—and possibly some content, such as headings—as the starting point for the new document.

Text box A movable resizable container for text or graphics.

Text control A content control that accepts only a text entry.

Text effects Decorative formats, such as shadowed or mirrored text, text glow, 3-D effects, and colors that make text stand out.

Text link A hyperlink applied to a selected word or phrase.

Text wrapping The manner in which text displays around an object.

Theme A predesigned set of colors, fonts, lines, and fill effects that look good together and that can be applied to your entire document or to specific items.

Theme template A stored, user-defined set of colors, fonts, and effects that can be shared with other Office programs.

Thesaurus A research tool that provides a list of synonyms.

Thumbnails A graphical representation of pages.

Title bar The bar at the top edge of the program window that indicates the name of the current file and the program name.

Toggle button A button that can be turned on by clicking it once, and then turned off by clicking it again.

Toolbar In a folder window, a row of buttons with which you can perform common tasks, such as changing the view of your files and folders or burning files to a CD.

Top-level points The main text points in a SmartArt graphic.

Track Changes A feature that makes a record of the changes made to a document.

Triple-click The action of clicking the left mouse button three times in rapid succession.

Trusted Documents A security feature in Office 2010 that remembers which files you have already enabled; you might encounter this feature if you open a file from an e-mail or download files from the Internet.

Two Pages A zoom setting that decreases the magnification to display two pages of a document.

Unformatted text Plain text without any special formatting applied.

USB flash drive A small data storage device that plugs into a computer USB port.

Vertical axis The axis that displays along the left side of a chart; also referred to as the *Y-axis*.

Vertical change bar Displays in the left margin next to each line of text that contains a revision.

View Side by Side Displays two open documents, in separate windows, next to each other on the screen.

Views button In a folder window, a toolbar button with which you can choose how to view the contents of the current location.

Visual Basic Editor (VBE) An editor that enables you to view and edit existing macro code or create a new macro.

Visual Basic for Applications (VBA) A programming language used to create macros.

Watermark A text or graphic element that displays behind document text.

Web browser Software that interprets HTML files, formats them into Web pages, and then displays them. Also referred to as a *browser*.

Web page A file coded in HTML that can be viewed on the Internet using a Web browser.

Web Page format A file type that saves a Word document as an HTML file, with some elements of the Web page saved in a folder, separate from the Web page itself.

Web site A group of related Web pages published to a specific location on the Internet.

Wildcard A special character such as * or ? that is used to search for an unknown term.

Window A rectangular area on a computer screen in which programs and content appear, and which can be moved, resized, minimized, or closed.

Windows Explorer The program that displays the files and folders on your computer, and which is at work anytime you are viewing the contents of files and folders in a window.

Windows taskbar The area along the lower edge of the Windows desktop that contains the Start button and an area to display buttons for open programs.

Word count A Word feature that indicates the number of pages, words, and characters in a document.

Word Options A collection of settings that you can change to customize Word.

WordArt A feature that applies combinations of decorative formatting to text, including shadows, reflections, and 3-D effects, as well as changing the line and fill color of text.

Wordwrap The feature that moves text from the right edge of a paragraph to the beginning of the next line as necessary to fit within the margins.

Works Cited In the MLA style, a list of cited works placed at the end of a research paper or report.

Writer's identification The name and title of the author of a letter, placed near the bottom of the letter under the complimentary closing—also referred to as the *writer's signature block*.

Writer's signature block The name and title of the author of a letter, placed near the bottom of the letter, under the complimentary closing—also referred to as the *writer's identification*.

X-axis See Horizontal axis.

XE Code identifying an index entry.

Y-axis See Vertical axis.

Zoom The action of increasing or decreasing the viewing area on the screen.

Index

14
Bibliography

SINGLE PC LICENSE AGREEMENT AND LIMITED WARRANTY

READ THIS LICENSE CAREFULLY BEFORE OPENING THIS PACKAGE. BY OPENING THIS PACKAGE, YOU ARE AGREEING TO THE TERMS AND CONDITIONS OF THIS LICENSE. IF YOU DO NOT AGREE, DO NOT OPEN THE PACKAGE. PROMPTLY RETURN THE UNOPENED PACKAGE AND ALL ACCOMPANYING ITEMS TO THE PLACE YOU OBTAINED THEM. *THESE TERMS APPLY TO ALL LICENSED SOFTWARE ON THE DISK EXCEPT THAT THE TERMS FOR USE OF ANY SHAREWARE OR FREEWARE ON THE DISKETTES ARE AS SET FORTH IN THE ELECTRONIC LICENSE LOCATED ON THE DISK:*

1. GRANT OF LICENSE and OWNERSHIP: The enclosed computer programs ("Software") are licensed, not sold, to you by Prentice-Hall, Inc. ("We" or the "Company") and in consideration of your purchase or adoption of the accompanying Company textbooks and/or other materials, and your agreement to these terms. We reserve any rights not granted to you. You own only the disk(s) but we and/or our licensors own the Software itself. This license allows you to use and display your copy of the Software on a single computer (i.e., with a single CPU) at a single location for academic use only, so long as you comply with the terms of this Agreement. You may make one copy for back up, or transfer your copy to another CPU, provided that the Software is usable on only one computer.

2. RESTRICTIONS: You may not transfer or distribute the Software or documentation to anyone else. Except for backup, you may not copy the documentation or the Software. You may not network the Software or otherwise use it on more than one computer or computer terminal at the same time. You may not reverse engineer, disassemble, decompile, modify, adapt, translate, or create derivative works based on the Software or the Documentation. You may be held legally responsible for any copying or copyright infringement which is caused by your failure to abide by the terms of these restrictions.

3. TERMINATION: This license is effective until terminated. This license will terminate automatically without notice from the Company if you fail to comply with any provisions or limitations of this license. Upon termination, you shall destroy the Documentation and all copies of the Software. All provisions of this Agreement as to limitation and disclaimer of warranties, limitation of liability, remedies or damages, and our ownership rights shall survive termination.

4. DISCLAIMER OF WARRANTY: THE COMPANY AND ITS LICENSORS MAKE NO WARRANTIES ABOUT THE SOFTWARE, WHICH IS PROVIDED "AS-IS." IF THE DISK IS DEFECTIVE IN MATERIALS OR WORKMANSHIP, YOUR ONLY REMEDY IS TO RETURN IT TO THE COMPANY WITHIN 30 DAYS FOR REPLACEMENT UNLESS THE COMPANY DETERMINES IN GOOD FAITH THAT THE DISK HAS BEEN MISUSED OR IMPROPERLY INSTALLED, REPAIRED, ALTERED OR DAMAGED. THE COMPANY DISCLAIMS ALL WARRANTIES, EXPRESS OR IMPLIED, INCLUDING WITHOUT LIMITATION, THE IMPLIED WARRANTIES OF MERCHANTABILITY AND FITNESS FOR A PARTICULAR PURPOSE. THE COMPANY DOES NOT WARRANT, GUARANTEE OR MAKE ANY REPRESENTATION REGARDING THE ACCURACY, RELIABILITY, CURRENTNESS, USE, OR RESULTS OF USE, OF THE SOFTWARE.

5. LIMITATION OF REMEDIES AND DAMAGES: IN NO EVENT, SHALL THE COMPANY OR ITS EMPLOYEES, AGENTS, LICENSORS OR CONTRACTORS BE LIABLE FOR ANY INCIDENTAL, INDIRECT, SPECIAL OR CONSEQUENTIAL DAMAGES ARISING OUT OF OR IN CONNECTION WITH THIS LICENSE OR THE SOFTWARE, INCLUDING, WITHOUT LIMITATION, LOSS OF USE, LOSS OF DATA, LOSS OF INCOME OR PROFIT, OR OTHER LOSSES SUSTAINED AS A RESULT OF INJURY TO ANY PERSON, OR LOSS OF OR DAMAGE TO PROPERTY, OR CLAIMS OF THIRD PARTIES, EVEN IF THE COMPANY OR AN AUTHORIZED REPRESENTATIVE OF THE COMPANY HAS BEEN ADVISED OF THE POSSIBILITY OF SUCH DAMAGES. SOME JURISDICTIONS DO NOT ALLOW THE LIMITATION OF DAMAGES IN CERTAIN CIRCUMSTANCES, SO THE ABOVE LIMITATIONS MAY NOT ALWAYS APPLY.

6. GENERAL: THIS AGREEMENT SHALL BE CONSTRUED IN ACCORDANCE WITH THE LAWS OF THE UNITED STATES OF AMERICA AND THE STATE OF NEW YORK, APPLICABLE TO CONTRACTS MADE IN NEW YORK, AND SHALL BENEFIT THE COMPANY, ITS AFFILIATES AND ASSIGNEES. This Agreement is the complete and exclusive statement of the agreement between you and the Company and supersedes all proposals, prior agreements, oral or written, and any other communications between you and the company or any of its representatives relating to the subject matter. If you are a U.S. Government user, this Software is licensed with "restricted rights" as set forth in subparagraphs (a)-(d) of the Commercial Computer-Restricted Rights clause at FAR 52.227-19 or in subparagraphs (c)(1)(ii) of the Rights in Technical Data and Computer Software clause at DFARS 252.227-7013, and similar clauses, as applicable.

Should you have any questions concerning this agreement or if you wish to contact the Company for any reason, please contact in writing:

Multimedia Production,
Higher Education Division,
Prentice-Hall, Inc.,
1 Lake Street,
Upper Saddle River NJ 07458.